Comparative Advantage, Growth, and the Gains from Trade and Globalization

A Festschrift in Honor of Alan V Deardorff

World Scientific Studies in International Economics

(ISSN: 1793-3641)

---

*Published**

Vol. 9 Globalization and International Trade Policies
by Robert M Stern (University of Michigan, USA)

Vol. 10 The First Credit Market Turnoil of the 21st Century: Implications for Public Policy
edited by Doughlas D Evanoff (Federal Reserve Bank of Chicago, USA, Philipp Hartmann (European Central Bank, Germany) & George G Kaufman (Loyola University, USA)

Vol. 11 Free Trade Agreements in the Asia Pacific
edited by Christopher Findlay (University of Adelaide, Australia) & Shujiro Urata (Waseda University, Japan)

Vol. 12 The Japanese Economy in Retrospect, Volume I and Volume II
Selected Papers by Gary R. Saxonhouse
by Robert M Stern (University of Michigan, USA), Gavin Wright (Stanford University, USA) & Hugh Patrick (Columbia University, USA)

Vol. 13 Light the Lamp
Papers on World Trade and Investment in Memory of Bijit Bora
edited by Christopher Findlay (University of Adelaide, Australia), David Parsons (KADIN Indonesia) & Mari Pangestu (Trade Minister of Indonesia)

Vol. 14 The International Financial Crisis: Have the Rules of Finance Changed?
edited by Asli Demirgüç-Kunt (The World Bank, USA), Douglas D Evanoff (Federal Reserve Bank of Chicago, USA) & George G Kaufman (Loyola University of Chicago, USA)

Vol. 15 Systemic Implications of Transatlantic Regulatory Cooperation and Competition
edited by Simon J Evenett (University of St Gallen, Switzerland) & Robert M Stern (University of Michigan, USA)

Vol. 16 Comparative Advantage, Growth, and the Gains from Trade and Globalization: A Festschrift in Honor of Alan V Deardorff
edited by Robert M Stern (University of Michigan, USA)

*The complete list of the published volumes in the series can be found at http://www.worldscibooks.com/series/wssie_series.shtml.

16 World Scientific Studies in International Economics

Comparative Advantage, Growth, and the Gains from Trade and Globalization

A Festschrift in Honor of Alan V Deardorff

Editor

Robert M Stern

University of Michigan, USA

World Scientific

NEW JERSEY · LONDON · SINGAPORE · BEIJING · SHANGHAI · HONG KONG · TAIPEI · CHENNAI

Published by

World Scientific Publishing Co. Pte. Ltd.
5 Toh Tuck Link, Singapore 596224
USA office: 27 Warren Street, Suite 401-402, Hackensack, NJ 07601
UK office: 57 Shelton Street, Covent Garden, London WC2H 9HE

Library of Congress Cataloging-in-Publication Data
Comparative advantage, growth, and the gains from trade and globalization : a festschrift in honor of Alan V. Deardorff / edited by Robert M. Stern.
p. cm. -- (World scientific studies in international economics, 1793-3641 ; v. 16)
Includes bibliographical references.
ISBN-13: 978-981-4340-36-6
ISBN-10: 981-4340-36-7
1. International trade. 2. Comparative advantage (International trade) 3. Globalization--Economic aspects.
I. Deardorff, Alan V. II. Stern, Robert M. (Robert Mitchell), 1927–
HF1379.C6556 2011
382--dc22

2011014104

British Library Cataloguing-in-Publication Data
A catalogue record for this book is available from the British Library.

In-house Editor: Juliet Lee Ley Chin

Typeset by Stallion Press
Email: enquiries@stallionpress.com

Printed in Singapore by B & Jo Enterprise Pte Ltd

PREFACE AND ACKNOWLEDGMENTS

Alan Deardorff was 65 years old on June 6, 2009. To celebrate this occasion, a Festschrift in Alan's honor was held on Friday and Saturday, October 2–3, 2009, in the Rackham Amphitheater at the University of Michigan in Ann Arbor. The Festschrift was entitled "Comparative Advantage, Economic Growth, and the Gains from Trade and Globalization: A Festschrift in Honor of Alan V. Deardorff." It was co-organized by two of Alan's former students, Drusilla Brown of Tufts University and Robert Staiger of Stanford University, together with Robert Stern representing the University of Michigan.

The first day of the Festschrift involved a series of panels in which invited participants reflected on Alan's contributions, including his writings on comparative advantage; trade and growth; the gains from trade and globalization; and computational modeling and trade policy analysis. The panel participants prepared written comments, setting out their evaluation of Alan's contributions combined with their own thoughts on the current state of knowledge and analysis of the particular topic. At the end of the first day, Paul Krugman of Princeton University and *The New York Times* delivered a Citigroup Foundation Special Lecture entitled "Reflections on Globalization: Yesteryear and Today."

The second day of the Festschrift involved "showcasing" the fruits of Alan's mentoring as an advisor. A number of Alan's former students were invited to present whatever paper they were currently working on and were most excited about presenting at the Festschrift. Those invited included Drusilla Brown, Tufts University; Peter Debaere, University of Virginia; David Hummels, Purdue University; Marc Melitz, Harvard University; Robert Staiger, Stanford University; and David Weinstein, Columbia University. Discussants were appointed to critique the individual papers. Day 2 of the Festschrift was therefore more like a research seminar, with the paper presentations, and the link to Alan simply being that these were contributions from his former students. These papers were but a small sample of work by Alan's former Ph.D. students.

The Festschrift was officially sponsored by the Gerald R. Ford School of Public Policy and the University of Michigan Department of Economics with generous support from the University of Michigan International Policy Center of the Ford School; College of Literature, Science, and the Arts, Office of the Vice President for Research; International Institute; the Stephen M. Ross School of Business; and from John W. Sweetland.

Robert M. Stern
Oakland, California
August 24, 2010

TABLE OF CONTENTS

FESTSCHRIFT PANELISTS

James E. Anderson, Boston College and NBER
Robert E. Baldwin, University of Wisconsin
Avinash Dixit, Princeton University
Wilfred J. Ethier, University of Pennsylvania and Tbilisi State University
Gene M. Grossman, Princeton University
Thomas W. Hertel, Purdue University
Ronald W. Jones, University of Rochester
Anne O. Krueger, Johns Hopkins SAIS and Stanford Center for International Development
Paul Krugman, Princeton University and *The New York Times*
James R. Markusen, University of Colorado and University College, Dublin
Will Martin, The World Bank
J. Peter Neary, University of Oxford and CEPR
Arvind Panagariya, Columbia University
T.N. Srinivasan, Yale University
Robert M. Stern, University of Michigan
John Sweetland, The Winsford Corporation

INTRODUCTION

A Tribute to Alan V. Deardorff

Robert M. Stern

Alan Deardorff is the John W. Sweetland Professor of International Economics and Professor of Economics and Public Policy in the Department of Economics and Gerald R. Ford School of Public Policy at the University of Michigan. He received his Ph.D. in economics from Cornell University in 1971 and has been on the faculty at the University of Michigan since 1970. He served as Chair of the Department of Economics from 1991 to 1995.

Professor Deardorff has also served as a consultant to many government agencies and international organizations, including the Departments of State, Treasury, and Labor of the United States Government, and the UN Conference on Trade and Development, and he is currently on the editorial boards of several academic journals. His many publications span a large variety of topics dealing with international trade theory and policy. His writings on international trade theory have dealt primarily with the theory of comparative advantage and the Heckscher–Ohlin and other models that explain the patterns and effects of international trade. His writings on trade policy have included analyses of anti-dumping laws, the safeguards clause of the General Agreement on Tariffs and Trade (GATT), and arguments for and against extending intellectual property protection to developing countries.

Together with Professor Robert Stern, he has developed a computer-based model of production, trade, and employment in 34 major countries of the world. This model has been used for a variety of purposes, including analysis of the Tokyo and Uruguay Rounds of multilateral trade negotiations and possible outcomes of the current World Trade Organization (WTO) Doha Round. Deardorff, Stern, and Drusilla K. Brown of Tufts University have also developed a series of models to evaluate the sectoral employment implications of various regional trading arrangements in North America, the Western Hemisphere, Asia, and Europe.

Over the course of his career, Professor Deardorff has authored/co-authored five books and monographs, six edited volumes, and nearly 90 academic papers. He has also published 84 conference papers in edited volumes.

Professor Deardorff currently maintains two widely used websites: *Family Tree of Trade Economists*, since 2001, and *The Terms of Trade and Other Wonders: Deardorff's Glossary of International Economics*, since 1998.

In recognition of his many accomplishments, Professor Deardorff has been honored and has delivered a number of special, invited lectures, including the Graham Lecture at Princeton University in 2006; Nottingham Lectures at the University of Nottingham in 2005; the Ohlin Lectures at the Stockholm School of Economics in 2003; and the World Economic Lecture at the University of Nottingham in 2002.

Professor Deardorff's recent and current topics of theoretical research include the role of trade costs in determining patterns of trade, the determinants of international specialization, and the mechanisms by which trade liberalization may stimulate industrialization and growth.

STRUCTURE OF THE VOLUME

In the chapters that follow, each of the major sections consists of the special lectures by John Sweetland and Paul Krugman and the brief papers that were prepared by invited participants on the occasion of the Festschrift that took place on October 2–3, 2009 at the University of Michigan.

John Sweetland's remarks provide an account of his experiences as a student at the University of Michigan, his business career, and his ongoing relationship with the Michigan Department of Economics over the years that includes the establishment of an endowed chair in international economics that Alan Deardorff has held for a number of years. In his special Citigroup Foundation Lecture delivered to a large audience at Hill Auditorium, Paul Krugman offers a panorama of the forces of globalization that have unfolded historically and how they have changed and are being manifested today.

The sections of the volume that follow include the panel papers devoted to reflections on Alan Deardorff's influential writings on a variety of topics, including comparative advantage, trade and growth, the gains from trade and globalization, and computational modeling and trade policy analysis. These papers were presented and critiqued in sessions during the Festschrift and subsequently revised and edited. In order to provide further perspective on the foregoing topics, each section includes reprints of a number of Professor Deardorff's most important papers that underlie the reflections on his work by the Festschrift panelists.

Alan Deardorff's truly remarkable intellectual and professional accomplishments are evident in what follows. Readers of this Festschrift volume are certain to be rewarded by the rigor, scope, and insights of his writings over a long and eminent career.

PART I

SPECIAL LECTURES

CHAPTER 1

Remarks: Deardorff Festschrift

John Sweetland

The Winsford Corporation

For years, the University of Michigan, as well as its colleges, schools, and departments, operated under the policy best described by Senator Moynihan as one of "benign neglect" toward its alumni. As a result, I had little contact with the College of LS&A, the Rackham School, or the Department of Economics from which I received both my bachelor's and master's degrees in the late '50s.

This began to change under President Harold Shapiro — formerly a professor of economics at Michigan — as he realized that the University had to look beyond state funding in major ways if it were to achieve its potential. Under his leadership, the Campaign for Michigan began and was carried out by his provost, then President Jim Duderstadt. Its goal was $1 billion — the largest ever sought by a state-supported university. It was a success at $1.4 billion, but more importantly, it brought out of the shadows thousands of loyal — and *generous* — alums. Since then, the recent $2.5 billion Michigan difference campaign, which ended last year, topped $3.2 billion and placed Michigan in the lead among state universities with the largest per student endowment among its peers.

It was this series of events that brought Alan and me into the same orbit. I had some reasonable degree of success ignoring what I was taught at Michigan by creating the largest cement import operation in the U.S. with facilities on the east and west coasts. Cement, I was taught, was too low value a commodity to be involved in international trade. By the early '90s when we sold our companies to Cemex and Lafarge, some 20% of the cement consumed in the United States was imported from Canada, Europe, and the Far East.

Shortly thereafter, I received a call from a Southern Californian alumnus who asked if he could bring Saul Hymans to my office for a visit. I knew who Saul was because the Research Seminar in Quantitative Economics was well known in national circles. Saul's visit was the first step in my reintroduction to Michigan and the economics department. To those here from the academic community, please don't turn down such opportunities. Former students that I have talked to uniformly feel honored by such a meeting — they want to hear what's happening!

Soon the romance became more serious. Would I consider a gift to the Campaign for Michigan? That grew into a request that I fund a Chair in Economics for a major number — at least for me! I decided to create the Chair in International Economics even though my field of concentration was industrial organization. My reason? I very much enjoyed my

Michigan experience, but the late '50s was a slow time in international trade. Europe and Japan were still recovering from World War II, most of the U.S. trade was exports — the first Volkswagen didn't appear until the late '50s and was viewed as a joke by the U.S. auto industry — and there was little evidence that change was coming quickly. My experience in developing new cement plants in Greece and Spain in the '60s, a time in the securities industry in the '70s bringing our investment products in Europe into compliance with the German equivalent of the Securities and Exchange Commission legislation, and extensive anti-dumping litigation brought by domestic cement companies against our operations in the '80s created an awareness that institutions like Michigan needed to look to the world and broaden the scope of their studies.

I then learned that the Department had the ideal candidate in mind to hold the first endowed Chair at Michigan in economics. Described as a scholar, a teacher, an author, a person with striking intelligence and a prodigious appetite for work, a recent chair of the department known for his collegial spirit — who else could it be but Alan Deardorff?

It has been a pleasure knowing Alan these past 12 years. I've had an opportunity to teach one introductory class in international economics for each of the past 10 years. From this vantage, I could sense the students' respect for Alan and the high regard they have for him. I'm honored to have a part in this celebration.

CHAPTER 2

Citigroup Foundation Special Lecture

Paul Krugman

Princeton University and The New York Times

INTRODUCTION[1]

Good afternoon and welcome. I am Susan Collins, the Joan and Sanford Weill Dean of the Gerald R. Ford School of Public Policy. And I am simply delighted to see all of you and welcome you here on behalf of the Ford School, the International Policy Center, and the Department of Economics. It is really wonderful to have so much interest in our speaker today, whom I will introduce in just a moment.

But as most of you know, we had to move the venue because of that interest, and I would like to thank Hill Auditorium for wedging us in, in the midst of performances by the University Symphony Band.

It is a great honor and a personal pleasure to welcome Paul Krugman to campus as the Ford School's 2009 Citigroup Foundation lecturer. This lecture series was established several years ago by the Citigroup Foundation as a gift in honor of Gerald R. Ford. We are very grateful to the Foundation for their generous gift, which has enabled us to bring distinguished policy leaders to campus, and we are extremely honored this afternoon to be able to add Professor Paul Krugman's name to the list of our Citigroup lecturers.

Today's lecture is the keynote address for an academic conference we are hosting on campus today and tomorrow. The conference was organized in honor of the distinguished career of our colleague and friend, Professor Alan Deardorff, who is currently the Associate Dean of the Ford School. Alan's wide-ranging and astute contributions have furthered our understanding of why countries trade, the implications for growth, and the impact of trade policy in a globalizing world. The conference has also brought many of the world's leading trade economists to Ann Arbor, and I am very pleased to welcome all of them here today as well.

Like many of those conference attendees, I am an international economist. And while I am very proud of my profession and its contributions, I do have to concede that there are not many economists whose work is followed closely by the general public, whose opinions

[1] This Introduction and Paul Krugman's lecture to follow are based on the editing of the transcript prepared for the occasion.

on economic matters stir great passions among lay people, and whose weekly writings are routinely discussed around the water cooler. Well, Paul Krugman is the exception. Whether they agree with him or not, people from all walks of life want to know what Paul has to say.

In just the past few days, for example, he has appeared in quite disparate settings such as the keynote speaker at a conference in Helsinki on Finland's economic competitiveness and as a guest on the HBO show, Real Time, with Bill Maher. Paul's even a hit over at YouTube where a little-known performer scored a quarter of a million views with his song — and I promise I won't sing it for you — "Hey, Paul Krugman." If you have not checked out the YouTube video, I encourage you to do so.

But of course they do not award Nobel Prizes for popularity or YouTube hits. Paul Krugman is one of the great economists of our time, and he was awarded the Nobel Prize for his analysis of trade patterns and the location of economic activity. Traditional theories of international trade emphasize why countries are different, and why they trade with each other, exporting and importing different products. Paul's work emphasized that much of the trade we see in the real world is between countries that are quite similar, and they are trading relatively similar products. His models highlight both that firms can take advantage of economies of scale, that is, produce more cheaply by producing large quantities, and that consumers value variety and choice. Thus, he pioneered models of trade in which firms produce similar products and compete in a globalizing marketplace. These models also link globalization to economic geography, helping us to understand where firms and people choose to locate and why. Paul's academic work stands out because of its insights about the real world, in packages that economists love because they are mathematically elegant and deceptively simple. His work on trade, like his work on financial crises and in so many other areas, has launched new avenues of research and literally thousands of academic papers.

Paul's work is also remarkable for its clarity. The lucidity of the writing in his many articles, books, and columns has significantly raised economic literacy around the globe, and as dean of a policy school, I particularly want to highlight his dedication to the importance of clear, analytic thinking as a guide for policy. On a more personal note, I can also attest to the fact that Paul has educated and inspired generations of international and policy-oriented economists. Nearly 30 years ago, his course on international trade was one of the first courses that I took in my doctoral studies at MIT, and I also had the great fortune to benefit from Paul's insights and perspective as a member of my dissertation committee and at numerous points during my career. For all of those reasons and more, I could not be more pleased to call to the stage our 2009 Citigroup Foundation lecturer. Please join me in welcoming Paul Krugman.

REFLECTIONS ON GLOBALIZATION: YESTERDAY AND TODAY

Well, thanks, Susan, and thank you all for coming. I would like to thank the Ford School and the Economics Department for organizing this event, and especially the Festschrift to celebrate the work of Alan Deardorff. Today is a kind of homecoming for me. This is the world in which I started. Because today's occasion is the conference honoring Alan Deardorff's work, I am going to try to address different things than what I mostly talk about these days. Everyone wants to know about the economic crisis, and I will talk about that a bit at the end, and I am sure it will come up in the questions. But at least for starters, I want to talk about my home territory, originally and academically, which is the topic of international trade and globalization.

And since today is really all about honoring Alan Deardorff, I thought I would reminisce for a moment. I got into international economics coming straight out of graduate school in the late 1970s and joined what was then the conference circuit where international economists would meet and many of whom are here now and somehow they all look older. That has not happened to me, of course. Alan Deardorff was at many of the meetings I attended in the late '70s, early '80s. He was extremely distinctive because he was an American, which at the time was quite rare. When I got into international economics, there were only a few Americans and most others came from other places. The way I thought about it was that it was a field dominated by colonials: some Indians, but mostly Canadians and Australians, it seemed at the time. That is probably not true literally, but there were an awful lot of them, which actually imparted a certain character to the conferences. I was later able to pinpoint this character.

Initially I would go to these meetings, and they were incredible. I would come home exhausted, even though I was much younger then, obviously. But even so, I really was having a hard time, and then I actually went to one with a bad cold and was taking cough and cold medicine and could not drink. I did not dare to drink, which is funny because there were all these Canadians and Australians and an awful lot of beer and alcohol at these meetings.

There was a reason why Americans were not that prevalent in international economics at the time: because even then international trade did not seem to be that big a deal for the United States. In 1970, which is about when a lot of people who were on the conference circuit then would have made their decision to be in international economics, imports were only about 5% of GDP. Now they are 17%. So we have had this explosion of international trade, which has turned what was at the time a little bit of a backwater within economics into something that has become enormously important. So I want then to talk about globalization and what it has done, and finish by talking about the role of globalization and the mess we are now in.

But I want to first talk a little bit about history, about the forces of globalization. The first thing you should know in terms of the history is that globalization is not a new phenomenon. It was ongoing in the late 19th century, encouraged by such key inventions as the railroad, steamship, and telegraph. There was a very extensive local economy created in the late 19th century. There is a lot to be learned even now from studying that period. But after World War I, the global economy went into abeyance for a long time. Between the two world wars, there was the Great Depression and protectionism, and a shift by much of the world to inward-looking strategies of economic development. Globalization receded significantly. By 1970, world trade as a share of gross world product was probably back to around what it had been in 1913. Other aspects of globalization were nowhere near their pre-World War I levels. There was not nearly as much flow of capital. Even now, despite all the talk about immigration, there is still less migration of people than there was earlier because there are many legal barriers now that did not exist then, and the legal barriers, although porous, do actually matter.

But just about the time that I was getting into international economics, just about the time that I first met Alan Deardorff, all that was about to change. Now there has been some return. While international trade had grown substantially in the '60s and '70s, it had done so in a kind of limited fashion. Most of what we would now consider the emerging markets were still inwardly turned in their economic policies. What was happening was that there were agreements that had opened up trade between quite similar countries. There was a lot of trade between the United States and Canada and within Western Europe. But much of what we now think of as globalization, certainly China, was not yet in the picture and even the smaller Asian economies were barely there. Things did not look the way they look now.

The analytical work that I and others did, which became a whole movement that ended up with the interesting event for me in Stockholm, was largely about growth and trade, trying to understand why the United States and Canada, which look so similar to each other, do so much trade. Why France and Germany ship automobiles back and forth to each other. It is kind of the way things tend to work in economics that as soon as you have a theory, the world starts moving in a way to make the theory less and less relevant, and so we have actually in some ways moved back to a completely different world, which in some ways, but not in all, resembles the kind of trade that we had in that first age of globalization, before World War I.

What has changed? Two things I think, really, and they were both happening together. When many of us were first involved in the *Handbook of International Economics* at a conference in Princeton in 1982, we had no idea in fact that the world was totally changing, and in a way that certainly I had no sense of at the time.

Two things were really changing. One was technology. The ability to ship things long distances fairly cheaply has been there since the steamship and the railroad. What was the big bottleneck was getting things on and off the ships. A large part of the cost of international trade was taking the cargo off the ship, sorting it out, and dealing with the pilferage that always took place along the way. So, the first big thing that changed was the introduction of the container. When we think about technology that changed the world, we think about glamorous things like the internet. But if you try to figure out what happened to world trade, there is a really strong case to be made that it was the container, which could be hauled off a ship and put onto a truck or a train and moved on. It used to be the case that ports were places with thousands and thousands of longshoremen milling around loading and unloading ships. Now longshoremen are like something out of one of those science fiction movies in which people have disappeared and been replaced by machines.

I have just been rereading a very good book called *The Box*, which is about the big change that occurred between the late 1970s and mid '80s, with a sharp drop in the cost of transactions. This opened up the world and made it possible to do what we do now, which is to produce a good in many different places with the different stages of production and different components. At this point, ask yourself where an iPod is made and the answer is that it is a really complicated question to answer.

The other thing that changed was policy. To some extent, in countries like the United States, we had actually already moved quite a long way towards free trade. What really changed was that many of the developing countries had followed, for 35 years after World War II, a policy of looking inward, of encouraging production for the domestic market. Whether by design or simply because that is the way the policy works, it ended up discouraging exports. What later followed was a great shift towards outward-looking policies, allowing foreign trade to become the engine for growth. The most extreme case, of course, was China, which went from virtually closed to the world to extremely open. And all of a sudden, with this explosion of world trade over a relatively short period of time, trade was no longer interesting just to Canadians, for whom it has always been of keen interest because they have their large neighbor to the south. It was also of great interest to all of us Americans.

What do we know about globalization? I think even now we do not have clear knowledge and are still adjusting our stories. In fact I have actually been changing my own story about globalization a little bit in the last few months because I have been noticing things that I was not paying sufficient attention to. I really should have been more aware, given my interest in globalization and trade. So let me now tell you what I did on my summer vacation. I actually took a vacation, "holidaying in Scotland," relatively recently, and it was kind of depressing. What can an economist do on vacation? They can go to museums that are focused on economics. So in Dundee, Scotland, there is the Verdant Works Museum, which is dedicated to the history of the Dundee jute industry.

If you have not been there, you may think of Dundee — with the name it sounds like some cute little town. But it is a grim, industrial city trying to claw its way back to what it once was. Industrially, it was "juteopolis," the center of the world's jute trade and a long way from its source of jute in the late 19th century. Taking the fibers, which came from India, treating them, drawing them, and eventually making them into burlap bags — it became a huge business. Dundee had more wealth per capita than any other place in Britain.

How should we think about Dundee? Part of it was comparative advantage, which has long pervaded our thinking, insofar as countries trade because they are different. They have different resources, different competencies, and they trade in effect to take advantage of these differences. Obviously Britain had to import the jute because it could not be grown in Scotland for sure. The manufacturing was taking place in Britain because Britain had the capital, the technological skill, and the certain kinds of skilled labor in a way that India at the time was lacking. Later on, actually, the industry moved back to India in the course of its development. But initially, at least, it was something that could be done more efficiently in Britain. But that is not the whole story because it does not say why you would be manufacturing in Dundee.

And there, the answer is much closer to the kinds of things that I have spent a lot of time thinking about in my career, which is the role of increasing returns. As is characteristic of these stories, there are some accidental historical factors that got the industry started. In the early stages, the process of treating the fibers relied on whale oil. While it later turned to mineral oil, initially it was whale oil, and Dundee was a whale importer. It also had ample supplies of flax. The clustering that took place eventually resulted in the production process feeding on itself.

Some years ago, many of us became interested in economic geography and rediscovered the works of the great Victorian economist Alfred Marshall, who focused on these industrial clusters that were very much a story of the time. Marshall emphasized three things. First, there was the creation of a thick market for specialized skilled labor. Second, there were specialized suppliers of equipment and services needed in industry, and, third, there was what we would now call technological spillover. Marshall referred to the mysteries of the trade, but there was no mystery as the developments were in the air. Basically, everybody in Dundee knew all about jute, and so you have this kind of clustering. And that is actually quite typical. If you go back, we tend to think of 19th century trade as having been straightforward. There were different countries, tropical and temperate. There were countries that knew how to do manufacturing and countries that did not — there was actually a lot of clustering going on, not only jute in Dundee, but hosiery and lace in Nottingham, and cutlery in Sheffield. This was the case in the United States as well. Although the United States was protectionist and relatively closed at the time, we also had Paterson, New Jersey, which was the equivalent of Nottingham, and Troy, New York, which was the detachable collar and cuff center. Well, I always love these historical examples.

What about today's world? Today's world is extraordinarily complex, with enormous volumes of trade. When I was first getting into this, we could say that, in some ways, globalization still fell short of what it was in the Edwardian era. We cannot say that now. Now, what we have that did not exist in the past are these complex supply chains in which there are many stages of production. Take the iPod. The iPod's final assembly point is in China, but that assembly involves only about $1.50 of the price of the iPod. For the rest, there are many other stages involving a large number of countries, which creates tremendous shipping back and forth. A lot of this now reflects again differences between countries. The wealthy countries still have advantages. They still have somewhat better technology. They have more skilled labor. They have all of the advantages of being in an advanced country environment in which there is quality control.

While I have not seen it, I understand that there is a new book called *Poorly Made in China*. While even now there are still differences in competence, on the other hand, developing countries have inexpensive labor and in some cases reasonably good productivity and manufacturing capability. Thus, we have trade going back and forth that is based upon these differences. The goods and stages are still required to be produced in advanced country environments, but other stages are done in developing countries. What is going on is similar to my story about Dundee. Except what is interesting these days is that if you want to find those clearly defined industrial clusters, those cities where a particular sort of narrow competence leads to a dominance of the whole city economy, you find them best in the emerging markets in the developing world.

If you go around China, you will find, comparable to Dundee that was the "juteopolis" in the late 19th century, the "underwear" city of Yanbu in the 21st century. There are these clusters. It is probably a foregone conclusion that we are going to have labor-intensive apparel produced in China or now moving down to even lower-wage countries like Vietnam. But the details depend a lot on whether some particular town or city can develop a specialty and derive the advantages of this clustering, that is, the advantages of the scale of production in a particular locality.

I should mention by the way, since again this is Alan Deardorff's Festschrift, that this whole process of fragmentation of production, which has made it possible to have this huge volume of world trade, is one of the areas in which he has done much. When we were just starting to see the surge in exports from smaller Asian countries, we used to say that there is only a limited amount of these labor-intensive manufactures that they can export. I remember specifically saying, "What will happen when China tries to do this?" There is not possibly enough labor-intensive manufactures to be able to segment the production of goods based on these labor-intensive stages of production.

Nonetheless, the process of fragmentation has gained a lot of momentum because of the interaction of technological and political changes. The technological changes meant that some countries could do very well by integrating with the global economy, which led other countries to be more willing to liberalize their policies and do the same thing, which resulted in the explosive growth of globalization. The question is whether this is a good thing or a bad thing. The answer, of course, is yes.

First of all, the world economy is richer because of the increased globalization. It is richer both because we have countries concentrating on the things they do relatively well. Note that this does not mean they do them absolutely well. Actually, for any given thing, it is almost certain that U.S. labor is more productive than Chinese labor, although this varies quite a lot. So by having the Chinese do the things in which they are relatively productive, we get the whole world producing efficiently, and this means that world wealth has increased. In addition, the world market makes it possible to do a lot of things on an efficient scale. In some cases, this is not just by having a really big factory, but in many cases having many factories in a place where the firms produce mutually reinforcing advantages.

Thus, in the end, the world is a richer place because the underwear makers of Yanbu are more efficient than any national, purely domestic, market-oriented underwear city could be. So we have a world that is clearly richer. That does not mean that everybody benefits equally, since there are many dislocations and distributional effects. The most obvious and the one that we worry about a lot is that workers with lower formal education in advanced countries are almost certainly hurt by imports. That inequality is wider to some extent because of globalization. I would argue that the evidence still suggests that this is a secondary factor. But inequality has widened, and globalization is probably part of it and has probably hurt workers in advanced countries.

If you take a global citizen point of view, though, you may want to say that those losses are less dramatic than the huge gains that many workers have achieved in the developing world. There is a real trap here for concerned people in the advanced world. That is, there is a tendency to compare the ugly reality of life for workers in today's developing countries with an abstraction of what some may think it ought to be or with an idealized picture of what it used to be like, rather than with reality. So sometimes it almost comes out as condescending thinking about happy peasants living their traditional lives in comparison with the actual lives of workers, which may be terrible. But the fact of the matter is, given the reality, that developing countries were incredibly poor in 1970, that some of them have now achieved a really large increase in their standard of living. Even if this still looks pretty bad to us, there has nonetheless been a tremendous amount of progress. Hundreds and perhaps billions of people now live better lives because of globalization. But it is a mixed picture, and it has also turned out to be much harder than I think many economists believed to actually reap those gains from globalization.

When the great takeoff of some East Asian economies took place, a lot of people thought that if you just opened yourself up to world markets, the benefits would be obvious. A number of countries, particularly in Latin America, did open themselves up to world markets and have not achieved great results. So it has turned out that there is a much more mixed and more uncertain picture than we were hoping it would be. But if you had asked me two years ago how globalization is going, I would have said, "Well, it is certainly not wonderful, but there are a lot of good things that have taken place." And that, on the whole, globalization has been a force for good.

But, as we all know, something happened to us recently, so we now have the world economy going through this terrible crisis. What can we say about the role of globalization in this and the future of globalization? Where are we currently? And by the way, of course — if you read your history — you cannot help but recall that the single biggest force killing the original global economy was the Great Depression of the 1930s. We are now in a world slump that bears a definite family resemblance to what happened in the early 1930s. Is it all going to happen again? What does it say about where we are going for now?

The current crisis has been awesome, of course. The first year of the crisis tracks the Great Depression very closely. It actually turns out that the initial fall in industrial production was not as big as it was in 1929 and 1930, but the initial fall in world trade in the current crisis was actually sharper than it was in 1929 and 1930. While the fall in GDP in the current crisis may have been of the Great Depression scale, it does appear to have stabilized. So it appears that Armageddon has been put on hold for at least a while. The apocalypse has been postponed, but it has been a pretty shocking crisis and of course we are nowhere near being out of the woods.

It is interesting to ask whether globalization paved the way for the crisis. Well, certainly not in the simple sense that all this increased trade was directly responsible for the crisis. In this case, if you want to look for causes of the crisis, you should look more at the financial side of globalization, which of course is not independent. So, if you are looking for where things went wrong, you might say that, as China became more deeply integrated into the world economy, it also stumbled into a policy of accumulating huge reserves, which led to a lot of cheap money in the United States that helped feed our housing bubble. This is an indirect chain but certainly is part of the story. You could also say that, in a more limited sense, we tend to think of this crisis as having been a primarily U.S. event. But actually, much happened in Europe as well, and their more localized globalization played a big role. That is, there was a lot of lending to Eastern European emerging nations that was in its own way as big and imbalanced as the U.S.-China imbalance and has ended in similarly severe grief.

So you can certainly say that the opening up of world capital markets, the opening up of world capital flows, played a definite role in generating the current crisis. Globalization has certainly therefore played a role in propagating the crisis.

One of the things that has been remarkable is that you know obviously the places of the financial excesses were in the United States, the United Kingdom, and arguably in different ways in some of the European countries that had enormous housing bubbles, such as Spain. But the punishment has not been borne, if you look cross-country, very much in relation to the crime. Thus, the steepest falls in GDP, at least initially, actually came in countries that did not have runaway financial sectors and did not have housing bubbles, in particular Japan and Germany. After all, what was their sin? Their sin was being deeply integrated in the world economy and being exporters of durable manufactured goods, which took the biggest hit. So the biggest declines in GDP, at least initially, have come in countries that were being hit through world trade, and all of this is possible because we have such an integrated global economy. And that contributes to what is in some ways the most troubling feature of this crisis looking forward, which is that it hit everybody.

There is another sense in which globalization helped lead to a synchronized crisis, and this is a little bit softer but still very important. One of the effects of globalization has been people looking for profit, which involves movement of goods and services and money. It also produces an integration of thought. More and more, we are all certainly culture-bound. There has been concern about the horrors of cultural homogenization, which is, whatever you think of it, very real. We certainly all dress alike around the world. We all watch the same kind of entertainment, and we all think alike. This means that with intellectual trends, the conventional wisdom at the moment is now a global convention rather than a national convention of wisdom. And, in particular, pretty much everyone around the world thought it was a great idea to deregulate banking at the same time so that when the house of cards came down, it came down everywhere, which makes this very difficult currently.

We have had an awesome financial crisis. It is not, now that we have seen it happen, that hard to understand. We look at it, and it is a more or less historically standard banking crisis but dressed in different clothes. So, if you go back to the early 1930s, there was a wave of banking failures and bank runs, and such things have happened in individual countries since then. This time, we had pretty good guarantees for banks as conventionally defined, that is, basically, big marble buildings that take deposits. The trouble was that we had failed to do anything about the growth of institutions that functionally are banks, borrowing short and lending long, but were not called banks, did not look like banks, and were not strictly speaking depository institutions. But once you take all of this into account, what we have had is the 21st century functional equivalent of 1931 around the world. So this time, bank runs do not consist of hordes of people out in the street banging on the doors. They consist of hordes of people on the internet clicking their mouses, but it has the same effect and is played out very similarly. And we have had, thank God, a pretty high-risk emergency response. We have learned something these past 75 years and appear to have contained it from being a total collapse.

But what comes next? Well, we have had a number of more localized banking crises around the world since the Great Depression. We have had Mexico and Argentina, and then Mexico again, and then Argentina again, and the Asian countries, and Sweden and Finland. All of these crises were very nasty. We know that the IMF has done a lot of reaching back in history to ask what happens in a crisis, and the answer is that financial crises not only are severe but may take a long time to recover from. There is one other thing that becomes very clear from the record, which is that with all modern financial crises, the economic recovery relies crucially on the same thing, which is that the crisis-afflicted country recovers to a large extent, at least for a while, by running big trade surpluses. It basically pulls itself out of its hole by selling a lot of goods and services to parts of the world that were not caught up in the crisis. I think you see the problem. Unless we can find another planet to export to, the normal exit from a financial crisis — not the stabilization itself, which I think has been achieved, but the actual return to something that looks like a reasonably fully employed economy — is not clearly available. I see crisis-afflicted countries like Argentina, the East Asian economies, or even Japan emerging temporarily from its lost decade of growth, being able to recover through export surpluses. But this may no longer be available under the present circumstances.

So if you are looking for a precedent for a world economy managing to emerge from a financial crisis and fully recovering from the effects of the crisis, where everybody is caught up in it and where countries are not able to do it by running trade surpluses, you actually have to go back to recovery from the Great Depression itself, when the full recovery was achieved through a large public spending program known as World War II. So it is not a very encouraging prospect.

The last time we had a global crisis in the Great Depression, one of the effects was to roll back globalization for a long period of time. This does not seem to be happening right now. Although, yes, there are tariffs being imposed on tires and other products, there has been nothing like the kind of protectionist response that took place in the 1930s, and not much sign that it is going to happen. The question I guess one might ask is, maybe, "Should it happen?" We seem to have a global economy in which our institutions have been lagging. We are not in a position in managing to find global solutions to the crisis. We are just managing to find ad hoc patches to keep the global economy from totally falling apart. We are to a certain extent holding the economy together with Scotch tape and chewing gum. But is there a reason, given the crisis, to roll back globalization? I think you could actually possibly make that case, but I do not think that it is going to happen because the advantages of globalization are still very real.

It is widely understood that protectionism was a major cause of the Great Depression. This is perhaps arguably not true, and in any case it stands out as a cautionary tale. This means that we need to find a way to deal with the crisis. One way to look at the world right now is that we actually created this global economy without creating the institutions that we need to manage it. We are still in a world of national policies. Even though we have supranational institutions, they are not functioning very well. So, for example, the European Union (EU) is looking awfully disunited when it comes to economic policies these days. While the EU members are highly interdependent, they do not seem to be able to make policies jointly.

We have had international cooperation with some of the emergency measures in the crisis, but they have been amazingly dependent on personal contact. You could argue that we managed to save the world basically because Jean-Claude Trichet, Mervin King, and Ben Bernanke were able to agree on things that needed to be done in the heat of the moment. And while I would like to have a rule that the believers of policies would always be in the hands of smart, bearded Princeton professors, that is not something we can really count on in the future. So we have not yet come to terms with this enormously moral degrading economy; this economy that I have to admit, 30 years ago, when I was getting into international trade, I never imagined would be this relevant; and we have no choice in the end. One could imagine rolling back trade flows in the face of a crisis. It is not technologically impossible to go back to a world of relatively inward-looking economies. But there are other ways in which we are globalized, like it or not. The atmosphere does not care where a ton of carbon dioxide gets emitted, and we are now at a stage where those global constraints bind enormously on all of us. In fact, we are globalized whether we like it or not.

It is an amazing and frightening time. I would like to think that we will come out of all this with the understanding that we really need to go beyond just trusting this vast, global economic machine to do the right thing and figure that we actually need to have some adult supervision of the entire system. Maybe it will actually happen. We are supposed to be optimistic, right? Otherwise, what is the point? So, amazing times. As a citizen of the world, I am quite horrified at what we are going through. A little less frightened than I was six months ago but still uneasy with the prospect.

But this is an occasion to analyze economic research and to celebrate the accomplishments of Alan Deardorff. As an economic researcher, I have to say that I am in clover. It is like watching Mount St. Helens erupt, a great time for study, unfortunately not a great time to live through. Thank you.[2]

---

[2] Following the lecture, there were a number of questions posed by the audience to which Professor Krugman responded. These questions covered a variety of issues, many of which were not germane to the subject of the lecture. The questions and Professor Krugman's responses are available on request.

PART II

COMPARATIVE ADVANTAGE IN A CHANGING GLOBAL ECONOMY

CHAPTER 3

Alan Deardorff on Comparative Advantage

James E. Anderson

Boston College and NBER

Alphabetical order puts me at the head of a distinguished panel with far more authority than I to speak on the subject of comparative advantage. I will be appropriately brief. But perhaps my perspective as a consumer rather than as a producer here will be useful.

In my opinion the writings of Alan Deardorff on comparative advantage are a great example of progress in economic theory and its connection to empirical confirmation. Almost 30 years later, it seems like we have always known these ideas. Appreciating the greatness of his 1980 and 1982 papers requires recalling the scene in which they appeared.

The theory of comparative advantage before 1980 was a compelling and beautiful insight essentially based on a toy world of two goods and two countries. The factor proportions theory of comparative advantage gave additional, compelling insights in special cases such as two factors or factor price equalization. Only a little more generality had been achieved.

Moreover, technical difficulties with the logic of comparative advantage in a world of costly trade were suggested by demonstrations that introducing or changing trade costs could reverse the direction of trade in some goods. The distance of the assumptions from the real world was so extreme that empirical confirmation seemed impossible.

Those of us teaching trade theory in the '70s felt there must be some truth to the logic, but comparative advantage was like a parable, not science. We might have been accused of mistaking mathematical beauty for economic truth, a charge Krugman recently leveled at the macro-economic work of the last 25 years.

Progress made in the '70s in refining the dual approach to modeling trade set the stage for using the mathematics of convex structure to analyze comparative advantage in high dimensions.

Alan discovered (more or less simultaneously with Dixit and Norman) the basic logic of comparative advantage extended to many goods and countries, many factors, without factor price equalization, and with costly trade. His propositions are an early example of the now common approach of looking for sufficient statistics that describe distributions of outcomes implied by models as opposed to a full catalog. On average, a country's trade vector will export goods that in autarky would be relatively cheap and import goods that in autarky would be relatively expensive. "On average" is defined as an easily interpreted covariance or correlation. On average, the factor content of a country's trade vector will export factors that in autarky would be relatively cheap and import factors that in autarky would be relatively expensive. Here the logic required "on average" to mean a covariance among three variables that Alan termed a "comvariance." His beautiful, spare expressions contained enough real-world complexity so that the theory could actually be tested. The work of Bernhofen and Brown (2004, 2009) shows that both the general theory of comparative advantage of 1980 and the factor proportions theory of 1982 are confirmed by the data.

On re-reading Alan's papers I was struck again by how general they are, and how much they look toward confirmation. In particular, I want to mention his treatment of costly trade in the 1980 paper and his treatment of the factor content of trade in the 1982 paper.

I have recently struggled with integrating trade costs with general equilibrium myself, so I especially appreciate his clean and very general model of resource costs of trade. The key insight is to model equilibrium, working backward from delivered products through the technology of distribution and production. I suspect there may be clues in Alan's 1980 paper for going beyond iceberg trade costs and yet still getting something like gravity to work with.

As to factor content, Alan's concern for measurement led him to analyze the consequences of what looked like several reasonable ways of defining factor content when techniques differ internationally. His discussion clarified what would be needed in a world without factor price equalization and paved the way for Bernhofen and Brown's 2009 paper.

REFERENCES

Bernhofen, Daniel and John Brown, 2004, A direct test of the theory of comparative advantage: The case of Japan, *Journal of Political Economy* 112(1), 48–67.

Bernhofen, Daniel and John Brown, 2009, Testing the general validity of the Heckscher–Ohlin theorem: The natural experiment of Japan, Nottingham University.

Deardorff, Alan V., 1980, The general validity of the law of comparative advantage, *Journal of Political Economy* 88(5), 941–957.

Deardorff, Alan V., 1982, The general validity of the Heckscher–Ohlin theorem, *American Economic Review* 72(4), 683–694.

CHAPTER 4

Comparative Advantage in a Changing Global Economy

Avinash Dixit

Princeton University

It is a special pleasure and privilege for me to be speaking at Alan Deardorff's 65th birthday celebration, and on the subject of comparative advantage. We have close connections in both respects. We were born only two days apart — he on D-day, and I on D + 2. And for a while we worked along closely parallel lines, albeit in total ignorance of each other's work. I still remember the pleasure I felt when I discovered his papers on generalizing comparative advantage: the fact that someone deeply immersed in the traditions of international trade had independently thought it useful to reformulate the question in the same way, and proceed to develop the theory very similarly, was comforting to Victor Norman and me, who were relative amateurs bumbling into the field.

So let me begin by recalling some of this work: Deardorff (1980, 1982) and Dixit and Norman (1980, pp. 94–102). The theory of comparative advantage used to be developed assuming that there were only two goods, implying that there was only one relative price. The country that had the lower relative price of a good in autarky would export that good when trade opened up. The theory then considered various determinants of the relative price in a closed economy, most notably productivities (Ricardo) and factor endowments (Heckscher–Ohlin). But when more goods were allowed, it was quickly found that strong generalizations of this prediction on a good-by-good basis were invalid, basically because with three or more goods, complementarity is possible, and that ruins monotonicity of the relationship between relative excess supplies and relative prices.

One way out of this would have been to assume gross substitutes, but that would be assuming away a significant real-world possibility. Alan, and independently Victor and I, came to the conclusion that the question had been wrongly posed. Instead of asking under what highly (and unrealistically) restrictive assumptions one could get a good-by-good generalization of the traditional result, one should ask how far one can get with economically sensible assumptions. It turned out that a simple and intuitively appealing result was available. The two-good result generalizes in the sense of an average: there is a positive correlation across goods between the standard determinants of comparative advantage and the pattern of exports.

Let P^a and P^{*a} denote the vectors of autarkic equilibrium prices in the home and foreign countries, and let X denote the vector of home's net exports. Then a simple revealed preference argument shows that

$$(P^{*a} - P^a) \bullet X \geq 0,$$

where • denotes inner product. When prices are suitably normalized, the inner product becomes a covariance. Therefore the home country on average exports those goods for which it has the lower autarkic relative price.

With many countries, Alan pushed the argument further. Stack the autarkic price vectors of all countries into a giant vector P, and similarly stack the vectors of their exports into a giant vector X. Then the revealed preference and market clearing arguments for all the countries can be combined into the result $P^a \bullet X \leq 0$, which has a similar correlation interpretation.

In the Ricardian model, each country's autarkic prices of goods are proportional to its labor requirement per unit output of those goods, so the result directly translates into the result that a country on average exports those goods for which it has lower unit labor requirements. In fact even stronger results are available in the Ricardian case. In the Heckscher–Ohlin model, we need a further step to get from factor endowments to autarkic relative prices, and again the generally valid result is a kind of correlation. The two lines of work on this were related but distinct.

Victor Norman and I worked with the GDP function $G(P, V)$ of output prices P and factor quantities V. Revealed preference arguments yield

$$G(P^{*a}, V^*) - G(P^{*a}, V) - G(P^a, V^*) + G(P^a, V) \leq 0.$$

For small differences in endowments, we have a Taylor approximation

$$(P^{*a} - P^a)' R(V^* - V) \leq 0,$$

where $R = G_{PV}$ is the matrix of the Rybczynski terms, and therefore related to factor intensities. This can be interpreted as saying that the home country on average has lower autarkic prices for those goods that use its relatively abundant factors relatively more intensively. This can be combined with the previous correlation between autarkic price differences and export quantities to get a vague sort of Heckscher–Ohlin conclusion.

Alan worked with factor prices and obtained a tighter result. With many countries, goods, and factors, he defined giant vectors ω, θ, and τ, where

$$\omega_{hij} = \frac{\bar{w}_h - w_h^{aj}}{\bar{w}_h},$$

the relative shortfall of country j's autarkic (a) price of factor h below the average across countries for this factor (the right-hand side is the same for all goods i);

$$\theta_{hij} = \frac{\bar{w}_h \, g_{hi}^{tj}}{p_i^w},$$

where g_{hi}^{tj} is the actual factor requirement matrix under trade (t) and p_i^w is the world prices of goods, so θ_{hij} is kind of the Jonesian factor shares; and

$$\tau_{hij} = p_i^w X_i^j$$

is net exports valued at world prices (the right-hand side is the same for all factors h). Then he showed that the "comvariance" between these three vectors, defined as

$$\text{com}(\omega,\theta,\tau) = \sum_{h,i,j} (\omega_{hij} - \bar{\omega})(\theta_{hij} - \bar{\theta})(\tau_{hij} - \bar{\tau}),$$

is non-negative (the bars indicate averaging across all three subscripts). This says that on average, countries export those goods which use their relatively cheaper (and more abundant, in this sense) factors relatively more intensively. This is a cleaner result, although there are the usual problems, which Alan recognizes and discusses, in going from factor abundance in the price sense to that in the quantity sense. A by-product of this analysis is the interesting and more widely useful notion of comvariance.

Alan recently returned to this topic (Deardorff, 2005), and gave a detailed overview of the literature. In the intervening years, conventional comparative advantage seemed to be on the way out. Trade among similar countries based on scale economies and product differentiation had attracted more interest from theorists and empirical economists alike. The traditional misunderstanding and suspicion of comparative advantage and gains from trade in the general public and special interests in policy debates were reinforced by these developments in the subject: they could now argue that the new ideas had rendered comparative advantage irrelevant. But the last decade or so has seen a revival of North-South trade based on differences in factor endowments and technologies, and therefore a revival of comparative advantage. To quote the prime mover of the new theories (Krugman, 2009):

> nobody doubts that trade between the United States and Mexico, where wages are only 13 percent of the US level, or China, where they are only about 4 percent, reflects comparative advantage rather than arbitrary, scale-based specialization. The old trade theory has regained relevance.

On rereading the material on comparative advantage after many years, I see some significant differences between Alan's work and the Dixit–Norman work, and must admit that they mostly favor Alan. He pursued the issues much more tenaciously, seeking results with many countries, under restricted trade, for different concepts of factor content, and so on, whereas Victor and I were content to establish just one main result for free trade between two countries. Alan also had a much deeper understanding and appreciation of the previous literature on the subject, and of the precise reasons for the anomalies that had been observed, and built his arguments on those foundations. More generally, Alan's writing shows, even at that young age, a mature and professional understanding of the subject, where Victor and I were amateur interlopers. I am happy to have participated in this line of research, and happier to acknowledge that Alan in many respects did better.

I want to mention another occasion when our research interacted, even though it is only indirectly connected to my assigned topic of comparative advantage. Victor Norman and I had developed the "integrated world equilibrium diagram" as a way to understand factor price equalization (Dixit and Norman, 1980, pp. 110–125, 289–292; see also Dixit, 2010). Our method gave a necessary and sufficient condition for factor price equalization in the case of two countries (and any number of goods and factors): the point representing the two countries' endowments in the Edgeworth-type world factor quantity diagram should lie within a set, often called a "lens," obtained by chaining together the factor requirements for the production of the integrated world equilibrium quantities of the goods. The rough intuition is that factor endowments should vary less across countries than factor intensities vary across goods. But extensions to many countries and many factors remained elusive. In Deardorff (1994), Alan took a major step forward. He constructed a corresponding lens composed of all countries' factor endowments, and proved that for factor price equalization it is necessary that the countries' factor endowment lens lies entirely inside the goods' factor requirement lens. His proof, following a suggestion by Bill Ethier, was very elegant. Subsequent work (Demiroglu and Yun, 1999) found further conditions under which the lens-inclusion property is also sufficient for factor price equalization.

International trade is not the first context in which I came across Alan's work. At the risk of departing even further from my remit and encroaching on the subject of the next panel, namely trade and growth, I want to mention one paper, because in this group I may be the only person who knows and remembers it.

Samuelson (1975) set out to find the "goldenest rule of growth." In an overlapping generations model with production, he sought to choose not only the saving rule for each generation and the steady state capital/labor ratio, but also the rate of growth of population, to maximize the steady state utility of each. But Alan (Deardorff, 1976) found that the great man had made a small mistake: under the usual assumption of such models, namely Cobb–Douglas production and utility functions, the second-order condition shows that Samuelson's solution minimizes utility: it is the worst steady state! Samuelson's reply (1976) begins: "*Mea culpa.*"

It ends: "Economists are in Professor Deardorff's debt, none more than I." This is the perfect occasion for all of us to join in Samuelson's encomium. And not only, or even primarily, for correcting Samuelson's error; no one would have chosen to implement his solution for population growth anyway. No; we applaud and thank Alan for his whole corpus of work.

REFERENCES

Deardorff, Alan V., 1976, The optimum growth rate for population: Comment, *International Economic Review* 17(2), 510–515.

Deardorff, Alan V., 1980, The general validity of the law of comparative advantage, *Journal of Political Economy* 88(5), 941–957.

Deardorff, Alan V., 1982, The general validity of the Heckscher–Ohlin theorem, *American Economic Review* 92(4), 683–694.

Deardorff, Alan V., 1994, The possibility of factor price equalization, revisited, *Journal of International Economics* 36(2), 167–175.

Deardorff, Alan V., 2005, How robust is comparative advantage?, *Review of International Economics* 13(5), 1004–1016.

Demiroglu, Ufuk and Kwan Koo Yun, 1999, The lens condition for factor price equalization, *Journal of International Economics* 47(2), 449–456.

Dixit, Avinash, 2010, The integrated world equilibrium diagram from international trade theory, Chapter 44, in Mark Blaug and Peter Lloyd, eds., Famous Figures and Diagrams in Economics (Edward Elgar, Cheltenham).

Dixit, Avinash and Victor Norman, 1980, Theory of International Trade (Cambridge University Press, Cambridge).

Krugman, Paul, 2009, The increasing returns revolution in trade and geography, *American Economic Review* 99(3), 561–571.

Samuelson, Paul, 1975, The optimum growth rate for population, *International Economic Review* 16(4), 539–544.

Samuelson, Paul, 1976, The optimum growth rate for population: Agreement and evaluation, *International Economic Review* 17(2), 516–525.

CHAPTER 5

Comparative Advantage Meets Alan Deardorff

Wilfred J. Ethier

University of Pennsylvania
International School of Economics at Tbilisi State University

We are here to praise Alan Deardorff — hopefully not yet to bury him. This is a delightful task (the praise, I mean), and not just because of his accomplishments, which I'll get to in a minute, but because Alan is one of the truly kind and decent people in our profession, and I feel privileged to have known him over these many years.

I am charged to address Alan's contributions to comparative advantage. This accounts for a considerable share of his total contribution.

Comparative advantage trade is trade to exploit international differences, whether differences in tastes, technology, or factor endowments, or whether differences due to national economic policies. More formally, a comparative advantage world is defined by the twin assumptions of perfect competition in all markets and no externalities.

The principle of comparative advantage describes the consequences of international trade in the classical setting where international factor markets do not exist. There are two aspects: the normative and the positive.

The normative component is the gains-from-trade theorem: If international trade replaces autarky, gainers gain more than losers lose in each country and therefore in the world as a whole. This result is a direct reflection of the basic nature of a comparative advantage world and, as such, remarkably free of other qualifications.

The positive component offers predictions of the pattern of trade and of the effect of trade, for each country, on relative prices and on the pattern of production. But, in contrast to the normative component, these predictions are quite sensitive to model detail: the number of goods, especially.

The principle of comparative advantage was derived as a response to basic concerns of economic policy. Its derivation was critical to the development of international trade theory and to classical economics more generally, and it remains the preeminent accomplishment of the theory of international trade.

For trade theorists, it's been all downhill ever since.

Alan's contributions to comparative advantage theory have been numerous and wide-ranging. These contributions were without doubt separately conceived, but, with the aid of hindsight, one can see that a remarkably coherent and wide-ranging research program was nevertheless accomplished.

First, nearly all of Alan's research — not just that directed explicitly at comparative advantage — has been conducted entirely in the framework of a comparative advantage world. Second, his work on comparative advantage trade theory has concentrated predominantly on the positive aspect of comparative advantage, not the normative. Third, that work has been successful in addressing the limitations of the positive approach in an impressively comprehensive way. Fourth, the whole effort has been characterized by an informed perseverance and clarity of vision consistent with a very large, deliberate, comprehensive, and early-conceived research program.

A fundamental contribution — both seminal in its own right and basic to Alan's larger accomplishment — was Alan's explication (Deardorff, 1980) of the general validity of the positive predictions of comparative advantage in higher dimensions. (Similar work was done contemporaneously and independently by Dixit and Norman, 1980). These predictions had previously been understood and expressed in simple two-good, two-country models. This fundamental contribution, which resolved questions that had lingered since the very inception of comparative advantage theory, was achieved relatively early in Alan's career.

So, for Alan also, it has been all downhill ever since.

Alan was able to generalize each of the positive predictions of traditional comparative advantage theory to a correlation among the relevant variables. Each correlation reduced to the standard textbook result in the 2×2 case. But, as a single constraint on the relevant set of variables, each correlation had less and less bite as the dimensionality increased. Thus the sensitivity of the result to dimensionality was rendered quite clear.

Since these results are basic, they must have wide applicability to trade theory. Alan has indeed done such application, extending the results to the relation between price and output changes (Deardorff, 1980a), considering the implications of transport costs (Deardorff, 1987) and of services (Deardorff, 1985), and considering in general the domain of relevance of comparative advantage (Deardorff, 2005a, 1994b). Not surprisingly, Alan's interventions have been especially effective when, as in Deardorff (1984, 1979), a multiplicity of goods is at center stage.

Comparative advantage trade can be generated by international differences in tastes, technology, or relative factor endowments. Alan explores them all, singly and in combination (*e.g.*, Deardorff, 1986, for preferences and Deardorff, 2005b, for technology), but the beauty is in the fruitful interplay with distinct and common features of basic trade models, an interplay for which Alan has always demonstrated an uncanny skill.

Alan utilized his basic correlation approach in deriving a general version (Deardorff, 1982) of the Heckscher–Ohlin theorem, which describes the pattern of trade in a comparative advantage world in which comparative advantage is determined solely by international differences in relative factor endowments. The Heckscher–Ohlin approach provides the framework for a wide array of contributions (*e.g.*, Deardorff, 2000, 1994b, 1974; Deardorff and Staiger, 1988).

In a series of papers (Courant and Deardorff, 1993, 1992, 1990; Deardorff, 1993) Alan, usually with Paul Courant, examines the trade, and general performance, of "lumpy" countries. These are countries that trade with the rest of the world and that may impose country-wide trade barriers, that are composed of distinct regions with limited interregional factor mobility (and thus regional disparities in factor endowments).

This is much in the spirit of Ohlin's (1967) notion of interregional economic relations. It contrasts with, but is a very natural complement to, the "new" economic geography (which differs most notably from the "old" in its choice of heroes). The latter endogenizes regional disparities, whereas the lumpy-trade models analyze the relation of such disparities to international trade. While Alan deliberately remains in a comparative advantage world, the economic geography literature consciously does not.

The theory of comparative advantage is central to trade theory and, indeed, is its crowning achievement. Alan has been outstanding in doing it justice. Sometimes nice guys do indeed finish first.

REFERENCES

Courant, P.V. and A.V. Deardorff, 1993, Amenities, nontraded goods, and the trade of lumpy countries, *Journal of Urban Economics* 34, 299–317.

Courant, P.V. and A.V. Deardorff, 1992, International trade with lumpy countries, *Journal of Political Economy* 100, 198–210.

Courant, P.V. and A.V. Deardorff, 1990, On the likelihood of factor price equalization with nontraded goods, *International Economic Review* 31, 589–596.

Deardorff, A.V., 2005a, How robust is comparative advantage?, *Review of International Economics* 13, 1004–1016.

Deardorff, A.V., 2005b, Ricardian comparative advantage with intermediate inputs, *North American Journal of Economics and Finance* 16, 11–34.

Deardorff, A.V., 2000, Factor prices and the factor content of trade revisited: What's the use?, *Journal of International Economics* 50(1), 73–90.

Deardorff, A.V., 1994a, Exploring the limits of comparative advantage, *Weltwirtschaftliches Archiv* 130, 1–19.

Deardorff, A.V., 1994b, The possibility of factor price equalization, revisited, *Journal of International Economics* 36, 167–175; reprinted in Rodney E. Falvey and Udo Kreickemeier, eds., *Recent Developments in International Trade Theory* (Edward Elgar, London), 2004.

Deardorff, A.V. and R.W. Staiger, 1988, An interpretation of the factor content of trade, *Journal of International Economics* 24, 93–107; reprinted in David Greenaway and Douglas R. Nelson, eds., *Globalization and Labour Markets* (Edward Elgar, Cheltenham).

Deardorff, A.V., 1987, The directions of developing countries' trade: Examples from pure theory, in Oli Havrylyshyn, ed., *Exports of Developing Countries: How Direction Affects Performance* (The World Bank, Washington), pp. 9–21.

Deardorff, A.V., 1986, FIRless FIRwoes: How preferences can interfere with the theorems of international trade, *Journal of International Economics* 20, 131–142.

Deardorff, A.V., 1985, Comparative advantage and international trade and investment in services, in Robert M. Stern, ed., *Trade and Investment in Services: Canada/U.S. Perspectives* (Ontario Economic Council, Toronto), pp. 39–71.

Deardorff, A.V., 1984, An exposition and exploration of Krueger's trade model, *Canadian Journal of Economics* 17, 731–746.

Deardorff, A.V., 1982, The general validity of the Heckscher–Ohlin theorem, *American Economic Review* 72, 683–694.

Deardorff, A.V., 1980a, The correlation between price and output changes when there are many goods, *Journal of International Economics* 10, 441–443.

Deardorff, A.V., 1980b, The general validity of the law of comparative advantage, *Journal of Political Economy* 88, 941–957; reprinted in J. Peter Neary, ed., International Trade (Edward Elgar Publishing Co., Aldershot), 1995; reprinted in Edward Leamer, ed., International Economics (Worth Publishers, New York), 2001.

Deardorff, A.V., 1979, Weak links in the chain of comparative advantage, *Journal of International Economics* 9, 197–209; reprinted in Jagdish N. Bhagwati, ed., International Trade: Selected Readings (M.I.T. Press, Cambridge, MA), 1981, and 2nd ed., 1987.

Deardorff, A.V., 1974, Factor proportions and comparative advantage in the long run: Comment, *Journal of Political Economy* 82, 829–833.

Deardorff, A.V., 1993, Directions of lumpy country trade, in W. Ethier, E. Helpman, and P. Neary, eds., Theory, Policy and Dynamics in International Trade (Cambridge University Press, Cambridge), pp. 55–72.

Dixit, A.K. and V. Norman, 1980, Theory of International Trade (Cambridge University Press, Cambridge).

Ohlin, B., 1967, Interregional and International Trade (Harvard University Press, Cambridge, MA).

CHAPTER 6

In Defense of Cones

Ronald W. Jones

University of Rochester

A basic question asked of any model dealing with a country engaged in international trade is "what does this country produce?" This is a question that must be raised even if there is a specified list of what commodities the country consumes and what commodities it is technologically capable of producing. The reason is that international trade allows a country's production pattern to be even more specialized than its consumption pattern and, in special cases, for this degree of specialization to reach the extreme limit in which only one commodity is produced, with this commodity exported in exchange for a myriad of imported commodities that are consumed. At the other end of possible scenarios is one in which, with a given number of inputs available at home, the number of commodities that a country produces in a competitive, free-trade equilibrium setting need not exceed the count of its productive factors. For example, in a labor-only Ricardian model a trading economy facing given world prices (given independently of its own technology and tastes) need only produce and export a single commodity in which it has its greatest comparative advantage (relative to the given world commodity prices), and will import the rest of its consumption bundle from its export proceeds. In the simple 2×2 form of the Heckscher–Ohlin scenario with, say, capital and labor the only two factors of production, the country may be specialized to produce a single commodity, or may be required to produce a mixture of both commodities in order to achieve full employment of both its productive factors. In this latter case there will typically exist an entire range of possible factor endowments for which both these same commodities will be produced in a trading equilibrium. Such a range is referred to as the *cone of diversification.*[1]

THE TWO-COMMODITY CASE

Figure 1 illustrates such a cone for a two-commodity case in which the two curves depend both upon the country's best technology for producing commodities 1 and 2 and

[1] For an early use of this phrase see the magisterial survey of international trade theory by John Chipman, *Econometrica* (1966), especially Part 3. The concept of a cone of diversification has frequently been used to good effect by Alan Deardorff, most recently in his article (2010) on the diagram made famous by Abba Lerner (1952) (after originally appearing as a student paper in 1933 at the London School of Economics).

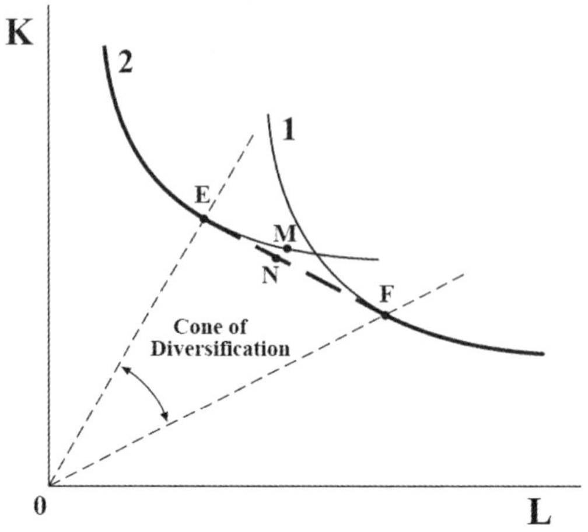

Fig. 1. Cone of diversification

upon world prices (and let the dollar be the unit of account), so that these curves represent the pair of *unit-value isoquants.* The inner convex hull of this pair, including the tangent cord *ENF*, is often referred to as the Hicksian composite unit-value isoquant, or the array of best ways of earning a dollar by producing for world markets for given world prices. The actual production choice depends, of course, on the country's endowment bundle of capital and labor. If the endowment ray lies in the *cone* determined by the tangency points *E* and *F*, the factor price ratio, *w/r*, will be given by the absolute value of the slope of the tangent cord. Should the endowment ray lie outside the cone, the country will be completely specialized to produce a single commodity, say, commodity 2 for a country with a high capital/labor endowment ratio, and the factor price ratio will be indicated by the slope of the isoquant. To see the importance and relevance of the tangent cord, *ENF*, consider an endowment ray that passes through point *M*. Producing just commodity 2 at point *M* would yield a dollar in world markets, and there is no other way in which a single commodity, whether the second commodity, or indeed the first commodity, could, by itself, result in a dollar earned with a smaller bundle of labor and capital. However, producing along the tangent cord, say, at point *N*, would also yield a dollar in world markets, and this entails producing *both* commodities, with, say, about 40 cents worth of the first commodity using the techniques at *F*, as well as 60 cents worth of the second commodity using the techniques at point *E*. The *cone of diversification* is the array of factor endowment ratios which would lead a country to produce along the *EF* flat.

An alternative way of illustrating a cone of diversification is shown in the right-hand quadrant of Fig. 2. The pair of upward-sloping curves shows that techniques chosen to produce either commodity (that is, the ratio of capital to labor selected) depend upon the market value of wages to rents on capital, and more capital-intensive techniques will be selected the higher the wage/rent ratio is. The left-hand side of the diagram illustrates the connection between the relative commodity price, p_1/p_2, and the

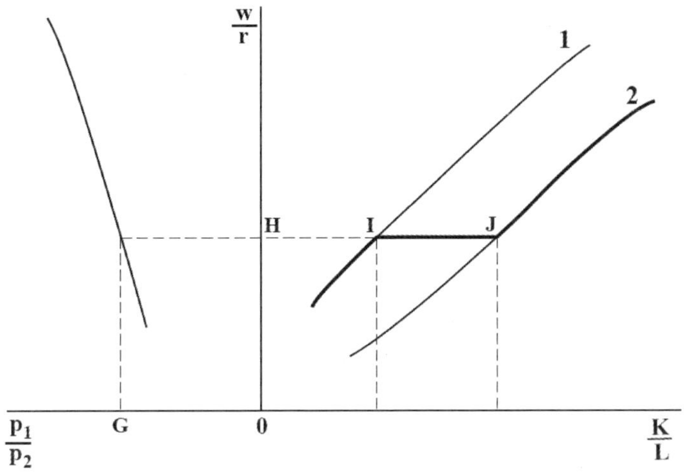

Fig. 2. Prices and factor intensities

wage/rent ratio, w/r, *if the country's endowment proportions were to allow diversified production.* Note that the sign of the slope of the locus reflects the assumption made in the right-hand side of the diagram that commodity 2 is the relatively capital-intensive commodity. A further often-assumed property of technology is exhibited in the left-hand side of the diagram: a ray from the origin always cuts the locus so that the ray is flatter than the locus at such a point. That is, an increase in the relative price of the first commodity would, if both commodities can be produced, result in a *greater than proportionate increase* in the ratio of wages to rents. This must be the case if, as is usually assumed, there is *no joint production*: each commodity is produced *separately* by using inputs of capital and labor.[2]

Suppose that the commodity price ratio is fixed at *0G* on the left-hand side of Fig. 2. If both commodities are produced, the ratio of wages to rents must be shown by *0H*, and the *flat* on the right-hand side displays the array of possible endowment rays, *IJ*, in which the economy can produce both commodities in a competitive equilibrium. These endowments are those shown in the cone of diversification shown in Fig. 1.

Figure 2 can be used to illustrate two possible scenarios. First, suppose the relative price of the first commodity should increase. Clearly there would emerge a different, higher flat in the right-hand side of the diagram. This can also be illustrated in Fig. 1 by shifting the unit-value isoquant for the first commodity radially towards the origin.[3] This would serve to rotate the cone of diversification counter-clockwise, with a corresponding steeper tangent cord (and an increase in w/r).

---

[2] As discussed in Jones (1965), there is a *magnification effect* whereby relative changes in each commodity price are flanked by the relative change in each factor price. Letting $\hat{x}$ represent dx/x, if commodity 1's relative price increases, $\hat{w} > \hat{p}_1 > \hat{p}_2 > \hat{r}$.

[3] For simplicity I assume that p_1 increases for a given value of p_2.

Second, keep the commodity/price ratio unchanged (at *0G*) and consider the changes in production patterns (and wage/rent ratios) either for an economy growing to ever higher capital/labor endowment proportions or for a comparison of the original economy (with an endowment ratio in the cone of diversification) with another economy that shares the same technology but has different factor endowments. In the first interpretation note that if the economy is very labor-abundant, it would be completely specialized to the first commodity and, as its relative capital endowment increases, so does its relative wage rate until it enters the cone of diversification. In the cone, until the extreme point *J* is reached, the economy's relative wage rate stays constant despite its growth in *K/L*. Although this rules out any accommodation in techniques or factor prices at the *intensive margin,* such growth will be accommodated by changes in the *extensive margin* — the change in the composition of outputs 1 and 2, with both capital and labor being released from production in the labor-intensive first commodity towards the capital-intensive commodity 2.[4] Further growth in the capital/labor endowment proportions will eventually lead to the economy becoming completely specialized in producing the capital-intensive commodity. The second interpretation introduces a second country, sharing the same technology. Again, suppose with trade that the equilibrium price ratio settles at the *0G* level in the left-hand part of Fig. 2, and the home country's endowment ray is in the cone of diversification. Will free trade result in the same factor price ratio in the two countries? To some this seemed unlikely since the assumption is being made that factors of production are not mobile internationally. However, such equality would indeed take place if the foreign country's endowment ratio were not too different from that at home, *i.e.*, if it also lay within the cone of diversification.[5] If the foreign country's endowment ratio lies even further from that at home, factor price equalization cannot take place.

FACTOR INTENSITY REVERSAL IN TECHNOLOGY

With this simple case in mind, we turn now to a different possible outcome, one that was discussed after Leontief (1953) cast doubt on Heckscher–Ohlin predictions by suggesting that American exports were more labor-intensive than American import-competing commodities. It was subsequently argued (*e.g.*, Jones, 1956) that even if countries shared the same technology and were both producing the same pair of commodities in a cone of diversification, the technology could allow more than one such cone to exist. Figure 3 illustrates this possibility. The technology for producing commodity 2 is assumed to be less flexible than that for the first commodity so that when labor is relatively inexpensive

[4] In Jones (2004) I showed how this was relevant to development in *open* economies, where even smooth aggregate growth can be hiding strong churning activity between sectors as resources are reallocated at the micro-level.

[5] The possibility of factor price equalization was shown in Samuelson (1948), but the general surprise shown in the profession led him to restate the argument the next year (1949) in the same journal.

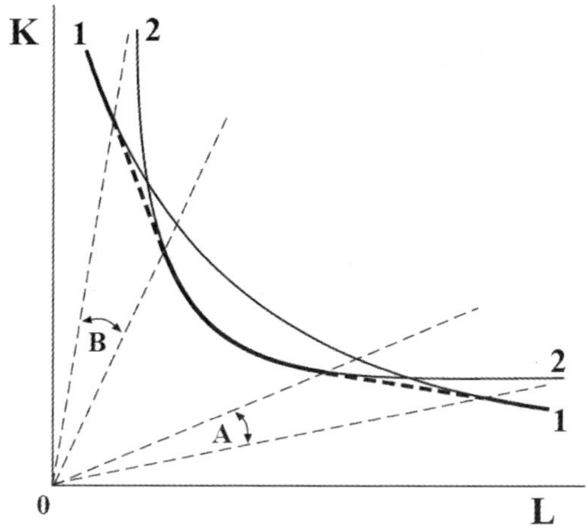

Fig. 3. Factor intensity reversal

the first commodity is labor-intensive (just as in Fig. 2), but at much higher relative wage rates the more flexible technology for producing the first commodity results in its becoming more capital-intensive than the second commodity.[6] There are two cones of diversification. The more labor-abundant home country might be incompletely specialized in cone *A* while the foreign country might also be incompletely specialized, but in cone *B*. If so, obviously these two countries, which both share a common set of production functions, would not have their factor prices equalized by free trade. As for the Leontief paradox, it is now a logical impossibility that for this pair of countries, each is exporting the commodity that is more intensive in its relatively abundant factor than is its import-competing commodity. Why? Either both countries export the commodity that is capital-intensive in its country, or each exports the commodity that is labor-intensive in its country (Jones, 1956).

The right-hand panel of Fig. 4 illustrates this phenomenon of *factor intensity reversal*. The two positively sloped curves are assumed to intersect each other (and there could be more than one intersection point), a reflection only of the comparison in technologies for the two commodities.[7] The relevant ranges of points along this pair of curves depend upon the value of the commodity price ratio, especially since each commodity price ratio may support more than one factor price ratio. The locus relating these two ratios is shown in the left-hand panel of Fig. 4, and is non-monotonic. Commodity price ratio *0G* is supportive

[6] Nonetheless, for an economy with a *given* endowment the commodity that is labor-intensive at some level of outputs must remain so for all possible outputs. That is, for constant returns to scale technology, the contract curve in a production box diagram either lies everywhere above the diagonal of the box, below it, or must itself be the diagonal.

[7] It is interesting to note that in subsequent decades much reliance was placed on a particular form for production functions: that of a constant elasticity of substitution (the CES function). When such functions have different elasticities, the kind of factor intensity reversal phenomenon discussed here becomes ubiquitous.

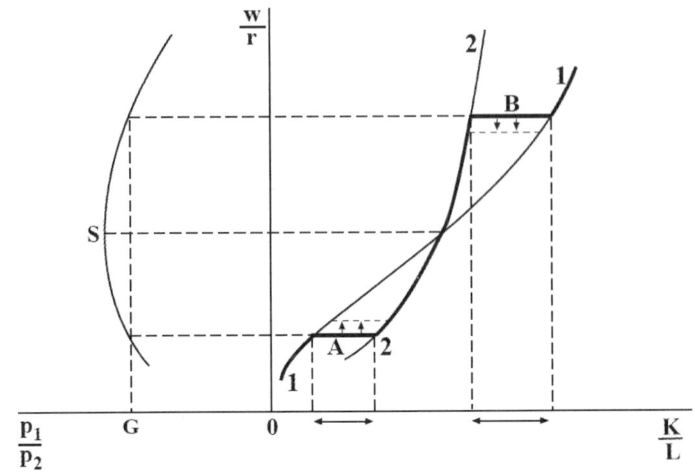

Fig. 4. FIR and price change

of two flats in the right-hand panel (or two cones of diversification in Fig. 3). The lower of the two factor price ratios supports the flat *A* in Fig. 4, and if two countries have endowment ratios on this flat, their factor prices would be equal. If commodity 1 should become a bit more expensive, flat *A* would be shifted upwards, commensurate with the first commodity being labor-intensive in this region. Along the upper flat (*B*) an increase in the relative price of the first commodity would lower the relative wage rate. Whereas factor price equality would prevail if both countries have endowments placing them on flat *B*, this would not be the case if the home country is relatively labor-abundant along flat *A* and the foreign country has its endowment ratio anywhere else. If this is in flat *B*, a commonly faced increase in commodity 1's relative market price would lower the foreign country's relative wage rate while wages would increase, relatively, in the home country. They share a common technology and face a common change in commodity prices and yet have factor prices moving in opposite directions.[8]

Finally, consider the case in which the home country starts off by being very labor-abundant, producing nothing but the first, labor-intensive commodity. Assuming the commodity price ratio stays the same when the home country experiences growth in its capital/labor endowment ratio, this country would experience the following changes in its production: Eventually it reaches flat *A* so that resources are gradually shifted out of producing labor-intensive commodity 1 towards the second commodity. When it becomes completely specialized to the second commodity and continues its capital growth, it remains specialized to commodity 2 until flat *B* is reached (*i.e.*, in Fig. 3 when the endowment ray, moving in a counter-clockwise manner, enters the cone of diversification *B*), until further capital

[8] Note that the factor price ratios in the two countries move together in the case in which the price rise is for the commodity that is more flexible in its technology. If, instead, there is a relative price rise for the commodity that has a less flexible technology, the factor price discrepancy is enhanced.

accumulation encourages it again to specialize in its capital-intensive commodity, which now is the first commodity. Thus in this two-commodity case in which there is a technological factor intensity reversal, steady growth in a country's capital/labor endowment proportions can witness a stage when it transfers resources from commodity 1 to commodity 2 and, following a period of complete specialization, once again produces both commodities but now switches resources back to the first commodity.

CONES IN THE MULTI-COMMODITY SETTING

The discussion of cones of diversification can be extended to the case in which many commodities can be produced and many countries engage in trade. However, a diagrammatic treatment is much easier to pursue while limiting the number of factors of production to two: labor and capital. Figure 5 displays a five-commodity case for a given technology and also a given set of commodity prices. Clearly this combination rules out production of commodity 5 for any country with this technology. Any of commodities 1–4 could be produced competitively by an economy with this technology if its factor endowments were appropriate. Given capital and labor as the only productive inputs, a country engaged in free trade at the given prices could concentrate on producing only a single commodity or a pair of commodities if its endowment ray should lie within cones *A*, *B*, or *C*.

Figure 6 displays this information in a different fashion.[9] With commodity prices given and fixed, production patterns depend upon factor endowments (as in Fig. 5), and the heavy locus charts out the path that would be taken if prices remain constant but the country is growing from low to high levels of capital per unit of labor. Note that I have assumed that there are no technological factor intensity reversals, such as that shown in Fig. 4.

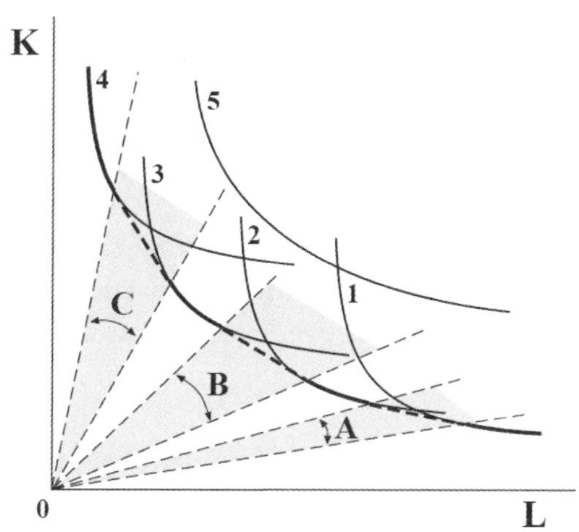

Fig. 5. Cones with many commodities

[9] An early use of this kind of diagram for the multi-commodity case is found in Jones (1974).

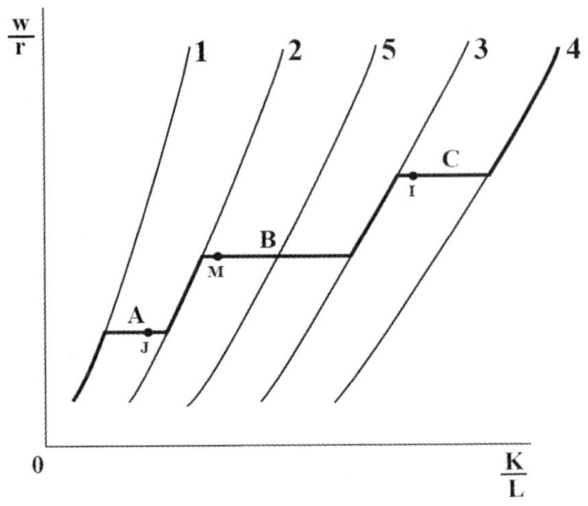

Fig. 6. Growth path with given prices

Steady growth leads to a production response that starts at an extremely labor-abundant stage, calling for complete specialization in the most labor-intensive commodity, 1, followed by diversified production in flat *A* during which growth favors production of the second commodity, aided by a reallocation of resources used to produce the first commodity. Note that production along every different flat is flanked by ranges in which only a single commodity is produced.[10]

As discussed earlier, such a diagram is also useful in comparing the activities undertaken, and relative factor prices established, in two economies that, although sharing the same technology and facing the same prices for commodities found on world markets, have different factor endowment bundles. Are their factor prices equalized in the global market? Yes, if endowments happen to be located in the same cone of diversification, producing the same pair of commodities, which presupposes that their endowment ratios are fairly similar. Otherwise the more capital-abundant region will, perhaps not surprisingly, have higher wage rates relative to the returns to capital, with a different pattern of production. In the spirit of the Heckscher–Ohlin theorem, it must then be the case that *all* capital/labor ratios found in production in the more capital-abundant country must exceed *any* found in the labor-abundant country. In particular this must imply that the capital-abundant country's exportable is produced by capital-intensive techniques compared to those utilized in producing exportables in a more labor-abundant country.[11] However, this was *not* the test used by Leontief (1953) in his examination of American input-output data. Instead, the Leontief procedure involves comparing factor intensities

[10] An exception has to be made for the case in which isoquants are right-angled, so that there is only a single way of producing a commodity regardless of changes in the wage/rent ratio.

[11] And this is the case whether or not these two countries trade with each other in a multi-country world, as long as they share a common technology and face the same set of world market prices.

used in American exports with those in American import-competing production. If, as he found, American import-competing products were more capital-intensive than those in the export sectors, would that necessarily imply that America was the more labor-abundant country? Figure 6 shows how, in a multi-commodity setting, such a conclusion is not warranted. Let Home be the capital-abundant country, with factor endowment proportions shown by point *I* on flat *C*, while Foreign, the more labor-abundant country, produces at point *J* on flat *A*. These two production points suggest that Home devotes most of its resources to produce commodity 3, for export as well as local consumption, and will be importing commodity 4 (as well as commodities 1, 2, and 5 since it does not produce any of them). Labor-abundant Foreign has an opposite kind of trading pattern — exporting its capital-intensive good, 2, and importing, *inter alia*, its import-competing commodity produced, commodity 1. The Leontief-type of procedure, inferring a factor abundance ranking by comparing (for each country) the ranking between the use of capital and labor in that country's exportable production with the ranking used in import-competing production, would judge Home to be the labor-abundant country![12]

In discussing the case in which there is a technological reversal of the factor intensity ranking in Fig. 4, I pointed out that an increase in the relative price of the first commodity would serve to raise relative wage rates in a country whose endowment ray lay in flat *A*, while lowering relative wages in a country sharing the same technology but possessing a capital/labor endowment proportion in flat *B*. In the current case there are no technological reversals, but much the same result occurs if in two countries factor endowment proportions result not in their sharing a common flat, but rather in having proportions relatively close so that they do share in the production of a common commodity, and with each producing a separate commodity that is not produced in the other. This is illustrated in Fig. 6 by endowment points *J* and *M*. A *decrease* in the price of the second commodity would serve to raise the relative wage rate in the labor-abundant country and lower it in the more capital-abundant country, much as in the illustration in Fig. 4 of a *technological* reversal of factor intensities in the two-commodity case even though there are no technological reversals in the many-commodity illustration in Fig. 6.

Another query that may be raised also concerns the effect of an increase in the price of one of the traded commodities, say, commodity 3 in Fig. 6. Although not shown, such a price increase would serve to raise the flat in cone *C* and lower it in cone *B*. Does such a price change encourage countries to specialize in production even further? The answer is typical: it depends. For a country at point *I*, originally producing commodities 3 and 4, a sufficient increase in p_3 would serve to induce the country to specialize completely in the third commodity, abandoning its production of the fourth commodity. By contrast, an economy with factor endowments that initially serve to promote specialization in the second commodity may, if the rise in p_3 is large enough, end up in cone *B*, becoming less specialized by producing both commodities 2 and 3. It all depends.

[12] This argument is developed in more detail in Jones (2008).

CONCLUDING REMARKS: THE SIGNIFICANCE OF CONES OF DIVERSIFICATION

A question that can be raised in any general equilibrium model depicting international trade is how a country can absorb a change in its relative factor endowments (say, growth in the labor force with no change in the capital endowment) if all commodity prices are determined in a larger world market. In principle there are two ways: (i) through a change at the *intensive margin, i.e.*, through an increase in the amount of labor used per unit of capital throughout the economy, and (ii) through a change at the *extensive margin, i.e.*, in the quantities of commodities produced. For example, consider a simple version of the *specific factors* model (*e.g.*, Jones, 1971) in which each of two sectors employs a type of capital utilized only in that sector along with labor drawn from a common pool available to both sectors. If, say, the labor supply expands, the wage rate must fall, serving to raise the return to capital in both sectors (remember that commodity prices are determined on world markets). At the *intensive margin*, new labor is absorbed in part by the use of more labor-intensive techniques in both sectors. At the *extensive margin*, outputs in both sectors increase, perhaps not in the same proportion.[13] However, in different model settings where the number of commodities produced is as large as the number of productive factors, such as in the 2×2 model illustrated in Figs. 1–4 in the cones of diversification, adjustment to endowment changes at given commodity prices is achieved by changes *only* at the *extensive margin.* No changes in factor prices (and in the *intensive margin*) are required. This is the basis for the factor price equalization theorem. With commodity diversification within cones, sufficient to provide the same number of competitive profit conditions (zero profits in equilibrium) as there are inputs, factor prices are completely determined by commodity prices.[14]

Finally, this discussion of the characteristics of the cones of diversification, even in the case of factor intensity reversals of a technological kind or in the multi-commodity case, reveals the *richness* of the Heckscher–Ohlin trade theory. Although the outcome in which factor price equalization for two countries sharing the same cone takes place at constant commodity prices, with both countries experiencing the same effect on factor prices if commodity prices change, is standard fare in the Heckscher–Ohlin trade theory, these results are no longer the only possibilities for the Heckscher–Ohlin model.

A *cone of diversification* entails a trading economy producing as many commodities as there are productive factors in an economy. This is not possible if the number of factors exceeds the number of commodities (as in specific factors models), in which case any alteration in factor endowments at given commodity prices must result in changes both in the intensive and extensive margins and factor prices must change in order to accommodate changes in factor proportions. However, if the number of commodities an economy is technologically capable of producing is at least as large as the number of its productive

[13] Output in the first sector increases relatively more if the first sector is more labor-intensive and/or has more flexible technology.

[14] Perhaps not uniquely, as Fig. 4 illustrates.

factors, one or more cones of diversification exist for each set of commodity prices. Alterations in factor endowments within these cones can be accommodated *without* making use of changes in factor prices and techniques of production, and this is a phenomenon not shared by any set of factor endowments outside these cones. The Heckscher–Ohlin theory is rich in its possibilities for income distribution as endowments and commodity prices change, with the consequences for income distribution depending critically on whether or not the economy's factor endowments lie within a *cone of diversification.*

REFERENCES

Chipman, John, 1966, A survey of the theory of international trade: Part 3, the modern theory, *Econometrica* 34, 18–76.

Deardorff, Alan, 2010, The Lerner diagram, in M. Blaug and P. Lloyd, eds., Famous Figures and Diagrams in Economics (Edward Elgar, Cheltenham).

Jones, Ronald W., 1956, Factor proportions and the Heckscher–Ohlin theorem, *Review of Economic Studies* 24, 1–10.

Jones, Ronald W., 1965, The structure of simple general equilibrium models, *Journal of Political Economy* 73, 557–572.

Jones, Ronald W., 1971, A three-factor model in theory, trade and history, in J.N. Bhagwati, R.W. Jones, R.A. Mundell, and J. Vanek, eds., Trade, Balance of Payments and Growth (North-Holland, Amsterdam).

Jones, Ronald W., 1974, The small country in a many-commodity world, *Australian economic papers* 13, 225–236.

Jones, Ronald W., 2004, Micro-churning with smooth macro growth: Two examples, in S. Dowrick, R. Pitchford, and S. Turnovsky, eds., Economic Growth and Macroeconomic Dynamics: Recent Developments in Economic Theory (Cambridge University Press, Cambridge).

Jones, Ronald W., 2008, Heckscher–Ohlin trade flows: A re-appraisal, *Trade and Development Review* 1, 1–6.

Leontief, Wassily, 1953, Domestic production and foreign trade: The American capital position re-examined, *Proceedings of the American Philosophical Society* 97, 4.

Lerner, Abba, 1952, Factor prices and international trade, *Economica* n.s. 19, 1–15.

Samuelson, Paul A., 1948, International trade and the equalisation of factor prices, *Economic Journal* 58, 163–184.

Samuelson, Paul A., 1949, International factor-price equalisation once again, *Economic Journal* 59, 181–197.

CHAPTER 7

Increasing Returns in a Comparative Advantage World

Paul Krugman

Princeton University and The New York Times

THE OLD NEW TRADE STORY

I like to begin classes on international trade by telling students that there are two basic explanations of international trade. The first is comparative advantage, which says that countries trade to take advantage of their differences — a concept that lies at the heart of Alan Deardorff's beautiful, classic paper, "The general validity of the law of comparative advantage" (1980). The second is increasing returns, which says that countries trade to take advantage of the inherent advantages of specialization, which allows large-scale production — which is what the "new trade theory" was all about.

I also like to illustrate these concepts from everyday experience. Everyday illustrations of comparative advantage are, of course, a staple of introductory textbooks — why sports stars shouldn't mow their own lawns, etc. But it's equally easy to illustrate the role of increasing returns. Even if two people are equally suited for the roles of rocket scientist and brain surgeon, it makes sense for one to specialize in surgery and the other in rockets, because mastering either skill takes years of study, and it would be wasteful for both people to master both disciplines.

So far, so good. But I have also usually tied this potted explanation of what trade theory is all about to a potted version of world economic history as a play in three acts: the fall and rise of comparative advantage. Act I goes as follows: before World War I there was a high level of world trade, and this trade fitted the comparative advantage paradigm pretty well; it was mainly between very different countries exporting very different goods. British trade, in particular, was mainly a matter of exporting manufactured goods and importing raw materials, and as a result most of the trade was with primary-product exporters that either had much higher land-labor ratios or were at a much lower level of economic development.

This first global economy was largely dismantled by wars and protectionism. Act II focuses on the recovery of trade after World War II, which took a very different form. Much of the growth of trade was the result of liberalization agreements among advanced countries, so that trade between similar countries came to dominate overall flows. And much of this trade between similar countries was also trade in similar goods — intraindustry trade — driven mainly by specialization due to increasing returns, a point noticed early on by Balassa (1966). The new trade theory — or, as my students tend to call it, the old new trade theory — began by using models of monopolistic competition to make sense of this similar-similar trade, essentially formalizing Balassa's original story.

Finally, in Act III comparative advantage staged a comeback. Trade liberalization in developing countries led to a sharp rise in North-South trade, which meant that once again much of world trade was taking place between very different countries. Unlike in the pre-WWI era, however, developing countries weren't mainly exporting primary products. Instead, they were exporting labor-intensive manufactures. This trade was able to grow so much in part because reductions in transport cost made it possible to fragment production into labor-intensive and skill-intensive stages (the subject of another line of Alan Deardorff's work, *e.g.*, Deardorff, 2001). So trade in today's world, like trade before World War II, is largely driven by comparative advantage, in which countries trade to take advantage of their differences.

As I said, this is the story I and many others have been telling for some time. And it's right in many respects. I now believe, however, that it misses an important point: the key role played by increasing returns, mainly in the form of localized external economies, even in times when the broad pattern of trade reflects comparative advantage. These localized externalities played a large role in the world economy of the early 20th century — and they play, if anything, an even larger role today.

COLLARS AND CUFFS, BUTTONS AND CIGARETTE LIGHTERS

The rise of the "new economic geography" and the increasing use of gravity-type relationships for empirical trade analysis (*e.g.*, Deardorff, 1998; Eaton and Kortum, 2002) have put space and distance into the mainstream of international economics. Yet we still tend, much more often than not, to model countries as dimensionless points. That's a strategic simplification that makes a great deal of sense for many purposes. But I have recently convinced myself that it's a habit that leads us to miss much of what was really going on in Acts I and III of the story described above.

Let's start by talking about the geography of industrial economies in the late 19th and early 20th century.

Many writers on economic geography have found inspiration in Chapter 10 of Alfred Marshall's *Principles of Economics* (1890), on "the concentration of specialized industries in particular localities." Marshall mentioned such examples as the Sheffield cutlery industry and the Staffordshire pottery industry, but there were many other examples that would have been familiar to his readers: the Nottingham lace industry, the Dundee jute industry, and so on.

On the other side of the Atlantic, the twelfth (1900) census included a quantitative assessment of industry localization (Hall, 1902), which demonstrated the extraordinary degree to which some industries were geographically concentrated: detachable collars and cuffs in Troy, NY, underwear in Cohoes, NY, costume jewelry in and around Providence, silk in Paterson, NJ, and more.

Some of these localized industries owed their origin to specific advantages of the site, but many were the result of historical accident — the blacksmith's wife who supposedly invented the detachable collar in Troy, the local entrepreneur named Egbert Egberts who installed the world's first power knitting machine in Cohoes. And regardless of origin, each localization was sustained by the trinity of agglomeration effects described by Marshall: information spillovers ("The mysteries of the trade become no mysteries; but are as it were in the air"), specialized suppliers, and thick labor markets. In short, external economies of scale.

And here's the thing: at least in the case of Britain, many of these localized industries were export-oriented, selling much of their production overseas. Dundee, for example, dominated global jute manufacturing — and since burlap bags were in demand everywhere, it was largely an export-oriented cluster.

Notice that I'm not asserting that increasing returns in the form of localized external economies actually caused international trade. It was probably the case that in the mid-19th century world economy only Britain had the right combination of resources, skills, and general technological competence to export many of the manufactured goods it did, in fact, export. In other words, comparative advantage determined the pattern of trade. Nonetheless, increasing returns were clearly evident in the local geography of production. And as I'll argue shortly, this has important implications for how we think about the gains from trade.

Before I get there, however, let me fast-forward to today's world — a world in which comparative advantage once again determines much of the pattern of trade. Thus, China's dominant role in the export of many labor-intensive manufactured goods surely reflects its combination of relatively abundant labor and relatively high manufacturing competence. There's not much historical accident in the fact that China makes the bulk of the world's buttons.

But there probably is a lot of historical accident and cumulative causation in the fact that 60% of the world's buttons are manufactured in the small town of Qiaotou, where, the story goes, three decades ago three brothers saw some discarded buttons lying in the gutter, realized there was a money-making opportunity, and planted the seed of an industrial cluster. And Qiaotou is characteristic of China's industrial landscape. As was the case for industrial Britain in the 19th century, many of China's manufactured exports are produced by highly localized industries whose geographical concentration shows clear evidence of the importance of external economies. Wenzhou produces 95% of the world's cigarette lighters; Yanbu is the underwear capital (the Cohoes of the 21st century!); and on and on.

Again, industrial localization within China probably has little if any impact on the pattern of trade measured at a national level, which basically reflects comparative advantage. But this does not, it turns out, mean that a pure comparative advantage approach tells the whole story. In particular, the story we should be telling about the gains from trade requires that we take account of the effects of external economies, even if these external economies don't affect the overall pattern of trade.

Actually, this should be obvious (but wasn't, at least to me, until I wrote this paper) from the everyday examples we use to illustrate the roots of trade. Suppose that Harry and Louise have to choose between rocket science and brain surgery — and that Louise has a clear advantage in the surgery department (Harry faints at the sight of blood). In that case, their pattern of specialization is fully determined by comparative advantage: Harry does rockets, Louise does brains. Yet the gains from trade are to a large extent the result not of the differences between the two individuals, but of the inherent advantages of specialization: because Harry can launch Louise while Louise fixes his brain, each of the two only needs to master one skill.

So how do we model this result — trade patterns determined by comparative advantage, but trade gains nonetheless including a strong element of increasing returns — more formally?

LOCALIZED EXTERNAL ECONOMIES AND THE GAINS FROM TRADE

When one tries to model the role of localized external economies in international trade, it turns out that the key strategic decisions involve what one assumes about factor prices. *Within* countries, should one assume that factors are perfectly mobile, and therefore equalize across industries, or should one think in terms of "lumpy" countries (Courant and Deardorff, 1992) across which wages and other factor prices differ? If factor prices are uniform within countries, what happens *between* countries? Should we assume that trade leads to factor price equalization, or should we model a world in which factor prices are unequal and in which countries that are lucky enough to get a disproportionate share of increasing-returns industries have higher wages?

In reality, there's a strong case for arguing that the lumpy-country representation is more realistic than the assumption of perfect internal mobility. China is famously still very much a dual economy, with an industrial coast and a still-backward interior. In fact, China still has legal restrictions on internal migration, even if these are largely ignored.

And with Chinese hourly compensation in manufacturing still only a tiny fraction of Western levels (Lett and Banister, 2009), it's obvious that factor price equalization does not prevail internationally.

But this paper is an exploratory effort, which means that simplicity is of the essence. So I'm going to do violence to reality and assume both that factors of production move freely to equalize factor prices within countries and that trade leads to factor price equalization internationally. (One can, if one likes, make a partial excuse by assuming that factors are measured in efficiency units, with the productivity of labor in particular varying across countries.) The meaning of the first assumption is obvious; the second will take a little explaining.

So let's bring on Samuelson's angel.

In 1949 Paul Samuelson sought to explain the fundamental logic of factor price equalization with a parable inspired by the story of the Tower of Babel (Samuelson, 1949). He asked readers to envision an original state of the world with no impediments to mobility of productive factors, so that all factor prices would be equalized. Then, he suggested, an angel came down to smite each unit of each factor on the forehead — that is, to divide labor, capital, and so on among nations, with the new rule that factors from each country could only work with other factors from the same country.

The question then becomes: How much damage did the angel do? And the answer is that if factors are not too unevenly divided among nations, none at all. For trade can, under certain circumstances, allow the world to produce the same quantity of each good, using the same factor inputs, as it would have if the angel had never made his visitation.

The basic logic is illustrated in Fig. 1, which shows a three-good world economy. I'll initially assume constant returns. There are assumed to be two factors of production, capital and labor, with the sides of the box representing the total world supply of each factor. There are three goods, A, B, and C. The vectors labeled A, B, C represent the factors that would have been employed in the production of each good in the integrated, pre-angel economy.

Now the angel does his smiting. This divides the world's productive resources between two countries, Home and Foreign. In Fig. 2, the sides of the box continue to represent total world resources; resources belonging to Home are measured from the southwest corner, resources belonging to Foreign from the northeast corner, so that the division of resources can be represented by the endowment point E.

Does this division do any damage? Not as drawn. In a constant-returns world, as long as the endowment point lies within the irregular hexagon shown, it is possible to allocate world production between Home and Foreign in such a way as to reproduce the integrated economy — producing the same quantities of each good, using the same factor inputs, as would have happened if there had been no avenging angel. In such a world equilibrium factor prices will be equalized. It's also straightforward to show that the pattern of trade will reflect factor abundances — specifically, if we look at the factor content of trade we will find each country exporting the factor in which it is abundant.

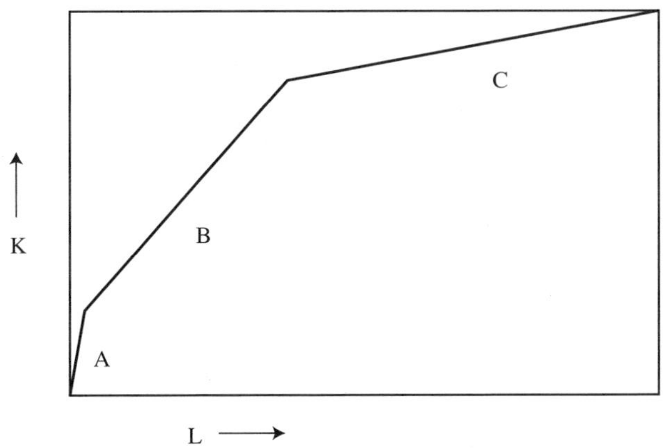

Fig. 1. The integrated economy

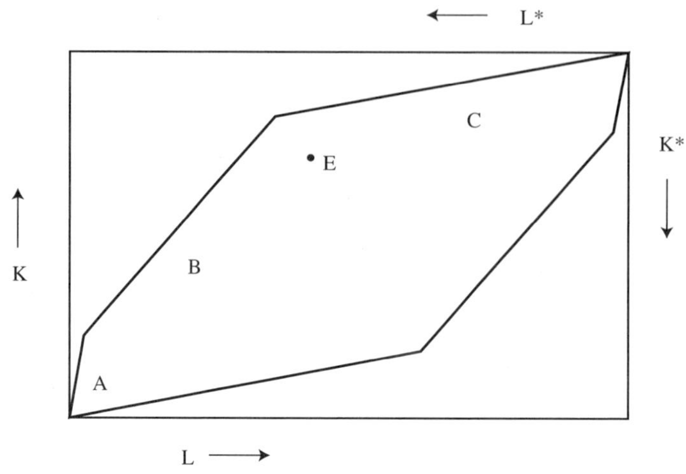

Fig. 2. After the angel smites

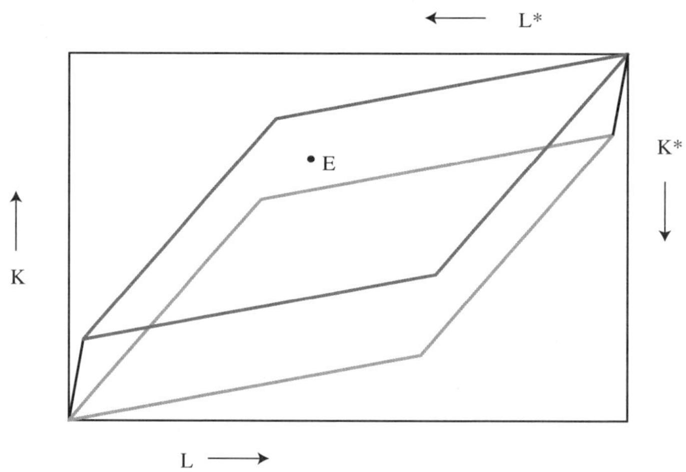

Fig. 3. Reproducing the integrated economy with localization

Now, how does this change if we introduce localized external economies? In the integrated economy, production of each good subject to such localized economies would be concentrated in a single location. To reproduce the integrated economy post-angel, this must continue to be true — which means that each good subject to localization economies must be concentrated in a single country. And this is a case already analyzed in Helpman and Krugman (1985).

Figure 3 shows how it works. Assume that good A is subject to localized external economies, while B and C remain constant returns. Then to reproduce the integrated economy, production of A must be concentrated either in Home or in Foreign, while B and C can be allocated between the countries. This in turn implies that the integrated economy can be reproduced as long as the endowment point lies within either the upper parallelogram — corresponding to concentration of industry A in Home — or within the lower parallelogram, corresponding to concentration of A in Foreign. In the figure as drawn, the endowment point lies in the upper but not the lower parallelogram, so that the only equilibrium that reproduces the integrated economy is one in which Home produces A. (There may be other equilibria that don't reproduce the integrated economy, but I disregard that possibility.)

The equilibrium portrayed in Fig. 3 may not look significantly different from the equilibrium shown in Fig. 2. In both cases the pattern of specialization and trade is determined by resources. In both cases factor prices are equalized, and the factor content of trade reflects national factor abundances. So one might be tempted to say that localized external economies don't matter for the story.

But that turns out not to be true once we turn to the gains from trade.

The standard proof of the gains from trade — the proof that lies behind Deardorff's generalized version of comparative advantage — is, of course, stated in terms of goods volume and goods prices. As Helpman and I pointed out (1985), however, when trade leads to factor price equalization it is also possible to think of gains from trade in terms of the dual. This isn't especially useful in most contexts. But it offers a convenient way to think about the role of localized external economies.

Figure 4 shows the constant returns case. Note that in this case we're not comparing pre- and post-angel situations — we're back to the more usual comparison between free trade and autarky. In this case the curve shows the unit isoquant for some good. The dotted line represents the vector of resources that *would have been used* to produce the good under autarky. When trade is opened, however, factor prices — which are, remember, assumed to become equalized internationally — are different from what they would have been under autarky. And what the figure shows is that at the new factor prices, the bundle

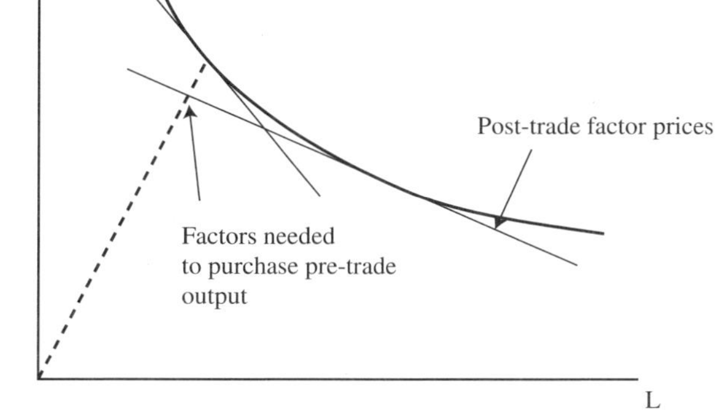

Fig. 4. Gains from trade in a constant-returns world

of resources that was used to produce one unit of each good in autarky now has a purchasing power that is more than enough to purchase that unit in a trading economy. Hence the nation as a whole, which consists of all its productive factors, is more than able to afford its pre-trade consumption: gains from trade.

So far, nothing new. But now introduce localized external economies. These shift the unit isoquant for each good subject to these externalities. The isoquant shifts outward in countries that don't end up producing the good, and therefore lose the external economies they had. But as long as factor prices are equalized, the only thing that matters for welfare is how a country's pre-trade isoquant compares with the post-trade isoquant in the country that ends up producing the good. And it's a reasonable presumption that this isoquant lies inside every country's pre-trade isoquant, since world production of the good and hence the strength of external economies will normally be larger than any individual country's production would have been in the absence of trade.

Figure 5 shows the implications. As before, the bundle of factors that would have produced a unit of the good in autarky are more than able to buy that unit after trade, showing that trade increases national purchasing power. But when goods are subject to localized external economies, there are two reasons for that gain. One is that countries are different, which leads to a change in factor prices. The other is that the concentration of world production in a single location allows greater exploitation of external economies, and hence raises efficiency. There are gains from trade due to the specialization of China in labor-intensive industries like button manufacture, but there are further gains from trade — gains that accrue to the world as a whole — from the concentration of world button production in the single small town of Qiaotou.

Over the past century world trade has gone through a great arc. At the beginning of the century trade was primarily between countries with very different resources exporting very different goods, so that it seemed to be a comparative advantage world. By the 1980s trade was largely between countries with similar resources exporting similar goods, so that economists turned to increasing-returns models to make sense of what they saw. But today, with the rise

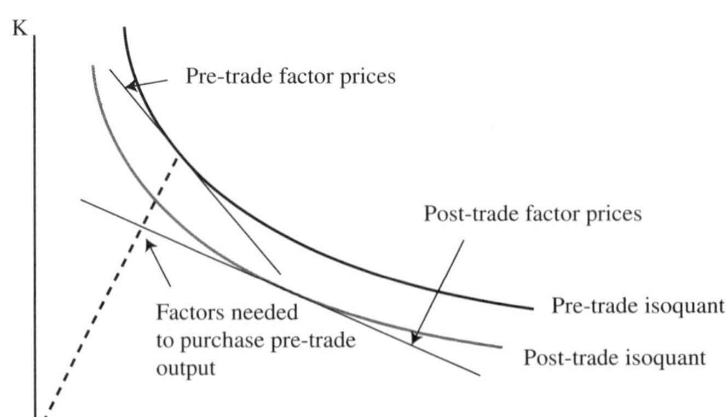

Fig. 5. The gains from trade with localized external economies

of China and other low-wage economies, we seem once again to be in a comparative advantage world, in which countries with very different resources export very different goods.

What I've argued in this paper, however, is that even during comparative advantage eras increasing returns in the form of localized external economies plays a significant role. In fact, the same eras in which comparative advantage seems to have ruled international trade are also the eras in which increasing returns has seemed to exert its strongest influence on *intra*-national economic geography. And this observation isn't irrelevant even in the trade context: gains from localization arguably are a significant source of gains from trade, even if they don't seem to affect the pattern of specialization.

Does this have any relevance to current policy disputes? Well, many people — myself included — have argued that imports of labor-intensive goods from developing countries exert a depressing influence on the real wages of less-skilled workers in advanced countries. This may still be true, but the role of local external economies may offer a partial offset: if Chinese buttons are cheap not just because of low wages but also because of the advantages of the Qiaotou cluster, U.S. imports of buttons have an ambiguous effect on low-skill wages rather than a definite Stolper–Samuelson effect.

I don't want to push this too far, however. The main point of this paper is simply to point out that increasing returns — made apparent by the localization of industries — have historically played an important role in world trade even in eras when comparative advantage seems to reign supreme.

REFERENCES

Balassa, B., 1966, Tariff reductions and trade in manufactures among the industrial countries, *The American Economic Review* 56, 466–473.

Courant, Paul N. and Alan V. Deardorff, 1992, International trade with lumpy countries, *Journal of Political Economy* 100(1), 198–210.

Deardorff, Alan V., 1980, The general validity of the law of comparative advantage, *Journal of Political Economy* 88(5), 941–957.

Deardorff, Alan V., 1998, Determinants of bilateral trade: Does gravity work in a neoclassical world?, in Jaffrey A. Frankel, ed., *The Regionalization of the World Economy* (University of Chicago Press, Chicago), pp. 7–28.

Deardorff, Alan V., 2001, Fragmentation in simple trade models, *The North American Journal of Economics and Finance* 12(2), 121–137.

Eaton, Jonathan and Samuel Kortum, 2002, Technology, geography, and trade, *Econometrica*, 70(5), 1741–1779.

Hall, Frederic S., 1902, The localization of industries, *Bulletin of the Twelfth Census of the United States.*

Helpman, Elhanan and Paul Krugman, 1985, Market Structure and Foreign Trade (MIT Press, Cambridge, MA).

Lett, Erin and Judith Bannister, 2009, China's manufacturing employment and compensation costs, 2002–2006, *Monthly Labor Review* 132, 30–38.

Samuelson, Paul A., 1949, International factor-price equalization once again, *The Economic Journal* 58, 181–197.

CHAPTER 8

Heckscher, Ohlin and Deardorff

J. Peter Neary[1]

University of Oxford and CEPR

It is a huge pleasure to contribute to this happy event. I have known Alan Deardorff for over 30 years and have enjoyed his company and savored his insights on countless occasions. He is not just a great scholar, but also a great guy, an indefatigable champion of the field of international trade, and a disinterested provider of public goods. We are all in his debt for his web resources, useful as well as fun, that shine like a good deed in a naughty world, or, to push the public goods analogy further, like a lighthouse towering over shark-infested seas. (I will refrain from naming any sharks.) Of course, we are also in his debt for his scholarship, and I want to make some remarks today inspired by rereading his classic papers on generalizing the theory of comparative advantage and the Heckscher–Ohlin theorem.[2]

I want to concentrate in particular on the generalization of Heckscher–Ohlin, since I believe that there is more that can be said about this. Alan derived the key result that the value at autarky factor prices of the factor content of trade (which I denote by w^0 and M^1 respectively) must be positive:

$$w^0 \cdot M^1 > 0 \tag{1}$$

where M is the vector of factors that would be needed to produce domestically the imports of goods. So, in a very general competitive framework, factors which are expensive in autarky will on average be imported: not directly, but embodied in the goods that are actually imported. However, Alan, and others subsequently, were very uneasy with this result. The problem is that we cannot be sure that the net imports of factors as measured by the vector M^1 have a zero mean, and so we cannot use (1) to derive a correlation between the two vectors. In a sense, the problem is that we have failed to address the question "Expensive

[1] Department of Economics, University of Oxford, Manor Road Building, Oxford, OX1 3UQ, U.K.; tel.: +44 (0)1865-271085; e-mail: peter.neary@economics.ox.ac.uk.

[2] Avinash Dixit and Victor Norman (1980) also deserve credit for their independent work on these topics: taken together, the work of these three made a huge advance in explaining what we know and what (ex ante) we cannot know about trade patterns in general equilibrium.

relative to what?" when we say that factors are expensive in autarky.[3] Alan's response to this was to seek implications of (1) which do yield correlation-type results, and he pursued some ingenious routes to deriving them. One of these was to consider all countries in the world together. Assuming that (1) holds for each, he showed that we can stack the autarky factor prices and net factor imports of all countries to form two giant vectors, and the world version of (1) now yields a true correlation since all countries overall cannot import factors on average, so the stacked world vector of M^1 must have a non-positive mean.

By contrast, I want to stick with Eq. (1) and to tease out its implications. One reason for this is empirical: we are unlikely ever to be able to observe autarky factor prices in all countries of a hypothetical non-trading world, so the stacked result is not going to help empirical work, despite its theoretical interest and importance. By contrast, in some exceptional cases we can observe autarky factor prices for a single country, which opens up the possibility of checking whether (1) holds in practice. This is exactly the approach which Daniel Bernhofen and John Brown adopt in an unpublished paper, which extends their earlier work on testing comparative advantage (see Bernhofen and Brown, 2004, 2009). They have access to an extremely rich data set on Japan for the periods just before and just after it opened up to trade in the 1860s, and are able to estimate autarky prices for a range of factors, as well as the net factor flows embodied in imports after trade. Reassuringly, they find that Eq. (1) holds, as the theory predicts. They also find some unexpected implications. For example, when they decompose the inner product to consider the contribution of different factors, they find that much of the implied value of embodied net imports is accounted for by female labor, pointing towards an unanticipated implication of Japan's opening up to trade, that the resulting shifts in industrial structure worked against this factor.

Turning from empirics to theory, I find it instructive to look at the implications of (1) in a number of special models. This shows both the usefulness of the result and its limitations. It is a result we had better like because, in many cases, it may be all we have. To pursue this approach, I use the tools that Albert Schweinberger and I adopted to derive (1) and some other corollaries in our 1986 paper. Like Dixit and Norman, this uses dual techniques, with the added feature that we introduced a single function to summarize the economy as a whole in its role as a virtual trader of factors. Thanks to Avinash and Victor, most of us are familiar with the GNP function, $g(p, v)$, as a shorthand summary of an economy's technology, giving the maximum value of GNP attainable facing given commodity prices p and with given factor endowments v. It is a tiny step from that to subtract GNP from national expenditure, represented by a consumer expenditure function $e(p, u)$, where u is aggregate welfare, to form what Albert and I called the trade expenditure function:

$$E(p, u, v) \equiv e(p, u) - g(p, v). \tag{2}$$

[3] Note that there is no problem of units of measurement: changing the units in which factors are measured can be thought of as pre-multiplying the M vector by a diagonal transformation matrix T. But then the factor prices must also be pre-multiplied by its inverse, T^{-1}, and when we form the inner product (1), T cancels so the result is unit-free.

This equals the difference between national expenditure and GNP, so not surprisingly its derivatives with respect to prices equal the vector of net imports of goods: $E_p = m$. The next step is to assume that prices equal unit costs in each sector, and to replace the goods prices p with the vector of unit cost functions $c(w)$. Now we can define a factor trade expenditure function:

$$\tilde{E}(w, u, v) \equiv E[c(w), u, v]. \tag{3}$$

This has the nice feature that its derivatives with respect to factor prices equal the net factor content functions, and shows explicitly that they equal the product of the unit factor requirements in each sector (given by the matrix of derivatives of the unit cost functions, c_w or A) and the vector of actual net imports of goods,[4] m:

$$\tilde{E}_w = c_w E_p = Am = M. \tag{4}$$

Armed with these tools, we return to (1) and ask why it does not extend easily to comparisons between countries. (Similar arguments apply to comparisons between autarky and free-trade equilibria in a single country. However, they require a little more notation and I am already above my quota.) Assume for simplicity that the rest of the world can be represented as a single country, and that it also exhibits a result such as (1), with asterisks denoting foreign variables:

$$w^{0*} \cdot M^{1*} > 0. \tag{5}$$

Now add this to the corresponding result for the home country (1) to get, after a little manipulation,

$$(w^0 - w^{0*}) \cdot M^1 + w^{0*} \cdot (M^1 + M^{1*}) > 0. \tag{6}$$

If we could show that the first term on the right-hand side is positive, we would have a significantly stronger generalization of the Heckscher–Ohlin theorem: this term equals the free-trade value of net factor imports, valued at the difference between the home and foreign autarky prices. The second term can therefore be interpreted as a measure of the deviation from Heckscher–Ohlin: factors that are more expensive in autarky at home relative to abroad may nevertheless be exported rather than imported on average if this term is sufficiently positive. Recall that, in deriving the general proof of comparative advantage, there is a parallel derivation with the big difference that it simplifies a lot, since it yields

$$(p^0 - p^{0*}) \cdot m^1 + p^{0*} \cdot (m^1 + m^{1*}) > 0. \tag{7}$$

Here the second term vanishes because, in this two-country world, the sum of the net goods trade vectors, $m^1 + m^{1*}$, is equal to zero. Hence we have a prediction about the direction of goods trade which can be reexpressed as a correlation: goods that are more

[4] All these derivatives are evaluated at domestic factor prices, which becomes important shortly.

expensive in autarky at home relative to abroad are always imported on average after trade. By contrast, the sum of the net factor trade vectors in (6), $M^1 + M^{1*}$, is not equal to zero in general. Substituting from (4) into (6) we can see why:

$$(w^0 - w^{0*}) \cdot M^1 + w^{0*} \cdot (A^1 - A^{1*})m^1 > 0. \tag{8}$$

The problem is that the net factor import vector M^1 in Eq. (1) must be evaluated using the techniques of production used in the home country, A^1, whereas M^{1*} in (5) must be evaluated using the techniques used in the foreign country, A^{1*}. Requiring these to be equal is a tall order, though there is one important special case where it holds: as every school girl knows (perhaps I exaggerate just a little), this is when technology is identical internationally and factor prices are equalized by free trade. In that case the second term in (8) vanishes, and we are in a Heckscher–Ohlin–Vanek world where factor content functions can be estimated directly, as long as both countries remain in the same cone of diversification. Equation (8) also implies a new result: if the home country uses more efficient techniques in all sectors than the foreign, then every term in $A - A^*$ is negative, and so the Heckscher–Ohlin correlation $(w^0 - w^{0*}) \cdot M^1$ is positive, even though factor prices need not be equalized.

I want to end with two other, less orthodox, applications of (1). Both involve models which are not usually thought of as having much in common with the Heckscher–Ohlin model. However, both have production sectors which can be represented by a GNP function, allowing the application of the tools developed so far.

The first is the specific-factors model, often seen as the antithesis of Heckscher–Ohlin, though of course it is just another special case of a general competitive model. Dixit and Norman derived the GNP function for this model, but it takes a much simpler and more tractable form in a special case recently introduced by Jim Anderson (2009). This assumes that production functions in each sector are Cobb–Douglas, and that each has the same share of labor. Thus the GNP function is the solution to the following maximization problem:

$$g(p,L,k) \equiv \max_{l_i} \left[\Sigma_i \, p_i x_i : x_i = \phi_i l_i^{\alpha} k_i^{1-\alpha}, \Sigma l_i = L \right] \tag{9}$$

where L is the scalar endowment of mobile labor, while k is the vector of the endowments of sector-specific capital stocks k_i. Now define $K \equiv \Sigma k_i$ as the aggregate capital endowment, and $\lambda k_i \equiv k_i / K$ as the share of capital in each sector. Jim's result is that the GNP function for this model can be expressed in a particularly simple form:

$$g(p,L,K,\lambda_k) = L^{\alpha} K^{1-\alpha} G \quad \text{where } G \equiv \left[\Sigma \lambda_{ki} (\phi_i p_i)^{\frac{1}{1-\alpha}} \right]^{1-\alpha}. \tag{10}$$

This is the product of two sub-functions, one a Cobb–Douglas aggregate of the overall factor endowments L and K, and the other a CES aggregate of goods prices, where the weights are the sectoral capital shares. The nice feature of this specification is that we can get explicit expressions for all variables in general equilibrium. In particular, we can evaluate the

Heckscher–Ohlin deviation term in (8) and explore the conditions under which we might expect to observe Heckscher–Ohlin properties even in a specific-factors world.

My second non-standard application is to the model of monopolistic competition with heterogeneous firms developed by Marc Melitz (2003). This model has already proved its usefulness as a guide to empirical work and as a workhorse for many exciting theoretical developments. Only recently, however, has it been shown that it is closely related to traditional general equilibrium models. I am referring in particular to the demonstration by Rob Feenstra and Hiau Looi Kee (2008) that the production sector of the Melitz model, with a Pareto distribution of firms, can be represented by a GNP function essentially identical to the one I have used above. Of course, goods prices are endogenous in a monopolistically competitive equilibrium, but we can take foreign demand parameters as exogenous and relate domestic goods prices to factor prices using standard properties of monopolistic competition with CES preferences. This allows a Heckscher–Ohlin-type result to be derived for a multisectoral version of the Melitz model too, by applying the approach I have used above.

It is appropriate to end by relating one of Alan's great results to the work of one of his students. I hope it shows that we have not heard the last of Heckscher and Ohlin, and also reminds us of another public good which Alan has provided through the outstanding students he has mentored, many of them here today. Heckscher and Ohlin have a lot to be grateful for to Alan, and so have we all.

REFERENCES

Anderson, James E., 2009, Gravity, productivity and the pattern of production and trade, NBER Working Paper No. 14642, January.

Bernhofen, Daniel M. and John C. Brown, 2004, A direct test of the theory of comparative advantage: The case of Japan, *Journal of Political Economy* 112, 48–67.

Bernhofen, Daniel M. and John C. Brown, 2009, Testing the general validity of the Heckscher–Ohlin theorem: The natural experiment of Japan, presented to the NBER Summer Institute, Cambridge, Mass.

Deardorff, Alan V., 1980, The general validity of the law of comparative advantage, *Journal of Political Economy* 88, 941–957.

Deardorff, Alan V., 1982, The general validity of the Heckscher–Ohlin theorem, *American Economic Review* 72, 683–694.

Dixit, Avinash K. and Victor D. Norman, 1980, Theory of International Trade (Cambridge University Press, London).

Feenstra, Robert C. and Hiau Looi Kee, 2008, Export variety and country productivity: Estimating the monopolistic competition model with endogenous productivity, *Journal of International Economics* 74, 500–518.

Melitz, Marc J., 2003, The impact of trade on intra-industry reallocations and aggregate industry productivity, *Econometrica* 71, 1695–1725.

Neary, J. Peter and Albert Schweinberger, 1986, Factor content functions and the theory of international trade, *Review of Economic Studies* 53, 421–432.

CHAPTER 9

Journal of International Economics 9 (1979) 197–209. © North-Holland Publishing Company

WEAK LINKS IN THE CHAIN OF COMPARATIVE ADVANTAGE

Alan V. DEARDORFF*

Institute for International Economic Studies, University of Stockholm, Stockholm, Sweden

University of Michigan, Ann Arbor, MI 48109, USA

Received October 1978

This paper examines the proposition that trade in many commodities can be explained by a chain of comparative advantage. It is first shown, in a two-country, two-factor model, that trade accords with the ranking of goods by factor intensity if there are unequal factor prices, free trade, and only final goods. This result continues to hold if either trade impediments or intermediate products are introduced. However, if both are present, the chain proposition breaks down. Finally, with many countries, it is shown that trade impediments alone can invalidate the chain proposition.

1. Introduction

My purpose in this paper is to investigate the proposition that trade in many commodities can be understood by first ranking the goods in order of factor intensities, then showing that all of a country's exports must lie higher on this list than all of its imports. A similar idea of a chain of comparative advantage was shown by Haberler (1936, p. 137) to be valid in a many-commodity extension of the classical theory of trade, the rankings there being of course in terms of comparative costs. The proposition was also stated for a two-factor, two-country version of the Heckscher–Ohlin model by Jones (1956–57), but was shown by Bhagwati (1972) to be incorrect if factor prices are equalized. Jones and Bhagwati apparently concurred, however, that the proposition would be valid whenever factor prices are not equalized, though neither provided a proof. Since a prime cause of unequal factor prices is the existence of tariffs, and since Travis (1964, 1972) has claimed that protection can account for the Leontief paradox, presumably by

*I would like to thank Jagdish Bhagwati, Ronald Jones, Richard Porter, Robert Stern and members of the Research Seminar in International Economics, University of Michigan, for their helpful comments.

altering the pattern of trade,[1] it seems that a concensus has not yet been reached as to just how general the chain-of-comparative-advantage idea is. In what follows, I explore the matter further and show that these differences of opinion can be reconciled.

Specifically, I show first that Jones and Bhagwati were right, so long as we remain in the model that they were considering, which excludes the possibility of produced goods being used as intermediate factors of production. That is, I will demonstrate the chain proposition in such a model whenever factor prices are unequal, whether that inequality is the result of complete specialization with no impediments to trade (section 2) or of tariffs and transport costs (section 3). Then I will introduce intermediate goods. This modification, it turns out, does not invalidate the chain proposition so long as there are unequal factor prices and free trade (section 4). But when impediments to trade are added as well, the chain proposition collapses. For I show, in section 5, that an increase in a tariff can cause a good that was previously exported to become imported and, at the same time, a good that was previously imported to become exported. It follows that no ranking of the goods is possible, on the basis of factor intensities, autarky prices, or anything else, that will permit separation of exports and imports via a single break in the chain.

It is ironic that Jones, Bhagwati, and others have found comfort in the presence of transport costs and other impediments to trade, which prevent factor-price equalization and thus remove the indeterminacy of production and trade. For the example in section 5 shows that, when there are intermediate goods, these same impediments to trade can invalidate the chain proposition when it would otherwise hold.

In the two-factor world considered here, the chain proposition is related to, but not identical to, the Heckscher–Ohlin theorem. The former merely says that some ranking of goods exists which suffices to determine trade. The latter says that the appropriate ranking is by factor intensities and, furthermore, that relative factor endowments determine which end of the chain contains a country's exports. However, in the cases considered here, the two propositions stand or fall together, so long as the price definition of factor abundance is used in stating the Heckscher–Ohlin theorem. For I will show in sections 2–4 that a country in which capital is relatively cheap, with trade, must export more capital intensive goods than it imports. And it can be shown, if there are only two countries, that relative factor prices must bear the same relationship with trade as without, so long as trade impediments

[1]Actually, it is difficult to be sure exactly what Travis was saying. He has never, to my knowledge, provided an example of a tariff that reverses the pattern of trade, though such an example is possible, as I show below in section 5. Nor is it clear whether Travis meant his remarks to be valid in a model of only two primary factors. In his (1972) article, he used and vigorously defended the two-factor assumption, but concluded that, if tariffs are high enough, the bulk of trade will be in goods requiring other primary factors.

are non-negative.[2] Thus, these sections also demonstrate the Heckscher–Ohlin theorem: that a country in which capital is relatively cheap in autarky must export relatively capital intensive goods. Also, of course, the counter example of section 5 shows that both propositions fail when there are both trade impediments and intermediate goods.

While most of the argument will be confined to a two-country world, it is of some interest also to show how the chain idea may extend to a world of many countries. This is not difficult, with the tools available, and, in section 6, I show that the chain of comparative advantage can be broken into several segments, one for each country. With the countries arranged along the chain in the same order as their relative factor endowments, each country will then export only goods within its segment of the chain and will import all others. That is true, however, only if trade is free and factor prices are unequal. Without the need, in this case, for intermediate goods, I will also show that tariffs can cause a rather dramatic rearrangement of the pattern of trade.

Considering the obvious importance, in the real world, of both trade impediments and intermediate goods, the results of this paper may seem to cast doubt on both the Heckscher–Ohlin theory and on the concept of comparative advantage itself. I therefore conclude in section 7 with a discussion of these more fundamental problems.

2. Free trade

Consider two countries, A and B, producing and trading n goods with no impediments to trade between them, so that the prices of the goods, $p_1, \ldots, p_n$, are the same in both countries. Production of each good requires the use of only two factors of production, capital (K) and labor (L), which are nontraded and available in each country in fixed supply. Production functions are identical between countries, and have the usual properties of concavity and homogeneity. Assume further that the goods can be ranked unambiguously in terms of capital intensity, X_1 being the most capital intensive and X_n, the least. Thus, there are no factor-intensity reversals between any pair of goods, and isoquants of different goods can intersect only once. Assume finally that perfect competition prevails in both countries,

[2]To see this, let t be a vector of ad valorem tariffs cum transport costs for each industry. Given technology, tastes, and factor endowments, the difference between the two countries' factor-price ratios, $\Omega = \omega^A - \omega^B$, must be a continuous function of t, $\Omega(t)$. Let t^0 be a particular vector of non-negative trade impediments, let t^a be a vector that would prevent trade entirely, and suppose that $\Omega(t^0) > 0$ (as in fig. 1 below) yet $\Omega(t^a) < 0$. Then by continuity there exists $t' > 0$ such that $\Omega(t') = 0$ and such that trade takes place. But if $\Omega = 0$, then factor prices are equal and so are commodity prices, and it is impossible for trade to take place over positive trade impediments, $t' > 0$. From this contradiction it follows that $\Omega(t^a) \geqq 0$. Since $\Omega(t^a) = 0$ can also be ruled out as implying that $\Omega(t) = 0$ for all t, it follows that $\Omega(t^0) > 0$ implies $\Omega(t^a) > 0$.

so that price equals average cost for any good that is produced and is less than or equal to average cost for any good that is not produced.

Suppose now that all that is known about a free trade equilibrium is that particular and unequal factor prices prevail in the two countries. What does this imply about the pattern of trade?

Begin by drawing the unit isocost lines for the two countries. These are shown in fig. 1 as the lines AA' for country A and BB' for country B, and represent the combinations of capital and labor which would cost, say, one dollar (or other international numeraire) in each of the two countries. They are shown as intersecting at a point M, with country A depicted as having a higher ratio of wage to rental (ω) than country B.[3]

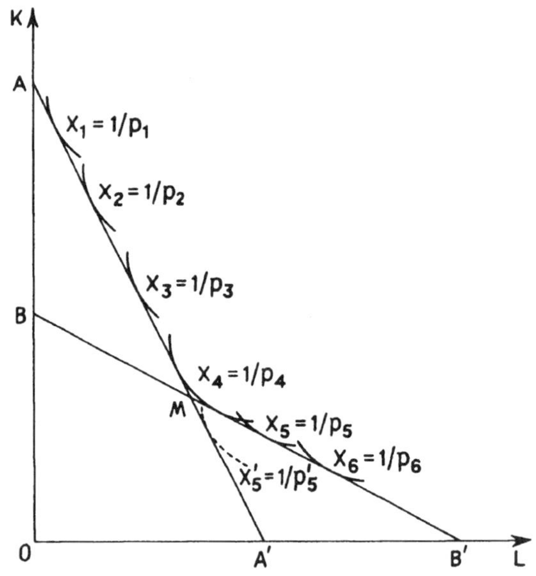

Fig. 1

From these isocost lines one can conclude what the free trade prices of each good must be. That is, the price of each good must be such as to place its unit-value isoquant exactly tangent to the outermost of the two unit-isocost lines, as shown by the (solid) isoquants drawn in fig. 1. For if a unit-value isoquant were to lie wholly outside both AA' and BB', the good would not be produced in either country, while if it lay anywhere inside either one of the lines, its production would yield a positive profit in the corresponding country. Furthermore, while it is possible for an isoquant to be tangent to

[3]Unequal factor prices do not, of course, ensure that the two isocost lines will intersect, as drawn, since one could lie wholly outside the other. In that case, as the analysis below indicates, the chain proposition holds trivially since all goods will be exported by the same country. Were balanced trade assumed, such a situation would of course be excluded.

both isocost lines (as good 4 in fig. 1), this need not happen for any good and, without factor intensity reversals, cannot happen for more than one.

It is now immediately evident from fig. 1 that the pattern of trade must agree with the ranking of the goods by factor intensity. The most capital intensive goods (1,2, and 3 in fig. 1) can only be produced in the high wage country, A, and must therefore be exported by A, while the most labor intensive (5 and 6) must be produced and exported by B. Good 4, in this case, may be produced in both countries and may be exported by either. It therefore constitutes the division of the chain of comparative advantage.

We have already noted that the high relative wage in A implies that it is capital abundant by the price definition.[4] It is also true in this case that A must be capital abundant by the physical definition as well. For we can see in fig. 1 that all production in A requires a higher ratio of capital to labor than all production in B. Thus, our result implies that every export of the capital abundant country, by either definition, must be more capital intensive than every one of its imports.[5]

Before extending this analysis to include tariffs, transport costs, and intermediate goods, it should be pointed out that the technique used here does not derive the trade equilibrium. Rather, it assumes that an equilibrium exists and merely examines a particular property of that equilibrium. Much more information would be needed to determine, for example, what the equilibrium factor prices should be and where, in the chain of comparative advantage, the division between the two countries should be located.

3. Impeded trade

If tariffs or transport costs permit different prices in the two countries, then the argument as given above is no longer valid, for there will be different unit-value isoquants in the two countries. But the argument can easily be salvaged if direct *subsidies* to trade are not permitted. For then a good will be exported only if its price is at least as high abroad as at home, and imported only if its price is at least as low abroad as at home, to compensate exporters and importers for the additional cost of tariffs and transport.[6]

[4]See footnote 2.

[5]Rather remarkably, no assumption has been needed about demand or about relative factor prices in autarky. However, if demand were so biased as to make the autarky relative wage in A less than the autarky relative wage in B, then factor prices would have to be equalized by free trade and the factor prices assumed in fig. 1 could not arise. This also follows from the argument given in footnote 2.

[6]In another context I have called this the assumption of 'natural' trade [see Deardorff (1977)]. This formulation is consistent with any of a variety of explicit assumptions about the nature of transport costs, so long as these costs are non-negative. However, the reader may prefer to think of a more explicit assumption, such as that of Samuelson (1954), who let a certain fraction of each good be used up in transport.

To see how this works, consider again the two countries whose unit isocost lines, with trade, are those shown in fig. 1. Suppose that some good, X_i, is exported by country A. To be exported it must be produced, and thus the unit-value isoquant of X_i in A must be tangent to AA'. Suppose it were tangent below the intersection M, like the dotted isoquant X_5' in fig. 1. For the good to be exported from A, it must also fetch at least as high a price in B (to cover any transport cost or tariff) and this would place B's unit-value isoquant for the same good still closer to the origin than X_5' and certainly inside the line BB'. The good would then yield a positive profit in B, and this is impossible. Thus, the unit-value isoquants of all of A's exports must be tangent to AA' above its intersection with BB' exactly as was the case with free trade. Applying a similar argument to exports from B, it follows as before that all of A's exports must be more capital intensive than all of A's imports.

This then validates the Bhagwati–Jones conjecture that a capital abundant country (using the price definition of abundance) will export only goods which are more capital intensive than any of its imports, if there are impediments to trade and unequal factor prices.[7,8]

4. Intermediate goods and free trade

Now suppose that any or all of goods $1,\ldots,n$ can be used as intermediate inputs in production. The argument of section 2 with free trade remains intact if unit-value isoquants are replaced by unit-value-*added* isoquants.

For any good X_i, let the production function be given by

$$X_i = F^i(K_i, L_i, X_{1i}, \ldots, X_{ni}),$$

[7]Note that if trade impediments were positive for all goods, then the qualification that factor prices be unequal would be unnecessary. For equal factor prices would mean equal commodity prices and thus no trade.

[8]I have called this a conjecture because I do not regard the argument provided by Bhagwati (1972) to be a proof, though naturally when a proposition is valid there can be some disagreement as to what constitutes proof. Bhagwati (p. 1054) argued that

> ...while a commodity in the middle of a chain of exportables may be priced out of the export market into being a nontraded good by high transportation costs, it is impossible for it to be turned into an imported good.

Now it is certainly true that the cost of transporting a given exportable cannot cause *it* to be imported. But I see no a priori reason why the cost of transporting some other good might not cause this to happen. Suppose, for example, that the cost of importing eggs were to raise their price so high as to cause substitution away from both bacon and eggs towards oatmeal. Then oatmeal could become imported and bacon exported, even if the reverse would be true if eggs could be imported cheaply. The proof in the text shows that this cannot happen in a two-factor model (where chickens and pigs – or the farmers that raise them – could be employed planting oats), but I see nothing in Bhagwati's remarks to rule this out.

where X_{ji} are the inputs of goods j into production of good i. Let

$$V_i(K_i, L_i, p_1, \ldots, p_n) = \max_{X_i, X_{ji}} \left[p_i X_i - \sum_{j=1}^{n} p_j X_{ji} \right]$$

$$\text{s.t. } X_i = F^i(K_i, L_i, X_{1i}, \ldots, X_{ni}).$$

For given values of all prices, the functions $V_i(K_i, L_i, \cdot)$ describe, in nominal terms, the maximum net revenue that can be earned and allocated to payment of the primary factors, capital and labor. They can therefore be used to determine the pattern of specialization, in exactly the same way that we earlier used production functions multiplied by prices.[9] That is, unit-value-added isoquants can be defined by setting $V_i = 1$, and production will require tangency between these and the unit-isocost lines.[10]

With free trade, all prices are the same in the two countries, which therefore share identical unit-value-added isoquants. The argument of section 2 can be repeated and the same result obtained. Thus, the chain of comparative advantage can still be used when there are intermediate goods, so long as trade is free and the prices of primary factors are not equalized. The factor intensities used in constructing the chain represent only direct capital and labor requirements, and do not include factors that are used indirectly by being embodied in intermediate inputs. For, as long as intermediate inputs are traded freely, they need not be produced within the country in which they are used.

5. Intermediate goods and impeded trade

If trade is not free, however, there is a problem. It arises because the

[9]Note that, since V_i is defined in nominal terms, we do not encounter the problem of defining either a natural unit for value added or a 'price' of value added, which has been a source of difficulty in the effective protection literature. In particular, our construction does not require the separability assumption that has been stressed by Bruno (1973) and by Bhagwati and Srinivasan (1973). It should also be mentioned that V_i, as functions of K_i and L_i, possess the same homogeneity and concavity properties that are assumed of the production functions, F_i. See Diewert's (1973) discussion of variable profit functions.

[10]In the special case, often assumed, of fixed coefficients between intermediate inputs and final output (so that $X_{ji} = a_{ji} X_i$) the function

$$V_i = \left(p_i \sum_{j=1}^{n} p_j a_{ji} \right) F^i(K_i, L_i).$$

The isoquants of V_i are then identical to the isoquants of F^i, and the unit-value-added isoquant is that for which

$$X_i = 1 \Big/ \left(p_i - \sum_{j=1}^{n} p_j a_{ji} \right).$$

position of a unit-value-added isoquant depends on *all* prices and not just on the price of the corresponding final good. Thus, when a tariff on, say, good 5 in fig. 1 raises its price in A above that in B, it does, as before, pull A's isoquant toward the origin to a position like X'_5. But it also pushes A's isoquants of other goods that use good 5 as an input out further from the origin than they are in country B. And this makes it impossible to infer individual relative prices from the positions of individual isoquants in the two countries as was done before. The same problem arises if prices differ due to transport costs, though for ease of exposition we will limit attention here to a tariff.

To see what can happen consider the following special case which will suffice to provide a counterexample to the chain proposition. Suppose there are only three goods, with goods 1 and 2 acting solely as final goods and with good 3 acting only as an intermediate input to production of good 1. Suppose further that country B is so large that we can take its prices as independent of trade with country A and that A is so capital abundant that it produces, in *free* trade, only the most capital intensive good 1. The free trade situation is depicted as the solid unit-value-added isoquants and isocost lines in fig. 2. The line AA' represents free trade factor prices in country A, which employs its entire endowment of capital and labor, K^A and L^A, in the production of good 1 at point a. Country B, with factor prices given by BB', produces all three goods using the unit-value-added isoquants, $V_1=1$, $V_2=1$, and $V_3=1$. Country A exports good 1 and imports goods 2 and 3.

Now suppose that country A levies a tariff on imports of good 3, raising its domestic price. This will pull A's unit-value-added isoquant for good 3 in

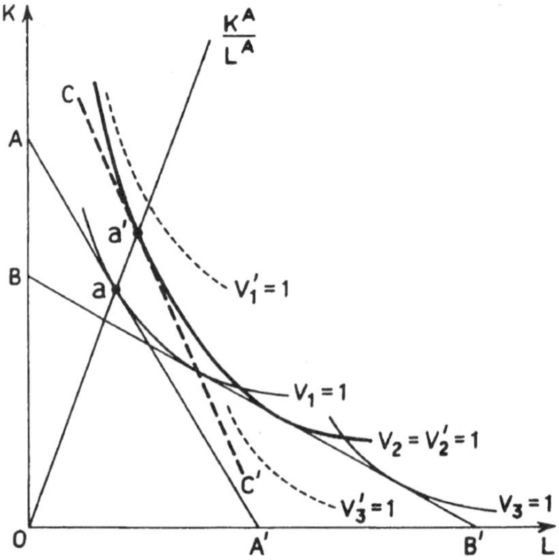

Fig. 2

toward the origin, to a position like $V_3' = 1$. The isoquant for good 2 will not be affected (since good 2 does not use good 3 as an input), but the unit-value-added isoquant of good 1 will be pushed out away from the origin, as additional production is required to cover the increased cost of the input of good 3 and leave a unit left over for value added.[11] If the tariff is large enough and if good 3 is a sufficiently important input into production of good 1, the new unit-value-added isoquant will be $V_1' = 1$ in fig. 2.[12]

It can now be seen from the figure that country A will specialize completely in production of good 2, at point a', with factor prices given by the line CC', since this is the only pattern of production and factor prices that can both yield zero profits and employ the factors in the ratio K^A/L^A. If both countries consume something of both goods 1 and 2, it follows that country A, with the tariff, will export good 2 and import good 1. The pattern of trade in these two goods has therefore been completely reversed by the tariff on good 3.[13]

The intuition behind this result is straightforward and is reflected in the diagram. When a tariff raises the price of the intermediate good, it also makes the final good more costly to produce, and since the intermediate good is itself very labor intensive, country A cannot reduce that cost by producing it itself. Instead, all production switches to good 2 which does not require the labor intensive, and now expensive, input of good 3.

Another way of seeing what is going on in this example is to look at effective rates of protection. With a tariff on the intermediate good and none on either final good, the effective rate of protection of industry 1 is negative. Thus, while the explicit effects of tariffs are only to tax trade, the tariff on the intermediate good has the implicit effect of subsidizing imports of, in this case, the capital intensive good.

[11]This may sound like a description of producers who take a loss on every unit but 'make it up in volume'. This need not be the case since there was initially a positive margin for value added, and hence a small enough input price increase will leave that margin positive. But it does point up the possibility that unit-value-added isoquants may not just move, but may disappear when input prices increase. This is particularly true when there is no possibility of substitution away from intermediate inputs, as in the fixed coefficients case of the preceding footnote. This possibility makes a counterexample even easier to obtain, however, since it means that a tariff increase can shift all production to good 2.

[12]It is essential for the counterexample that the isoquant, $V_1' = 1$, lie outside the line CC', which is tangent to the $V_2 = 1$ isoquant where it crosses the K^A/L^A ray. In the figure, this requires a substantial movement of the V_1 isoquant, but this need not be the case. If good 2 were only slightly more labor-intensive than good 1, CC' would lie very close to AA' and a small movement of the V_1 isoquant would suffice.

[13]I am indebted to Jagdish Bhagwati for suggesting this construction of the counterexample, which is more direct than was used in an earlier version of this paper. The earlier construction drew upon a result of Batra and Casas (1973) who showed that a nontraded intermediate good of extreme factor intensity can cause the Heckscher–Ohlin theorem to be violated. Thus, if we begin, as in this example, with the theorem holding under free trade, a prohibitive tariff on an intermediate good can reverse the pattern of trade.

The counterexample of this section shows that a ranking by capital intensities cannot suffice to determine trade.[14] But more importantly, it shows that a ranking by *any other criterion* must fail as well. In the example, any ranking that places all of A's exports above all of A's imports with free trade will fail to do so when a tariff is applied. For good 1 has changed from an export to an import and good 2 has done just the reverse.

6. Many countries

Analysis of the free trade cases, both with and without intermediate goods, extends readily to the case of many countries, though naturally one cannot expect a single division of the chain of comparative advantage to delineate correctly the trade of all countries. Since the analysis is similar to what has gone before, it will be left to the reader to imagine or draw the appropriate diagrams. Simply insert, as in fig. 1, the unit isocost lines for all countries. World prices – common to all countries – must then give rise to unit-value (-added) isoquants that are tangent to the outer envelope of all of these isocost lines. Each country will then produce and export only those goods with isoquants tangent to its own isocost line, the intersections of which with adjacent cost lines therefore provide upper and lower limits on the factor intensities of its exports.

Thus, the chain of goods ranked by capital intensity is broken into segments, one for each country, and the segments are ordered identically with the relative capital abundance of the countries. As in the two-country case, adjacent segments may contain one good in common, if the isoquant for such a borderline good happens to touch two countries' isocost lines in the manner of good 4 in fig. 1. Otherwise the division between segments of the chain occurs between goods. Each country must export all goods which appear only in its segment of the chain and must import all goods which do not appear in its segment. Borderline goods may be exported by either or both of the countries in whose segments they appear. It follows that each of a country's exports must be at least as capital intensive as each of the exports of all less capital abundant countries and at least as labor intensive as each of the exports of all less labor abundant countries.

This conclusion, however, is extremely sensitive to the assumption of free trade. Even without intermediate goods, impediments to trade can drastically alter the pattern of trade.

To see this, return to the two-country configuration of fig. 1 and add a tiny third country, C, with a factor endowment ratio lying between the ratios

[14]Note that direct-plus-indirect capital intensities do not work either. For when the intermediate good in our example was traded freely, then good 2 was imported even though it may be the most capital intensive on the direct-plus-indirect basis.

employed by A and B in industry 4. With free trade, such a country will specialize completely in production of good 4, exporting it in exchange for imports of all other goods. Now suppose, however, that it levies a large tariff on imports of the most capital intensive good, 1. The tariff will raise the price of good 1 in C, pulling its unit value isoquant in towards – and past – C's unit isocost line. Country C will begin production of good 1 and the relative wage in C will fall. However, good 1 is so capital intensive that much of it cannot be produced with the factors available in C and, if demand is also fairly inelastic, imports of good 1 will continue. Thus, there is nothing to prevent a further increase in the tariff from raising its price still more, to bring its unit-value isoquant inside BB'. When that happens, a new isocost line must appear in C, tangent only to isoquants of goods 1 and 6. Production of good 4 (C's original export good) ceases entirely and production of good 6 begins instead. And good 6 must also be exported, since good 1 cannot be, and imports of goods 2, 3, 4, and 5 must continue. Thus, country C, because of a tariff, has changed from being an exporter of a good of intermediate factor intensity to become an exporter of the most labor intensive good that there is.

It should perhaps be noted that this extreme response of the trade pattern to a tariff is only possible for a country whose factor abundance is intermediate between those of other countries. This explains why this result was not possible in the two-country case.

7. Conclusion

It would indeed be useful if we could construct some ranking of commodities, by some criterion, which would enable us to predict the pattern of trade, even if only in the sense of saying that each of a country's exports must lie higher on this list than each of its imports. I have shown that such a ranking is possible in certain cases. But it is impossible both in Bhagwati's 'not unimportant' case of factor price equalization and in the obviously important case of positive trade impediments and intermediate goods. This does not mean, however, that trade theorists should abandon the Heckscher–Ohlin theorem or the Law of Comparative Advantage. What it does mean is that we should search for alternative statements of these propositions that will retain their validity and still tell us something useful about the pattern of trade in the real world.

One such formulation has been developed, as a statement about the 'factor content' of trade. Vanek (1968) showed that, under certain assumptions, the factor content of a country's trade can be inferred from a chain of factor endowment rankings, very much like the chain of comparative advantage in trade of goods discussed here.[15] The assumptions used to prove this result, however, include factor price equalization. It is therefore not known, yet, whether the factor content version of the Heckscher–Ohlin theorem can be extended to the troublesome case considered here of trade impediments and intermediate goods.[16] This is an important issue, since it was implicitly the factor content of trade that was the focus of Leontief's (1954) famous calculations.

The result in section 5, in which an export good and an import good exchange roles, is as critical for the theory of comparative advantages as it is for the Heckscher–Ohlin theory. For it implies that no ranking of goods can suffice to determine trade, not even one based on relative autarky prices. Yet this does not mean that comparative advantage plays no role in determining the pattern of trade. Rather, the role that it does play is not as strong as the chain proposition would suggest. I have shown elsewhere that relative autarky prices must be negatively correlated with net exports [Deardorff (1977)]. The result of section 5 is consistent with such a correlation, so long as the relative autarky price of good 1 is higher than that of good 2.

Finally, I would like to point out a use that has been made of the Bhagwati–Jones proposition of section 3, a use which turns out to be inappropriate in view of the result of section 5. Harkness and Kyle (1975) motivated their use of logit analysis in an empirical test of the Heckscher–Ohlin theorem on the grounds that the theorem predicts only the direction, not the extent, of trade. They acknowledged Bhagwati's (1972) observation that even the prediction of direction fails if factor prices are equalized, but argued that transportation costs are such a fact of life that Bhagwati's counterexample cannot arise in the real world. Yet intermediate goods are just as much a fact of life as transportation costs. The counterexample which the two together permit can therefore not be dismissed so easily.

[15]Melvin (1968) also stated this proposition for the two-factor case. Vanek's demonstration, which has been generalized to bilateral trade by Horiba (1974), allows for any number of factors.

[16]Baldwin (1971, p. 130) states in a footnote that 'tariffs can weaken the pattern of indirect factor trade in a Heckscher–Ohlin model but cannot alone produce paradoxical results'. It is unclear from the context, however, just what model he has in mind and thus whether this is any more than a statement of the (later) Bhagwati–Jones proposition that was proved above in section 3.

References

Baldwin, Robert E., 1971, Determinants of the commodity structure of U.S. trade, American Economic Review 61, 126–146.

Batra, Raveendra N. and Francisco R. Casas, 1973, Intermediate products and the pure theory of international trade: A neo-Heckscher–Ohlin framework, American Economic Review 63, 297–311.

Bhagwati, Jagdish H., 1972, The Heckscher–Ohlin theorem in the multi-commodity case, Journal of Political Economy 80, 1052–1055.

Bhagwati, Jagdish H. and T.N. Srinivasan, 1973, The general equilibrium theory of effective protection and resource allocation, Journal of International Economics 3, 259–281.

Bruno, M., 1973, Protection and tariff change under general equilibrium, Journal of International Economics 3, 205–226.

Deardorff, Alan V., 1977, Comparative advantage and natural trade in general equilibrium, Seminar Discussion Paper no. 83, Research Seminar in International Economics, University of Michigan.

Diewert, W.E., 1973, Functional forms for profit and transformation functions, Journal of Economic Theory 6, 284–316.

Haberler, Gottfried von, 1936, The theory of international trade with its applications to commercial policy (William Hodge & Co., London).

Harkness, Jon and John F. Kyle, 1975, Factors influencing United States comparative advantage, Journal of International Economics 5, 153–165.

Horiba, Y., 1974, General equilibrium and the Heckscher–Ohlin theory of trade: The multi-country case, International Economic Review 15, 440–449.

Jones, Ronald W., 1956–57, Factor proportions and the Heckscher–Ohlin theorem, Review of Economic Studies 24, 1–10.

Leontief, Wassily, 1954, Domestic production and foreign trade: The American capital position re-examined, Economia Internazionale 7, 3–32.

Melvin, James, 1968, Production and trade with two factors and three goods, American Economic Review 58, 1249–1268.

Samuelson, Paul A., 1954, The transfer problem and transport costs: Analysis of the effects of trade impediments, Economic Journal, 264–289.

Travis, William P., 1964, The theory of trade and protection (Harvard University Press, Cambridge, Mass.).

Travis, William P., 1972, Production, trade, and protection when there are many commodities and two factors, American Economic Review 62, 87–106.

Vanek, Jaroslav, 1968, The factor proportions theory: The *n*-factor case, Kyklos 4, 749–756.

CHAPTER 10

The General Validity of the Law of Comparative Advantage

Alan V. Deardorff

Institute for International Economic Studies, University of Stockholm, and University of Michigan

It is well known that the law of comparative advantage breaks down when applied to individual commodities or pairs of commodities in a many-commodity world. This paper shows that the law is nonetheless valid if restated in terms of averages across all commodities. Specifically, a theorem and several corollaries are derived which establish correlations between vectors of trade and vectors containing relative-autarky-price measures of comparative advantage. These results are proven in a general many-commodity model that allows for tariffs, transport costs, and other impediments to trade.

The purpose of this paper is to demonstrate, in a general model, the validity of a weak form of the Law of Comparative Advantage, that is, that the *pattern of international trade is determined by comparative advantage.* This is surely the oldest proposition in the pure theory of international trade and is common both to the Ricardian comparative-costs theory and the Heckscher-Ohlin factor-proportions theory, so long as comparative advantage is measured by relative autarky prices. As such, one might think that the proposition requires no further comment except in the basic textbooks whose job it is to explain important truths in simple terms.

Yet this proposition, like other more recent theorems of trade theory, has proven somewhat difficult to extend beyond the simple

I would like to thank Ted Bergstrom, Paul Courant, Ronald Jones, Robert Stern, Lars Svensson, and Hal Varian for their helpful comments on an earlier draft of this paper, originally titled "Comparative Advantage and Natural Trade in General Equilibrium."

[*Journal of Political Economy,* 1980, vol. 88, no. 5]

models in which it was first formulated. Three examples should suffice to illustrate this difficulty. First, when Jones (1961) extended the doctrine of comparative advantage to a classical model with many goods and countries, he was forced to restate the concept of comparative costs in a form that lacked most of the simplicity and intuitive appeal of the original. Second, in the context of the Heckscher-Ohlin model, Melvin (1968) showed that if there are more goods than primary factors of production then the indeterminacy of the structure of production, that had been noted previously by Samuelson (1953), implies that any good may be exported by any country. This, it would seem, destroys altogether any determinate relationship between the pattern of trade and anything else. And third, Travis (1964, 1972) has argued that the introduction of impediments to trade, and particularly of tariffs, can alter the pattern of trade, causing goods that would have been exported to be imported and vice versa. Thus, it appears that if the two-commodity, two-country, free-trade model is extended or modified in plausible ways, it then ceases to be possible to explain the pattern of trade by simple comparisons of autarky prices. Most recently, this impossibility has been shown by Drabicki and Takayama (1979).

I will show in this paper, however, that a version of the comparative-advantage proposition *does* hold in a general model that allows for all of the complications just mentioned. This is not to say that the authors cited in the last paragraph were wrong. Instead, what is needed is to relax somewhat the rigidity of the proposition itself and require only that it hold in the sense of an appropriate average rather than for each commodity individually. While several forms of the proposition will be proved below, all may be summarized by the following statement: There must exist a negative correlation between any country's relative autarky prices and its pattern of net exports. Thus, on average, high autarky prices are associated with imports and low autarky prices are associated with exports.

This proposition will be demonstrated in a model that includes a variety of impediments to trade, as well as free trade, as special cases. I allow in a general way for transport costs, and I allow domestic and world prices to differ by additional amounts to reflect such artificial trade impediments as tariffs and quantitative restrictions. Unlimited interference with trade is not allowed, however, since it is clear that sufficient use of trade *subsidies* could lead to any pattern of trade and thus invalidate the law of comparative advantage. For ease of reference, and to distinguish it from the more restrictive case of free trade, I will refer to this combination of assumptions as defining "natural trade." Thus a natural trade equilibrium is one in which there are no trade subsidies or other artificial stimulants to trade, but in which trade impediments of any sort may or may not be present. Free trade is then a special case of natural trade.[1]

My treatment of transport costs is somewhat unusual and should therefore also be mentioned in this introduction. Rather than postulate an explicit form for transport costs, I will distinguish goods on the basis of where they are delivered and incorporate transportation technology into a more general specification of the technology of production. For each country, a single production possibility set will define the constraints on its ability to produce for delivery at home and for delivery abroad. Thus any resources used up in transportation will be taken into account when the competitive producers and traders of the economy maximize the value of net delivered output. In the body of the paper I will simplify notation somewhat by assuming that all world trade passes through a single international port, though in an Appendix I show that most of my results carry over to a world of any number of such ports.

With this introduction the analysis can proceed. In Section I, I will state and discuss the assumptions of the model, which are broad enough to encompass a wide variety of models that have appeared in the literature. In Section II, I will first prove a basic theorem, which uses autarky prices to value the vector of goods that a country trades in a natural trade equilibrium. This result then leads readily to four corollaries which provide alternative statements of the law of comparative advantage in the average sense discussed above. In Section III, I discuss several ways that these results can be strengthened or modified. Finally, I return in Section IV to the particular issues raised above and show how my results contribute to an understanding of the various phenomena noted by other authors.

I. The Model

Consider a world of m countries, $i = 1, \ldots, m$, and n goods, $j = 1, \ldots, n$. The list of goods includes all final goods, intermediate goods, and services of primary factors of production. Each good may be delivered either on the country's home market or at the international port. Let Q^i be an n-vector of net supplies to country i's home market and T^i be an n-vector of net supplies by country i to the international port. Thus positive elements of Q^i represent goods available for consumption in country i, while negative elements represent net use of goods or factor services by production processes in country i. Similarly, the elements of the vector T^i represent the country's trade in each of the n goods: exports if positive and imports if negative. The country's total

[1] Natural trade also includes autarky as another special case, though my results are, of course, of interest only in situations in which some trade actually does take place.

production, net of goods and resources used up in production and transport, is then $X^i = Q^i + T^i$.

Each country has its own net production possibility set, F^i, defined as the set of all feasible pairs of n-vectors, Q^i and T^i, given its technology and any constraints it may face on endowments of primary factors. Of the sets, F^i, I assume whatever is necessary to permit existence of the equilibria I will be studying. Thus, they must be closed, convex, and, in some weak sense, bounded from above.[2] In addition, I make the following assumption that says essentially that transport costs are nonnegative: If

$$(Q^i, T^i) \in F^i,$$

then

$$(Q^i + T^i, 0) \in F^i, \tag{1}$$

where 0 here represents an n-vector of zeros. This says that any total net output vector that is feasible with trade is also feasible without, since resources can only be used up, but never created, by transporting goods between the domestic market and the international port. Thus if it is feasible to produce a good and deliver it abroad, $T_j^i > 0$, then it is also feasible to produce it and deliver it at home. Likewise, if it is feasible to import a good, $T_j^i < 0$, then it is also feasible not to import it and to reduce deliveries on the home market by the same amount.[3]

To represent demand in each country, stronger assumptions will be used. I assume that preferences in each country can be represented by a family of n-dimensional community indifference curves, which it will be convenient to represent by a community utility function, U^i. These utility functions are assumed to have the property of local nonsatiation: For any Q^{i0} there exists a Q^{i1} arbitrarily close to Q^{i0} such that

$$U(Q^{i1}) > U(Q^{i0}). \tag{2}$$

This assumption will be used to rule out "thick" indifference curves.

Both producers and consumers are assumed to behave competitively, so that they maximize, respectively, the value of net output and the utility of consumption, subject to the prices that they face in each country.[4] In autarky equilibrium, production is for the domestic

[2] It would be sufficient, though not necessary, to assume the existence of a vector $\bar{X}^i$ such that $Q + T \leq \bar{X}^i$ for all $(Q, T) \in F^i$.

[3] Note that this assumption includes, as a special case, the more explicit assumption made by Samuelson (1954), who specified that some fraction, α_j, of each good be used up in transport. If I let G be a more conventional production possibility set in which location of delivery is not specified, then my $F = \{(Q, T)$ such that $\bar{X} \in G$ where $\bar{X}_j = Q_j + T_j + \alpha_j |T_j|\}$. Assumption (1) then follows immediately.

[4] In order for producers to maximize the value of net output, I make the standard assumptions that domestic economies are competitive and that there are no externalities, production taxes, or other domestic distortions. Increasing returns to scale must also be ruled out.

market only, while with trade, producers maximize the sum of the value of output delivered at home and the value of output delivered abroad, the prices of which will in general be different due to transportation costs. The price of output delivered abroad will also in general be different from the world price, due to impediments to trade such as tariffs. Equilibrium in the home market requires that the vector of net supplies to the home market be consumed. Equilibrium in international trade requires in addition that the sum of all countries' net supplies to the international port be zero and that each country's trade be balanced at world prices.

I begin by characterizing autarky equilibrium. Let Q^{a^i} be a vector of net outputs both supplied and demanded on the domestic market of country i under autarky, and let p^{a^i} be a corresponding vector of autarky prices. Then the following three assumptions require that Q^{a^i} be feasible, maximal, and preferred, given the prices p^{a^i}:

$$(Q^{a^i}, 0) \in F^i, \tag{3}$$

$$p^{a^i}Q^{a^i} \geqslant p^{a^i}Q \text{ for all } (Q, 0) \in F^i, \tag{4}$$

$$U^i(Q^{a^i}) \geqslant U^i(Q) \text{ for all } Q \text{ such that } p^{a^i}Q \leqslant p^{a^i}Q^{a^i}. \tag{5}$$

Here, and throughout the paper, all products of vectors represent inner products.

To characterize a natural trade equilibrium, more notation is needed. Let Q^{n^i} and T^{n^i} be vectors of net supply by country i to domestic and foreign markets in a natural trade equilibrium. Let p^{q^i} and p^{t^i} be corresponding vectors of prices facing domestic producers, consumers, and traders in these markets, defined in terms of a single international numeraire. Thus the elements of p^{q^i} are simply the domestic prices in country i, while those of p^{t^i} are the prices paid or received by domestic traders at the international port and will be referred to as traders' prices. In particular, p^{t^i} includes any tariffs that must be paid on domestic imports and is net of any export taxes paid on exports. The two vectors of prices will have to differ by enough to cover transport costs if trade is to take place, but this will be assured by the maximization assumption below. Assumptions analogous to those above require that production, trade, and consumption be feasible, maximal, and preferred given these prices:

$$(Q^{n^i}, T^{n^i}) \in F^i, \tag{6}$$

$$p^{q^i}Q^{n^i} + p^{t^i}T^{n^i} \geqslant p^{q^i}Q + p^{t^i}T \text{ for all } (Q, T) \in F^i, \tag{7}$$

$$U^i(Q^{n^i}) \geqslant U^i(Q) \text{ for all } Q \text{ such that } p^{q^i}Q \leqslant p^{q^i}Q^{n^i}. \tag{8}$$

Within the international port, there is also a vector of world prices, p^w, also measured in terms of the international numeraire. It represents the price at which international exchange actually takes place and may differ from the national traders' prices, p^{ti}, to the extent that countries levy tariffs or export taxes. Each country's trade is assumed to be balanced at these world prices:

$$p^{w}T^{ni} = 0. \tag{9}$$

The relationship between world prices and national traders' prices can in general be complicated, depending both on the precise nature of trade impediments and on the direction of trade itself. However, all I need to characterize natural trade is to rule out trade subsidies, and this is done by the following simple assumption:

$$(p_j^w - p_j^{ti})T_j^{ni} \geqslant 0 \text{ for } \quad j = 1, \ldots, n. \tag{10}$$

What this says is that if a good is exported, $T_j^{ni} > 0$, then the world price must be at least as large as the price the exporter receives, any differences between the two representing an export tax levied by country i. And if a good is imported, $T_j^{ni} < 0$, then the world price must be no greater than the price the importer pays, any difference representing a tariff. Of course, if there were no policies interfering with trade, then (10) would be an equality.

Finally, I require that the world market for each good clear:

$$\sum_{i=1}^{m} T^{ni} = 0. \tag{11}$$

Assumptions (1) through (11) are sufficient for most of my results. However, later in the paper I will have occasion to make comparisons among autarky and world prices. For that purpose it will be convenient to normalize world prices and each country's autarky prices to lie on the unit simplex:

$$\sum_{j=1}^{n} p_j^w = \sum_{j=1}^{n} p_j^{ai} = 1 \qquad i = 1, \ldots, m. \tag{12}$$

This is equivalent to taking, as numeraire, a bundle containing one unit of each good.

It may be well to note, before I proceed, that my list of assumptions does *not* include a number that are often made in trade theory. The utility functions have not been assumed to be differentiable and neither have the boundaries of the production possibility sets. The latter have not been assumed to be convex, nor the former to be homothetic. And neither have been assumed to be in any sense identical across countries. Thus the countries can differ arbitrarily in tastes, technologies, and factor endowments. None of this should be too surprising, however, since, while some of these assumptions may make certain modes of analysis more convenient, they are not really needed for establishing the role of comparative advantage.

More surprising, perhaps, is the limited amount I have had to say about the role of, and availability of, factor endowments in the model. Since the assumption of natural trade permits any of the "goods" to be nontraded, one can as well include the services of any or all factors of production as elements in the vector of n goods and even allow them to be in variable supply. One could even allow some or all of them to be traded internationally, so that the concept of comparative advantage is then extended to trade in the services of factors of production. Or, at the other extreme, one could identify as separate factors those which are employed in different industries and thus allow for various degrees of interindustry factor immobility. Finally, with some care one can allow for dynamic factor accumulation by interpreting the sets F as constraints on steady-state net output per capita.[5]

The point is that, while the list of assumptions earlier in this section was a long one, the assumptions themselves are much less restrictive than one often meets in models of international trade. With some care and ingenuity in interpreting the model, the results I am about to derive can shed light on the mechanism of international trade in quite a variety of contexts.

II. A Theorem and Its Corollaries

Now consider any one of the countries described in Section I. I will show first that if one uses autarky prices to evaluate its net trade vector in a natural trade equilibrium then that value must be less than or equal to zero. That is, the value of what a country gives up in trade is no greater, at autarky prices, than the value of what it acquires. While this may not seem to be a very surprising property, its proof uses most of the assumptions that were introduced in Section I. And once it is established, it leads fairly easily to a variety of results concerning comparative advantage.

The meaning of the theorem can be illustrated with the simple offer-curve diagram of figure 1. For a country which trades only two goods, the curve COC' shows the various possibilities for exports and imports of both goods with free trade. My theorem says that any trade which takes place will have a negative value when valued at autarky prices. But since autarky prices are given by the slope of the line tangent to the offer curve at the origin, POP', this means merely that

[5] Care is needed here in assuring that a competitive economy will still, in a dynamic context, maximize the steady-state value of net output per capita. If technology permits inputs and outputs at different times, then it is the discounted value of the input-output stream that is maximized by a competitive economy. This can be resolved for one's purposes either by assuming that the interest rate equals the natural rate of growth or, more generally, by making a distinction between rental markets for the services of stocks of goods and the markets for their flow as final sales.

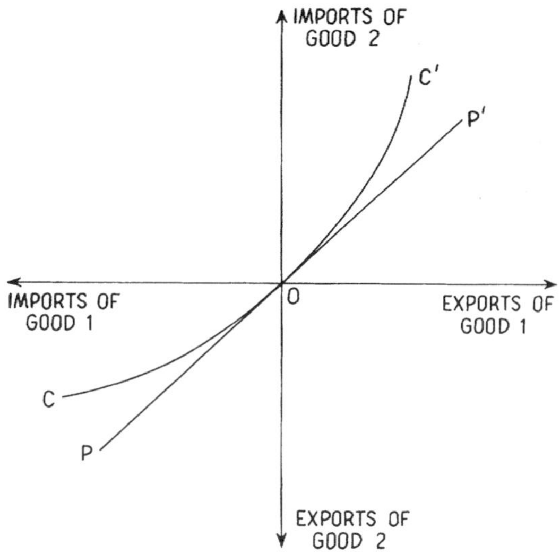

FIG. 1

COC' lies wholly to one side of this line. Well-behaved offer curves will have this property, and the reader may recognize a number of my assumptions as necessary to prevent the offer curve from "bending backward." Of course my model is far more general than figure 1, since it allows an arbitrary number of goods and does not require free trade. Still, one can interpret the theorem as saying that autarky prices provide a supporting hyperplane for the set of all possible trades.

Theorem.—If prices and quantities in autarky and trade satisfy assumptions (1)–(10) for a particular country, i, then

$$p^{a^i}T^{n^i} \leqslant 0. \tag{13}$$

Proof.—Since I am dealing with only a single country, I will omit the country superscript in what follows. I begin by adding up the inequalities in (10) to get

$$p^wT^n - p^tT^n \geqslant 0, \tag{14}$$

from which, using (9),

$$p^tT^n \leqslant p^wT^n = 0. \tag{15}$$

From (3) and (7) it then follows that

$$p^qQ^a \leqslant p^qQ^n + p^tT^n \leqslant p^qQ^n, \tag{16}$$

and this, from (8), implies

$$U(Q^n) \geqslant U(Q^a). \tag{17}$$

Thus the vector of goods consumed in natural trade is at least as preferred as that consumed in autarky. It follows from (2) and (5) that

$$p^a Q^n \geqslant p^a Q^a, \tag{18}$$

for if this were not the case, (2) would permit one to find another vector, $\bar{Q}$, in the neighborhood of Q^n, that would also cost less at autarky prices than Q^a but would be strictly preferred, violating (5).

Now (6) and (1) imply that $(Q^n + T^n, 0) \in F$, so that (4) implies

$$p^a Q^a \geqslant p^a (Q^n + T^n). \tag{19}$$

Rearranging and using (18) one gets the desired result:

$$p^a T^n \leqslant p^a Q^a - p^a Q^n \leqslant 0. \tag{20}$$

Q.E.D.

The theorem has been stated in the form of a weak inequality. Still it should be clear, from the chain of reasoning used in its proof, that there are many ways that the inequality can be strengthened. Some of these will be mentioned in Section III.

Consider, now, the issue of comparative advantage. My theorem is already very suggestive in this regard: For the autarky-price value of trade to be negative, it would have to be true that the autarky prices of exports are low compared with those of imports, and thus the country is exporting those goods with relatively low autarky prices as the principle of comparative advantage would suggest. To make this relationship more precise, I will now examine several correlations between particular vectors of relative autarky prices and net exports. By showing these correlations to be less than or equal to zero, I establish a *tendency* for high-autarky-priced items to be imported and for low-autarky-priced items to be exported. I do not attempt to say anything about the pattern of trade in any particular commodity, or pair of commodities, for it is known from the work of others that such statements are likely to be invalid in a model as general as mine. Still, if I can show a negative correlation such as just described, I will have demonstrated that comparative advantage is nonetheless valid as at least a partial determinant of the pattern of trade overall.

The sign of a correlation between two vectors is, of course, the same as the sign of their covariance. For any two n-vectors, x^1 and x^2, by definition

$$\text{cor}\,(x^1, x^2) = \frac{\text{cov}\,(x^1, x^2)}{\sqrt{\text{var}\,(x^1)\,\text{var}\,(x^2)}} \tag{21}$$

where

$$\text{cov}\,(x^1, x^2) = \sum_{j=1}^{n} (x_j^1 - \bar{x}^1)(x_j^2 - \bar{x}^2), \tag{22}$$

$$\text{var}\,(x^i) = \sum_{j=1}^{n} (x_j^i - \bar{x}^i)^2 \quad \text{for } i = 1, 2, \tag{23}$$

and

$$\bar{x}^i = \frac{1}{n}\sum_{j=1}^{n} x_j^i \quad \text{for } i = 1, 2. \tag{24}$$

Since the denominator of (21) is nonnegative (and nonzero if the correlation is defined), the correlation and covariance must have the same sign.[6] Furthermore, the covariance can be rewritten as follows:

$$\text{cov}\,(x^1, x^2) = x^1x^2 - n\bar{x}^1\bar{x}^2. \tag{25}$$

Thus if either of the vectors sums to zero, so that it has zero mean, then the sign of their correlation is just the sign of their inner product. Since I will use this property several times, I state it formally for ease of reference: If

$$\sum_{j=1}^{n} x_j^i = 0 \quad \text{for } i = 1 \quad \text{or} \quad i = 2, \tag{26}$$

then

$$\text{cor}\,(x^1, x^2) \gtreqless 0 \qquad \text{as } x^1x^2 \gtreqless 0.$$

In stating the role of comparative advantage, my first problem is to decide what is meant by "relative autarky prices." With many countries, there is no single set of foreign autarky prices with respect to which one country's can be compared. I will resolve this problem first by using world prices with trade as the basis for comparison. This gives corollaries 1 and 2 below. Then I show in corollary 3 that if in fact there are only two countries, so that a single vector of foreign autarky prices can be identified, then a comparison of the two vectors of autarky prices also yields the appropriate correlation with the vector of trade. Finally, in corollary 4 I establish a correlation between trade and autarky prices for a world of many countries without reference to world prices.

Corollary 1.—For any country let ρ be the vector of ratios of its autarky prices to the world prices that prevail with trade,

$$\rho_j = p_j^a/p_j^w \qquad j = 1, \ldots, n, \tag{27}$$

[6] I ignore, in what follows, the possibility of either vector having a zero variance so that the correlation is undefined. When that happens, as it will when there is no trade or when relative autarky prices are all identical, my conclusions about correlations can be restated as conclusions about the corresponding covariances only.

and let e be the vector of the country's net exports, valued at world prices,

$$e_j = p_j^w T_j^n \qquad j = 1, \ldots, n. \tag{28}$$

Then if assumptions (1)–(10) are satisfied for that country, it must be true that

$$\text{cor}\,(\rho, e) \leqslant 0. \tag{29}$$

Proof.—From balanced trade (9),

$$\sum_{j=1}^{n} e_j = p^w T^n = 0 \tag{30}$$

so that (26) permits one to consider only the inner product, ρe. But

$$\rho e = \sum_{j=1}^{n} \frac{p_j^a}{p_j^w} p_j^w T_j^n = \sum_{j=1}^{n} p_j^a T_j^n = p^a T^n \leqslant 0 \tag{31}$$

by the theorem. Q.E.D.

Here I have used ratios of autarky to world prices as the basis for comparison of industries. A slightly different comparison is also possible using the difference between autarky and world prices. For this difference to be meaningful, I assume that both price vectors are normalized to lie on the unit simplex, as stated in assumption (12).

Corollary 2.—If assumptions (1)–(10) are satisfied for any country and if prices are normalized as in (12), then

$$\text{cor}\,(p^a - p^w, T^n) \leqslant 0. \tag{32}$$

Proof.—For the inner product I have

$$(p^a - p^w)T^n = p^a T^n - p^w T^n = p^a T^n \leqslant 0 \tag{33}$$

by (9) and the theorem. Since, by (12),

$$\sum_{j=1}^{n} (p_j^a - p_j^w) = \sum_{j=1}^{n} p_j^a - \sum_{j=1}^{n} p_j^w = 0, \tag{34}$$

(26) permits one to deduce (32) from (33). Q.E.D.

Notice that both of these results obtain for any particular country without any assumptions whatever about behavior in the rest of the world. Also, no use has been made of the requirement that world markets clear, assumption (11). This, of course, is because I have not yet tried to make comparisons across countries. I now make such a comparison for a two-country world.

Corollary 3.—If the world contains only two countries, $i = 1, 2$, both satisfying (1)–(10), and if (11) is also satisfied, then

$$\text{cor}\,(p^{a1} - p^{a2}, T^{n1}) \leqslant 0, \tag{35}$$

where p^{a^1} and p^{a^2} are both normalized to the unit simplex (12).

Proof.—From (11) with $m = 2$ note that

$$T^{n^1} = -T^{n^2}. \tag{36}$$

Thus

$$(p^{a^1} - p^{a^2})T^{n^1} = p^{a^1}T^{n^1} + p^{a^2}T^{n^2}, \tag{37}$$

which is seen to be nonpositive by applying the theorem to each of the two terms on the right-hand side separately. The normalization (12), together with (26), then implies (35). Q.E.D.

This result, though derived only for a two-country world, has the advantage of placing a clear restriction on the possible pattern of natural trade. Given the two vectors of autarky prices, it says that, of all the conceivable patterns of trade that might emerge, only those which yield the indicated nonpositive correlation will be observed. Corollaries 1 and 2, on the other hand, do not embody such a clear restriction on the pattern of trade, since they contain the world-price vector which must be determined simultaneously with the pattern of trade.

To obtain a similar restriction for a many-country world I now prove a final corollary which deals with all countries and industries simultaneously. Let P^a be a vector of length mn containing the autarky prices of all countries and all industries, and let E be a vector of the same length containing the net exports of all countries and all industries, arranged in the same order as in P^a.

Corollary 4.—If the world contains m countries, all satisfying assumptions (1)–(10), and if (11) is also satisfied, then

$$\text{cor}\,(P^a, E) \leq 0. \tag{38}$$

Proof.—From the construction of E, it is clear that

$$\sum_{k=1}^{mn} E_k = \sum_{j=1}^{n}\left(\sum_{i=1}^{m} T_j^{n^i}\right) = 0 \tag{39}$$

by (11). Thus (26) allows one to look only at the inner product of P^a and E. But

$$\begin{aligned} P^aE &= \sum_{k=1}^{mn} P_k^a E_k = \sum_{i=1}^{m}\left(\sum_{j=1}^{n} p_j^{a^i} T_j^{n^i}\right) \\ &= \sum_{i=1}^{m} p^{a^i}T^{n^i}. \end{aligned} \tag{40}$$

From the theorem, each term in this summation is nonpositive, implying (38). Q.E.D.

To summarize, the first two corollaries provide alternative explanations of a single country's trade, one in value terms, the other in terms of quantities, with comparative advantage measured by comparisons of autarky prices with world prices. The third corollary provides the general analogue to the traditional comparative-advantage proposition for two countries in terms of a good-by-good comparison of the two countries' autarky prices. Finally, the fourth and last corollary provides the most general statement of comparative advantage for the world as a whole.

III. Refinements

In this section I point out two ways that the proofs above can be modified, either to strengthen the results or to alter the assumptions needed for their validity.

Strong Inequalities

The theorem and its corollaries are stated in terms of weak inequalities. These can be strengthened by any of several additional assumptions which serve to contribute a strict inequality somewhere in the chain of reasoning used to prove the theorem. I leave it to the reader to verify that any of the following assumptions would serve this purpose. (1) Transport costs are strictly positive for nonzero trade. (2) Tariff or export tax revenues are strictly positive in the natural trade equilibrium. (3) The optimal consumption bundle given any positive price vector is unique and different in natural trade and autarky. (4) The production possibility set is strictly convex, and trade and autarky prices differ.

While the first of these assumptions, especially, is realistic, I have chosen not to use any of them throughout the paper since they would exclude one of the best-known models and results of trade theory. That is the classical Ricardian constant-costs model with two countries of different size. In that model a trade equilibrium can arise in which the world prices equal the autarky prices of the large country, which then alters production, but not consumption, when it moves from autarky to trade. In that case the value of its trade at its own autarky prices is of course zero, as are the correlations of corollaries 1 and 2 for the large country. However, aside from this and perhaps other equally special cases, one can expect strictly negative correlations to be the normal result.

Relation to the Gains from Trade

The reader will already have noted that part of the proof of the theorem bears a marked similarity to the proof of the gains from trade (Samuelson 1939). I showed first that natural trade would be preferred to autarky (inequality [17]) and then that this implies the theorem. An alternative proof could have begun, then, with the assumption that trade is beneficial.

While this would not really be an improvement over the present analysis, since it would leave unanswered the question of whether there would indeed be gains from trade, this modification does suggest an alternative proof that does not rely on the fiction of community preferences.[7] Suppose that each country contains many individuals, each with his own preferences, and that a move from autarky to trade is accompanied by suitable redistribution of income so as to leave all individuals better off. Then an inequality like (18) can be obtained for each consumer individually, and (18) itself can be obtained by adding these up. The rest of the proof then follows.

IV. Discussion

At the beginning of the paper I noted that familiar simple statements about the role of comparative advantage become difficult or impossible when models are complicated in a variety of realistic ways. I have now developed an alternative way of representing the relationship between autarky prices and trade by looking at correlations between the two. This has enabled me to state a variety of simple propositions regarding comparative advantage, and I have proved these propositions in a very general model. I will now compare these results with others that have appeared in the literature.

Consider first the classical model of constant costs. Here it must be admitted that my contribution is limited, for the role of comparative advantage is already well understood in the classical model. The familiar proposition for a two-country world, that goods can be ranked in terms of comparative advantage with one end of the chain being exportable and the other importable, is considerably stronger than my own corollary 3 for the same case.[8] I note only what has sometimes been doubted: that while the classical theory predicts only the direction and not the magnitude of trade, it nonetheless permits one to infer a negative correlation between relative costs and net exports.[9]

[7] This alternative proof was suggested by Ted Bergstrom.

[8] The explanation of trade in terms of a chain of comparative advantage was apparently first demonstrated by Haberler (1936).

[9] Doubt that this should be true has been expressed, e.g., by Bhagwati (1964, p. 11) in criticizing empirical tests of the comparative-costs theory. Similar doubts in the context of the factor-proportions theory also led Harkness and Kyle (1975) to employ logit analysis, rather than least-squares regression, to test that theory. While my results do not deal directly with factor endowments or factor intensities, they nonetheless suggest that tests for simple correlations may not, after all, be inappropriate.

With both many countries and many goods, the classical model has been examined in detail by Jones (1961). His results, again, allow a much more precise determination of the pattern of international specialization than does, say, my corollary 4. Still, my results do show that a straightforward comparison of costs does have something to say about the pattern of trade without going all the way to the solution of a mathematical programming problem as is done by Jones.[10]

Turning now to generalizations of the factor-proportions theory of trade, one sees that my model is consistent with the 3-good, 2-factor model in which Melvin (1968) found the pattern of trade to be indeterminate. But this indeterminacy has not prevented me from obtaining meaningful correlations. What I have done, in a sense, is to exploit those limitations that Melvin *was* able to place, implicitly, on the pattern of trade, as he did in his elegant figure 8, and to show that these limitations are enough to assure that the pattern of trade still, in a general sense, follows the dictates of comparative advantage. In his figure, Melvin showed that trade could be represented by any of an infinite number of lines, connecting two other parallel lines and passing through a single point representing demand. The clue to the validity of my correlations is that the two parallel lines must lie on opposite sides of the demand point in a manner that is prescribed by relative autarky prices. Thus in Melvin's model, and in more general multicommodity, multifactor models, the law of comparative advantage is weakened but not destroyed by the indeterminacy of the pattern of production.

Finally, a great advantage of my model is that it allows for a considerable amount of interference with the free flow of trade by such impediments to trade as transport costs and tariffs. It is true, as Travis (1964, 1972) has suggested, that such impediments can cause particular goods to be exported that would have been imported and vice versa.[11] But while this is possible for particular goods, my analysis shows that it cannot be true of so many goods as to reverse the average relationship that must hold between comparative advantage and trade. Only by subsidies could this average relationship be made not to hold—subsidies either of production, which would violate my assumptions (4) and (7), or of trade, which could violate my assumption (10).

[10] In a further discussion of his results, Jones (1977) remarks that "alternative and equivalent criteria in two-by-two cases may not prove equivalent in more general settings. But knowledge of the general case can aid in recasting criteria in the simple model so that it can generalize." My results provide another example of this phenomenon, for my correlations, when applied to the two-by-two case, are equivalent to alternative statements of the comparative advantage criterion.

[11] An example of this is given in Deardorff (1979) and requires the presence of intermediate goods, as well as tariffs or transport costs, in a multicommodity model.

Appendix

Instead of the single international port assumed in the body of the paper, let there now be an arbitrary number of ports, l, indexed $h = 1, \ldots, l$. While it is not necessary, these could now be identified with the countries of the model, in which case one would have $l = m$. Instead of a single trade vector for each country, I must now distinguish trade vectors for each of the l destinations. Let ${}^h t^i$ represent country i's vector of net supplies to port h. Then the total trade vector, $T^i = \Sigma_{h=1}^{l} {}^h t^i$. In addition I must now distinguish separate world-price vectors at each port, ${}^h p^w$, and separate vectors of traders' prices facing country i's traders at each port, ${}^h p^{t^i}$. A country's production possibilities set, F^i, now contains all feasible collections of the $l + 1$ vectors $(Q^i, {}^1 t^i, \ldots, {}^l t^i)$.

The following assumptions now replace those in Section I:

$$\text{If } (Q^i, {}^1 t^i, \ldots, {}^l t^i) \in F^i, \quad \text{then} \quad \left(Q^i + \sum_{h=1}^{l} {}^h t^i, 0, \ldots, 0\right) \in F^i, \tag{A1}$$

$$(Q^{a^i}, 0, \ldots, 0) \in F^i, \tag{A3}$$

$$p^{a^i} Q^{a^i} \geq p^{a^i} Q \text{ for all } (Q, 0, \ldots, 0) \in F^i, \tag{A4}$$

$$(Q^{n^i}, {}^1 t^{n^i}, \ldots, {}^l t^{n^i}) \in F^i, \tag{A6}$$

$$p^{a^i} Q^{n^i} + \sum_{h=1}^{l} {}^h p^{t^i h} t^{n^i} \geq p^{a^i} Q + \sum_{h=1}^{l} {}^h p^{t^i h} t \quad \text{for all } (Q, {}^1 t, \ldots, {}^l t) \in F^i, \tag{A7}$$

$$\sum_{h=1}^{l} {}^h p^{w h} t^{n^i} = 0, \tag{A9}$$

$$({}^h p_j^w - {}^h p_j^{t^i}) {}^h t_j^{n^i} \geq 0 \quad \text{for } j = 1, \ldots, n; h = 1, \ldots, l, \tag{A10}$$

$$\sum_{i=1}^{m} {}^h t^{n^i} = 0 \quad \text{for } h = 1, \ldots, l, \tag{A11}$$

$$\sum_{j=1}^{n} p_j^{a^i} = 1 \qquad i = 1, \ldots, m. \tag{A12}$$

The remaining assumptions are unchanged.

The statement of the theorem is unchanged, but its proof must be modified. Inequality (14) is obtained for each port individually, and thus from (A9), I get

$$ {}^h p^{t h} t^n \leq 0 \quad \text{for } h = 1, \ldots, l. \tag{A15}$$

Inequality (16) then follows from (A7) as before; (17) and (18) are unchanged, while (19) follows from (A1), (A6), and (A4) as before; (20) follows, and the theorem is proved.

Corollaries 1 and 2 no longer make sense, as there are now many vectors of world prices. However, corollaries 3 and 4 can still be proved by using the theorem and (A11).

Thus most of the results of the paper continue to be valid in a world of many ports, and the fiction of a single port was needed only to simplify notation.

References

Bhagwati, Jagdish N. "The Pure Theory of International Trade: A Survey." *Econ. J.* 74 (March 1964): 1–84.

Deardorff, Alan V. "Weak Links in the Chain of Comparative Advantage." *J. Internat. Econ.* 9 (May 1979): 197–209.

Drabicki, John Z., and Takayama, Akira. "An Antinomy in the Theory of Comparative Advantage." *J. Internat. Econ.* 9 (May 1979): 211–23.

Haberler, Gottfried von. *The Theory of International Trade, with Its Applications to Commercial Policy.* London: Hodge, 1936.

Harkness, Jon, and Kyle, John F. "Factors Influencing United States Comparative Advantage." *J. Internat. Econ.* 5 (May 1975): 153–65.

Jones, Ronald W. "Comparative Advantage and the Theory of Tariffs: A Multi-Country, Multi-Commodity Model." *Rev. Econ. Studies* 28 (June 1961): 161–75.

———. " 'Two-ness' in Trade Theory: Costs and Benefits." Special Papers in International Economics no. 12, Princeton Univ., Internat. Finance Sec., April 1977.

Melvin, James R. "Production and Trade with Two Factors and Three Goods." *A.E.R.* 58 (December 1968): 1249–68.

Samuelson, Paul A. "The Gains from International Trade." *Canadian J. Econ. and Polit. Sci.* 5 (May 1939): 195–205.

———. "Prices of Factors and Goods in General Equilibrium." *Rev. Econ. Studies* 21 (February 1953): 1–20.

———. "The Transfer Problem and Transport Costs, II: Analysis of Effects of Trade Impediments." *Econ. J.* 64 (June 1954): 264–89.

Travis, William P. *The Theory of Trade and Protection.* Cambridge, Mass.: Harvard Univ. Press, 1964.

———. "Production, Trade, and Protection When There Are Many Commodities and Two Factors." *A.E.R.* 62 (March 1972): 87–106.

CHAPTER 11

The General Validity of the Heckscher-Ohlin Theorem

By ALAN V. DEARDORFF*

Despite a number of attempts to extend it, the Heckscher-Ohlin Theorem remains woefully restricted in terms of the generality of the assumptions needed for its proof. In its traditional form as a statement about the commodity composition of trade, the theorem is valid only in the highly abstract environment of the two-factor, two-good, two-country model that has been the mainstay of trade theory for half a century.[1] A weaker version of the theorem, involving the factor content of trade rather than its commodity composition, has been proved for any number of factors, goods, and countries. But this generality has so far been bought only at the cost of other and perhaps equally restrictive assumptions.[2] The purpose of this paper is to provide statements and proofs of the Heckscher-Ohlin (H-O) Theorem that are more general than those currently available.

The approach taken is similar to that used in my 1980 article for an extension of the theory of comparative advantage in terms of correlations between autarky prices and trade. In Section I, I lay out the assumptions on which the analysis is based. These assumptions provide the outlines of a reasonably general model in which there may be any numbers of goods and factors and in which factor prices may be equalized or not. Trade impediments in the form of tariffs or export taxes are permitted, though transportation costs are not.[3] In Section II, I discuss the difficulty of inferring the factor content of trade in a world of unequal factor prices, and I provide several alternative definitions of that concept for use later in the paper. These, together with the assumptions of Section I, are used in Section III to prove a theorem on the value, at autarky prices, of the factor content of trade.

In Section IV this theorem is used to prove a first corollary that makes a more direct statement about the pattern of trade. It says that, worldwide, there must be a negative correlation between the factor content of trade by factor and country, and the corresponding autarky factor prices. It is precisely these autarky factor prices that constitute the Ohlin measure of factor scarcity. Therefore, the corollary provides a formal statement of the general idea that countries tend to export the services of those factors which they have in relative abundance, and it may be regarded as a generalization of the factor-content version of the H-O Theorem.

Finally, a generalization of the commodity version of the theorem is proved in Section V. The concept of a covariance is generalized

*University of Michigan. I have benefitted greatly from the comments of Paul DeGrauwe, Wolfgang Mayer, Michael Mussa, Carl Simon, and Robert Stern, as well as others who participated in seminars at the Universities of Michigan, Chicago, and Cincinnati and at the National Bureau of Economic Research. An anonymous referee also made valuable comments.

[1]With additional goods and factor-price equalization, the theorem runs afoul of the indeterminacy of production and trade noted by Paul Samuelson (1953) and James Melvin (1968). Without factor-price equalization, trade impediments and intermediate production can cause reversals of the pattern of trade, as shown in my 1979 article. If additional factors and countries are also added, it becomes difficult even to state the theorem, let alone to prove it.

[2]Melvin stated such a theorem for the three-good, two-factor case, and Jaroslav Vanek (1968) proved it for the general case, but only by assuming factor-price equalization. Trent Bertrand (1972) and Jon Harkness (1979) were able to drop the factor-price equalization assumption, but replaced it with restrictions on consumption of either goods or factors by country of origin. It is unclear to me, however, that these restrictions can ever be met in a model that is otherwise plausible. Harkness (1978) has also used the factor-content version of the theorems as the motivation for a regression equation relating commodity trade to factor intensities. This bears some resemblance to my analysis below in Section V. See, however, James Anderson (1981) and Edward Leamer and Harry Bowen (1981), who have criticized his result, with a reply by Harkness (1981).

[3]For ease of exposition I do not allow here for transportation costs. These were included in an earlier version of this paper, following the technique in my 1980 article.

to relate three variables rather than two. It is then shown that this generalized covariance, or "comvariance," among certain measures of factor abundance, factor intensity, and trade must be positive. This result may be interpreted as the general mathematical expression of the notion that countries tend to export those goods which use intensively their abundant factors. A concluding Section VI discusses further the concept of factor intensity and the particular definition of it that is required for this result.

I. Assumptions

I consider a world in which l primary factors combine to produce m goods in n countries. Factors cannot be traded but goods, at least potentially, can. A country's production, consumption, and trade are described by a pair, $(\mathbf{L}^j, \mathbf{X}^j) = (\mathbf{L}^j, \mathbf{C}^j + \mathbf{T}^j)$, where $\mathbf{L}^j = (L_1^j, \ldots, L_l^j)$ is an l-vector representing country j's employment of the l factors; $\mathbf{X}^j = (X_1^j, \ldots, X_m^j)$ is an m-vector of net outputs of goods in country j; $\mathbf{C}^j = (C_1^j, \ldots, C_m^j)$ is an m-vector of final demands for goods in country j; and $\mathbf{T}^j = (T_1^j, \ldots, T_m^j)$ is an m-vector of country j's net exports. Elements of $\mathbf{T}^j$ will be negative for goods which are imported.

Technology is characterized by a set $\mathcal{H}$ of all feasible pairs, $(\mathbf{L}, \mathbf{X})$, and is common to all countries. Of this set, I implicitly assume whatever is necessary to permit the existence of the equilibria I will be studying.[4] This assumption of internationally identical technologies is consistent with the spirit of the H-O model, which directs attention to factor endowments rather than technologies as the incentive for trade.

Demand is characterized for each country, j, by a vector-valued demand function $D^j(\mathbf{p}^j, Y^j)$, where $\mathbf{p}^j$ is an m-vector of domestic goods prices in some numeraire and Y^j is income in the same units. Demands are assumed to be homogeneous of degree zero in prices and income, and to satisfy the weak axiom of revealed preference:[5]

Assumption 1:

$$(1) \quad [\mathbf{p}^1 D(\mathbf{p}^1, Y^1) \geq \mathbf{p}^1 D(\mathbf{p}^2, Y^2)] \Rightarrow [\mathbf{p}^2 D(\mathbf{p}^1, Y^1) > \mathbf{p}^2 D(\mathbf{p}^2, Y^2)]$$

where superscripts denote any two alternative price and income combinations for the given country, j (country superscript omitted). Demanders, incidentally, are assumed always to spend all of their incomes, so that the extreme left-hand and extreme right-hand products in (1) are equal to Y^1 and Y^2, respectively.

Primary factors of production are available in fixed supply in each country, and are given by vectors $\bar{\mathbf{L}}^j$. Equilibrium will require that factors be fully employed. Goods may also serve as intermediate inputs to production, and if that is ever their sole use, then particular C_i will be zero in equilibrium.

An autarky equilibrium for any country consists of vectors of net output, $\mathbf{X}^a = \mathbf{C}^a$, of prices (of goods), $\mathbf{p}^a$, and of wages (of factors), $\mathbf{w}^a$, that are feasible, demanded, and that maximize profits.[6] These requirements are captured in the following three assumptions:

Assumption 2:

$$(2) \quad (\bar{\mathbf{L}}, \mathbf{C}^a) \in \mathcal{H};$$

Assumption 3:

$$(3) \quad \mathbf{C}^a = D(\mathbf{p}^a, \mathbf{p}^a \mathbf{C}^a);$$

[4]They must be closed, convex, and, for any given $\mathbf{L}^j$, bounded from above.

[5]To assume that this axiom holds for a country as a whole is of course very strong, almost as strong as the usual trade-theoretic assumption of community indifference curves. Though without theoretical justification, the assumption now has some very tentative empirical support in Hal Varian (1980) and Steven Landsburg (1981), who both searched for violations of the strong axiom of revealed preference and failed to find any.

[6]For Assumption 4, as well as 7 below, to follow from profit maximization, I also assume perfect competition and the absence of increasing returns to scale, externalities, production taxes and other domestic distortions.

Assumption 4:

$$(4) \qquad \mathbf{p}^a\mathbf{C}^a - \mathbf{w}^a\bar{\mathbf{L}} \geqslant \mathbf{p}^a\mathbf{C} - \mathbf{w}^a\mathbf{L} \quad \text{for all } (\mathbf{L},\mathbf{C}) \in \mathcal{H}.$$

A trade equilibrium is somewhat more complicated. There is first a vector of world prices, $\mathbf{p}^w$, which is not associated with any particular country and is defined relative to some international numeraire. In addition, residents of each country, j, face a vector of domestic prices, $\mathbf{p}^{tj}$, that may differ from $\mathbf{p}^w$ due to their country's taxes on trade. A trade equilibrium, then, consists of these vectors of world and domestic prices, the latter for each country, plus vectors of goods produced, traded, and demanded by each country, $\mathbf{X}^{tj} = \mathbf{C}^{tj} + \mathbf{T}^{tj}$, and finally vectors of factor wages, $\mathbf{w}^{tj}$. Assumptions analogous to those made above require that production and trade be feasible, that demands be met, and that profits be maximized:

Assumption 5:

$$(5) \qquad (\bar{\mathbf{L}}, \mathbf{C}^t + \mathbf{T}^t) \in \mathcal{H};$$

Assumption 6:

$$(6) \qquad \mathbf{C}^t = D(\mathbf{p}^t, \mathbf{p}^t\mathbf{C}^t);$$

Assumption 7:

$$(7) \qquad \mathbf{p}^t(\mathbf{C}^t + \mathbf{T}^t) - \mathbf{w}^t\bar{\mathbf{L}} \geqslant \mathbf{p}^t\mathbf{X} - \mathbf{w}^t\mathbf{L}; \quad \text{for all } (\mathbf{L},\mathbf{X}) \in \mathcal{H}.$$

In addition it is assumed that trade is balanced at world prices and that differences, if any, between world and domestic prices result, on average, more from taxes on trade than from subsidies:

Assumption 8:

$$(8) \qquad \mathbf{p}^w\mathbf{T}^t = 0;$$

Assumption 9:

$$(9) \qquad (\mathbf{p}^t - \mathbf{p}^w)\mathbf{T}^t \leqslant 0.$$

This last assumption is a weaker version of what I have called elsewhere (1980) the assumption of natural trade. It limits the use of trade subsidies that might otherwise artificially give rise to any conceivable pattern of trade. It says that the total revenue from taxes on trade, plus rents arising from other forms of trade restriction, must be at least as great as the total paid out in subsidies to trade.[7] Thus trade policy constitutes on average more of an impediment to trade than a stimulant.

Finally, equilibrium in international trade for the world as a whole requires that world markets clear.

Assumption 10:

$$(10) \qquad \sum_{j=1}^{n} \mathbf{T}^{tj} = 0.$$

It should be noted that the assumptions made here are not intended to be sufficient to determine an equilibrium. I have not, for example, specified the quantitative size of the tariffs that may be implicit in Assumption 9, or even their form as ad valorem or specific. I have only made those assumptions that are needed for the results I intend to prove, and that means that the results will be valid for a variety of more explicit models such as might be used for other purposes.

II. The Factor Content of Trade

If techniques of production are everywhere the same, then there is no difficulty defining the factor content of trade as just the factors required directly and indirectly to produce the vector of traded goods, using these common techniques. This is the case, for exam-

[7]To see this, consider each term in the expansion of the inner product in (9). Negative terms indicate either exports ($T_i^t > 0$) for which traders receive less than the world price ($p_i^t < p_i^w$), or imports ($T_i^t < 0$) for which traders pay more than the world price ($p_i^t > p_i^w$). In either case, such price differences represent either taxes on trade or the rents that accrue to the holders of scarce import or export licenses, and the total of the negative terms is the total tax revenue plus rent. Positive terms similarly indicate either exporters getting more than the world price or importers paying less, both of which require subsidies to trade.

ple, if technologies are homogeneous and internationally identical and factor prices are internationally equalized, as assumed by Vanek (1968). But if factor prices may be unequal, as permitted here, then there exists a variety of techniques that might be used to impute factor content to each good, and the factor content of trade may therefore be defined in a corresponding variety of ways.

Rather than limit myself throughout to a specific definition of factor content of trade, I will instead state two more assumptions that deal with it, one or both of which will be required in proving results later in the paper. Then I will describe three specific ways that the factor content of trade might be defined, illustrating different concepts of factor content when techniques of production differ internationally. Only one of these definitions, it turns out, is appropriate for the most general result to be proved later in the paper, but all three satisfy the first of the two assumptions below and that is all that is needed for the basic theorem of Section III.

In general terms I represent the factor content of a country's trade by an l-vector of factors, $\mathbf{S}^j$. Each element of the vector, S_h^j, represents the net export of factor h, or import if negative, that is said to be embodied in country j's total vector of trade in goods. The first assumption made about this vector is that, if these amounts of factors could be traded instead of goods, then this factor trade could substitute for the commodity trade in terms of permitting the same levels of consumption to be achieved. Formally, $\mathbf{S}^j$ is assumed to satisfy the following condition

Assumption 11:

$$(\bar{\mathbf{L}}^j - \mathbf{S}^j, \mathbf{C}^{tj}) \in \mathcal{H}. \tag{11}$$

That is, if endowments of factors are reduced by the amounts of factors regarded as exported, and increased by the amounts regarded as imported, it would become possible to produce entirely domestically the same vector of goods that is consumed with trade. With this assumption, since $\bar{\mathbf{L}}^j - \mathbf{S}^j$ is a vector of factors capable of producing $\mathbf{C}^{tj}$, one may also think of $\mathbf{S}^j$ as the difference between factor endowments and the factor content of consumption, just as trade in goods is the difference between production and consumption of goods.

The second assumption that I will sometimes need about the factor content of trade is that net exports of each factor by the world as a whole, as measured by $\mathbf{S}^j$, are nonnegative. That is, what all countries together are regarded as exporting of each factor is at least as great as what they regard themselves, in the aggregate, as importing.

Assumption 12:

$$\sum_{j=1}^{n} S_h^j \geq 0; \; h=1,\ldots,l. \tag{12}$$

This condition, which would hold with equality if $\mathbf{S}^j$ represented actual trade in factors, will be shown in a moment to hold for two specific definitions of the factor content of trade.

To construct such specific definitions of factor content I need the additional assumptions of constant returns to scale and the absence of joint production, so that techniques of production can be represented by the amount of inputs used per unit of output of each good. I can then represent various production techniques with $(l \times n)$ matrices, $\mathbf{G}$, whose elements g_{hi} denote the direct-plus-indirect requirement of factor h per unit of output of good i. Various such matrices may be used to represent techniques in use in different locations and circumstances.

Factor content based on domestic coefficients: Perhaps the simplest specific definition of the factor content of trade would impute factors to goods on the basis of domestic techniques of production. Let $\mathbf{G}^{dj}$ be the direct-plus-indirect factor requirements matrix based on techniques of production actually in use in country j with trade, or, for those goods not produced, the cost-minimizing techniques given j's domestic factor prices. I then define the domestic factor content of trade $\mathbf{S}^{dj}$ as

$$\mathbf{S}^{dj} = \mathbf{G}^{dj}\mathbf{T}^j. \tag{13}$$

Note that this definition clearly satisfies Assumption 11, since (5) implies

$$\mathbf{G}^{dj}(\mathbf{C}^{tj}+\mathbf{T}^{j})\leq\bar{\mathbf{L}}^{j},$$

which in turn implies $\mathbf{G}^{dj}\mathbf{C}^{tj}\leq\bar{\mathbf{L}}^{j}-\mathbf{S}^{dj}$.

Actual factor content of trade: A second specific definition imputes to traded goods those factors actually used in their production wherever that took place. Let $\mathbf{G}^{tj}$ be the actual factor requirements matrix for country j's trade. It is constructed by tracing backwards through the complete production history of each good that enters $\mathbf{T}^{j}$, and adding up the factors actually used in its production, plus those used in producing intermediate inputs to its production, perhaps in a different country, and so on. Once this matrix is constructed, I define the actual factor content of trade, $\mathbf{S}^{tj}$, as simply:

$$\mathbf{S}^{tj}=\mathbf{G}^{tj}\mathbf{T}^{j}. \tag{14}$$

This definition of factor content also satisfies Assumption 11, since technologies are everywhere identical.

Factor content based on actual content of consumption: The factor content of trade need not always be measured as a matrix times the vector of traded goods. To see this, consider repeating the process described above of measuring the factors actually used in producing goods, but apply it to the vectors of goods consumed by countries rather than those traded. Letting $\mathbf{G}^{cj}$ represent this actual factor requirements matrix for country j's consumption bundle, I can then define a third measure of the factor content of trade as follows:

$$\mathbf{S}^{cj}=\bar{\mathbf{L}}^{j}-\mathbf{G}^{cj}\mathbf{C}^{tj}. \tag{15}$$

This is just the difference between country j's endowment of factors and the factors that may be said to be embodied in its consumption. Like (14), (15) is consistent with (11) due to the identical technology assumption.

To see how these three definitions compare to one another, and also to check whether they satisfy Assumption 12, consider the sum across all countries of various factor trade vectors. Taking the last one first, one can be sure that the actual content of worldwide consumption is no greater than world factor endowments,

$$\sum_{j=1}^{n}\mathbf{G}^{cj}\mathbf{C}^{tj}\leq\sum_{j=1}^{n}\bar{\mathbf{L}}^{j}, \tag{16}$$

since these are the factors actually used. It follows that

$$\sum_{j=1}^{n}\mathbf{S}^{dj}\geq\mathbf{0}, \tag{17}$$

with equality if factors are fully employed.[8]

What I have called the actual factor content of trade, $\mathbf{S}^{tj}$, has a similar but even stronger property. Since every exported good of one country is an import of another, and since the actual factor content is the same for both, it must follow that

$$\sum_{j=1}^{n}\mathbf{S}^{tj}=\mathbf{0}. \tag{18}$$

Finally, the domestic factor content of trade may be of either sign for the world as a whole, since imports tend to be inefficient to produce domestically and thus "contain" large amounts of factors that enter negatively in $\mathbf{S}^{dj}$. Thus

$$\sum_{j=1}^{n}\mathbf{S}^{dj}\gtreqless\mathbf{0}. \tag{19}$$

Assumption (12), then, is satisfied by both $\mathbf{S}^{c}$ and $\mathbf{S}^{t}$, but may not be satisfied by $\mathbf{S}^{d}$. The use of domestic techniques of production to impute factor content of trade may therefore lead to difficulties in generalizing the H-O Theorem. Why this is true will be explained further in Section VI below.

There are of course other ways that might be used to measure the factor content of trade, some of which would undoubtedly satisfy one or both of Assumptions 11 and

[8]Inequality would arise even with full employment, however, if transport costs were included in the model, for then S^{c} would include as exports all factors used up in transporting goods.

12. But not all methods work, as may be seen by considering the method that is probably most common in practice: that is to use the techniques employed by a single country to impute factor content in all countries. The difficulty with this single country method is that it is likely to impute excessive factor content to other countries' exports, making it impossible for them to produce their with-trade consumption bundles if these resources were removed. Thus the single country method of imputing factor content need not satisfy Assumption 11.

III. A Theorem on the Factor Content of Trade

I can now prove that, for any country, the value at autarky factor wages of the factor content of trade must be negative.

THEOREM: *If Assumptions* 1 *through* 9 *hold, and if* $\mathbf{S}^j$ *is defined so as to satisfy* (11), *then*

$$\mathbf{w}^{aj}\mathbf{S}^j < 0. \tag{20}$$

PROOF:

I omit the superscript j in what follows. Begin by rearranging (9) and using (8) to get

$$\mathbf{p}^t\mathbf{T}^t \leqslant \mathbf{p}^w\mathbf{T}^t = 0. \tag{21}$$

Next, use (7) to evaluate autarky production, (2), at trade-equilibrium prices:

$$\mathbf{p}^t\mathbf{C}^t + \mathbf{p}^t\mathbf{T}^t - \mathbf{w}^t\bar{\mathbf{L}} \geqslant \mathbf{p}^t\mathbf{C}^a - \mathbf{w}^t\bar{\mathbf{L}}. \tag{22}$$

Rearrange and use (21):

$$\mathbf{p}^t\mathbf{C}^t - \mathbf{p}^t\mathbf{C}^a \geqslant -\mathbf{p}^t\mathbf{T}^t \geqslant 0. \tag{23}$$

Thus

$$\mathbf{p}^t\mathbf{C}^t \geqslant \mathbf{p}^t\mathbf{C}^a. \tag{24}$$

Substituting (6) and (3) for $\mathbf{C}^t$ and $\mathbf{C}^a$, (1) then implies

$$\mathbf{p}^a\mathbf{C}^t > \mathbf{p}^a\mathbf{C}^a. \tag{25}$$

Finally, (11) entitles one to use (4) to get

$$\mathbf{p}^a\mathbf{C}^a - \mathbf{w}^a\bar{\mathbf{L}} \geqslant \mathbf{p}^a\mathbf{C}^t - \mathbf{w}^a(\bar{\mathbf{L}} - \mathbf{S}) \tag{26}$$

or

$$\mathbf{w}^a\mathbf{S} \leqslant \mathbf{p}^a\mathbf{C}^a - \mathbf{p}^a\mathbf{C}^t. \tag{27}$$

But the right-hand side of this is strictly negative from (25), which implies (20).

What this theorem says may perhaps be better understood by rewriting (20) in terms of $\hat{\mathbf{L}}^j = \bar{\mathbf{L}}^j - \mathbf{S}^j$, which from (11) may be thought of as the factor content of $\mathbf{C}^{tj}$. The theorem implies

$$\mathbf{w}^{aj}\bar{\mathbf{L}}^j < \mathbf{w}^{aj}\hat{\mathbf{L}}^j \tag{28}$$

which says that the factors needed to produce the trade consumption bundle would have cost more, at autarky factor prices, than the endowment of factors available. The result is surely plausible once it is shown, in equation (24), that the trade consumption bundle is revealed preferred to that of autarky. Most of the proof consists of demonstrating this revealed preference, and is therefore quite similar to Murray Kemp's (1962) demonstration of the gains from trade.[9]

IV. Implication for the Pattern of Factor-Content Trade

The theorem of Section III is markedly similar, both in content and in method of proof, to one I proved in my 1980 article. This does for the factor content of trade what the other did for the commodity composition of trade. However, implications of this theorem for the pattern of trade do not follow quite as readily for two reasons. In the earlier paper I derived four corollaries involving various correlations between trade and autarky prices for particular countries and for the world as a whole. Some of these used world prices for reference and some

[9]It is worth noting that (24), which is analogous to Kemp's inequality (5), therefore provides a slight generalization of Kemp's theorem on the gain from trade. Kemp allowed only for restrictions on trade. My Assumption 9 permits some use of trade subsidies so long as trade policy does not subsidize trade on average. By the same token, Kemp's theorem can also be extended to allow for real transportation costs, as implicit in my 1980 article.

depended on the assumption of balanced trade. For the factor content of trade, however, there do not in general exist world factor prices, and trade in factor content need not be balanced. Fortunately the most general of my earlier corollaries did not require either of these assumptions, and an analogous result can be established for the factor content of trade.

Let $\mathbf{W}^a$ be a vector of length nl containing the autarky factor prices of all countries and factors:

$$(29)\quad \mathbf{W}^a = \left(w_1^{a^1},\ldots,w_l^{a^1},w_1^{a^2},\ldots,w_l^{a^n}\right).$$

Also let $\mathbf{E}^S$ be a vector of the same length containing the net exports by each country of each factor, arranged in the same order:

$$(30)\quad \mathbf{E}^S = \left(S_1^1,\ldots,S_l^1,S_1^2,\ldots,S_l^n\right).$$

Then the corollary states that these two vectors must be negatively correlated:

COROLLARY 1: *If the world contains n countries, all satisfying Assumptions* 1 *through* 9, *and if the factor content of trade also satisfies Assumptions* 11 *and* 12, *then*

$$(31)\quad Cor(\mathbf{W}^a,\mathbf{E}^S) < 0$$

where Cor( ) is the simple correlation between the elements of the two vectors that are its arguments.

PROOF:

The sign of the correlation is the same as that of the corresponding covariance. That, in turn, depends on the inner product of the two vectors minus the product of their means multiplied by their length. Thus the corollary will be proven if it can be established that

$$(32)\quad \mathbf{W}^a\mathbf{E}^S - nl\;\overline{\mathbf{W}}^a\overline{\mathbf{E}}^S < 0$$

where a bar over a vector denotes its mean. Now $\overline{\mathbf{W}}^a$ must be positive for the model to be meaningful. And it follows easily from (12) and (30) that

$$(33)\quad \overline{\mathbf{E}}^S \geqslant 0.$$

Thus the second term in (32), including its sign, is nonpositive. Finally, the inner product, $\mathbf{W}^a\mathbf{E}^S$, is just the sum of the n inner products, $\mathbf{w}^{a^j}\mathbf{s}^j$, that were shown in the theorem to be negative. This proves (32) and thus Corollary 1.

This result gives substance to a very general statement of the H-O Theorem in its factor-content interpretation. Recalling that autarky factor prices inversely reflect the abundance of those factors in the Ohlin sense, equation (31) says that countries will on average tend to be net exporters of their abundant factors and net importers of their scarce factors. Proof of this proposition does not depend on factor-price equalization or on any peculiar characteristic of demand behavior as have other attempts to generalize the theorem. On the contrary, the present model even allows for tariffs and requires of demand only the weak axiom of revealed preference.

The result does, however, require that the imputation of factor content to trade be consistent with both Assumptions 11 and 12. The specific definitions in Section II that accomplish this are those that rely on techniques of production actually used, wherever that production takes place. In particular, the factor content of imports is to be measured by the factors which produce them aboard. This is in contrast to what has usually been done in testing the factor proportions theory empirically. Wassily Leontief's (1953) test and others like it have always used domestic input-output tables to evaluate the factor content of imports as well as exports.

V. Implications for the Pattern of Commodity Trade

The link between the factor content of trade and the commodity composition of trade is seen most easily by looking at an implication of the factor content of trade for a particular factor.

Suppose in general that a country's factor content of trade is measured as some matrix of factor requirements, $\mathbf{G}^j$, times its vector of commodity trade, $\mathbf{T}^j$,

$$\mathbf{S}^j = \mathbf{G}^j \mathbf{T}^j, \tag{34}$$

as in either the domestic factor content or actual factor content definitions of Section II. Letting g^j_{hi} be the elements of $\mathbf{G}^j$, the factor content of trade for a particular factor $\hat{h}$ becomes

$$S^j_{\hat{h}} = \sum_{i=1}^{m} g^j_{\hat{h}i} T^j_i. \tag{35}$$

Now g^j_{hi} are direct plus indirect per unit factor requirements, and can be used to construct measures of factor intensity. A particular measure that will be convenient here is the following:

$$\theta_{hij} \equiv \overline{w}_h g^j_{hi} / p^w_i, \tag{36}$$

where $\overline{\mathbf{w}}$ is any vector of factor wages. These θ's have the form of "factor shares," since they relate values of factor inputs to values of outputs. However, since neither the wages nor the prices used in equation (36) are necessarily those faced by the producers in choosing g's, the θ's may not be observable as factor shares. Still, they provide a better measure of factor intensities than the g's alone, since they are unit free.

In any case, equation (35) can be multiplied through by $\overline{w}_{\hat{h}}$, and each term in the summation can be both multiplied and divided by world prices to yield the following result:

$$\overline{w}_{\hat{h}} S^j_{\hat{h}} = \sum_{i=1}^{m} \theta_{\hat{h}ij} \left(p^w_i T^j_i \right). \tag{37}$$

From Assumption 8, balanced trade, the mean of the terms in parentheses is zero. It follows that the inner product on the right-hand side of equation (37) also gives the sign of the correlation between the θ's and the values of commodity trade. It therefore implies the following:

> If a country is a net exporter (importer) of a particular factor content, then there must be a positive (negative) correlation across commodities between the value of its net exports at world prices and the intensity with which commodities use the factor.

More intuitively, this means that countries tend to export those goods which are intensive in the factors whose content they export.

This connection between commodity and factor-content trade, together with the results of earlier sections of the paper, suggest that it should be possible to construct another corollary that would correlate commodity trade with factor intensity and factor abundance and thus generalize the commodity version of the H-O Theorem. The difficulty here is the need to correlate three variables symmetrically, and I am not aware of any standard method of doing this.

I therefore define a generalization of the concept of the covariance. Let $\mathbf{x}$, $\mathbf{y}$, and $\mathbf{z}$ be three vectors all of length N, and let $\bar{x}$, $\bar{y}$, and $\bar{z}$ be their respective means, $\bar{x} = \sum_{i=1}^{N} x_i / N$, etc. I define the *comvariance*[10] among $\mathbf{x}$, $\mathbf{y}$, and $\mathbf{z}$ as follows:

$$com(\mathbf{x},\mathbf{y},\mathbf{z}) = \sum_{i=1}^{N} (x_i - \bar{x})(y_i - \bar{y})(z_i - \bar{z}). \tag{38}$$

I will show below that this definition characterizes the kind of relationship that is stated in the H-O Theorem.

To measure factor abundance, I first define a vector of world-average autarky prices as follows:

$$\overline{w}_h = \sum_{j=1}^{n} w^{aj}_h / n. \tag{39}$$

I then define factor abundance for each factor h and country j in terms of the relative deviations of the country's autarky factor price from this world average:

$$\omega_{hj} = \left(\overline{w}_h - w^{aj}_h \right) / \overline{w}_h \tag{40}$$

[10] This name was suggested by Kathe Courant, who pointed out that "covariance" is actually an incorrect use of the prefix whose root is *cum* = "with." Properly, the prefix should be "co" only before vowels (as in "coalesce") and "com" before consonants (as in "commingle").

where the sign has been chosen so that ω will be high (positive) for countries with relatively cheap, and hence abundant, factors.

For factor intensity, I use the measure θ_{hij} defined above in (36), with $\bar{w}_h$ now explicitly defined in (39), and using the actual-factor-requirements-of-trade matrix $\mathbf{G}^{tj}$ defined in Section II.

$$\theta_{hij} = \bar{w}_h g_{hi}^{tj} / p_i^w. \tag{41}$$

Finally, for trade I again use the value of net exports at world prices:

$$\tau_{ij} = p_i^w T_i^j \tag{42}$$

Now let ω, θ, and τ be vectors of length $N = lmn$ whose elements are $\omega_{hij} = \omega_{hj}$ for all i, θ_{hij}, and $\tau_{hij} = \tau_{ij}$ for all h. The elements in ω are repeated m times and those in τ are repeated l times, in order to conform to the dimension of θ. I can then state the following corollary:

COROLLARY 2: *If the factor requirements matrix, $\mathbf{G}^{tj}$, has the property that $\mathbf{S}^{tj} = \mathbf{G}^{tj}\mathbf{T}^{tj}$ satisfies both* (11) *and* (12), *and if Assumptions* 1–10 *are also satisfied, then*

$$com(\omega, \theta, \tau) > 0. \tag{43}$$

PROOF:

It is easily derived from (38) that

$$com(\mathbf{x},\mathbf{y},\mathbf{z}) = \sum_{i=1}^{N} x_i y_i z_i + 2N\bar{x}\bar{y}\bar{z} - \bar{x}(\mathbf{y}\cdot\mathbf{z}) - \bar{y}(\mathbf{x}\cdot\mathbf{z}) - \bar{z}(\mathbf{x}\cdot\mathbf{y}). \tag{44}$$

From (39) and (40) it follows that $\bar{\omega} = 0$, while $\bar{\tau} = 0$ from either (8) or (10). Thus all but two terms in (44) disappear for evaluating (43), which becomes

$$com(\omega, \theta, \tau) = \sum_{h=1}^{l} \sum_{i=1}^{m} \sum_{j=1}^{n} \omega_{hij}\theta_{hij}\tau_{hij} - \bar{\theta} \sum_{h=1}^{l} \sum_{i=1}^{m} \sum_{j=1}^{n} \omega_{hij}\tau_{hij}. \tag{45}$$

Since $\omega_{hij} = \omega_{hj}$, the summation over i in the second term can be moved to its right, leaving $\Sigma_{i=1}^{m}\tau_{hij} = \Sigma_{i=1}^{m}\tau_{ij} = 0$ by balanced trade, (8). Thus, substituting from (40)–(42),

$$\begin{aligned} com(\omega, \theta, \tau) &= \sum_{h=1}^{l} \sum_{i=1}^{m} \sum_{j=1}^{n} \left\{ \left(\frac{\bar{w}_h - w_h^{aj}}{\bar{w}_h} \right) \times \left(\frac{\bar{w}_h g_{hi}^{tj}}{p_i^w} \right) \left(p_i^w T_i^j \right) \right\} \\ &= \sum_{h=1}^{l} \sum_{i=1}^{m} \sum_{j=1}^{n} \left(\bar{w}_h - w_h^{aj} \right) g_{hi}^{tj} T_i^j \\ &= \sum_{h=1}^{l} \bar{w}_h \sum_{j=1}^{n} S_h^{tj} - \sum_{j=1}^{n} \sum_{h=1}^{l} w_h^{aj} S_h^{tj}. \end{aligned} \tag{46}$$

The first term here is nonnegative, from (12), while the sum over h in the second term is the inner product that was shown to be negative in the theorem of Section III. Thus, from (12) and (20),

$$com(\omega, \theta, \tau) \geqslant - \sum_{j=1}^{n} w^{aj} S^{tj} > 0. \tag{47}$$

To interpret this result, rewrite it in terms of the definition in equation (38):

$$com(\omega, \theta, \tau) = \sum_{k=1}^{N} (\omega_k - \bar{\omega})(\theta_k - \bar{\theta})(\tau_k - \bar{\tau}) > 0, \tag{48}$$

where the triple subscript has been replaced by a single subscript k. Each k represents a particular factor-good-country combination for which there are abundance, intensity, and trade observations. For the summation in (48) to be positive, the N terms must on average be positive. And for the product that is each term to be positive, either all three factors must be positive or exactly two must be negative.

Consider what this means for the pattern of trade. Goods that are exported ($\tau_k > \bar{\tau} = 0$), must on average use relatively intensively ($\theta_k > \bar{\theta}$) those factors in relative abundance

$(\omega_k > \bar{\omega})$ and use relatively unintensively $(\theta_k < \bar{\theta})$ those factors that are relatively scarce $(\omega_k < \bar{\omega})$. Likewise imported goods $(\tau_k < \bar{\tau} = 0)$ must on average use scarce factors intensively and abundant factors unintensively. Together, then, (48) gives mathematical substance to the H-O Theorem as an explanation of the pattern of commodity trade in an average sense.

VI. Factor Intensity Ambiguities

I have so far given very little attention to the difficulties of measuring "factor intensity," even though this concept is crucial to the H-O Theorem. Traditionally, ambiguities in the definition of factor intensity, as typified by "factor intensity reversals" (*FIR*s) have interfered with the proof of the theorem in even the simple two-factor case. With more factors one might expect the difficulties to be compounded. Yet my Corollary 2 above generalizes the theorem without any additional restrictions on technology and is therefore valid even in the presence of *FIR*s. How is this possible?

In fact the definition of factor intensity is subject to many of the same ambiguities that are discussed above for measuring the factor content of trade. Indeed, the two concepts are intimately related, since both are defined in terms of techniques of production. In a world of variable factor proportions and unequal factor prices, a variety of techniques exist and might plausibly be selected for measuring both the factor content of trade and the factor intensity of production of any given good. To prove my results in this paper I have required that the particular techniques chosen for these purposes satisfy rather restrictive conditions. These conditions lead me to measure factor intensity in a way that gets around such problems as *FIR*s.

Specifically, Corollary 2 requires that the factor-requirements matrix used for measuring factor intensity in equation (41) be such that the implied factor content of trade satisfy both (11) and (12). The only matrix for which I have been able to verify that both of these properties hold is $\mathbf{G}^{tj}$, which represents the actual factor requirements of country j's trade. This means that the factor intensity of imports is defined by the techniques used to produce them abroad, which may be quite different from those used at home. And it also means, if factor prices are unequal, that the factor intensities of exports and imports are measured at different factor prices.

It is apparently this definition of factor intensity that has allowed me to bypass the pitfall of *FIR*s. Consider the traditional $2\times2\times2$ model. If one or more *FIR*s separate the two countries, then it is well known that each country may export either good. But it will also be true that the capital-abundant country will employ a higher ratio of capital to labor in production of whatever it exports than will the labor-abundant country in whatever *it* exports. It follows that, in terms of actual techniques used in producing both exports, the capital-abundant country's exports will be more capital intensive than its imports, and this is what Corollary 2 implies.

To see this, examine Figure 1 which is familiar from Harry Johnson (1957). It shows, for two countries, A and B, their autarky relative commodity prices, p_A and p_B, relative factor prices, and relative factor employments in two industries, X and Y. A single *FIR* is assumed and the positions of the countries are such that B has a comparative advantage in X and A in Y. If factor content and factor intensities were measured in both countries on the basis of techniques used in country A, then the resulting trade would appear to run counter to the H-O Theorem in any of its interpretations. It is therefore fortunate that this single country method of measuring factor intensity fails to satisfy Assumption 11 as explained in Section II. For otherwise the results of this paper would contradict this well-known implication of *FIR*s.

That the actual factor content and intensities of trade avoid this problem can also be seen from Figure 1. In a trade equilibrium (not shown), A exports Y which it produces with a factor ratio of approximately k_Y^A and imports X which is produced in B at approximately k_X^B. Thus with these measurements, the capital-abundant country A does export a good that is more capital intensive than its import. Of course, the same would be true if the trade pattern were reversed,

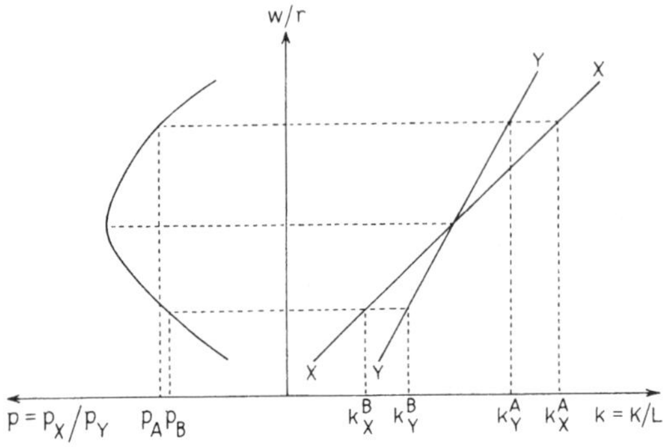

FIGURE 1

since all production in A will in this case be more capital intensive than all production in B.

My Corollary 2 is therefore a somewhat weaker statement of the H-O Theorem than has traditionally been understood. It would perhaps be desirable to relate trade to measures of factor intensity that are independent of that trade, or that at least refer to common factor prices for all goods. But that must evidently be impossible without ruling out some generalized notion of *FIR*s, and I have as yet no certain way of doing this.

I would note, however, one possible method that may be worth pursuing in further research. In Section II, I mentioned the possibility of using the domestic factor requirement matrix, $\mathbf{G}^{dj}$, but I made no further use of it because the implied factor content vectors, $\mathbf{S}^{dj}$, could not be shown to satisfy Assumption 12. Still, if 12 could be made as an *additional* assumption, then $\mathbf{G}^{dj}$ could be used to measure factor intensity in Corollary 2. The H-O Theorem would then be generalized to relate trade, factor abundance, and the domestic factor intensity of production.

I should note in closing that none of these problems arise if techniques of production happen to be internationally identical. If there is factor-price equalization, then Vanek's strong results hold on the factor content of trade, and my Corollary 2 explains the average pattern of commodity trade in spite of the Samuelson-Melvin indeterminacy. And if, alternatively, technology requires fixed proportions among primary factors everywhere regardless of factor prices, then Corollaries 1 and 2 both provide useful extensions of existing versions of the Heckscher-Ohlin Theorem without any ambiguity as to the meanings of factor content and factor intensity. Only when techniques differ internationally do such ambiguities arise, and for such a world the corollaries spell out which of the alternative definitions of content and intensity are appropriate for formulating valid statements about the pattern of trade.

REFERENCES

Anderson, James E., "Cross-Section Tests of the Heckscher-Ohlin Theorem: Comment," *American Economic Review*, December 1981, *71*, 1037–39.

Bertrand, Trent J., "An Extension of the *N*-Factor Case of Factor Proportions Theory," *Kyklos*, July 1972, *25*, 592–96.

Deardorff, Alan V., "Weak Links in the Chain of Comparative Advantage," *Journal of International Economics*, May 1979, *9*, 197–209.

______, "The General Validity of the Law of Comparative Advantage," *Journal of Political Economy*, October 1980, *88*, 941–57.

Harkness, Jon P., "Factor Abundance and Comparative Advantage," *American Economic Review*, December 1978, *68*, 784–800.

______, "The Factor-Proportions Model with Many Nations, Goods and Factors: Theory and Evidence," discussion paper no. 358, Institute for Economic Research, Queen's University, August 1979.

______, "Cross-Section Tests of the Heckscher-Ohlin Theorem: Reply," *American Economic Review*, December 1981, *71*, 1044–48.

Johnson, Harry G., "Factor Endowments, International Trade and Factor Prices," *Manchester School of Economic and Social Studies*, September 1957, *25*, 270–83.

Kemp, Murray C., "The Gain from International Trade," *Economic Journal*, December 1962, *72*, 803–19.

Landsburg, Steven E., "Taste Change in the United Kingdom, 1900–1955," *Journal of*

Political Economy, February 1981, *89*, 92–104.

Leamer, Edward E. and Bowen, Harry P., "Cross-Section Tests of the Heckscher-Ohlin Theorem: Comment," *American Economic Review*, December 1981, *71*, 1040–43.

Leontief, Wassily W., "Domestic Production and Foreign Trade: The American Capital Position Re-examined," *Proceedings of the American Philosophical Society*, September 1953, *97*, 332–49.

Melvin, James R., "Production and Trade with Two Factors and Three Goods," *American Economic Review*, December 1968, *58*, 1249–68.

Samuelson, Paul A., "Prices of Factors and Goods in General Equilibrium," *Review of Economic Studies*, February 1953, *21*, 1–20.

Vanek, Jaroslav, "The Factor Proportions Theory: the *N*-Factor Case," *Kyklos*, October 1968, *21*, 749–56.

Varian, Hal R., "The Nonparametric Approach to Demand Analysis," CREST discussion paper C–22, department of economics, University of Michigan, July 1980.

CHAPTER 12

Comparative advantage and international trade and investment in services†

Alan V. Deardorff

University of Michigan

My purpose in this paper is to evaluate the theoretical validity of the principle of comparative advantage as it applies to international trade in services. I will focus only on the positive issue of whether trade, if undistorted by policy, will conform to a pattern that is explainable by comparative advantage, and I will not treat, except tangentially, the welfare effects of such trade. Even so, as I will explain in a moment, it is probably impossible to provide a conclusive answer to the question of whether services trade follows comparative advantage. Instead, I will confine my attention to two distinctive characteristics of trade in services, and use these as the basis for theoretical models. Within these models I will show that, while there exist ways of defining comparative advantage and trade such that the principle of comparative advantage holds quite nicely, there is nonetheless at least one case in which trade will appear to violate the principle. Thus it is not clear that comparative advantage is necessarily the most useful criterion for explaining international trade in services.

The difficulty that arises in evaluating trade in services – and this applies to the problem in both its positive and normative aspects – is the lack of consensus as to what constitute services. Most can agree on a list of real-world activities that are services, and with some exceptions there is no difficulty in distinguishing the items on the list from goods. But it is harder to identify what it is economically that distinguishes all goods from all services, and then to use this difference as the basis for theoretical analysis.

At one extreme, economists are accustomed to lumping all goods and services together, assuming implicitly that there are no economically meaningful differences between them: It then follows of course that what is said of goods applies equally well to services, and in particular that the principle of comparative advantage is as valid for services as for goods. But this follows from the failure to distinguish between them in the first place, and it proves nothing. The opportunity remains for someone to point out a difference between goods and services and to object that this difference has not been taken into account. Without explicitly considering models of all possible characteristics that might distinguish goods and services, as well as all possible combinations thereof, one cannot claim to have proved one's case conclusively. Since there is no end to the list

† Post-printed from Robert M. Stern, ed., *Trade and Investment in Services: Canada/US Perspectives*, Toronto: Ontario Economic Council, 1985, pp. 39–71.

of characteristics that might be advanced as distinguishing at least some goods and services, I conclude that the issue of this paper is one that can never be resolved once and for all.

On the other hand, just as we often know intuitively which things are goods and which are services, we also know intuitively that some of the differences between goods and services are unimportant for the issue of comparative advantage. Hindley and Smith (1984) illustrate this in the following comment on the view that services have been ignored in theories of comparative advantage:

> The underlying premise is that services are different from goods, which may indeed be so. But a bunch of flowers and a ton of coal and a jet airliner are very different things also. It may be true that no economist has discussed international trade in brussels sprouts or used that vegetable to illustrate comparative advantage. That surely does not raise any substantial question as to whether the conceptual and theoretical apparatus of comparative cost theory is applicable to brussels sprouts.

Even this, of course, presumes our agreement that the brussels sprout is just another vegetable. Were it known, instead, that brussels sprouts are addictive, or that their production fouls the environment, or that they are valued primarily as collectables, then we might recognize that some of the postulates that are normally assumed in proving comparative advantage are violated by brussels sprouts, and we would not be so sanguine.

Thus the only way to proceed on an issue like this, I believe, is piecemeal. Select, one at a time, various characteristics that distinguish services from goods, characteristics that intuition suggests *may* have a bearing on trade and comparative advantage. Build a model that can capture these characteristics and examine its implications. Finally, base one's conclusion, first, on a judgement as to the empirical relevance of those characteristics, if any, that do seem to undermine comparative advantage, and second, on the comprehensiveness of the list of characteristics that do not. In all, one must keep an open mind: there always remains the possibility that some other characteristic, so far unexamined, will be found to overturn the results.

In subsequent sections, then, I will follow this approach, examining in theoretical terms three separate characteristics that seem important for at least a portion of the international trade in services. The sections are largely independent, since different techniques turn out to be useful in each. I will try only at the end to tie them together in some fashion.

The first characteristic that I will consider is also the least general: the fact that traded services often arise as a byproduct of trade in goods. While trade services, such as transportation, cargo insurance, and trade financing, are not the only kind of services that are traded, there is reason to think that they fail to satisfy one of the standard assumptions of trade theory, and thus may make a re-examination of comparative advantage worthwhile. It turns out that comparative advantage continues to work quite well to explain such trade, but the exercise is nonetheless fruitful in providing other insights.

In the next section, I turn to another characteristic that is often regarded as more general, and also more likely to transcend comparative advantage. This is the fact that trade in services frequently requires, or is at least accompanied by, international direct investment. If comparative advantage explains only trade in goods, and if trade in services is really a form of trade in the factors of production, then one might question the relevance of comparative advantage for explaining trade in services. It turns out, however, that international factor movements are just as much the creatures of comparative advantage as is trade in goods. This is implicit in some of the theoretical writings on comparative advantage, and can be made explicit quite easily. Thus if services trade were really just a disguised form of international factor movement, it would still be determined by the principle of comparative advantage.

However, it is my view that the characterization of services trade as factor trade is overly simple and perhaps misleading. In the last section, therefore, I will suggest an alternative interpretation in which services are distinct from goods in terms of the location requirements of production. Loosely following Hill (1977), I will assume that while goods can be produced elsewhere from where they are consumed, services cannot. In contrast, however, and to make trade in services (as distinct from factors) possible in these circumstances, I will also assume that production of services is possible even though some of the factors of production from which they are produced are not present but instead make their contribution from a distance, perhaps even from a different country.

To formalize this concept, I look at a simple 2x2x2 model in which one of the sectors is identified as producing a service. The labour in this sector can produce only for domestic demand, but the second input – call it management – can be provided from abroad.[1] If we think of the ownership of the firm as abiding with management, then it is natural to think of the firm as exporting the service, even though the actual production takes place within the importing country using local labour. Since management itself does not move, one would not observe international investment occurring here, except perhaps if one were to infer such investment from the repatriation of earnings that are necessary to pay the managers at home. Furthermore, it turns out that, depending on the factor intensities of production in the two sectors, one can easily get a case in which the service is exported from a country in which it would have been relatively expensive in autarky, thus violating comparative advantage.

Before beginning, I should mention one characteristic of some services trade that I will not consider. I will not look at any models of imperfect competition, and even in the last section, where I model what might be viewed as multinational corporations, I continue to assume that these corporations behave competitively. My reason for this is twofold. First, I wish to give comparative advantage a fair chance of working, and existing models of trade, even in goods, have not established that comparative advantage is descriptively correct for all of the possible imperfectly competitive market structures. Presumably, if comparative advantage has difficulty in my competitive model, as it does in the last section, then it would have no less difficulty in a model of imperfect competition.

Second, while it is true that many of the multinationals that deal in services are too large to be regarded as competitive, this is equally true of those that deal in goods.

[1] One might be uncomfortable with the idea that managers never set foot in the country where production takes place. Presumably, the presence of managers when a subsidiary is first established may be necessary, even if the subsidiary can function without them present later on.

Thus it is hard to see that imperfect competition is an identifying characteristic of trade in services per se. With that in mind, I prefer to look at the simplest models that do incorporate such identifying characteristics, and for this the competitive framework seems appropriate.

TRADE IN TRADE SERVICES

Not all services are rendered directly to consumers. Many services are intermediate inputs to production, and some are inputs to other activities such as trade. Indeed, trade in goods inevitably requires that goods be moved from one country to another, and the provision of that transportation is a service. In the modern world, other services too are used by traders, such as cargo insurance, trade financing, and legal help in dealing with different countries' regulations. Thus one can say that trade in goods constitutes a source of demand for a variety of services that I will call trade services.[2]

Now these trade services are not themselves inevitably traded. Exporters and importers could, if they wished, deal only with transporters, insurers, banks, and lawyers from their home countries. But it is also natural for traders to be aware of the availability of these services from other countries, and thus one might expect trade in trade services to arise earlier in history than trade in services of other kinds and for other uses. Thus trade in trade services, if it is distinct at all from other forms of service trade, seems worthy of examination.

Furthermore, trade in trade services does have one very special property that distinguishes it from other forms of trade: the demand for it arises solely from other trade. Why is this important for our discussion of comparative advantage?

A first reason is that comparative advantage is customarily measured in terms of autarky prices. Yet trade services by definition are not demanded in autarky, and therefore their autarky prices do not exist. Thus we must look elsewhere for an indicator of comparative advantage in trade services, and this alone makes them of some interest. One possibility, if the services are produced using factors of production that have well-defined autarky prices, would be to measure comparative advantage in terms of their minimum costs of production at autarky factor prices.[3] Yet even this may be suspect, since the autarky factor prices in no way reflect the demands for them that may arise when they are used to produce trade services.

A second reason is that trade services violate an assumption that is often made in trade theory, and to the extent that demonstrations of comparative advantage rest on that assumption, they need at least to be reconsidered. The assumption in question is that demand conditions are identical across countries; that is, that faced with identical prices consumers in different countries will demand goods in identical proportions. This assumption is sometimes used in proofs of the Heckscher-Ohlin theorem, and when it is not, differences in demand are incorporated in comparisons of relative autarky prices. But as just noted, autarky prices are not obviously available in the case of trade services.

---

[2] These are services that Stern (1985) calls complementary to goods.

[3] Another possibility, in some cases, would be to use the autarky prices of similar services that are used within the domestic market even in autarky. This may be misleading, however, since the requirements of international trade are often different from those of domestic trade.

There is a final problem that would seem on the face of it to cause problems: trade in trade services itself is not well defined. We are not accustomed in trade theory to worrying about where, in the process of trade in a good, the ownership of that good changes hands. But in defining trade in trade services this may make a difference. Consider, for example, the case of a good that is sold by a domestic exporter to a foreign importer, and that must be transported from one to the other. Suppose further that the transportation service is provided by a firm based in the importing country.[4] If that transportation is purchased by the importing firm, then the transaction involves no trade in transportation services. But if it is purchased by the exporting firm, our country will be regarded as importing these services. The actual production that takes place, including the production of the transportation service, is the same in both cases, but the recording of how much trade has occurred is quite different. Clearly there are similar problems whenever a trade service is provided, since there are always two parties to the goods-trade transaction and either may be the demander of the service.

What difference could all of this make for comparative advantage? A couple of interesting possibilities suggest themselves.

Consider, for example, a country with a cost advantage in providing transportation services. By the usual argument of comparative costs, this country should become a net provider of these services to the world, once trade is allowed. Suppose however that the country is very remote from world markets, and that as a result it is also an unusually great demander of transportation services, once it enters into trade. We may then find it being an importer of transportation, in spite of its comparative cost advantage. Note too that the country's distance from world markets will not be reflected in its autarky costs of transportation, as would be the case if it had an unusual demand for a good or factor instead, since in autarky its demand for transportation is not revealed to any market.

A second difficulty that might be expected to arise from trade services has to do with the effect that restrictions on trade in services may have on patterns of trade in goods. Suppose, for example, that a country has a comparative advantage in a particular good that happens to require a large dose of some trade service, say insurance, if it is to be traded. This in itself need not interfere with its exporting the good, so long as all countries pay the same price for trade insurance. But suppose instead that trade in insurance is not permitted and that the country has a strong comparative disadvantage in providing this service. Then the cost to it of exporting, should it be required to insure its trade itself, could be prohibitive of its exporting the good at all. Thus it appears that acknowledging the existence of trade services in a model of trade in goods may alter what we can say even about the latter.

In fact, however, trade in trade services does not make as much difference for comparative advantage as all of this suggests. To see this, I introduce the following formal model.

Consider a world of n countries and m goods and let there be also s services that will be useful only if there is trade in goods. In vectors of appropriate lengths, and omitting implicit country superscripts, let X be a particular country's outputs of goods, C its final demands for these goods, and thus $T=X-C$ its net exports of goods. Similarly, let

---

[4] Similar problems arise if transportation is provided by the exporting country or even by a third country.

S be the trade services it produces, U the trade services that it uses in the course of trade, and $V=S-U$ its net exports of trade services.

In order to characterize the technology of production and trade, I must first define the physical meaning of trade, and as I have done before in Deardorff (1980) I will make use of the convenient fiction of a single world port. That is, suppose that there exists a single point on the globe through which all trade must pass. Further, to resolve the ambiguity mentioned above in the definition of trade in trade services, I will assume that each country's own traders are responsible for getting its goods to and from the world port, so that if a foreigner provides trade services between a country and the port, this will be regarded as imports of those services.[5] These assumptions are not as restrictive as they seem, as I argued in the appendix to Deardorff (1980).

Technology can now be defined quite simply. For production, let $F=\{(X,S)\}$ be the set of all feasible outputs of goods and services that can be produced by a country given its technology and factor endowments. It is a production possibility set of the usual sort, and it admits negative values for elements of X, representing the net use of goods as intermediate inputs. Only non-negative values of S are in the set, however, since the services here are useful in trade only, and not in domestic production. The manner in which they may be used is described by another set, $G=\{(T,U)\}$, the set of all possible vectors of net trade in goods and (non-negative) vectors of trade services used. If a particular service, U_1, were required in fixed proportion to the amount of trade in a particular good, T_1, for example, then a cross-section of the set G would be as indicated in Figure 1. That is, U_1 must be at least as great as the appropriate constant times the absolute value of T_1. In general, of course, more complicated shapes are possible, and I assume only sufficient boundedness on the technology to make the relevant maximization problems possess solutions. These sets, F and G, may differ in general from country to country.

I turn now to characterization of equilibria, making such assumptions, familiar in trade theory, as perfect competition, the weak axiom of revealed preference, profit maximization, and balanced trade. I will consider only three types of equilibrium: autarky, in which there is no trade in either goods or services; free trade, in both goods and services; and what I will call semi-autarky, in which there is free trade in goods but no trade at all in services, so that, for example, each country's own transportation firms must move its exports to the port and its imports from the port. More general cases of nonprohibitive tariffs and other restrictions on the two kinds of trade could easily be allowed with additional notation.

An autarky equilibrium consists of vectors of prices of goods, p^a, prices of services, q^a, and outputs of goods, X^a, which are feasible to produce, are demanded by consumers facing these prices, and maximize the value of the country's output:

$$p^a X^a \geq p^a X + q^a S \quad \text{for all}\,(X,S) \in F \tag{1}$$

[5] A more realistic but more cumbersome specification would be to define all trade services produced as exported and all trade services used as imported, since trade statistics typically measure a country's trade from its own border. Obviously the results here, which relate to net trade, would not be affected by this specification.

Note that, while the output of trade services is zero in autarky equilibrium, we can still speak of equilibrium prices for these services as long as these are prices at which profit-maximizing producers of services would be content not to produce. However, since negative values of S are excluded from F, .this is likely to mean that these prices are not unique. Indeed, for any equilibrium that satisfies (1), any other prices of services not greater than q^a will also be an autarky equilibrium.

A free-trade equilibrium is somewhat more involved. It consists, for a given country, of both domestic and world prices, p^d and p^w, the latter being the prices of goods at the international port, together with world prices of services, q^w, as well. In addition, there are quantities of goods produced and consumed, X^f and C^f respectively, and quantities of services produced and used, S^f and U^f. To be an equilibrium, all of these quantities must be feasible, the goods consumed must be willingly demanded at the prices p^d, and production and trade must yield as great a value as any other available opportunity. Thus

$$p^d X^f + q^w S^f \geq p^d X + q^w S \quad \text{for all } (X,S) \in F \tag{2}$$

and

$$(p^w - p^d)T^f - q^w U^f \geq (p^w - p^d)T - q^w U \quad \text{for all } (T,U) \in G \tag{3}$$

Finally, I require balanced trade:

$$p^w T^f + q^w V^f = 0 \tag{4}$$

To complete the specification of the free-trade equilibrium, I would need the requirement that world markets clear for both goods and services. I would also note that world prices of goods and services are the same for all countries, while domestic prices need not be.

A semi-autarky equilibrium, as described above, requires essentially the same conditions as (2), (3), and (4), though in this case the quantities of services produced and used, call them S^S and U^S, must be the same, and the prices of services, p^S, can vary across countries. I will not bother to write down the analogous conditions.

I am now in a position to examine the role of comparative advantage in these equilibria. As in Deardorff (1980), the crucial relationship involves the value of trade at autarky prices. Since this value is the inner product of the vector of net trade with the vector of autarky prices, its sign turns out to give us various correlations between autarky prices and trade. And it is easy to show, much as in Deardorff (1980), that

$$p^a T^f + q^a V^f \leq 0 \tag{5}$$

To see this, first note that

$$\begin{aligned} p^d C^a &= p^d X^a \\ &\leq p^d X^f + q^w S^f \\ &\leq p^d X^f + q^w S^f + \left[(p^w - p^d)T^f - q^w U^f\right] \\ &= p^d C^f + p^w T^f + q^w V^f \\ &= p^d C^f \end{aligned} \tag{6}$$

where the first inequality follows from (2), the second inequality follows from (3) using $T=U=0$ on the right-hand side of (3), and the last two equalities use the definitions, $T=X-C$ and $V=S-U$, and equation (4). Relation (6) says that free-trade consumption is revealed preferred to autarky consumption, and thus the weak axiom of revealed preference implies that

$$p^a C^a \leq p^a C^f \tag{7}$$

Finally, the autarky value of trade can be evaluated as follows:

$$\begin{aligned} p^a T^f + q^a V^f &= p^a X^f + q^a S^f - p^a C^f - q^q U^f \\ &\leq p^a X^a - p^a C^f - q^q U^f \\ &= p^a C^a - p^a C^f - q^q U^f \\ &\leq -q^a U^f \\ &\leq 0 \end{aligned} \tag{8}$$

where the first inequality follows from (1), the second from (7), and the last from the fact that both q and U must be non-negative vectors. This completes the proof of (5).

The inequality in (5), then, establishes that the principle of comparative advantage holds in this model of trade in both goods and trade services. That is, it must be true on average that the goods and services a country exports must be worth less to it in autarky than the goods and services it imports. Of course, this average relationship permits individual goods and services to be traded in ways that seem contrary to comparative advantage, and thus some examples such as those I discussed above are possible. But there is nothing special about services in this respect: similar examples can be found also for trade in goods alone, as I showed in Deardorff (1979). Thus it seems that this particular characteristic of trade in services – the fact that much of it is demanded only as a byproduct of trade in goods – does not after all undermine the usual result of comparative advantage.

There is, however, more that one can say in this particular model. First, recall that the autarky prices of services that appear in (5) are to a large extent arbitrary. Given any prices for which (2) holds, (2) will also hold if these prices are replaced by prices of services that are closer to zero, and even if they are replaced by zero itself. Thus it follows as a corollary to (5) that

$$p^a T^f \leq 0 \tag{9}$$

This looks exactly like the traditional result from a model without services, but it applies to this model in which the trade in goods that is included in T is only a part of the trade that is going on. Thus the principle of comparative advantage, it turns out, applies to trade in goods alone, even when trade services are also being traded.

There is yet another corollary that follows in turn from (9). It is possible in general for a country to exchange goods for services and vice versa. But in a model like this, in which all services are trade services, it is impossible for there to be net trade in just one good in exchange for services. For if there were, then p^aT^f would be positive for the country that exports the good, thus violating (9).

Finally, consider what would happen in a semi-autarky equilibrium in which there is trade in goods but not in services. All of the conditions used above still apply, with the superscript 'f' replaced by 's'. Thus the result in (5) continues to hold in a semi-autarky equilibrium, and

$$p^aT^s \leq 0 \tag{10}$$

since V^s is zero by definition. Thus comparative advantage continues to explain trade in goods, even if trade in traded services is not permitted. Evidently, my example above, showing how prohibition of trade in services might undermine a country's comparative advantage in a good that it finds expensive to trade, indicates only how trade can be reduced or eliminated by this phenomenon, but not that its pattern can be reversed.[6]

To conclude this section, then, allowing for trade in trade services leads to some interesting possibilities as far as the trade in particular goods and services may be concerned, but it does not in any way undermine the principle of comparative advantage as the general indicator of the patterns of trade that can take place. On the contrary, the principle is strengthened in a sense, for it now applies even to the subcategory of trade in goods alone, as well as to trade in goods and services together.

SERVICES TRADE AS INTERNATIONAL FACTOR MOVEMENTS

A notable feature of much of the trade in services is that it may require a *presence,* on the part of the exporting firm, within the importing country. This means that some employees of the exporting firm may have to be present to administer, market, or oversee the service. Or it may mean the need to establish a physical plant in which or from which the service can be provided in the importing country. Either way, this suggests the need for labour, capital, or both to move from the exporting country to the importing country in order to provide the service. I will argue in the next section that such factor movements are not in fact an inevitable feature of trade in services, but they certainly can occur in conjunction with it and have been identified by many as a crucial aspect of services trade. Therefore, it seems sensible at this point to ask if factor movements do give reason to doubt the validity of comparative advantage as it applies to services.

---

[6] Note that (10) is consistent with T^s=0. That is, even though trade in goods is permitted in semi-autarky, it may be that none will occur, if the costs of domestically produced trade services turn out to be prohibitive.

The answer, fortunately, is easily found. Quite independently of whether they involve services or not, international factor movements fit neatly into the theory of comparative advantage. It is true, of course, that factor movements can reduce – even to zero – the amount of trade in goods that occurs in response to comparative advantage. But it is also true that trade in goods and factors together conforms to the principle of comparative advantage in the usual sense that those goods and factors that are exported will, on average, have been cheaper in autarky than those that are imported.

It is unnecessary to prove this result here since it has appeared elsewhere. In my own article (1980), this result was implicit, since the goods in that model were defined to include 'all final goods, intermediate goods, and services of primary factors of production', any or all of which could be traded or nontraded. The result has also been made explicit by Ethier and Svensson (1983) as one of many theorems of trade theory that they extend to a model with factor mobility.

Thus to observe that trade in services often involves international direct investment, for example, in no way suggests that it should therefore fail to conform to comparative advantage. On the contrary, if the export of certain services requires the export of capital, then one would expect the countries that export these services to be also those in which capital is relatively cheap. Similarly, if other services require the movement of certain types of labour in order for them to be traded, then those countries where this labour is readily available will be the most likely to export them.

As always in general discussions of trade patterns, one can find cases in which particular goods, services, or factors appear to be traded perversely. This is usually either a result of the greater importance of some other determinant of relative costs, or the result of some form of complementarity with another good or service. For example, suppose that a service relies heavily on both skilled and unskilled labour, and is relatively expensive in the United States because the scarcity of the latter outweighs the abundance of the former. If trade in the service requires that only skilled labour move internationally, the necessary unskilled labour being taken from the local labour market in the importing country, then one could easily find the service being exported by the United States in spite of its relatively high autarky cost here. In this example, the trade in the service alone appears to run counter to comparative advantage, but the trade in goods and services together, including the trade in skilled labour, would not. A proper evaluation of comparative advantage requires only that we succeed in taking into account all of the trade that is actually taking place.

On the other hand, this example is very similar to the situation that I will describe in the next section. For suppose that the skilled labour just mentioned could make its contribution to production without actually moving to the country to which the service is being exported. Trade in the service would continue to occur but trade in skilled labour would not. Since the trade in the service is what appeared perverse, we would then be left with an apparent violation of comparative advantage without any offsetting trade in factors. Thus it may not be movement of factors internationally, but rather the possibility that they need not move in order to make a contribution, that causes the greatest difficulty for the principle of comparative advantage as it applies to services. This is what I will examine more formally in the next section.

SERVICE TRADE WITH ABSENT FACTORS

I noted above the tendency for service trade to require the presence of the service exporting firm in the importing country. This is a general property of services trade, especially if one follows Hill (1977) in defining services as marketable activities in which production must take place in the presence of the demander. Hill argues that services in general cause a change in either the person or the property of the consumer of the service. If the change is in a person, then obviously that person must be present during production, but even if the change is in some good owned by the consumer, the need to maintain that ownership intact during whatever transformation occurs makes it unlikely that production can take place too far removed from the consumer. In any case, I will from now on let this property be one of the defining characteristics of a service: that its production must take place in the same location (or at least the same country) as is occupied by the person or firm that purchases it.

In the previous section, this characteristic led to the association of services trade with international factor movements, on the assumption that a firm can produce in a foreign country only if it also moves some of its factors of production there. But this is not a good assumption, as recent observation of the behaviour of multinational corporations makes clear. To produce in a foreign country, a firm needs to employ factors of production there. But these need not be factors that it brought from its home country; they can be hired on local factor markets. Indeed for many years trade theorists felt that we had covered the subject of multinational enterprises implicitly in our studies of international capital movements, and only recently have we explicitly recognized that such enterprises typically organize much of their financial and other activities locally, in the same countries where they produce. Furthermore, even when they do raise funds on international capital markets, their decisions are truly international, and have little to do with where their home offices are located.

Thus a firm that wishes to export a service may do so by setting up a branch in a foreign country, hiring local labour, and financing any necessary local capital expenditures within the local market of the foreign country as well. If it does all of this, one may then wonder what it is that is actually being exported. The answer in general is that there is some other factor that contributes to the profitability of the firm. This may be a unique method of management, a proprietary product or brand name, or a technique of production to which only it has access. In any case, if the export of the service is truly an export at all, there must be something that is provided by the home office of the firm that contributes to its profitability. Otherwise, it would pay its entire revenue to local factors, and no international transactions would take place at all.

To capture this idea I will follow Markusen (1984) and Helpman (1984) in their models of multinational corporations, and assume that production of services requires inputs of at least some factors that need not be physically present at the same location where production takes place. These 'absent factors' can encompass all of the contributions described above that a multinational can make to its subsidiaries, but for ease of reference I will, from now on, simply call them management.

Markusen and Helpman both go well beyond what I want to do here, in their pursuit of explanations for multinationals. For one thing, they make no distinction between goods and services, and their multinationals may implicitly produce both. In addition, they assume that what I am calling absent factors are also, in a sense, public goods within the firm, which is able to provide services to additional numbers of subsidiaries without additional effort in the home office. This in turn leads them also to assume that multinationals are large and noncompetitive. I will make neither of these assumptions, since I do not view imperfect competition as more likely for services than for goods, and I want therefore to remain in an environment where small competitive firms are possible. Thus my factor, management, is just like any other factor in a neoclassical production function, except that it need not be located where production of services takes place.

Notice, then, the dichotomy that I am assuming in the technologies of goods and services. Production of goods, I assume, requires the simultaneous presence of all factors of production, but does not require the presence of those who will consume or otherwise use the goods once they are produced. Services, on the other hand, do require the presence of consumers, but do not require the presence of all factors of production. Naturally, real-world activities are not so clearly separated. There are services in which there is no absent factor contribution, but these can be dispensed with as unable to enter international trade. There are also goods that can make use of absent factors, and this could complicate the analysis a bit since their location of production might then be indeterminant. But it will be convenient here to consider only the two extremes.

In fact, what seems to be crucial for the results that follow is not that some factors can be absent, but rather that some factors must be present, and that for services this presence must be in the same location as the consumer of the service. Since goods can be transported, it is hard to think of examples of exports of goods for which some factor of production must be present in the importing country.[7]

To show what this view of goods and services can imply for comparative advantage, I turn now to a very simple model of international trade that incorporates this view. The model is like the standard textbook Heckscher-Ohlin (H-O) trade model of two goods, two factors, and two countries. However, in this case I make one of the goods a service, and require that it be produced where it is consumed. Further, as just explained, I call one of the two factors of production management, and let it contribute to services production *in absentia*. Otherwise, the assumptions of the model are exactly those of the H-O model.

In autarky this model looks exactly like the H-O model. Since autarky constrains all factors, production, and consumption to locate within the same closed country, the special location requirements of services are unimportant. Thus, for example, the autarky relative price of the service will depend on demand for the service relative to the good, the endowments of the two factors, labour and management, and the intensities with which these two factors are required in production of the good and the service. In particular, comparing two countries, A and B, I will assume that the autarky relative price of the service is lower in Country A than in Country B. With identical homothetic demands and identical technologies, this could either mean that services are management-intensive and that Country A has a relative abundance of management, or that services are labour-intensive and A is well endowed with labour. Alternatively, the price

---

[7] On the other hand, Bob Staiger has pointed out to me that local content legislation has precisely this effect. It is interesting to speculate on whether, given the findings below, such legislation can undermine comparative advantage even in goods.

difference could result from differences in technology. In any case, Country A has a comparative advantage in services by the usual criterion of relative autarky prices, and we wish to see if this advantage is reflected in its trade, once trade is allowed.

In the H-O model, free trade equates the prices of traded goods across countries. This in turn equates factor prices across countries as well, if the other assumptions of the factor-price-equalization theorem are satisfied, in particular if technologies are identical and if both goods are produced in both countries. In the model here, things are different but the outcome may be the same.

Free trade directly equates the price, across countries, of only the good, not the service. If the producer of a service were to observe a higher price abroad than at home, that in itself would not induce it to export, since to serve the foreign market it must produce there and must employ at least some local factors. The fact that it can produce more cheaply at home using domestic factors is of no help, since those factors cannot in general be used for production abroad.

On the other hand, I assume that one of the domestic factors, management, *can* be used for production abroad, since it is not required to be present where production takes place. Under what circumstances, then, will a service firm be able to compete successfully abroad? Obviously the answer depends on technology and the price of management in the two countries, not on the price of the service itself. If management is cheaper in Country A than in Country B, and if technologies are everywhere the same, then producers from A will be able to undercut the prices charged by producers in B, since they will have access to the same labour market in B, but will be able to use cheaper management. In fact, the same would be true for producers in B, were we to permit them to hire managers from A, but I will assume that the identity of the firm lies with its managers and exclude this possibility.

Continue to assume, for the time being, identical, constant-returns technologies. Clearly, then, trade in services will take place, if it is permitted, whenever the price of management differs between the countries. This could lead to specialization of various sorts, for example, all of the services in Country B being provided by Country A's firms. But if it does not, then such trade will equate the prices of management in the two countries, just as trade in a good equates the price of the good. Further, once the price of the one good and the price of the one factor, management, are equated across countries, then the logic of the factor-price-equalization theorem will work to equate the remaining prices; those of the other factor, labour, and of the service. Thus free trade will tend to equate the price of services in the two countries, but not because of arbitrage in the markets for services themselves. The requirement that services be produced where they are consumed prevents such arbitrage. Instead the prices of services are equated indirectly, just as factor prices are equated in the H-O model.

Formally, let the countries produce a good, X, and a service, S, using factors of production labour, L, and management, M. Prices of the good, p, and of the service, q, will equal the minimum unit costs of whatever firms produce them, and these costs are functions of the wage of labour, w, and the salary of management, s:

$$p = c_X(w,s); \quad q = c_S(w,s) \tag{11}$$

where each of the four prices should bear appropriate superscripts to indicate which country's good, service, and factors are being described. With free trade in the good, we must have $p^A=p^B$, and thus, if the good is produced in both countries,

$$p^A = c_X(w^A, s^A) = c_X(w^B, s^B) = p^B \tag{12}$$

With free trade in the service industry, Country A's producers will expand their operations in B's market whenever $c_S(w^B, s^A) < q^B$, since they can use their own managers and B's workers. If in equilibrium producers from both countries continue to serve B's market, this relationship must hold with equality, and thus

$$c_S(w^B, s^A) = c_S(w^B, s^B) \tag{13}$$

which, given the nature of the unit cost functions, will be true only if

$$s^A = s^B \tag{14}$$

Similar reasoning implies (14) if service producers from both countries share *A's* market, so that it is only if a single country's producers take over the provision of services in both countries that salaries will fail to be equalized.

Furthermore, once salaries are equalized, it follows from (12) that wages will be equalized as well, and then from (11) that prices of services will be equalized. Thus, with incomplete specialization, free trade in this model implies complete factor price and service price equalization, much as in the H-O model.

In order to examine further the nature of the free-trade equilibrium, it is helpful to use diagrams. In Figure 2, I show the two countries' transformation curves between *X* and *S* as they would appear if both countries were to use their labour and management only in domestic production. These are conventional transformation curves, and I have drawn them to reflect my assumption that Country A has an apparent comparative advantage in services. Thus if services could be traded directly, a world relative price of services, q^f, would prevail in both countries.[8] Production and consumption would take place at points *H* and C respectively, and Country A would export *S* to Country B in exchange for *X*.

In the present model, such direct trade in services is not possible, but if there is factor price equalization as just described, the same price, q^f, will clear the market. To make this possible, some of the management in one of the countries will be withdrawn from production of domestic services, and put into use instead as an absent factor in production of services abroad. While the factor does not actually move internationally, the production possibilities in the two countries will be affected exactly as if it did.

Which country's management will do this? To determine this, one could either look at the autarky prices and the incentives they provide, or look at the changes in output that take place as production possibilities shift and see if they take us toward or away from equilibrium. Fortunately, both approaches yield the same result, as the reader can

[8] I am now taking the price of the good as numeraire, $p^A = p^B = 1$.

verify. But the result does depend on relative factor intensities, and so I now consider two cases. A third case, with unequal technologies, will follow.

Case I: Services are management intensive

In this case, for Country A to have the assumed comparative advantage in services, it must also have a relative abundance of the factor, management. Thus in autarky, the salary of managers in A would be less than those in B, and there would be an incentive, as described above, for A's service producers to export services: they will set up operations in B and provide services using labour that they hire there, while continuing to use managers located within A. These managers, while they remain physically in A, are no longer contributing to production there, and A's production possibilities contract exactly as though the managers had moved abroad. As a result, A's transformation curve shifts inward in Rybczynski fashion. At the constant relative price, q^f, Country A's production point in Figure 2 will move to the left and upward, following the Rybczynski line R^A. Likewise, as these managers begin to contribute to production in Country B, that country's production possibilities will expand and its production point will follow the parallel Rybczynski line, R^B, down and to the right.

When will this process end? Since services must be produced where they are consumed, it will end when the outputs of services in both countries exactly equal what the countries' own consumers demand. Thus the equilibrium is found in A and B along the Rybczynski lines vertically below and above, respectively; the consumption points, C^A and C^B.

In this equilibrium, Country A imports good X, paying for it with what it earns from the provision of services in Country B's market. These services, which amount physically to the quantity $S_2 - S_1$ in Figure 2, are worth a good deal more than the imports of X that Country A gets in return. The difference, of course, is paid to labour in Country B.

It is a bit unclear how one should measure what is going on here. It seems clear that Country A is exporting services, but what is the quantity of services that is being exported? If we measure it as the total produced abroad, $S_2 - S_1$, then we either appear to have unbalanced trade or we must say in addition that service firms in A are *importing* labour from B. The latter is peculiar, since B's workers are neither moving to A, nor providing input to production there. Alternatively, one could measure the export of services by the amount that the service firms repatriate, and which they use in turn to pay their managers. This, in units of services, is $S_3 - S_1$ in Figure 2 and is equal in value to the imports of X, but it gives the appearance of measuring an input rather than an output. Finally, one could give up trying to measure trade in services at all, on the grounds that services cannot, strictly speaking, be traded, and measure instead the export of factor services – management in this case – that is taking place implicitly within the service firms. This would give the same value as the second alternative.

In any case, whatever its amount, if there is trade in services here at all, it is clearly Country A that is doing the exporting. This is not surprising, since I assumed at the outset that A had a comparative advantage in services. But in fact comparative advantage has nothing to do with this result, as the next case I consider will make clear.

Case II: Services are labour intensive

If services are labour intensive, then Country A's assumed low relative price must be the result of an abundance of labour. This case is shown in Figure 3, where the transformation curves and free-trade price lines are the same as in Figure 2. What is different is the incentive for trade in services.

As a result of its abundance of labour, it is the wage, not the salary, that must be relatively lowest in Country A in autarky. Attempts therefore by A's service producers to penetrate B's market will be frustrated, since they will find themselves employing B's more expensive labour as well as their own more expensive managers, the worst of both worlds. Instead, it is B's producers of services that will have the incentive to trade, and they will begin to use their managers together with Country A's labour to produce services in A.

This causes A's production possibility curve this time to shift outward, and B's to shift inward, their production points as before moving along Rybczynski lines until markets are cleared. But this time, since services are now labour-intensive, these Rybczynski lines are steeper than the transformation curves rather than flatter, and the equilibria in Figure 3 are found above C in Country A and below C in Country B. This is as it should be, since A is now importing services, paying for them in part with its own labour, and in part with its exports of the good, X.

Thus, we have a case in which trade in services appears to run counter to comparative advantage. Labour-scarce Country B exports labour-intensive services in spite of the fact that these services cost more in B than in Country A in autarky. The reason for this result is that direct competition in the service industry is ruled out by the need to produce in the presence of consumers, together with the inability to move labour internationally. Instead, the only thing that matters for this kind of trade is the price of the only factor whose services can, in a sense, be traded: the factor I have called management whose productive services can operate from a distance. Since management is the abundant factor in B, this pattern of trade makes sense.

Whether this pattern of trade should in fact be thought of as violating the principle of comparative advantage is another question, however. It turns out that by carefully reinterpreting what we mean by the principle, we can assure that it remains valid even in this model.

One possibility, in line with the third method of measuring trade mentioned above, would be to say that services are not being traded at all, and that what is being traded is the productive contribution of the factor, management. Since in both cases I and II considered above, services are exported by the country in which management has the lower relative autarky salary, trade then follows comparative advantage.

Another possibility, more in line with modern interpretations of the generalized Heckscher-Ohlin model, is to focus not on trade itself but on the factor content of that trade. In that case, since the activity of producing the service abroad incorporates a contribution from only one domestic factor, management, the factor content of that trade is exclusively management. It follows again that each country tends to export, in factor content terms, its abundant factors.

Unfortunately, neither of these interpretations is particularly useful when it comes to explaining what is commonly meant by trade in services. For that, the model of this section has to suggest that the principle of comparative advantage is of little use, largely because in this model trade in services is not trade in the conventional sense.

Case III: Differences in technology

A final case should be briefly considered, since it casts doubt on even the successful interpretations of comparative advantage mentioned above. Suppose that factor endowments are the same in the two countries and that autarky prices differ instead because Country A has a different technology for producing services than does Country B. There are many ways that technologies could differ, and the nature of the difference can be important, as is well known even in the conventional H-O model.[9] I will assume simply that A has a Hicks-neutral technological advantage in the industry. It is also important, in this model, whether the superior technology continues to be available to a firm if it produces abroad. There are some interesting possibilities here, but I will assume that a country's managers know their technology, so that its use abroad is possible.[10]

Consider first how the autarky equilibria in the two countries will compare. If the two countries were to face the same price, A would clearly produce more services and less goods than B. If demands are identical, it follows that the autarky price of services in A must be lower than in B, and thus that the relative amount of services that is produced and consumed in A will be greater than in B. What this means for factor prices depends both on the degree of substitution between goods and services in demand and on the relative factor intensities of the two industries.[11] It is enough to consider one possibility. It may be that the salary of management in A, measured in units of X, is higher than in B, but by less than the full extent of A's technological advantage.

If that is the case, then when trade is permitted, A will clearly export services to B. For A's producers have a superior technology, and their managers, though paid more than managers in B, are not paid enough to offset their firms' competitive edge.

Now this is as far as we need to go to see the implications of this example for comparative advantage. On the one hand, comparative advantage in the usual sense now seems to be working quite well: A is exporting services, which it produced more cheaply than B in autarky. On the other hand, consider the alternative interpretations of comparative advantage that were used above to reconcile case II with comparative advantage. In this case the autarky price of management is higher in A than in B, but with trade Country A nonetheless appears to export the services of management. Thus the suggestion above that this model really involves trade in management, not services, and that this trade is in accord with comparative advantage, fails to work once differences in technology are introduced.

---

[9] See Findlay and Grubert (1959), for example.

[10] With this in mind one might prefer to think of the technology as embodied in the managers, so that it would be factor-augmenting instead of Hicks neutral. I do not believe that alternative specifications of the technological advantage would make much difference for the point that I wish to make here.

[11] If preferences were Cobb-Douglas, for example, A and B, with their identical factor endowments, would produce the same amount of the good, X, in autarky and factor prices would be the same in the two countries in units of X. If the elasticity of substitution in demand is other than one, on the other hand, demand for X will be either larger or smaller in A than in B, and factor prices will differ also, in accordance with the relative factor intensity of X.

Summary of the cases

Note, then, what these three cases together suggest about the validity of various versions of the principle of comparative advantage:

Version 1: *Countries tend to export those goods and services for which their relative autarky prices are lowest.* This version is false in case II above, where services make intensive use of the factor that must be employed locally where the service is provided. The reason is that a low autarky price in this case primarily reflects the cheapness of this factor at home, and this is of no use in exporting the service.

Version 2: *Countries cannot trade service outputs, since these must be produced where they are consumed, but can only trade those inputs to the production of services whose contribution can be made internationally. Thus countries tend to export those goods and those international service inputs for which their relative autarky prices are lowest.* This version is true in both case I and case II above, where countries share identical technologies. But if technologies differ, as in case III, then this version is no longer necessarily true. Service inputs such as management may be highly paid as a result of a technological advantage, and may nonetheless, because of that advantage, be able to compete in producing services abroad.

Version 3: *In terms of the factor content of trade, countries tend to export those factors (embodied in both goods and services) for which their relative autarky prices are lowest.* This version, like version 2, is true in both case I and case II, but may be false in case III.

Thus, no version of the principle of comparative advantage that I have been able to find is valid in all three cases. It is interesting that version 3 is a form of what is usually regarded as the Heckscher-Ohlin theorem, rather than the principle of comparative advantage. Since we have always known that the H-O theorem is valid only with identical technologies, one can say that it is made no less valid by introducing services. On the other hand, the conventional principle of comparative advantage, which version I probably comes closest to expressing, has been presumed to be much more generally true than the H-O theorem.[12] Thus it seems that allowing for services in the manner done here has much more serious implications for comparative advantage than it does for the factor proportions theory as embodied in the H-O theorem.[13]

---

[12] Compare the treatments in Deardorff (1980) and Deardorff (1982).

[13] In his comment below, Ron Jones suggests that something like version 2 of comparative advantage can be salvaged even in the case of nonidentical technologies if one either allows managers in the two countries to be viewed as different factors, or regards managers in one country as embodying more units of management services than managers in the other. I am attracted by this interpretation, but I am also uneasy with it for a number of reasons. First, since the technological advantage need not, in the technical sense, be factor-augmenting (as in general the Hicks-neutral advantage assumed above is not), the difference between the management factors in the two countries may not be well defined. Second, in the case III example, the technological advantage exists only in the service industry, and the management factor is the same in the two countries when employed in the goods industry. Thus it is not the case that one country's managers unambiguously embody more units of management services than the others, but only if employed in a particular industry. And third, I am generally leery of attempts to rescue comparative advantage by defining goods traded by different countries as different goods, and my reservations extend to doing the

CONCLUSION

I have looked in this paper at three different characteristics of trade in services, to see in each case what they suggest for the validity of the principle of comparative advantage. These characteristics were, first, that traded services often are demanded as a byproduct of trade in goods; second, that trade in services often goes hand in hand with international movement of factors; and third, that services may be provided internationally by transnational firms, some of whose factors of production make their contributions from a distance. The first two of these characteristics, I argued, do not in any way undermine the usefulness of comparative advantage in explaining trade, but the effect of the third is more troublesome. While it may be possible to reconcile trade with comparative advantage in this case, to do so requires a reinterpretation of trade in a way that interferes considerably with the usefulness of comparative advantage as a guide to empirical reality. Furthermore, when comparative advantage results from differences in technology rather than differences in factor endowments, then the reinterpretation actually makes matters worse. I am left with the uneasy feeling that the principle of comparative advantage may not be as robust as many, including myself, have thought.

The question remains as to whether the model of the last section, which led to this conclusion, has any validity itself. That many corporations transcend national boundaries is clear, and that activities in the home office might contribute to the productivity of subsidiaries seems to me to be eminently reasonable. The particular form assumed for this contribution in the model is of course far too simple, but as an illustration of how this phenomenon might matter for trade, I feel it is appropriate. In any case, I look forward to the impressions of others as to the usefulness of the approach taken here.

I do find the troublesome case II especially interesting because of the way it seems in one sense to correspond to reality. It has been observed that services tend to be relatively expensive in the United States relative to the world at large.[14] Nonetheless, as is evident from the US concern with trade liberalization in services, many regard the United States as at least a potentially important exporter in these industries. Now admittedly, this apparent contradiction of comparative advantage may result entirely from an aggregation problem: the particular services that we are likely to export are quite different from the bulk of very labour-intensive services that even the United States would be more than content to see remain largely nontraded or restricted. But it is interesting that Country B in the case II example was also a labour-scarce Country and that it nonetheless could profit from exporting services that were, in comparison with goods, labour-intensive.

A final remark is in order regarding the welfare implications of what I have said about trade in services. Nothing that I have done here should be regarded as casting doubt on the potential for countries to gain from free trade, in services as well as goods. Even in the case II example, where trade might be said to run counter to comparative advantage, there is still a very clear gain from trade for both the countries involved.

---

same thing with factors. This practice, it seems to me, comes close to making the principle of comparative advantage tautological.

[14] See, for example, Stern's (1985) contribution to this conference.

REFERENCES

Deardorff, Alan V. (1979) 'Weak links in the chain of comparative advantage' *Journal of International Economics* 9, 197-209 (May)

– (1980) 'The general validity of the law of comparative advantage' *Journal of Political Economy* 88, 941-57 (October)

– (1982) 'The general validity of the Heckscher-Ohlin theorem' *American Economic Review* 72, 683-94 (September)

Ethier, Wilfred J. and Lars E.O. Svensson (1983) 'The theorems of international trade with factor mobility' Working Paper No. 1115, National Bureau of Economic Research (May)

Findlay, R. and H. Grubert (1959) 'Factor intensities, technological progress and the terms of trade' *Oxford Economic Papers* 11, 111-21

Helpman, Elhanan (1984) 'A simple theory of international trade with multinational corporations' *Journal of Political Economy* 92

Helpman, Elhanan and Paul R. Krugman (1984) *Increasing Returns, Imperfect Competition, and International Trade.* In process (May)

Hill, T.P. (1977) 'On goods and services' *Review of Income and Wealth* 23, 315-38 (December)

Hindley, Brian and Alasdair Smith (1984) 'Comparative advantage and trade in services' Presented at a Conference on Restrictions on Transactions in the International Market for Services, Wiston House, West Sussex, England, 30 May – 2.June

Markusen, James R. (1984) 'Multinational, multi-plant economies, and the gains from trade' *Journal of International Economics* 16

Stern, Robert M. (1985) 'Global dimensions and determinants of international trade and investment in services'

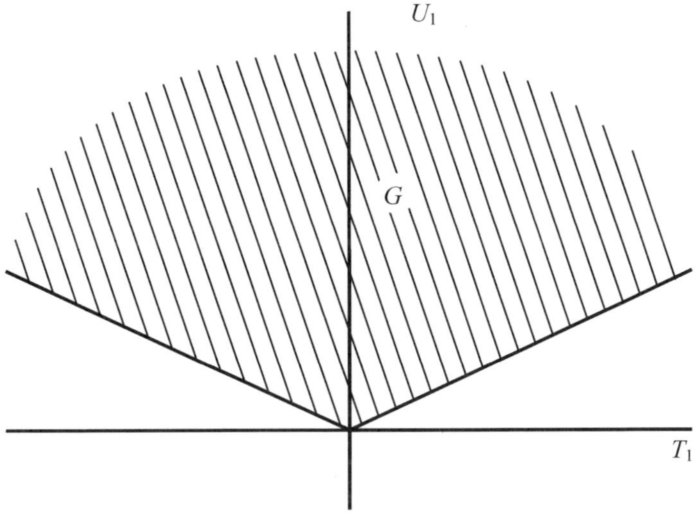

FIGURE 1

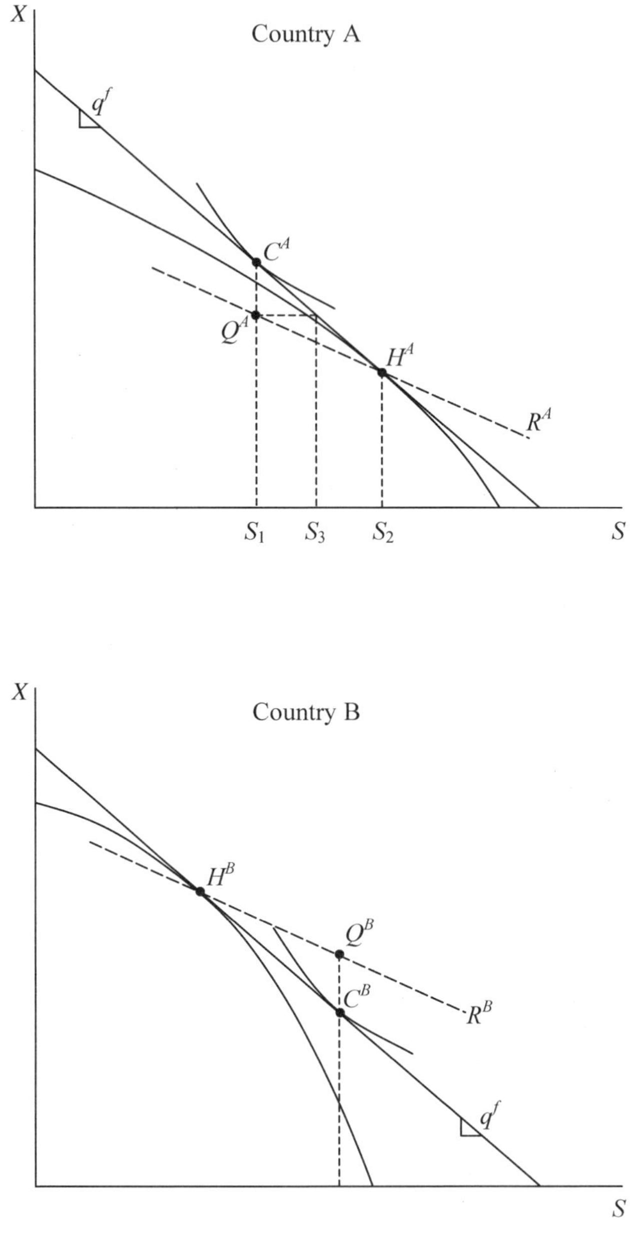

FIGURE 2

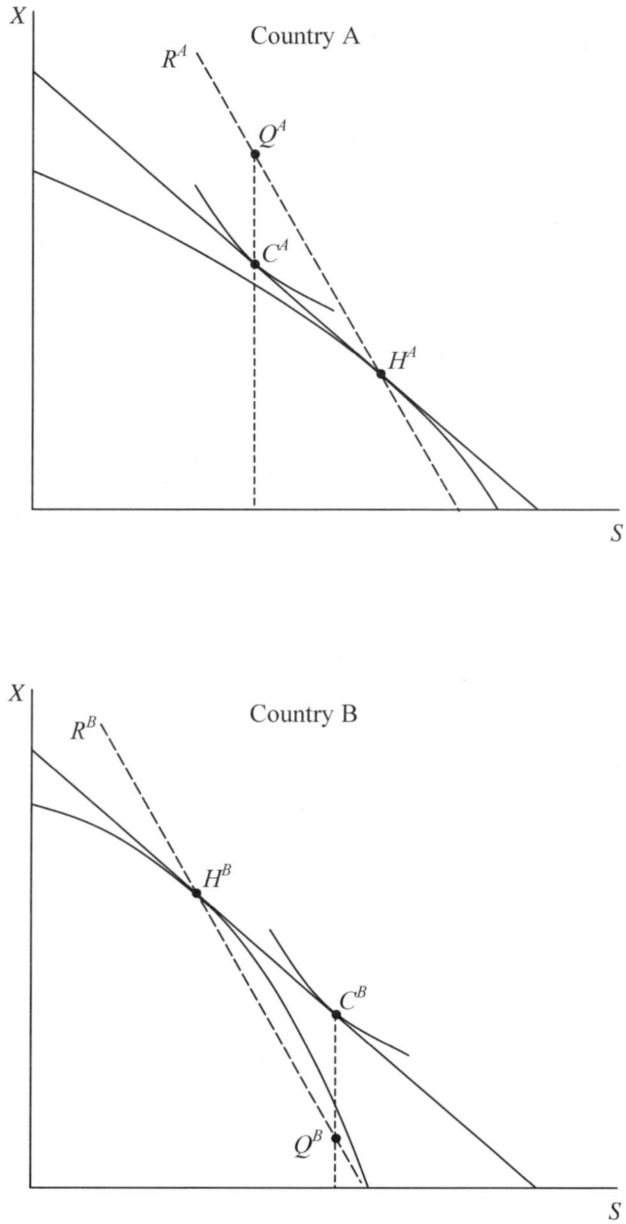

FIGURE 3

CHAPTER 13

Journal of International Economics 20 (1986) 131–142. North-Holland

FIRLESS FIRWOES: HOW PREFERENCES CAN INTERFERE WITH THE THEOREMS OF INTERNATIONAL TRADE

Alan V. DEARDORFF*

University of Michigan, Ann Arbor, MI 48109, USA

Received April 1984, revised version received May 1985

An example is presented of a two-country, two-factor, four-good trade model in which free trade causes factor prices to be drawn farther apart than they were in autarky. The example is equivalent to a two-good model with a double factor intensity reversal (FIR), and thus demonstrates that the problems associated with FIRs can arise in many dimensions without them. These problems include the undermining of other trade theorems as well, and can be avoided only by making some assumption about demand as well as about technology. For example, the model becomes well-behaved if preferences and technology are both Cobb–Douglas.

1. Introduction

It is well known that factor intensity reversals (FIRs) can play havoc with the theorems of the Heckscher–Ohlin–Samuelson (HOS) model of international trade. It is therefore customary to exclude FIRs by assumption, with or without a solid empirical basis for doing so.[1] The standard $2 \times 2 \times 2$ HOS model then performs nicely. While other difficulties have sometimes arisen in efforts to extend theorems to higher dimensions, some success has been achieved, as surveyed by Ethier (1984). However, I would suggest that further extensions will be difficult, at least until we come to terms with the problems posed in two dimensions by FIRs. For the same *kinds* of problems also arise in many dimensions, even when FIRs themselves are absent. The problem is that certain properties of preferences among many goods can replicate arbitrarily closely the *effects* of FIRs. Thus, until we can find an acceptable

*This paper is based on Deardorff (1983), a short paper which failed to generate the interest I thought it deserved. In the spirit of the Washington bureaucracy, I have responded to the failure of that paper by making it larger and changing its name. I would like to thank Ted Bergstrom, Jon Eaton, Bob Stern and two anonymous referees for their helpful comments, as well as other members of the Research Seminar in International Economics at Michigan and those who participated in the trade theory conference at the University of Western Ontario, 17 March, 1984. Support in writing this paper was provided by the Ford Foundation.

[1]Minhas (1962) claimed to have identified enough empirically relevant FIRs to make the HOS model questionable. His methodology was criticized by a number of authors, surveyed by Bhagwati (1969), but Stern (1975) noted more recent work that leaves the empirical importance of FIRs still up in the air.

regularity assumption that applies simultaneously to both technology and preferences, our efforts to characterize behavior in a many dimensional HOS model will be of only limited success.

The basis for these concerns consists of an example in section 2. Free trade in four goods between two countries with two factors can cause factor prices to move farther apart than in autarky. This occurs without FIRs, but for reasons best understood by looking first at a two-good model with a double FIR. The factor-price equalization theorem is violated in the extreme in this example, since there is not even a tendency toward factor prices being equalized. This is not a complete novelty, since Land (1959), with an assist by Stewart (1976), has also shown such an example. But in my example, unlike Land's, factor prices move apart in opposite directions, providing a more dramatic and easily understood picture of their effects.

These effects are discussed further in section 3, where I examine major propositions of pure trade theory. While some of these have been extended in various forms to higher dimensions, I argue that the intuition behind them all is undermined in this example. Thus, the example represents more than just a curious possibility. It goes to the heart of the economic intuition that has underlain trade theory since Heckscher (1919) and Ohlin (1933).

Their insight, as I understand it, was that factor prices are determined by factor scarcity, and that trade, by opening factor markets to indirect competition with factors abroad, alters this relative scarcity. Thus, a country's scarce factor is relatively expensive in autarky, earning the usual scarcity rent. With trade, however, the products produced by that scarce factor must compete with counterparts produced by the same factor abroad, where it is relatively more abundant. This trade erodes the scarcity rent of the factor, causing its originally high relative return to fall. Similarly, a country's relatively abundant factor will have its relatively low autarky price raised by trade, as it finds new markets for what it can best produce. Thus, the tendency for factor prices to converge with trade is a straightforward implication of supply and demand, and has nothing to do with the particular mathematical properties of homogeneous production functions that seem, almost coincidentally, to give rise in special cases to full factor-price equalization.

Given this strong economic reason for factor prices to converge, why then do they fail to do so in my example? The reason is that factors of production face competition, indirectly through the goods they produce, not just with identical goods producible with identical factors abroad. Instead, in a world of many goods, complex relationships in demand matter as well. Specifically, in my example a scarce factor competes through trade with goods produced abroad that are not identical to what it produces at home, but are only close substitutes. If these close substitutes happen to be relatively expensive abroad, compared with other goods produced there, then the domestic scarce factor may win this competition in spite of its own scarcity. Likewise, if competition through close substitutes pits a domestic abundant factor against other products that are relatively cheap abroad, then its relative return may fall. Since this competition is with different goods whose factor intensities are unrelated to those used at home, knowledge of relative scarcity and abundance of factors alone is not enough to determine how this competition will work itself out.

The particular example below focuses on goods that are close substitutes, but extremes of complementarity in demand no doubt could also lead to similar results. The point is that once one moves beyond the simplicity of a two-good model where interesting patterns of substitutability and complementarity cannot arise, the issue of how factors compete with one another through international trade depends crucially on these aspects of demand. One result of this is that even the tendency toward factor-price equalization is not assured in a general many-good model. This in turn, as I will show in section 3, causes other aspects of economic performance, such as trade itself and real factor incomes, to depart from what one would have expected on the basis of the simple HOS model.

Another implication of these results is that existence or nonexistence of FIRs is not the issue. To clinch this point I show in section 4 that one can turn any model with FIRs into one without, and vice versa, simply by redefining goods. FIRs are meaningful only in the textbook two-good model, where the limited number of goods constrains the relationships that can exist among them. For a many-good model to be well behaved we need some other assumption about preferences, together with technology.

What assumption should this be? I do not know, and I hope others will be induced to look for one by my example. All I offer now is an assumption that is far too extreme: that all utility and production functions are Cobb–Douglas. In section 5 I show that this assumption guarantees factor-price convergence. Thus my example and its disturbing implications cannot occur in such a Cobb–Douglas world.

2. The example

Because Samuelson's (1949) factor-price equalization theorem requires very restrictive assumptions, it would be useful to have a weaker but more generally valid result, such as that factor prices are drawn closer together by trade.[2] Unfortunately, Land (1959) has shown that this need not be the case.[3] Here, I provide a more dramatic example of factor-price divergence

[2]This was Ohlin's (1933) proposition, which Samuelson (1971) argues is correct in a specific-factors model.

[3]Johnson (1967) objected that Land's counterexample was inconsistent with equilibrium in all markets. Stewart (1976), however, showed how demands could respond to price differences so as to validate Land's example.

that is simpler and more useful for my later analysis.[4] In my example, the structure of preferences for four goods leads to behavior like a two-good model with a double FIR, in which factor prices may move apart in opposite directions with trade.

First consider the familiar two-good HOS model with two FIRs. The relationship between relative factor prices, ω, and the relative price of two goods, $p = p_I/p_{II}$, is S-shaped as in fig. 1.[5] If factor endowments of two countries, A and B, differ appropriately, then autarky factor prices may be ω^A and ω^B, as shown. As drawn, the relative autarky price of good I is higher in A, even though good I is locally labor-intensive in both countries and A is abundantly endowed with labor.[6] Thus, with trade, as prices of goods come together, prices of factors are driven farther apart.

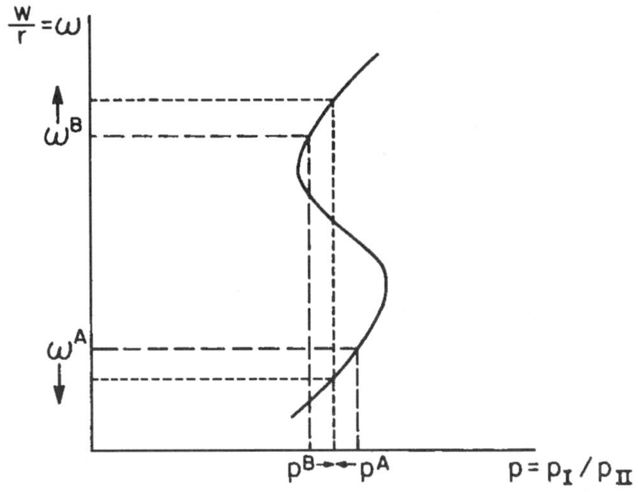

Fig. 1

Now consider a different model, with no FIRs but four goods, whose unit isoquants are those in fig. 2. Suppose the following very special preferences: goods X_1 and X_3 are perfect substitutes, as are goods X_2 and X_4. With this

[4]In the Land–Stewart counterexample, free trade can lower the wage–rental ratio in both countries, and the fall can be greater where the ratio was initially lower. Comparing these changes may be sensitive to units of measurement. Dixit and Norman (1980, p. 102) mention the difficulty of measuring distance between vectors of factor prices. This difficulty is avoided when factor-price ratios move apart in opposite directions.

[5]See Samuelson (1949) for this relation without FIRs. See Chacholiades (1978, pp. 273–280) and the references cited therein for cases of single and multiple FIRs.

[6]Relative factor intensities determinine the slope of the curve, since a rise in the relative wage raises the relative price of the labor-intensive good. Thus in fig. 1, good I is labor intensive for both high and low wage–rental ratios, but capital intensive in between. Relative factor abundance can be measured either by relative autarky factor prices or by relative physical endowments. In this case the two definitions agree.

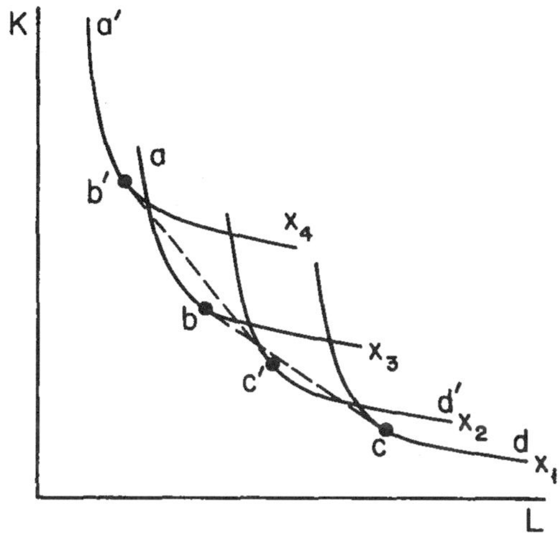

Fig. 2

assumption the two pairs of goods can be aggregated, and the model is equivalent to a model with only two goods.

The feasible inputs for a unit of the X_1–X_3 aggregate include all convex combinations of inputs for producing one unit of X_1 and one unit of X_3, thus the convex hull of the separate X_1 and X_3 isoquants: the curve *abcd*. Similarly, the unit isoquant for the X_2–X_4 aggregate is the curve *a'b'c'd'*. These two aggregate unit isoquants intersect three times, displaying two FIRs, just as in fig. 1. Thus, the four-good model with these particular pairwise perfect substitutes will behave exactly like the two-good model with a double FIR, and factor prices may diverge with trade, as in fig. 1.

What can happen, more fully, is this.[7] Since prices of perfect substitutes must be the same, let $p_1 = p_3 = p_{\rm I}$ and $p_2 = p_4 = p_{\rm II}$, and call goods X_1 and X_3 type I, goods X_2 and X_4 type II. In autarky, if country A is sufficiently labor abundant, it will satisfy demands for the two types of goods by producing only X_1 and X_2, while with enough more capital country B will produce only X_3 and X_4. Furthermore, if A's and B's endowments are sufficiently close to the factor requirements of X_2 and X_3, respectively, then the price of type I goods relative to type II goods, $p_{\rm I}/p_{\rm II}$ in fig. 1, will be higher in A than in B.

When trade is opened up, demanders in A find it cheaper to import X_3 from B than to buy X_1 domestically. Likewise, demanders in B import X_2 from A to replace domestic production of X_4. Thus, A exports X_2 in exchange for X_3 from B, and the relative price $p_{\rm I}/p_{\rm II}$ falls in A and rises in B.

[7]The following discussion can be illustrated with an elaboration of Samuelson's diagram relating relative prices of goods and factors to factor intensities. Space does not permit including that diagram here, but it is available on request.

Since X_2 is more capital intensive than X_1, the fall in $p_I/p_{II} = p_1/p_2$ in A and the shift of production toward X_2 causes the wage–rental ratio there to fall, while the opposite happens in B.

As resources shift toward the exports of the two countries, output of both X_1 (in A) and X_4 (in B) will fall, and one or both of the countries may completely specialize. If this happens in a country, relative factor prices there stop adjusting, but this does not interfere with them having been driven farther apart by trade.[8]

This particular example is made tractable by having goods be perfect substitutes, but a similar result could occur if they were only very close substitutes. What seems to be important is the asymmetry in substitution, goods being closer substitutes for some goods than for others, and the way this asymmetry interacts with factor intensities.[9]

3. Implications for other theorems of trade

Implicit in the example of section 2 are several disturbing implications for theorems of the HOS model, besides the factor-price equalization theorem itself.

3.1. The Heckscher–Ohlin theorem

One might expect the Heckscher–Ohlin theorem to collapse in this example, but instead, general versions of the theorem are still valid. In Deardorff (1982) I proved two such versions – one for the factor content of trade, the other for its commodity composition – by defining factor content and intensity using country-of-origin production techniques. In the example here, country A exports X_2 and B exports X_3, other goods not being traded at all. Each country thus exports a good that is more intensive in the use of its abundant factor than what it imports, and this satisfies the theorem.

However, the example does point out the limited usefulness of the theorem in this form, since it fails to tell what trade will be, starting from autarky. Each country produces only two goods in autarky, and either one could be exported and the other displaced by imports.

Since imports displace production not only of goods identical to themselves, but also of goods that are close substitutes in demand, a theorem cannot tell us how industries will be affected by trade without first considering properties of demand.

[8]Complete specialization here is made more likely by the endowments of the two countries being somewhat closer together, since this drives apart their autarky price ratios, p_I/p_{II}.

[9]The example is consistent with the familiar assumption of internationally identical, homothetic preferences.

3.2. The Stolper–Samuelson theorem

At one level, the Stolper–Samuelson theorem is a technical and local relationship between prices of goods and factors, and its validity in a two-factor model depends mainly on whether goods are produced. Generalizations of Stopler–Samuelson, surveyed in Ethier (1984), mostly look for similar local relationships.

At a more intuitive level, however, the theorem says simply that free trade lowers the real wage of the scarce factor, and raises the real wage of the abundant factor, compared to autarky. Since free trade opens factor markets to indirect competition from abroad, the idea that it should cause a lessening of scarcity rents has great appeal. This suggests a more useful generalization of the Stolper–Samuelson theorem in terms of, say, a negative correlation between changes in factor returns and a measure of their relative scarcity.

Unfortunately, even this weak relationship does not hold generally, since it fails in the example here. As long as two goods are produced in a country, real returns still follow relative returns, ω. Since relative returns move apart with trade, so do real returns, and thus real returns to scarce factors rise and real returns to abundant factors fall with trade. The reason is again that factors compete not with identical factors abroad, but rather with whatever factors produce the closest substitutes for what they produce at home.

3.3. The Rybczynski theorem

Like its dual, the Stolper–Samuelson theorem, the Rybczynski theorem could have both local and global versions. The global version would be that further accumulation of a country's already abundant factor will worsen its terms of trade, while accumulation of its scarce factor will improve it. This is what happens in the 2×2 model with no FIRs if both goods are normal in consumption and both are produced, and it seems plausible that the same would happen in higher dimensions. If countries trade embodied factor services, it is natural to think of accumulation of the scarce factor, say, as reducing the demand for imports of its services and thus lowering their price.

Unfortunately, once again, my example indicates that this is not generally true. If country A produces both X_1 and X_2 with free trade, then a greater endowment of labor will increase its output of X_1 and reduce its output of the less labor-intensive X_2. Since A exports X_2, this change is therefore ultra-biased against exports and will improve the terms of trade.[10] Analogously, accumulation of A's scarce factor, capital, will worsen its terms of trade.

How can accumulation of the abundant factor fail to worsen the terms of trade? It is not that such accumulation fails to cheapen the factor itself. Instead, what is happening is a consequence of the unusual pattern of trade. While A's exports are more labor intensive than her actual imports, they are

[10] See Corden (1956).

not more labor intensive than her import substitutes. When A accumulates labor, production of import substitutes expands and production for export declines, leading to an improvement in the terms of trade.

3.4. The Mundell theorem

A final result to consider is Mundell's (1957) result that trade substitutes for international factor mobility. In the 2×2 model, in addition to equalizing factor prices, greater trade also reduces the movement of factors, while greater factor movement reduces the volume of trade.

In my example here these results are overturned. Trade moves relative and absolute factor prices farther apart than in autarky and thus increases the incentive for international factor movement. Also, within limits, some international movement of factors increases the volume of trade. Start from free trade with A producing X_1 and X_2 and exporting X_2. If a small amount of labor moves from the low-wage A to high-wage B, at initial prices A's outputs of X_1 will fall and of X_2 will rise, tending to increase trade. After adjustment of prices to restore equilibrium, it is likely that the new equilibrium will involve larger quantities of X_2 and X_3 being exchanged.

4. Do FIRs really matter?

In spite of the importance attached to them in the textbook HOS model, the absence of FIRs is neither necessary nor sufficient for the validity of the theorems of trade in higher dimensions.[11] To emphasize this point I now note that FIRs can be made to appear and disappear at will, just by redefining goods. Thus, FIRs seem to be harmless little beasts in general, and, if they appear, are mere figments of our aggregation.[12]

Suppose first that a FIR exists in the technologies of goods X and Y, occurring at capital–labor ratio k_0, and suppose that at or near k_0 good X has the larger elasticity of substitution.[13] Redefine X as two different goods depending on whether it is produced with more or less capital per worker than k_0.[14] Letting these two goods be perfect substitutes in demand, we now have an exactly equivalent model with no FIRs.[15]

[11]That it is not sufficient follows from my example. That it is not necessary is well known even in two dimensions.

[12]For another example of this, see Jones (1974), where a model of many traded goods and one nontraded good without FIRs becomes a two-good model with one FIR when the traded goods are aggregated.

[13]Goods cannot have the same elasticity of substitution over an interval and still have a FIR within that interval.

[14]Let X produced with $k \geq k_0$ be X' and X produced with $k < k_0$ be X''. The X' and X'' isoquants are portions of the original X isoquant, supplemented with horizontal or vertical segments beginning at k_0.

[15]Alternatively, convert each good to a continuum of goods, each using a different and fixed technique of production chosen from the original isoquants.

By a similar procedure, FIRs can be created by redefining goods. Take any good, X, with a conventional curved isoquant. Pick two arbitrary capital–labor ratios, k_1 and k_2, and define two different goods depending on whether they use the factors in a ratio that is between these or not. That is, define X as X' for $k \in [k_1, k_2]$ and as X'' otherwise. The X' isoquant will be vertical or horizontal outside this interval, while the X'' isoquant will have a downward-sloping straight segment within it. With X' and X'' perfect substitutes, these constructed portions of their isoquants will never be used, and the new model will behave exactly like the old model. Yet these two newly defined goods do display a FIR.[16]

Thus, if the definition of a 'good' is flexible,[17] the concept of a FIR should not play a compelling role in trade theory. The qualifications imposed by FIRs on the theorems of trade are appropriate however, as section 3 makes clear. Unless further analysis suggests an acceptable alternative assumption to the absence of FIRs – one that will get rid of the problems they cause even with many goods – we should take these problems seriously. In fact, I would suggest that FIRs be given increased attention in teaching, since they conveniently illustrate in two dimensions the problems posed by complementarities and substitutabilities in higher dimensions.

5. An alternative to the absence of FIRs?

If the absence of FIRs is neither necessary nor sufficient for trade in many dimensions to be well behaved, what alternative assumption might serve the purpose better? Traditionally, extensions of trade theorems have relied on factor-price equalization and incomplete specialization, which in turn require countries to have sufficiently similar endowments. Like Krueger (1977), I find these assumptions to be overly restrictive as descriptions of the world, and they rule out cases I find most interesting. Allowing specialization instead, the problems of section 3 need to be dealt with on their own terms. My example suggests that problems arise when goods are closer substitutes for some goods than for others, and I expect similar problems with analogous variations in complementarity.[18] To rule these out completely is too restrictive, but may help to start the search for a more empirically acceptable assumption.

Consider, then, a model with two countries, two factors, and any number of goods, n. Let all utility and production functions be Cobb–Douglas and

[16]Again we could achieve the result with a continuum of goods. Turn just one of two goods into a continuum of goods with fixed techniques, as in the preceding footnote. Each of the new goods displays a FIR relative to the other original good.

[17]Redefining goods would be unacceptable if a particular definition of a 'good' were universally accepted, but this is hardly the case. Nor is differentiating goods on the basis of how they are produced unusual, since this is a common feature of industrial classification systems.

[18]It was complementarities that provided the 'weak link in the chain of comparative advantage' in Deardorff (1979).

identical across countries.[19] All elasticities of substitution are then unity, and thus such extremes of substitutability as were assumed in section 2 are ruled out. In this Cobb–Douglas world, factor prices must be drawn together by free trade, even when they are not completely equalized.

To see this, note first that Cobb–Douglas preferences and production functions together imply indirect Cobb–Douglas preferences for factors. That is, if consumers spend a fraction b_i on good i, and if the labor share in producing good i is a_i, then the fraction of consumer expenditure that is paid to labor producing good i is $c_i = a_i b_i$. Also, for any $n' \leqq n$, the fraction of expenditure on the subset of goods $1, \ldots, n'$ is constant, as is the fraction $\theta(n')$ of that that goes in turn to labor,

$$\theta(n') = \sum_{i=1}^{n'} c_i \Big/ \sum_{i=1}^{n'} b_i. \tag{1}$$

The wage–rental ratio of a country in autarky, ω_0^j, $j = \mathrm{A, B}$, can be derived by comparing shares of labor and capital, to yield:

$$\omega_0^j = \frac{w_0^j}{r_0^j} = \frac{\theta(n)}{1-\theta(n)} \frac{K^j}{L^j}, \quad j = \mathrm{A, B}, \tag{2}$$

where K^j and L^j are the respective capital and labor endowments.

With free trade and unequal factor prices, labor-abundant A will produce only goods more labor intensive than those produced in B.[20] Ranking the goods by labor intensity,

$$a_1 > a_2 > \cdots > a_n, \tag{3}$$

one can again compare capital and labor shares to derive

$$\omega^{\mathrm{A}} = \frac{w^{\mathrm{A}}}{r^{\mathrm{A}}} = \frac{\theta(i')}{1-\theta(i')} \frac{K^{\mathrm{A}}}{L^{\mathrm{A}}}, \tag{4}$$

where i' is the most capital-intensive good produced only in country A.[21] The wage–rental ratio in B with trade, ω^{B}, is analogous to (4) but with θ replaced by $(1-\theta)$.

To compare wage–rental ratios, note from (2) that autarky wage–rental ratios depend only on the capital–labor endowment ratios, K/L, since $\theta(n)$ is the same in both countries. Thus, $\omega_0^{\mathrm{A}} < \omega_0^{\mathrm{B}}$, since A is labor abundant.

[19]Dornbusch, Fischer and Samuelson (1980) use Cobb–Douglas utility and production functions in part of their analysis of the Heckscher–Ohlin model with a continuum of goods.

[20]See Deardorff (1979). A single good, i_c, may be produced in common.

[21]If there is a good, i_c, produced in common, then ω^{A} lies between that of eq. (4) and the value that would be obtained replacing i' in (4) with i_c. The argument still goes through.

Next note in (1) that $\theta(n')$ is a weighted average of the a_i from $i=1,\dots,n'$. From (3) it follows that $\theta(n')$ declines as n' increases. Comparing (2) and (4), since $i'<n$, it follows that $\omega_0^A<\omega^A$. By similar reasoning for B, one can complete the following chain of inequalities:

$$\omega_0^A<\omega^A<\omega^B<\omega_0^B. \tag{5}$$

Thus, wage–rental ratios *are* drawn closer together by trade in this special Cobb–Douglas model, and none of the problems noted in section 3 arises.

6. Conclusion

I view this paper as calling attention to a problem that needs to be solved. The example in section 2 is not implausible, but I doubt that it is representative of the world. The particular pattern of substitutability in the example is quite asymmetric and thus, I suspect, unlikely to occur. What we need is some assumption on preferences and technology together, similar in spirit but less restrictive than the Cobb–Douglas assumption of section 5, that will rule out such an extreme result. I hope that this paper will stimulate others to search for such an assumption.

After decades in which trade theory has focused primarily on properties of production functions,[22] it is important that we now give equally careful attention to the demand side. of the economy. We have not done so before largely because there is little room for preferences to matter in a two-good model. But as we now extend trade theory into higher dimensions, preferences may come into their own as, if nothing else, an irritating complication in the analysis.

[22]See however Jones (1980) who has explored the roles of various assumptions about demand in trade theory. Also, Melvin (1969) has explored implications of a particular demand assumption in a Ricardian model, and Melvin (1983) has looked at taste differences within a country with transport costs.

References

Bhagwati, Jagdish, 1969, The pure theory of international trade: A survey, in: J.N. Bhagwati, Trade, tariffs and growth (M.I.T. Press, Cambridge, MA) 3–122.

Chacholiades, Miltiades, 1978, International trade theory and policy (McGraw-Hill, New York).

Corden, W.M., 1956, Economic expansion and international trade: A geometric approach, Oxford Economic Papers 8.

Deardorff, Alan V., 1979, Weak links in the chain of comparative advantage, Journal of International Economics 9, 197–209.

Deardorff, Alan V., 1982, The general validity of the Heckscher–Ohlin theorem, American Economic Review 72, 683–694.

Deardorff, Alan V., 1983, An example of international factor-price divergence, Research seminar in international economics, Seminar discussion paper no. 116, University of Michigan.

Dixit, Avinash K. and Victor Norman, 1980, Theory of international trade (Cambridge University Press, London).

Dornbusch, Rudiger, Stanley Fischer and Paul A. Samuelson, 1980, Heckscher–Ohlin trade theory with a continuum of goods, Quarterly Journal of Economics 95, 203–224.

Ethier, Wilfred J., 1984, Higher dimensional issues in trade theory, in: Ronald W. Jones and Peter B. Kenen, eds., Handbook of international economics, vol. I (North-Holland, Amsterdam) 131–184.

Heckscher, E., 1919, The effect of foreign trade on the distribution of income, Ekonomisk Tidskrift, 497–512.

Johnson, Harry G., 1967, The possibility of factor-price equalization when commodities outnumber factors, Economica 34, 282–288.

Jones, Ronald W., 1974, The small country in a many-commodity world, Australian Economic Papers 13, 225–236.

Jones, Ronald W., 1980, Demand behavior and the theory of international trade, in: J.S. Chipman and C.P. Kindleberger, eds., Flexible exchange rates and the balance of payments (North-Holland, Amsterdam).

Krueger, Anne O., 1977, Growth, distortions and patterns of trade among countries, Princeton Studies in International Finance No. 40 (Princeton, NJ).

Land, A.H., 1959, Factor endowments and factor prices, Economica 26, 137–142.

Melvin, James R., 1969, On a demand assumption made by Graham, Southern Economic Journal 36, 36–43.

Melvin, James R., 1983, Domestic taste differences, transportation costs and international trade, in process.

Minhas, B.S., 1962, The homohypallagic production function, factor-intensity reversals and the Heckscher–Ohlin theorem, Journal of Political Economy 60, 138–156.

Mundell, Robert A., 1957, International trade and factor mobility, American Economic Review 47, 321–335.

Ohlin, Bertil, 1933, Interregional and international trade (Harvard University Press, Cambridge, MA).

Rybczynski, T.M., 1955, Factor endowments and relative commodity prices, Economica 22, 336–341.

Samuelson, Paul A., 1949, International factor-price equalization once again, Economic Journal 59, 181–197.

Samuelson, Paul A., 1971, Ohlin was right, Swedish Journal of Economics 73, 365–384.

Stern, Robert M., 1975, Testing trade theories, in: Peter B. Kenen, ed., International trade and finance: Frontiers for research (Cambridge University Press, New York) 3–49.

Stewart, Doug, 1976, Can trade widen the difference between factor rewards?, American Economic Review 66, 671–674.

Stolper, Wolfgang and Paul A. Samuelson, 1941, Protection and real wages, Review of Economic Studies 9, 58–73.

CHAPTER 14

International Trade with Lumpy Countries

Paul N. Courant and Alan V. Deardorff

University of Michigan

This paper explores the implications for the pattern of international trade of differences among regions within countries—what we call "lumpiness." If factors of production are sufficiently unevenly distributed across regions, then the pattern of trade of the country as a whole may depart from what it would have been had factors been evenly distributed. Thus lumpiness in the geographical distribution of factors can be a determinant of trade. We show in particular that if other determinants of trade are absent, then a country will tend to export the good that intensively uses its lumpier (i.e., more unevenly distributed) factor.

I. Introduction

International trade theory customarily assumes that countries are homogeneous entities. That is, trade theory abstracts from geographical, intracountry differences in factor endowments, consumer incomes and tastes, access to technology and resources, and the conditions of the environment affecting both producers and consumers.[1] Such differences are assumed either not to exist or not to matter, even though it is precisely these kinds of differences, when they arise among countries rather than within them, that give rise to trade itself.

We have received helpful suggestions from many colleagues in writing this paper. These include, but are not limited to, Jim Levinsohn, Joel Slemrod, Alasdair Smith, Bob Stern, Jerry Thursby, Marie Thursby, and many others who participated in seminars at Carleton, Columbia, Michigan, North Carolina, Purdue, Queen's, Toronto, Union College, Wayne State, Western Ontario, and Yale. An anonymous referee also provided helpful suggestions. Deardorff received partial support in writing this paper from the Ford Foundation.

[1] See, however, Melvin (1985*a*, 1985*b*) for treatments that do include some of these differences.

[*Journal of Political Economy*, 1992, vol. 100, no. 1]

In effect, it has been said, the countries of trade theory are points, with no physical dimension across which such differences could arise.[2]

This neglect of intranational differences may be justified if such differences are in fact small compared to the analogous differences that exist between nations. But casual observation suggests that in many cases there are far greater differences among regions of a single country than there are between comparable regions of different countries. It is the purpose of this paper to explore some of the implications of such differences for the pattern of international trade. In particular, we shall show that various differences among regions within a country—what we call the "lumpiness" of countries—if they are large enough, can be a cause of international trade that is distinct from other more traditional determinants of trade such as differences in overall factor endowments and technologies.

The simplest class of regional differences to consider consists of regional differences in factor endowments.[3] If factors of production are distributed unevenly over the countryside, then trade will arise among regions within the country, exactly as predicted by the Heckscher-Ohlin (factor proportions) theory of international trade. We shall argue further, however, that if such differences among regions are sufficiently large, then complete specialization of the regions themselves will occur. This will lead the country as a whole to produce different quantities of goods than it would if factors were more evenly distributed. This, in turn, can alter the quantities, and even the direction, of trade, compared to what they would have been in a more traditional model in which regional differences play no role.

Throughout the paper, in order to focus clearly on the effects of lumpiness on trade and to abstract from other factors that might give rise to trade, we shall confine our attention to a very special case: a small open economy that, if it were regionally homogeneous, would not trade even if it could. That is, we consider as a benchmark case a country whose autarky prices, in the absence of differences among regions, would be identical to world prices. If introducing lumpiness then causes the country to trade, we can ascribe that trade to the effects of the lumpiness. Naturally, a corollary of all our results is that a country that *would* trade if it were homogeneous could have its pattern of trade altered, perhaps even reversed, by lumpiness.

[2] Herbert Giersch, e.g., made this observation in a conversation a few years ago.

[3] Others include differences in amenities and in the production possibilities for non-traded goods. As we show in another paper (Courant and Deardorff 1990), analysis of these other cases follows from the analysis of unequal factor endowments here.

We also make several other assumptions throughout the paper. Preferences of all consumers are identical and homothetic, so that consumer preferences can be aggregated independently of the distribution of income. All markets for both goods and factors are perfectly competitive, and prices of both goods and factors adjust freely to equate supply and demand. Factor supplies are perfectly inelastic, except where we explicitly consider movements of factors across regions, and factors are also internationally immobile. These assumptions keep the analysis simple, and they also serve to make it comparable to most of the existing literature on the Heckscher-Ohlin trade model so that the distinctive role of lumpiness can be appreciated.

II. An Example of Trade Due to Uneven Factor Allocation

We begin with the familiar case of a small open economy that produces only two goods, both traded, using two factors of production, labor and land. Both factors are initially assumed to be distributed across the (only) two regions of the economy in identical proportions. As our benchmark case, we assume that preferences and world prices are such that, with free international trade, the country's trade in both goods is zero.

Figure 1 shows the transformation curve of the country as a whole, for producing goods X and Y, as the curve TT'. The relative price of good X on the world market is given by the slope of the dashed line labeled P (which is parallel to all other similarly dashed lines in the figure), tangent to TT' at Q^0. A community indifference curve is also tangent to P at Q^0, which is therefore also the country's consumption point, C^0.

The country is divided into two regions, A and B, which for the moment are assumed to possess the factors of production in the same proportions as the country as a whole. This is illustrated by drawing the transformation curve of region A as $T_A T'_A$, relative to the same origin as TT', and the transformation curve of region B upside down as $T_B T'_B$ relative to point Q^0 as an origin. Because these two regions have the same relative factor endowments as the country as a whole, their transformation curves are identical in shape to TT' and are tangent at a point, Z^0, with the same relative outputs as Q^0.

Now suppose that the relative factor endowments of the two regions are made unequal by moving, say, some of the labor endowment out of region B and into region A. If, as we now assume, good X is the relatively labor-intensive good, then it is well known that such an expansion of the labor force in region A will cause its output of X to rise and its output of Y to fall, along the "Rybczynski line," RR'.

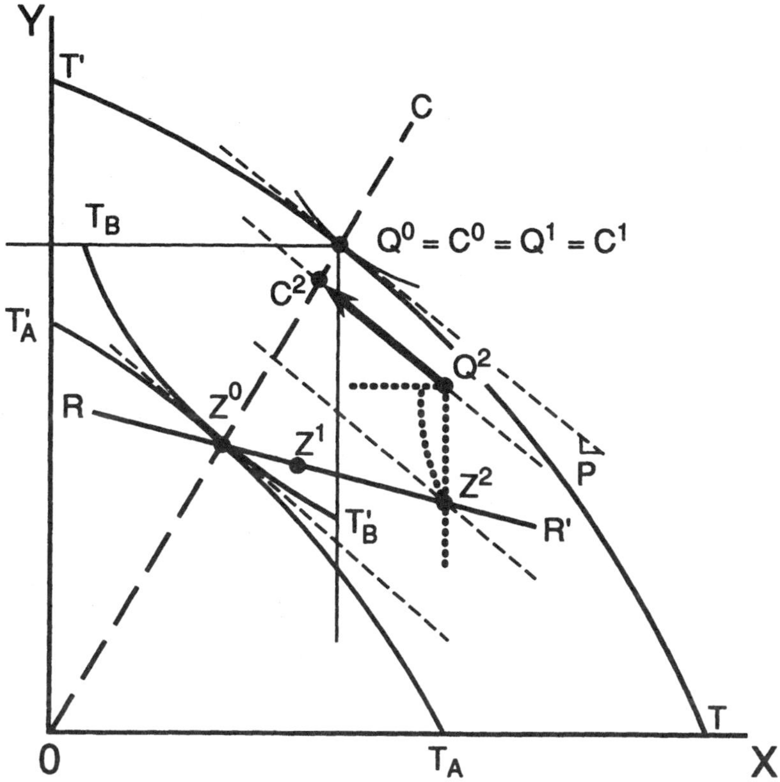

FIG. 1

Suppose that the new output of region A is given by the point Z^1. In region B a similar process is occurring, but in reverse. Its output too will move along a Rybczynski line, but in the direction of reducing its output of X and increasing that of Y. In fact, with identical, linearly homogeneous technologies in both regions, it is well known that the changes in outputs of the two regions will be equal and opposite, so that point Z^1 also represents the new output of region B, drawn relative to the same set of axes as Z^0.

Clearly the output of the entire country is unchanged by this exercise, and it continues to be represented by point Q^0. There is interregional trade, of course, each region trading with the other the difference between the outputs at Z^1 and their regional consumption bundles along the ray OC. But there is no international trade.[4]

[4] Interregional trade has generally been explained along the same lines as international trade, drawing heavily itself on the Heckscher-Ohlin theory of trade. See Moroney and Walker (1966) for the seminal empirical analysis of interregional trade along

This result of no trade arises only because we did not go far enough. Suppose instead that even more labor is reallocated between the regions, so that the output of region A moves further down RR' to point Z^2. It is now impossible for an equal and opposite change in outputs to occur in region B, for that would require output of good X to become negative there. What happens instead, once enough labor is withdrawn from region B so that it completely specializes in good Y, is that further reductions in labor reduce only its output of Y. The result is that region B's transformation curve becomes the dotted one, shown together with a set of dotted axes in the figure, perched on its tip above the point Z^2.

The output of the country as a whole is now Q^2, which is below and to the right of Q^0. Since world prices have not changed, the country will continue to consume the goods in the same ratio as before, though subject to the somewhat reduced income that it earns by producing Q^2. It therefore consumes at C^2 and trades the differences between C^2 and Q^2, as shown by the arrow in the figure.

Thus we see by this example that a sufficiently uneven allocation of factors between regions can indeed give rise to international trade. It remains to be seen, though, how general this result may be and what it is that has determined the pattern of the country's trade.

III. The Role of Regional Factor Allocation in International Trade

To explore further how the country's trade depends on the allocation of factors between regions, we turn to factor space in figure 2, an elaboration of the familiar Edgeworth production box diagram.[5] The horizontal dimension of the box is the labor endowment of the country as a whole, and the vertical dimension is the land endowment. If one measures the factor endowments of region A from the lower left (O_A) and of region B from the upper right (O_B), any point in the box indicates a particular allocation of factors between the regions.

As is well known from the Heckscher-Ohlin model, given the world prices of goods X and Y and with the absence of factor intensity reversals, there will exist a single set of factor prices consistent with incomplete specialization and a corresponding pair of least-cost tech-

Heckscher-Ohlin lines, and see Ho (1987) for a recent treatment and references to other literature. There is also a quite different literature on interregional trade, focusing on the role of cities as "central places" among which trade takes place (see, e.g., Tinbergen 1968; Ahn and Nourse 1988).

[5] The Edgeworth box was used to illustrate the Heckscher-Ohlin model by Lancaster (1957) and was extended to two countries by Dixit and Norman (1980) and Helpman and Krugman (1985) to map out regions of country specialization and nonspecialization. It is applied here for the latter purpose, but for regions of a single country.

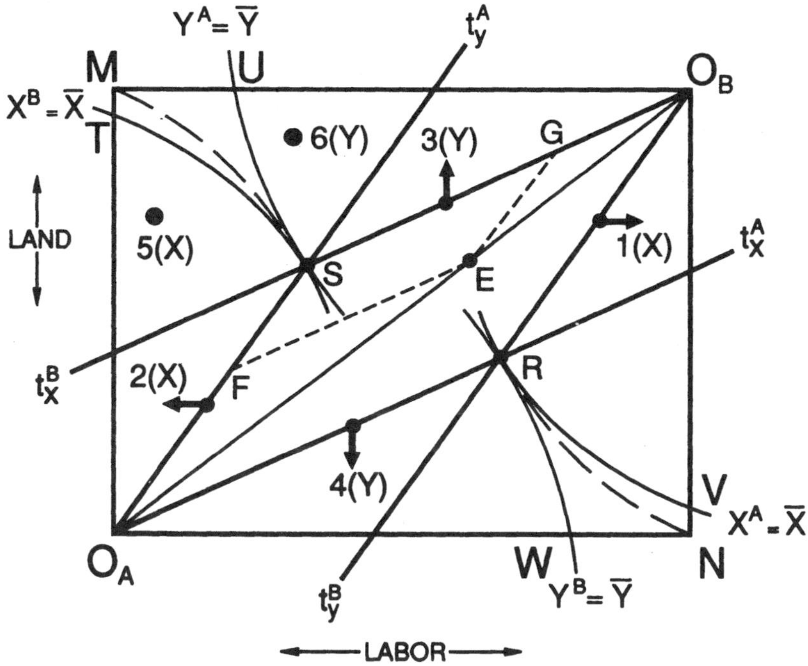

FIG. 2

niques of production for producing goods X and Y. Letting the ratios of land to labor employed by these techniques be denoted t_X and t_y, we draw rays t_X^A and t_y^A from O_A and t_X^B and t_y^B from O_B. Those factor allocations for which both regions can be incompletely specialized lie in the parallelogram O_ARO_BS. Since factor prices are also equalized (and constant) within this area, we refer to it as the factor-price-equalization (FPE) parallelogram.

The initial case considered in figure 1 is now represented by an allocation such as E on the diagonal of the box. Here both regions are endowed with the factors in the same proportions, and each produces outputs in the same proportions.[6] Throughout the parallelogram, factor prices remain equalized and the total outputs of X and Y for the country remain constant. Below the diagonal, however, region A produces proportionately more X than region B does, and A therefore exports X to B, even though the country as a whole does not trade. Point Z^1 in figure 1 would correspond to an allocation inside the FPE parallelogram to the right of E.

[6] Outputs of X and Y in A and B are proportional to the lengths EF, O_AF, O_BG, and EG, respectively.

We now consider what the patterns of output and trade will be for allocations outside the parallelogram. The diagram is divided into several sections, within each of which we have identified representative locations by the numbers 1–6. We have also recorded in parentheses next to these numbers the good, X or Y, that the country as a whole exports at that location.

Consider for example point 1. As indicated by the small arrow leading to it, it can be reached from the parallelogram of nonspecialization by reallocating labor from region B into region A, leaving region A to produce both goods but region B to produce only Y. This is exactly the reallocation considered in figure 1, where we saw that the country would export good X as a result. The result may be recalled here by noting that, as one traverses the small arrow adjacent to point 1, output of X will rise in region A and remain constant at zero in region B, whereas the output of Y will fall in both. Hence the ratio of X to Y produced in the country as a whole will rise, leading it to export X. The same reasoning, with the names of the regions interchanged, will imply that the country will also export X at point 2. Similarly, points 3 and 4 in the top and bottom of the figure yield analogous conclusions if one considers the change in land allocation needed to reach them.[7] For example, moving to point 3 from the border of the FPE parallelogram entails a reduction of X production in both regions and an increase in Y production in region A. On the other hand, points 5 and 6 (and their unmarked counterparts in the lower right of the figure) must be handled somewhat differently. The allocations at *S* and *R* are just on the verge of complete specialization, with, at *S* say, all the country's good Y produced in region A and all its X produced in B. These points are still within the parallelogram, and thus the outputs at these points are the same as those for the country as a whole throughout the parallelogram. We label isoquants drawn through *S* and *R*, $\overline{X}$ and $\overline{Y}$, indicating these outputs. With these isoquants for reference, it can then be seen directly that at point 5 region A produces less Y than $\overline{Y}$ whereas region B produces more X than $\overline{X}$. It follows that the country exports X. A similar argument shows that the country exports Y at point 6, with analogous results in the figure's lower right.

In the space between the two isoquants, we cannot know the pattern of trade. However, since outputs rise continuously and monotonically as one moves away from the origin, we do know that there will exist

[7] Land is of course assumed to be immobile throughout this paper. When we "change land allocations" in our analysis, we are really asking the hypothetical question of what the equilibrium would have been if more of the land had been located in, say, region A.

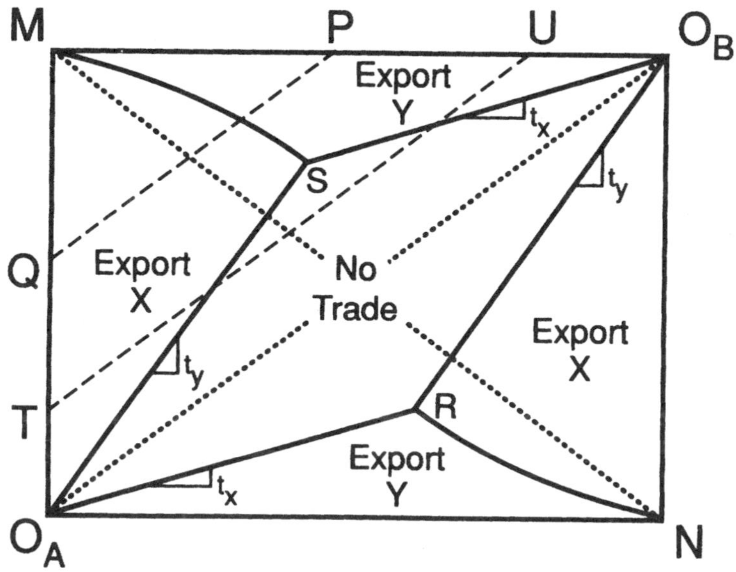

FIG. 3

a well-defined locus of points in that space in which the ratio of the two regions' outputs of X and Y is the same as the ratio $\overline{X}/\overline{Y}$. This locus is drawn as the dashed curve *SM* in figure 2. Below it the country exports X, above it the country exports Y, and along the locus there is no trade.[8]

This, then, completely maps out the patterns of trade for the country. The results are summarized in figure 3, where the several areas with different trade patterns are separated by solid lines, and the more cumbersome details of figure 2 are omitted. The figure demonstrates that there exists a considerable variety of factor allocations across regions that will cause the country to trade, and it also allows us to learn something about how these allocations matter for trade.

It is clear from the figure that there will always be trade if the factors are sufficiently *unevenly* distributed across regions. Regardless of the sizes of the two regions (as reflected by distances from the respective origins O_A and O_B), if the distribution of one or both factors is sufficiently uneven, then there will be trade.

The next problem is to infer from the figure what determines the pattern of this trade. Noting that the areas in which X is exported are near the right and left sides of the box, whereas the areas in

[8] The locus *SM* is drawn in fig. 2 as extending to the corner of the box. This is assured if both factors are required to produce any output, which we assume for the remainder of the paper.

which Y is exported are near the top and bottom, and recalling that good X is labor intensive, we suggest that the country tends to export the good that uses relatively intensively the factor that is *more unevenly distributed* across regions.

This is not a very rigorous statement, for we do not have a precise idea of what is to be meant by the term "more unevenly distributed." Certainly if one were to consider variations in technologies, in world prices, and in the preferences of the country's consumers for the two goods, the shapes and sizes of the various areas in figure 3 could change markedly. A precise definition of "unevenly distributed" would therefore have to be formulated relative to these technological and demand considerations. However, unevenness of factor distribution, or lumpiness, does seem to describe, if only in a loose way, something that is important about the economics of the situation.

We can make it more precise. First, notice in figure 3 that if one specifies the allocation of one factor arbitrarily and the other factor is allocated sufficiently unevenly, the country can be made to export the good that uses that other factor intensively.[9] This provides a more formal interpretation of the result just stated. That is, if we assume that nothing can be produced in either industry without the services of both factors, then one output must be zero anywhere along the edge of the box, so that the ratio of outputs can equal $\overline{X}/\overline{Y}$ only at the corners. Proposition 1 then follows from the diagram.

PROPOSITION 1. If both factors are essential in both industries, then for any given allocation of either factor between regions, a sufficiently uneven allocation of the other factor will cause the country to export the good that intensively uses that other factor.

A second way of looking at this same issue requires that we introduce two rather different measures of lumpiness. The first, which we call "overall (relative) factor lumpiness," measures the extent to which the ratios of the two factors fail to be identical in the two regions. There are several ways that such a discrepancy could be measured, but it will be convenient for our purposes to define it as follows.

DEFINITION. *Overall factor lumpiness* is the fraction of either factor endowment that would have to be reallocated to make the ratios of factors the same in the two regions.

Clearly, this measure of overall lumpiness is zero everywhere along the upward-sloping diagonal of the box, and it is constant along straight lines parallel to that diagonal. In figure 3, all points along the locus *QP* are equally lumpy in this sense, as are all points on the locus *TU*. An economy with an allocation on *QP* is unambiguously lumpier, in this sense, than one with an allocation on *TU*. Indeed, all

[9] We are indebted to the anonymous referee for pointing out this interpretation.

points on *QP* lie entirely outside the FPE parallelogram, implying that the *QP* economy is so lumpy that it always exports one good or the other. Overall factor lumpiness alone, therefore, can cause trade, as noted in proposition 2.

PROPOSITION 2. There always exists a level of overall factor lumpiness such that all allocations that meet or exceed that level will lead to trade.

Looking next at individual factors, we also define "individual (absolute) factor lumpiness" as the extent to which a given factor departs from being equally allocated across regions.

DEFINITION. *Individual factor lumpiness* is the fraction of the endowment of a given factor that would have to be reallocated to make endowments of that factor the same in the two regions.

Evidently, the individual lumpiness of labor is zero along the vertical line bisecting the box, while the lumpiness of land is zero along the horizontal line bisecting the box. More useful, however, is the comparison of these individual measures of lumpiness for the two factors. Labor and land are equally lumpy both along the upward-sloping diagonal of the box and along the downward-sloping diagonal. These two diagonals, which are shown in the figure as dotted lines, divide the box into four triangular quadrants. In the left and right of these quadrants, the individual lumpiness of labor is greater than that of land; in the top and bottom quadrants, land is lumpier than labor.

We can now combine these two definitions of lumpiness to formulate another sense in which the country tends to export the good that intensively uses its lumpier factor. Consider all allocations along a locus of constant overall lumpiness such as *TU*. As we vary the sizes of the two regions along this locus from *T* to *U*, we necessarily pass from an allocation in which the country exports X and labor is the lumpier factor to an allocation in which it exports Y and land is the lumpier factor. Along the way, it may or may not pass through an interval of allocations in which there is no trade. Thus we have the following proposition.

PROPOSITION 3. For any nonzero degree of overall factor lumpiness, if the sizes of the two regions differ sufficiently, then the country will export the good that intensively uses the more individually lumpy factor.

To understand these results, it is helpful to realize first that what we have here is an aggregation problem. Both regions of the country are behaving, individually, exactly like the familiar countries of the Heckscher-Ohlin model. Trade of the country as a whole is then the sum of the trade of the two regions. Within the limits of nonspecialization, the allocation of factors between the regions does not matter for the country's trade, since the movement of a factor from one region to the other causes outputs to rise and fall by equal amounts in the two regions.

However, if a factor is so unevenly allocated that one of the regions is completely specialized, producing nothing of the good that uses that factor intensively, this process breaks down. A further reallocation of the factor in the same direction cannot reduce the output of that good where it is already zero, and can only increase it in the region that is receiving the factor. Therefore, making the allocation of a factor still more uneven in this way tends eventually to increase the country's output of the good that uses it intensively and causes it to be exported.

Two-Country Trade

Until now we have considered a small open economy facing fixed prices. We should pause at this point, however, to indicate what trade patterns would look like in a two-country world.

Suppose, therefore, that we have two countries with identical relative factor endowments, both initially with these factors identically distributed across their internal regions so that trade is zero between them at their common (autarky) prices. If factors were now shifted between regions within only one of the countries, then our analysis above would indicate not the equilibrium pattern of trade, but rather the direction of the disequilibrium in world markets that would arise at the initial prices. For example, if labor were reallocated sufficiently between regions in one country as in figure 1, then that country would come to have an excess supply of the labor-intensive good X.

World markets would therefore have to adjust. As there is nothing in our model that is peculiar in terms of the shapes of the countries' supplies and demands (their offer curves), it follows that the new equilibrium will be found with a lower relative price of X. The lower price of X will induce the country in which factors remain evenly distributed to import X, and it will also reduce somewhat the amount of X that the first country exports. Naturally our pictures will no longer apply exactly to either country since the world prices will not be the autarky prices for either.

The point of mentioning all this is only to acknowledge that it is not only *uneven* distribution of factors in a country that will cause it to trade, but also a *more even* distribution of factors than elsewhere in the world. In this two-country example, the country with the even distribution of factors nonetheless trades as a result of the world price adjustment that has been induced by the uneven distribution of factors elsewhere. In particular, we can say that a country with an even distribution of factors will export the good that uses intensively in production the factor that is more evenly distributed elsewhere.

Finally, we should note that this model is in no way a departure from the traditional principle of comparative advantage. While it is true that a lumpy country may trade in a direction that is contrary to the Heckscher-Ohlin theorem, this trade is nonetheless completely consistent with the law of comparative advantage. As the two-country example illustrates, the country with more unevenly distributed labor will have a lower relative autarky price for the labor-intensive good and hence a comparative advantage in it.[10]

Factor Mobility

The results so far seem to depend crucially on the interregional immobility of both factors of production. If even one factor were mobile and could move across regions to seek the highest return, then trade would no longer occur.

For example, suppose again that labor were initially allocated disproportionately into region B sufficiently to cause region A to produce only Y and the country to export X. Then the wage of labor in region A would be higher than in region B, where continued nonspecialization would still determine a wage equal to that abroad. If labor could move, it would presumably depart from B and move into A, moving us to the right in figure 3. This movement would continue until wages became equalized, which can occur only in the FPE parallelogram. Thus this parallelogram, which we already identified as the region of no trade, becomes the set of equilibrium factor allocations if factors move to equalize their factor prices across regions.

This result can be turned on its head, however, if workers respond to something else in addition to wages in deciding where to live and if this something else differs across regions. Obvious candidates for this "something else" are the prices of nontraded goods and utility-relevant amenities that differ in availability across regions. In another paper (Courant and Deardorff 1990), we explore these and other phenomena that lead mobile factors to prefer one region over the other, all other things equal. The striking result of these analyses is that in many cases equilibrium requires that factor returns differ by region, ensuring that the economy is outside the FPE parallelogram and, hence, requiring that lumpiness of factors be sufficient to cause international trade.

The basic story behind these results can be illustrated by supposing

[10] This model is, like many others, a special case of the model examined by Deardorff (1980).

that region B is a nicer place to live than region A. Workers will then move to region B, and equilibrium will occur, not when wages are equalized, but instead when there is a sufficient real wage differential to induce them to be indifferent to locating in either of the two regions. Such a wage differential implies directly that the economy will be outside the FPE parallelogram and that there will therefore be international trade due to lumpiness.

IV. Conclusion

Intranational lumpiness of economic resources (by which we mean differences across regions of a country that may cause the regions to produce or to consume differently) can cause trade. In this paper we have shown that lumpiness of factor endowments can cause trade directly. We also note here, and prove elsewhere, that lumpiness of consumption amenities, production amenities, and the provision of nontraded goods can cause factor endowments to become sufficiently lumpy in equilibrium that the mechanisms explored in this paper will cause trade.

References

Ahn, J. K., and Nourse, H. O. "Spatial Economic Interdependence in an Urban Hierarchy System." *J. Regional Sci.* 28 (August 1988): 421–32.

Courant, Paul N., and Deardorff, Alan V. "Amenities, Nontraded Goods, and the Trade of Lumpy Countries." Manuscript. Ann Arbor: Univ. Michigan, 1990.

Deardorff, Alan V. "The General Validity of the Law of Comparative Advantage." *J.P.E.* 88 (October 1980): 941–57.

Dixit, Avinash K., and Norman, Victor. *Theory of International Trade: A Dual, General Equilibrium Approach.* Cambridge: Cambridge Univ. Press, 1980.

Helpman, Elhanan, and Krugman, Paul R. *Market Structure and Foreign Trade: Increasing Returns, Imperfect Competition, and the International Economy.* Cambridge, Mass.: MIT Press, 1985.

Ho, Chih-chin. "Determinants of U.S. Interregional Trade Patterns: An Empirical Assessment." Ph.D. dissertation, Univ. Michigan, 1987.

Lancaster, Kelvin. "The Heckscher-Ohlin Trade Model: A Geometric Treatment." *Economica* 24 (February 1957): 19–39.

Melvin, James R. "Domestic Taste Differences, Transportation Costs, and International Trade." *J. Internat. Econ.* 18 (February 1985): 65–82. (*a*)

———. "The Regional Economic Consequences of Tariffs and Domestic Transportation Costs." *Canadian J. Econ.* 18 (May 1985): 237–57. (*b*)

Moroney, John R., and Walker, James M. "A Regional Test of the Heckscher-Ohlin Hypothesis." *J.P.E.* 74 (December 1966): 573–86.

Tinbergen, Jan. "The Hierarchy Model of the Size Distribution of Centres." *Papers Regional Sci. Assoc.* 20 (1968): 65–68.

CHAPTER 15

Journal of International Economics 36 (1994) 167–175. North-Holland

The possibility of factor price equalization, revisited

Alan V. Deardorff*

Department of Economics, The University of Michigan, 240 Lorch Hall, Ann Arbor, MI 48109-1220, USA

Received July 1992, revised version received March 1993

This paper derives a condition for factor price equalization (FPE) in a Heckscher–Ohlin model with many goods, factors, and countries. Using Dixit and Norman's integrated world economy (IWE), two sets, called lenses, are constructed: one spanned by the factor vectors used to produce goods in the IWE; the other spanned by the countries' factor endowments. If the factor–endowment lens ever passes outside the factor–use lens, then FPE is impossible. In this sense, therefore, FPE requires that factor endowments vary less across countries than factor intensities vary across industries.

1. Introduction

Much depends, in modern international trade theory, on whether prices of factors are equalized internationally. With factor price equalization (FPE), industries in different countries with identical, constant-returns-to-scale technologies use identical techniques of production, and the analysis of trade and production is greatly simplified.[1] Even when there are elements of increasing returns to scale, Helpman and Krugman (1985) have gotten great mileage out of the assumption of FPE in simplifying otherwise intractable problems. In constrast, without FPE, trade patterns are perhaps more starkly de-

Correspondence to: Alan V. Deardorff, Department of Economics, The University of Michigan, 240 Lorch Hall, Ann Arbor, MI 48109-1220, USA.

*My thanks to Paul Krugman, who has probably forgotten encouraging me to write an earlier version of this several years ago. I have also received useful comments from Bob Stern and other participants in the Research Seminar in International Economics at Michigan, and from participants at the 10th Annual Conference on International Trade at the University of Western Ontario. Several anonymous referees have also made extremely helpful suggestions. One of them, later identified as Bill Ethier, provided the method of proof that I now use for the result. It is more elegant, more general, and considerably shorter than the cumbersome proof I used before, and I thank him. Partial support in writing this paper was provided by a grant from the Ford Foundation.

[1]For example, the factor content version of the Heckscher–Ohlin Theorem, introduced to the theoretical literature by Vanek (1968) and to the empirical literature by Leamer (1980), depends in its simplest form on the assumption of FPE.

SSDI 0022-1996(93)01285-M

limited,[2] but the different techniques of production used in different countries make comparisons across them much more difficult.[3] As a contribution, therefore, to understanding the presence or absence of FPE, this paper presents a necessary condition for FPE, stated in terms of the allocation of factor endowments across any number of countries relative to the demands for, and the factor intensities of, any number of goods.[4]

Our knowledge of the conditions for FPE has evolved over the years. Samuelson (1949) identified the crucial condition for FPE in a two-factor model – that the two countries should produce at least two goods in common – and he recognized that this in turn requires that countries' factor endowments differ by less than the factor intensities of the industries. McKenzie (1955) generalized this idea to arbitrary numbers of factors (and at least as many goods) by focusing on the sets spanned by input requirement vectors and factor endowments. In current terminology, he showed that FPE required that factor endowments lie in the diversification cone. These conditions and others have been used over the years to try to ascertain the 'likelihood' of FPE and whether that likelihood rises or falls with the numbers of goods and factors.[5]

Perhaps the most useful and enlightening approach to FPE, though, and the one that I will build upon here, was presented by Dixit and Norman (1980, pp. 110–122). They spoke in terms of an 'integrated world economy' (IWE), in which both factors and goods are perfectly mobile across countries.[6] In an IWE the world as a whole attains an equilibrium with a single set of prices of goods, prices of factors, and techniques of production, and with certain equilibrium quantities of all goods demanded on world markets. Then in the same world but with immobile factors, if it is possible to allocate factors within countries to industries, using the techniques of production of the IWE, in such a way as to duplicate the world outputs of the IWE, then FPE is possible and this allocation is one that could arise with FPE. If it is not possible to allocate the given factor endowments in this way, then FPE is not possible.

[2]See Jones (1974) and Deardorff (1979) who show how, with free trade but without FPE, countries specialize in production of a small number of traded goods and import all others.

[3]In Deardorff (1982), for example, I was able to prove generalizations of both the factor-content and commodity versions of the Heckscher–Ohlin Theorem even in the absence of FPE. Without FPE, however, the measurement of factor intensity for these purposes becomes cumbersome.

[4]Wu (1987) has provided a necessary condition for *the absence* of FPE in a model with two factors, two countries, and many goods. His condition, which therefore implies an analogous sufficient condition for FPE, is quite different from the necessary condition derived here.

[5]Samuelson (1949, p. 192) started this discussion himself with the claim that adding more than two goods 'increases the likelihood of complete factor-price equalization'. This was followed by McKenzie (1955), Land (1959), Johnson (1967), Vanek and Bertrand (1971), Wu (1987) and Deardorff and Courant (1990).

[6]Samuelson (1949) had also used this device, though without the name or the accompanying diagram, to motivate and explore the conditions for FPE. Helpman and Krugman (1985) have also used it for a variety of problems.

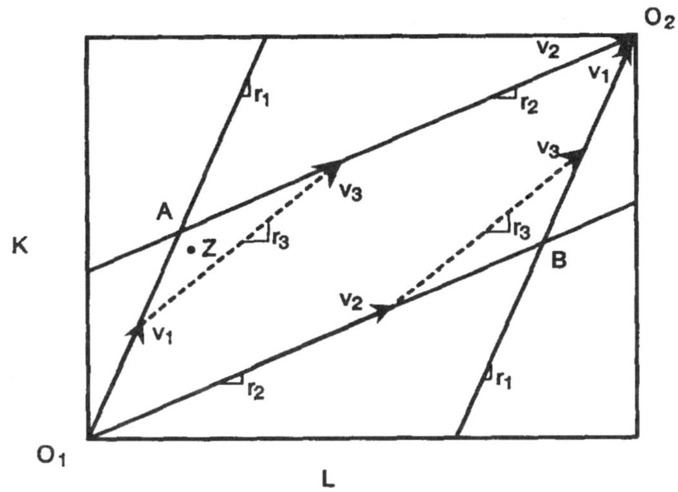

Fig. 1. FPE with two and three goods and two countries.

2. The model

With two factors, two goods, and two countries, this formulation leads to the simple and familiar visual representation of FPE factor allocations shown by the solid lines in fig. 1.[7] It shows a box diagram, the dimensions of which are L and K, the world factor endowments of labor and capital. Letting the lower-left corner at O_1 be the origin for measuring factor endowments of country 1, and the upper-right corner at O_2 be the origin for measuring factor endowments of country 2, any point in the box describes an allocation of the world's factor endowments between the two countries. Inserting into this diagram rays from both O_1 and O_2 with slopes equal to the ratios of capital to labor employed in the two industries, r_1 and r_2, Dixit and Norman (1980) have shown that FPE occurs if and only if factor endowments lie within the parallelogram formed by these rays, O_1AO_2B.

With a third good (here assumed to be of intermediate capital intensity, between goods 1 and 2), factor intensities alone are not enough to determine where FPE is possible; one needs also to know the outputs of each good in the IWE, and the amounts of the factors needed to produce them. Let X_i, $i=1,\ldots,3$, be the quantities of the goods demanded on the world market in the IWE, and let v_i be the vectors of factors needed to produce them. Since these vectors of factors must exhaust the world endowments, if placed end to end in the box diagram they must extend from one origin to the other. In fig.

[7]This diagram is often attributed to Lancaster (1957), who used (p. 31) something similar to show that two countries trading with FPE are equivalent to a single closed economy.

1, these vectors are drawn both in decreasing order of capital intensity, v_1, v_3, v_2, and in increasing order of capital intensity, v_2, v_3, v_1.

Together these vectors outline the hexagonal area $O_1v_1v_3O_2v_3v_2$, which is the only portion of the box in which FPE can occur. To see this, consider a point such as Z, inside the two diversification cones but above the path $v_1v_3v_2$. At such a point both countries are capable of keeping both factors fully employed using the three available techniques, but only by producing too much of two of the goods. Country 1, for example, must use more than the vector v_1 in industry 1, or else it would have too much capital per worker left over to be fully employed in the more labor-intensive industries 2 and 3.[8]

Thus it is not enough that countries have their endowments inside the same diversification cone. In addition they must be far enough inside of it to be able to produce the quantities of goods demanded on the world market. In the case shown in fig. 1, the danger is that if both countries are too near the opposite sides of the diversification cone, then both will need to produce larger quantities of goods of extreme factor intensity than are demanded on the world market. Correspondingly, the output of the good of intermediate factor intensity will be too small.

This technique can easily be extended to additional goods. Let there be n goods, $j=1,\dots,n$. Define X_j for each good to be the quantities demanded on the world market in the IWE, and define $v_j=(l_j,k_j)$ as the vectors of labor and capital needed to produce these quantities using the techniques of the IWE. Again these vectors could be laid end-to-end in a box like fig. 1, and they would reach exactly from O_1 to O_2. By arranging them first in decreasing order of capital intensity (as measured by the ratio $r_j=k_j/l_j$), and then a second time in increasing order of capital intensity, two paths can be constructed between which lie all possible allocations of two countries' factor endowments that are consistent with FPE. The space between these two paths, which are shown as the solid lines in fig. 2, has roughly the shape of a lens. All of this has been shown, or at least suggested, by Dixit and Norman (1980, p. 117).

In order to extend this technique to more than two countries and more than two factors, as well as more than two goods, it is useful to reinterpret slightly what has just been said. The area in the box between the two strings of vectors – what I will call a polyhedral lens – is the set of all points that can be reached by the vectors, or by parts of them. One could also form an analogous shape using the endowment vectors of the countries. With only two of them, this would be a parallelogram; with more it too would be a polyhedral lens as shown by the broken lines in fig. 2. With two countries, it

[8]This can be verified geometrically by drawing lines parallel to v_2 and v_3, down and to the left from point Z. See Dixit and Norman (1980, pp. 116–117).

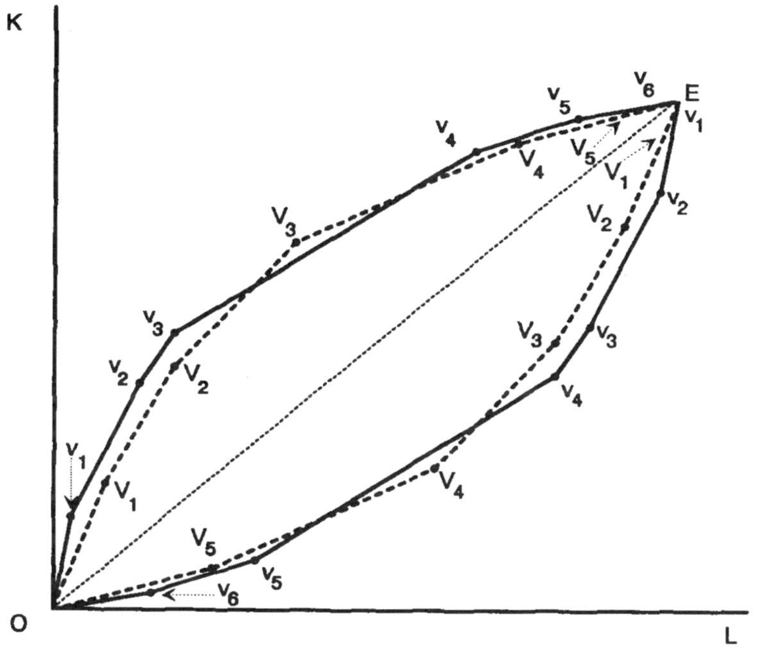

Fig. 2. Factor use (solid) and endowment (broken) lenses with six goods and five countries.

is clear that if the endowment point lies inside the factor intensity lens, then this endowment parallelogram will lie inside it as well. My claim is that even with more countries and more factors, a necessary condition for FPE is that the lens formed by the factor–endowment vectors must be a subset of the lens formed by the factor–use vectors.

To make the idea of these lenses precise, consider any collection of m n-dimensional row vectors, $a_i=(a_{i1},\dots,a_{in})$, arranged as rows of an $m\times n$ matrix $a=(a_{ij})$. Then the (polyhedral) lens spanned by these vectors is defined by

Definition (lens):

$$\mathscr{L}(a)=\{x\in\mathbb{R}^n \mid x=ba \text{ for some } m\text{-vector } b\ni 0\leqq b_i\leqq 1, \text{ where } a \text{ is } m\times n\}. \qquad (1)$$

Now suppose that there are m countries indexed i, n goods indexed j, and f factors indexed h. Define the $n\times f$ matrix $v=(v_{jh})$, where v_{jh} is the amount of factor h required for production of the world demand for good j in the IWE. Similarly, define the $m\times f$ matrix $V=(V_{ih})$, where V_{ih} is country i's endowment of factor h. Factor price equalization is possible if and only if the rows of v can be allocated across the m countries so as to exhaust the factor endowments in V. That is, letting u_m and u_n represent vectors of lengths m and n consisting entirely of ones,

Definition (factor price equalization). The factor–use vectors in v and the factor–endowment vectors in V permit FPE only if $\exists$ an $m \times n$ matrix $\lambda = (\lambda_{ij})$, with $0 \leqq \lambda_{ij} \leqq 1$, such that

$$\lambda v = V, \tag{2}$$

$$u_m \lambda = u_n. \tag{3}$$

With these definitions, it can then be shown that FPE implies that the factor–endowment lens lies wholly inside the factor–use lens:

Theorem.

$$\text{FPE} \Rightarrow \mathscr{L}(V) \subseteq \mathscr{L}(v). \tag{4}$$

Proof. Consider any vector of factors $x \in \mathbb{R}^f$ such that $x \in \mathscr{L}(V)$. From (1) $\exists$ an m-vector b, with $0 \leqq b_i \leqq 1$, such that

$$x = bV. \tag{5}$$

From FPE $\exists \lambda$, with $0 \leqq \lambda_{ij} \leqq 1$, satisfying (2) and (3). Let

$$c = b\lambda. \tag{6}$$

Then from (5) and (2),

$$x = bV = b\lambda v = cv. \tag{7}$$

From (3), elements of c are weighted averages of elements of b. Since the latter are between zero and one, the same is true of c, and it follows from (1) that $x \in \mathscr{L}(v)$. Q.E.D.

This is a general result. With only two factors, but arbitrarily many goods and countries, the factor–use and factor–endowment lenses are easily depicted as in fig. 2. In each case, the vectors are laid end to end, in decreasing order of their slopes to get the top of the lens and in increasing order of their slopes to get the bottom of the lens. The case shown is one in which FPE does not hold, because the endowment vectors of three of the five countries, 1, 2, and 3, extend outside of the factor–use lens.[9]

With more than two factors, the lenses are of higher dimension and cannot easily be graphed. However, for one lens to be inside another it must also be true that the projections of the first lens onto any plane must also be inside the projection of the second onto the same plane. Therefore, FPE also implies that these projections for any pair of factors will display the factor–endowment lens lying inside the factor–use lens. Thus, if a picture like fig. 2 arises for any pair of factors, with those two factor endowments for a subset of countries extending outside the limits that can be reached by factor–use vectors for those same factors, then FPE is not possible.

The theorem provides only a necessary condition for FPE, not a sufficient condition. It seems plausible to me that the same condition may in fact be sufficient for FPE, but I have as yet been unable to show that. All I know at this point is that the condition is sufficient for the case of two countries (and arbitrarily many goods and factors) as shown in the appendix, and that I have been unable to construct a counter-example in the easily graphed case of two factors (and arbitrarily many goods and countries). I would note only that the necessary condition mentioned in the preceding paragraph, involving not the full lenses but only their projections onto the various two-factor planes, is surely not sufficient for FPE since higher dimensional lenses could easily intersect without that ever showing in these projections.

3. Discussion

This result gives analytical content to the idea from the $2\times2\times2$ Heckscher–Ohlin model that FPE requires factor endowments to differ across countries by less than factor intensities differ across industries. With only two goods and two countries, this merely means that the endowments must lie in the same diversification cone. That is, the difference in endowment ratios of the two countries must be literally smaller than the difference in factor intensity ratios of the two industries. With additional goods this simple result no longer holds, as was seen in fig. 1, and with additional countries and factors the requirements of FPE become even more stringent, as was shown here. It is now necessary to compare not only the extremes of factor endowments with the extremes of factor intensities, but also to account for differences in the distribution of both endowments and intensities for goods and countries that are not extreme.

[9]In Deardorff (1991) I examined the two-factor case in more detail and showed somewhat more explicitly how the placement of point V_3 above the upper edge of the factor–use lens was inconsistent with FPE.

The comparison of the two lenses in the theorem does this. For example, if all vectors contributing to a lens pointed in the same direction, then the lens would be a straight line with no thickness. Thus if factor intensities do not differ across industries, the factor–use lens will be such a line, and any variation at all in relative factor endowments will preclude FPE. Likewise, if relative factor endowments were all the same and factor intensities were not, then the factor–endowment lens would be such a line and would necessarily lie within the factor–use lens. In either case the extent to which the lens is bowed out away from its diagonal depends on how different are the vectors that contribute to it. Thus, for the factor–endowment lens to lie wholly within the factor–use lens as required for FPE, the variation across countries in relative factor endowments must be less, in some sense, than the variation across industries of factor intensities.[10]

4. Conclusion

I have deliberately not attempted here to draw conclusions about the 'likelihood' of FPE. Such conclusions are often difficult to interpret in any case, and in this case they would require a prior sense of the likelihood, in the real world, of various distributions of factor intensities, factor endowments, and demands for goods. What is really needed is to measure these distributions and to match them against the requirement of the theorem. However, since the theorem deals with factor intensities and demands as they would appear in the IWE, and since we certainly do not observe that kind of equilibrium in the world, that empirical exercise cannot be done.

Appendix: Sufficiency with two countries

To see that $\mathscr{L}(V) \subseteq \mathscr{L}(v) \Rightarrow$ FPE in the case of two countries, n goods and f factors, let V_1 and V_2 be the endowment vectors of the two countries. $V_1 \in \mathscr{L}(V)$ since $V_1 = (1\,0)V$, and $\therefore$ $V_1 \in \mathscr{L}(v)$. From (1) $\exists$ n-vector b, with $0 \leqq b_j \leqq 1$, such that $V_1 = bv$. Define

$$\lambda = \begin{pmatrix} b \\ u_n - b \end{pmatrix}.$$

[10]These variations must also be weighted by levels of output in the IWE and by country size. Wu (1987) argued that FPE is made less likely if demands are greatest for goods of intermediate rather than extreme factor intensity. That is clear here, as well, where high demand for such goods in the IWE will make the factor–use lens thin. Similarly, if the largest countries tend to have extreme factor endowments, then this will thicken the factor–endowment lens and also make the condition for FPE more stringent.

It is then easily checked that the conditions for FPE are satisfied: $0 \leqq \lambda_{ij} \leqq 1$ by construction; $u_m\lambda = b + (u_n - b) = u_n$; and

$$\lambda v = \begin{pmatrix} bv \\ (u_n - b)v \end{pmatrix} = \begin{pmatrix} V_1 \\ V - V_1 \end{pmatrix} = \begin{pmatrix} V_1 \\ V_2 \end{pmatrix} = V.$$

References

Deardorff, A.V., 1979, Weak links in the chain of comparative advantage, Journal of International Economics 9, 197–209.

Deardorff, A.V., 1982, The general validity of the Heckscher–Ohlin theorem, American Economic Review 72, 683–694.

Deardorff, A.V., 1991, The possibility of factor price equalization, revisited, Research Seminar in International Economics Discussion Paper No. 277 (Department of Economics, The University of Michigan).

Deardorff, A.V. and P.N. Courant, 1990, On the likelihood of factor price equalization with nontraded goods, International Economic Review 31, 589–596.

Dixit, A.K. and V. Norman, 1980, Theory of international trade (Cambridge University Press, London).

Helpman, E. and P.R. Krugman, 1985, Market structure and foreign trade (MIT Press, Cambridge, MA).

Johnson, H.G., 1967, The possibility of factor-price equalisation when commodities outnumber factors, Economica 34, 282–288.

Jones, R.W., 1974, The small country in a many-commodity world, Australian Economic Papers 13, 225–236.

Lancaster, K., 1957, The Heckscher–Ohlin trade model: A geometric treatment, Economica 24, 19–39.

Land, A.H., 1959, Factor endowments and factor prices, Economica 26, 137–142.

Leamer, E.E., 1980, The Leontief paradox, reconsidered, Journal of Political Economy 88, 495–503.

McKenzie, L.W., 1955, Equality of factor prices in world trade, Econometrica 23, 239–257.

Samuelson, P.A., 1949, International factor price equalisation once again, The Economic Journal 59, 181–197.

Vanek, J., 1968, The factor proportions theory: The *n*-factor case, Kyklos 4, 749–756.

Vanek, J. and T.J. Bertrand, 1971, Trade and factor prices in a multi-commodity world, in: J. Bhagwati, R. Jones, R. Mundell and J. Vanek, eds., Trade, balance of payments and growth: Papers in international economics in honor of Charles P. Kindleberger (North-Holland, Amsterdam).

Wu, H., 1987, The equalization of factor prices in general equilibrium when commodities outnumber factors, Journal of International Economics 23, 343–356.

NORTH-HOLLAND

North American Journal of
Economics and Finance 12 (2001) 121–137

THE NORTH AMERICAN
JOURNAL OF
ECONOMICS
AND FINANCE

Articles

Fragmentation in simple trade models

Alan V. Deardorff

Department of Economics, The University of Michigan, Ann Arbor, MI 48109-1220, USA

Received 30 March 2001; accepted 13 April 2001

Paper presented in a session on "Globalization and Regionalism: Conflict or Complements?" North American Economics and Finance Association, Chicago, IL, January 4, 1998, revised January 8, 1998.

Abstract

This paper examines the effects of "fragmentation," defined as the splitting of a production process into two or more steps that can be undertaken in different locations but that lead to the same final product. Introducing the possibility of fragmentation into simple theoretical models of international trade, the paper finds the effects of fragmentation on national welfare, on patterns of specialization and trade, and on factor prices. Models examined include the Ricardian Model and the Heckscher-Ohlin Model, both for small open economies and for a two-country world. Results are as follows: 1. If fragmentation does not change the prices of goods, then it must increase the value of output of any country where it occurs and that of the world. 2. If fragmentation does change prices, then fragmentation can lower the welfare of a country by turning its terms of trade against it. 3. Even in a country that gains from fragmentation, it is possible (but not necessary) that some factor owners within that country will lose. 4. To the extent that factor prices are not equalized internationally in the absence of fragmentation, fragmentation may be a force toward factor price equalization.

JEL classification: F11

Keywords: Fragmentation; Outsourcing

Tel.: +1-734-764-6817; fax: +1-734-763-9181.
E-mail address: alandear@umich.edu; http://www.econ.lsa.umich.edu/~alandea (A.V. Deardorff).

1062-9408/01/$ – see front matter
PII: S1062-9408(01)00043-2

1. Introduction

The subject is fragmentation: the splitting of a production process into two or more steps that can be undertaken in different locations but that lead to the same final product. Also called "intraproduct specialization" by Arndt (1998) and by the more loaded term "outsourcing" in some economic literature as well as in the popular press, fragmentation occurs both within countries and across countries.[1] Within countries, if domestic factor markets are well integrated and markets are competitive, then fragmentation would be expected to occur only if the combined resources used by the fragmented steps were less than those used by the original process, in which case fragmentation would also represent a technological improvement. In this paper I will assume instead that fragmentation does not economize on resources, and therefore I will focus on fragmentation that occurs across countries.[2]

Internationally, fragmentation has become increasingly common in recent years as barriers to international trade and investment have fallen and as an increasingly competitive world environment has forced producers to look outside their own borders for ways to reduce costs. In the debate over the causes of increased wage inequality in the United States in the 1980s and 90s, "globalization" and technology have both been suggested as important causes of the increased wage differential paid to skilled labor, globalization being represented variously by international trade, foreign direct investment, factor mobility, and outsourcing.[3] In fact, fragmentation may be thought of as a manifestation of globalization and technology combined, since in many industries it is only advances in technology that have made the splitting of production processes and the coordination of the resulting parts possible.

In any case, with the exception of Arndt (1997) and Jones and Kierzkowski (2001), the economic effects of fragmentation do not seem to have been given the theoretical treatment they deserve, and in this paper I will attempt to correct that.[4] Using several familiar and simple models of international trade, I will examine the implications of fragmentation on trade, patterns of specialization, and factor markets, looking especially at its effects on factor prices and on the overall welfare of the countries involved.

I will examine the effects of fragmentation first in a Ricardian model in section 2, then in a Heckscher-Ohlin model in section 3. Section 4 concludes.

2. Fragmentation in Ricardo

I will look first at the effects of fragmentation on a small open economy, then at a large country in a two-country world.

2.1. A small open Ricardian economy

Consider first the textbook case of only two goods. The country is endowed with a fixed amount of labor, L, and it can use this labor to produce either of two (final) goods, X and Y. The unit labor requirements of each are fixed at a_X and a_Y respectively. As a small open economy, the country faces fixed prices of the two goods on a world market, p_X and p_Y, at which it can buy or sell unlimited quantities. As usual, if the wage in the country were w, then the supply prices of the two goods would be wa_X and wa_Y respectively, and profits would be made if either of these were below the corresponding world price. Therefore the market equilibrium wage is instead

$$w_0 = \max\left(\frac{p_X}{a_X}, \frac{p_Y}{a_Y}\right) \tag{1}$$

The country specializes in whichever good yields this highest wage, exporting X if $p_X/a_X > p_Y/a_Y$ and vice versa. Equivalently, if

$$\frac{a_X}{a_Y} < \frac{p_X}{p_Y}, \tag{2}$$

then the country has a comparative advantage in X and will export it. I will assume this to be the case.

Now suppose that fragmentation becomes possible in the X industry. In general, this means that the process for producing one unit of good X can be split into multiple parts, $i = 1, \ldots, n_X$, each requiring an amount of labor a_{Xi}, and since I do not want to conflate fragmentation with technological progress, I assume that $\Sigma_{i=1}^{n_X} a_{Xi} \geq a_X$. Coordination of these fragmented parts might in general require oversight by a single entity such as a multinational enterprise (whose function could itself be represented by one of the parts), but to consider explicitly how the parts are organized would take me too far afield.[5] Instead I will define each part as producing one unit of an intermediate good, Z_{xi}, that is also an intermediate input to the next part that produces one unit of Z_{xi+1}, the final step producing a unit of good X itself: $Z_{Xn_X} = X$. Thus production of a unit of each intermediate input except the first requires, in addition to the labor a_{Xi}, one unit of the preceding intermediate good, Z_{xi-1}.

In general not all of these intermediate goods need be regarded as tradable; their tradability indicates whether two adjacent parts of the fragmented production process can take place in different countries. However, if they are not tradable, then their separate identities will play no role in the model here with an integrated competitive domestic labor market, and they could be combined into one. Therefore, I will assume that all of these intermediate goods are internationally tradable.

What I have described is a fairly general formulation of fragmentation, but in the spirit of my initial 2-good model, let me start with the simple case of $n_X = 2$. That is, let production of X be fragmented into just two parts, requiring amounts of labor a_{X1} and a_{X2}, the first of which produces an intermediate good Z, that is required one-for-one with production of good X in the second part. The result is simply a 3-good Ricardian model, where the three goods are X, Y, and Z, and where the demand for Z is the quantity of X that is produced using the fragmented technology. Since Z is tradable, introduction of fragmentation also requires that the world market provide an additional price for it, p_Z. The question is, what does all of this do to the small open economy facing this and the other prices?

The answer depends in part on whether those other prices—p_X and p_Y—also change as a consequence of fragmentation. This is an issue that will come up more clearly in the 2-country model below, so for now I simply assume that they do not. This will in fact be the

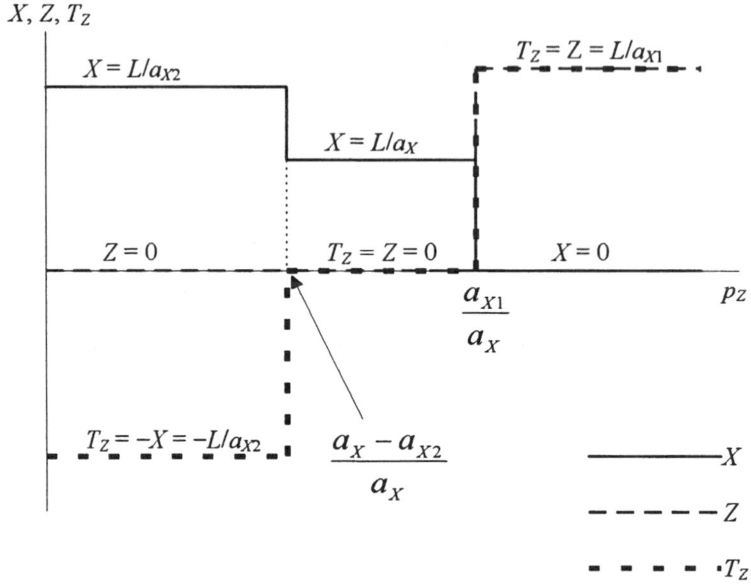

Fig. 1.

case if the large rest-of-world with which our small country trades is itself a fully integrated economy. In that case, there is a single wage of labor prevailing throughout the rest-of-world, and fragmentation that does not lower total labor requirements cannot lower the price of *X*. Its price cannot rise, either, since the original unfragmented technology is still available.

What matters for the small country, then, is the price of *Z*, which will depend on the parameters of the fragmented technology in the rest-of-world. Since this is a Ricardian model, these are not necessarily the same as in the small country, and I will therefore just examine how behavior in the small country depends on p_Z.

The answer is simple. Labor now has two additional options for employment, in addition to producing *X* from scratch and producing *Y*. It can produce *Z*, earning a wage p_Z/a_{X1}, or it can produce *X* from *Z*, earning a wage $(p_X - p_Z)/a_{X2}$. Labor will therefore engage in whichever of the four activities earns it the most, and it will do more than one thing only if two or more of the activities yield the same wage. Thus the equilibrium wage in the fragmented small open economy, w_F, is

$$w_F = \max\left(\frac{p_X}{a_X}, \frac{p_Y}{a_Y}, \frac{p_Z}{a_{X1}}, \frac{(p_X - p_Z)}{a_{X2}}\right) \tag{3}$$

The country will engage in whichever activity or activities yields this maximum wage.

The country's production and trade are summarized in Fig. 1. By assumption (2) that it has a comparative advantage in good *X*, it will never produce good *Y*. Whether and how it produces good *X*, however, depends on the price of the intermediate input. Taking good *X* as numeraire, comparison of the arguments in (3) shows that if p_Z is sufficiently low—below

$\frac{a_X - a_{X2}}{a_X}$—then the country will employ only the second fragmented part of the new technology for producing X, importing all it needs of good Z from the rest-of-world. For a somewhat higher price of the intermediate input, however—above $\frac{a_X - a_{X2}}{a_X}$ but below $\frac{a_{X1}}{a_X}$—it will continue to produce X from scratch with the old technology. Finally, if the price of the intermediate is high enough—above $\frac{a_{X1}}{a_X}$—then it will produce only Z. In the latter case, since it does not produce X and therefore does not need Z, it exports all of its output of Z. The figure shows these responses of output to price as the heavy solid line for X and the heavy dashed line for Z. In addition, it shows net trade in Z (exports if positive, imports if negative) as the heavy dotted line.[6]

For some prices, then, Fig. 1 shows the fragmented technology not being used at all. This occurs only if $\frac{a_{X1}}{a_X}$ is in fact greater than $\frac{a_X - a_{X2}}{a_X}$, which it may not be. This requires that

$$a_{X1} + a_{X2} > a_X, \tag{4}$$

or in other words that the fragmented technology use more resources than the original, or that fragmentation is, in this sense, "costly." I will take this to be the normal case in this section, although the justification for doing so most easily relies on transportation costs, which I am assuming away in the rest of the model.

In any case, the model says that if fragmentation is costly, then for some parameters and prices it will not be used, but for other parameters it will. Also, if fragmentation is not costly, then the middle range of behavior in Fig. 1 collapses to a single price, and fragmentation is used at all prices but one, $\frac{a_{X1}}{a_X}$, where all are indifferent between producing Z, producing X from scratch, and producing X from Z.

It might seem in the case of costly fragmentation that welfare might fall, since the country is using part of what seems to be an inefficient technology. In fact, however, we see immediately from (3) that welfare cannot fall with the introduction of fragmentation in this Ricardian Model. The entire population is labor, and everyone earns a common wage that is at least as great as it was before, in real terms since prices of consumer goods are fixed. The reason, of course, is that while using both parts of the fragmented technology would indeed be inefficient, the country does not do that. On the contrary, it uses only one part of it, and the other part is not used anywhere. It is the latter part that is really inefficient at prevailing prices.

So far I have assumed that fragmentation occurs only in the export industry. That, of course, need not be the case. If fragmentation were to become possible in producing good Y instead, then the above analysis would be modified but only slightly. Parameters a_{Y1} and a_{Y2} would replace their X counterparts, and Y would replace X in the third and fourth arguments of (3). The result is again a range of prices of the intermediate good Z for which fragmentation is not observed, although in this case it will continue to be good X, not the potentially fragmented good Y, that is produced in the midrange.[7] If the price of the intermediate is outside this range, however, good X, will not be produced at all, and the country will either produce and export the intermediate or produce and export Y. Thus fragmentation may give a country a comparative advantage in a good where it had no comparative advantage before.

This is about all that the simple Ricardian model of a small economy can tell us, but the results are pretty clearly robust to expansion of the model to include, say, more goods or more degrees of fragmentation. With both of these arbitrarily large, the wage is set as

$$w_F = \max_{\substack{j=1,\ldots,n \\ i_j=1,\ldots,n_j}} \left(\frac{p_j}{a_j}, \frac{(p_{ji_j} - p_{ji_j-1})}{a_{ji_j}} \right) \tag{5}$$

where the technology for producing each of n goods j is potentially fragmented into n_j parts, the last of which produces the final good itself. p_j, a_j are the prices and unit labor requirements for producing the jth good, $j = 1,\ldots,n$, using the original Ricardian technology. p_{ji_j}, a_{ji_j} are the prices and unit labor requirements for the i_jth intermediate input to good j, $i_j = 1,\ldots,n_j$, with $p_{j0} = 0$ and $p_{jn_j} = p_j$.

From this, it follows that the country will tend to specialize in using only one fragment of one technology, unless parameters and prices coincidentally align so that more than one process yields the same wage. Comparative advantage now refers most appropriately to processes, not goods, although we may identify them with the intermediate goods that they produce. As in the 2-good model, as long as prices of final goods in the rest-of-world are given and unchanged by the introduction of fragmentation, the small country cannot lose from it. Patterns of production and trade will not be determined quite as simply as in the 2-good model, but one of the patterns suggested in Fig. 1 will continue to hold: given the prices of all other goods and fragments, a particular fragment will be employed and its intermediate product exported if its price is high enough. A low price, on the other hand, will not necessarily assure that it will be imported, since that also requires a high price in the next stage of production.

2.2. A two country Ricardian world

A small country in the Ricardian model, then, cannot lose from fragmentation so long as prices of final goods remain fixed. And fixity of prices has a certain plausibility if the rest-of-world is integrated, as noted above. However a large country can surely not take prices as given, and the problems that arise for a large country are also those that arise for a nonintegrated rest-of-world. We therefore need to look at a two-country world in order to explore these problems. In that context, I will focus only on one issue: whether a country can lose from fragmentation. Along the way we will incidentally see a bit more about how fragmentation affects specialization and trade.

For a country to lose from fragmentation, prices must turn against it, and this requires that it be trading initially so that there is scope for its terms of trade to worsen. I will consider, therefore, a country that specializes initially in good X, and try to see whether fragmentation can lower the relative price of good X sufficiently for it to lose. I will consider the same simple form of fragmentation that I looked at before, splitting production of good X into two parts. For simplicity and to avoid the costs of fragmentation itself being the source of any

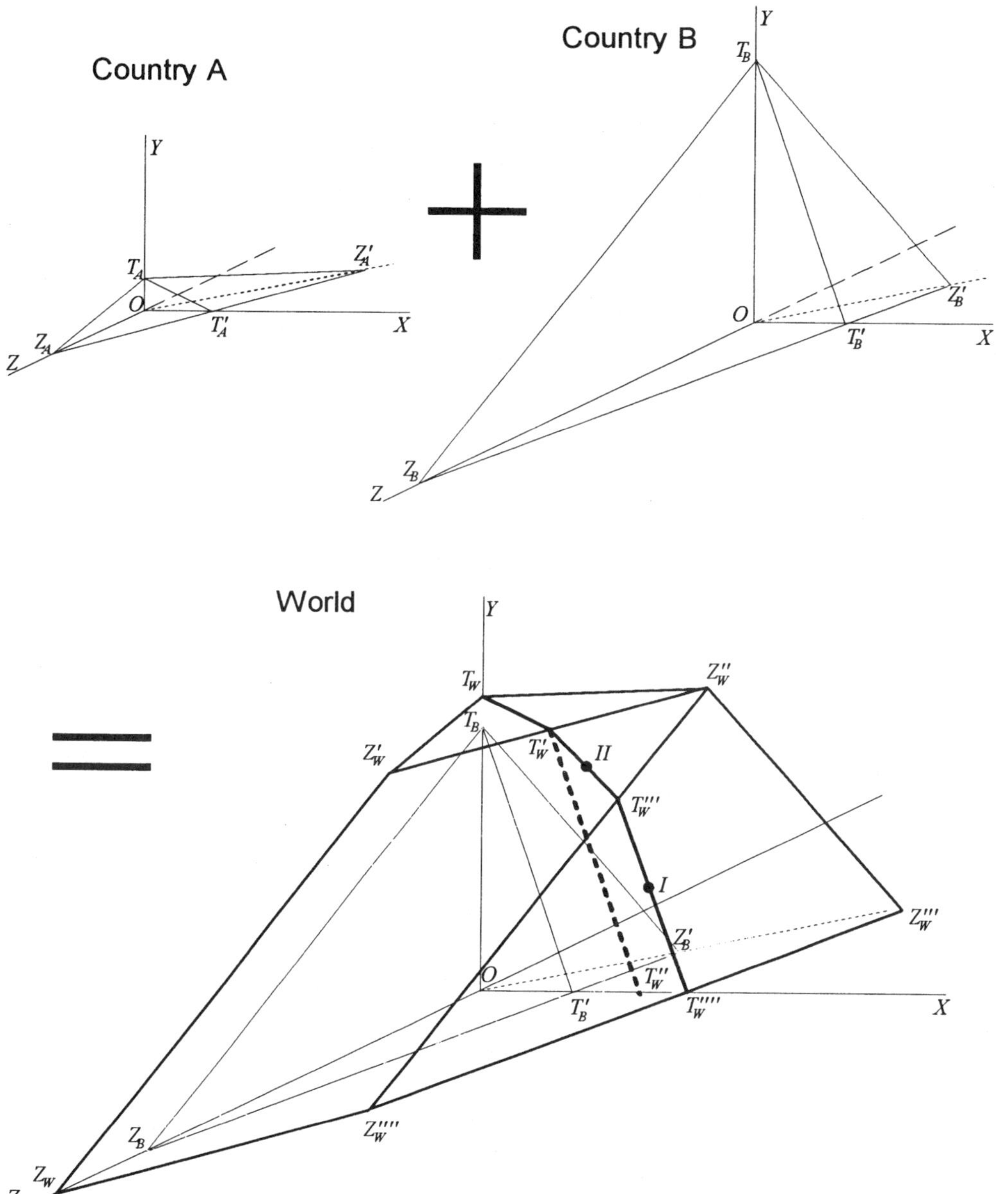

Fig. 2.

loss, I will now assume that fragmentation is costless. Analogous other cases should not be hard to find.

Fig. 2 tells us most of what we need to know, although some explanation is required. In the upper left corner is drawn the production possibility frontier (PPF) for the country of interest, Country A, which is assumed again to have a comparative advantage in good *X*. Its customary Ricardian transformation curve is T_AT_A' in the *X-Y* plane, showing the maximum amounts of goods *X* and *Y* that it can produce without fragmentation. Fragmentation expands its production possibilities into a third dimension, with the *Z* axis measuring its net output of intermediate good *Z*, positive if it produces it, negative if it is a net user of *Z* in production of *X*. Point Z_A shows the maximum amount that can be produced if all labor is devoted to production of good *Z*. Production possibilities include the triangular plane through Z_A, T_A, and T_A'. It is also possible to be a net user of *Z* in producing *X*, and the maximum amount of *X* that can be produced that way is graphed together with the equal negative input of *Z* at point Z_A' (which is on the dotted 45° line in the horizontal (*X*,–*Z*) plane). Again, linear technologies also permit production anywhere on the triangular plane through Z_A', T_A, and T_A'. If fragmentation were costly, the surface combining these two triangles would be kinked along T_AT_A' (i.e., the straight line connecting Z_A and Z_A' would pass to the left of T_A'). But with costless fragmentation as I assume here, the two triangles are part of the same plane, and the full PPF of country A with fragmentation consists of the larger triangle $T_AZ_AZ_A'$. To assure that Country A will have a comparative advantage in *X* both with and without fragmentation, I have drawn these production possibilities as skewed in the *X* direction.

The top right portion of Fig. 2 shows the PPF for Country B, with its greatest productivity being in the directions of final good *Y* and intermediate good *Z*. Otherwise the graph for Country B has exactly the same interpretation as for Country A.

Now combine these two PPFs, to get the PPF of the world in the bottom part of the figure. The construction is a little messy but actually not all that difficult if you draw it carefully. As is familiar in the 2-good Ricardian model, one simply places the origin for one PPF on the surface of the other, then slides it around in all possible ways to generate the largest outputs possible. In two dimensions only, this process of adding together T_AT_A' and T_BT_B' would yield the world frontier $T_WT_W'T_W''$ that appears in the *X-Y* plane in the bottom graph. It is linear with just one kink (at T_W'), and the two linear segments are exact replicas of the transformation curves of the two individual countries.

To construct the PPF in three dimensions, I place the origin of Country A's PPF on the surface of Country B's PPF, $T_BZ_BZ_B'$. As a result of the shapes of the two PPFs, point Z_A' of A's PPF traces out a duplicate of B's PPF: the triangle $Z''_WZ'''_WZ''''_W$. The bottom edge of A's PPF, Z_AZ_A' traces out the parallelogram $Z_WZ'_WZ''_WZ''''_W$ as its origin traverses T_BZ_B. And A's PPF itself becomes the topmost facet of the world PPF, the triangle $T_WZ'_WZ''_W$. Note that the parameters underlying these figures are such that only three patterns of specialization are possible: County B produces only good *Y* (the top triangle); Country A produces only good *X* using the fragmented technology and imported inputs of good *Z* (the lower triangle); and Country B produces a mix of *Y* and *Z* while Country A produces only *X*, mixing the original and the fragmented technology (the parallelogram).

However, the world cannot be in equilibrium just anywhere on the three-dimensional surface. By assumption, good *Z* has no use except in producing *X*, so the world's net output of *Z* must be zero. Therefore the only relevant part of the world PPF is the solid heavy kinked line, $T_WT'_WT'''_WT''''_W$. Just where on this curve the equilibrium will be found depends on preferences of consumers in both countries for consuming goods *X* and *Y*.

The potential gains for the world from fragmentation are now evident. Without fragmentation, the world was confined to the output combinations on $T_W T_W' T_W''$, and if preferences put the equilibrium on the steeper segment, $T_W' T_W''$, then fragmentation permits an increase in the world consumption of both goods. These gains should not be surprising: they are simply the result of comparative advantage being followed within the fragmented technology for producing good *X*.

What are prices in the world equilibrium? They are given by the slopes of a plane tangent to the world PPF wherever the equilibrium is located. As usual in a Ricardian model, these may be determined mostly by preferences if the equilibrium is at one of the kinks, T'_W or T''_W, or they may be determined entirely by parameters of production if the equilibrium is in one of the straight segments. Note that if demand for *X* is sufficiently high so that the equilibrium is in the steeper of these segments, $T'''_W T''''_W$, then prices are those of Country B in autarky and do not change with fragmentation. That is the situation addressed in our analysis of the small country above, thus indicating that the assumptions made there were appropriate. Of course in this case, represented for example at point *I* in Fig. 2, Country A does not lose from fragmentation, as already noted.

The possibility of loss arises in the other segment, $T'_W T''''_W$, at points like the one marked *II*. Here the relative price of good *X* falls as a result of fragmentation, and since Country A initially exported *X*, this constitutes a fall in its terms of trade. This is not enough to show that it loses, however, since it would have gained a positive amount from the fragmentation itself had prices not fallen. It turns out, though, that Country A *must* lose from fragmentation in this case. Segment $T'_W T''''_W$ is part of the parallelogram traced out by the lower edge of Country A's PPF as its origin traverses the upper left edge of B's PPF. Therefore the price plane tangent to the world PPF in this segment includes the entire bottom edge of A's PPF. This is enough to assure that there are no gains to it from shifting resources toward fragmented production, and the reduced terms of trade therefore causes an unambiguous loss.

Both results are illustrated in Fig. 3. In the top panel, prices remain fixed with fragmentation and country A gains unambiguously. Initially trading only *X* and *Y*, it consumed at point *C* along the two-dimensional price line given it by Country B. With fragmentation prices do not change, but Country A shifts all of its labor to producing good *X* with inputs of *Z* and the fragmented technology. Production moves to point Z_A' and it trades from there to point C' along the price plane, also given it by Country B. The nature of the trade, incidentally, is that it imports both *Y* and *Z*, since it produces neither.

The other case is shown in the bottom part of the figure. Here again Country A starts at point *C*, but now with fragmentation it trades along a price plane that is both flatter (lower p_X/p_Y) and rotated clockwise from above (lower p_X/p_Z), as shown. The loss in welfare is unambiguous. Production, incidentally, is somewhere on the bottom edge between points T_A' and Z_A', and the country imports *Y* and *Z*. The main difference between this and the case above is that the country also produces some of good *X* from scratch, and indeed it is this that requires prices that make the two processes for producing *X* equivalent and prevents any gain to Country A from using the fragmented technology. Country B, of course, now does gain.

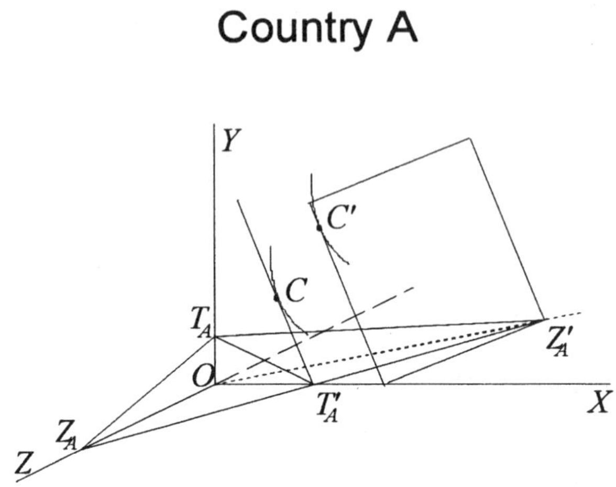

3-1: Equilibrium at *I* in Figure 2

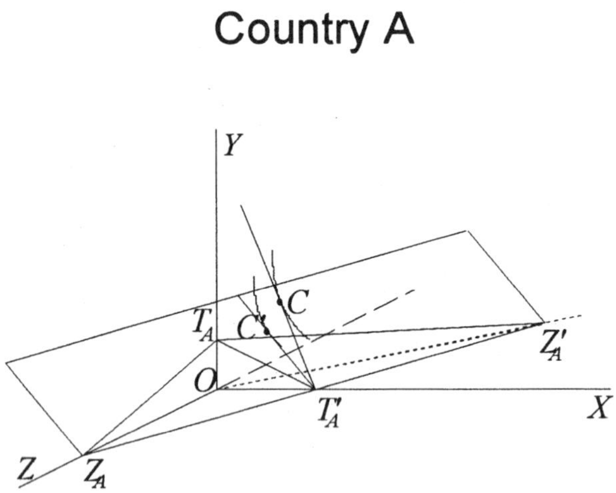

3-2: Equilibrium at *II* in Figure 2

Fig. 3.

3. Fragmentation in Heckscher-Ohlin

The simplicity of the Ricardian model is valuable for the insights that it can yield into the behavior of more complicated models. For example, a Heckscher-Ohlin (H-O) model can approximate arbitrarily closely to the Ricardian model of Section 2, and therefore we can conclude immediately that a large country can lose from fragmentation, even in a H-O world. However, there are other details that are assumed away in a Ricardian model that it therefore cannot address. The most obvious and important is the existence of separate factors of production and the possibility that some factors may gain while others may lose from a change such as fragmentation. I will explore that possibility here.

The first thing to note about a H-O model, however, is that fragmentation as defined here will not occur in the kinds of equilibria most often considered in the H-O literature. That is, if prior to fragmentation there is factor price equalization (FPE), and if fragmentation is costly, then there will be no incentive to fragment production. Therefore, in order for the issue of fragmentation to be interesting, we must start with a world economy in which factor prices are different. That is, I will assume that factor endowments differ sufficiently across countries that they are unable, in free trade, to produce enough goods in common to cause FPE. I will also assume, for simplicity, that fragmentation is costless, although one could easily think of there existing an infinitesimal fragmentation cost, ϵ, that is too small to show up in the diagrams. Again, I will start with a small country and then move to a 2-country model.

3.1. A small open H-O economy

Fig. 4 shows what can happen in a 2-good model. The solid lines show the initial situation before fragmentation. It is a familiar Lerner diagram with good X chosen as numeraire so that the unit value isoquant for X is also its unit isoquant.

A small country trades with a large rest-of-world in which prices of the two goods, X and Y, are given and imply the unit value isoquants shown. The diversification cone is given by the rays k_X and k_Y, with corresponding factor prices $\tilde{w}$ and $\tilde{r}$. The small country, however, is not inside the cone. Its endowment point is E, and it therefore specializes in good X with factor prices w_0 and r_0.

Now fragmentation becomes possible everywhere. The technology for producing good X now includes the possibility of producing an intermediate input, Z, one unit of which requires the factors shown by the new isoquant labeled $Z = 1$.[8] A unit of good Z can be used together with additional inputs of capital and labor to produce a unit of X. Since I am now assuming that fragmentation is costless, the isoquant for producing a unit of X from Z is simply the factors that are left over out of the original $X = 1$ isoquant. That is, the isoquant for producing X from Z can be drawn upside down relative to, say, point O_{XZ} as an origin, and it will then be just tangent to the $Z = 1$ isoquant.[9]

Note that I have drawn the technology for producing Z as more capital intensive than for producing X. With that assumption, the activities available to the world now include one whose factor requirements (at the rest-of-world's factor prices) are given by the ray k_Z. The

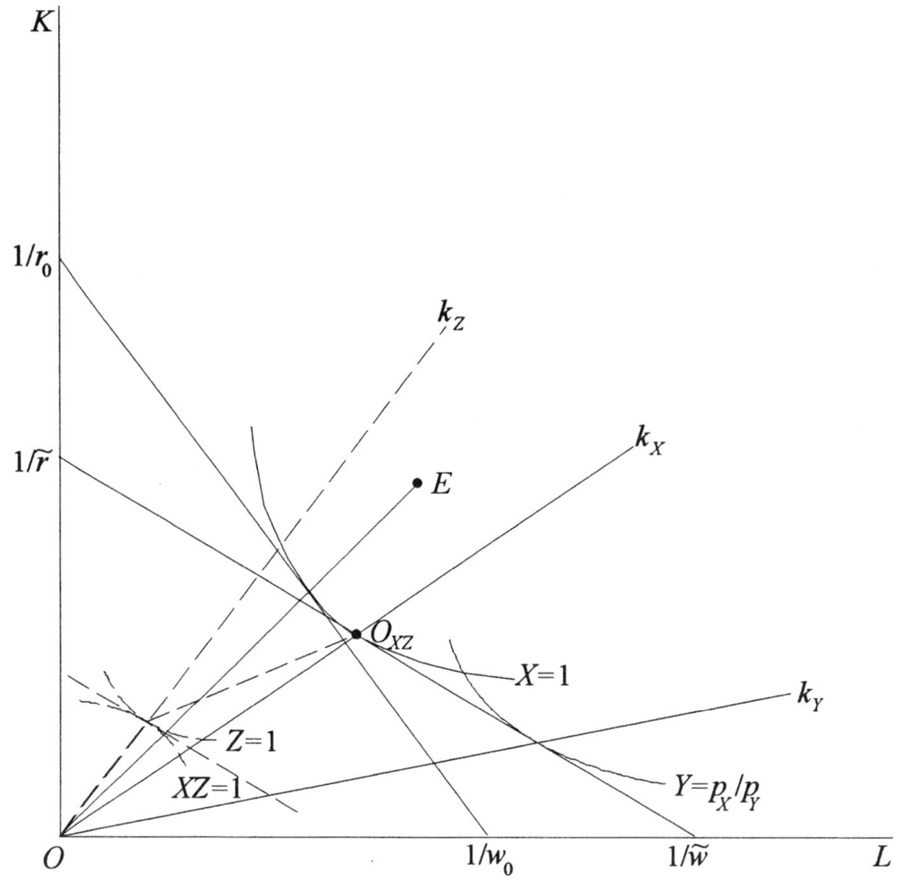

Fig. 4.

diversification cone is therefore enlarged by fragmentation. In the case shown, the small country is now inside it, and it will therefore now be able to fully employ its factors at the world's factor prices. This is now a 3-good, 2-factor H-O model, so exact outputs and the pattern of trade are indeterminate *à la* Melvin (1968). But we can be sure in this case that the small country will produce some of intermediate good *Z* together with some of either *X* and/or *Y*.

More important here, however, is what happens to factor prices. Evidently from the figure, the wage has fallen from w_0 to $\tilde{w}$, while the rental on capital has risen from r_0 to $\tilde{r}$. Since prices are fixed, these changes are real as well as nominal.

Thus we have a case here where a country gains from fragmentation,[10] but not all factor owners within that country share in the gain. On the contrary, workers here are made worse off as the production process for their product fragments into a capital-intensive and a labor-intensive part, only the former of which necessarily remains viable within their country.

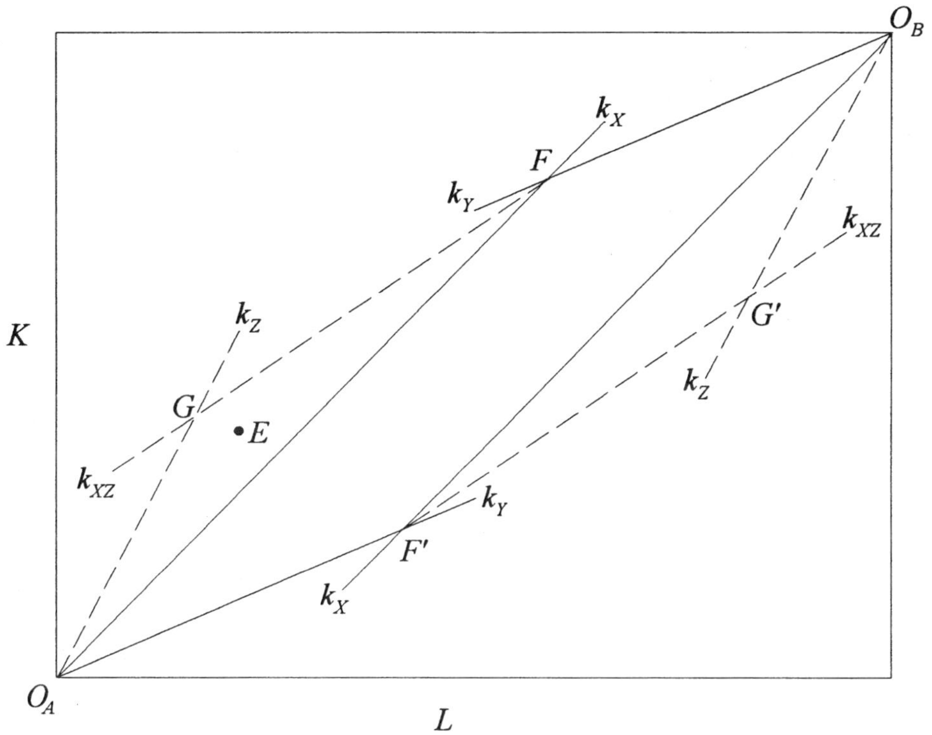

Fig. 5.

3.2. A two-country H-O world

What happened in Fig. 4 did not really require that the country in question be small. To see this, consider a two-country world of the same sort. Fig. 5 shows the Travis-Dixit-Norman[11] integrated world economy (IWE) diagram that Helpman and Krugman (1985) exploited so successfully for a variety of purposes. Without fragmentation, the FPE region is the parallelogram O_AFO_BF'. Fragmentation, which makes it possible to duplicate the X output of factor vector O_AF with the two fragmented vectors O_AG and GF, expands the FPE region to $O_AGFO_BG'F'$. Thus, for some allocations of the world's factors for which FPE would not have been possible, fragmentation leads to FPE.

For example, if the allocation were at point E, then there could not have been FPE without fragmentation. What exactly would have happened instead we don't know, since prices would not have been those prevailing in the IWE, but it seems plausible that Country A would have produced only good X and Country B would have produced a mix of X and Y.[12] Fragmentation again permits Country A to shift resources into the most capital-intensive fragment of producing Z, and again it is likely to raise the return to capital and lower the wage. There may also be small effects on factor prices in Country B, as market clearing prices of X and Y change, but these are difficult to determine.

This result illustrates the more general phenomenon that fragmentation enhances the possibility of factor price equalization. With arbitrary numbers of goods, factors, and countries, I showed in Deardorff (1994) that FPE requires that factor endowments be more similar than factor intensities in a certain well-defined sense: the set of vectors that can be constructed from parts (or all) of the factor endowment vectors—called the "factor endowment lens"—must lie inside the analogous set of vectors defined by the factors used in the IWE—the "factor use lens." Costless fragmentation unambiguously enlarges the factor use lens and thus makes FPE possible for factor allocations for which it was not possible before.

To see this, note that a factor use lens is defined as

$$\mathcal{L}(v) = \{x \in \mathbb{R}^f \mid x = bv \text{ for some } g\text{-vector } b \in I^g\} \tag{6}$$

where there are f factors and g goods, I^g is a set of g-vectors whose elements are in the unit interval, [0,1], and v is a $g \times f$ matrix of factor-use row vectors. Then let v^0 be the matrix of factor uses without fragmentation, $v_j^0, j = 1,\ldots,g$, and let v^1 be the matrix of factor uses in which some or all goods have been fragmented into 2 or more parts. Numbering the rows of v^1 ji, $i = 1,\ldots,n_j$, the cost of fragmentation will be zero if $v_j^0 = \Sigma_{i=1}^{n_j} v_{ji}^1$. It is then easily shown that[13,14]

$$\mathcal{L}(v^1) \subseteq \mathcal{L}(v^0) \tag{7}$$

This tells us that the possibility of FPE is increased by fragmentation. That is, there may be allocations of the world's factor endowments for which FPE is not possible without fragmentation and for which FPE becomes possible with fragmentation. It also says that if FPE is possible without fragmentation, then it must remain possible if fragmentation is introduced. If one were comfortable thinking of the world's allocations of factors as being somehow randomly determined given its total endowments and the parameters of technology and tastes, then it would say that the likelihood of FPE either rises or stays the same with fragmentation; it cannot fall.

Thus fragmentation may well cause factor prices to become equalized across countries. The analysis here does *not* say, however, that, failing that, factor prices will be drawn closer together by fragmentation. Fig. 4 certainly suggests that result in a special case. There, if the endowment point were above the k_Z ray rather than below it as drawn, then indeed factor prices in the country would remain different from those in the world after fragmentation but would be drawn closer to them.[15] As far as I know, however, that is not a general result. In fact, we are surprisingly ignorant (or at least I am) of how the higher-dimensional H-O model behaves outside of the FPE region, or when the lens condition of Deardorff (1994) is not satisfied.

4. Conclusion

The underlying question addressed in this paper is, "Does fragmentation matter?" Or, since this is a theoretical piece, not empirical, "Can it matter?" The answer seems to be a relatively strong "Yes."

Of course, fragmentation will *not* matter if factor prices are equal everywhere, for then the fragmented technologies will at best duplicate what was done without them and there will be no reason to use them. But if factor prices are not equal across countries, either because technologies differ as in the Ricardian model or because factor endowments are less similar than factor intensities in the H-O model, then fragmentation can certainly make a difference. The main effects of fragmentation, at least as I have been able to identify them from these simple models, are as follows (all assuming that fragmented technologies are used at all):

1. If fragmentation does not change the prices of goods, then it must increase the value of output of any country where it occurs and that of the world.
2. If fragmentation does change prices, then fragmentation can lower the welfare of a country by turning its terms of trade against it.
3. Even in a country that gains from fragmentation, it is possible (but not necessary) that some factor owners within that country will lose.
4. To the extent that factor prices are not equalized internationally without fragmentation, fragmentation may be a force toward factor price equalization.

Notes

1. The term "fragmentation" comes from Jones and Kierzkowski (2001). Several other terms for this phenomenon were also suggested at the NAEFA session, none seeming to generate a consensus.
2. Even without any saving in resources, fragmentation could occur within a country for a variety of reasons. Perhaps the most obvious is if labor markets are not competitive, so that wages are bid up in some sectors by the bargaining power of unions. Fragmentation in order to divert some parts of a production process outside the purview of the union then makes obvious economic sense. Even with perfect competition, if a country is "lumpy"—that is, if different equilibrium wages are paid in different regions within the country as in Courant and Deardorff (1992)—then fragmentation may occur across regions for much the same reasons as the international fragmentation I will examine here.
3. There have been many surveys of this voluminous "trade and wages" literature, most recently by Johnson and Stafford (1997). One pair of papers that has focused attention on outsourcing is Feenstra and Hanson (1996, 1997).
4. The literature now also includes two of the other papers prepared for the NAEFA session for which this was written. Not coincidentally, they are by the same authors: Arndt (1998) and another paper by Jones and Kierzkowski for which I do not have the exact citation. The empirical literature on fragmentation has also been expanded with a new paper by Slaughter that I also don't have.
5. The analysis here is general enough, both in this section and the next, to include the sorts of disembodied contributions to a firm's operations that Helpman (1984) took to be the hallmark of a multinational corporation. Although I will define each fragmented part of the production process as producing an intermediate input that is then used in the next stage of production, this intermediate input can be a fiction, at least until one attempts to apply this approach to the data.
6. Trade in X and Y are not shown, since they depend on preferences and income. Good

Y, which is not produced, must be imported for all p_Z, although the quantity imported will be somewhat larger when the fragmented technology is being used, due to the country's higher income, and it will fall with p_Z for low p_Z and rise with p_Z for high p_Z due to changes in the terms of trade in *Z*. When only good *X* is produced, then part of it must be exported in exchange for Y, while it must be imported when it is not produced. Again, the quantities kept or imported depend on real income, which is larger when the fragmented technology is being employed and depends then on the p_Z.

7. This midrange will exist even if fragmentation in the import-competing good is costless, since fragmented production must now overcome the comparative disadvantage in (2).
8. Again, this intermediate input need not be a physical entity, and therefore could represent, say, the "headquarter services" that Helpman (1984) and others have used to model multinational corporations. For my purposes, it is immaterial (literally) whether the different fragments of production are performed within a single firm or between firms. This generality is desirable, of course, but it also means that none of the results of this section are really new. They are merely extensions of what was shown by Helpman (1984) and Helpman and Krugman (1985). I am grateful to Steve Matusz for pointing this out.
9. If these were drawn correctly, then the $X = 1$ isoquant could be traced out by the origin for the $XZ = 1$ isoquant as it slides around the $Z = 1$ isoquant. The construction is much the same as we used to use to construct Scitovsky indifference curves. Remember them?
10. I have not shown that gain, but I hope it is clear. Fragmentation has expanded the small country's production possibilities, and at fixed prices this can only help.
11. Years ago, I incorrectly attributed this diagram to Helpman and Krugman in the presence of both Elhanan Helpman and Avinash Dixit and had my attention gently directed toward Dixit and Norman (1980). More recently, Bob Baldwin has sent me further back, to Travis (1964). While Travis did not speak by that name of an "integrated world economy," he certainly used the concept and drew the diagram (on p. 16) for exactly the purpose of identifying a factor price equalization region. Travis in turn called it an Edgeworth box, although I am not aware (never having read Edgeworth) that Edgeworth ever used his boxes quite this way, with factor endowments measured from the corners. All of this is surely known to scholars, but the rest of us have to pick it up wherever we can.
12. If we assume fixed-coefficient technologies, then this is necessarily the case, since good and factor prices will leave the factor use vectors unchanged. Of course in that case, part of the capital in Country A of Fig. 5 would be unemployed and the rental on capital would be zero. However the changes in factor prices identified in Fig. 4 would still occur, in amplified form.
13. Suppose $x \in \mathcal{L}(v^0)$. Then from (6) $\exists b \ni x = bv^0 = b\Sigma v_i^1$ which implies $x \in \mathcal{L}(v^1)$.
14. See Debaere and Demiroglu (1997), who note the same thing in a different context. Their result is that the measured factor use lens will lie within the true one if measured industries are aggregated.
15. Such a result may exist, but I am pessimistic. After wasting several years trying to

show that free trade must draw factor prices closer together, only to find the counter-example presented in Deardorff (1986), I will not be surprised if fragmentation admits of equally poorly behaved possibilities in a general model.

Acknowledgments

I have benefited from discussions on this topic with Peter Debaere, Sven Arndt, and other participants in the Globalization workshop held at Claremont in January 1997, as well as participants in the NAEFA session for which the paper was initially written, including my discussant, Matthew Slaughter.

References

Arndt, Sven W. (1997). Globalization and the open economy. *North American Journal of Economics and Finance, 8* (1).

Arndt, Sven W. (1998). Super-specialization and the gains from trade. *Contemporary Economic Policy, XVI* (October).

Courant, Paul N., & Deardorff, Alan V. (1992). International trade with lumpy countries. *Journal of Political Economy, 100* (February), 198–210.

Deardorff, Alan V. (1986). FIRless FIRwoes: how preferences can interfere with the theorems of international trade. *Journal of International Economics, 20* (February), 131–142.

Deardorff, Alan V. (1994). The possibility of factor price equalization, revisited. *Journal of International Economics, 36,* 167–175.

Debaere, Peter, & Demiroglu, Ufuk (1997). On the similarity of country endowments and factor price equalization among developed countries. In process, November 1.

Dixit, Avinash K., & Norman, Victor (1980). *Theory of international trade.* London: Cambridge University Press.

Feenstra, Robert C., & Hanson, Gordon H. (1996). Globalization, outsourcing, and wage inequality. *American Economic Review, 86* (May), 240–245.

Feenstra, Robert C., & Hanson, Gordon H. (1997). Productivity measurement, outsourcing, and its impact on wages: estimates for the U.S., 1972–1990. NBER Working Paper No. 6052, June.

Helpman, Elhanan (1984). A simple theory of international trade with multinational corporations. *Journal of Political Economy, 92* (June), 451–471.

Helpman, Elhanan, & Krugman, Paul R. (1985). *Market structure and foreign trade: increasing returns, imperfect competition, and the international economy.* Cambridge, MA: MIT Press.

Johnson, George E., & Stafford, Frank (1997). The labor market implications of international trade. In O. Ashenfelter & D. Card (Eds.), *Handbook of labor economics,* vols. III and IV. North-Holland.

Jones, Ronald W., & Kierzkowski, Henry (2001). Globalization and the consequences of international fragmentation. In R. Dornbusch, G. Calvo, & M. Obstfeld (Eds.), *Money, factor mobility and trade.* Cambridge, MA: MIT Press.

Melvin, James R. (1968). Production and trade with two factors and three goods. *American Economic Review, 58* (December), 1248–1268.

Travis, William Penfield (1964). *The theory of trade and protection.* Cambridge, MA: Harvard University Press.

CHAPTER 17

Review of International Economics, 13(5), 1004–1016, 2005

How Robust is Comparative Advantage?

*Alan V. Deardorff**

Abstract

This paper reviews the theoretical development of the concept of comparative advantage, starting with the two-good model of Ricardo and the two-good extension and reinterpretation by Haberler. In both, the presence of comparative advantage provides the scope for countries to gain from trade by specializing, and the pattern of that trade is explained by the pattern of comparative advantage. These strong results of the two-good model can be extended under certain circumstances to multiple goods and countries, but under more general assumptions such strong results no longer are assured. Instead one can derive much weaker results, usually in the form of correlations between comparative advantage and trade, and these weaker results hold in a much wider variety of circumstances. The paper examines those assumptions that permit such generalizations, but then also examines when those assumptions are most likely to fail, and what happens as a result.

1. Introduction

Comparative advantage is certainly one of the most basic ideas in economics, underlying much of our understanding both of why countries trade the way that they do and why they benefit from doing so. But it is also a difficult concept for many people to understand, and seemingly even more difficult for them to believe once they do understand it (and especially if they don't). It is common to hear critics of trade say that comparative advantage may have been valid two centuries ago when David Ricardo first proposed it, but that for various reasons it is wrong or irrelevant in the world of today. Therefore it is perhaps worthwhile to restate just what comparative advantage means, and what it does and does not imply. In this paper I will review what I think we know, from the standpoint of economic theory, about the meaning and the generality of comparative advantage.

I will start, in section 2, by recalling the simplest models in which comparative advantage plays its strongest role: the Ricardian model in terms of labor costs and Haberler's model in terms of opportunity cost, both in the two-good context in which simple diagrams provide compelling illustrations. I will then explore some simple generalizations of these results, especially to more goods and countries, in section 3. But I will also note the limitation of these generalizations for making strong statements about the pattern of trade. In section 4 I recall my own result from 25 years ago, showing that a particular definition of comparative advantage suffices under quite general assumptions to provide a very weak explanation of patterns of trade in the sense of a correlation, and I examine the assumptions under which this result both does, and does not, hold. I conclude in section 5 with—what else?—my conclusion from all of this.

---

*Deardorff: Department of Economics, University of Michigan, Ann Arbor, MI 48109-1220, USA. Tel: 734-764-6817; Fax: 734-763-9181; E-mail: alandear@umich.edu. I have benefited from the comments of participants at the January AEA session, including especially Daniel Bernhofen, Bill Ethier, and Ron Jones. Jonathan Eaton also alerted me to an error in my thinking that I have since corrected.

2. Comparative Advantage with Two Goods: Ricardo, Haberler

Ricardo presented comparative advantage with a numerical example of two goods and two countries. Production required labor only, and in fixed amounts per unit of output. Comparative advantage was therefore defined naturally in terms of the unit labor requirements (or equivalently, labor productivities) in the two industries and two countries. Letting a_g^c be the amount of labor needed to produce one unit of good g in country c, then country 1 has a comparative advantage in producing good 1, compared to country 2 and good 2, if it can produce it with less labor relative to good 2, compared to country 2:

$$\frac{a_1^1}{a_2^1} < \frac{a_1^2}{a_2^2}. \tag{1}$$

The importance of this can be shown in several ways. One is to look at the possible world outputs of the two goods by the countries together, assuming that each has a fixed endowment of labor. It can then be shown that world output is increased if one or both specialize in producing only the good in which it has a comparative advantage. Equivalently, one can show that an appropriate marginal reallocation of labor in both countries, in the direction of their respective comparative advantages, will increase world output of one or both goods. Both of these results can also be illustrated in terms of production possibility frontiers (PPFs) as in Figure 1, where the left and middle panels show PPFs for countries 1 and 2 respectively. The right panel shows their sum—that is, the set of all possible world outputs obtained by adding feasible output vectors from countries 1 and 2. Condition (1) implies that the PPF of country 1 is flatter than that of country 2, as drawn. And this in turn implies, as seen in the figure, that the world PPF can be reached only by one or both countries specializing completely in the good in which it has a comparative advantage.

Arguments such as these show that, for the world to enjoy more of goods 1 and 2 than are available in autarky, specialization in accord with comparative advantage is necessary. That does not, in and of itself however, imply either of the properties that we normally associate with comparative advantage: that countries individually gain from comparative-advantage-determined trade, and that free trade will in fact lead to countries specializing in this way. For these implications, we need not just the presence of comparative advantage, but also an economic structure that induces the countries to take maximal advantage of their production and trade possibilities. Such a structure is provided by perfect competition, with profit-maximizing producers and utility-maximizing consumers interacting atomistically to achieve maximum value and

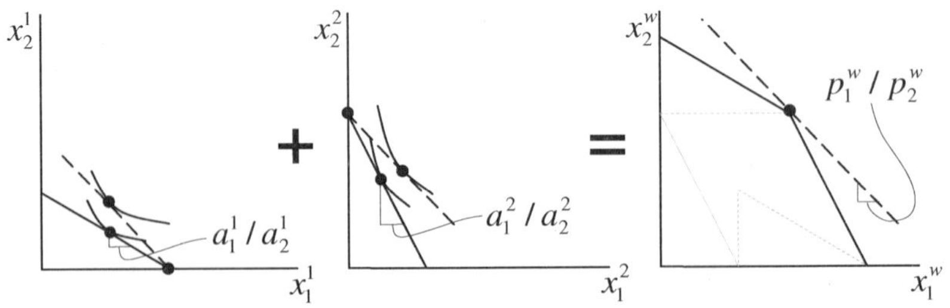

Figure 1. The Ricardian Model: Production Possibilities and a Free-Trade Equilibrium

utility at given prices, which are in turn determined so as to clear markets. In that case, and assuming also free and frictionless trade, world prices will be determined to support production on the world PPF with one or both countries therefore specializing in its comparative-advantage good and therefore necessarily exporting it to the other country. Such a free-trade equilibrium is shown by the dashed lines in Figure 1.

A strict gain from trade in this case is not assured, since one country may find that equilibrium world prices are exactly equal to its autarky prices, and therefore that it neither gains nor loses from trade. And indeed we cannot really ascribe the avoidance of loss from trade to the presence of comparative advantage, since the competitive structure assures it. On the other hand, it is true that if a Ricardian economy does gain from trade, consuming therefore outside its PPF, then in a perfectly competitive market economy it can only do so if it does in fact export the good in which it has a comparative advantage.

Thus the gains from trade and the pattern of trade are related, but not in the sense that trade according to comparative advantage is necessarily strictly beneficial. Rather it is the gain from trade that implies the pattern of trade, not the reverse. A country that gains from trade at some particular world prices must, in this model, specialize in the good whose world relative price is higher than its autarky relative cost, while a country that neither gains nor loses from trade must face world prices equal to its costs. Thus if one or both countries gain from trade, while neither lose, world prices must lie at or between their relative costs, implying that each country exports the good in which it has comparative advantage.

The Ricardian model is special in many ways, but the most obvious difference from more standard modern trade models is the assumption of constant costs. Both the Heckscher–Ohlin model and the specific factors model have marginal costs that increase as more of a good is produced, leading to production possibilities that are concave to the origin, as in the left and middle panels of Figure 2. In such a framework, which was considered by Haberler (1930), comparative costs are not uniquely defined, since they depend on the particular points on two countries' respective PPFs that are selected for comparison. Nonetheless the behavior of countries in such a model is not that much different from the Ricardian model, except for the fact that countries can now continue to produce both goods even at prices that differ from autarky.

Haberler's contribution here was to recognize that what was important for trade, the gains from trade, and comparative advantage, even in the Ricardian model, was not labor costs *per se*, but rather the opportunity cost, at the margin, of producing one good instead of another. If this varies with levels of output, as in Figure 2, then marginal opportunity costs may become equalized as a result of trade (if it is free), and

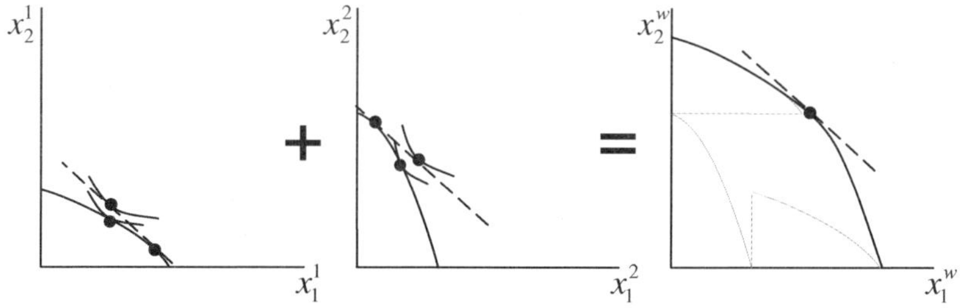

Figure 2. Haberler Model: Production Possibilities and a Free-Trade Equilibrium

thus become unhelpful as a guide to trade. But marginal opportunity costs in autarky, given by the slope of the PPF at the autarky equilibrium, are in any case the more relevant indicator, both of the potential for gain from trade and of the direction of specialization needed to achieve it. For if opportunity costs differ between two countries in autarky, then a small reallocation of resources increasing the output in each country of the good for which its opportunity cost is smaller than abroad, will again permit a rise in world output. Under the Ricardian assumption of constant labor requirements, low opportunity cost is equivalent to low relative unit labor requirements, and it therefore provides an equivalent definition of comparative advantage. In more general models, a comparison of marginal opportunity cost at the autarky equilibria is the more valid and useful definition of comparative advantage.

As in the Ricardian model, the existence of comparative advantage by the opportunity-cost definition has its most direct implication for the gains from trade. If opportunity costs differ in autarky, then with perfect competition free trade will lead to gains from trade for one or both countries. Indeed strict gains for both countries now occur so long as both PPFs are strictly concave—i.e. if marginal opportunity cost is strictly increasing as output rises. On the other hand, if opportunity costs do not differ in autarky, so that neither country has a comparative advantage in either good, then there is no scope for gain from trade in this model.

The implication for the pattern of trade then follows from the gains from trade. If, for example, a country were to export the good in which it does not have a comparative advantage, perhaps by subsidizing its production or its export, then it would necessarily lose from trade. This is illustrated in Figure 3, where a country faces a world relative price of good 1 that is higher than its autarky price, so that it has a comparative advantage in good 1. But here I suppose that it nonetheless produces less of good 1, and more of good 2, than in autarky, resulting in exporting good 2. As can be seen, its loses from this trade. Thus, in order to gain from trade such a country must export the good in which it has comparative advantage.[1]

It should be noted too that while trade in accord with comparative advantage is necessary for the gains from trade, it is not sufficient, even in this simple model. Figure 4 shows a case of a country with comparative advantage in good 1 that expands production too far in the direction of good 1—perhaps due to a subsidy to its production

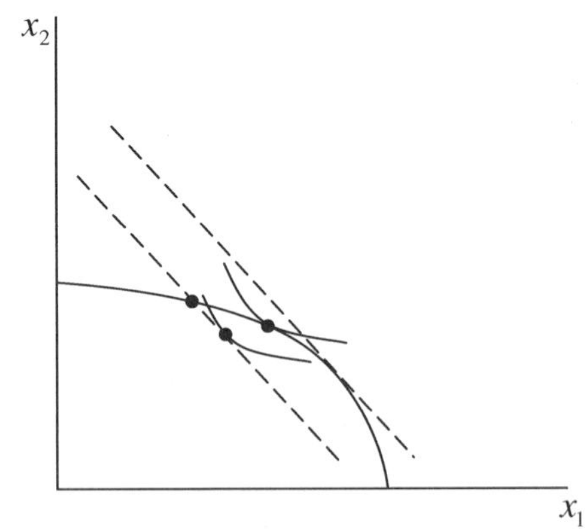

Figure 3. Trade Contrary to Comparative Advantage Reduces Welfare

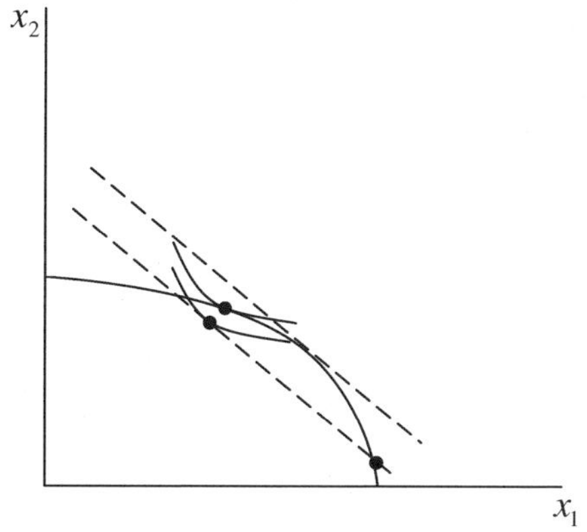

Figure 4. Too Much Trade in Accord with Comparative Advantage Reduces Welfare

or export—and as a result makes itself worse off by trade, even though that trade is in the direction dictated by comparative advantage.

The conclusion, then, from both the Ricardian and the Haberler two-good models, is that comparative advantage can be usefully defined in terms of a comparison of relative autarky prices, which also represent marginal opportunity costs in autarky. A difference in relative autarky prices, and thus the presence of comparative advantage, implies the potential to increase world output by reallocating resources within the two countries. Combined with market structures of perfect competition, comparative advantage also implies that unless policies interfere with market incentives, countries stand to gain from trade in the sense that at least one country will gain and neither will lose. And this gain from trade is achievable only if countries each export the good in which they have comparative advantage.

3. Strong Generalizations

The Ricardian model generalizes easily to more than two of either goods or countries, though not quite so easily to more than two of both together. The strong generalization is in terms of a "chain of comparative advantage." This was shown first, it seems, by Haberler (1930) himself, for the Ricardian model. That is, suppose that there are two countries, as before, but multiple goods $g = 1, \ldots, G$. Number the goods in order of country 1's relative labor requirements:

$$\frac{a_1^1}{a_1^2} < \frac{a_2^1}{a_2^2} < \cdots < \frac{a_G^1}{a_G^2}. \tag{2}$$

Then it can be shown that all of country 1's exports will lie to the left in this chain of all of country 2's exports. With free trade there will exist a single "break" in this chain, either between two goods or exactly at one of them, such that country 1 will export all goods to the left of this break and import all goods to its right. Indeed, this result is easily extended to an infinite number of goods, as done by Dornbusch et al. (1977).

Similarly, if there are only two goods but multiple countries, $c = 1, \ldots, C$, then a similar ranking can be constructed over the countries' relative labor requirements for producing the two goods:

$$\frac{a_1^1}{a_2^1} < \frac{a_1^2}{a_2^2} < \cdots < \frac{a_1^C}{a_2^C}. \tag{3}$$

Now all exporters of good 1 will lie to the left of all exporters of good 2, and with free trade a single break in this chain will separate all exporters of good 1 on the left from all importers of good 1 on the right.

These are nice results, but their generality is of course limited by the fact that the world inconveniently seems to contain more than two of *both* goods and countries. This can be gotten around, perhaps, by aggregating either goods or countries, although the assumptions needed to do that cleanly are unlikely to be believable. The two-country chain in (2) at least has the advantage that one of the countries can be taken to represent the rest of the world, especially if the country concerned is small. In that case, labor requirements in the large country 2 can be replaced by world prices:

$$\frac{a_1^1}{p_1^w} < \frac{a_2^1}{p_2^w} < \cdots < \frac{a_G^1}{p_G^w}. \tag{4}$$

This permits a single country's trade in all goods to be determined by this ranking of its labor costs relative to world prices.

Also, both of these chain results can be used to make partial statements about patterns of trade in just two goods or two countries, even when there exist more than two of both. For example, using (2), if countries 1 and 2 are any two of a larger number of countries in the world, we can still say that with free trade all of the goods that country 1 exports (to country 2 or otherwise), and that country 2 does not export, will lie to the left in this chain of all of the goods that country 2 does export. Of course, any number of the goods may not be exported by either country, and these may lie anywhere in the chain. So this result does not as fully specify the pattern of trade as in the two-country case. But it still shows some role for comparative advantage.

Similarly, (3) can be used with more than two goods to clarify which of many countries may export a particular pair of goods, 1 and 2. That is, all of the countries that export good 1 and not good 2 must lie to the left in this chain of all of the countries that export good 2. Again this tells us nothing about the positions of countries that export neither good.

A more complete specification of the patterns of specialization and trade in the Ricardian model with many goods and countries was provided by Jones (1961). He showed that an efficient assignment of countries to goods in a many-good, many-country Ricardian model is to minimize the product of countries' unit labor requirements. This is a bit less complete than it sounds, however, because the question of how many countries produce each good must be solved separately. Nonetheless it shows compellingly that specialization is associated somehow with low unit labor requirements. Also "low" here must be interpreted in comparison to other countries and other goods, much as in (1), since the model requires that each country produce something, and thus contribute at least one of its unit labor requirements to one of these products.

Allowing for increasing costs, as in Haberler's model, the chain result in (3)—for two goods and multiple countries—is easily extended. Simply replace the a's with autarky prices, $\tilde{p}_g^c$, for good g in country c:

$$\frac{\tilde{p}_1^1}{\tilde{p}_2^1} < \frac{\tilde{p}_1^2}{\tilde{p}_2^2} < \cdots < \frac{\tilde{p}_1^C}{\tilde{p}_2^C}. \tag{5}$$

The result then holds exactly as in the Ricardian case: all of the countries that export good 1 will lie to the left of all countries that import it. This follows easily from the fact that each country has an excess supply of, say, x_1 for any world relative price of x_1 that is above its autarky price, and an excess demand below.

The result for multiple goods is harder to get, since in general the relative supplies of two goods may depend on the price of a third. However, in the special case of the Heckscher–Ohlin model with multiple goods but just two factors of production, the multi-good chain result generalizes easily for countries whose factor endowments place them in different cones of specialization. Such countries will specialize in different goods, and under free trade those goods will be distinct in terms of the intensity with which they use the factors. That is, goods can be ranked in terms of, say, their relative capital intensity compared to labor, in much the same way that they are ranked in (2). Indeed, that ranking also corresponds to their relative autarky prices, and thus to their marginal opportunity costs, exactly as in Haberler's model with increasing costs. And that ranking suffices to determine trade in the same manner as the chain proposition: all of the exports of a country in a more capital-abundant cone of specialization will be more capital-intensive than all of the exports of a country in a less capital-abundant cone. Indeed, this is also true in this model under free trade with large numbers of both goods and factors. All of this was shown, for example, in Deardorff (1979).

That paper also shows, however, that this strong relationship may break down if we move away from free trade. Without free trade countries face different prices, and with multiple goods, prices of one good can alter the viability of producing another good in ways that interfere with comparative advantage. The simplest such case—shown in Deardorff (1979) for the Heckscher–Ohlin model and in Deardorff (2005) for the Ricardian model—is when some goods serve as intermediate inputs to the production of other goods. Then a trade barrier on an input that raises its price can make production of the corresponding final good too costly to survive, even though the country might otherwise possess a relatively low cost of producing the final good. Also, and even without intermediate inputs, the combination of both multiple countries and multiple goods can, in the presence of trade barriers, alter factor prices sufficiently to change the entire set of goods in which a country can compete with its many trading partners. Thus, although comparative advantage provides rather strong predictions of trade patterns in simple cases, it fails to do so in models that allow for even a small amount of realistic complication, such as trade barriers, intermediate inputs, and large numbers of both countries and goods.

This is *only* true, however, of the ability of comparative advantage to predict trade patterns. It should not be forgotten that another implication of comparative advantage—and arguably the more important one—is that it predicts and explains gains from trade. This implication is not in the least undermined by the difficulties just mentioned of using comparative advantage to predict trade patterns.

Admittedly this is partly because an important part of the gains-from-trade result has nothing to do with comparative advantage, but arises simply from perfect competition. One of the theorems of welfare economics tells us that, if an economy has perfect competition and a convex technology, then a market equilibrium will be Pareto-optimal. A corollary of that result is the basic gains-from-trade result of Samuelson (1939) that free trade cannot make a country worse off compared to autarky, and will make it better off as long as it faces prices, with trade, that differ from those in autarky. All that comparative advantage does is to provide a reason for prices with trade to differ from autarky, and thus to assure that the gains from trade are positive rather than zero.

But even though this contribution may be small, it is nonetheless important. While as trade economists we may be very interested in explaining the pattern of trade, the important message of comparative advantage theory for the world is that trade is beneficial. And it is this message that the public most often distrusts. We must be careful not to let any failures of theory to predict trade patterns suggest that we also have doubts about the welfare implications of comparative advantage. There may be good reasons to doubt that trade in the real world is beneficial, but these reasons should rest on departures from the assumptions of the basic welfare theorem—market failures, non-convex technologies, etc.—not on the sorts of things that may cause comparative advantage to mis-predict the pattern of trade.

4. Weak Generalizations

The failure of chain propositions to survive the introduction of trade barriers and intermediate inputs does not mean that comparative advantage can say nothing at all about the pattern of trade. What is needed, however, is to weaken what we attempt to say. Instead of trying to make statements that apply to every good, for example ("every export lies to the left of every import"), we might look for only average relationships ("exports lie on average to the left of imports"). This, in effect, is what has been found to be theoretically true as indicated by correlations.

Such results were first derived independently by Dixit and Norman (1980) and Deardorff (1980). Using autarky prices as indicators of comparative advantage, and letting T_g^c be the net exports of good g by country c, both showed that

$$\tilde{p}^c T^c = \sum_g \tilde{p}_g^c T_g^c < 0. \tag{6}$$

On its face, since the vector T^c is a mixture of both positive and negative elements (exports and imports), and since autarky prices are all positive, this result suggests that exports have on average lower autarky prices than imports.

For a simple example, consider a small open economy that faces given world prices p_g^w and whose trade is balanced at those prices. Then separating the vector T_g^c into its positive and negative components, $X_g^c = \max\{T_g^c, 0\}$ and $M_g^c = \max\{-T_g^c, 0\}$, (6) implies:

$$\sum_g \frac{\tilde{p}_g^c}{p_g^w} \frac{p_g^w T_g^c}{\overline{X}^c} < \sum_g \frac{\tilde{p}_g^c}{p_g^w} \frac{p_g^w M_g^c}{\overline{M}^c}, \tag{7}$$

where $\overline{X}^c = \overline{M}^c = \Sigma_g p_g^w X_g^c$. That is, the trade-weighted average of the country's autarky prices of goods it exports, relative to world prices, is less than the trade-weighted average of the relative prices of its imports.

An equivalent but more flexible way to formalizing such averages is to examine correlations. In Deardorff (1980) I derive four of them, the broadest being a negative correlation across all goods and countries between autarky prices and quantities of net exports.[2]

These results are certainly weak, since they do not tell us whether any particular good will be exported or imported by any particular country. That is appropriate, however, since the assumptions needed to derive these results are general enough to include those features—intermediate inputs and trade barriers, in particular—that could potentially cause any particular good to be traded in either direction. I will discuss those assumptions in a moment.

But before I do, let me note that, in an important sense, these correlation results are just as strong as what the Ricardian and Haberler models are able to say in the two-good, two-country case. In those simple models, there are really only two ways that (balanced) trade can proceed: country 1 exports good 1 and imports good 2; or it exports good 2 and imports good 1. Comparative advantage cuts the set of possible outcomes in half: given inequality (1), only the first of these possibilities can arise. The correlation result also cuts the set of possible trade patterns—which is of course much larger when there are many goods and countries—in half: only those trade patterns that give rise to the specified negative correlation can arise.

Under what assumptions do these results obtain? This is important, because the whole point of the exercise is that it is more general than the other formulations discussed earlier. Although these assumptions are stated in Deardorff (1980), and also in a sequel that relaxed some of them in Deardorff (1994), it may be worthwhile to give them more explicit attention. The following are the assumptions that are accommodated in these two papers, and thus that are consistent with the theoretical validity of at least some version of the comparative-advantage correlation result:

Assumptions Consistent with Comparative-Advantage Correlation

- **Multiple goods and countries:** this is of course the assumption that I have stressed here, since it presents the most immediate difficulty for extending the graphical kinds of analysis in Figures 1 and 2. It is also the assumption that was most glaringly needed when others attempted to take the trade theory of two-dimensions to the data.
- **Tariffs and other artificial trade costs:** in two-good models, tariffs only reduce the volume of trade but cannot change its direction. With many goods this is not the case, for particular goods as already noted. But it turns out that artificial barriers to trade cannot overturn the correlation result unless they act, on net, to encourage trade rather than limit it. Thus sufficiently large export subsidies could overturn comparative advantage, as we saw in Figure 3, but as long as trade policies restrict trade rather than promoting it, both the gains from trade and the average relationship between comparative advantage and trade will continue to hold. This is perhaps important, if only because of the common public perception that if other countries are restricting trade, then the theory of comparative advantage is somehow undermined and that therefore our country should restrict trade as well.[3]
- **Transport costs and other real trade costs:** transport costs have effects similar to tariffs, and they serve to discourage trade, not to promote it, so it is not surprising that they too leave the weak version of the law of comparative advantage unscathed. Their analysis is somewhat trickier than tariffs, however, because of their use of real resources.[4] Only recently have transport costs been given much attention in the trade field,[5] and in theoretical models they are still often formulated in the clever but unrealistic form of "iceberg costs," following Samuelson (1952). Fortunately, that simplification is not necessary for the correlation result, which permits all manner of resources to be used in accomplishing trade over all manner of routes.[6]
- **Intermediate inputs:** as noted above, it is the combination of trade costs with intermediate inputs that creates the most obvious problems for strong formulations of comparative advantage. Fortunately, the correlation result is proved for a formulation of technology that imposes no meaningful restriction on the use of goods as inputs to other goods. Thus all goods may be final goods, intermediate goods, or both. This aspect of the result seems to be increasingly important as "foreign outsourcing," or "offshoring," leads to increasing trade in intermediate inputs.

- **Arbitrary preferences:** results in trade theory sometimes require rather strong assumptions about preferences, most commonly that they be homothetic. That is not the case for comparative advantage, which remains valid for all possible shapes of preferences. The result does require the Weak Axiom of Revealed Preference, which amounts essentially to assuming that countries behave as if they have well-defined community preferences. That is restrictive. But once you have those preferences, they may take any form.
- **Goods may be services:** although the items produced and traded in the formal model are called goods, they can just as well be services. In Deardorff (1985) I allow for services explicitly, taking account of various features that might differentiate services from goods, and I show there that the correlation result continues to hold.
- **Goods may be dated:** one can, in principle, treat goods produced in different years as different goods, and then view the model as describing equilibrium over time. This poses no problem for the correlation result, although it does perhaps limit its usefulness, since by saying nothing about trade in particular goods it now also says nothing about trade in particular years, such as the present.
- **Goods may be differentiated:** more generally, any amount of product differentiation can be allowed, simply by defining differentiated products as different goods (though subject to the strong restriction that markets for these differentiated goods still be perfectly competitive).
- **Trade may be unbalanced:** in Deardorff (1994) I dropped the assumption of balanced trade and found two ways that the correlation result would still hold. One was the aforementioned dating of goods, extending the correlation across time, the usefulness of which is that it allows a comparative-advantage explanation of why countries may run trade deficits and surpluses at different points in their life cycles. The other was to look at trade at a single time, at which it can still be shown to conform to comparative advantage even with a trade imbalance under the additional assumption that preferences are homothetic.
- **Countries may be lumpy:** failure of markets to be perfect within countries can certainly interfere with comparative advantage, as I will note below. However, one kind of imperfection does not seem to cause problems. If factors are immobile across geographical regions within a country—what in Courant and Deardorff (1992) we called "lumpy countries"—then I show in Deardorff (1994) that the comparative advantage correlations still go through.

This list of assumptions is rather long, intended to suggest that the law of comparative advantage really is quite robust. And importantly it should be understood that the proof of the correlation result starts, in all these cases, with showing the gains from trade, from which the pattern of trade then follows just as in the simpler models. However, there are plenty of assumptions that are not included in this list, and these suggest ways that, most importantly, countries may lose from trade and, less importantly, that the pattern of trade may not accord with comparative advantage. The most important of these seem to be the following:

Assumptions Inconsistent with Comparative-Advantage Correlation

- **Domestic distortions:** the perfectly competitive paradigm rests, of course, on the assumption that prices reflect true marginal costs and benefits. If there are external economies or diseconomies in production or consumption, or if market power causes prices to exceed marginal costs, then this will not be true. And if it is not, then economies will fail to maximize the value of their output, perhaps both with and without trade, and the arguments for comparative advantage do not go through. In Deardorff (1994) I briefly addressed this issue and showed that comparative advantage can be salvaged under a particular assumption about how distortions correlate with the changes in output that occur with trade. Unfortunately, this assumption is not particularly plausible. Therefore, for now at least, I think we must accept that domestic distortions interfere with the case for comparative advantage working its magic.

- **Increasing returns:** similarly, and often related to distortions, technologies may not be convex. If they are not, then this too interferes with the ability of a market economy to maximize value, especially globally, and as is well known this can lead countries to lose from trade. This is true even if the increasing returns are external to the firm, permitting markets to remain perfectly competitive. But in fact increasing returns are also likely to lead to market power of large firms and therefore cause domestic distortions along with non-convexity. In any case, my impression is that increasing returns are hard to reconcile with comparative advantage.

These assumptions undeniably cause problems for the theory of comparative advantage, both as a source of gains from trade and as a predictor of patterns of trade. And unfortunately there is also no denying that both domestic distortions and increasing returns are pervasive facts of economic life. What should be stressed, however, is that neither of these assumptions works systematically *against* comparative advantage, thus making its role less and less likely the more common they are. Rather, what these assumptions do is to complicate the story, not reverse it, and to complicate it to the point that we can no longer make confident predictions based on current knowledge.

A particular distortion such as a negative externality from production, for example, if it occurs in an export sector may reverse the gains from trade. But if the same distortion occurs in an import-competing sector, it will increase the gains from trade. And since a given sector must exist as both export and import competing in different countries, there may be no presumption that the existence of this distortion reduces the gains from trade worldwide. Likewise, the presence of increasing returns is known to increase gains from trade in some countries at the same time that it decreases or reverses them in others. Therefore, the very fact that distortions and increasing returns are ubiquitous may mean that their positive and negative effects on the gains from trade in different countries and industries will cancel out.

Or maybe not. Perhaps there is structure that we have not explored that will bias the net effects of all these complications in one direction or the other, either for or against trade. I don't know. My point here is just that the mere presence of frequent instances of distortion and increasing returns suggests only that we are ignorant, not necessarily that we are wrong.

5. Conclusion

Where does all this leave us? My own stake in this discussion probably would make it impossible for me to accept that comparative advantage is a useless concept. But I hope that the arguments reviewed here will convince others, too, that the concept of comparative advantage tells us something fundamentally important about the effects and determinants of international trade. A single concept can hardly be expected to explain every aspect of something as widespread and complicated as trade. But the theory gives good reason to believe that comparative advantage works, on average, to provide the potential for gain from trade and to explain what the nature of beneficial trade is likely to be.

References

Anderson, James E. and Eric van Wincoop, "Trade Costs," *Journal of Economic Literature* 42 (2004):691–751.

Courant, Paul N. and Alan V. Deardorff, "International Trade with Lumpy Countries," *Journal of Political Economy* 100 (1992):198–210.

Deardorff, Alan V., "Weak Links in the Chain of Comparative Advantage," *Journal of International Economics* 9 (1979):197–209.

———, "The General Validity of the Law of Comparative Advantage," *Journal of Political Economy* 88 (1980):941–57.

———, "Comparative Advantage and International Trade and Investment in Services," in Robert M. Stern (ed.), *Trade and Investment in Services: Canada/US Perspectives*, Toronto: Ontario Economic Council (1985):39–71.

———, "Exploring the Limits of Comparative Advantage," *Weltwirtschaftliches Archiv* 130 (1994):1–19.

———, "Ricardian Comparative Advantage with Intermediate Inputs," *North American Journal of Economics and Finance* 16 (2005):11–34.

Dixit, Avinash K. and Victor Norman, *Theory of International Trade*, London: Cambridge University Press (1980).

Dornbusch, Rudiger, Stanley Fischer, and Paul A. Samuelson, "Comparative Advantage, Trade, and Payments in a Ricardian Model with a Continuum of Goods," *American Economic Review* 67 (1977):823–39.

Haberler, Gottfried, "The Theory of Comparative Cost and Its Use in the Defense of Free Trade" (1930); originally published in German in *Weltwirtschaftliches Archiv* 32 (1930):349–70; translated and reprinted in Anthony Y. C. Koo (ed.), *Selected Essays of Gottfried Haberler*, Cambridge, MA: MIT Press (1985):3–19.

Jones, Ronald W., "Comparative Advantage and the Theory of Tariffs: a Multi-Country, Multi-Commodity Model," *Review of Economic Studies* 28 (1961):161–75.

Samuelson, Paul A., "The Gains from International Trade," *Canadian Journal of Economics and Political Science* 5 (1939):195–205.

———, "The Transfer Problem and Transport Costs," *Economic Journal* 62 (1952): 278–304.

Notes

1. In this case and the next, the figures show the case of a production subsidy, not an export subsidy. An export subsidy would cause a further drop in welfare as the consumption choice would also be distorted.

2. To get from an inner product of two vectors like (6) to a correlation, one works through the covariance, which is also the difference between the inner product and a product of the two vectors' means. The correlation therefore has the same sign as the inner product if one of the vector means is zero. In the four corollaries of Deardorff (1980), I formulate relationships that have this property by several devices, including normalization of prices, use of a condition of balanced trade, and in the most general result referred to here, use of the market-clearing condition that the sum of net trades across all countries must be zero.

3. Having said that, though, and having noted that export subsidies *can* undermine comparative advantage, the public might be justified in thinking that foreign export subsidies *do* justify trade intervention. In fact, while a foreign subsidy might cause us to trade contrary to our true underlying comparative advantage, it does not undermine our gain from doing so. It is only the subsidizing country that loses.

4. I am still indebted to Lars Svensson for drawing my attention to my failure to recognize this in an early version of Deardorff (1980).

5. See Anderson and van Wincoop (2004).

6. The text of Deardorff (1980) uses an artificial assumption that all trade must pass through a single world "port," with respect to which transport technologies are defined. However, an appendix generalizes this to an arbitrary number of such ports, which can be located anywhere.

PART III

INTERNATIONAL TRADE AND ECONOMIC GROWTH

CHAPTER 18

Alan Deardorff's Contributions on Trade and Growth

Gene M. Grossman

Princeton University

It has been a pleasure to re-read some of Alan Deardorff's papers on trade and growth, and to read others for the first time. These papers are typical of Alan's work; they artfully tease new insights on important issues from simple, familiar models.

It is fitting to begin my review with "A Geometry of Growth and Trade." Alan loves diagrams, and given his skill in developing them, it is easy to see why. His diagrammatic analyses are as incisive as any algebraic treatment and more pleasing to the eye.

Deardorff (1974) provides a simple geometric tool for analyzing trade and growth in a small open Solovian economy. Consider a small economy that produces a single consumer good and a single investment good from two factors of production, capital and labor. For simplicity, take the labor force as fixed.[1] Suppose that households save a constant fraction s of income and that capital depreciates at constant rate δ. In Fig. 1, $R(p, K)$ represents the *revenue* or *national-product* function for an economy facing world relative price p of the consumer good and having a stock of capital K. As is well known from microeconomic theory, a competitive economy maximizes the value of national output given prices. Therefore, the equilibrium allocation of capital and labor is such that $R(p, K)$ is the economy's national income. And, as is well known from trade theory, a two-sector economy facing a given relative price will specialize in producing the labor-intensive good when its capital stock is small, specialize in producing the capital-intensive good when its capital stock is large, and will produce both goods in an intermediate "cone of diversification." Therefore, the national-product function has two curved portions that depict the diminishing returns to capital when only one good is being produced, and a linear segment whose slope represents the constant marginal product of capital within the diversification cone.

With a constant savings propensity, $sR(p, K)$ represents national savings, which fully finances national investment in an economy that cannot borrow or lend internationally. The dashed line, δK, represents aggregate depreciation, and the gap between the two is net investment. The capital stock grows when $sR(p, K)$ exceeds δK and shrinks when it is

[1] The original paper incorporates constant, exogenous population growth by treating the capital-to-labor ratio as the state variable.

smaller. The intersection of the two curves depicts the steady state. The diagram readily yields predictions about the evolution of the trade pattern and about the effects of changes in savings behavior or world prices on the growth path and the ultimate steady state. For example, an increase in the savings propensity leads to a larger steady-state stock of capital, more output of the capital-intensive good, and greater exports (or fewer imports) of that good.

Deardorff (1974) employs the simple assumption that national savings is a constant fraction of national income. But a similar tool to his can be used to study transitional dynamics in an open economy with optimal savings behavior. Suppose the representative consumer allocates spending to maximize an intertemporal utility function of the form[2]

$$\int_t^{\infty} e^{-\rho(\tau-t)} \log c(\tau) d\tau$$

where $c(\tau)$ is consumption at time τ and ρ is a constant discount factor. Then, as is well known, the Euler equation implies

$$\frac{\dot{E}}{E} = i - \rho; \tag{1}$$

i.e., the households adjust expenditure $E = pc$ so that the rate of growth of spending is equal to the difference between the interest rate and the discount rate. Capital is the only asset in the model and the investment good is numeraire, so the rate of interest i must equal the

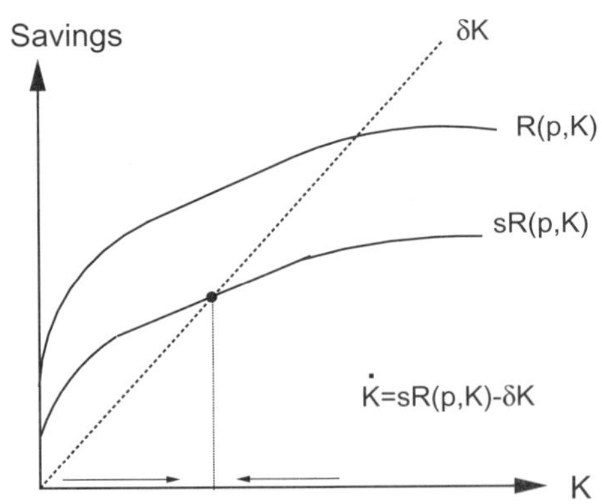

Fig. 1. Two-sector Solovian trade and growth

[2] It is easy to handle the case of a constant elasticity of intertemporal substitution; the text describes the special case where this elasticity is equal to one.

real return on capital net of depreciation, *i.e.*, $i = r(p, K) - \delta$, where $r(p, K) = \partial R/\partial K$ is the rental rate on capital. Finally, savings — which is the difference between national income and spending — finances net investment as in Deardorff (1974):

$$\dot{K} = R(p, K) - E - \delta K. \tag{2}$$

Equations (1) and (2) can be used to construct a phase diagram that bears a strong similarity to the Deardorff diagram. In Fig. 2, the $\dot{K} = 0$ curve represents the equation $E = R(p, K) - \delta K$. The qualitative properties of this curve follow from those of the national-product function, which Deardorff has discussed. The $\dot{E} = 0$ curve depicts the values of K and E such that $r(p, K) = \delta + \rho$. Two comments are in order about this curve. First, the level of spending E does not affect anything in this equation, so the "curve" is in fact a vertical line. Second, the factor-price equalization theorem implies a single value of r for all values of K in the diversification cone. If this value of r does not happen to equal $\delta + \rho$, as it generally will not for arbitrary p, then the $\dot{E} = 0$ curve will not be located at any value of K in the diversification cone.

The figure shows the "arrows" of adjustment that apply to either side of each curve. It is readily seen that the system exhibits saddle-path stability. For a given initial K, there is a single value of the initial level of spending that avoids $K \to 0$ and $K \to \infty$ as time progresses. This initial value of E is the only one that allows for satisfaction of the intertemporal budget constraint and the transversality condition for optimization of lifetime utility. The economy approaches the steady state along the stable arm, denoted by SS in the figure.

The figure can be used much as Deardorff's original diagram. It is easy to track the evolution of the trade pattern and to perform comparative statics with respect to changes in the discount rate or the international relative price. One conclusion differs from that in the Solovian world: a small open economy with optimal savings and a constant discount rate is quite unlikely to remain incompletely specialized in the long run.

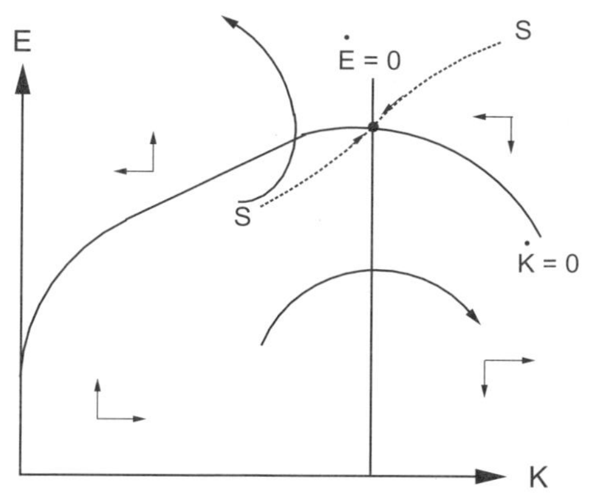

Fig. 2. Two-sector neoclassical trade and growth

I see several important substantive themes in Alan's other writings on trade and growth that have gained traction in the more recent literature. First, trade may be harmful to a growing economy in some circumstances. Second, and related, an open economy may be trapped in poverty in a world with multiple steady states. Third, growth may be sustained by trade in a neoclassical economy that would be doomed to stagnation if it remained closed to international exchange. I take up each point in turn.

In Deardorff (1973), Alan analyzed the effects of trade on *per capita* consumption in steady state and in the approach to steady state. He considered an open economy capable of producing a single consumer good and a single investment good that saves a constant proportion of its income, as in Deardorff (1974). He proved, for example, that a small economy that saves in excess of the golden rule savings ratio will experience a reduction in steady-state consumption if the world relative price of the consumption good is a bit above its autarky price.[3] If its savings rate falls short of the golden rule savings ratio, then steady-state consumption falls with an opening to trade if the world relative price of the consumption good is a bit below the autarky price. Intuitively, steady-state consumption increases if a country starts in autarky with less investment than is needed on the margin to maintain a unit of capital and it exports the investment good, or if it starts with more capital than is needed on the margin to maintain a unit of capital and it imports the capital good.

The paper also considers the effects of trade on *per capita* consumption in the short run; that is, in the moments after an opening of trade. If trade causes the relative price of the consumption good to rise, thereby generating exports of this good, then *per capita* consumption will initially fall. If the relative price moves in the opposite direction and the country exports the investment good, *per capita* consumption will rise.

This analysis suffers from two shortcomings. First, as Alan himself recognized, it is not typically optimal for households to consume a constant fraction of their current income. Alan thus relates his findings to the theory of the second best. But convincing second-best arguments that question the gains from trade usually refer to realistic market failures, not to empirically unsupported and somewhat arbitrary assumptions of sub-optimal behavior. Second, it is impossible to evaluate the welfare effects of an opening of trade that induces short-run gains and long-run losses (or *vice versa)* without reference to some intertemporal utility function. The Solow model offers no such utility function and therefore no metric for welfare comparisons. Subsequent to Deardorff (1973), Samuelson (1975) and Smith (1979, 1984) showed rigorously that a neoclassical economy with well-functioning markets always gains from trade when savings decisions derive from utility maximization, no matter what the form of its intertemporal utility function is.

[3] The golden rule savings rate is the value of s that generates the golden rule capital-to-labor ratio as its steady state. The golden rule capital-to-labor ratio, in turn, is the value of K/L that makes the marginal product of capital equal to the sum of the population growth rate and the depreciation rate.

But the possibility of losses from trade has been emphasized in recent writings on trade and growth in non-neoclassical settings. Most common are models in which growth is driven by local knowledge spillovers. These can be spillovers in human capital accumulation, as in Lucas (1988) and Stokey (1991), or spillovers in the R&D process, as in Young (1993), Feenstra (1996), and Grossman and Helpman (1991, Ch. 8; 1994).

The idea is quite simple. Consider a two-sector economy, one in which technology is static and another in which technology can improve with the accumulation of human capital or knowledge. There are spillovers in the accumulation process that offset the private diminishing returns, so that growth can be sustained. In the autarky equilibrium, the economy is incompletely specialized and the ongoing activity in the dynamic sector ensures the continuing accumulation of knowledge. Although the autarky allocation of resources to the dynamic sector will be sub-optimally small in the absence of a Pigouvian subsidy that addresses the externality, growth is sustained. Now open the economy to trade and suppose that the country has a comparative disadvantage in the dynamic sector, either due to its relatively unsuitable resource endowments or to an initial disadvantage of history that gives its trade partner a technological head start. In either case, the opening of trade will cause the country to specialize relatively and perhaps fully in the industry with a static technology. Its growth in output will slow and perhaps cease as a result of trade. Even so, trade may be gainful, since the country will be able to import the good produced in the dynamic sector at a lower price than in autarky. But it is easy to construct examples in which trade is harmful in these circumstances, for reasons to do with the theory of the second best. Inasmuch as the autarky equilibrium entails too little production of the dynamic good, if trade drives resources out of this industry it can generate losses by exacerbating a pre-existing distortion. Of course, losses from trade would not be possible if the opening of trade were accompanied by an appropriate Pigouvian subsidy to the externality-generating activity.

Deardorff (2001) makes a related but different point, drawing on work by Galor (1996). He considers a neoclassical economy that potentially can produce three goods, one investment good and two consumption goods, with capital and labor. The industries differ in their factor intensities, so there are two cones of diversification. Following Galor, he supposes that savings are approximately proportional to the wage bill, perhaps because there are overlapping generations and each generation earns capital income only in the last period of life, when it consumes all. Figure 3 — analogous to Fig. 1 — shows the aggregate savings for this economy as a function of its capital stock. For low values of K, the economy is incompletely specialized and the wage bill rises as capital is accumulated. The region between K_1 and K_2 represents the first diversification cone, where the country produces the two least capital-intensive goods. In this range, factors prices are insensitive to factor endowments, so the wage bill is constant, as is aggregate savings. Further capital accumulation leads to a range of specialization in the intermediate good, again with a rising wage bill, and then a second region of diversification, for capital stocks between K_3 and K_4. Finally, if capital were to accumulate beyond K_4, the economy would specialize in producing the most capital-intensive good, and savings would rise with K.

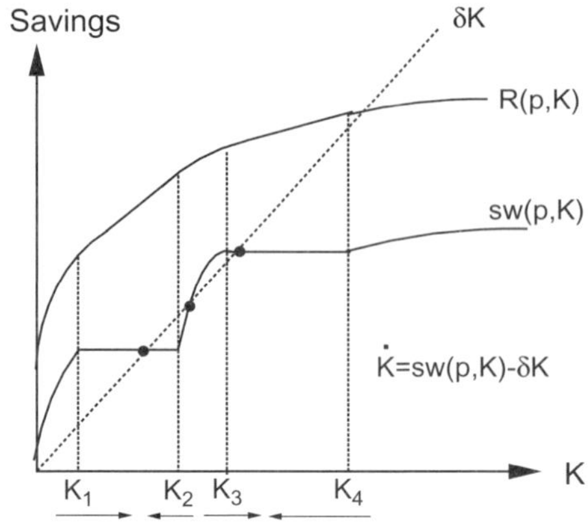

Fig. 3. Multiple steady states

As is clear from the figure, this economy can have three distinct steady states, the first and third of which are locally stable. In other words, an economy such as this can get stuck in a "poverty trap." If it starts with a capital stock less than K_1 and trades with an otherwise identical economy that begins with more capital, then it will accumulate capital until it reaches the first steady state, whereupon its growth will cease at a relatively low level of *per capita* income.[4] Differences in initial conditions are sufficient to generate long-run differences in income and welfare for countries that are otherwise the same in terms of their technologies and savings behavior.

This is an interesting finding inasmuch as multiple equilibria are not common in neoclassical growth models. The allusion to an overlapping-generations setup is intriguing, as it seems possible to have a poverty trap together with fully optimal savings behavior and convex technologies.

The potential for multiple equilibria among identical countries also arises in non-neoclassical settings. In fact, this possibility is quite natural in models with static or dynamic increasing returns to scale. Azariadis and Drazen (1990) offer an example with multiple steady states even in the closed economy. They consider an economy with "threshold externalities," *i.e.*, externalities generated by human capital that are relatively weak when the stock of human capital is small, but grow stronger as the skill level increases. In such a setting, an economy can get trapped in an equilibrium with low skills, despite the fact that it has the potential for sustained growth were it to manage somehow to escape the trap.[5] Young (1993), Feenstra (1996), Grossman and Helpman (1991, Ch. 8) and others

[4] If the economy is large, the equilibrium prices may be changing in the transition, in which case the national income and aggregate savings curves will be shifting about. Nonetheless, the point remains that there can be multiple steady states and a stable equilibrium at a low level of national income. With more than three goods, the number of steady states can increase.

[5] One way out might be with a "big push," as emphasized by Murphy, Shleifer and Vishny (1989).

show the possibility for trade to generate permanent income (or growth rate) differences between otherwise identical countries that differ in their initial levels of technological development. They consider an international equilibrium with trade between countries that differ only in their initial levels of technological development. Were the countries to remain closed, they would converge upon similar long-run steady state growth paths. However, with trade, the leading country gains an initial advantage in the more dynamic sector, and the advantage is perpetuated (or even extended) over time.

In neoclassical growth models, diminishing returns to capital typically spell the stagnation of growth in *per capita* incomes as increases in the capital-to-labor ratio drive down the marginal return to investment. Growth need not peter out, however, as Solow (1956) himself noted, if the return to capital is bounded from below. This idea of bounded long-run returns to capital has featured prominently in a branch of the literature on endogenous growth, where models with such features have been termed "*AK* models." See, for example, Jones and Manuelli (1990) for an application to the open economy. However, many have questioned the plausibility of the assumption that marginal returns will be bounded from below as the capital-to-labor ratio grows indefinitely.

Deardorff (1994) was one of the first to point out that growth can be sustained in some circumstances in an *open* neoclassical economy even if the technology does not admit a lower bound on the return to capital. His explanation relies on cross-country differences in population growth rates and the opportunities afforded by international investment.[6]

Consider a pair of Solovian economies that each produce a single good. Let the population growth rates and the savings rates be exogenous and country-specific. Alan refers to the country with the slower population growth as the North and the country with the faster population growth as the South. Technologies are such that both the North and the South will approach constant steady levels of *per capita* income in their autarkic equilibria. But suppose now that the North can invest its savings in the South. Then, for some savings rates, it avoids the otherwise inevitable rise in the capital-to-labor ratio by making use of the ever-larger Southern labor force. When the North has slower population growth and a sufficiently large savings rate, *per capita* income in the North grows forever. For even higher Northern savings rates, national income growth in the North matches the rate of population growth in the South, and residents of the North come to own a significant portion of the world's capital despite being a vanishing fraction of the world's labor force. Deardorff (1994) observes that, in circumstances in which the North enjoys sustained growth in *per capita* income but national income growth less than the rate of population growth in the South, a change in the North's savings propensity will change its long-run growth, just as in models of endogenous growth. In short, Alan points out that, by investing abroad, a relatively small country (in terms of population) can escape diminishing returns at home.

[6] Deardorff (1999) uses a similar framework to study the evolution of international inequality in *per capita* incomes.

This argument bears a family resemblance to a related point made by Ventura (1997). He considers a small, Heckscher–Ohlin economy that trades freely at fixed prices. The economy has two sectors with diminishing (and non-bounded) returns to capital in each, and savings derived from intertemporal utility maximization. Without trade, this economy would approach a steady state. With trade, it will do so as well, as was illustrated in Fig. 2. But, Ventura points out, the country will experience a potentially long growth phase when its endowments are within the diversification cone during which the return to capital will remain constant. The constancy of returns to capital reflects the factor-price equalization theorem which applies during this phase. But as long as the country remains incompletely specialized, it is as if it had access to an *AK* technology. So the growth experience for a long time might mimic that which would be predicted by such a model. And, of course, changes in policy and in savings behavior will alter the growth rate during this episode.

Deardorff's (1994) story of sustained growth is an interesting one that deserves further attention and development. To me, it seems to beg for the endogenization of population growth. Can populations diverge forever? Might the South of Deardorff's model experience a demographic transition at some stage? Or might trade postpone or even prevent such a transition? Going further, can we justify sustained differences in savings behavior? Are these differences "cultural" or do they reflect the growth experience? There is much to be done with endogenous preferences and endogenous procreation in models of trade and growth.[7]

Let me end this review where I began. I have long been a big fan of Alan Deardorff, whose work is always clean, crisp, and elegant. His papers on trade and growth complement the many other areas to which he has contributed, including his brilliant work on comparative advantage and his very useful applied research on trade policy. I am happy to be part of this celebration and look forward to his continued productivity for many years to come!

REFERENCES

Azariadis, Costas and Allan Drazen, 1990, Threshold externalities in economic development, *Quarterly Journal of Economics* 105, 501–526.

Deardorff, Alan V., 1973, The gains from trade in and out of steady-state growth, *Oxford Economic Papers* 25, 173–191.

Deardorff, Alan V., 1974, A geometry of trade and growth, *Canadian Journal of Economics* 7, 295–306.

Deardorff, Alan V., 1994, Growth and international investment with diverging populations, *Oxford Economic Papers* 46, 477–491.

Deardorff, Alan V., 1999, Diverging populations and endogenous growth in a model of meaningless trade, *Review of International Economics* 7, 359–377.

[7] See Galor and Weil (2000) for a very interesting contribution of this sort.

Deardorff, Alan V., 2001, Rich and poor countries in neoclassical trade and growth, *Economic Journal* 111, 277–294.

Feenstra, Robert C., 1996, Trade and uneven growth, *Journal of Development Economics* 49, 229–256.

Galor, Oded, 1996, Convergence? Inferences from theoretical models, *Economic Journal* 106, 1056–1069.

Galor, Oded and David N. Weil, 2000, Population, technology and growth: From Malthusian stagnation to the demographic transition and beyond, *American Economic Review* 90, 806–828.

Grossman, Gene M. and Elhanan Helpman, 1990, Trade, innovation, and growth, *American Economic Review (Papers and Proceedings)* 80, 86–91.

Grossman, Gene M. and Elhanan Helpman, 1991, Innovation and Growth in the Global Economy (MIT Press, Cambridge).

Jones, Larry E. and Rodolfo Manuelli, 1990, A convex model of equilibrium growth: Theory and policy implications, *Journal of Political Economy* 98, 1008–1038.

Lucas, Robert E., Jr., 1988, On the mechanics of economic development, *Journal of Monetary Economics* 22, 3–42.

Murphy, Kevin M., Andrei, Shleifer, and Robert W. Vishny, 1989, Industrialization and the big push, *Journal of Political Economy* 97, 1003–1026.

Samuelson, Paul A., 1975, Trade pattern reversals in time-phased Ricardian systems and intertemporal efficiency, *Journal of International Economics* 5, 309–363.

Smith, Alasdair, 1979, Intertemporal gains from trade, *Journal of International Economics* 9, 239–248.

Smith, Alasdair, 1984, Capital theory and trade theory, in R.W. Jones and P.B. Kenen, eds., Handbook of International Economics, Vol. 1 (North-Holland, Amsterdam).

Solow, Robert M., 1956, A contribution to the theory of growth, *Quarterly Journal of Economics* 70, 65–94.

Stokey, Nancy L., 1991, Human capital, product quality, and growth, *Quarterly Journal of Economics* 106, 587–616.

Ventura, Jaume, 1997, Growth and interdependence, *Quarterly Journal of Economics* 112, 57–84.

Young, Alwyn, 1993, Invention and bounded learning by doing, *Journal of Political Economy* 101, 443–472.

CHAPTER 19

Alan Deardorff Festschrift Remarks

Anne O. Krueger

Johns Hopkins School for Advanced International Studies
Stanford Center for International Development

I am pleased and honored to participate in this celebration of Alan Deardorff. He has contributed enormously to the profession through his research, his teaching, his policy contributions, and his good citizenship in the profession. I won't comment on his teaching and good citizenship except to say that I've encountered many of Alan's former students, both graduate and undergraduate, and all speak enthusiastically about his support and role in their education, including in some cases their decision to go on to graduate school in economics. And many of his former students, who are participating in this symposium, have continued down paths opened up by Alan and, of course, his colleagues.

One of the many impressive things about Alan has been the breadth of his interests and contributions, as the organization of today's program attests. And not only have his interests and contributions been broad, they have encompassed both positive and normative theoretical and empirical work.

The marching orders for these comments included the request that we reminisce a bit about the development of the field of international economics. In thinking about comparative advantage and growth, that is almost a natural starting point.

Recall that the Heckscher–Ohlin model has been around for a long time. Even Ellsworth's classic 1938 textbook presented it, suggesting that there would be a "tendency" toward factor price equalization as labor-abundant countries exported their labor-intensive goods and capital-abundant countries their capital-intensive goods. The Heckscher–Ohlin model was very attractive intuitively. It seemed to fill in a hole left by the Ricardian model by explaining — apparently — why there were differences in relative costs and prices between countries.

But in the late 1940s, Paul Samuelson contributed his paper showing that with incomplete specialization (and the other assumptions well known to all of us) there would be factor price equalization. And, at about the same time, Leontief came up with his famous paper on the factor content of trade now referred to universally as the Leontief paradox.

Both of these papers raised enormous and challenging questions about the HOS model, as it was soon called, which occupied much of the intellectual energy of international trade theorists and empiricists over the next several decades. For, while the HOS model was appealing in its original "tendency to" form, the logical conclusions that derived from careful examination of the underpinnings of the model seemed entirely at variance with the facts, and Leontief's empirical findings were even more challenging. When the workhorse model seemed to fly so much in the face of reality, it was small wonder that we focused on trying to figure out why.

Efforts were theoretical and empirical. On the theoretical side, more goods and factors, specific factors (at the extreme there was a paper with one specific factor for each good, which seemed somewhat tautological), constant or varying elasticities of substitution (with the possibility of factor intensity reversals), many countries (was Germany labor-abundant relative to the U.S. or capital-abundant relative to developing countries?), and many more variants were tried. While examination of the bilateral factor content of trade was shown theoretically not to be the correct test, empirically many pairwise countries' trade patterns were examined with mixed results.

Alan's early contributions focused on this central range of issues (although, to his credit, he never forgot that comparative advantage and the arguments for free trade rested on differences in relative autarkic prices and not on the reasons for them in many plausible models). Much of his early work, "Weak Links in the Chain of Comparative Advantage," "The General Validity of the Law of Comparative Advantage," "The General Validity of the Heckscher–Ohlin Theorem," and "An Interpretation of the Factor Content of Trade" with Bob Staiger were all of this ilk, as was his masterful contribution, "Testing Trade Theories and Predicting Trade Flows," to the Jones–Kenen handbook. That interest has continued, as perusal of his C.V. shows, with his 2001 EJ paper producing a three-good model permitting two cones of diversification with factor price equalization in each cone but divergence between them. He believes that the "two-cone" world economy better fits the facts than a single factor-price-equalization outcome, and has contributed significantly to understanding some North-South issues on that basis, arguing that as the South now attempts development, countries in the North are threatened in a way they were not earlier in the growth of the world economy.

But Alan has also delved into issues of trade and growth going way beyond the HOS model (which, of course, could immediately be transformed into a growth model). Perhaps because of his focus on many-goods models, his range of interests has covered a wide area: intellectual property, outsourcing, sources of the rich-poor divide in trade negotiations, political economy, and, of course, the impact of alternative proposed liberalizations of trade under the WTO.

In addition to twists and turns of HOS models, of course, we have in recent years begun to understand other sources of gains from trade: imperfect competition when the variety and quality of goods can be greatly increased, while costs are lowered, through trade; the effects of increased competition resulting from international trade on individual firms' incentives to produce more efficiently; and much more. I doubt that any of us now thinks that any one model fully explains the pattern of trade. But I also doubt that any would deny that factor proportions are part of the overall explanation. Alan's contribution to our understanding of the power and the limits of factor proportions in multi-commodity, multi-country models has contributed significantly to, and advanced, that understanding.

In each of these areas, and many more to be covered in other panels, Alan has been thoroughly professional in seeking to understand the underlying sources of comparative advantage, the benefits of international trade, and the effects of alternative policies on trade. His work is cited in professional journals, in policy analyses, and in textbooks. A perusal of two textbooks that I happened to have on my shelf showed Alan cited for several of his early papers on the HOS model, for his "Weak Links in the Chain of Comparative Advantage," for much of his work with Bob Stern on the impact of trade liberalization in the various MTN rounds, and for much that will be discussed in other panels.

Alan, I salute you for your intellectual contributions, your thorough professionalism, and for your many advances in our understanding of the international economy. This celebration is well deserved.

CHAPTER 20

International Trade and Economic Growth[1]

T. N. Srinivasan

Yale University

Let me begin by saluting Alan Deardorff for his enormous contributions to trade theory per se and importantly to parts of theory that have served as formulations for empirical analysis. There are many I could cite from his large body of work. I will cite just three: Alan Deardorff (1998) is among those which provided a theoretical foundation for the workhorse of empirical analysis of bilateral trade flows, namely the gravity model that goes back to Jan Tinbergen (1962) and Hans Linneman (1966) of the Tinbergen School. The others are his classic papers on the general validity of comparative advantage, one (Deardorff, 1980) based on the Ricardian model and the other (Deardorff, 1982) based on Heckscher–Ohlin–Samuelson (HOS). Alan embeds each in a multi-country, multi-factor, multi-commodity Arrow–Debreu competitive general equilibrium model and then asks and answers a well-posed question: which of the basic propositions of the simple Ricardian or HOS models survive in more general settings, and if they do, in what form. More generally, Alan, like many distinguished theorists, uses propositions of theories with their strong and unrealistic assumptions, about consumer and producer behavior, and the markets as benchmarks for asking and answering in a systematic and coherent way the implications of well-specified departures from the strong assumptions. Thus, in his use, the role of theories and their conclusions is only as a device for generating propositions rigorously which serve as benchmarks for systematic analyses of reality. He does not have to believe the theories literally for this purpose. I doubt whether he or any distinguished theorist ever did.

Recently there has been a flood of critiques by economists and the media, sometimes by economists serving as newspaper columnists, of macroeconomic theory and policy making prior to the onset of the financial crisis. It would seem that the critics show little understanding of the proper role of theory in thinking about policy making in the real world. Some, including distinguished theorists of trade and open economy macroeconomics, who ought to know better, charge those theorists, from whom they apparently differ for other reasons possibly including political beliefs, as literal believers in the conclusions of their theory, be it of efficient markets or of dynamic stochastic general equilibrium,

[1] In preparing these remarks, I have drawn on Srinivasan (2001), Srinivasan (2008), and Srinivasan and Wallack (2004).

unbounded rationality or what have you! Some even go as far as basing their charges on a "pithy" quote or two in and out of context from those they criticize. Clearly such economist critics and their critiques do not advance our discipline.

Recent contributions to trade theory are exciting and continue their traditional base on general equilibrium theory. Unfortunately, trade policy making and debates, for example, on globalization, continue to be prime examples of what Alan Blinder calls Murphy's Law of Economics, namely, that economists have the least influence on policy in areas such as trade where they know more than others and are least divided.

Turning to the topic of this panel, I want to draw attention to an important and policy-relevant distinction between economic growth and economic development. Although the two have important linkages and openness to international trade and investment contributes to both, they are not the same. In many ways the objectives of development go beyond the objective of accelerating growth, and achieving the former often depends on overcoming or alleviating domestic institutional constraints, including governance, much more intensively than for achieving growth objectives. In addition, both sets of objectives are multidimensional, involving different characteristics, different time horizons, and so on. Lack of understanding of this distinction and its complexity has led to the misnaming of the Doha Round of Multilateral Trade Negotiations as the Development Round, this has led, on one hand, to unrealistic expectations that once the Doha Round is successfully concluded with an agreement with a "balanced outcome," then the development problems would be solved and its goals achieved as well, and, on the other hand, to fears, if not despair, that if Doha fails, achievement of development goals will be stalled forever. Neither the expectations nor the fears are warranted. This is because the sources of most constraints that inhibit faster development are domestic. A successful conclusion of the Doha Round could, though not necessarily would, ease some of the external constraints on development; it certainly would not ensure development success if the domestic constraints are not addressed.

On the relation between economic growth and international trade, long ago Dennis Robertson (1940) described "trade as an engine of growth," meaning that greater openness to trade would trigger faster growth. On the other hand, Irving Kravis (1970) described "trade as a handmaiden of growth," meaning that faster growth would lead to greater trade. The existence of a possible two-way relationship between the two, that is, the endogeneity of outcomes of openness and growth means the results of empirical analyses based on a single equation, a "reduced form" kind with one of them as the variable to be explained and the other as one of the explanatory variables, could vary depending on how the endogeneity is addressed. This opens the door for the search for clever instruments, a search that has unduly occupied some of the creative members of our profession recently! Apart from this, most empirical studies do not recognize the results of the "second best" theory, as applied to trade and domestic distortions. For example, removing some distortions on trade while keeping intact others on trade and also non-trade-related ones need not lead to the "first best" expectations of improvements in efficiency. Moreover, whether or not it would depends on the local context.

Simply put, there are basically three sources of aggregate real GDP growth in an economy: growth of inputs into the production process, efficiency in the allocation of inputs across the production of goods and services, and technical progress in the sense of successful innovation in discovering new products and more and more productive technologies and in their adoption into production. Openness could potentially contribute to all three sources: first by separating the domestic use of inputs from their domestic endowments or supply. For example, a country which wishes to use more or less of its endowment of capital (or labor of any type) can import or export some of it. By exporting its excess capital endowment, for example, it could earn more from its use abroad than at home. Thus, trade in inputs yields gains for both trading partners. The link between improvement in efficiency through exploitation of comparative advantage, by shifting use of inputs towards goods and services in which the domestic economy has a comparative cost advantage, and growth is straightforward. To the extent the gains in efficiency through such reallocation of inputs are in part saved and invested, obviously such efficiency gains from trade contribute to growth. Even if the efficiency gains are fully consumed, their contribution to increasing welfare is evident. Finally, the mechanisms through which openness serves as a source of innovation in the domestic economy are several: horizontal and vertical spillovers of knowledge from foreign direct investment, learning of new products, or more productive ways of producing existing products by domestic exporters and others.

Whether or not the potential contribution of greater openness to the three sources of growth are realized will depend on the functioning of domestic institutions, including importantly the financial and legal systems, the domestic political economy, the existence of relevant markets, their depth and efficiency and so on. Distortions in any of these could limit the beneficial effects of openness and could even reverse them. Unfortunately, much of the recent empirical literature on globalization on growth, poverty, employment, etc., does not often explicitly build the various mechanisms by which globalization could have effects and test for their absence or presence, but taking into effect any constraints that may inhibit their full use. I am deeply skeptical of the "dummy variable" approach for assessing the effects of domestic factors. In my view, the dummy variables are mute and dumb on the mechanisms or factors through which they might have contributed to the observed effects.

In saying all this, I am not dismissing the very impressive recent theoretical developments on foreign trade, investment and growth based on preference for variety, economic geography of agglomeration effects, the development of process-based trade as compared to trade in products and the related phenomena of outsourcing and off-shoring, and, above all, shifting the analysis to the incentives operating at the firm level for participating in foreign trade and increasing the extent of their participation, if they decide to participate. Nor do I dismiss the surprisingly few empirical studies which rest on sound theoretical foundations. I expect to see in future the recent trend in exciting theoretical developments to continue now that more of the recent Ph.D. cohorts have entered trade theory, and not only theory, but also theory with a focus on the empirical applicability and policy relevance. By their research these cohorts would be paying a fitting tribute to Alan Deardorff and his contributions.

REFERENCES

Deardorff, Alan, 1980, The general validity of the law of comparative advantage, *Journal of Political Economy* 88(5), 941–951.

Deardorff, Alan, 1982, The general validity of the Heckscher–Ohlin theorem, *American Economic Review* 72(4), 683–694.

Deardorff, Alan, 1998, Determinants of bilateral trade: Does gravity work in a neoclassical world?, in Jeffrey Frankel, ed., The Regionalization of the World Economy (University of Chicago Press, Chicago), pp. 7–28.

Kravis, Irving, 1970, Trade as a handmaiden of growth: Similarities between the nineteenth and twentieth centuries, in C. Nick Harley, ed., The Integration of the World Economy 1850–1914, Vol. 1 (Edward Elgar, Cheltenham), pp. 402–424.

Linnemann, Hans, 1966, An Econometric Study of World Trade Flows (North-Holland, Amsterdam).

Robertson, D., 1940, Essays in Monetary Theory (P.S. King, London).

Srinivasan, T.N., 2001, Trade, development and growth, *Essays in International Economics*, No. 225, International Economics Section (Princeton University, Princeton, NJ).

Srinivasan, T.N., 2008, Globalization and poverty, in E. Dinopoulos, P. Krishna, A. Panagariya, and K.-Y. Wong, eds., Trade, Globalization and Poverty (Routledge, New York).

Srinivasan, T.N. and Jessica Wallack, 2004, Globalization, growth and the poor, *De Economist* 152(2), 251–272.

Tinbergen, Jan, 1962, Shaping the World Economy (The Twentieth Century Fund, New York).

CHAPTER 21

OXFORD JOURNALS
OXFORD UNIVERSITY PRESS

THE GAINS FROM TRADE IN AND OUT OF STEADY-STATE GROWTH[1]

By ALAN V. DEARDORFF

In recent years growth theory and trade theory have converged in a flurry of articles which analyse growth of open economies and trade among growing economies. The first of these, in the tradition of modern growth theory, used mathematical techniques.[2] More recently, several authors have applied geometric techniques, familiar to trade theorists, to the problem.[3] Several of these authors have pointed out that growing economies may suffer a loss in steady-state *per capita* consumption as a result of opening to trade, though it has not always been clear how likely or how serious this result would be.

In this paper we use geometric techniques to analyse the effect of trade on *per capita* consumption in steady state and during the approach to steady state. The method used has the advantage that a single diagram yields results for a number of different cases without requiring difficult manipulations of the curves.

We will assume throughout that an economy saves and invests a constant fraction of its income. There need be nothing optimal, of course, about such proportional saving, and therefore the conclusions we draw about gains and losses from trade are only second-best results.

In Sections I and II we will define the model we will use and derive the geometric tools from which our results will follow.[4] In Section III we will discuss in detail the effect of a change in the terms of trade on steady-state *per capita* consumption, and show that a closed economy can suffer from free trade. In Section IV we look at trade between two countries with identical technologies but different propensities to save. In Section V we look at trade between countries with different technologies. Throughout Sections II to V we assume that the consumption good is always more capital-intensive than the investment good. In Section VI we look at what happens if this assumption is reversed. Finally, in Section VII we drop the assumption that economies are always in steady states, and look at *per capita* consumption as the economy adjusts towards its steady state.

[1] This paper originated as part of the author's Ph.D. thesis submitted to Cornell University. The author has benefited from discussions with Jaroslav Vanek, Trent Bertrand, Edwin Burton, and Jay Levin and from extensive comments and suggestions provided by W. M. Corden. Thanks are due also to Robert M. Stern and the Research Seminar in International Economics at the University of Michigan.

[2] Oniki and Uzawa (1965), Bardhan (1965), and Stiglitz (1970).

[3] Johnson (1971), Vanek (1971), and Bertrand (1971).

[4] This paper had been written before the appearance of the articles by Stiglitz (1970), Johnson (1971), and Bertrand (1971). We will refer occasionally in footnotes to relationships between this paper and the works of those authors.

I. The closed economy

We consider a two-sector economy which can produce two goods: a consumption good and an investment good. To produce these it employs capital and labour subject to production functions which are neoclassical—that is, they are homogeneous of degree one and have positive but diminishing marginal products.[1] These functions are assumed to be continuous and differentiable everywhere. The labour force grows at a constant rate, n. The capital stock depreciates at a constant rate, μ, but is augmented at each moment in time by the amount of investment. Investment is always equal to savings which is in turn equal to a constant fraction, s, of national income.

The economy is in a steady state when its capital stock is growing at the same rate, n, as the labour force. Letting K be the capital stock, L be the labour force, and I be investment in units of the investment good, we have as our definition of a steady state that

$$\dot{K}/K = (I/K) - \mu = n, \tag{1}$$

where the dot over K indicates its derivative with respect to time. Letting $k = K/L$ be the capital-labour ratio we can solve (1) to get

$$I/L = (\mu + n)k \tag{2}$$

as the equation for *per capita* investment in a steady state.

Because we have assumed neoclassical production functions in both sectors, it follows that we can represent these functions as in Fig. 1, where sectoral *per capita* output is shown as an increasing concave function of the sectoral capital-labour ratio alone. Here k_i is the capital-labour ratio in the ith industry, L_i is the labour force employed in the ith industry, $\bar{I}$ is the output of the investment good, and $\bar{C}$ is the output of the consumption good. Of course if the economy is completely specialized in production of either good then the corresponding curve gives *per capita* output for the whole economy, in units of that good, as a function of the economy's capital-labour ratio, k.

For any given capital-labour ratio the economy can produce anywhere along a transformation curve such as that shown in Fig. 2 as TT'. The endpoints of this curve are given directly by the curves in Fig. 1. The economy will choose to produce at a particular point on the transformation curve, such as P in Fig. 2, only if the marginal rate of transformation between the two goods equals the ratio of their prices. That is, it will produce at P only if the price ratio is that given by the slope of the tangent, AB. All of this is familiar from traditional trade theory.

[1] In order to assure the existence of steady states, we assume the 'Inada conditions': that in both industries the marginal product of capital is infinite if the industry capital-labour ratio is zero and approaches zero as the capital-labour ratio becomes infinite.

Let C be consumption. If the economy is closed, then its consumption must equal its production of the consumption good, so that $C/L = \bar{C}/L$. If the economy is open and faces prices given by the slope of AB in Fig. 2, then it can consume anywhere along the line AB. Exactly where this consumption point will lie depends of course on the propensity to save, s.

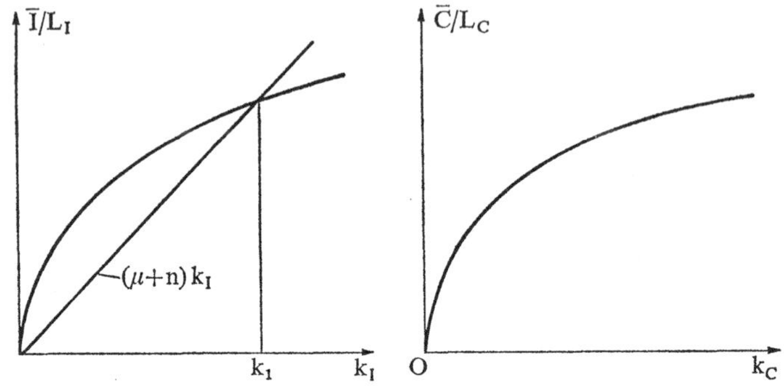

FIG. 1a, 1b

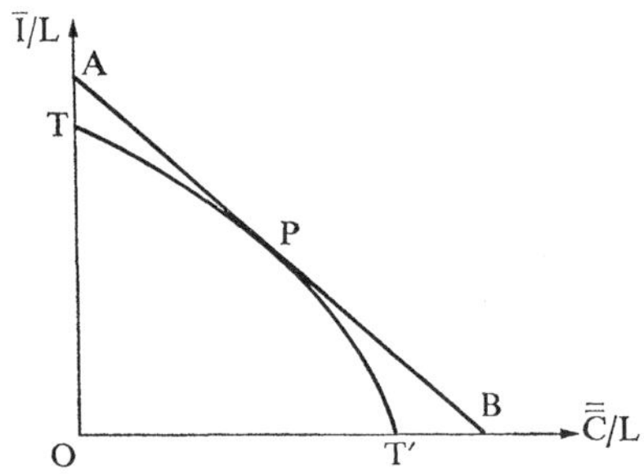

FIG. 2

Our object is to study *per capita* consumption, C/L, when the economy is in various steady states. To do this we begin with a curve representing the level of *per capita* consumption that a closed economy could attain at each capital-labour ratio, assuming investment at each point to be just enough to keep the economy in steady-state growth. This consumption possibility curve is the curve labelled $[C/L]$ in Fig. 3, where the square brackets remind us that it refers to a closed economy. We will explain its properties in a moment, but first a comment on its interpretation is in order.

The $[C/L]$ curve does not represent a functional relationship between C/L and k. The steady-state values of both of these variables are determined, though not necessarily uniquely, by the propensity to save as well as the other parameters of the model. Thus the $[C/L]$ curve represents a locus of the steady-state values of both variables corresponding to all possible savings propensities.

We can get a good deal of information about the nature of this locus by looking at the *per capita* production function for the investment good shown in Fig. 1*a*. It tells us the *per capita* production of the investment good that is possible if the economy completely specializes. We have also drawn a ray from the origin, $(\mu+n)k_I$, which we know from equation 2 to be the amount of the investment good needed to maintain steady growth at each capital-labour ratio. Comparing these two curves we see immediately that not all capital-labour ratios are consistent with steady growth. If, as drawn in Fig. 1*a*, the curves intersect at a positive capital-labour ratio, k_1, then

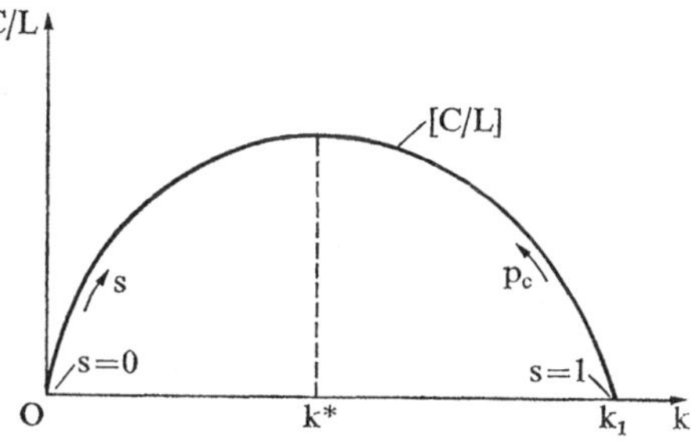

FIG. 3

capital-labour ratios greater than k_1 cannot possibly be maintained. To do so would require a greater amount of the investment good than the closed economy is capable of producing, even with complete specialization. Furthermore, we are assured that the two curves will intersect in the manner shown if either the rate of population growth, n, or of depreciation, μ, is positive, and if the Inada conditions are satisfied.[1] Thus steady states are possible only for capital-labour ratios between zero and k_1 inclusive, and the $[C/L]$ locus in Fig. 3 takes on values only in this interval.

We note also from Fig. 1*a* that a steady state at $k = k_1$ requires complete specialization in the investment good. Since the two production functions together rule out positive *per capita* production of any good if $k = 0$, we conclude that steady-state *per capita* consumption must be zero at both $k = 0$ and $k = k_1$. At capital-labour ratios between zero and k_1, however, complete specialization would yield more of the investment good than necessary to maintain steady growth. There will therefore be resources left over for production of the consumption good, and steady-state consumption will be positive inside the interval. Thus the closed economy's steady-state *per capita* consumption will be as drawn in Fig. 3: zero at $k = 0$ and $k = k_1$, positive at $0 < k < k_1$, and undefined at $k > k_1$.[2]

[1] See footnote 1, p. 174.

[2] We have also drawn the curve as concave from below, a property which we will show later to be correct. Concavity is suggested, of course, by the concavity of the production function in Fig. 1*a*, if we identify the vertical distance between the two curves with the

The $[C/L]$ locus describes all of the steady states that a closed economy can attain. Which point on that locus the economy actually does attain will depend on its savings propensity. Furthermore, to different points on the locus there will normally correspond different price ratios needed to clear the markets for the investment and consumption goods.[1] It will be useful for our later analysis to know how the savings ratio and the price ratio vary along the curve.

The role of the savings ratio is easy to determine. If savings were zero, then no investment would take place and the steady-state capital-labour ratio would also have to be zero. If the savings ratio were unity, on the other hand, only the investment good would be produced, and we see from Fig. 1*a* that the steady-state capital-labour ratio would be k_1. Since our model is continuous, it follows that the savings propensity, s, that underlies the $[C/L]$ locus, must vary continuously from zero at $k = 0$ to unity at $k = k_1$. This relationship between k and s will also be monotonic, s increasing with k, if we make a further assumption, namely that the steady state corresponding to any given savings ratio is unique.[2] Making this assumption, we indicate with an arrow in Fig. 3 that s increases as we move to the right along the $[C/L]$ locus.

Finally, consider the behaviour of prices along the $[C/L]$ locus. As the capital-labour ratio rises, the price of the capital-intensive good will fall. This is necessary in order to maintain *per capita* production of the investment good that is proportional to k, as required in equation (2) for steady-state growth. Otherwise, if prices were to remain unchanged, the Rybczynski Theorem tells us that $\bar{I}/L$ would either fall absolutely or rise by a greater percentage than k, depending on the relative factor intensities.

We will assume, except in Section VI, that the investment good is labour-intensive. Thus in Fig. 3 we indicate with an arrow that the relative price of the consumption good, p_c, falls as we move to the right along $[C/L]$. The direction of this arrow will simply be reversed when we assume the investment good to be capital-intensive in Section VI.

The $[C/L]$ locus of Fig. 3, together with the indicated behaviour of s and p_c along it, provide us with as complete a picture of the steady states of the

resources left over for consumption after steady-state investment requirements are satisfied. This identification is correct, however, only if factor intensities in the two sectors happen to be identical.

[1] If factor intensities in the two industries happen to be identical then there will exist a unique price ratio consistent with incomplete specialization. In that case the equilibrium price would be the same at all points on the $[C/L]$ locus. If factor intensities are not identical, however, prices must vary along the locus.

[2] Uzawa (1963) has shown such uniqueness under the assumption that production of the investment good is relatively labour-intensive. Drandakis (1963) has shown that steady states will be unique regardless of factor intensities if the elasticities of factor substitution in the production functions are sufficiently large. Thus either of these assumptions suffices to give us monotonic variation of s along the $[C/L]$ locus.

closed economy as we need for our analysis. It will be convenient, however, before we go on to the open economy, to identify one further property of the closed economy. Since $[C/L]$ is zero at $k = 0$ and $k = k_1$ and is positive in between, it follows that it must reach a maximum at some $k = k^*$ in that interval.[1] The savings ratio, s^*, to which this k^* corresponds is the familiar golden rule savings ratio. Therefore we will call k^* the golden rule capital-labour ratio and the corresponding p_c^* the golden rule terms of trade.

II. The open economy

We now consider an open economy that has some given savings ratio, but which may face any of a variety of international prices. To each price that such a country faces, there will correspond a steady-state capital-labour

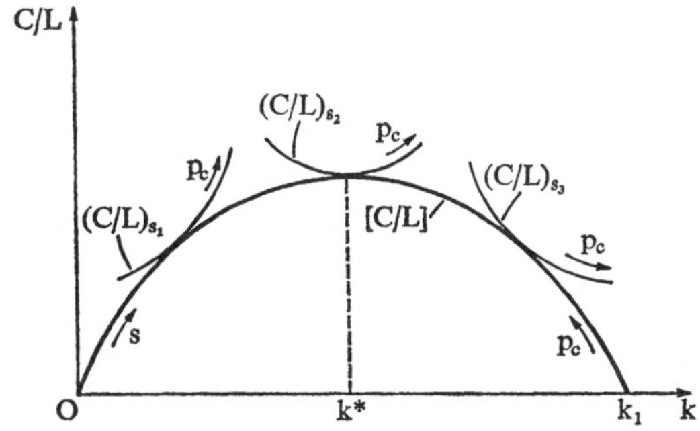

FIG. 4

ratio and some amount of consumption per head in that steady state. Thus we can imagine a locus, $(C/L)_s$, of *per capita* consumption for all steady-state capital-labour ratios attainable with the given savings ratio but with different prices, p_c. We have drawn three such loci in Fig. 4, each corresponding to a different savings ratio. We must now show that they are drawn correctly.

First we note that any $(C/L)_s$ locus must coincide at one and only one point with the $[C/L]$ locus of Fig. 3. This point of coincidence would be reached if the world price equalled the price that would prevail in steady state in a closed economy with the same savings ratio. It is therefore the point of no trade along the $(C/L)_s$ locus. Its existence and uniqueness

[1] k^* can be identified, as in one sector growth models, by the equality of the marginal product of capital with $(\mu+n)$. This marginal product must, of course, be measured in units of the investment good in order for it to be of the same dimension as $(\mu+n)$. To verify the criterion we merely assume the contrary. If the marginal product of capital were greater than $(\mu+n)$ then only part of an additional unit of capital would have to be employed in the investment good industry to maintain steady growth at the new higher capital-labour ratio. That part of the additional capital which is left over can be used to increase *per capita* consumption. A similar argument can be used to show that if the marginal product of capital is less than $(\mu+n)$, a small decrease in the capital-labour ratio will increase steady-state *per capita* consumption.

follow from the continuous monotonic variation of s from zero to one along $[C/L]$.

Next we note that a $(C/L)_s$ locus cannot pass below $[C/L]$. This follows directly from the familiar static gains from trade. We know that trade permits a combination of consumption and investment outside of a country's transformation curve. In general, of course, this gain from trade need not imply an increase in consumption, since the gain could be absorbed entirely into increased use of the investment good. However, the loci $(C/L)_s$ and $[C/L]$ both represent steady-state solutions. This means that at any given capital-labour ratio, *per capita* investment must be the same on both curves. It follows that the static gain from trade must be devoted entirely to an increase in *per capita* consumption in the open economy over what it would be in a closed economy with the same steady-state capital-labour ratio. Notice, however, that this does not mean that an economy with a fixed savings ratio must gain from trade. We have compared open and closed economies with identical steady-state capital-labour ratios, and they must therefore have different savings ratios if the open economy actually trades. But we have established the desired result that the $(C/L)_s$ locus lies above $[C/L]$ except at the unique point where they coincide.

Finally, we note that at any strictly positive $[C/L]$ the closed economy must be incompletely specialized. It should be clear from the nature of our model that its solution must be continuous and smooth except possibly at points verging on complete specialization. Thus the $(C/L)_s$ locus must be smooth where it touches the $[C/L]$ locus, and since the two cannot cross they must be tangent. This establishes the essential features of the $(C/L)_s$ loci as drawn in Fig. 4.

Jaroslav Vanek has shown that when the price of the consumption good rises, an open economy like the one we are discussing will move to a higher steady-state capital-labour ratio. This is easily understood. An increase in p_c raises national income in units of the investment good for any given capital-labour ratio. Since a constant fraction of this income is saved, investment must increase and so must the steady-state capital-labour ratio. From this it follows that p_c must be rising as we move to the right along any $(C/L)_s$ locus. This we have again indicated with arrows in Fig. 4.

There is one more locus that will be of some use to us later on. That is the locus of steady-state *per capita* consumption for an open economy with fixed terms of trade but variable savings ratio.

Two such loci denoted $(C/L)_p$, have been drawn in Fig. 5.[1] Each is shown as a straight line in the neighbourhood of the autarky point where it touches

[1] These loci correspond exactly to the open economy investment requirements curves which Johnson (1971) labelled PQ in his article and which Bertrand (1971) corrected and further analysed. Ours are drawn as functions of K/L instead of I/L, but the transformation is straightforward, since in steady state K/L and I/L are related by equation (2).

$[C/L]$. This is a result of the homogeneity of the production functions. According to Euler's Theorem, the value of each sector's output equals the value of inputs used in the sector. The value of the country's output, then, must be the value of the country's factor supplies, K and L. In *per capita* terms

$$Y/L = r(K/L)+w, \tag{3}$$

where r and w are the prices of capital and labour respectively and Y is the value of national output. From factor-price equalization theory we know

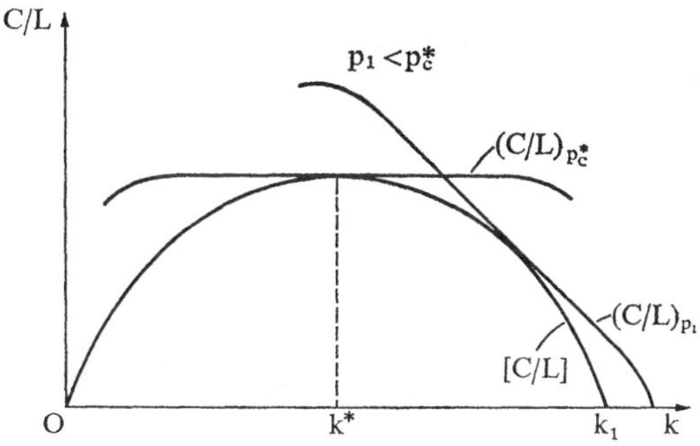

FIG. 5

that constant commodity prices imply constant factor prices as long as both goods are produced. Thus in equation (3), *per capita* income is a linear function of the capital-labour ratio in a region of nonspecialization. Since the *per capita* investment needed for steady growth is also a linear function of k, it follows that the difference between the two—steady-state consumption per head—must be a linear function of k in the neighbourhood of the autarky point.

Incidentally, the same argument we used to show that no $(C/L)_s$ locus can pass below $[C/L]$ applies as well to $(C/L)_p$. The gains from trade can influence only consumption when we compare two economies in steady state at the same capital-labour ratio. Thus, it follows that the $[C/L]$ locus can never pass above any straight line drawn tangent to it at any point. This means that it must be concave—a fact which we have always considered when drawing it but have not, until now, proved.

III. The possibility of gains and losses from trade

We are now ready to assert our fundamental result regarding gains from trade. Consider any closed economy in steady state. Its capital-labour ratio and *per capita* consumption must be those indicated by the point on the $[C/L]$ locus corresponding to its savings ratio. At that point there is a $(C/L)_s$ locus which is tangent and which gives us the *per capita* consumption it can reach if it opens to trade at various prices. It is immediately obvious from Fig. 4 that there will almost always be some prices at which trade would be harmful.

Suppose, for example, that the economy's savings ratio is s_3 in Fig. 4. Then a small increase in p_c must cause its steady-state capital-labour ratio to increase and its *per capita* consumption to fall. This follows because at s_3 $[C/L]$ is downward sloping and $(C/L)_{s3}$, being tangent to it and smooth, must also be downward sloping. Similarly, if s_1 is its savings ratio, small decreases in p_c will cause a fall in *per capita* consumption. Indeed, only when $s_2 = s^*$ is *per capita* consumption already at a minimum in autarky.

Next we notice that when a closed economy enters into trade at a higher price for the consumption good, it must, in trade, be exporting the consumption good and importing the investment good. Combining this fact with the observations in the preceding paragraph, we can state the following theorem:

> *Theorem*: If an economy's savings ratio is equal to the golden rule savings ratio s^* which maximizes steady-state *per capita* consumption when the economy is closed, then any trade will increase its steady-state *per capita* consumption. If $s < s^*$, then a little trade is worse than no trade at all if it involves exporting the investment good. If $s > s^*$, a little trade is worse than no trade at all if it involves exporting the consumption good.

The words, 'a little trade', in the above are essential. In the previous section we considered properties of the $(C/L)_s$ locus only in the neighbourhood of its tangency with $[C/L]$. As the difference between the trade price and the autarky price becomes large we leave the neighbourhood of such a tangency and the curve is quite likely to turn back up.[1] Thus, our theorem is valid only for small changes in the price from autarky.[2]

The theorem is the central result of this paper. In the following sections we will merely ask under what circumstances free trade might be expected, according to this theorem, to be detrimental. Thus, it is desirable, before we go on, to be sure that we understand why the theorem is true.

A good clue to what is happening here is the important role played by the golden rule savings ratio, s^*. As explained earlier, the golden rule

[1] In fact it must turn back up. When the economy is producing only the investment good, a further fall in p_c has no effect on the steady-state capital-labour ratio and can only increase *per capita* consumption; when the economy is producing only the consumption good a further rise in p_c can affect C/L only by changing K/L, and K/L must rise with an increase in p_c, thereby increasing C/L.

[2] Our theorem agrees completely with Johnson's (1971) conclusions regarding *per capita* consumption, so long as one looks only at savings less than the golden rule. His failure to consider what happens when savings is greater than the golden rule has also been pointed out by Bertrand (1971).

capital-labour ratio in the closed economy is characterized by the equality of the marginal product of capital with the investment per unit of capital needed to maintain steady growth.[1] Thus, if a closed economy starts in a steady state below k^*, the marginal product of capital must be greater than the investment necessary to maintain a unit of it. If the economy were then to export the investment good, it would lose more in productivity than it would gain by not having to maintain the investment good as capital. Alternatively, at $k > k^*$, the marginal product of capital is too small, so that imports of the investment good add less in productivity than is needed to maintain the increased capital-labour ratio.

We see, then, that a country will incur a decrease in steady-state *per capita* consumption whenever it moves away from the golden-rule capital-labour ratio. This is true regardless of whether the movement results from a change in the economy's savings ratio or from a change from autarky to trade. In the latter case, however, the conclusion holds only if the volume of trade is small. For as the volume of trade becomes large, the usual static gains from trade become significant and outweigh the loss due to the non-optimal capital-labour ratio.

IV. Trade generated by different savings propensities

We now consider two countries with identical technologies but different savings ratios, and attempt to determine how steady-state *per capita* consumption in the two countries will be affected by trade between them. In order for steady states to exist under free trade it is necessary that we assume the rates of population growth to be the same in both countries.[2] With these assumptions the various loci that we derived in Sections I and II relating steady-state C/L to the capital-labour ratio will be identical for the two countries.

We denote the countries by A and B, and their savings ratios by s_a and s_b, with $s_b > s_a$. We can determine the effect on steady-state C/L of the opening of trade by first identifying on the $[C/L]$ curve the two closed economy steady states and the corresponding steady-state prices. Noting the arrows connected with $[C/L]$ in Fig. 4 we see that steady-state p_c will be lower in country B than in country A since $s_b > s_a$. Therefore, free trade will cause a fall in p_c for country A and rise in p_c for country B. If these changes are small enough, our theorem tells us that the effect on steady-state C/L in each country will depend on whether their respective savings

[1] See footnote 1, p. 178.

[2] See Vanek (1971). Actually, as he argues there, if the population growth rates differ in the two countries the faster growing country will eventually become so large relative to the other that it may be regarded as closed, while the slower growing country may eventually be regarded as facing terms of trade given from outside.

ratios are smaller than, equal to, or greater than the golden rule savings ratio, s^*. Since p_c falls for country A it will move to the left along its $(C/L)_{s_a}$ locus. If $s_a < s^*$, then this movement implies a fall in steady-state C/L, while if $s_a \geqslant s^*$ it implies a rise. Similarly, p_c rises for country B, requiring movement to the right along its $(C/L)_{s_b}$ locus. Thus, in country B, C/L will rise if $s_b \leqslant s^*$ and fall if $s_b > s^*$.

If s_a and s_b lie on the same side of s^* (and if they are close together so that price changes will be small enough to apply the theorem) then the country whose savings ratio is closest to s^* will gain from trade while the other will lose. Of course, if the two savings ratios are far apart, then the change in price from autarky to free trade may be large and both countries may gain from trade.

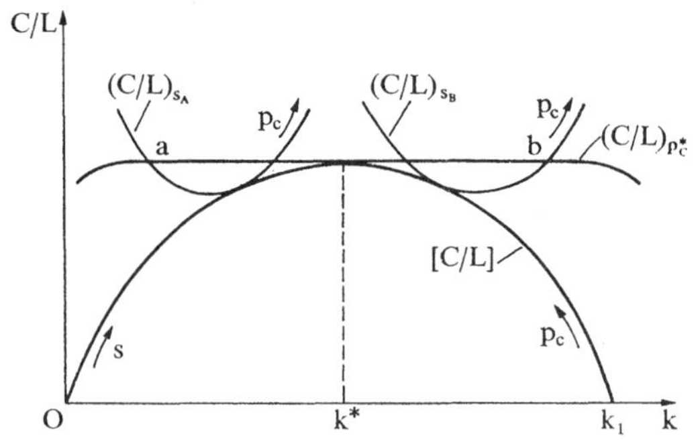

FIG. 6

If the savings ratios lie on opposite sides of s^* ($s_a < s^* < s_b$), then if our theorem applies it will mean a fall in C/L for *both* countries. It is not clear, however, that in this case the price changes can be assumed small enough to apply the theorem. To see this we employ the $(C/L)_p$ locus discussed at the end of Section II. In Fig. 6 we have drawn two appropriate $(C/L)_s$ loci, one on either side of s^*, and in addition have added the $(C/L)_{p_c^*}$ locus of Fig. 5. It should be clear that if, with the opening of trade, p_c should happen to settle precisely at p_c^*, then country A must move to the point a and country B must move to the point b. Thus, both countries will have increased C/L through trade. If the free trade p_c differs from p_c^*, then one country will end up above the $(C/L)_{p_c^*}$ locus and one country will end up below it. In any case, as long as both curves intersect $(C/L)_{p_c^*}$ in its linear segment, it is impossible for both to lose from trade.

The linear segment of any $(C/L)_p$ locus corresponds, as we have seen before, to incomplete specialization. Outside of this region both ends of the locus curve toward the k-axis. Thus if two countries have savings ratios that are sufficiently far apart, both may completely specialize with trade operating on the curved portions of a $(C/L)_p$ locus. This suggests the possibility that steady-state *per capita* consumption could be lower with trade than without for both countries. Unfortunately most of our information about both the $(C/L)_p$ and the $(C/L)_s$ curves is valid only with incomplete specialization, since it was based on continuity and smoothness of functions in the neighbourhoods of autarky points. Thus we are not equipped either to prove or disprove this possibility that both countries might lose from trade.

We can, however, give intuitive plausibility to such an occurrence. If neither country completely specializes in free trade, then factor prices will be equalized between them and world production will be efficient. If, on the other hand, either country does specialize, then factor prices will remain unequal in free trade. This means that world production is inefficient as compared to a world with perfect factor mobility. Now in a static context, this inefficiency cannot negate the gains from trade, since it must be compared to the even greater inefficiency of autarky. But in the dynamic model we consider here, free trade leads the capital-labour ratios of the two countries to move further apart than they were in autarky, thus increasing the production inefficiency that results from complete specialization.

We have been interested here in gains from trade. However, our analysis also demonstrates clearly the effect of trade on capital accumulation. Manipulation of Fig. 4 shows us that with the opening of trade the steady-state capital-labour ratios in the two countries must move in opposite directions and become further apart than they were under autarky. The reason for this result is straightforward. The country with the higher savings propensity attains a higher capital-labour ratio in steady state as a closed economy. This gives it a comparative advantage in the capital-intensive consumption good. Trade, therefore, decreases the price of the investment good in the high-saving country and increases it in the low-saving country. This causes investment—and therefore steady-state capital-labour ratios—to rise in the former and fall in the latter.

This, in a sense, is an extension of familiar comparative advantage results. A country which has a comparative advantage in production of one good will, with the opening of trade, shift its production towards that good. Similarly, a country which, because of its higher propensity to save, has an advantage in the accumulation of capital, will, with the opening of trade, be able to support an even higher ratio of capital to labour. We will see in Section VI, however, that this result holds only if the consumption good is relatively capital-intensive. If the reverse is true, then capital-labour ratios will be drawn closer together by trade, since a high savings rate will now generate comparative advantage in the investment good instead of the consumption good.

V. Trade generated by different technologies

We have just seen how the gains from trade will behave if that trade is generated by differences in propensities to save. We look now at the same problem when trade results from differences in technologies.

Suppose that two countries, A and B, have identical savings ratios and that the technology is Hicks-neutral more efficient by the same percentage in both industries in country B than in country A. It is not hard to see that the steady-state autarky price of the consumption good will be lower in B than in A as long as the consumption good is relatively capital-intensive. To see this, suppose that initially both countries have the same capital-labour ratio. B's transformation curve will then be a uniform radial expansion of A's. Since their savings ratios are identical they will both find short-run equilibrium at the same price, with B producing more of both goods than A. If A happens to be in its steady state, then B must necessarily be growing, since their steady-state capital requirements, $(\mu+n)k$, are the same. This shows that the autarky steady-state capital-labour ratio must be higher for B than for A. We need then only use the familiar result that an increase in the capital-labour ratio lowers the relative price of the capital-intensive good to conclude that the autarky steady-state p_c must be lower in B than in A.

We now know that free trade will cause an increase in p_c for the more efficient country, B, and a decrease for A. Using our theorem it then follows that if the difference in technologies is small—so that the price change is small—then the more efficient country, B, can lose from trade if its savings ratio is above s_b^*, while country A can lose from trade if its savings ratio is below s_a^*, where s_a^* and s_b^* are the golden rule savings ratios corresponding to the two different technologies.

A second possibility that is easily analysed is that of a Hicks-neutral technical advantage in only the consumption goods industry. In that case, for a given capital-labour ratio, the more efficient country's transformation curve will be a horizontal percentage expansion of the other country's transformation curve, assuming the consumption good to be measured on the horizontal axis. It is easily verified that the autarky steady-state capital-labour ratios will be identical in the two countries, but the p_c will be lower in the more efficient country. Thus, our application of the theorem in the previous case continues to hold.

If there is Hicks-neutral technical advantage in only the investment goods industry, then no general statement can be made. The net effect will be a combination of the two just mentioned: a uniform technical advantage in both industries plus a technical disadvantage of the same percentage in only the consumption good. Since the first of these means a lower p_c and the second means a higher p_c, the net difference between autarky prices in the two countries will depend on which effect is stronger.

VI. The case of the capital-intensive investment good

We have assumed, since the end of Section I, that production of the consumption good is relatively capital-intensive compared with production of the investment good. This is the familiar capital-intensity condition used by Uzawa to assure stability and uniqueness of the steady state for a closed economy with a given savings ratio. It is not, however, a necessary condition for stability and uniqueness.[1] Nor is there any reasonable economic justification for assuming that it is satisfied. Therefore, in this section we will outline the changes that must be made in our analysis if we make the reverse capital intensity assumption.[2]

Actually, very few changes are necessary. We observed in Section II that a capital-intensive investment good causes the price of the consumption good, p_c, to rise rather than fall as we move to the right along the $[C/L]$ locus. All other properties of the $[C/L]$ locus are maintained, including the movement of s along $[C/L]$, since we continue to assume that a unique steady state is associated with each savings ratio. Furthermore, the arguments used to derive the $(C/L)_s$ loci and their properties were independent of the capital-intensity assumption.[3]

We see then that the only difference between the picture in Fig. 4 and the picture we need for our new capital-intensity assumption is that the direction of the arrow indicating price change along $[C/L]$ is reversed. It is easily seen that our theorem as stated in Section III continues to be true. It did not rely on the direction of price change along $[C/L]$.

Our application of the theorem in Section IV does, however, require revision. Now if two closed economies are in steady state, the one with the higher savings ratio will also have a higher p_c, and thus will experience a fall in p_c when trade is opened between them. It is easily verified that if the savings ratios of the two countries are on the same side of the golden rule s^*, then the one closer to s^* will lose from trade while

[1] See footnote 2, p. 177.

[2] For completeness we should, perhaps, mention what happens if factor intensities in the two sectors are identical. As mentioned in footnote 1, p. 177, there would then be only one price ratio consistent with incomplete specialization, regardless of the capital-labour ratio. It follows that operation anywhere above the $[C/L]$ locus with trade requires complete specialization. Each $(C/L)_s$ locus then has a kink where it touches $[C/L]$, and our arguments which rely on the smoothness of these loci do not work. In fact it appears that the $(C/L)_s$ loci are essentially V-shaped, rather than U-shaped, and any trade is beneficial. This case is rather pathological, however, since the two production functions are presumably independent.

[3] Actually, it turns out that while the $(C/L)_s$ loci must be convex from below when C is K-intensive, they may be concave from below when I is K-intensive, at least in the neighbourhood of their tangencies with $[C/L]$. However, since our results do not depend on the curvature of these loci, we can ignore this technicality.

the one further from s^* will gain from trade. If, on the other hand, the savings ratios are on opposite sides of s^*, then both must necessarily gain from trade.

VII. The adjustment towards steady state

We have occupied ourselves so far in this paper entirely with steady states. Unfortunately, steady states are remote at best. To discuss gains and losses from trade that will not be realized for decades or even centuries may seem a waste of effort. In recognition of this quite valid objection we look briefly in this section at the behaviour of the model when it is not in a steady state. We restrict attention here to a single small economy which, if it trades, faces a terms of trade that is given and fixed through time.

(*a*) *Initially in steady state*

Suppose that initially the economy is closed and in its appropriate steady state as given by a point on the $[C/L]$ locus. Then suppose that it opens itself to trade with a world in which the international price p_c is higher than its domestic price. It will of course begin to export the consumption good. But more important for our purposes is the fact that its *per capita* consumption will fall. The reason for this is that its output as a closed economy must have contained some of the investment good whose price has fallen. Its national income in terms of the consumption good has therefore also fallen, and consumption is a constant fraction of that national income. This result holds even after the economy has shifted resources into production of the consumption good, as may easily be verified with a transformation curve and several price lines.

The opposite result holds if p_c falls with trade. That is, *per capita* consumption will rise initially.

These results may be added to the diagram in Fig. 4, and we have done so in Fig. 7. There we have drawn, for each of three savings ratios, the paths of *per capita* consumption as the economy adjusts to prices higher and lower than autarky. In every case the initial effect of the price change and the long-term effect of the change in the capital-labour ratio act in opposite directions. If the long-run effect is not sufficient to offset the initial effect, then the gain or loss from trade is unambiguous. For example, with $s = s_3$ and a fall in p_c, *per capita* consumption rises immediately above its autarky value and stays above it. Similarly, with $s = s_3$ and a rise in p_c, C/L is ever after lower than it was in autarky. In either case it turns out that our decision as to gains from trade looking only at steady states was correct: the short-run effects only strengthen the conclusion.

On the other hand, if the long-run effect more than offsets the initial effect, then whether or not there have been gains from trade depends on the time horizon one wishes to use. When $s = s_1$ and p_c rises, then there is initially a fall in C/L but over time it rises again and eventually surpasses its autarky value. To say that there has been a gain from trade is to take a very long-run view of the welfare of the economy. Still, if we take the short-run view, it is not clear that *per capita* consumption is the appropriate index of welfare—at least if saving is taking place voluntarily.[1]

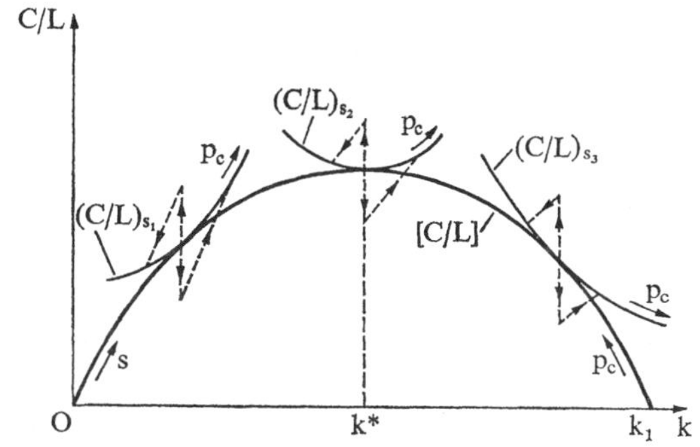

FIG. 7

(*b*) *Not initially in steady state*

Before we leave this section we relax the assumption that the closed economy is initially in a steady state. In its place we assume that the world price is identical to that which would prevail for the closed economy in steady state. In these circumstances trade can have an effect only during the approach to steady state, but not in the steady state itself. We then ask under what circumstances it would be desirable to open the economy to trade during that approach.

Consider, for example, a closed economy with savings ratio $\bar{s}$. Let $\bar{k}$ be the steady-state capital-labour ratio associated with $\bar{s}$ for the closed economy, and $\bar{p}_c$ be the corresponding steady-state price of the consumption good. Suppose, however, that the economy is not initially in steady state, but that it starts with a capital-labour ratio, k^0, less than $\bar{k}$. If the consumption good is capital intensive, then the fact that k^0 is below $\bar{k}$ implies that p_c in the closed economy must initially be higher than the world price. This means that if the economy were to open to trade, the price of the

[1] Stiglitz (1970), using a model similar to ours but with different savings assumptions, found the possibility that steady-state *per capita* consumption would fall with trade, but he commented: 'Should we, therefore, conclude that the opening of trade may have lowered social welfare ? Obviously not.' 'What has happened is that the opening of trade has changed the pattern of consumption over time and more consumption may be taken earlier. . . .' His comment applies as well to our model if savings is less than the golden rule. But if savings is greater than the golden rule we see that a loss in steady-state consumption follows an even greater loss in consumption in the short run. Stiglitz did not get this result because his savings assumptions prevented savings from ever being greater than the golden rule.

consumption good would fall and *per capita* consumption would rise immediately. This immediate gain from trade extends—in a sense—to the entire period of adjustment, since p_c would remain above $\bar{p}_c$ for all time if the economy remained closed, approaching $\bar{p}_c$ from above as the closed economy approached steady state. By opening to trade, then, the economy will enjoy greater *per capita* consumption at each capital-labour ratio than it would have if it were to remain closed.

This does not mean, however, that the economy necessarily gains from trade. For the price change which increases *per capita* consumption also reduces *per capita* investment. Thus, while the economy's capital-labour ratio must rise towards the same steady state regardless of whether it is open or closed, it will approach that steady state more slowly if it is open. Since *per capita* consumption increases with the capital-labour ratio, the initial gain from trade may be offset by the faster growth of the capital-labour ratio under autarky. Thus we must compare a short-run gain from trade with a possible long-run loss. The desirability of trade during the approach to steady state must then depend on the country's attitude toward time preference.

In the case just considered the economy begins its adjustment from a capital-labour ratio below the steady state, $\bar{k}$. If instead k^0 is initially above $\bar{k}$, then the results are reversed. With $k^0 > \bar{k}$, and the consumption good capital intensive, the world price, $\bar{p}_c$, must be above the initial autarky price. Opening to trade will then cause an initial loss of *per capita* consumption. At the same time, however, *per capita* investment will increase, so that the economy's capital-labour ratio will fall towards $\bar{k}$ more slowly than it would if it remained closed. Thus the initial loss from trade might possibly be offset after some time by a higher capital-labour ratio.

If the investment good is capital intensive, then all of these conclusions are again reversed. The price of the consumption good will then be below the world price when k^0 is less than $\bar{k}$ and above the world price when k^0 is above $\bar{k}$. For all cases, however, we can say the following:

> If opening to trade involves a fall (rise) in the price of the consumption good, then the economy will gain (lose) from trade initially; this immediate effect of trade may be offset later in the adjustment process, however, since the open economy's capital-labour ratio will be less than (greater than) what it would have been had it remained closed.

It should be noted, in comparing the paths followed by the closed and open economies, that the capital-labour ratios of the two can differ at each point in time even though they approach the same steady state, $\bar{k}$. Of course, this difference must itself approach zero, but it will never actually be zero.

VIII. Conclusion

We have devoted most of this paper to showing various ways that a growing economy may lose from trade. These results may seem to contradict the traditional static gains from trade analysis, but actually they do not. It is still true that an economy *can* gain from trade if it behaves optimally. As Trent Bertrand (1971) has shown, the locus of steady-state consumption possibilities with free trade dominates that of the closed economy.[1] By suitably adjusting the savings propensity the economy will never lose from free trade and will usually gain. We conclude, therefore, with an attempt to identify which of the assumptions of our model were responsible for the loss from trade that we derived. The most obvious of these is the constant savings propensity, but we defer its consideration for a moment.

First consider the many other assumptions used in our model. These included: constant exponential growth of the labour force, depreciation which is a constant fraction of the capital stock, and neoclassical production functions which are subject to the Inada derivative conditions. These or similar assumptions are needed in order that steady states may exist. For example, if population does not grow and if capital does not depreciate, then the capital-labour ratio would grow without bound.[2] There would be no steady state and questions concerning steady-state *per capita* consumption would be meaningless.

Our model also follows the tradition of neoclassical growth models in assuming that markets work perfectly. Specifically, we assume full employment of factors. Since our purpose has been to show that an economy may lose from trade, the fact that we have done so without invoking such market imperfections is probably an advantage.

We turn, then, to the savings assumption. As mentioned earlier, trade will never decrease steady-state *per capita* consumption if the economy saves appropriately. Our assumption that savings is a constant fraction of income is therefore the major reason for our result that the economy can lose from trade. But the same would be true for any savings assumption that is not based on individual maximizing behaviour. If, for example, savings were a constant fraction of profits rather than of income, it would still be true that steady-state *per capita* consumption could fall with trade.[3] Thus our proportional savings assumption is by no means the only savings assumption that can generate a steady-state loss from trade.

[1] These loci correspond in our analysis to $(C/L)_p$ and $[C/L]$ respectively.

[2] This could also happen if the Inada conditions fail to hold, or if depreciation, though positive, fails to increase in proportion to the capital stock.

[3] This has been shown by Stiglitz (1970) and is true only if the fraction of profits saved is less than one.

Our reason for assuming proportional savings is rather that it simplifies the analysis and that it permits a greater variety of autarkic steady states. The assumption that only profits are saved, for example, leads to a discontinuity in steady-state behaviour that makes the kind of analysis we used impossible. And in addition, if only profits are saved, the closed steady-state capital-labour ratio cannot exceed the golden rule capital-labour ratio, k^*. Thus all of the solutions associated with an economy which over-saves are ruled out from the start.

Thus our proportional savings assumption has allowed us to demonstrate quite simply the possibility of a steady-state loss from trade. Such a loss is likely to be possible with any savings assumption that is not inherently optimal, though to prove this would require a much more difficult analysis than we attempted here. In any case, the constant savings propensity does occupy a prominent place in economic literature—especially in growth theory—and its implications deserve to be explored.

University of Michigan, Ann Arbor

REFERENCES

1. Bardhan, P. K., 1965, 'Equilibrium growth in the international economy', *Quarterly Journal of Economics*, **79**, 455–64.
2. Bertrand, Trent J., 1971, 'The gains from trade: an analysis of steady-state solutions in the open economy', mimeographed, Johns Hopkins University.
3. Drandakis, Emanuel M., 1963, 'Factor substitution in the two-sector growth model', *Review of Economic Studies*, **30**, 217–28.
4. Johnson, Harry G., 1971, 'Trade and growth: a geometrical exposition', *Journal of International Economics*, **1**, 83–101.
5. Oniki, H., and Uzawa, H., 1965, 'Patterns of trade and investment in a dynamic model of international trade', *Review of Economic Studies*, **32**, 15–38.
6. Stiglitz, Joseph E., 1970, 'Factor price equalization in a dynamic economy', *Journal of Political Economy*, **78**, 456–88.
7. Uzawa, Hirofumi, 1963, 'On a two-sector model of economic growth II', *Review of Economic Studies*, **30**, 105–18.
8. Vanek, Jaroslav, 1971, 'Economic growth and international trade in pure theory', *Quarterly Journal of Economics*, **85**, 377–90.

CHAPTER 22

A geometry of growth and trade*

ALAN V. DEARDORFF / *University of Michigan*

I INTRODUCTION

The literature on growth of open economies has been enriched recently by several authors who have applied geometric techniques to the problem (see Johnson, 1971; Vanek, 1971; and Bertrand, 1971). In their articles, traditional tools of pure trade theory were adapted to the growing economy. In this paper we offer an alternative, and considerably simpler, geometric technique for analyzing growth of a small open economy. The same technique can also be used for a number of other similar problems, though we limit our attention here to the problem of trade and growth (see Deardorff, 1971).

The basis of this technique is a diagram which brings together a number of important features of a competitive two-sector economy with homogeneous production functions. We present and explain the diagram in section II. In section III we add the assumption that savings is proportional to income and study the dynamics of growth in a small open economy.[1] In section IV we conclude with a brief description of several other applications of the technique.

* The analysis presented here is drawn mainly from my Ph.D. dissertation, Deardorff (1971). Financial support in writing the present paper was provided by NSF grant, GS 3073, for research in international economics at the University of Michigan. For their helpful comments on earlier versions of this paper, I am indebted to Angelo Mascaro, Richard Porter, Bruce Reynolds, Robert Stern, and Jaroslav Vanek, as well as to other members of my thesis committee at Cornell and of the Research Seminar in International Economics at Michigan. Finally, I have benefited from the comments of two anonymous referees.

1 Our technique can also be adapted to handle the 'classical' savings assumption that only profits are saved (see Deardorff, 1971).

Canadian Journal of Economics/Revue canadienne d'Economique, VII, no. 2
May/mai 1974. Printed in Canada/Imprimé au Canada.

II THE DIAGRAM

The tools which pure trade theorists have most frequently used to depict the production side of an economy are the Edgeworth box and the transformation curve. Because these tools were intended for static problems, they are drawn for given factor endowments. Changes in these endowments can be handled only by shifting the curves. In problems of growth, therefore, where changes in factor endowments are the central feature and occur continuously, these traditional tools are cumbersome.

The standard model involves production of two goods with two factors. Technology is specified by two production functions which are homogeneous of degree one in both factors, and which display positive but diminishing marginal products for the individual factors. The two factors are capital, K, and labour, L. From these are produced an investment good, I, and a consumption good, C.[2] (Demands for the two goods are denoted without bars as I and C respectively.) The homogeneous production function can be written in terms of outputs per worker as follows:

$$\bar{I}/L_I = f_I(K_I/L_I = f_I(k_I) \text{ and} \quad (1)$$

$$\bar{C}/L_C = f_C(K_C/L_C) = f_C(k_C). \quad (2)$$

Here K_j and L_j $(j = I, C)$ are the stocks of capital and labour employed in producing the jth good. The functions f_j (...) are strictly increasing and strictly concave. We will assume occasionally that they satisfy the 'Inada Conditions' that their marginal products, f_j' decline from infinity to zero as k_j rises from zero to infinity.[3]

Diagrams representing single production functions of this form have been used extensively in the analysis of growth models. The reader is no doubt familiar with the interpretation of such curves: at the point of operation, the slope is the competitive capital rental and the vertical intercept of the tangent is the competitive wage.[4] In a one-sector economy, such a curve represents per capita national income as a function of the capital/labour ratio, and is very useful in analysing growth. In a two-sector economy, a similar curve can be constructed from (1) and (2), and it also represents, *for given prices* of the two goods, per capita national income in units of the numeraire as a function of the economy's capital/labour ratio. It yields the same information about factor prices, and, in addition, can be adapted to show per capita outputs of each sector.

2 Identification of the goods by their uses in investment and consumption is necessary only in section III dealing with growth. In this section, I and C may represent any arbitrary pair of goods.

3 The association of these conditions with Inada has become traditional in growth literature, and refers to Inada (1963).

4 For proof of these properties and others, see Hahn and Matthews (1964).

This curve is constructed in Figure 1. We begin by drawing the per capita production functions, $f_j(k_j)$, each multiplied by its given price, p_j, so that the two may appear in a single diagram, with vertical dimension revenue per

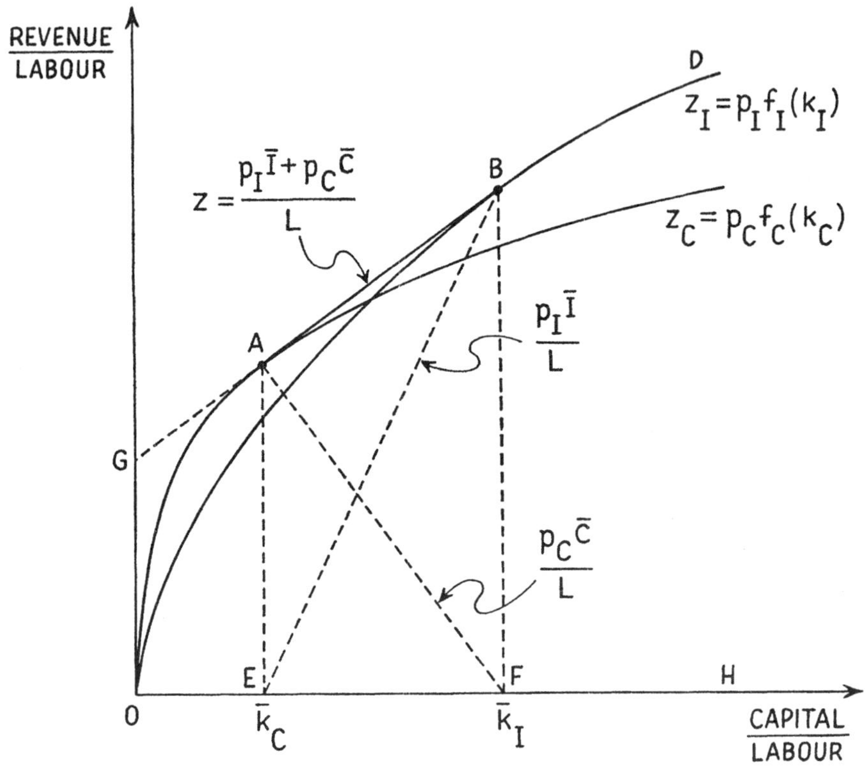

FIGURE 1

head, z_j. These are then connected by their common tangent, AB, and perpendiculars AE and BF, are dropped from the points of tangency to the horizontal axis.[5] Finally, the diagonals of the resulting trapezoid, AF and EB are drawn in.

We can now read off various economic variables as functions of the economy's capital/labour ratio, given the prices for which the curves have

5 If no common tangent exists, then given the Inada conditions, one of the sectoral revenue curves, z, must be above the other for all k. Thus, at the given prices, only one of the goods would be produced regardless of the capital/labour ratio and the economy can be treated as having only one sector. It is also possible that more than one common tangent can be found if the sectoral revenue curves intersect more than once. A necessary, though not sufficient, condition for such multiple intersections is the existence of factor-intensity reversals. In this paper, we assume that neither of these complications arise. They are analysed more fully in Deardorff (1971).

been drawn. The envelope, *OABD*, is the value of total output per head, or per capita national income,

$$z = (p_I I + p_C C)/L.$$

The feet of the perpendiculars, *E* and *F*, are of special significance since they provide the bounds on the economy's capital/labour ratios within which it will produce both goods and outside of which it will completely specialize. These same points also tell us the capital/labour ratios employed in the two sectors, $\bar{k}_C$ and $\bar{k}_I$, so long as both goods are produced.[6] Thus, the outputs per unit of labour *employed* in the two sectors are given by the distances *EA* and *FB*, for any economy-wide capital/labour ratio between $\bar{k}_C$ and $\bar{k}_I$. Of more interest, however, are the values of each sector's output divided by the *total* labour force. These are given, for all economy-wide capital/labour ratios, k_j, by the curves *OAFH* for the consumption good and *OEBD* for the investment good. Finally, we can find the factor prices of capital and labour as the slope and intercept, respectively, of the tangent to the point of operation on *OABD*.

Thus, if the economy's capital/labour ratio, *k*, lies between *O* and *E*, it will produce only the consumption good, and the per capita output of that good will be given by the curve *OA*. Similarly, if *k* lies to the right of *F*, only the investment good will be produced. But if *k* lies between the 'specialization points,' *E* and *F*, both goods will be produced and the per capita outputs of each will be given by the diagonals, *AF* and *EB*.

The diagram and the properties we have described can be most readily understood if we recall that a competitive economy maximizes the value of national output at prevailing prices. Thus we need only show that the curve *OABD* gives the maximum per capita value, or revenue, that could be produced at each capital/labour ratio, and that the diagonals *AF* and *EB* correctly describe the sectoral behaviour needed to reach the maximum.[7]

Now national revenue possibilities certainly include the sectoral revenue curves themselves, z_I and z_C, since the economy could always completely specialize. It could, in addition, divide its resources between the two sectors, and produce at an arbitrary pair of points on the two curves. Let K_I, L_I, K_C, and L_C be the amounts of the factors employed in the two industries. Then the ratio of total capital to labour is

$$k = (K_I + K_C)/(L_I + L_C) = l_I k_I + (1 - l_I)k_C, \qquad (3)$$

6 Since $\bar{k}_I$ is larger than $\bar{k}_C$ in Figure 1, we are assuming good *I* to be capital-intensive compared to good *C*. Throughout the paper, the labeling of these specialization points as sectoral capital/labour ratios makes it easy to determine which good is being assumed capital-intensive in each application of the diagram.

7 As long as the labour force is given, maximizing total output is equivalent to maximizing per capita output.

where $l_I = L_I/L$ and $k_j = K_j/L_j$, $j = I, C$, and both factors are assumed to be fully employed. At the same time, total revenue per capita is

$$z = (p_I\bar{I} + p_C\bar{C})/L = l_I z_I + (1 - l_I) z_C. \tag{4}$$

Solving (3) for l_I and substituting into (4) we get

$$z = [(k - k_C)/(k_I - k_C)]\, z_I + [(k_I - k)/(k_I - k_C)]\, z_C. \tag{5}$$

The specification of an arbitrary pair of points on the sectoral revenue function determines all k_j and z_j.[8] But then (5) is linear in k. Thus, the revenue possibilities include straight lines between any pair of points on the two curves. Among such straight lines, the one which maximizes revenue is clearly the common tangent, AB.

If we now let points A and B determine the k_j and z_j of (5), we notice that the two terms on the right-hand side of (5) are the per capita revenues generated in the two sectors when we operate between A and B. These, too, are linear in k, so that per capita sectoral revenues are indeed given by the straight diagonals in Figure 1.

The diagram as it stands in Figure 1 is useful for a variety of purposes. The fact that it is drawn for given prices is actually an advantage when we wish to compare two countries which, because they trade freely, do face identical prices.[9] It is also an advantage when we analyse the dynamic behaviour of a small open economy which faces prices that are given from outside.

Naturally there are other problems for which prices cannot be taken as given. But we can also use the construction of Figure 1 to analyse the effects of price changes. It is merely necessary to shift one of the sectoral revenue curves and repeat the construction of the trapezoid and its diagonals. Thus if, for example, p_I rises, p_C remaining the same, the effect is to shift the z_I curve of Figure 1 proportionally upward. This, as the reader can verify, causes both specialization points to move to the left, so that a new trapezoid appears to the left of the old one.[10]

8 Though not k itself, since l_I in (3) is still free to vary.

9 Thus Figure 1 provides a framework for unusually simple proofs of several well-established results from the pure theory of international trade. For example, the role of the common tangent, AB, in determining factor prices in the region of non-specialization, leads almost immediately to the factor price equalization theorem. Similarly the diagonals of the trapezoid, AF and EB, lead directly to proofs of the Rybczynski and Heckscher-Ohlin theorems.

10 We do not, at this point, include a figure illustrating this shifting of curves because it would be extremely cluttered and thus difficult to interpret. The interested reader, who is not confined to using a single colour of ink, can perform the construction for himself. Later in the paper, we will illustrate the effects of price changes for specific problems, but we will then be interested in only a few of the economic variables. Incidentally, the reader may find it an interesting exercise to use the diagram to

III GROWTH IN THE SMALL OPEN ECONOMY

We turn to the analysis of growth in a small open economy. If an open economy is small, then it faces prices that are given from outside. If these prices are also constant over time, we can use Figure 1 to describe the economy's production possibilities over time. The advantage of this approach is that the curve *OABD* in Figure 1 plays the same role in the two-sector small open economy as does the single per capita production function of a one-sector closed economy. We can therefore analyse growth of the former by the same simple method used by Solow (1956) in his one-sector growth model.

The standard neoclassical growth model assumes constant proportional rates of population growth, n, and capital depreciation, μ. As capital depreciates, it is also augmented by investment, I. Thus,

$$\dot{L} = nL \quad \text{and} \tag{6}$$

$$\dot{K} = I - \mu K, \tag{7}$$

where dots over variables denote time derivatives. Equations 6 and 7 imply the following differential equation for the capital/labour ratio:

$$\dot{k} = (I/L) - (\mu + n)k. \tag{8}$$

If assumptions are available that make per capita investment depend only on k, then equation 8 can be analysed by graphing the two terms on its right-hand side as functions of k. The direction of movement of k is then determined by their relative heights, and the stationary solutions – or 'steady states' – by their intersections.

We assume then that investment always equals savings, and that savings is a constant fraction, s, of national income.[11] Since per capita national income has already been found in Figure 1 to be a function of the capital/labour ratio, these assumptions assure that per capita investment is also a function of k. More than that, the curve representing I/L must have the same shape as *OABD* in Figure 1, reduced to a fraction, s, of its height. Now, the vertical dimension of Figure 1 was revenue per head, revenue being expressed in units of money or some arbitrary numeraire. But I/L must be expressed in units of the investment good per head in order to compare it with $(\mu + n)k$

determine the effect of a change in relative commodity prices on factor prices, and thus to verify a version of the Stolper-Samuelson theorem. By taking first good I, and then good C, as numeraire, the result in terms of real factor prices may be seen to be unambiguous.

11 This is the same savings assumption used by Oniki and Uzawa (1965), Johnson (1971), and Vanek (1971).

in (8). We therefore must take the investment good as numeraire, setting $p_I = 1$.[12]

All of this is illustrated in Figure 2. The per capita income curve, *OABD*, and the production diagonals, *AF* and *EB*, are reproduced from Figure 1. *OABD* is then multiplied by the fraction, *s*, to yield the per capita investment curve. Finally we add a straight line from the origin with slope $\mu + n$ to represent the second term of (8).

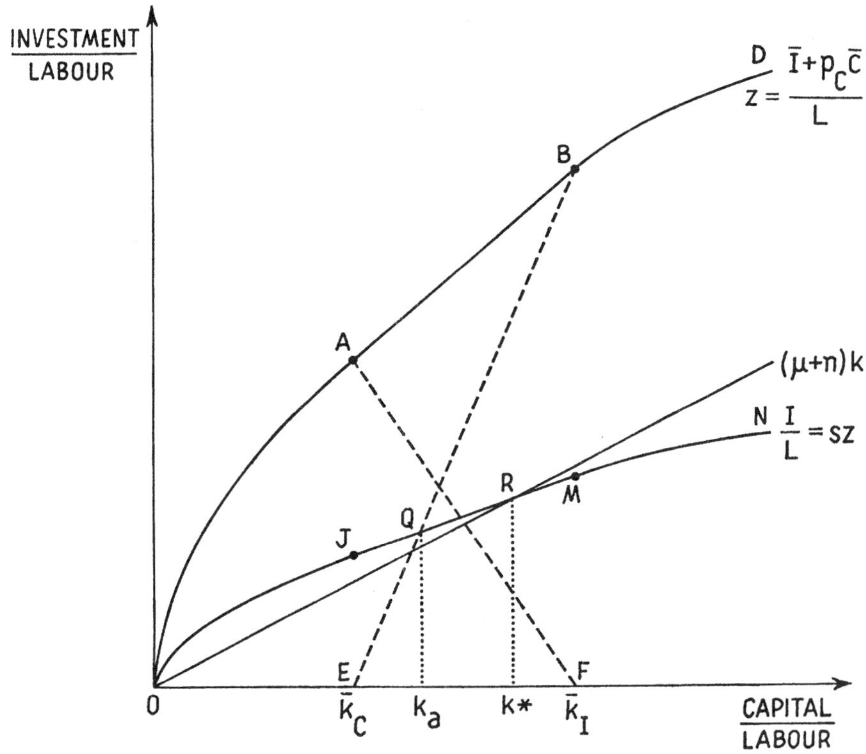

FIGURE 2

The dynamics of k are determined completely by the two curves I/L and $(\mu + n)k$. If k lies initially below k^*, then I/L is greater than $(\mu + n)k$, and k must be increasing. Similarly if k is initially above k^*, it will fall over time. In either case, k must approach k^*, which is the steady state. Existence, uniqueness, and stability of steady-state growth can be examined with these two

12 This restriction is unimportant as long as prices do not change, and, when they do, it merely means that all relative price changes must be represented through changes in p_C.

curves, and the conclusions are the same as in Solow's one-sector growth model.[13]

We can investigate the behaviour of trade over time by comparing the I/L curve, which represents demand for the investment good, with the curve *OEBD*, which, if the investment good is relatively capital-intensive, represents supply of the investment good. Consider the particular case drawn in Figure 2. Suppose k were initially less than k_C. Then the economy would initially produce only the consumption good, and would of course import the investment good. The capital/labour ratio would rise over time, however, eventually surpassing $\bar{k}_C$, and the economy would begin producing the investment good. As k continues to increase, imports of the investment good fall, and when k reaches k_a, the trade pattern reverses. Ultimately, in the steady state, k^*, the economy is an exporter of the investment good and an importer of the consumption good.

What we have described is of course only a special case. Different values of the parameters, μ, n, and s, would yield different steady states, and therefore different patterns of trade and production in, and during the approach to, steady state. Furthermore, if the investment good were labour-intensive, the above description would be reversed, and k_a would be found at the intersection of I/L with *AF* rather than *EB*. The influence of the various parameters on the dynamics of trade and growth, under different assumptions about factor intensities, can easily be analysed in Figure 2.

A more interesting problem, however, concerns the effects of price changes on the model. Since the investment good is our numeraire, we can only alter p_C. Now any change in p_C will change a large portion of the per capita income curve, *OABD*, as it was derived in Figure 1. The change in *OABD* will in turn cause a similar change in the I/L curve of Figure 2 and thus, generally, a change in the steady-state capital/labour ratio. In addition, the production diagonals also move, and this may have further effects on production and trade initially and in the new steady state.[14]

All this seems fairly complicated, but one general conclusion is easy to obtain: if the price of the consumption good changes, then the steady-state capital/labour ratio must change in the same direction unless the economy

13 Existence is guaranteed (for positive μ or n) by the Inada conditions, while uniqueness and stability follow from the fact that the ratio of income to capital declines continuously as k rises. The latter is true in spite of the linear portion of the I/L curve, since the construction of *OABD* guarantees that the extension of that linear portion has a positive intercept with the vertical axis.

14 In addition to the effects on production and trade, one would also like to determine the effect of a price change on per capita consumption. Unfortunately, our diagram is not well suited to this problem, since use of it for growth analysis requires the investment good as numeraire. This means that the difference between national income and investment must be adjusted whenever prices change to get consumption. For an analysis of this problem with a different, more appropriate, geometric technique, see Deardorff (1973).

specializes completely in production of the investment good, both before and after the price change, in which case the steady-state capital/labour ratio remains unchanged. This is true regardless of which good is capital-intensive.

This conclusion is easily derived from our geometry. Let p_C increase in Figure 1. This raises the z_C curve and thus also raises the portions OA and AB of the per capita income curve. Only that part of the latter corresponding to complete specialization in $\bar{I}$ remains unchanged. But these changes are reflected exactly in changes of the I/L curve of Figure 2. And when I/L rises, its intersection with $(\mu + n)k$ – and thus the steady-state capital/labour ratio – must move to the right. If, contrary to Figure 1, the investment good were labour-intensive, then the increase in p_C would cause an upward shift of the right-hand portions of the per capita income curve rather than the left-hand portions. But the shift would still be upward except where there is complete specialization in the investment good.[15]

This is illustrated in Figure 3 for the case of the labour-intensive investment good. An increase in p_C shifts the national income curve from $OABD$ to $OA'B'D'$. Thus, the per capita investment curve also shifts from $OJMN$ to $OJ'M'N'$. Since the latter is above the former to the right of J, the steady state moves from k^* to $k^{*\prime}$.

We may determine the effect of the price change on steady-state trade by adding the production diagonals for the investment good and comparing the steady-state values of I/L. In Figure 3, since the investment good is labour-intensive, $\bar{I}/L$ would be given by the diagonals AF and $A'F'$ (not shown) before and after the price change.[16] It is clear that $A'F'$ lies uniformly to the left of AF, while $k^{*\prime}$ lies to the right of k^*. Since both AF and $A'F'$ are downward-sloping, production of the investment good is lower in the new steady state, while demand for it is higher. Thus the rise in p_C causes exports of the investment good – if there are any – to fall, or imports of it to rise.

If the investment good is capital-intensive, then the effect on trade is less clear-cut. In this case, the diagonal representing production of the investment good, EB in Figure 2, is upward-sloping and moves to the right. The steady state, k^*, also moves to the right, so that the increase in p_C may cause production of the investment good to rise, in steady state, relative to demand. This raises the possibility, noticed by Johnson (1971), that a country which opens to trade may ultimately export the good whose price has fallen.[17]

15 This can be explained intuitively, as follows. As long as the economy does not produce only the investment good, an increase in the price of the consumption good raises the investment-good-equivalent of its national income (since its production of C can now be exchanged for more of $\bar{I}$). Since part of this increase in income is saved, the result is an increase in its capital/labour ratio.

16 Points F and F' are the specialization points for the consumption good and lie directly below points B and B' respectively.

17 Since the economy will initially import the good whose price has fallen, this means that the direction of trade may reverse during the transition from one steady state

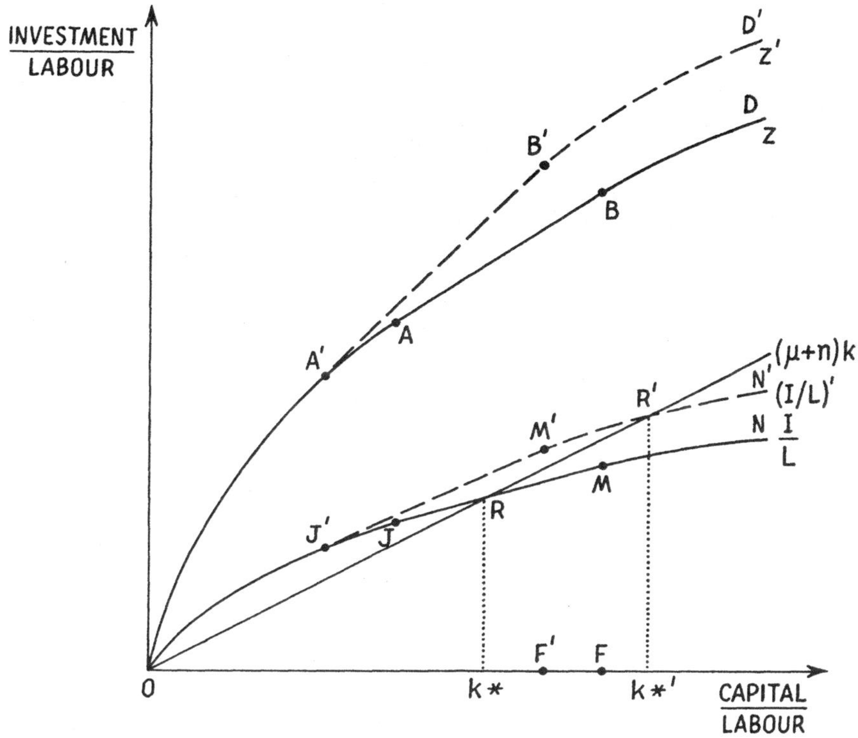

FIGURE 3

IV OTHER APPLICATIONS

In this paper, we have applied our geometry only to the problem of growth in a small open economy. A number of other applications are possible, however, and in this section we mention several of them, leaving it to the interested reader to work out the details.[18]

One such application arises when, in section III, we drop the assumption that savings is proportional to income. If, in its place, we assume that only profits are saved, then we can use the profit rate indicated by the slope of the national-income curve to derive a new curve representing profits, and therefore savings and investment, per capita. This curve can then be used to analyse growth in much the same manner as was used in this paper for an open economy with proportional savings. It is easily shown for example that

to another. Such trade reversals have been analysed more fully, and in a more general model, by Deardorff (1974). There, it is shown that if the initial steady state involves no trade, so that the price change reflects a shift from autarky to free trade, then trade reversal requires some instability in the growth process prior to trade.

18 These applications are more fully considered in Deardorff (1971).

an open economy with such 'classical' saving is very likely to specialize in production of only one of the goods once it reaches a steady state (as noted by Bertrand, 1971 and Stiglitz, 1970).

Next, we note that our diagram is particularly well suited to the analysis of an economy with more than two commodities. For each additional commodity, we simply add the appropriate per capita revenue curve to the diagram, and derive national income by maximizing over the convex combinations of all such curves. The conditions for factor-price equalization in the n-commodity case can then be illustrated, as well as the indeterminacy of production and trade noted by Melvin (1968).

Once additional goods are included in the diagram, our analysis of growth in a small open economy can easily be extended to an economy with any number of goods. The only restriction is that we must continue to assume only one investment good. Existence, uniqueness, and stability of steady states can still be proved. The comparative steady-state effects of changing the growth, savings, and price parameters are unchanged from the two-good case, except for the discontinuous effects that prices can now have on the pattern of specialization.[19]

Finally, the diagram can also be used to examine growth models of a closed two-sector economy, of the kind introduced by Uzawa (1961 and 1963). The fact that our diagram is drawn for given prices makes its application to a closed economy more difficult than its application to a small open economy, of course, since prices must adjust in a closed economy to clear the markets. But the problem can still be handled by shifting the curves and tracing out a locus of short-run equilibria. This locus can then be used intact to describe growth over time.

REFERENCES

Bertrand, Trent J. (1971) 'The Gains from Trade: An Analysis of Steady-State Solutions in the Open Economy.' Mimeographed, Johns Hopkins University

Deardorff Alan V. (1971) 'Growth and Trade in a Two-Sector World.' Unpublished Ph.D. dissertation, Cornell University

Deardorff, Alan V. (1973) 'The Gains from Trade In and Out of Steady State Growth.' *Oxford Economic Papers* 25, 173–91

Deardorff, Alan V. (1974) 'Trade Reversals and Growth Stability.' *Journal of International Economics*

Findlay, Ronald (1970) 'Factor Proportions and Comparative Advantage in the Long Run.' *Journal of Political Economy* 78, 27–36

Hahn, F.H. and R.C.O. Matthews (1964) 'The Theory of Economic Growth: A Survey.' *Economic Journal* 74, 779–902

Inada, Ken-ichi (1963) 'On a Two-Sector Model of Economic Growth: Comments and a Generalization.' *Review of Economic Studies* 30, 119–27

19 It is not necessary that all the goods be traded. The geometry adapts readily to Findlay's (1970) model in which the investment good itself is non-traded.

Johnson, Harry G. (1971) 'Trade and Growth: A Geometrical Exposition.' *Journal of International Economics* 1, 83–101
Melvin, J.R. (1968) 'Production and Trade with Two Factors and Three Goods.' *American Economic Review* 58, 1249–68
Oniki, H. and H. Uzawa (1965) 'Patterns of Trade and Investment in a Dynamic Model of International Trade.' *Review of Economic Studies* 32, 15–38
Solow, Robert M. (1956) 'A Contribution to the Theory of Economic Growth.' *Quarterly Journal of Economics* 70, 65–94
Stiglitz, Joseph E. (1970) 'Factor Price Equilization in a Dynamic Economy.' *Journal of Political Economy* 78, 456–88
Uzawa, Hirofumi (1961) 'On a Two-Sector Model of Economic Growth.' *Review of Economic Studies* 29, 40–7
Uzawa, Hirofumi (1963) 'On A Two-Sector Model of Economic Growth II.' *Review of Economic Studies* 30, 105–18
Vanek, Jaroslav (1971) 'Economic Growth and International Trade in Pure Theory.' *Quarterly Journal of Economics* 85, 377–90

CHAPTER 23

Growth and International Investment with Diverging Populations
Author(s): Alan V. Deardorff
Source: *Oxford Economic Papers*, New Series, Vol. 46, No. 3 (Jul., 1994), pp. 477-491
Published by: Oxford University Press
Stable URL: http://www.jstor.org/stable/2663577
Accessed: 05/05/2010 13:55

Oxford Economic Papers 46 (1994), 477–491

GROWTH AND INTERNATIONAL INVESTMENT WITH DIVERGING POPULATIONS

By ALAN V. DEARDORFF

Department of Economics, University of Michigan, Ann Arbor, MI 48109, USA

1. Introduction

The neoclassical theory of growth, pioneered by Solow (1956) and Swan (1956), has long been regarded as unsatisfactory because of its steady-state implications. In models where growth is driven solely by capital accumulation, and where there are sufficiently diminishing returns to capital per worker, continued long-run growth is impossible in *per capita* terms. This is thought to be particularly inappropriate in an international context, where experience seems to suggest that countries differ systematically in their abilities to sustain long-run per capita growth. Thus neoclassical growth theory, and especially its application to models of international trade, fell into disfavor after a flurry of activity in the late sixties and early seventies, and was widely regarded as a dead-end theoretical undertaking.[1]

More recently, Romer (1986) and Lucas (1988) have revived the growth theory of a closed economy by incorporating into their models aspects of economies of scale. This turns out to permit countries to sustain *per capita* growth even in the long run, and indeed it allows the long-run growth rate of a country to depend endogenously on its saving behavior. Other authors, most notably Grossman and Helpman in a series of papers and a book, have picked up this theme and applied it in an international context.[2] In their models, growth rates not only are endogenous, but they can differ across countries and be influenced by policy, including trade policy. This is an exciting development, not only because it revives an undeniably important but previously stagnant area of economic inquiry, but also because it may, at long last, permit economic theory to contribute to the debate on the link between liberal trade and economic development.

Jones and Manuelli (1990) have recently suggested that the neoclassical model is not quite as deficient as it seemed. Expanding on a point made originally by Solow (1956), they show that if diminishing returns are limited by a lower bound on the marginal product of capital, then sustained *per capita* growth is possible after all, and the growth rate of a country does depend on policies that influence its saving behavior. Thus while the introduction of

[1] See Findlay (1984) and Smith (1984) for surveys of this traditional literature on trade and growth.

[2] See Grossman and Helpman (1990, 1991a, 1991b). Helpman (1988) has provided an excellent and intuitive introduction to this literature.

economies of scale into growth models may well be extremely important in its own right, it is not a necessary condition for achieving these two desirable theoretical outcomes.

In this paper I show that the same results obtain for any country whose population grows less rapidly than populations elsewhere in the world. This is true in a neoclassical growth model, without any restriction on diminishing returns. By allowing for both the international mobility of capital as well as differences across countries in their rates of population growth—what I call diverging populations—I show that a country can use growth elsewhere in the world to limit the decline in its return to capital and thus to get the same benefits as in Jones and Manuelli (1990). Those authors were correct that 'the crucial feature to attain sustained growth seems to be that the marginal product of capital remains bounded away from zero'. However that boundedness need not depend on a perhaps implausible feature of technology, but can arise simply and economically from differences in population growth rates.

In addition, my model displays a property that is familiar in another context from the early growth literature but that has received little attention of late. In the manner of the capitalist class in the two-class Pasinetti (1962) growth model, my country with the slower population growth rate can, if it saves sufficiently, come to dominate the determination of the world return to capital and thus the world growth path. In achieving this result, that country comes to own a significant share of world capital, even though its share of world population becomes negligible. This, therefore, has important and perhaps disturbing implications for the long run distribution of world income and wealth.[3]

All of this depends crucially, as will become clear, on the assumption that population growth rates differ across countries. This possibility has been neglected in the international growth literature, both old and new, not because it is unlikely to arise in the real world, but because it has been considered

[3] Avinash Dixit has pointed out to me another parallel in the literature. Marx (1967, p. 212), quoted in Junankar (1982, p. 93), like Solow but for different reasons, predicted a falling rate of profit:

> ... the gradual growth of constant capital in relation to variable capital must necessarily lead to a *gradual fall in the general rate of profit*, so long as the rate of surplus value, or the intensity of exploitation of labour by capital, remain the same.

Lenin, like me but also for different reasons, redirected attention to the ability of a capitalist country to export its capital, and thus avoid or at least postpone the trap of the falling rate of profit. According to Griffin and Gurley (1985, p. 1097), Lenin (1939)

> ... ascribed growing capital exports, a principal mark of the new imperialism, to 'the fact that in a few countries capitalism has become "over-ripe" and (owing to the backward stage of agriculture and the impoverished state of the masses) capital cannot find a field for "profitable" investment'. Lenin also (1939, pp. 124–5) provided an intriguing picture of the 'imperialist' countries that come to live off of their foreign capital:
>
> More and more prominently there emerges, as one of the tendencies of imperialism, the creation of the 'bondholding' (rentier) state, the usurer state, in which the bourgeoisie lives on the proceeds of capital exports and by 'clipping coupons'.

uninteresting.[4] It is argued that the high-population-growth country, which for convenience I will call South,[5] will become infinitely large relative to the low-population-growth country, which I will call North, and South will therefore behave ultimately like a closed economy. North, on the other hand, will become so small relative to South as to be unable to affect its terms of trade, and it will therefore behave like the small open economy whose growth has been analyzed extensively in the early literature.[6] This argument is valid, however, only if international capital flows are excluded from the model.[7] If capital flows are allowed, then the fact that North's labor force becomes negligible relative to South's does not necessarily imply that it also comes to own a negligible share of world capital.

The reason for this, as well as an indication of the way my model will behave, may be found in the literature on two-class growth models that has grown on the foundation laid by Pasinetti (1962). Pasinetti's model included, in a closed economy, a class of capitalists who earned no labor income but instead derived their entire income from capital. Likewise in my model, North's share in world labor income must eventually be zero because of its low population growth rate. North therefore becomes analogous to Pasinetti's capitalist class and, like the capitalists, may continue indefinitely to own a positive share of world capital.

[4] The surveys by Findlay (1984) and Smith (1884), for example, make no mention of the possibility that countries may differ in their population growth rates. Khang and Kemp (1973) do construct a two-country model in which population growth rates may differ, and their model in addition allows for two sectors and a variety of savings assumptions. Therefore the model of the present paper is really a special case of theirs. However, Khang and Kemp do not proceed very far with the solution to their model, and in particular they do not derive any of the major results that are derived here.

[5] The labels North and South are used in this paper purely for ease of exposition. The model is not a 'North-South' model in the sense, say, of Findlay (1984). On the other hand, this model does bear some resemblance to the North-South model of Findlay (1980). The higher population growth rate in my South is not that different from the unlimited supply of labor in Findlay's South, which was based on the dual economy of Lewis (1954). Burgstaller and Saavedra-Rivano (1984) introduced capital mobility into Findlay's model and, as I will not note below, found results that are essentially the same as one of the cases presented here.

[6] Oniki and Uzawa (1965) handled only the case of identical population growth rates, claiming (p. 16) that 'the general case of constant but different rates of population growth is handled without much difficulty'. Bardhan (1966. p. 39) disputed this claim on the grounds that 'growth equilibrium does not exist' unless population growth rates are equal, as he had proved in Bardhan (1965). Since Bardhan defined growth equilibrium as having the property that all variables, including exports and imports, grow at the same rate as population, his claim was quite correct. However, it misses the point that the model does possess a well-defined asymptotic solution in which quantities traded grow at a rate equal to the smaller of the two population growth rates and thus become negligible relative to population in the faster growing century. Kemp (1969, p. 226) seems to have been the first to recognize explicitly this tendency for a two-country growth model to resolve itself into the polar cases of small open and large closed economies.

[7] There are no international capital flows in the models cited in the preceding footnote. Kemp (1969, chap. 11) also looked at a model with international investment, but in that model he assumed from the outset that population growth rates were identical. Other treatments of growth and trade in a small open economy, such as Johnson (1971), Vanek (1971), and Deardorff (1974) have also excluded capital flows. Buiter (1981) looked at capital flows in a two-country overlapping-generations model but again assumed that population growth rates were identical. Jones and Manuelli (1990) also allowed international capital flows, but held all populations constant.

This result depends, as Samuelson and Modigliani (1966) pointed out, on a sufficiently large propensity to save by the capitalist class.[8] Without that, the capitalists' share of total capital becomes negligible, and in a closed economy they may be disregarded. In my model this means that North does become small, in terms of its shares of both labor and capital. It is still worth studying, however, since the growth behavior of a small open economy with mobile capital turns out to be markedly different from that of the small open economy with immobile capital that has previously been studied.

When North saves enough that it does not become small, then several conclusions about the behavior of my two-country model may be obtained directly from the two-class literature. The most important of these has come to be called the Pasinetti Paradox, which states that the steady-state return to capital equals the ratio of the population growth rate to the savings propensity of the capitalist class alone. It is therefore independent of the savings behavior of the workers. In my two-country model this means that the return to capital depends, in a steady state, on the larger of the two population growth rates and on the savings propensity of North, but it is independent of savings in South.

Samuelson and Modigliani (1966) noted that this result holds only if the capitalists save enough to maintain their ownership of a positive share of total capital. In the dual case of low capitalist savings, they obtain the similar but less remarkable result that the steady-state average product of capital equals the ratio of the population growth rate to the worker's propensity to save. Since this is a property that holds for a closed economy with a single class of savers, it merely verifies, in the model here, that South eventually behaves as though it were closed if savings in North are sufficiently low.

While these conclusions follow immediately from the two-class literature, that literature does not answer all of the questions one might wish to ask about the two country model. How, for example, do growth rates in the two countries separately depend upon their savings propensities and population growth rates? What influence does the ability to invest savings internationally have on *per capita* consumption in the two countries? Such questions have not been considered in the two-class literature because of the omission from the two-class model of any reference to the population of the capitalist class.[9] Yet the answers to these questions are interesting, as I may indicate by listing the results that follow from my model:

Proposition 1 The steady state of the model divides into three cases, according to the relative size of the savings propensity in North. In Case 1, with a low

[8] The model will be formulated through most of the paper in terms of constant propensities to save out of income. In Deardorff (1990), however, I discuss how the model would behave with a form of rational saving instead.

[9] This omission is understandable, considering the original purposes of such models, since factor returns and shares do not depend, in steady state, on the size or rate of growth of the capitalist population.

savings propensity, North grows only as fast as its own population growth rate and thus remains small relative to South. In Case 2, with a somewhat higher savings propensity, North grows more rapidly than its own population forever, but nonetheless continues to own only a negligible share of world capital. In Case 3, with an even higher savings propensity, North grows as rapidly as population in South, and North also owns a significant share of world capital.

Proposition 2 North can, by changing its savings propensity, affect its own steady-state growth rate within the limits imposed by the two population growth rates.

Proposition 3 Steady-state *per capita* consumption in South is unaffected by the savings propensity of North in Cases 1 and 2, and increases with that savings propensity in Case 3.

Proposition 4 *Per capita* consumption in North approaches a constant steady-state level only in Case 1. In Cases 2 and 3, *per capita* consumption in North grows exponentially forever, with a rate of exponential growth that increases with its savings propensity in Case 2 and remains constant (equal to the difference between the two population growth rates) in Case 3.

These propositions are in striking contrast to the results of early neoclassical growth models, both of closed and of open economies, and they are much more reminiscent of the recent literature on endogenous growth with economies of scale. Throughout the neoclassical literature, it has been accepted that a country cannot sustain growth of its income at a rate greater than its population growth rate, unless there is some form of technical progress or a lower bound on the marginal product of capital. It follows that a country with sufficiently diminishing returns cannot affect that rate of growth through its savings behavior, unless the rate of technical progress in turn depends in some way on its rate of savings. Now it appears, in Propositions 1 and 2 above, that a country, even with a stationary, constant-returns-to-scale, diminishing returns technology, can use investment in a more rapidly growing economy to sustain growth more rapid than its own population growth rate, and also that it can influence its growth rate through its savings propensity. The Solow phenomenon still operates, of course, but it is now the foreign population growth rate that limits a country's rate of growth. It is clear from Proposition 4 that this has important implications for the welfare of the country that has this opportunity. Furthermore, the benefits in terms of *per capita* consumption that North obtains by investing abroad are not obtained at the expense of South, as is clear in Proposition 3.

In subsequent sections of this paper I will present the model more formally and prove Propositions 1 and 2. Propositions 3 and 4 are straightforward and can be found in Deardorff (1990). I will also indicate the dividing lines that separate the three cases. The model I use for this purpose is a simplified version of Kemp's (1969, chap. 11) model of trade, investment, and growth. I simplify his model considerably, however, by abstracting from trade and assuming that there is only one good, which is produced everywhere in the world.[10] This simplification makes the extension of the model to countries with different population growth rates more manageable.

In Section 2 I begin by analyzing growth of a small economy with mobile capital. A small economy is one whose shares of both world labor and world capital are negligible, so that it faces a rate of return to capital that is given from outside. It therefore may correspond to either of Cases 1 and 2 mentioned earlier. In Section 3 I present the more general two-country model, derive its asymptotic properties, and complete the proofs of Propositions 1 and 2.

This model is primarily intended as a description of the growth of countries with internationally mobile capital. It is, however, formally identical to a two-class model of a single economy, and it has straightforward implications for the origin and behavior of the classes in such a model. I discuss these implications in Section 4.

2. The small country case

Consider first the growth of a small country that has access to a large international capital market. By abstracting from trade, this model becomes a modification of Solow's (1956) growth model of a closed one-sector economy. The modification, of course, is to include as income its earnings invested abroad.

Denoting the country as Country 1 for later inclusion in a two-country model, I make the familiar neoclassical assumptions that gross investment equals savings, that savings is a constant fraction, s_1, of income, and that the labor force grows exponentially at a constant rate n_1. With these assumptions the country's dynamic behavior is described by the following pair of differential equations

$$\mathrm{d}L_1/\mathrm{d}t = n_1 L_1 \tag{1}$$

$$\mathrm{d}K_1/\mathrm{d}t = s_1[wL_1 + rK_1] \tag{2}$$

where K_1 and L_1 are the country's labor force and capital stock respectively.[11]

The bracketed expression in (2) is the country's income. Note that (2) does not distinguish between capital invested domestically and capital invested abroad. This will be appropriate if there is perfect international capital mobility[12] and perfect domestic factor markets. This assumption, together with a linearly homogeneous production function for domestic output, also allows w to be uniquely determined by r. Thus both w and r are parameters given by the rest of the world.

The system (1, 2) reduces to a single differential equation in the capital-labor

[10] In Deardorff (1990) I examine the possibility of two traded goods, as well as the possibility of a sector producing nontraded goods.

[11] Capital does not depreciate here, though a constant rate of depreciation could be incorporated without substantively altering the results.

[12] The possibility that capital is less than perfectly mobile is discussed in Deardorff (1990) and is modelled numerically in Deardorff (1987).

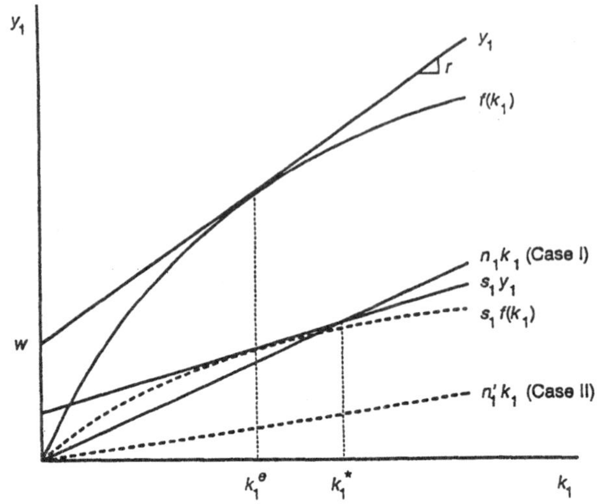

FIG. 1.

ratio, $k_1 = K_1/L_1$

$$dk_1/dt = s_1[w + rk_1] - n_1k_1 \tag{3}$$

The behavior of this differential equation is easily seen in Fig. 1, which is largely familiar from expositions of the Solow closed economy growth model $f(k_1)$ is the production function in intensive form. Given r from the world market, enough capital per head will be employed at home, k_1^e, to equate $f'(k_1^e) = r$. The economy's *per capita* income, y_1—including income from capital invested abroad—is then the straight line tangent to $f(k_1)$ with slope r. *Per capita* savings, which is the first term on the right-hand side of (3), is the fraction of this line s_1y_1, and need only be compared to a ray from the origin, n_1k_1, to determine where k_1 is rising, falling, or stationary over time.

For the value of n_1 shown, this means that k_1 is driven over time toward the steady state level, k_1^*. The only difference from the Solow model in this case is a slightly higher steady-state capital-labor ratio (compare the intersection of n_1k_1 with the curve $s_1f(k_1)$, which would be *per capita* savings in a closed economy) and the fact that the country invests $k_1^* - k_1^e$ of its capital abroad.[13] In this case, the model retains the important characteristics of Solow's closed-economy growth model. The growth rates of capital and income both ultimately converge to the population growth rate, n_1, and there is no sustained growth of the economy in *per capita* terms. This corresponds to Case 1 mentioned in Proposition 1 of the introduction.

For other parameters, however, the result can be different. Consider the lower

[13] Of course, for higher n_1 or lower s_1, steady state would be to the left of k_1^e and the country would import capital.

population growth rate, n'_1. In this case, $n'_1 k_1$ does not intersect $s_1 y_1$ and the economy accumulates capital without bound. There is no steady state, in the usual sense of a constant capital-labor ratio. But the model does possess well-defined asymptotic properties. To see this, solve eq. (3) explicitly as follows

$$k_1(t) = (k_1^0 - k_1^*) \exp[(s_1 r - n_1)t] + k_1^* \tag{4}$$

where k_1^0 is the initial capital-labor ratio, and

$$k_1^* = \frac{-s_1 w}{s_1 r - n_1} \tag{5}$$

The behavior of this solution clearly depends on the expression $(s_1 r - n_1)$. If $s_1 < n_1/r$, then the exponential term in (4) disappears over time, and the economy converges to k_1^*. This is Case 1 as just described.

The rate n'_1 in Fig. 1, on the other hand, corresponds to the more interesting case where r and s_1 are large enough to make $(s_1 r - n'_1) > 0$. In that case k_1 must grow indefinitely, and it is the constant term in (4), k_1^*, that becomes insignificant. The term $(s_1 r - n_1)$ is now the asymptotic rate of growth of the capital-labour ratio. It follows that $s_1 r$ is the asymptotic rate of growth of both capital and income—the latter since the wage component of income becomes insignificant.

It is here then—in what I called Case 2 in the introduction—that this growth model exhibits behavior that is radically different from traditional neoclassical models. Not only is it possible for a country to grow indefinitely at a rate greater than its population growth rate, but it can also increase this rate of growth by increasing its savings propensity. The reason for this, of course, is that the country is freed, by the international capital market, from the usual constraint of diminishing returns. In a completely closed economy with constant returns to scale, the productivity of capital is limited by its own labor force, and diminishing returns normally prevent the economy from increasing its capital-labor ratio indefinitely. In this small country model, on the other hand, the return to capital that it can earn by investing abroad is constant. This solution to the Solow model was recognized by Solow (1956) when the technology includes a positive lower bound on the marginal product of capital. From here on, I assume that such a positive lower bound does not exist, so that it is only by investing abroad that a small country can escape diminishing returns.

It remains to be seen, however, whether the small-country assumption can possibly be valid. In the asymptotic solution the small country invests an ever increasing fraction of its ever increasing capital stock abroad. Is it possible for the rest of the world to absorb this much capital without it affecting the rate of return? If population abroad grows no more rapidly than at home, then the answer must certainly be no. For then the small country's capital stock would be growing faster than world population, and diminishing returns would have to set in just as in a closed economy.

But if the population growth rate is higher abroad than at home, then the smaller country can increase its capital stock faster than its own population and rely on the more rapid population growth in the rest of the world to keep the return to capital from falling.[14] This possibility is explored further in the next section.

3. The two-country case[15]

In the two-country model the behavioral assumptions for each country are the same as those used for the small country in Section 2. The return to capital and the wage rate, however, are determined by factor productivities in the two countries, together with the condition that the return to capital be the same in both.

Let the two countries have identical linearly homogeneous production functions, so that the average product of labor in both is the same function, f, of only the capital-labor ratio employed. With competitive factor pricing and perfect capital mobility, it follows that the ratios of capital to labor employed in each country will equal the world capital-labor ratio. The competitive return to capital then depends only on the world capital-labor ratio, K/L.[16]

$$r = f'(K/L) \tag{6}$$

as does the competitive wage

$$w = f(K/L) - rK/L \tag{7}$$

The dynamic equations of the two-country cases consist of eqs (1) and (2) of Section 2, repeated for each country

$$\mathrm{d}L_i/\mathrm{d}t = n_i L_i, \qquad i = 1, 2 \tag{8}$$

$$\mathrm{d}K_i/\mathrm{d}t = s_i[wL_i + rK_i], \qquad i = 1, 2 \tag{9}$$

K_i, of course, is the capital owned by country i, not necessarily the capital

[14] This possibility of endogenous growth would also arise if foreign labor were available in unlimited supply, as in the Lewis (1954) duel economy. Burgstaller and Saavedra-Rivano (1984) have examined growth of a Solow economy that was able to invest abroad into such a dual economy, and they found, with the two countries producing distinct goods, that steady-state growth displayed several distinctive features. Implicitly, however, they looked only at equilibria analogous to my Case 1, for they assumed (their eq. (43′), p. 224) that $s_1 r < n_1$. They dismissed the alternative case as dynamically unstable, not realizing that a well defined asymptotic solution of endogenous growth would emerge in that case. Of course, with distinct goods being produced in the two countries and no mechanism for expanding demand faster than the population of the North, this solution would have to involve an ever falling terms of trade of the South. This is an even more disturbing outcome than they identified.

[15] If there are more than two countries, as discussed in Deardorff (1990), all but those with the highest savings and population growth rates disappear asymptotically into the small country cases of Section 2.

[16] Variables without subscripts pertain to the world.

installed in that country. Notice that there may be different population growth rates, n_i, as well as different savings propensities, s_i, in the two countries. In particular, I assume without loss of generality that

$$n_1 < n_2 \tag{10}$$

so that country 1 is North of the introduction.

Equations (8) and (9), with substitution from (6) and (7), form a system of four differential equations in the four unknowns, K_i, L_i, $i = 1, 2$. The system is more readily analyzed, however, by introducing the following new variables. Let

$$\lambda = L_1/(L_1 + L_2) \tag{11}$$

be country 1's (North's) share of the world labor force; let

$$\rho = K_1/(L_1 + L_2) \tag{12}$$

be the ratio of country 1's capital to the world labor force; and let

$$k = K/L = (K_1 + K_2)/(L_1 + L_2) \tag{13}$$

be the world capital-labor ratio.

Then with some manipulation, the system (8–9) becomes

$$\mathrm{d}\lambda/\mathrm{d}t = \lambda(1 - \lambda)(n_1 - n_2) \tag{14}$$

$$\mathrm{d}\rho/\mathrm{d}t = (s_1 r - n_2)\rho + [s_1 w + (n_2 - n_1)\rho]\lambda \tag{15}$$

$$\mathrm{d}k/\mathrm{d}t = s_2(w + rk) - n_2 k + (s_1 - s_2)r\rho + [(s_1 - s_2)w + (n_2 - n_1)k]\lambda \tag{16}$$

Since r and w are functions only of k in (6) and (7), the eqs (14), (15), and (16) form a closed system of three differential equations in the three unknowns, λ, ρ, and k.

To see the asymptotic properties of this sytem, observe first that λ must go to zero over time in (14), since n_1 has been assumed less than n_2. Thus, the asymptotic equations of motion for ρ and k can be simplified considerably by letting $\lambda = 0$ in (15) and (16)

$$\mathrm{d}\rho/\mathrm{d}t = (s_1 r - n_2)\rho \tag{17}$$

$$\mathrm{d}k/\mathrm{d}t = [s_2 f(k) - n_2 k] + (s_1 - s_2)r\rho \tag{18}$$

This system of two differential equations can be analyzed in terms of the phase diagram that is derived as the lower quadrant of Fig. 2.

First, $\mathrm{d}\rho/\mathrm{d}t = 0$ in (17) requires either that $\rho = 0$ or that $s_1 r = n_2$. Since r depends only on k, the latter fixes a vertical line at a value k^* such that $s_1 f'(k^*) = n_2$. This in turn is identifiable in the upper quadrant by the curve $s_1 f(k)$ being parallel to the ray $n_2 k$.

Solution to $\mathrm{d}k/\mathrm{d}t = 0$ in (18) is more complex, since it involves both k and ρ. However, it is easy to anchor the solution along the k-axis, where $\rho = 0$ and what remains of (18) is the growth equation of the closed-economy Solow

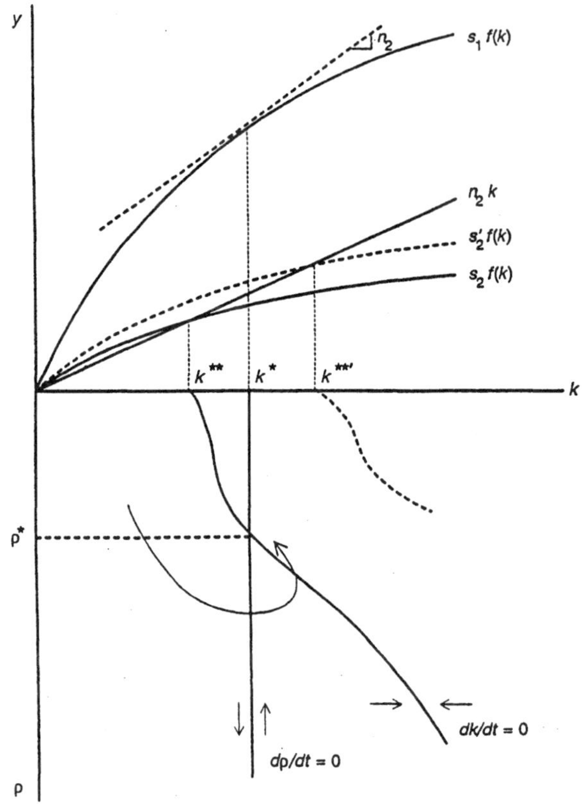

FIG. 2.

growth model. Thus $\mathrm{d}k/\mathrm{d}t = 0$ along the k-axis at k^{**}, where $s_2 f(k)$ crosses $n_2 k$ in the upper quadrant

$$s_2 f(k^{**}) = n_2 k^{**} \tag{19}$$

For k larger than k^{**}, (18) can be solved with $\mathrm{d}k/\mathrm{d}t = 0$ to yield

$$\rho = \frac{n_2 k - s_2 f(k)}{(s_1 - s_2) f'(k)} \tag{20}$$

which rises with k as long as $s_1 > s_2$, which I assume. Thus the $\mathrm{d}k/\mathrm{d}t = 0$ locus in the lower quadrant of Fig. 2 slopes down and to the right, starting at k^{**}, and, if $k^{**} < k^*$, crosses $\mathrm{d}\rho/\mathrm{d}t = 0$ at some value $\rho^* > 0$.

The dynamics of ρ and k are shown by the arrows, and they lead to convergence—not necessarily monotonic—to the intersection at (k^*, ρ^*).[17] This

[17] The stability of this dynamic process will be discussed further below.

is the Case 3 solution described in the introduction. North now comes to own a permanently non-negligible share of world capital, even though North's share of world labor, λ, goes to zero. Since $\rho = K_1/(L_1 + L_2)$ becomes a positive constant, K_1 must grow asymptotically at the same rate as world population, n_2.

An important property of this Case 3 solution is that, while ρ depends on s_2, k^* does not. Thus r and w, which depend only on k, are also independent of s_2 in the Case 3 steady state. This is clear directly from (18), where $d\rho/dt = 0$ is consistent with a positive solution for ρ only if $r = n_2/s_1$. And this is the familiar result mentioned earlier from two-class growth models, and known as the Pasinetti Paradox. Indeed this model is formally identical to the two-class model, since North's low population growth rate drives its share of labor income to zero, and thus it acts as if it earned only profits.

The Case 3 solution shown in Fig. 2 for the growth rate n_2 arises only because $k^{**} < k^*$, so that the two curves do intersect at strictly positive ρ. If they do not—as shown by the larger $k^{**\prime}$ implied by a higher s_2'—then the dynamics of the model take it to $k^{**\prime}$ itself, and k^* becomes irrelevant.[18] In that case the world capital stock is determined entirely in country 2 as though it were a closed economy, and country 1 can be in either of the small-country cases, 1 or 2, discussed in Section 2.

It is now possible to delineate the bounds on parameters that will give rise to each of the three cases. Let $r^{**} = f'(k^{**})$ be the rental rate that would arise in country 2 as a closed economy, and that will arise in Cases 1 and 2 if they occur. In Section 2 it was already observed that Case 1 requires $s_1 r^{**} < n_1$, while Case 2 requires the opposite. Now, since k^* is defined by $f'(k^*) = n_2/s_1$, it follows that[19]

$$k^* \lesseqgtr k^{**} \quad \text{as} \quad n_2/s_1 \gtreqless r^{**} \tag{21}$$

Thus the three cases arise as follows

$$\text{Case 1:} \quad s_1 < n_1/r^{**} \tag{22}$$

$$\text{Case 2:} \quad n_1/r^{**} < s_1 < n_2/r^{**} \tag{23}$$

$$\text{Case 3:} \quad s_1 > n_2/r^{**} \tag{24}$$

With $n_2 > n_1$, all that is required for all these cases to be consistent with fractional values of s_1 is that $n_2/r^{**} < 1$. Thus each of the three cases can arise, depending on the values of the various savings and population growth parameters, as long as $r^{**} > n_2$.[20]

[18] Recall that the entire k-axis is also consistent with $d\rho/dt = 0$. In Case 3 the point $(k^{**}, 0)$ was also a steady-state solution, but it was dynamically unstable.

[19] Since $k^{**} = f'^{-1}(r^{**})$ while $k^* = f'^{-1}(n_2/s_1)$, and f' is monotonically decreasing.

[20] The importance of each case also depends on the solution being dynamically stable. Samuelson and Modigliani (1966) have proved both local stability of the Pasinetti equilibrium (my Case 3) and global stability of their 'dual' equilibrium (my Cases 1 and 2). In addition, Guha (1972) has proved global stability of the Pasinetti equilibrium if the elasticity of factor substitution is greater than $\frac{1}{2}$.

Since r^{**} is the steady-state return to capital for country 2 as a closed economy, this condition, $r^{**} > n_2$, requires that country 2 save less than the 'golden rule' of savings. It is well known that, in order to maximize its steady-state *per capita* consumption, a closed economy must save enough to set its steady-state return to capital equal to its rate of population growth. That is, golden rule savings by country 2 will yield $r^{**} = n_2$. If country 2 fails to follow the golden rule by saving less than the rule indicates, then it will indeed be true that $r^{**} > n_2$, and Case 3 will be possible for values of s_1 less than unity.

4. Implications for two-class growth models

I already noted the fact that my model is formally identical to a two-class growth model of a closed economy. Thus by simply replacing the word 'country' with 'class' throughout the preceding sections, one can reinterpret the results as properties of a two-class model.

The most important, and also the simplest, implication of applying this model to a two-class economy is its interpretation of the meaning of classes. When Pasinetti (1962, p. 272) introduced the two-class model, he defined the capitalist class as 'a category of individuals who—owing to the position they occupy in the production process—derive all their incomes . . . exclusively from profits . . .'. The model here shows, however, that the special role that capitalists play in growth depends not on their earning no labor income at all, but on their share of total labor income being negligible. This can be the case even if capitalists as individuals do provide labor, so long as the number of capitalists remains small compared to the total labor force, due to their lower than average rate of population growth or reproduction. Thus Samuelson and Modigliani's (1966, p. 297) '. . . difficulty of identifying a class whose sole source of income is income from capital . . .' may not be so difficult after all. One needs merely to identify classes that differ in the rates at which their populations grow.

There is, of course, a more serious difficulty with the concept of ongoing classes. This was also noted by Samuelson and Modigliani, and my approach does nothing to alleviate it. The classes, however they are defined, must maintain their identities and their ownership of capital from generation to generation. Thus the model breaks down if capital is transferred from one class to another when individuals or their descendants change classes. This objection to the two-class model applies as well as to my two-country version, though it is surely less serious in the two-country case, to the extent that international migration is limited.[21]

Finally, my model of a two-class economy also yields an interesting and disturbing implication for the distribution of income between classes. From Proposition 1 it follows that, if the capitalists' propensity to save is large enough, then the capitalists will enjoy an ever increasing *per capita* income, while the

[21] On the other hand, even a large amount of labor migration would be consistent with my model if the migrants typically take no capital with them.

per capita income of workers remains constant. Thus *per capita* income inequality between classes grows indefinitely.[22] Applied, again, in the international context, the implication of ever-increasing international income inequality is equally disturbing.

[22] This result may be compared to those of Stiglitz (1969) who examined a variety of sources both of equality and of inequality, in the distribution of income and wealth. While Stiglitz did consider, separately, differences in both reproduction and savings rates between classes, he never put the two assumptions together as I do here.

ACKNOWLEDGEMENTS

The original version of this paper was written with financial assistance provided by NSF Grant GS-3073. Support more recently has been provided by the Ford Foundation and the Donner Foundation. I am indebted for their comments especially to Bob Barsky, Avinash Dixit, Jon Eaton, Jim Levinsohn, Matthew Shapiro, T. N. Srinivasan, Bob Stern, and Tom Weisskopf as well as to participation in seminars at the University of Western Ontario, Harvard University, The University of Michigan, and a meeting of the Mid-West International Economics Group at Ohio State University. Several anonymous referees have also contributed helpful comments.

REFERENCES

Bardhan, P. K. (1965). 'Equilibrium Growth in the International Economy', *Quarterly Journal of Economics*, **74**, 455–64.

Bardhan, P. K. (1966). 'On Factor Accumulation and the Pattern of International Specialization', *Review of Economic Studies*, **33**, 39–44.

Buiter, W. H. (1981). 'Time Preference and International Lending and Borrowing in an Overlapping-Generations Model', *Journal of Political Economy*, **89**, 769–97.

Burgstaller, A. and Saavedra-Rivano, N. (1984). 'Capital Mobility and Growth in a North-South Model', *Journal of Development Economics*, **15**, 213–37.

Deardorff, A. V. (1974). 'A Geometry of Growth and Trade', *Canadian Journal of Economics*, **7**, 295–306.

Deardorff, A. V. (1987). 'Trade and Capital Mobility in a World of Diverging Populations', in D. G. Johnson and R. D. Lee (eds), *Population Growth and Economic Development: Issues and Evidence*, University of Wisconsin Press, Madison, WI, 561–88.

Deardorff, A. V. (1990). 'Growth and International Investment with Diverging Populations', CREST Working Paper No. 90–15, University of Michigan.

Findlay, R. (1980). 'The Terms of Trade and Equilibrium Growth in the World Economy'. *American Economic Review*, **70**, 291–9.

Findlay, R. (1984). 'Growth and Development in Trade Models', in R. W. Jones and P. B. Kenen (eds), *Handbook of International Economics*, **I**, North-Holland, Amsterdam.

Griffin, K. and Gurley, J. (1985). 'Radical Analyses of Imperialism, the Third World, and the Transition to Socialism: a Survey Article', *Journal of Economic Literature*, **23**, 1089–143.

Grossman, G. M. and Helpman, E. (1990). 'Comparative Advantage and Long-Run Growth', *American Economic Review*, **80**, 796–815.

Grossman, G. M. and Helpman, E. (1991a). *Innovation and Growth in the Global Economy*, MIT Press, Cambridge, MA.

Grossman, G. M. and Helpman, E. (1991b). 'Quality Ladders and Product Cycles', *Quarterly Journal of Economics*, **106**, 557–86.

Guha, A. (1972). 'The Global Stability of Two-Class Neoclassical Growth', *Quarterly Journal of Economics*, **86**, 687–90.

Helpman, E. (1988). 'Growth, Technological Progress, and Trade', *Empirica—Austrian Economic Papers*, **1**, 5–25.

Johnson, H. G. (1971). 'Trade and Growth: A Geometrical Exposition', *Journal of International Economics*, **1**, 83–101.

Jones, L. E. and Manuelli, R. (1990). 'A Convex Model of Equilibrium Growth: Theory and Policy Implications', *Journal of Political Economy*, **98**, 1008–38.

Junankar, P. N. (1982). *Marx's Economics*, Philip Allen Publishers Ltd, London.

Kemp, M. C. (1969). *The Pure Theory of International Trade and Investment*, Prentice-Hall Englewood Cliffs, NJ.

Khang, C. and Kemp, M. C. (1973). 'International Trade and Investment between Countries with Different Natural Rates of Growth', *Metroeconomica*, **25**, 215–28.

Lenin, V. I. (1939). *Imperialism: The Highest Stage of Capitalism*, International Publishers, New York (originally published in Russian, 1917).

Lewis, W. A. (1954). 'Economic Development with Unlimited Supplies of Labor', *The Manchester School*, **22**, 139–91.

Lucas, R. E. Jr. (1988). 'On the Mechanics of Economic Development', *Journal of Monetary Economics*, **22**, 3–42.

Marx, K. (1967). *Capital*, **III**, International Publishers, New York (originally published in German, 1894).

Oniki, H. and Uzawa, H. (1965). 'Patterns of Trade and Investment in a Dynamic Model of International Trade', *Review of Economic Studies*, **32**, 15–38.

Pasinetti, L. (1962). 'The Rate of Profit and Income Distribution in Relation to the Rate of Economic Growth', *Review of Economic Studies*, 267–79.

Romer, P. M. (1986). 'Increasing Returns and Long-Run Growth', *Journal of Political Economy*, **94**, 1002–37.

Samuelson, A. and Modigliani, F. (1966). 'The Pasinetti Paradox in Neoclassical and More General Models', *Review of Economic Studies*, 269–302.

Smith, A. (1984). 'Capital Theory and Trade Theory', in R. W. Jones and P. B. Kenen (eds), *Handbook of International Economics*, **I**, North-Holland, Amsterdam.

Solow, R. M. (1956). 'A Contribution to the Theory of Economic Growth', *Quarterly Journal of Economics*, **70**, 65–94.

Stiglitz, J. E. (1969). 'Distribution of Income and Wealth Among Individuals', *Econometrica*, **37**, 382–97.

Swan, T. W. (1956). 'Economic Growth and Capital Accumulation', *Economic Record*, **32**, 334–61.

Vanek, J. (1971). 'Economic Growth and International Trade in Pure Theory', *Quarterly Journal of Economics*, **85**, 377–90.

CHAPTER 24

Determinants of Bilateral Trade: Does Gravity Work in a Neoclassical World?*,†

Alan V. Deardorff

The University of Michigan

ABSTRACT

This paper derives equations for the value of bilateral trade from two extreme cases of the Heckscher-Ohlin Model, both of which could also represent a variety of other models as well. The first case is frictionless trade, in which the absence of all impediments to trade in homogeneous products causes producers and consumers to be indifferent among trading partners. Resolving this indifference randomly, expected trade flows correspond exactly to the simple frictionless gravity equation if preferences are identical and homothetic or if demands are uncorrelated with supplies, and they depart from that equation systematically when there are such correlations. The second case is of countries that each produce distinct goods, as in the H-O Model with complete specialization or a variety of other models. Expressions are derived for bilateral trade, first with Cobb-Douglas preferences and then with CES preferences. The standard gravity equation with trade declining in distance continues to be a central tendency for these trade flows, with departures from it that are easily understood in terms of relative transport costs. The main lessons from the paper are two. First, it is not all that difficult to justify even simple forms of the gravity equation from standard trade theories. Second, because the gravity equation appears to characterize a large class of models, its use for empirical tests of any of them is suspect.

Keywords: Bilateral Trade
Gravity Equation

JEL Subject Code: F11

Correspondence:

Alan V. Deardorff
Department of Economics
University of Michigan
Ann Arbor, MI 48109-1220

Tel. 313-764-6817
Fax. 313-764-2769
E-mail: alandear@umich.ed

* I have benefited greatly from comments and conversations with Don Davis, Simon Evenett, Jeffrey Frankel, Jon Haveman, David Hummels, Jim Levinsohn, and Bob Stern, as well as from the comments of my discussants, Jeffrey Bergstrand and Gene Grossman.

† Paper presented at a conference on Regionalization of the World Economy, sponsored by the National Bureau of Economic Research, held in Woodstock, Vermont, October 20–21, 1995.

I. Introduction

It has long been recognized that bilateral trade patterns are well described empirically by the so-called gravity equation, which relates trade between two countries positively to both of their incomes and negatively to the distance between them, usually with a functional form that is reminiscent of the law of gravity in physics. It also used to be frequently stated that the gravity equation was without theoretical foundation. In particular, it was claimed that the Heckscher-Ohlin (H-O) Model of international trade was incapable of providing such a foundation, and perhaps even that the H-O Model was theoretically inconsistent with the gravity equation. In this paper I will take another look at these issues. It is certainly no longer true that the gravity equation is without a theoretical basis, since several of the same authors who noted its absence went on to provide one. I will briefly review their contributions in a moment. Since none of them build directly on an H-O base, it might be supposed that the empirical success of the gravity equation is evidence against the H-O model, as at least one researcher has implied by using the gravity equation as a test of an alternative model incorporating monopolistic competition. I will argue however that the H-O model, at least in some of the equilibria that it permits, admits easily of interpretations that accord readily with the gravity equation. At the same time, developing these interpretations can yield additional insights about why bilateral trade patterns in some cases depart from the gravity equation as well.

There are two keys to these results, which once stated may make the rest of the paper obvious to those well-schooled in trade theory. The two keys open doors to two different cases of H-O model equilibria, one with frictionless trade and one without.

With frictionless trade — that is, literally zero barriers to trade of all sorts, including both tariffs and transport costs — the key is that trade is just as cheap, and therefore no less likely, than domestic transactions. Therefore, instead of thinking as we normally do of countries first satisfying demands out of domestic supply and then importing only what is left, we should think of demanders as being indifferent among all equally priced sources of supply, both domestic and foreign. Suppliers likewise should not care about to whom they sell. The H-O model (and other models based solely on comparative advantage and perfect competition) is usually examined only for its implications for net trade, and we then jump to the conclusion that gross trade flows are equal to net. But with no trade impediments, there is no reason for trade to be this small. If instead we allow markets to be settled randomly among all possibilities among which producers and consumers are indifferent, then trade flows will generally be larger and will fall naturally into a gravity-equation configuration, in a frictionless form without a role for distance. With identical preferences across countries, this configuration is particularly simple. With non-identical preferences it is a bit more complex, but it is also more instructive.

The other key is to the case of trade in the presence of trade impediments. If there exist positive impediments to all trade flows, however small, then the H-O model cannot have factor price equalization (FPE) between any two countries that trade with each other. For if they did have FPE, then their prices of all goods would be identical and neither could overcome the positive barrier on its exports to the other. Since we do observe trade between every pair of countries that we care about, it follows that the H-O equilibria we look at with impeded trade should be ones without FPE between any pair of countries. If we assume also that the number of goods in the world is extremely large compared to the number of factors, it will be true that for almost all goods only one country will be the least-cost producer. With trade barriers this does not imply complete specialization by countries in largely different goods, but it makes such a case more plausible than might have been thought otherwise. In any case, motivated by this observation, I will study bilateral impeded trade under the assumption that each good is produced by only one country. With that assumption, bilateral trade patterns in the H-O model are essentially the same as in other models with differentiated products, and it is no surprise that the gravity equation emerges once again. My contribution here will be to derive bilateral trade in terms of incomes and trade barriers in a form that may be more readily interpretable than has been seen before.

None of this should be very surprising, although I admit that this is much clearer to me now than it was when I started thinking about it. All that the gravity equation says, after all, aside from its particular functional form, is that bilateral trade should be positively related to the two countries' incomes and negatively related to the distance between them. Transport costs would surely yield the latter in just about any sensible model. And the dependence on incomes would also be hard to avoid. The size of a country obviously puts an upper limit on the amount that it can trade (unless it simply re-exports, which one normally excludes), so that small countries necessarily trade little. For income not to be positively related to trade, it would therefore have to be true also that large countries trade very little, at least on average. Therefore, the smaller are the smallest countries, the less must all countries trade in order to avoid getting a positive relationship between size and trade. Looked at in that way, it would therefore be very surprising if some positive relationship between bilateral trade and national incomes did not also emerge from just about any sensible trade model. The H-O model has some quirky features, but in this respect, at least, it turns out to be sensible.

As for the functional form, a simple version of the gravity equation — what I will call the standard gravity equation — is typically specified as

$$T_{ij} = A\frac{Y_i Y_j}{D_{ij}} \tag{1}$$

where T_{ij} is the value of exports from country i to country j, the Y's are their respective national incomes, D_{ij} is a measure of the distance between them[1], and A is a constant of proportionality. While this particular multiplicative functional form may not be obvious, the easiest alternative of a linear equation clearly would not do, for trade between two countries must surely go to zero as the size of either goes to zero. None of this constitutes a derivation of the gravity equation, of course, but it does suggest why one would expect something like it to hold in any plausible model.

---

[1]Clearly this measure should not go to zero for adjacent countries, or (1) would yield infinite trade between them. Empirical work typically uses distance between national capitals. For theoretical purposes below, it is convenient to use a measure that starts at one (such as one plus distance) to accommodate transactions of a country with itself.

I turn now to a brief review of the literature in Section II, followed by the two cases just mentioned: frictionless trade in Section III and impeded trade in Section IV.

II. Theoretical Foundations for the Gravity Equation

As has been noted many times, the gravity equation for describing trade flows first appeared in the empirical literature without much serious attempt to justify it theoretically. Tinbergen (1962) and Pöyhönen (1963) did the first econometric studies of trade flows based on the gravity equation, for which they gave only intuitive justification. Linnemann (1966) added more variables and went further toward a theoretical justification in terms of a Walrasian general equilibrium system, but the Walrasian model tends to include too many explanatory variables for each trade flow to be easily reduced to the gravity equation. Leamer and Stern (1970) followed Savage and Deutsch (1960) in deriving it from a probability model of transactions. Their approach was very similar to what I will suggest below, but they applied it only to trade, not to all transactions, and they did not make any explicit connection with the H-O model. Leamer (1974) used both the gravity equation and the H-O model to motivate explanatory variables in a regression analysis of trade flows, but he did not integrate the two approaches theoretically.

These contributions were followed by several more formal attempts to derive the gravity equation from models that assumed product differentiation. Anderson (1979) was the first to do so, first assuming Cobb-Douglas preferences and then, in an appendix, CES preferences. In both cases he made what today would be called the Armington Assumption, that products were differentiated by country of origin. His framework was in fact very similar to what I will examine here with impeded trade, although I motivate the differentiation among products, as already noted, by the H-O model's case of non-FPE and specialization rather than by the Armington Assumption. Anderson modeled preferences over only traded goods, while I will assume for simplicity that they hold over all goods. Anderson's primary concern was to examine the econometric properties of the resulting equations, rather than to extract easily interpretable theoretical implications as I seek here.

Finally, Jeffrey Bergstrand has explored the theoretical determination of bilateral trade in a series of papers. In Bergstrand (1985) he, like Anderson, used CES preferences over Armington-differentiated goods to derive a reduced form equation for bilateral trade involving price indices. Using GDP deflators to approximate these price indices, he estimated his system in order to test his assumptions of product differentiation. For richness his CES preferences were also nested, with a different elasticity of substitution among imports than between imports and domestic goods. His empirical estimates supported the assumption that goods were not perfect substitutes and that imports were closer substitutes for each other than for domestic goods.

In Bergstrand (1989, 1990) he departed even further from the H-O model by assuming Dixit-Stiglitz (1977) monopolistic competition, and therefore product differentiation among firms rather than among countries. This was imbedded however in a two sector economy in which each monopolistically competitive sector had different factor proportions, thus being a hybrid of the perfectly competitive H-O model and the one-sector monopolistically competitive model of Krugman (1979). In the first paper, Bergstrand used this framework to derive yet again a version of the gravity equation, and in the second he examined bilateral intra-industry trade.

Bergstrand's later work therefore serves to bring together the earlier Armington-based approaches to deriving the gravity equation with a second strand of literature in which gravity equations were derived from simple monopolistic competition models. Almost from the start of the New Trade Theory's attention to such models, it was recognized that they provided an immediate and simple justification for the gravity equation.[2] Indeed, Helpman (1987) used this correspondence between the gravity equation and the monopolistic competition model as the basis for an empirical test of the latter. That is, he interpreted the close fit of the gravity equation with bilateral data on trade as supportive empirical evidence for the monopolistic competition model. For this to be correct, of course, it would need to be true, as Helpman apparently believed, that the gravity equation does not also arise from other models. He remarked (p. 63) that "The factor proportions theory contributes very little to our understanding of the determination of the volume of trade in the world economy, or the volume of trade within groups of countries," and he went on to demonstrate geometrically that the volume of trade under FPE in the 2x2x2 H-O model is independent of country sizes.[3] Helpman was, I would like to think, in good company. No less an authority than Deardorff (1984, pp. 500–504) noted several of the empirical regularities that are

[2]One such was apparently Krugman (1980), cited in Helpman (1987).

[3]This argument appeared first in Helpman and Krugman (1984). I would argue that Helpman's locus for comparisons, which are along straight lines parallel to the diagonal of a Dixit-Norman-Helpman-Krugman factor allocation rectangle, is inappropriate. Along these straight lines, the differences in relative factor endowments of the two countries also change, becoming more pronounced (and leading to greater trade) at the same time that countries are becoming more different in size (leading to less trade). A better comparison would have been along a locus for which the percentage difference in factor endowment ratios remains constant. This would be a curve bowed out from the diagonal of the box, and along this curve the trade volume would be largest where country incomes are equal, just as in the gravity equation.

captured in the gravity equation and pronounced them paradoxes, inconsistent with, or at least not explainable by, the H-O Model.

Helpman applied his test to data on trade of the OECD countries, where most would agree that monopolistic competition is plausibly present. Hummels and Levinsohn (1995) decided to attempt a sort of negative test of the same proposition by looking for the same relationship in the trade among a much wider variety of countries, including ones where monopolistic competition is less plausibly a factor. To their surprise, they found that the test worked just as well for that group of countries, thus leading one to suspect that perhaps the relationship represented by the gravity equation is more ubiquitous, and not unique to the monopolistic competition model. It might be thought that the work by Anderson and Bergstrand cited above would have already suggested this, since they derived gravity equations from a variety of models other than the monopolistic one that Bergstrand eventually incorporated into his analysis. But in fact the versions of the gravity equation that Anderson and Bergstrand obtained were somewhat complex and opaque, and it was not obvious that they would lead to the success of the very simple gravity equation tested by Helpman.

My point in this paper, of course, is that one can get essentially this same simple gravity equation from the H-O model properly considered, both with frictionless and with impeded trade. This does not mean that the empirical success of the gravity model lends support to the H-O model, any more than it does to the monopolistic competition model. For reasons I have already indicated, I suspect that just about any plausible model of trade would yield something very like the gravity equation, whose empirical success is therefore not evidence of anything, but just a fact of life.

III. Frictionless Trade

Consider now an H-O model with any numbers of goods and factors. In fact, for most of what I will say in this section,[4] the argument is more general and could apply to any perfectly competitive trade model with homogenous products, including a Ricardian model, a specific-factors model[5], a model with arbitrary differences in technology, and so forth. For this model, consider a frictionless trade equilibrium — that is, an equilibrium with zero transport costs and no other impediments to trade — with each country a net exporter of some goods to the world market and a net importer of others. This equilibrium need not be unique, as it will not be in the H-O model with FPE and more goods than factors. If the model is H-O, then there may be FPE among some or all countries, but there need not be. We need merely have some vectors of production, consumption, and therefore net trade in each country that are consistent with maximization by perfectly competitive producers and consumers in all countries, facing the same prices (due to frictionless trade) for all goods, and such that world markets clear.

It is customary to note that patterns of bilateral trade are not determined in such a model, and indeed they are not. But the reason for this indeterminacy is itself important: both producers and consumers are indifferent, under the assumption of frictionless trade and homogeneous products, among the many possible destinations for their sales and sources for their purchases.

---

[4]The only exception is the penultimate paragraph of this section, where bilateral trade is related to per capita incomes using an assumption about preferences and factor intensities of goods.

[5]Of course the specific-factors model is just a special case of the H-O model with many goods and factors.

Therefore, while it is true that a wide variety of outcomes is possible, we can get an idea of the average outcome by just allowing choices among indifferent outcomes to be made randomly.

Thus, having already found the equilibrium levels of production and consumption, let the actual transactions be determined as follows: producers each industry put their outputs into a world pool for their industry; consumers then choose randomly their desired levels of consumption from these pools. If consumers draw from these pools in small increments, then the Law of Large Numbers will allow us to predict quite accurately what their total choices will be by using expected values. In general, these expected values will be appropriate averages of the wide variety of outcomes that are in fact possible in the model.

Homothetic Preferences

All of this works extremely simply if preferences of consumers everywhere are identical and homothetic, which I will now assume as a first case. Let x_i be country i's vector of production and c_i its vector of consumption in a frictionless trade equilibrium with world price vector p.[6] It's income is therefore $Y_i = p'x_i = p'c_i$, where I also assume balanced trade so that expenditure equals income. Now consider the value of exports from country i to country j, T_{ij}. With identical, homothetic preferences all countries will spend the same fraction, β_k, of their incomes on good k, so that country j's consumption of good k is $c_{jk} = \beta_k\, Y_j/p_k$. Drawing randomly from the world pool of good k, to which country i has contributed the fraction $\gamma_{ik} = x_{ik}/\Sigma_h x_{hk}$, country j's purchases of good k from country i will be $c_{ijk} = \gamma_{ik}\, \beta_k Y_j/p_k$. Let $x_k^w = \Sigma_i x_{ik}$ be world output of good k. Note that, with identical fractions of income being spent on good k by all countries, that fraction

[6]All vectors are column vectors unless transposed with a prime, $'$.

must also equal the share of good k in world income, Y^w: $\beta_k = p_k x_k^w / Y^w$. The value of j's total imports from i is therefore

$$\begin{aligned} T_{ij} &= \sum_k p_k c_{ijk} = \sum_k \gamma_{ik} \beta_k Y_j \\ &= \sum_k \frac{x_{ik}}{x_k^w} \frac{p_k x_k^w}{Y^w} Y_j = \sum_k p_k x_{ik} \frac{Y_j}{Y^w} \\ &= \frac{Y_i Y_j}{Y^w} \end{aligned} \tag{2}$$

Thus with identical, homothetic preferences and frictionless trade, an even simpler gravity equation than (1) emerges immediately, with constant of proportionality $A = 1/Y^w$. Distance, of course, plays no role here since there are no transport costs, and I will call (2) the simple frictionless gravity equation. To get this, all that is needed is to resolve the indeterminacy of who buys from whom by making that decision randomly.

Arbitrary Preferences

If preferences are not identical and/or not homothetic, then the equilibrium may have each country spending a different share of its income on each good, and the simple derivation above does not work. Let β_{ik} now be the share of its income that country i spends on good k in the equilibrium, and also let α_{ik} be the share of country i's income that it derives from producing good k. The first and second equalities of (2) still hold, but with β_k replaced by β_{ik}. The value of world output of good k is $p_k x_k^w = \Sigma_i \alpha_{ik} Y_i$, and therefore the fraction of world output of good k that is produced by country i is $\gamma_{ik} = \alpha_{ik} Y_i / \Sigma_h \alpha_{hk} Y_h$. Country j, again drawing randomly from the pool for good k an amount equal to its demand $\beta_{jk}Y_j$, will get that fraction from country i. Thus the value of sales by country i to country j of good k will be

$$T_{ijk} = \frac{\alpha_{ik}Y_i}{\sum_h \alpha_{hk}Y_h}\beta_{jk}Y_j \tag{3}$$

Summing across goods k, we get

$$T_{ij} = \sum_k T_{ijk} = \sum_k \frac{\alpha_{ik}Y_i}{\sum_h \alpha_{hk}Y_h}\beta_{jk}Y_j = Y_iY_j\sum_k \frac{\alpha_{ik}\,\beta_{jk}}{p_k x_k^w} \tag{4}$$

This is not the gravity equation, since the summation could be quite different for different values of i and j. As an extreme example, if country i happens to specialize completely in a good that country j does not demand at all, then T_{ij} will be zero regardless of Y_i and Y_j.

However, it is possible to simplify (4) further if one can assume that the fractions that exporters produce and that importers consume are in some sense unrelated. Let $\lambda_k = p_k x_k^w/Y^w$ be the fraction of world income accounted for by production of good k. Then

$$T_{ij} = \frac{Y_iY_j}{Y^w}\sum_k \frac{\alpha_{ik}\,\beta_{jk}}{\lambda_k} \tag{5}$$

Clearly, since each country's good-shares of both production (α_{ik}) and consumption (β_{jk}) sum to one, this will reduce to the simple frictionless gravity equation (2) if either the exporter produces goods in the same proportions as the world ($\alpha_{ik} = \lambda_k$) or if the importer consumes goods in the same proportion as the world ($\beta_{jk} = \lambda_k$, as was true in the case of identical, homothetic preferences), but not in general. If the λ_k were equal for all k, thus each being $1/n$ where n is the number of goods, we would also get back to (2) if α_{ik} and β_{jk} were uncorrelated. With goods having unequal shares of the world market, we can still get this if we define correlations on a weighted basis, using the λ_k as weights.

That is, let

$$\tilde{\alpha}_{ik} = \frac{\alpha_{ik}-\lambda_k}{\lambda_k}, \qquad \tilde{\beta}_{jk} = \frac{\beta_{jk}-\lambda_k}{\lambda_k}$$

be the proportional deviations of country i's production shares and of country's consumption shares from world averages. Then

$$\sum_k \lambda_k \tilde{\alpha}_{ik} \tilde{\beta}_{jk} = \sum_k \frac{1}{\lambda_k}(\alpha_{ik} \beta_{jk} - \lambda_k \beta_{jk} - \lambda_k \alpha_{ik} + \lambda_k^2) = \sum_k \frac{\alpha_{ik} \beta_{jk}}{\lambda_k} - 1 \qquad \textbf{(6)}$$

and we can rewrite (5) as

$$T_{ij} = \frac{Y_i Y_j}{Y^w} (1 + \sum_k \lambda_k \tilde{\alpha}_{ik} \tilde{\beta}_{jk}) \qquad \textbf{(7)}$$

This is the main result of this section of the paper. The sign of the summation in (7) is the same as the sign of the weighted covariance between $\tilde{\alpha}_{ik}$ and $\tilde{\beta}_{jk}$. Thus if these deviations of exporter production shares and importer consumption shares from world averages are uncorrelated, then once again the simple frictionless gravity equation (2) will hold exactly.

Perhaps more importantly, equation (7) also states simply and intuitively when two countries will trade either more or less than the amounts indicated by the simple frictionless gravity equation. If an exporter produces above average amounts of the same goods that an importer consumes above average, then their trade will be greater than would have been explained by their incomes alone. On the other hand, if an exporter produces above average what the importer consumes below average, their trade will be unusually low. These statements presume that the simple frictionless gravity equation describes what is "usual." This is in fact the case here, since across all country pairs (i, j) the average of bilateral trade is equal to what the simple frictionless gravity equation prescribes:

$$
\begin{aligned}
\sum_{ij}\left(T_{ij} - \frac{Y_iY_j}{Y^w}\right) &= \sum_{ijk}\frac{Y_iY_j}{Y^w}\lambda_k\,\tilde{\alpha}_{ik}\,\tilde{\beta}_{jk} \\
&= \sum_{ik}\frac{Y_i}{Y^w}\tilde{\alpha}_{ik}\sum_j\left(Y_j\,\beta_{jk} - Y_j\,\lambda_k\right) \\
&= \sum_{ik}\frac{Y_i}{Y^w}\tilde{\alpha}_{ik}\left(\sum_j c_{jk} - \lambda_k Y^w\right) \\
&= 0
\end{aligned}
\qquad \textbf{(8)}
$$

To sum up, with frictionless trade the values of bilateral trade are on average given by the simple frictionless gravity equation, Y_iY_j/Y^w. If expenditure fractions differ across countries because preferences are not identical and/or not homothetic, then individual bilateral trade flows will vary around this frictionless gravity value. If one country tends to overproduce what another overconsumes, then exports of the former to the latter will be above that value, and if one tends to underproduce what another overconsumes, then these exports will be below that value.

It is important for these results that sales of a country to itself, T_{ii}, be included along with international trade. In this form the gravity equation holds on average even in the special case of countries who each demand only their own products. Their above average "exports" to themselves then offset their below average (zero) exports to each other to leave the average unaffected.

Combined with what we already know about the H-O model and what we may suspect about preferences, this also leads us loosely to a corollary that I suspect could be made more formal with additional effort. Suppose that preferences are internationally identical but not homothetic, and suppose further that high-income consumers tend to consume larger budget shares of capital-intensive goods. Then capital abundant countries will have higher than average per capita incomes and will therefore consume capital-intensive goods in disproportionate amounts. At the same time, from the H-O Theorem, they will also produce disproportionate amounts of these same goods. Therefore we would expect to find these countries trading more than average with each other and less than average with low-income labor-abundant countries. This is the same result that Markusen (1986) found in his "eclectic" model and for essentially the same reason. Although Markusen had increasing returns and monopolistic competition in his manufacturing sectors, these features served primarily to generate intraindustry trade. His volume-of-trade result was driven by a high income elasticity for capital-intensive goods.

Such a disproportionately high volume of trade among high income countries happens to accord well with trade patterns in the real world. On the other hand, under the same circumstances the theory here also predicts that labor abundant (hence poor) countries will trade disproportionately with each other as well. This is the same conclusion that Linder (1961) came to from a quite different theoretical model, but the empirical evidence in its favor is less clear.[7]

IV. Impeded Trade

I turn now to the case of impeded trade, assuming instead that there not only exist barriers to trade, such as transport costs, but that these exist for every good. These barriers needn't be large, but I will assume them to be strictly positive on all international transactions. The case that I will consider will in addition have the property that every country produces and exports different goods. Indeed this extreme specialization is the only property that I actually need in this section — the trade barriers are incidental.[8] I thought briefly that this case was the only one that could arise with positive transport costs, but I now realize that my thinking was flawed. I will nonetheless try to motivate the specialization assumption along the lines of that argument, but ultimately I can only claim to be considering a special case.

As mentioned in the introduction, the H-O Model has a striking implication in the presence of strictly positive transport costs: While in general the H-O Model permits equilibria with both FPE and non-FPE among groups of countries, no two countries that have the same factor prices can trade with each other. The reason is that with identical factor prices (recall that the FPE

---

[7]As I understand it, Jeffrey Frankel and his co-authors have found in several studies, such as Frankel, Stein, and Wei (1994), that high-income countries trade disproportionately more than the gravity equation would suggest with all trading partners and not just among themselves, while low income countries trade less.

[8]Thus the results in this section would also obtain in an H-O model with frictionless trade if factor endowments differed sufficiently to yield such specialization, as well as in a Ricardian model with specialization. They would also hold in any Armington model and any monopolistic-competition model, in both of which product differentiation in effect implies specialization.

Theorem equates factor prices absolutely, not just relatively) they will have identical costs of production. With perfect competition, neither country's producers could compete with domestic producers in the other's market, since the exporters would have to overcome the positive transport cost and domestic suppliers would not.

Now this is not a very appealing property of the H-O model, I admit, and this by itself might be enough to make you prefer a model with some sort of imperfect competition. But it is a property of the H-O Model nonetheless, and I will take advantage of it. Since we do in the real world observe virtually every country trading with every other, if we are to give the H-O Model a chance to apply in the real world we must assume unequal factor prices in each pair of countries.

Now suppose also that there are many more goods than there are factors, perhaps even an infinite number of goods as in Dornbusch et al. (1977, 1980). If trade were frictionless, having unequal factor prices would severely limit the number of goods that any two countries could produce in common. With trade impediments this is no longer the case, since goods can become nontraded, and they can also compete in the same market if the difference in transport costs exactly equals the difference in productioncosts. But if transport costs for a given good are constant between any pair of countries (not varying with the amount transported), then I think the case can be made that only a negligibly small subset of all goods will be sold by any two countries to the same market. Thus for almost all trade, a country's consumers will be buying each good from only a single country's producers, either their own domestic industry or from the industry of a single foreign exporter.

This is not quite the same as saying that there only exists a single exporter of each good anywhere in the world, but that is nonetheless the case that I will consider. Indeed, I will go one step further and assume that each good is not only exported by only one country but is also produced in only that one country. That being the case, the products of each country will be distinct in the eyes of consumers, not because of an Armington Assumption that national origin matters, but because they really are different goods. One could argue that this is just as unrealistic as the case I dismissed above of countries not trading with each other at all, since for any industrial classification one observes production in multiple countries of goods that are classed the same. However, just as in the debate over the existence of intra-industry trade, where the phenomenon is sometimes argued to be an artifact of aggregation,[9] it may be that multiple producing countries may simply be producing different goods.

Suppose then that every good is produced by a different country in a particular international trading equilibrium. As long as we consider only that equilibrium, we can identify each good with the country that produces it and enter them into a utility function as imperfect substitutes. Let transport costs be of Samuelson's "iceberg" form, with the transport factor (one plus the transport cost) between countries i and j being t_{ij}. That is, a fraction $(t_{ij} - 1)$ of the good shipped from country i is used up in transport to country j.

With perfect competition, sellers from country i will not discriminate among markets to which they sell, and they will therefore receive a single price, p_i, for their products in all markets. Buyers however must pay the transport cost, and therefore the buyers' price in market j will be $t_{ij}\, p_i$.

What can we say about the pattern of bilateral trade? That depends on preferences, which I will assume first to be identical and Cobb-Douglas. That is, consumers in each country spend a

[9]See Deardorff (1984, p. 501) for a discussion.

fixed share, β_i, of their incomes on the product of country i. Let x_i be the output of country i. Country i's income, Y_i, is

$$Y_i = p_i\, x_i = \sum_j \beta_i Y_j = \beta_i Y^w \tag{9}$$

from which $\beta_i = Y_i/Y^w$. Trade can be valued either exclusive of transport costs (f.o.b.) or inclusive of transport costs (c.i.f). On a c.i.f. basis we get immediately

$$T_{ij}^{cif} = \beta_i Y_j = \frac{Y_i Y_j}{Y^w} \tag{10}$$

With Cobb-Douglas preferences, therefore, we once again get the simple frictionless gravity equation for c.i.f. trade, with no role for transport costs or distance. On an f.o.b. basis, however, these flows must be reduced by the amount of the transport cost:

$$T_{ij}^{fob} = \frac{Y_i Y_j}{t_{ij} Y^w} \tag{11}$$

To the extent that transport cost is related to distance, this immediately gives a result very similar to the standard gravity equation, (1), which includes distance.

This Cobb-Douglas formulation is nonetheless not very satisfactory, because the bilateral expenditures on international trade do not decline with distance. To allow for that to happen, and as the last model that I will consider, let preferences be instead CES. Let consumers in country j maximize the following CES utility function defined on the products of all countries i (including their own):

$$U^j = \left(\sum_i \beta_i c_{ij}^{\left(\frac{\sigma-1}{\sigma}\right)} \right)^{\frac{\sigma}{\sigma-1}} \tag{12}$$

where $\sigma > 0$ is the common elasticity of substitution between any pair of countries' products. Facing c.i.f. prices $t_{ij}p_i$ of the goods, j's consumers, maximizing this function subject to their income $Y_j = p_j x_j$ from producing x_j, will consume

$$c_{ij} = \frac{1}{t_{ij}\, p_i} Y_j\, \beta_i \left(\frac{t_{ij} p_i}{p_j^I} \right)^{1-\sigma} \tag{13}$$

where p_j^I is a CES price index of landed prices in country j:

$$p_j^I = \left(\sum_i \beta_i\, t_{ij}^{1-\sigma} p_i^{1-\sigma} \right)^{1/(1-\sigma)} \tag{14}$$

Therefore the f.o.b. value of exports from country i to country j is

$$T_{ij}^{fob} = \frac{1}{t_{ij}} Y_j\, \beta_i \left(\frac{t_{ij}\, p_i}{p_j^I} \right)^{1-\sigma} \tag{15}$$

Note that the c.i.f. value of trade is this same expression multiplied by t_{ij}, which is therefore now decreasing in t_{ij} if $\sigma > 1$.

The parameter β_i is no longer country i's share of world income, as it was in the Cobb-Douglas case, so this does not reduce as easily to the standard gravity equation. However, if we let θ_i be country i's share of world income, we can relate it to β_i as follows, and then solve for β_i:

$$\theta_i = \frac{Y_i}{Y^w} = \frac{p_i x_i}{Y^w}$$

$$= \frac{1}{Y^w} \sum_j \beta_i p_j x_j \left(\frac{t_{ij} p_i}{p_j^I} \right)^{1-\sigma} \tag{16}$$

$$= \beta_i \sum_j \theta_j \left(\frac{t_{ij} p_i}{p_j^I} \right)^{1-\sigma}$$

from which

$$\beta_i = \frac{Y_i}{Y^w} \frac{1}{\sum_j \theta_j \left(\frac{t_{ij} p_i}{p_j^I} \right)^{1-\sigma}} \tag{17}$$

Using this in (16) we get

$$T_{ij}^{fob} = \frac{Y_i Y_j}{Y^w} \frac{1}{t_{ij}} \left[\frac{\left(\frac{t_{ij}}{p_j^I} \right)^{1-\sigma}}{\sum_h \theta_h \left(\frac{t_{ih}}{p_h^I} \right)^{1-\sigma}} \right] \tag{18}$$

To simplify this and facilitate interpretation, first select units of goods so that each country's product price, p_i, is normalized at unity. Then p_j^I becomes a CES index of country j's transport factors as an importer, what I will call its average distance from suppliers δ^s:

$$\delta_j^S = \left(\sum_i \beta_i t_{ij}^{1-\sigma} \right)^{\left(\frac{1}{1-\sigma} \right)} \tag{19}$$

What matters for demand along a particular route is the transport factor t_{ij} relative to this average distance from suppliers, what I will call the relative distance from suppliers ρ_{ij}:

$$\rho_{ij} = \frac{t_{ij}}{\delta_j^S} \tag{20}$$

With this notation, the trade flow in (18) becomes

$$T_{ij}^{fob} = \frac{Y_i Y_j}{Y^w} \frac{1}{t_{ij}} \left[\frac{\rho_{ij}^{1-\sigma}}{\sum_h \theta_h \rho_{ih}^{1-\sigma}} \right] \tag{21}$$

This is the main result of this section of the paper. It says the following: If importing country j's relative distance from exporting country i is the same as an average of all demanders' relative distances from i, then exports from i to j will be the same as in the Cobb-Douglas case. That is, c.i.f. exports will be given by the simple frictionless gravity equation, while f.o.b. exports will be reduced below that equation by the transport factor from i to j, much as in the standard gravity equation with the transport factor (one plus transport cost) measuring distance. If j's relative distance from i is greater than this average, then c.i.f. (resp. f.o.b.) trade along this route will be correspondingly less than the simple frictionless (resp. standard) gravity equation, while if j's relative distance from i is less than this, trade will be correspondingly more. Since the transport factor for a country from itself is always unity and therefore less than any such average, countries' purchases from themselves will always be more than would appear warranted by the simple frictionless gravity equation.

The result also says that the elasticity of trade with respect to these relative distance measures is $-(\sigma - 1)$. Thus, the greater is the elasticity of substitution among goods, the more will trade between distant countries fall short of the gravity equation and the more will trade among close countries (and transactions within countries themselves) exceed it.

Likewise, a general reduction in the transport factors themselves, such as might occur with an improvement in transportation technology, will pull trade closer to the amounts predicted by the simple frictionless gravity equation. This does not therefore mean that all bilateral trade flows will expand with a drop in transport costs. Rather, trade between distant countries will expand, while trade between close countries — neighbors — will contract, since the latter lose some of their advantage relative to distant countries. Of course a country is its own closest neighbor, and therefore purchases of a country from itself also contract. It follows that total international trade expands.

V. Conclusion

In this paper I have derived equations for the value of bilateral trade from two extreme cases of the H-O Model, both of which also characterize a variety of other models as well. The first case was frictionless trade, in which the absence of all barriers to trade in homogeneous products causes producers and consumers to be indifferent among trading partners, including their own country, so long as they buy or sell the desired goods. Resolving this indeterminacy with a random drawing, I derived expected trade flows that correspond exactly to the simple frictionless gravity equation whenever preferences are identical and homothetic. Generalizing the result to arbitrary preferences, I found that this gravity equation would still hold on average, but that individual trade flows would exceed or fall short of it depending on a weighted correlation between the exporter's and the importer's deviations from the world average supplies and demands. This in turn was suggestive of how particular non-homotheticities in demand could interact with factor endowments and factor proportions to cause countries to trade excessively (compared to the simple frictionless gravity equation) with countries like themselves.

The second case considered was of countries that each produce different goods. This is also a possible equilibrium of the H-O Model, though of course it is a property as well of other models that have been used in the literature to derive the gravity equation, such as models with Armington preferences and models with monopolistic competition. Here I derived expressions for bilateral trade, first with Cobb-Douglas preferences and then with CES preferences. The former is almost too simple, yielding the simple frictionless gravity equation exactly for trade valued c.i.f. and the standard gravity equation, with division by a transport factor, for trade valued f.o.b. The CES case is more cumbersome, but it too reduces to something not all that different: bilateral trade flows are centered around the same values found in the Cobb-Douglas case, but they are smaller for countries that are a greater than average distance apart as measured by transport cost, and larger for countries that are closer than average. The latter includes purchases of a country from itself, which are increased above the Cobb-Douglas case by the greatest amount. The extent of these departures from the simple Cobb-Douglas gravity equation depends on the elasticity of substitution among goods, being larger the greater is that elasticity.

The lesson from all of this is twofold, I think. First, it is not all that difficult to justify even simple forms of the gravity equation from standard trade theories. Second, because the gravity equation appears to characterize a large class of models, its use for empirical tests of any of them is suspect.

References

Anderson, James E. 1979 "A Theoretical Foundation for the Gravity Equation," *American Economic Review* 69, (March), pp. 106–116.

Bergstrand, Jeffrey H. 1985 "The Gravity Equation in International Trade: Some Microeconomic Foundations and Empirical Evidence," *Review of Economics and Statistics* 67, (August), pp. 474–481.

Bergstrand, Jeffrey H. 1989 "The Generalized Gravity Equation, Monopolistic Competition, and the Factor-Proportions Theory in International Trade," *Review of Economics and Statistics* 71, (February), pp. 143–153.

Bergstrand, Jeffrey H. 1990 "The Heckscher-Ohlin-Samuelson Model, the Linder Hypothesis and the Determinants of Bilateral Intra-Industry Trade," *Economic Journal* 100, (December), pp. 1216–1229.

Deardorff, Alan V. 1984 "Testing Trade Theories and Predicting Trade Flows," in Ronald Jones and Peter Kenen, eds., *Handbook of International Economics* Volume 1, New York: North-Holland, Chapter 10.

Dixit, Avinash K. and Joseph E. Stiglitz 1977 "Monopolistic Competition and Optimum Product Diversity," *American Economic Review* 67, pp. 297–308.

Dornbusch, Rudiger, Stanley Fischer, and Paul A. Samuelson 1977 "Comparative Advantage, Trade, and Payments in a Ricardian Model with a Continuum of Goods," *American Economic Review* 67, pp. 823–839.

Dornbusch, Rudiger, Stanley Fischer, and Paul A. Samuelson 1980 "Heckscher-Ohlin Trade Theory with a Continuum of Goods," *Quarterly Journal of Economics* 95, (September), pp. 203–224.

Frankel, Jeffrey, Ernesto Stein, and Shang-Jin Wei 1994 "Continental Trading Blocs: Are They Natural, or Super-Natural," in process, (August 30).

Helpman, Elhanan 1987 "Imperfect Competition and International Trade: Evidence from Fourteen Industrial Countries," *Journal of the Japanese and International Economies* 1, pp. 62–81.

Helpman, Elhanan and Paul R. Krugman 1984 *Increasing Returns, Imperfect Competition, and International Trade,* in process (May).

Hummels, David and James A. Levinsohn 1995 "Monopolistic Competition and International Trade: Reconsidering the Evidence," *Quarterly Journal of Economics* 110, (August), pp. 799–836.

Krugman, Paul R. 1979 "Increasing Returns, Monopolistic Competition, and International Trade," *Journal of International Economics* 9, pp. 469–479.

Krugman, Paul R. 1980 "Differentiated Products and Multi-lateral Trade," mimeo.

Leamer, Edward E. 1974 "The Commodity Composition of International Trade in Manufactures: An Empirical Analysis," *Oxford Economic Papers* 26, pp. 350–374.

Leamer, Edward E. and Robert M. Stern 1970 *Quantitative International Economics,* Boston: Allyn and Bacon.

Linder, Staffan Burenstam 1961 *An Essay on Trade and Transformation,* New York: John Wiley and Sons.

Linnemann, Hans 1966 *An Econometric Study of International Trade Flows,* Amsterdam: North-Holland.

Markusen, James R. 1986 "Explaining the Volume of Trade: An Eclectic Approach," *American Economic Review* 76, (December), pp. 1002–1011.

Pöyhönen, Pentti 1963 "A Tentative Model for the Volume of Trade Between Countries," *Weltwirtschaftliches Archiv* 90, pp. 93–99.

Savage, I. R. and K. W. Deutsch 1960 "A Statistical Model of the Gross Analysis of Transactions Flows," *Econometrica* 28, (July), pp. 551–572.

Tinbergen, J. 1962 *Shaping the World Economy: Suggestions for an International Economic Policy,* New York: The Twentieth Century Fund.

CHAPTER 25

The Economic Journal, **111** (*April*), 277–294. © Royal Economic Society 2001. Published by Blackwell Publishers, 108 Cowley Road, Oxford OX4 1JF, UK and 350 Main Street, Malden, MA 02148, USA.

RICH AND POOR COUNTRIES IN NEOCLASSICAL TRADE AND GROWTH*

Alan V. Deardorff

A neoclassical growth model provides an explanation for a 'poverty trap', 'club convergence', or 'twin peaks', in terms of specialisation and international trade. The model has many countries with identical linearly homogeneous technologies for producing three goods using capital and labour. With diverse initial endowments, initial equilibrium has unequal factor prices and two diversification cones. With savings out of wages, following Galor (1996), there may easily be multiple steady states. Poor countries converge to a low steady state while rich countries converge to a high one, even though all share identical technological and behavioural parameters.

Why do some countries become rich and seem to stay that way, while others remain mired in poverty? The simple neoclassical growth model of Solow (1956) and Swan (1956) seems poorly suited to answering this question, since in the absence of some *deus ex machina* like exogenous technological progress, it seems to predict zero long-run per capita growth for all countries, as well as per capita incomes that differ in steady state only due to differences in saving. Unless the world is divided quite radically into some countries that save a lot and others that save very little, with few in between, the model seems unable to explain the growing polarisation of the world economy into nations that are rich and nations that are poor.

In a recent paper, Galor (1996) notes that a comparatively minor modification of the neoclassical growth model can change this conclusion. If all saving is done out of wages, as Galor motivates with a simple overlapping generations model, then with an appropriately shaped technology the neoclassical model can generate multiple steady states. Here, even if all countries are alike in technologies and behavioural parameters, large enough differences in initial conditions will divide them into separate groups, one converging to a lower steady state and the other to a higher. Galor calls this phenomenon 'club convergence', and he notes a body of empirical evidence in its favour, also reviewed by Quah (1996), who describes the phenomenon as 'twin peaks' in the international distribution of income. There also exist other more elaborate theoretical growth models that can yield club convergence, but a strong point of Galor's explanation is, with one exception, its simplicity.

The exception, I think, is the contortions that one must go through to get the technology of the simple model to yield the desired multiple steady states. As I will show, in order to get multiple steady states with positive income even

* I owe an obvious debt to Oded Galor, whose presentation of his results from Galor (1996) at a conference in Helsingor, Denmark, in August 1996 gave me the idea for this paper. I have also benefited greatly from conversations on this topic with colleagues and participants at seminars too numerous to mention. A very incomplete list includes Susanto Basu, Andy Bernard, John Boyce, Ron Cronovich, Pat Deardorff, John Laitner, Ramakishen Rajan, Karan Singh, Bob Stern, Jaume Ventura and Henry Wan. I also have had good comments from two referees.

in the poor one, the technology cannot be Cobb-Douglas or even constant elasticity of substitution (CES), but must have an elasticity of substitution that varies with the capital-labour ratio in a very particular way. Thus the Galor model shows that club convergence is possible, but it does not make it seem particularly likely.

Another feature of Galor's model, in common with a surprising amount of the literature on growth convergence, is that the economy is closed, or at least there is no explicit role for international trade.[1] Yet it turns out that by allowing for trade much as in the early neoclassical trade and growth literature, we can transform his model into something not much more complex, but that easily yields his special shape for per capita savings. The trick is only to recognise the role of specialisation in international trade. By including multiple goods (the model here has three) in a Heckscher-Ohlin (HO) model of production and trade, the same heterogeneity in initial factor endowments that starts Galor's countries toward different steady states can also prevent world-wide factor price equalisation. There emerge instead two separate cones of diversification, into which different countries are drawn by growth, and in which they then remain, due to the international factor price differences themselves.

That, then, is the message of this paper: that a model comprising three components – simple neoclassical growth, savings primarily out of wages due perhaps to overlapping generations, and multi-good HO trade – provides a compact explanation of why countries that start out different may remain so. Interestingly, the model does not suggest that trade is necessarily a force for making countries more alike, but rather the opposite. Without trade, these countries seem more likely to converge, although not to a steady state that is desirable. Furthermore, the model also has implications for how policy, including trade policy, will change a steady state. A temporary increase in savings can allow a poor country to escape the poverty trap of a low initial capital stock. Trade restrictions, however, can only make matters worse.

I will begin in Section 1 by briefly recapitulating the Solow growth model and Galor's variant of it yielding multiple steady states and thus poverty traps and club convergence. Then I will recall, in Section 2, the extension of the Solow model to a two-sector trading economy, such as was the focus of the early neoclassical literature on trade and growth. In Section 3, this model will be modified to include three goods and thus the possibility of multiple cones of diversification. Multiple steady states are then shown to arise naturally from Galor's saving assumption. Comparative static and comparative steady state properties are explored in Section 4, trade policy in Section 5, and I conclude in Section 6.

[1] It is one-sector model and could therefore be a country that completely specialises and exports one good in exchange for all others.

1. Poverty Traps, Club Convergence, and Galor's Modification of Solow Growth

It is hardly news that countries are very unequal in their per capita incomes. Using data from Maddison (1982), Baumol (1986) and Abramovitz (1986) documented this inequality and how per capita incomes have changed over time. Baumol, in particular, noted the apparent convergence of incomes among a group of high-income countries, which he called a 'convergence club'. Others have sought to explain this phenomenon in various ways, including the use of dynamic growth models with multiple steady states. These generate growth paths in which groups of countries that start in the neighbourhood of a given steady state converge to it, while other groups with different initial conditions converge to other steady states.[2]

The example that I will build on here is Galor (1996). He adapted the Solow (1956) one-sector growth model to a two-period overlapping generations context in which savings, of necessity, came only out of wages. In the familiar Solow model, national income, Y, is generated from the employment of labour L and capital K in a function F that is homogeneous of degree one:

$$Y = F(K, L). \tag{1}$$

F is a production function, although it could represent, and will below, a more general relationship between factors and income. For later use, Y should be measured in the same units as investment and the capital stock.

The labour force grows at a constant proportional rate, n, while the capital stock grows due to investment, which is in turn equal to saving, S:[3]

$$\dot{L} = nL. \tag{2}$$

$$\dot{K} = S. \tag{3}$$

Letting $k = K/L$ be the capital-labour ratio, its change over time, $\dot{k} = dk/dt$, is

$$\dot{k} = S/L - nk. \tag{4}$$

That is, change over time in the capital-labour ratio is critically dependent on the specification of per capita saving, S/L. In Solow's formulation, saving was a constant fraction, s, of total income, so that $S = sY = sF(K, L)$. The homogeneity of F could then be exploited to express per capita saving in terms of per capita income, $y = Y/L = F(K, L)/L = F(K/L, 1) = f(k)$:

$$S/L = sf(k). \tag{5}$$

The dynamic behaviour of the model is then seen graphically, as in Fig. 1, where the positive and negative terms in (4) are graphed separately. The first, per capita saving, is just the fraction s of the per capita production function, $f(k)$, which is also shown. The second term in (4) is a ray from the origin with

[2] Examples include Azariadis and Drazen (1990), Galor and Zeira (1993), Barro and Sala-I-Martin (1995), Quah (1996, 1997), and others surveyed by Azariadis (1996).

[3] A constant rate of depreciation is also easily incorporated.

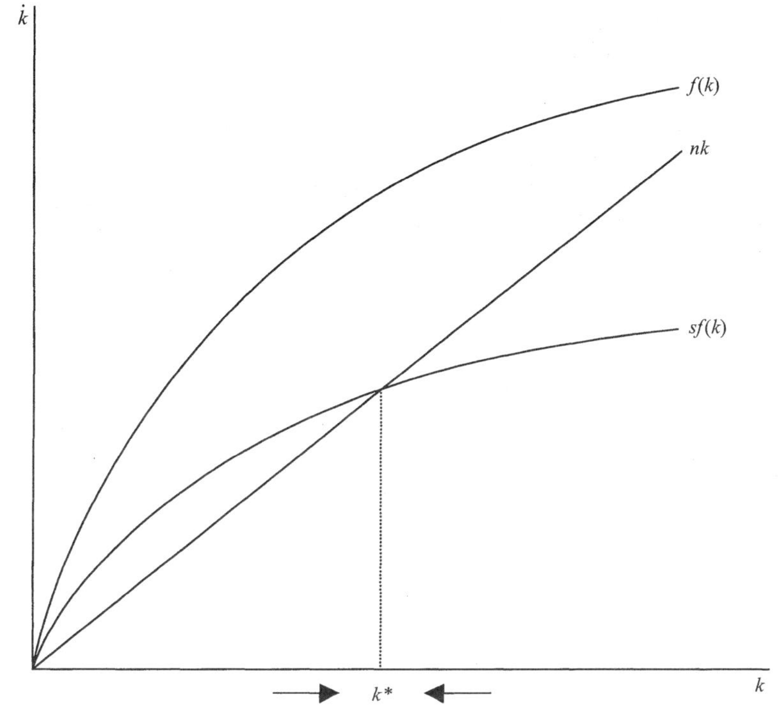

Fig. 1 *One Sector, Proportional Saving*

slope n. The time derivative of the capital-labour ratio is the vertical distance between these two curves. Under standard assumptions about production functions,[4] per capita saving in this formulation is above nk at low k and below it at high k, crossing nk only once. That intersection is the steady state capital-labour ratio, k^*. The dynamics of the model cause k to converge to k^* over time, as shown by the arrows.

It is this behaviour that has led interpreters to associate the Solow model with what has been called (conditional) convergence. That is, any two countries with the same technology, f, and the same savings and population growth parameters (hence 'conditional') but different initial factor endowments will converge over time to the same capital-labour ratio, k^*, and therefore to the same level of per capita income. The strong result can be weakened, as noted by Solow himself, by permitting a technology for which output per unit of capital, $f(k)/k$, is always above a lower bound greater than n.[5] This raises the possibility of indefinite endogenous per capita growth as in the recent endogenous growth literature. But it does not help to explain a case that may be more relevant empirically: countries whose growth does level off, but at vastly different levels of per capita income.

[4] These assumptions include the Inada (1963) conditions that $f'(0) = \infty$ and $f'(\infty) = 0$.
[5] Thus violating the second Inada Condition.

Galor's (1996) suggested modification of the Solow model to create this possibility is very simple: assume that savings occurs only out of wages, not out of total income. He motivates this assumption by placing the Solow model in a two-period, overlapping generations context, with only the first generation working and no bequests. In such a model, only the first generation can save, and its income is solely from labour, so savings is a fraction, s_w, of labour income. That fraction could depend on a variety of things, including the rate of return on capital, but for simplicity we can take it to be a constant.[6] Per capita savings is then this fraction of the wage: $S/L = s_w w$.[7]

In a closed economy, the wage must rise with capital accumulation,[8] but it need not do so smoothly. It may rise quickly to a relatively high level for low values of k and then rise only slowly as k rises further. This will happen, for example, with a CES production function with an elasticity of substitution, σ, greater than one. Alternatively, the wage may be a constant fraction of per capita income, like the savings function in Fig. 1, as it will with a Cobb-Douglas production function. Or it may stay very low until some critical k is approached, then rise rapidly to level off much higher, as it will with a CES production function if σ is sufficiently less than one. This last possibility is shown in Fig. 2.

As seen there, savings out of wages can, in the case shown, lead to multiple steady states, k_1^*, k_2^* and k_3^*. The middle steady state is unstable, and the economy approaches either k_1^* or k_3^* over time depending on whether initial k is below or above k_2^*. This is more or less the club-convergence phenomenon, but it takes an extreme form here, since $k_1^* = 0$. That is, countries end up either rich or, in effect, dead.

To get multiple steady states that start above zero is quite possible in this simple model, but it requires that the wage, as a function of k, wiggle even more than the one shown in Fig. 2. Perhaps such a function could be justified, although at this point Galor's model may begin to strain the bounds of plausibility.

In any case, the Galor model has another characteristic that seems manifestly inappropriate for addressing growth of different countries: These countries do not seem to trade. Each produces a single good that it uses for both consumption and investment, and it has no use for exports or imports. The model could be reinterpreted to correct this, having each country produce a

[6] This would be the case, for example, if consumers in the two-period overlapping generations model had Cobb-Douglas preferences for first and second period consumption.

[7] This is different from Solow's assumption that savings is a constant fraction of output, and it also differs from the alternative of savings out of capital income that was sometimes used in early growth models. The fact that it may be optimal with overlapping generations is important, but not decisive, since optimisation by an infinitely lived representative consumer yields a different result, and neither model is at all realistic. Mankiw (1995), in a beautiful survey of growth theories, considers this issue and sees no basis for preferring one or the other (and himself then chooses the simple proportional saving of Solow). Aiyagari (1985) argues that the two models are observationally equivalent, but that is clearly not the case here.

[8] In a small open HO economy, it need not, which is the message of Samuelson's (1949) factor price equalisation theorem.

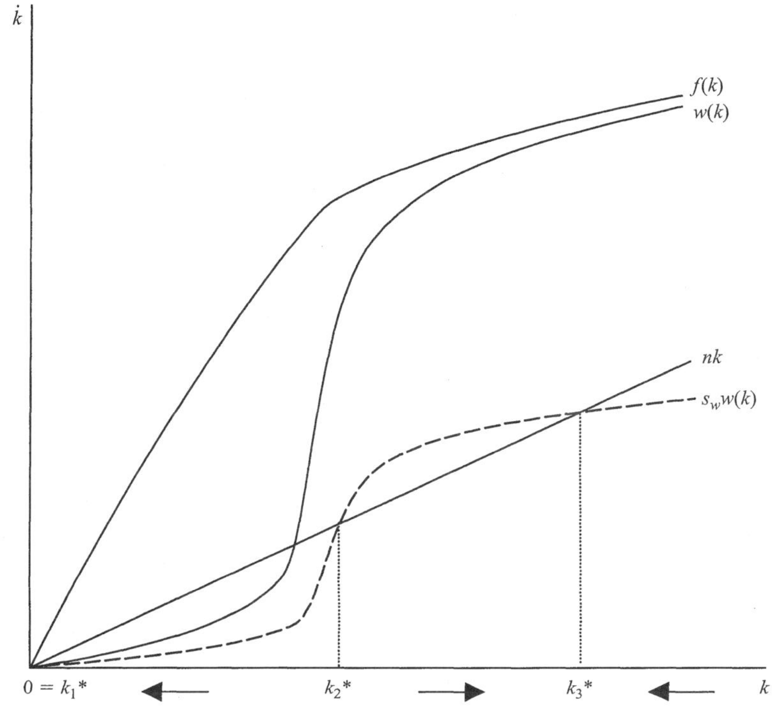

Fig. 2. *One Sector, Saving out of Wages*

single good and exchange it for many others, but that degree of specialisation is also extreme. I will look next at growth in a HO trade model, where patterns of specialisation and diversification will be endogenous.

2. Neoclassical Trade and Growth

Among the many extensions of neoclassical growth theory in the 1960–70s, extensions to incorporate trade were among the most prominent. After Uzawa (1961, 1963) first built and solved a two-sector neoclassical growth model of a closed economy, Oniki and Uzawa (1965) took the natural next step of allowing two such countries to trade. They had one sector produce a consumption good and the other an investment good, in an elegant hybrid of Solow growth and $2 \times 2 \times 2$ HO trade. The model was a bit cumbersome, however, and was not itself the basis for many extensions.

I will work here with this model as exposited in Deardorff (1974). There I showed that, given prices of the two goods, per capita income of a country can be constructed from the per-worker production functions of the two industries, each multiplied by its price. As shown in Fig. 3 for two goods, labour-

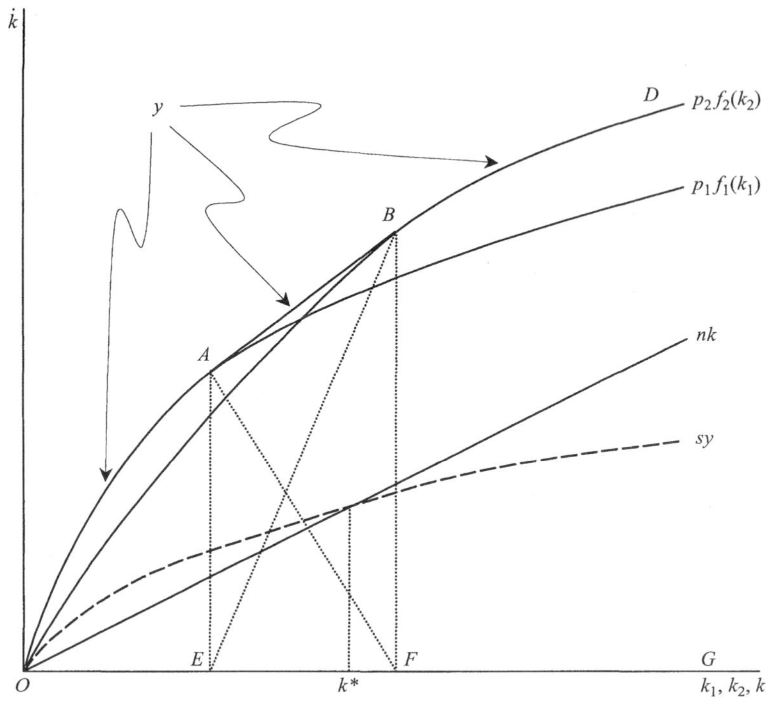

Fig. 3. *Two Sectors, Proportional Saving*

intensive X_1 and capital-intensive X_2, the per-worker production functions, f_1 and f_2, are first drawn as functions of their respective sectoral capital-labour ratios, k_1 and k_2. Per capita income of the country, y, as a function of the country's capital-labour ratio, k, is then the convex hull of f_1 and f_2. That is, a straight line tangent to both sectoral curves is drawn from A to B, and y is then given by the uppermost of the two curves and this straight segment, *OABD*. Per capita outputs of the two sectors are also given, by curves *OAFG* and *OEBD*, which include the diagonals of the trapezoid formed by *AB* and the perpendiculars from A and B to the horizontal axis.

Using Solow's (and Oniki and Uzawa's) proportional savings assumption, per capita saving, $S/L = sy$, is then simply a replica of *OABD*, scaled vertically downward, itself including a straight segment between the vertical lines *EA* and *FB*. If prices remain fixed over time, then this per capita savings curve can be used along with ray, *nk*, to infer the dynamics of growth. In the case shown in Fig. 3, the steady state at k^* has the country producing both goods, although if it had started its growth at a much lower capital-labour ratio, it would first have specialised in the more labour-intensive good, X_1. Under the assumption of Oniki and Uzawa that one of the goods is the investment good, the pattern of trade can also be inferred by comparing the per capita output of that good, given above, to the demand for investment given by *sy*.[9]

With proportional saving, this two-sector, open-economy growth model evidently behaves much like the one-sector closed-economy Solow growth model, with the same implication of conditional convergence of the countries of a trading world. Indeed, one could have many countries all looking like Fig. 3 and trading with the same world economy whose prices anchor the figure, and all would then converge eventually to the same k^* regardless of their initial conditions.[10]

Also like the Solow model, this model can be modified following Galor to generate a form of club convergence. I do not pursue that modification here, because I do not find the results as plausible as those of the next section, where I also allow for more goods and failure of factor price equalisation. But the interested reader may wish to investigate them.[11]

3. More Goods

In the years since the heyday of neoclassical growth theory, attention to the HO model has extended beyond the two-good textbook version to allow more goods. At the same time, the role of factor price equalisation (FPE) in HO models has been clarified. If the factor endowments of all the countries in the world are sufficiently similar, then free and frictionless trade will lead to complete FPE, with all countries able to produce all goods. But if factor endowments differ enough, then FPE will be impossible, and the world will sort itself into at least two groups of countries with different factor prices.[12] One such arrangement has countries in just two groups, each group of countries producing a different group of goods. Such an equilibrium suggests itself for the problem here, where for a different reason we are also looking at groups of countries that may have different factor endowments. I will therefore

[9] In the case shown, for example, if the investment good is the capital-intensive X_2, an initially very poor country will first produce none of it and instead import all that it requires in exchange for the consumption good. Then, at some point in time, it will begin to produce it, and eventually, in steady state, it will export it.

[10] Of course the world market-clearing prices would be likely to change over time as the world factor endowments evolve, but at any point in time the picture would look enough like Fig. 3 to generate convergence. Also, if all countries share the same technology and parameters, then the common steady state must have no trade. That is, unlike Fig. 3, if X_2 is the investment good *sy* must intersect *nk* where it also intersects *EB*.

[11] With only wages saved, the two-good case of Fig. 3 will generate club convergence somewhat like Fig. 2, so long as the elasticity of substitution of one sector is sufficiently small. If that is the capital-intensive sector, and with, say, a Cobb-Douglas other sector, per capita saving behaves as follows: it rises in proportion to national income to the left of *E*, is constant between *E* and *F*, then rises quickly to include almost all income somewhere to the right of *F*. For appropriate parameters s_w and *n*, there will be positive stable steady states to the left of *F* and also far to the right of *F*. In this scenario, the poor club does survive with positive income, and it may even produce both goods, while the rich club necessarily specialises completely in the capital intensive good. By making the labour-intensive good also substitution inelastic, another stable steady state at zero can also be obtained.

[12] See Deardorff (1994*b*).

extend the analysis of the previous section to a model of three goods, which is the minimum that permits these two groups.

Suppose, then, that goods X_1, X_2, and X_3 have different capital intensities, and that world prices happen to be such that FPE is not possible. Trade theorists are familiar with this situation, which is usually depicted in the Lerner-Pearce diagram with unit-value isoquants that imply two cones of diversification, one for producing goods X_1 and X_2, the other for producing X_2 and X_3.[13] In the per capita income diagram used here and applied to this case, the convex hull of the three per-worker production functions now includes two straight segments that correspond to these diversification cones. Fig. 4 shows this hull and the two cones, one between *A* and *B*, and another between *C* and *D*. To reduce clutter I have omitted the portions of the per worker production functions that are not part of the hull, but the reader can visualise them.[14]

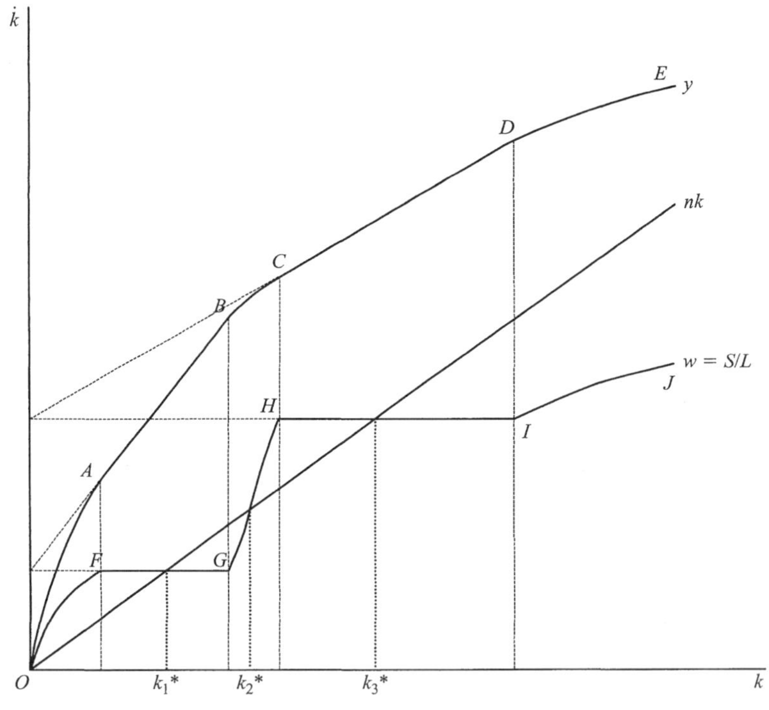

Fig. 4. *Three Sectors, Saving out of Wages*

[13] See Deardorff (1979).

[14] The production function for X_1 simply continues the smooth curve begun by *OA*. That for X_2 is a curve from *O* to *B* (starting flatter than *OA*), includes the short curved segment *BC*, and then continues in another smooth curve to the right of *C* and below the hull. That for X_3 is an even flatter smooth curve from *O* to *D* and then follows the hull along *DE*.

This three good model would again behave very like the Solow one-sector model if savings were proportional to income. The per capita savings curve would be just a scaled down version of the per capita income curve, and could cross the nk ray only once. But with Galor's assumption of savings out of wages, this shape has startling implications. Throughout each straight segment of the per capita income hull, factor prices are constant due to FPE. In particular, the wage is constant at the level given by the vertical intercept of the (extended) straight segment.[15] And where the per capita income curve is not straight, following a per worker production function, the wage rises with k at a rate that depends essentially on the elasticity of substitution of that particular sectoral production function. Thus a curve representing the wage for all levels of k is like the one shown: rising from O to F, flat from F to G, rising from G to H, flat again at a higher level from H to I, and finally rising thereafter.

This unusual shape for w is also, under Galor's assumption, the shape of the per capita savings curve, since that is the same curve scaled down by the fraction s_w. Rather than draw yet another curve in Fig. 4, I assume implausibly that s_w is unity (or alternatively that the entire vertical dimension of the figure has been scaled by s_w), and I therefore treat the wage curve itself as the per capita savings curve. Inserting a population growth ray, nk, it is then not hard to get two stable steady states, both in cones of diversification.[16,17] These are shown as k_1^* and k_3^*, and there is also an unstable steady state at k_2^*. Thus it is not only easy to get multiple steady states – and thus club convergence – once one allows for multi-good, HO trade; the model even seems to suggest them as likely.

This is a bit of an overstatement, however, for in drawing Fig. 4 I have implicitly made several assumptions that contribute to this result. First, I have drawn the wage curve as quite steep between points G and H. This will only be the case if the elasticity of substitution in good X_2 is sufficiently less than one. In contrast, a Cobb-Douglas function would have had the wage just proportional to per capita output, and the resulting wage curve would cross rays from the origin only from above, preventing the unstable crossing at k_2^*. But with inelastic substitution in this good of intermediate factor intensity, the wage

[15] This is a standard feature of two-factor production functions written in intensive form. Per worker output is $y = f(k)$, the rental price of capital is $r = f'(k)$, and the wage is $w = f(k) - rk$, which is the vertical intercept of the tangent to the curve $f(k)$.

[16] As long as the segment GH is steep enough to cut rays from the origin from below, as drawn in Fig. 4 and as discussed further below, then there will exist values of n such that there are multiple steady states. However these will not necessarily occur in cones of diversification. The latter property is easy to get by drawing the production functions appropriately, as shown, but it is also not hard to draw the functions so that a steady state in one cone can only be accompanied by other steady states outside of either cone. Of course, the per capita income curve on which this is all based depends not only on the sectoral production functions, but also on world prices, and these will have adjusted so that all goods are produced somewhere and world markets clear. To me that suggests that configurations such as Fig. 4, with both steady states in cones of diversification, are more likely than configurations in which one steady state involves specialisation. However, 'likely' here has no rigorous meaning. In any case, the behaviour of the model is pretty much the same in either case.

[17] If the production function of the most capital-intensive good has low elasticity of substitution, then the wage will rise rapidly to the right of point I, and additional steady states will exist with complete specialisation.

curve can cross rays from below as shown. Indeed, if good X_2 were Leontief, points B and C would coincide and GH would be vertical.

I have also implicitly selected prices of the goods that yield the desired picture. However, this is not as arbitrary as it might seem. World prices must be such as to give equilibrium in all markets. If initial factor endowments are sufficiently different across countries to prevent FPE, then prices must adjust so that all goods are produced somewhere. This does not itself assure that all countries diversify, but positive production of all goods is easiest if prices adjust so that both diversification cones include at least some countries.

I am treating the figure and the prices that underlie it as though they were fixed over time, but they will probably not be fixed as long as a nontrivial portion of the world economy is still adjusting toward steady state. Nonetheless, it seems likely that at each time along the way, the picture will look something like Fig. 4, with countries below some dividing-line converging on a low k and others above it converging on a high k. What will matter ultimately will be the prices that prevail when all countries have reached steady state. Since the two groups of countries are not themselves becoming closer together along the way, it will not be surprising if they remain too far apart for FPE in the steady state. Then steady state prices that permit all goods to be produced could easily give rise to the picture in Fig. 4.

Let me summarise what this model, together with HO trade theory, says. Suppose that countries have identical technologies and identical behavioural parameters (n and s_w), but different initial factor endowments. If those differences are not too large, then world equilibrium entails FPE and we are in something like the situation of Section 2, with only a single diversification cone and a single flat in the wage curve. Convergence of all factor endowments to a single steady state is not assured, because multiple steady states can arise here just as in Galor's one sector model. But they do not appear particularly likely.

However, if countries begin with endowments too diverse to permit FPE, then market-clearing prices will necessarily imply multiple cones of diversification and a wage curve that wiggles as in Fig. 4. As long as the good of intermediate factor intensity that is produced between cones has sufficiently low elasticity of substitution, the wiggles *must* be big enough to yield multiple steady states for a range of other parameter values. Thus the initial differences in factor endowments may remain indefinitely, and the world will evolve toward a permanent situation in which countries remain divided into two groups, one rich and one poor.

4. Comparative Statics and Comparative Steady States

Suppose now that we start in such a world steady state, with many countries that are technologically and behaviourally identical but which, because of history and the dynamics described above, have sorted themselves into two such groups. What will happen to one of the countries if its behaviour changes? The solid lines in Fig. 5 reproduce the per capita savings and population growth curves from Fig. 4. If we are in a world steady state, some

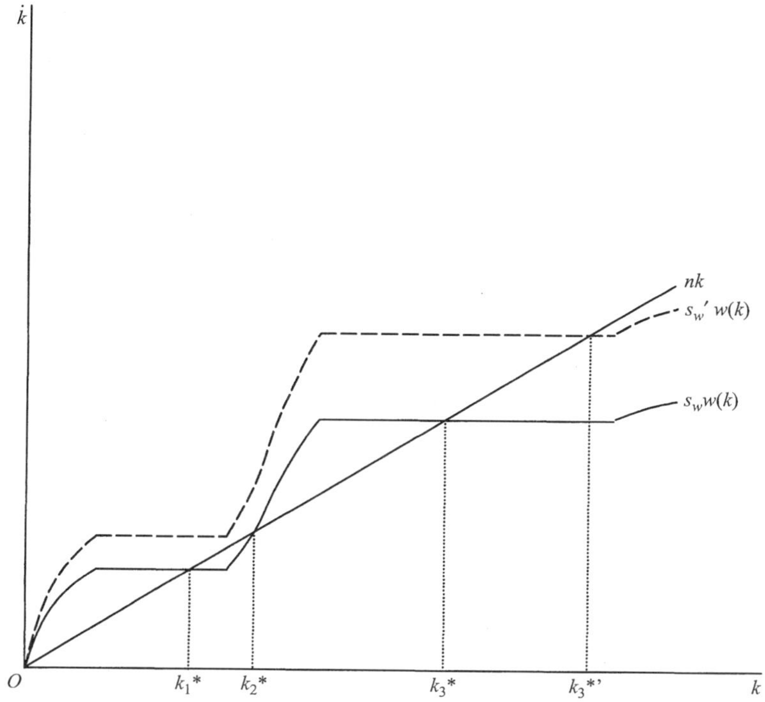

Fig. 5. *An Increase in the Saving Rate*

countries are at k_1^* and others are at k_3^*. What happens if a poor country, starting at k_1^*, increases the fraction of its wages that it saves, from s_w to s_w'? A small increase will move its steady state only slightly to the right, and it will get a small increase in its per capita income over time, just as in the Solow model.[18] But a larger increase in s_w, like the one shown, will shift the savings curve enough to eliminate the lower steady state. The capital-labour ratio of the country will therefore begin to rise over time and, if s_w remains high, eventually approach a steady state $k_3^{*'}$ even higher than k_3^*. Thus a comparatively small change in behaviour can lead to a large change in the country's situation. Poor countries need not be condemned to poverty indefinitely, it seems, and the cure for poverty here is the usual one: more savings. But the increase has to be large enough to eliminate the poor steady state entirely, not just move away from it.

What's more, the increase in saving does not even have to be permanent. If the country saves at the higher rate s_w' just long enough for k to grow past k_2^*,

[18] As in the Solow model, this increase in per capita income need not imply higher per capita consumption, since savings has increased. However, such a poor country is likely to be well below the golden rule of saving – that is, its return to capital is likely to exceed its population growth rate – and therefore per capita consumption will rise as well in steady state.

then returns to saving only s_w, growth will continue to k_3^*. The unstable steady state, k_2^*, acts as a threshold that the poor country merely needs to get past in order to continue growing like a rich country.

All of this assumes that a single, negligibly small poor country attempts to increase savings. What would happen if an entire group of poor countries tried this? Prices would then have to change, and use of the diagram would be considerably more complicated. Results depend in part on which is the investment good, since it must be the numeraire for comparison with nk. But a likely answer is clear in the plausible case where the investment good is an import of the poor countries. As the poor countries all increase their saving out of wages, they will all begin to grow. As they do, their output of the most labour-intensive good will fall at initial prices.[19] For equilibrium, the price of that good will rise relative to the others. As it does, the first curved segment of the per capita income curve in Fig. 4 will shift up, the straight portion from A to B becoming flatter. This raises the wage and shifts per capita saving up even further for the poor countries. Fig. 6 shows just the second part of this process, the price increase for good X_1. The total effect combines Figs. 5 and 6. Clearly, and to me surprisingly, a smaller increase in savings by poor countries is needed for them to escape poverty together than would be needed for them to do it individually!

Likewise, if only some poor countries save more, prices change to help the growth of others who do not. Indeed, other poor countries may conceivably escape the poverty trap if the price increase is large enough, without increasing their own propensities to save out of wages.

What holds for the savings rate holds equally, in reverse, for the population growth rate, n. By lowering its population growth rate below that of the world, a single negligibly small country can also grow in per capita terms, and it may be able to eliminate the lower steady state entirely.

Analogous results obtain for rich countries, who by saving less, or reproducing faster, may destroy the rich steady state that has sustained them.[20]

5. Trade and Trade Policy

The multiple equilibria that may arise with free trade in the absence of FPE may suggest that free trade somehow enhances the possibility of a poverty trap. After all, in a closed economy prices would have to permit the production of all goods, and while the analysis of the one-sector closed economy above indicates that multiple steady states can arise even there, without multiple

[19] From the Rybczynski Theorem, indicated by the downward diagonal of the trapezoid under AB in Fig. 4.

[20] One needs to be careful about increases in population growth rates, however, since a country that raises its population growth above that of the world will not be able to remain negligibly small, and there will have to be effects on prices. Neoclassical growth with differences in population growth rates is explored in Deardorff (1994a). With international investment as well as trade, a country with a population growth rate lower than the world's can achieve endogenous sustained per capita growth. Its growth rate depends on its savings, much as in endogenous growth models, but without increasing returns to scale or improvement in technology.

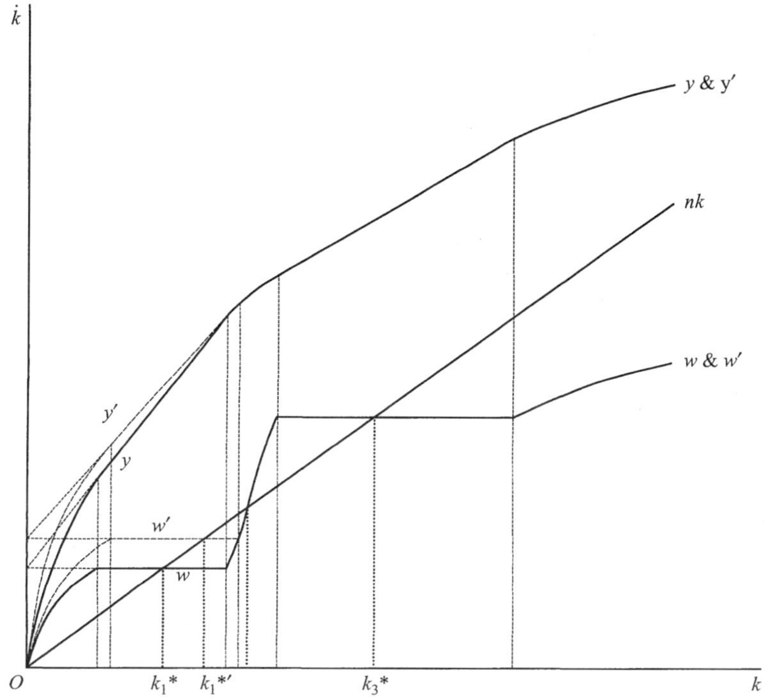

Fig. 6. *An Increase in the Price of the Most Labour-intensive Good*

cones of diversification this seems distinctly less likely. I therefore ask here whether trade intervention may improve the lot of a poor country in this model.[21]

To consider trade policy, we must first be careful about how price changes are introduced into this model. It is critical that per capita savings must be measured in the same units as capital, since savings is to provide the amount of new capital needed to sustain steady-state growth along the ray *nk*. Thus we must identify which of our goods is used for investment, and then hold its price constant. Since the factor intensity of the investment good is not known, we may need to consider three cases of any price change.[22]

In addition, there are two types of country to consider, rich and poor, as well as more than one possible pattern of trade between them. Allowing all these possibilities would be tedious, and I therefore look only at a tariff levied by a

[21] It is already known that a tariff can have different effects in a static model with multiple cones than in the traditional HO model. Davis (1996) shows the effects of protection and trade liberalisation in a static model like the one here.

[22] Uzawa (1961, 1963) found that if the investment good were capital intensive, this could cause instability, either in the disequilibrium dynamics of price adjustment at a point in time, or in the approach to steady states over time. That has led some to prefer the opposite factor intensity assumption, for reasons analogous to Samuelson's (1948) Correspondence Principle. However it is precisely such instabilities that may cause multiple equilibria such as we study here, and I therefore would not rule them out.

poor country, leaving rich-country protection to the reader. I ask whether a single poor country, in a world of many countries both rich and poor, can grow any more successfully by restricting trade.

Start, then, in a free-trade steady state with many technologically and behaviourally identical countries that have sorted themselves into rich and poor groups as above, due to different initial factor endowments.[23] In this equilibrium, the poor countries must export good X_1 and the rich countries must export X_3. Either group could export X_2, depending on the group sizes and their steady-state factor endowments. Thus the poor countries may import only X_3, or they may import both X_2 and X_3. For brevity, I will consider only the first of these cases.

That is, our chosen poor country, small and one of many importers of X_3, now levies a tariff, raising its domestic price of X_3 above the constant world price. If X_3 is not the investment good (whose domestic price we must hold fixed), then the curve $p_3 f_3$ that underlies y would shift upward in Fig. 4 due to the tariff, raising y and rotating it counterclockwise to the right of C. If instead, good X_3 *is* the investment good, then the rise in its price above the world price would appear as a *downward* shift of both $p_1 f_1$ and $p_2 f_2$ and thus of the y curve in Fig. 4 from O to D. These two possibilities are shown in panels (b) and (a) respectively of Fig. 7.

In both, I have kept savings constant, as a fraction of the wage, assuming that tariff revenue is not saved.[24] Where X_3 is the investment good, panel (a), the proportional downward shift of both $p_1 f_1$ and $p_2 f_2$ causes the wage in the lower diversification cone to fall. There is also a larger change in the wage in the upper cone, since the tangency at C moves down and to the left, and the vertical intercept of the tangent (not shown) falls substantially. This does not matter for the poor country, however, since its endowment is in the lower cone. What does matter is that the wage in the lower cone falls (by the percent of the tariff). Because this reduces saving, the country's steady state capital-labour ratio falls. Thus when X_3 is the investment good, the tariff levied by the poor country just increases its poverty in steady state. This is not surprising, since X_3 is also the import good, and what the tariff is doing is making investment more expensive.

If X_3 is *not* the investment good, the outcome is only slightly better, as shown in panel (*b*) of Fig. 7. Now the tariff does shift a portion of the per capita income curve upward, to the right of C, also moving the tangency at C to the left. However, the vertical intercept of that tangency falls, and therefore the wage is reduced in the upper cone of diversification. This does not matter for the poor country, however, since it is not there. Instead, in this case the wage in the lower cone is left unchanged by the tariff, and there is no effect on the poor country's steady state. The tariff here has not hurt growth, but it has

[23] There is no reason why one could not also examine a country that is different from the others in technology or behavioural parameters.

[24] If tariff revenue is saved, then this slightly improves the chance that the tariff may be beneficial. But as usual in second best analysis, any less distorting tax could provide revenues to be saved and yield a superior outcome.

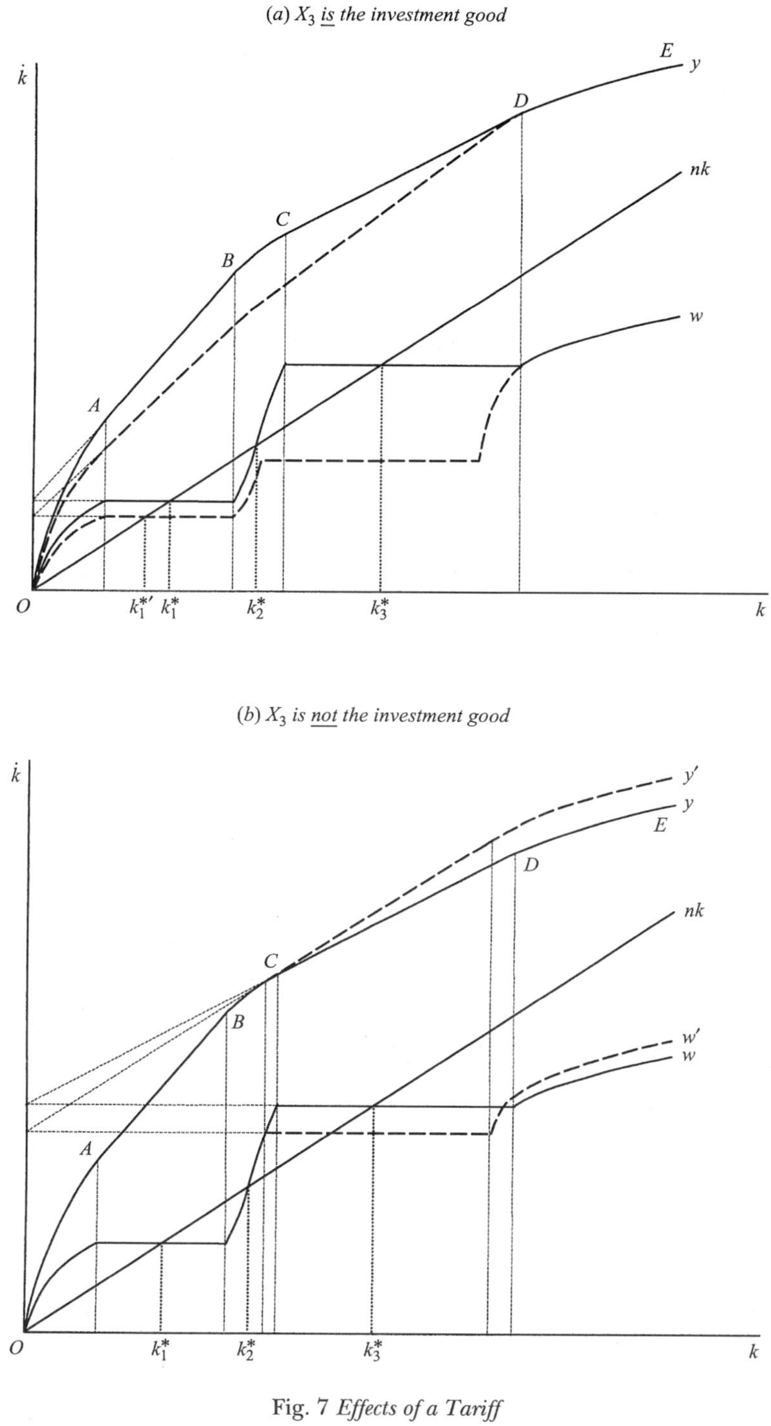

Fig. 7 *Effects of a Tariff*

not helped either.[25] Thus in neither case does a small tariff – one that leaves the poor country still not producing good X_3 – help it to escape the impoverished steady state.

But what if the tariff were raised still higher, to the point that production of good X_3 were to become viable? This would draw factors out of good X_2, until either X_2 would be imported or a tariff would be placed on imports of it as well. In the working paper version of this paper, Deardorff (1997), I assumed the latter, and therefore examined broad protection that moves the country all the way to autarky. The analysis becomes somewhat tedious, since it is necessary to consider separately each of the three cases in which the investment good is X_1, X_2, and X_3. But it turns out that in all three cases, protection lowers the wage in units of the investment good in the neighbourhood of the lower steady state. It therefore reduces saving and causes this steady state to move to a still lower capital-labour ratio. The result that protection hurts growth in this model therefore extends all the way to autarky.

Thus, protection by a poor country, prohibitive or not, usually leads it to an even more impoverished steady state than was attainable with free trade and at best leaves the steady state unchanged while lowering static welfare.[26] It is therefore not international trade that should be faulted for this sad steady state in free trade. The solution to such poverty will not be found in withdrawal from the world market, but rather in finding some way to increase saving as discussed in the previous section.

6. Conclusion

The world of this paper is not a happy one, for it condemns whole populations to permanent poverty, not because they behave any differently from more fortunate folk, but only because of their place in history. If that is the case in the real world as well, then it is very important to find out why, and what can be done to change it. I find it rather surprising that the HO model of international trade, which I tend to think of as quite well behaved, can yield this result in one of its more plausible equilibria.

[25] Of course static welfare, were we to look at it, would still be reduced by the tariff due to the usual inefficiency that it causes in choices between X_3 and other goods. This is an example of Mazumdar's (1996) point that trade liberalisation, even though it may increase static welfare by reducing inefficiency, will increase growth only if it lowers the price of the investment good, contrary to the claim of Baldwin (1992).

[26] One must be careful, however, in drawing conclusions about welfare across steady states, since to get from one steady state to another one traverses a non-steady-state growth path where welfare can be quite different. See Deardorff (1973).

References

Abramovitz, Moses. (1986). 'Catching up, forging ahead, and falling behind', *Journal of Economic History*, vol. 46 (June), pp. 385–406.
Aiyagari, S. Rao. (1985). 'Observational equivalence of the overlapping generations and the discounted dynamic programming frameworks for one-sector growth', *Journal of Economic Theory*, vol. 35 (April), pp. 201–21.
Azariadis, Costas. (1996). 'The economics of poverty traps, part I: complete markets', *Journal of Economic Growth*, vol. 14 (December), pp. 449–96.
Azariadis, Costas and Drazen, Allan (1990). 'Threshold externalities in economic development', *Quarterly Journal of Economics*, vol. 105 (May), pp. 501–26.
Baldwin, Richard E. (1992). 'Measurable dynamic gains from trade', *Journal of Political Economy*, vol. 100 (February), pp. 162–74.
Barro, Robert and Sala-I-Martin, Xavier (1995). *Economic Growth*. New York: McGraw Hill.
Baumol, William J. (1986). 'Productivity growth, convergence, and welfare: what the long-run data show', *American Economic Review*, vol. 76 (December), pp. 1072–85.
Davis, Donald R. (1996). 'Trade liberalisation and income distribution', NBER Working Paper no.5693, National Bureau of Economic Research, (August).
Deardorff, Alan V. (1973). 'The gains from trade in and out of steady-state growth', *Oxford Economic Papers*, vol. 25 (July), 173–91.
Deardorff, Alan V. (1974). 'A geometry of growth and trade', *Canadian Journal of Economics*, vol. 7 (May), pp. 295–306.
Deardorff, Alan V. (1979). 'Weak links in the chain of comparative advantage', *Journal of International Economics*, vol. 9 (May), pp. 197–209.
Deardorff, Alan V. (1994*a*). 'Growth and international investment with diverging populations', *Oxford Economic Papers*, vol. 46 (July), pp. 477–91.
Deardorff, Alan V. (1994*b*). 'The possibility of factor price equalisation, revisited', *Journal of International Economics*, vol. 36 (February), pp. 167–75.
Deardorff, Alan V. (1997). 'Rich and poor countries in neoclassical trade and growth', Research Seminar in International Economics Discussion Paper No. 402, University of Michigan, June 29.
Galor, Oded. (1996). 'Convergence? Inferences from theoretical models', ECONOMIC JOURNAL, vol. 106 (July), pp. 1056–69.
Galor, Oded and Zeira, Joseph (1993). 'Income distribution and macroeconomics', *Review of Economic Studies*, vol. 60 (January), pp. 35–52.
Inada, Ken-ichi. (1963). 'On a two-sector model of economic growth: comments and a generalisation', *Review of Economic Studies*, vol. 30 (June), pp. 119–27.
Maddison, Angus. (1982). *Phases of Capitalist Development*. New York: Oxford University Press.
Mankiw, N. Gregory. (1995). 'The growth of nations', *Brookings Papers on Economic Activity 1:1995*, pp. 275–310.
Mazumdar, Joy. (1996). 'Do static gains from trade lead to medium-run growth?' *Journal of Political Economy*, vol. 104 (December), pp. 1328–37.
Oniki, H. and Uzawa, H. (1965). 'Patterns of trade and investment in a dynamic model of international trade', *Review of Economic Studies*, vol. 32 (January), pp. 15–38.
Quah, Danny T. (1995). 'Galton's fallacy and tests of the convergence hypothesis', *Scandinavian Journal of Economics*, vol. 95 (December), pp. 427–43.
Quah, Danny T. (1996). 'Twin peaks: growth and convergence in models of distribution dynamics', ECONOMIC JOURNAL, vol. 106 (July), pp. 1045–55.
Quah, Danny T. (1997). 'Empirics for growth and distribution: stratification, polarisation, and convergence clubs', *Journal of Economic Growth*, vol. 2 (March), pp. 27–59.
Samuelson, Paul A. (1948). *Foundations of Economic Analysis*. Cambridge: Harvard University Press.
Samuelson, Paul A. (1949). 'International factor-price equalisation once again', ECONOMIC JOURNAL, vol. 59 (June), pp. 181–97.
Solow, Robert. (1956). 'A contribution to the theory of economic growth', *Quarterly Journal of Economics*, vol. 70 (February), pp. 65–94.
Swan, T. W. (1956). 'Economic growth and capital accumulation', *Economic Record*, vol. 32, pp. 334–61.
Uzawa, H. (1961). 'On a two-sector model of economic growth', *Review of Economic Studies*, vol. 29 (October), pp. 117–24.
Uzawa, H. (1963). 'On a two-sector model of economic growth: II', *Review of Economic Studies*, vol. 30 (June), pp. 105–18.

CHAPTER 26

Comments on Alan Deardorff's Contributions on the Subject of the Gains from Trade and Globalization

Robert E. Baldwin[†]

University of Wisconsin

It is an honor to participate in a Festschrift for Alan Deardorff. Alan is a master theorist. He has made major contributions to our understanding of so many economic concepts and relationships in international economics with his modeling and analytical skills. Moreover, he has done so in an exceptionally clear manner, often using geometry as well as algebra to make his points.

I have been asked to comment on Alan's contributions on the topic of gains from trade and globalization. Very rightly, I think, Alan takes a very broad view of what constitutes globalization. He takes globalization to mean the increase in international transactions in markets for goods, services, some factors of production, plus the growth and expanded scope of institutions that straddle national borders such as firms, governments, international organizations, and nongovernmental organizations. As he and Bob Stern say in one of their papers, globalization is not only growth in international trade but expansion of foreign direct investment, multinational corporations, integration of world markets and resulting financial capital flows, extraterritorial reach of government policies, attention by NGOs to issues that span the globe, and the constraints imposed on government policies by international institutions.

Alan has written a number of papers exploring the welfare and other economic effects of some of the newer and less familiar forms of globalization such as fragmentation, business and social networking, and outsourcing.[1] Let me summarize some of his contributions on these topics. Following Jones and Kierzkowski (2001) who first introduced the term, Alan defines fragmentation as the splitting of a production process into two or more steps. We generally think of a two-step fragmentation process as arising because of technological progress that permits a country to specialize in the fragmented segment in which

[†] Robert Edward Baldwin, born in Buffalo New York on July 17, 1924, died in Madison on April 7, 2011. He was Hilldale Professor of Economics, Emeritus, at the University of Wisconsin-Madison. A lifelong academic, Baldwin was one of the world's most influential thinkers on international trade, an adviser to governments and international organizations, and an inspiring teacher much beloved by generations of students who carry forward his light as renowned scholars in their own right.

[1] See References for a listing of Alan's papers covered in this comment.

it has a comparative advantage and import the other intermediate input. This enables the country to produce a larger amount of the final good than formerly possible and thus move to a higher budget line than it faced before that fragmentation process. If the country is small so that world prices are fixed, the country cannot lose in welfare terms, as Alan shows. However, as we know from the Stolper–Samuelson relationship, particular groups within a country can lose even if the country as a whole gains. Moreover, if a country is large so that world prices can change as a result of the fragmentation process, he also shows that it is possible for the country's terms of trade to worsen sufficiently for it to end up at a lower welfare level. However, he concludes that fragmentation is more likely to benefit countries rather than make them worse off.

In his analysis of networking, which he regards as a decline in trade costs, Alan disagrees with the pioneer in this topic, namely, Jim Rauch, when it comes to the question of whether an increase in networking can reduce a country's welfare. Rauch (2001) argues that this is possible whereas Alan argues that it is not, at least in an undistorted world economy. The reason is simply that trade costs are real costs, using up real resources, whereas, in contrast, tariffs do not. Because real costs use real resources, a reduction in these costs permits the world economy to do exactly what it did before and still have some resources left over. As he says, a competitive economy will then use these released resources to produce more and yield a world output that is worth more at the new equilibrium prices than the outputs previously produced. But perhaps Rauch has in mind an economy in which there already exist economic distortions.

Before leaving the topic of the welfare effects of such activities as fragmentation, I want to discuss briefly just what economists mean when they say that a country or the world gains from trade. As Alan points out, our current understanding of what is meant by a country gaining from trade dates from two articles by Samuelson, one in 1939 and another in 1962, almost 25 years later. Assuming for simplicity that there are only two individuals and two goods in a distortion-free economy, Samuelson in his 1962 article introduces the notion of *point* and *situation utility possibility frontiers* that depict, respectively, the maximum ordinal utility reached by each individual by distributing between the two individuals a particular quantity of goods attainable under autarky or free trade in every possible manner and by distributing between the two individuals the sets of optimal quantities of the goods that can be obtained under autarky or free trade. The situation utility possibility frontier is the envelope of all the optimal collections of goods that could be obtained under one of these policies, *i.e.*, all the point utility possibility curves attainable under autarky or free trade.

Since the maximum quantities of the two goods achievable under a policy of free trade is greater (except for one point) than under a policy of autarky, the utility possibility curve based on the free trade situation lies entirely outside the utility possibility curve based on the autarky situation. This means that by appropriate lump sum redistribution (assumed to be costless) that would change production and trade levels it is possible to make everyone better off under the free trade situation than under the autarky situation, no matter what the initial free trade distribution of goods is. This is the sense in which it can be said that the policy of free trade is potentially welfare-improving for a country compared to a policy of autarky. For similar reasons, it can be said that a policy of imposing optimum tariffs is welfare-improving compared to a policy of free trade. However, free trade in the sense of the particular collection of goods obtained under this policy is not potentially welfare-improving compared to the particular collection of goods obtained under autarky. The point utility possibility curves obtained in these cases may intersect.

It seems to me that trade economists (but not Alan) too often fail to be clear that when they say free trade is better than autarky, they are talking about the policy of free trade and the policy of autarky, and not the particular collection of goods obtained by following these policies.

The last topic in Alan's writings on the gains from trade and globalization that I want to discuss briefly is his interesting analysis of the making of rules of globalization in political economy terms. He points out that corporations have played a significant role in formulating these rules in international organizations such as the GATT, the WTO, and NAFTA. For example, the stimulus to focus the Tokyo Round of trade negotiations on nontariff trade barriers came mainly from business interests. Similarly, the political pressure to include trade-related intellectual property rights as a negotiating subject in the Uruguay Round came mainly from the business sector. We know from direct observation and assume in our economic models that corporations are not interested in promoting general economic welfare but rather their own welfare, namely, profits. As Alan points out, while economic theory is reassuring about the effects of the profit motive when it drives behavior in competitive marketplaces, there is no such reason to trust its effects in the political arena. In short, there is no reason to expect the invisible hand to guide governments that are under the influence of corporations toward desirable outcomes in political markets.

Alan cited two instances where he believes corporations have shaped the rules of globalization in a manner that increased their profits at the expense of the general public. One is the TRIPS agreement in the Uruguay Round and the other is Chapter 11 of NAFTA. The TRIPS agreement requires all countries to enact and enforce intellectual property laws that are comparable to those that exist in developed countries. This, in his view, is a change that can only benefit rich-country owners of intellectual property and harm poor-country consumers.

Chapter 11 of NAFTA requires that any expropriation of the property of a foreign investor be accompanied by appropriate compensation. What Alan finds particularly objectionable is that the victim of such expropriation can bring a case before a NAFTA tribunal against the national government of the country in which the expropriation took place. Moreover, it seems that it is being used not just against direct expropriation but against governments whenever they introduce a policy or regulation that reduces a corporation's profits. Alan believes that both of these provisions go too far in giving corporations power over foreign governments, a conclusion with which I think most of us would agree. Thus, I think that Alan's broadening of his studies of the gains from trade and globalization to include investigations into the political economy of how the rules for globalization are determined is very worthwhile, and encourage him and other economists to pursue this line of investigation further.

REFERENCES

Deardorff, Alan V., 2001a, Fragmentation in simple trade models, *North American Journal of Economics and Finance* 12, 121–137.

Deardorff, Alan V., 2001b, Fragmentation across cones, in Sven W. Arndt and Henryk Kierzkowski, eds., Fragmentation: New Production Patterns in the World Economy (Oxford University Press, Oxford), pp. 35–51.

Deardorff, Alan V., 2001c, International provision of trade services, trade, and fragmentation, *Review of International Economics* 9, 233–248.

Deardorff, Alan V., 2001d, Trade and welfare implications of networks, *Journal of Economic Integration* 16, 485–499.

Deardorff, Alan V., 2002, What might globalization's critics believe?, World Economy Lecture, December 5, 2002, University of Nottingham, Nottingham, United Kingdom.

Deardorff, Alan V., 2004a, Who makes the rules of globalization?, Paper prepared for a Globalization Workshop at the CESifo Venice Summer Institute, included in Elias Dinopoulos, Pravin Krishna, Arvind Panagariya, and Kar-yiu Wong, eds., Trade, Globalization, and Poverty, (Routledge, New York), pp. 173–186.

Deardorff, Alan V., 2004b, A trade theorist's take on skilled-labor outsourcing, *International Review of Economics and Finance* 14, 259–271.

Deardorff, Alan V., 2005a, Ricardian comparative advantage with intermediate inputs, *North American Journal of Economics and Finance* 16, 11–34.

Deardorff, Alan V., 2005b, Gains from trade and fragmentation, Research Seminar in International Economics, Discussion Paper No. 543, July.

Deardorff, Alan V. and Robert M. Stern, 2002, What you should know about globalization and the world trade organization, *Review of International Economics* 10, 404–423.

Deardorff, Alan V. and Robert M. Stern, 2004, Globalization's bystanders: Does trade liberalization hurt countries that do not participate?, Paper prepared for the UNU/WIDER Project of the Impact of Globalization on the World's Poor, Oct. 29–30, Helsinki.

Jones, Ronald W. and Henryk Kierzkowski, 2001, Globalization and the consequences of international fragmentation, in R. Dornbusch, G. Calvo, and M. Obstfeld, eds., Capital Mobility and Trade: Essays in Honor of Robert A. Mundell (MIT Press, Cambridge, MA).

Rauch, James E., 2001, Business and social networking in international trade, *Journal of Economic Literature* 39, 1177–1203.

Samuelson, Paul A., 1939, The gains from international trade, *Canadian Journal of Economics and Political Science* 5, 195–205.

Samuelson, Paul A., 1962, The gains from trade once again, *The Economic Journal* 72, 820–829.

CHAPTER 27

On Some Aspects of Globalization

Arvind Panagariya[1]

Columbia University

In his wide-ranging World Economy Lecture, Alan Deardorff (2003) embarks upon a journey into the writings of globalization critics. In the course of the journey, he identifies the complaints with which he agrees, those with which he disagrees but understands within the context of the standard trade models, and those that do not fit the conventional theory. In the latter case, he goes on to develop alternative models that may better capture the concerns of the critics. In addition to his usual analytic clarity, rigor, and originality, the lecture also brings to fore a most admirable characteristic of Alan's personality: his eagerness to listen to the opposite view and, if persuaded by it, a willingness to modify his own thinking. For the benefit of his friends who may have missed reading this lecture, I can scarcely resist quoting from its concluding section:

> In preparing for this talk, I read more than I ever had before of the writings of globalization critics, including several books and numerous items on the web. …
>
> As I mentioned to colleagues along the way, I sometimes felt that I was brainwashing myself by reading the works of globalization critics. Particularly, perhaps, because I was determined to keep an open mind to their point of view rather than constantly marshalling my economist's presumptions against them, I found as I read that I too sometimes became appalled at the state of the world that they described. I too sometimes easily accepted that it was globalization that had in some manner contributed to this situation.
>
> In the end, what I realized was that my previous defensive posture towards the critics of globalization had perhaps prevented me from giving proper weight to the flaws in the world system that even defenders of globalization have long deplored. I tended, before this, to dismiss those flaws as exceptional and to focus instead on much broader good that I thought globalization could do and had done. The latter, I still think, was appropriate, but the flaws deserve attention too.

My objective in this short paper is to honor Alan by imitation, "the sincerest of flattery" in the immortal words of Charles Caleb Colton. As in his lecture, I select a set of themes underlying the writings of globalization critics. Given the scarcity of time and space, it is

[1] The author can be reached at ap2231@columbia.edu.

not possible to touch on all the themes Alan has covered in his World Economy Lecture and elsewhere. Instead, I limit myself to issues relevant to developing countries — my current preoccupation — on which I have something new or different to say.

DEVELOPED COUNTRY PROTECTION AND SUBSIDIES IN AGRICULTURE

Globalization critics have often pointed out that while preaching liberalization to the developing countries, developed countries have themselves retained high levels of protection and subsidies in agriculture. They not only accuse the developed countries of hypocrisy but also vehemently criticize them for hurting the poorest developing countries by driving down the prices of agricultural products in which the latter enjoy comparative advantage. Most economists embrace this criticism and gladly join the globalization critics in calling for the removal of agricultural protection and subsidies.

Yet, as I discuss in Panagariya (2003, 2005), while tariffs and subsidies in agriculture deserve to be criticized and removed for their usual trade-distorting effects, criticisms by globalization critics and some economists, most notably Stiglitz (2002), focusing on the hypocrisy of developed countries and injury to the poorest countries are misplaced for at least four reasons.

First, regarding hypocrisy, the truth of the matter is that until the launch of the Uruguay Round, the developing countries themselves had no interest in market access in agriculture. They sought to industrialize and therefore were focused on either import substitution or market access in industrial products, often through trade preferences rather than reciprocal bargaining in the General Agreement on Tariffs and Trade (GATT) rounds of multilateral negotiations.

Second, in so far as the effects of the subsidies and protection are concerned, the facts are largely the other way around: they benefit rather than hurt the poorest countries. European tariffs and subsidies have the effect of driving down the world prices of most agricultural products and raising them internally within Europe. Whether an outside country loses or benefits from this depends on whether it is an exporter or importer of agricultural products. It turns out that an overwhelming majority of the Least Developed Countries (LDCs) are net food importers and a significant majority are net agricultural importers. The decline in the world prices of agricultural products therefore benefits the majority of the LDCs at least at the national level.

This point became apparent recently when food inflation struck the world economy. Rather than celebrate the price hike as a boon to the fortunes of the poor countries, virtually all saw it as a curse for the poor countries. There was near universal outrage that the poor countries suffered the most from food inflation!

Third, once we take account of the trade preferences available to the LDCs in the European Union (EU) market, it can be shown that virtually all LDCs benefit from the existing system of protection and subsidies. Under the Everything But Arms (EBA) initiative, the EU permits the products of LDCs to be sold free of duty in its markets. This means the LDCs sell their exports at the high internal EU price and buy their imports at the low external world market price. On both counts, they benefit.

Finally, agricultural protection is not purely a developed country phenomenon. True, the Cairns Groups of developing countries have a comparative advantage and low protection in agriculture. But many developing countries that are net importers do have high agricultural protection. Recall that it is the Indian demand for a very generous special safeguard in agriculture that has been one of the important stumbling blocks to the conclusion of the Doha Round.

Before I conclude this section, an objection to the above points as also an exception to which these points do not apply may be noted. The objection is that even if the LDCs gain from the low world prices because they are net agricultural importers, the poor may be hurt because they must compete against the subsidized imports. Deardorff (2003), who has clearly thought through this issue more deeply than most critics, clearly anticipates this point when he writes,

> As a trade economist, I am fond of pointing out that in the aggregate such subsidies hurt the country whose government pays them and actually benefit the rest of the world. And if the subsidies were in fact delivering affordable food to the world's hungry, I would not mind them at all as long as they could be depended on to continue. But in fact, as I understand it, most of the hungry in the developing countries are in rural areas where, instead of benefiting from this cheap food, they have to compete with it for livelihood. In the long run, that may or may not be best use of their labor, but in the short run these subsidies are simply driving small developing country farmers further into poverty. That is inexcusable.

But even this objection is subject to two qualifications. First, in principle, the LDC farmers can access the internal EU price under the EBA. Their competition is not with the subsidized external world price but instead with the EU internal price. Second, even if competition with the subsidized external price is a problem, the LDCs are far better off employing a countervailing duty on imports, which is entirely legal under the WTO rules. Such duty would allow the LDCs to realize a higher price for their farmers while also contributing to their revenue kitties.

The exception to the proposition that developed-country subsidies benefit the LDCs arises in the case of cotton. As it turns out, the EU produces no cotton and therefore applies no subsidies and tariffs to it. As a result, its internal cotton price equals the border cotton price and the EBA offers no relief to LDC exporters of the product. The culprit in this case is the United States, which subsidizes cotton production and drives down its world price. Four small West African countries are net exporters of the product and are hurt by the low price. But even here, the subsidy benefits Bangladesh, which is a net importer of cotton. Unsurprisingly, cotton is the only product cited as an example of rich-country subsidies hurting the poor countries. Even sugar turns out to be a mixed case.

INTELLECTUAL PROPERTY RIGHTS, LABOR STANDARDS AND RULE MAKING

The issue of geographical expansion of intellectual property rights (IPR) protection to include all countries in the world has been another important contentious issue in recent years. A key component of the Uruguay Round Agreement was the Agreement on Trade-Related Aspects of Intellectual Property Rights (TRIPS), which extended the approximate intellectual property protection standards in the United States to the entire world. All countries except the LDCs were required to introduce these standards in their domestic laws latest by January 1, 2005. The LDCs were given a temporary reprieve in the pharmaceuticals sector but they too must introduce them by January 1, 2016.

The key contentious element of TRIPS negotiations related to the extension of the 20-year patent protection to both process and product in the area of pharmaceuticals. By maintaining a weak intellectual property regime that recognized only process patents, some developing countries, most notably India, had successfully created substantial indigenous low-cost medicine industries. Local firms in these countries could alter the production process of medicines still under patent in the developed countries and sell the generic version so produced at a fraction of the price of the original medicines. These countries opposed the extension of product patent in pharmaceuticals to them.

Deardorff (1992) provides a formal model that brilliantly captures the sources of tensions associated with the TRIPS negotiation. The model hypothesizes a fixed cost of each medicine to be invented, of which there are potentially numerous. These medicines may be ranked based on their present value of the consumer surplus net of production costs and the cost of innovation. Ideally, one would want all medicines with zero or positive net present value to be innovated and produced. But since innovations are a public good they must be supported by either a government subsidy or patent protection. Because government subsidies bring their own problems, patent protection remains the principal viable practical option under most circumstances. The social cost of patent protection is, of course, the monopoly distortion in the product market. The patent gives the innovator the sole right to manufacture and sell the medicine. The longer the patent, the more medicines are innovated. But the longer the patent, the higher the social cost of monopoly distortion in medicines that are innovated even under a shorter patent. The optimal patent is one that equates the gain from the last medicine innovated to the increased social cost of distortion on intra-marginal medicines. It is evident that the optimal patent is finite. For producers, a longer patent is almost always better than a shorter patent since it gives them monopoly rights for a longer period. The consumers must weigh the benefits from additional innovation on the margin against the monopoly cost incurred on the intra-marginal medicines.

The tension between costs and benefits, which arises when the patent is extended over time, also arises when it is extended in space. When the intellectual property protection of a given length of time is extended to another country, it brings more innovation on the margin but it also extends the monopoly distortion in all existing innovations to that country. Such extension may or may not be beneficial from the global welfare viewpoint. Even if it is beneficial, it will turn harmful as we keep adding more and more countries. If innovating firms are concentrated in the countries already covered by the patent and the newly included country is relatively poor so that the beneficial impact on new innovations is minimal, the former gain while the latter loses.

This simple Deardorff model of intellectual property protection neatly brings out all the tensions at work in extending intellectual property rights to the poor countries: pharmaceutical firms acquire the right to collect royalties in the poor countries, developed countries that do much of the innovation also benefit, and the poor countries stand to lose since they losing royalty-free access to patented medicines.

The only possible source of significant gain to the poor countries is the possibility that the patent would stimulate innovation in medicines specifically relevant to them such as those relating to malaria and tuberculosis. But even this gain will fail to materialize, as has been the case so far, if the purchasing power in the poor countries is insufficient to support the research necessary to innovate the medicines. This is likely to be the case since the initial cost of research in an area in which pharmaceutical companies have not been engaged before are likely to be large while the ability to pay for medicines in the poor countries is likely to be small.

The central theme of Alan's World Economy Lecture is that globalization critics view globalization as benefiting corporations and hurting workers. Deardorff (2008) picks up this theme and develops the idea that a key avenue through which corporations exploit the globalization process to their advantage is through rule writing. In this latter paper, he offers the TRIPS Agreement as an example of rule writing by corporations.

There is no doubt that the United States pharmaceutical firms were the key driving force behind pushing and perhaps even drafting some of the language of the TRIPS Agreement. By extending the patent protection to the developing countries, these firms stood to reap extra rents on the innovations they would have undertaken anyway to serve the developed country markets. They also had the necessary political muscle to get the United States Trade Representative to negotiate the desired agreement on their behalf.

Nevertheless, it was perhaps the North-South rather than the capital-labor tension that dominated rule writing in the TRIPS negotiations. Benefits from the TRIPS Agreement were to accrue to the United States pharmaceutical firms not so much at the expense of the United States labor or labor anywhere for that matter as the developing country consumers. The corporations could exercise their muscle in the TRIPS negotiations principally because the United States government was backing them up. And the counterweight to the corporations was provided not by the United States or other countries' labor lobbies but, instead, the developing country governments.

As it turns out, at least as of now, the AFL-CIO (2008) officially supports the pursuit of intellectual property protection in the international trade negotiations. A statement by the Executive Council of the organization dated March 4, 2008, explicitly endorses this position. To quote from this statement,

> The AFL-CIO has worked to ensure that intellectual property protection is pursued as a key component of our international trade agenda. Foreign intellectual property rights infringement robs the U.S. of tens of billions of dollars in sales, with the resulting loss of jobs and income for America's workers.

Indeed, asymmetry in the negotiating power in favor of the United States gives all of its powerful lobbies greater clout in rule writing than their developing country counterparts. The AFL-CIO support for the pursuit of intellectual property rights protection is not an accident. They want to gain the same benefit from rule writing for workers as corporations at the expense of the developing countries. As a result, they have made common cause with corporations and sought their support for extending U.S. labor standards to the developing countries. While they remain some way from achieving this goal in the WTO, they have made significant progress in the free trade area (FTA) negotiations with small Southern countries that have virtually no negotiating power *vis-à-vis* the United States. The process of labor groups jumping into rule writing had already begun in the North American Free Trade Agreement (NAFTA) when the Clinton administration insisted on a side agreement on labor rights before giving it final approval. Subsequently, the labor clauses have been a central element of FTA agreements signed by the United States.

In a similar vein, it is the North-South rather than the capital-labor dimension of rule writing that provided the counterforce to the promotion of corporate interests in the Doha negotiations. Driven by its corporations, the EU had strongly pushed for a multilateral investment agreement in the Doha negotiating agenda. But a more or less united offensive by the developing countries forced it to withdraw this demand immediately following the 2003 WTO ministerial meeting in Cancun. While corporations have thus used rule writing to advance their interests as globalization proceeds, Northern labor has not been too far behind. In both cases, the counterweight has come from the developing countries that too have learned the importance of rule writing and actively participate in the process.

THIRD-COUNTRY EFFECTS OF TRADE LIBERALIZATION

An important policy question is how non-discriminatory trade liberalization among developed countries impacts developing countries. The specific context is the multilateral liberalization prior to the Uruguay Round Agreement that was confined to developed countries. Most developing countries eschewed active participation in the negotiations until the Uruguay Round, choosing to benefit from free-riding the developed country liberalization. Was this a wise choice?

Deardorff and Stern (2006) provide a neat theoretical analysis of this question, answering it in the negative. They use a multi-product, multi-country, political economy model with additively separable preferences, a constant marginal utility from the consumption of the numeraire good, and production functions that allow one specific factor and one common factor in all non-numeraire goods and only the common factor in the numeraire good. This model has the property that all substitution in production as well as consumption is between individual non-numeraire goods and the numeraire good. Alternatively put, it fully validates the partial equilibrium analysis, allowing welfare conclusions to be drawn from the sum of the consumers' and producers' surplus and tax revenue.

The political economy component of the model postulates that liberalization is driven solely by producer profits. This is not a necessary assumption but it suffices to obtain the key results while simplifying the analysis. In this setting, it is straightforward that developed countries choose not to liberalize any product exported exclusively by the developing countries. Such liberalization produces no benefits for producers in the developed countries undertaking liberalization. On the other hand, goods exported exclusively by developed countries are most likely to be liberalized. In so far as such liberalization expands within-developed-country trade, it is likely to divert supplies from developing countries. This will raise the price paid by the developing countries for these products or, equivalently, worsen their terms of trade. This benefits developed country producers. Therefore, the countries have an incentive to liberalize trade in products in which they are able to expand their mutual trade by diverting it from developing countries. The action will hurt the developing countries.

Most trade economists will appreciate the message underlying this conclusion: developing countries choose to stay out of the negotiating process at their own peril. Nevertheless, I suspect that the outcome in the real world is somewhat different: developing countries that are themselves keen to take advantage of the opportunities offered by trade and chose to be open on a unilateral basis probably benefited from developed country trade liberalization via the Kennedy and Tokyo Rounds. It is inconceivable that South Korea and Taiwan did not benefit from the liberalization by developed countries in the 1960s and 1970s.

The Deardorff–Stern model obtains its strong conclusion by choosing a model in which it is possible to force liberalization from spilling over to the outside countries despite the Most Favored Nation (MFN) nature of liberalization. I suspect that in practice this is not possible. Liberalization within the GATT-WTO system must follow a tariff nomenclature that does not allow product categories to be defined according to the origin. This fact combined with the observation that in reality countries source most products from both developed and developing countries makes it nearly impossible to avoid spillover of developed country liberalization to developing countries.

We know from the recent work of Schott (2004) that even as we go down to the 10-digit products within the harmonized tariff system, we observe the United States continuing to import a very large number of products from both developed and developing countries.[2] Typically, the former send overwhelmingly high-unit-value varieties and the latter low-unit-value varieties of the same product. This pattern makes the exclusion of developing countries from developed country liberalization envisaged in the Stern–Deardorff model highly unlikely.

An early study by Michael Finger (1976) confirms the favorable trade effects of the Kennedy Round on the developing countries: it concluded that "tariff cuts of each importer (EEC, United States, Japan) caused a significant increase of imports, from developing and from other developed countries." A more recent study by Romalis (2007) finds very strong growth effects of the opening up of the developed countries via the Kennedy Round on the developing countries.

---

[2] Also see Mukerji and Panagariya (2009) in this context.

Before I conclude this section, let me hasten to add that in one sense my points reinforces the underlying message of Deardorff and Stern: only countries that are themselves open will reap the benefits of liberalization by developed countries. Therefore, the qualifications to the Deardorff–Stern analysis I have put forward do not in any way undermine their key message: it pays to be open. And in so far as participation in multilateral negotiations leads to the opening up of one's own economy, such participation can only enhance the scope for benefiting from developed country liberalization.

CORPORATIONS AND GLOBALIZATION

Given the central focus on the role played by corporations in the process of globalization in Alan's writings, it is appropriate to end by asking whether he regards them as a positive or negative force on balance. The answer in Deardorff (2003, p. 657) is refreshingly unequivocal and worthy of reproduction in near entirety:

> Perhaps more than most economists, I am personally predisposed to see corporations as beneficial to the society. It seems obvious to me that corporations have made possible a level of well-being throughout most of the world that far exceeds what could have been achieved without them. The invisible hand of the market only partly accounts for this, since large corporations clearly have far more power over markets than we assume in our competitive models. But as long as these large corporations are forced to compete with one another and also with small new entrants that may at any moment emerge — a level of competition that requires the active vigilance and sometimes enforcement by government competition authorities — I have no doubt but that they do far more good than harm for the vast majority of the world's population. And indeed, within the markets in which they operate, corporations are much more vulnerable to public opinion and therefore powerless than is often thought.

The history of economic policies in India, which I have discussed in detail in my recent book (Panagariya, 2008), lends a great deal of support to Alan's view. Motivated by fears of the concentration of wealth in the hands of corporations, India went on to tie their hands (and feet too!) in the 1960s and 1970s in ways that will be incomprehensible to Americans. The result was growth at a pace that was considerably below the country's potential. Eventual restoration of the freedom of corporations to operate in a business-friendly environment has led to dramatic improvements in the well-being of many within a relatively short span of time, with poverty at last declining significantly as well.

REFERENCES

AFL-CIO, 2008, Innovation and patent reform, AFL-CIO Executive Council Statement, March 4, San Diego. Accessed on September 30, 2009, at http://www.alston.com/files/docs/AFL%20CIO%20March%204%202008.pdf.

Deardorff, Alan V., 1992, Welfare effects of global patent protection, *Economica* 59, 35–51.

Deardorff, Alan V., 2003, What might globalization's critics believe?, The World Economy Annual Lecture, Leverhulme Center, University of Nottingham, December 5, 2002, published in *The World Economy* 26, 639–658.

Deardorff, Alan V., 2008, Who makes the rules of globalization?, in Elias Dinopoulos, Pravin Krishna, Arvind Panagariya, and Kar-yiu Wong, eds., Trade Globalization, and Poverty (Routledge, New York), pp. 173–186.

Deardorff, Alan V. and Robert M. Stern, 2006, Globalization's bystanders: Does trade liberalization hurt countries that do not participate?, *World Development* 34, 1419–1429.

Finger, J. Michael, 1976, Effects of the Kennedy Round tariff concessions on the exports of developing countries, *Economic Journal* 86(341), 87–95.

Mukerji, Purba and Arvind Panagariya, 2009, Within- and across-product specialization revisited, Columbia University, New York.

Panagariya, Arvind, 2003, Trade liberalization and food security: Conceptual links, in Trade Reforms and Food Security (Food and Agriculture Organization of the United Nations, Rome), pp. 25–42.

Panagariya, Arvind, 2004, TRIPS and the WTO: An uneasy marriage, in Keith Maskus, ed., The WTO, Intellectual Property Rights and the Knowledge Economy (Edward Elgar, London) [Originally in the informal volume Bhagwati, J., ed., The next negotiating round: Examining the agenda for seattle, Proceedings of the Conference held at Columbia University, July 23–24, 1999, pp. 91–102.

Panagariya, Arvind, 2005, Agricultural liberalization and the least developed countries: Six fallacies, *World Economy* 28 (Special Issue on Global Trade Policy), 1277–1299.

Panagariya, Arvind, 2008, India: The Emerging Giant (Oxford University Press, New York).

Romalis, John, 2007, Market Access, Openness and Growth, *NBER* Working Paper No. 13048, April.

Schott, Peter, 2004, Across-product versus within-product specialization in international trade, *Quarterly Journal of Economics* 119(2), 647–678.

Stiglitz, Joseph, 2002, Globalization and its discontents (W. W. Norton & Company, New York).

CHAPTER 28

Economica, **59**, 35–51

Welfare Effects of Global Patent Protection

By Alan V. Deardorff

University of Michigan

Final version received 15 October 1990. Accepted 23 May 1991.

This paper uses a simple model of invention and patent protection to examine the welfare effects of extending patent protection from the country where invention takes place to another country that is only a consumer of invented products. It is shown that, while the welfare of the inventing country certainly rises with the extension of patent protection, that of the other country probably falls, and may well fall by more than the increase in welfare of the inventing country. In particular, as patent protection is extended to a larger and larger portion of the world, the effect on the welfare of the world as a whole of extending it to the rest of the world becomes negative.

Introduction

The Uruguay Round of Multilateral Trade Negotiations has included a major effort by the industrialized countries especially to bring the protection of intellectual property rights under the auspices of the General Agreement on Tariffs and Trade (GATT). The purpose is primarily to extend such protection to countries that currently provide it only weakly or not at all, particularly certain developing countries. This paper will explore one aspect of the economics of this issue, emphasizing in particular the possible adverse welfare effects that would be caused by extending intellectual property protection to all countries of the world. The argument will be formalized in terms of a particularly simple model of patent protection, though the principles apply as well to other forms of intellectual property protection such as copyrights.[1]

As is well known, a primary reason for providing patent protection is to permit inventors to earn a return on their inventions, and therefore to provide an incentive for technology to advance. The cost of providing patent protection, however, is that it permits the patent-holder to exercise monopoly power over the market for the new product, and this prevents the benefits of the new product from being enjoyed optimally by consumers. It is for this reason, some have argued, that patent protection is granted for only a limited time, so as to achieve a desirable balance between incentives to invent and gains to consumers from products after they have been invented.[2] I will argue that the same sort of trade-off may also justify limiting patent protection geographically, as well as over time.

Such a geographical limitation on the coverage of patents is most likely to be desirable when inventive activity is concentrated in one part of the globe, while the benefits from inventions can be enjoyed equally by consumers worldwide. To make the point, I will therefore focus on a particular very simple theoretical model of inventions and patents that has these properties in extreme form.

In the context of this model, I will show first that the trade-off between incentives to invent and the subsequent enjoyment of inventions does justify the use of patent protection, at least as a second-best policy in the country where invention occurs.[3] Thus, the principal motive most often discussed for extending patent protection around the world is indeed present in my model. However, I will then show that extending this protection to other countries is very likely to be harmful to them, in spite of the fact that they will benefit from increased inventive activity. In those circumstances, if the world as a whole does gain from extending patent protection, it is only in the inventing countries that these gains are experienced, and in fact, they gain even more than the world as a whole because they gain at the rest of the world's expense.[4]

Finally, I show that it is even possible for the world as a whole to lose from extending patent protection, and that such a loss *must* occur, in the context of my model, as the coverage of patent protection is extended to the entire world. Thus, a case can be made, in terms of world welfare, for limiting the coverage of patent protection to less than the entire world.

I recognize that the model in which I demonstrate this result is far from general, and that there are many considerations that are absent from the model that could undermine it. I will discuss several of these in the concluding section. Nor would I argue by any means that the efforts in the Uruguay Round have been misguided. I do not doubt that a good case can be made for extending patent and other intellectual property rights into a number of countries where they currently do not exist, or are only laxly enforced. However, the case for universal patent protection is not a clear one, as my analysis demonstrates, and the concerns of some developing countries that they will be exploited by patent protection are not without foundation.

I. An Economic Analysis of Patent Rights

A single invention in a single country

Consider first the case of a single invention. At a research cost of R, an inventor has designed a new product that can be produced by anyone at a constant marginal production cost of c. Individual consumers have a demand for the new product that is described by their inverse demand function,

(1) $$p = a - bq.$$

With n identical consumers, the inverse market demand function is

(2) $$p = a - (b/n)q.$$

which is graphed in Figure 1 as the curve DD.

Competitive production. Suppose first that the inventor is *not* granted a patent. Then anyone at all will be able to produce the new good, and a perfectly competitive market price equal to the marginal cost, c, will be established. The competitive output will be

(3) $$q^c = n\frac{a-c}{b},$$

and consumers will earn a surplus of

(4) $$s^o = \int_0^{q^c} [a - (b/n)q - c]\,\mathrm{d}q = \frac{n}{2}\frac{(a-c)^2}{b}.$$

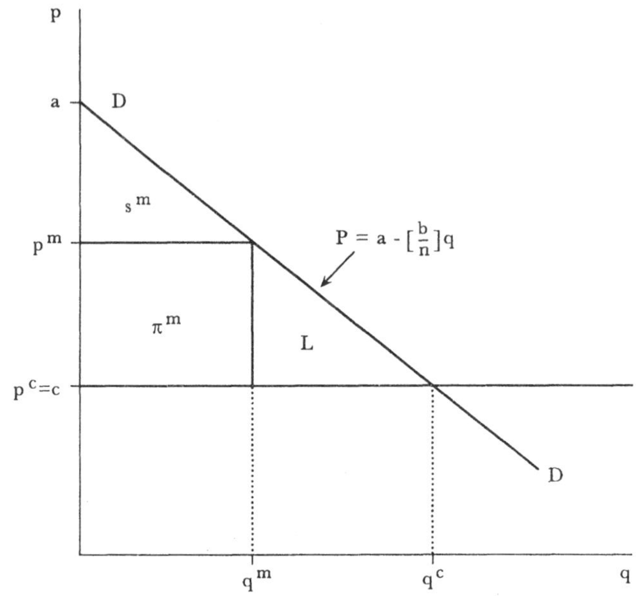

FIGURE 1. Welfare effects of monopoly pricing of a single invention.

There will be no monopoly profits earned on the invention, and the inventor will have lost entirely the cost of research, *R*. None the less, given that the product has already been invented, this competitive outcome is also optimal in the sense of maximizing joint consumer and producer welfare, and the consumer surplus in equation (4) is therefore superscripted with an *o* for optimal.

Monopolized production. Now suppose instead that a patent is granted to the inventor. The inventor will now be able to charge a monopoly price that maximizes the monopoly profit on production,

$$(5) \qquad \pi = (p - c)q,$$

where p is given by the market demand function, (2). It is seen that, because demand is linear and marginal cost is constant, the monopoly output will be exactly half of the competitive output,

$$(6) \qquad q^m = \tfrac{1}{2} n \frac{a - c}{b}$$

with a monopoly price halfway between cost c and the demand parameter a,

$$(7) \qquad p^m = \tfrac{1}{2}(a + c),$$

and monopoly profit

$$(8) \qquad \pi^m = \tfrac{1}{4} n \frac{(a - c)^2}{b} = \tfrac{1}{2} s^o.$$

As noted here and as illustrated in Figure 1, monopoly pricing in this linear case extracts exactly half of the optimal consumer surplus in the form of monopoly profit.

Consumers in this monopoly situation derive an even smaller surplus:

$$(9)\qquad s^m = \int_0^{q^m} [a-(b/n)q-p^m]\,\mathrm{d}q = \tfrac{1}{8}n\frac{(a-c)^2}{b} = \tfrac{1}{4}s^o,$$

that is, only one-quarter of what they would have obtained with perfect competition. The benefit to society as a whole of having the invention produced by a monopoly includes both the monopoly profit and the consumer surplus, and is therefore three-quarters of the benefit that would have acrued under competition:

$$(10)\qquad b^m = \pi^m + s^m = \tfrac{3}{4}s^o.$$

Therefore, there is a deadweight loss of one-quarter of the optimal consumer surplus that is attributable to monopoly pricing.

This is illustrated in Figure 1, where the demand curve DD and the constant marginal cost c give rise to a competitive (and optimal) output of q^c at a price $p^c = c$. A patent that grants monopoly power to the patent-holder cuts output in half, raises price, and creates a deadweight loss that is labelled L. However, the advantage of the patent is also indicated in that the patent holder now earns the monopoly profit π which then provides some return on the cost of the invention.

Unfortunately, even this return may not be enough to compensate the inventor for a worthwhile invention. If we now consider the *ex ante* problem of whether the invention was worthwhile, it is clear that the invention would have been worth the cost to society as long as the optimal consumer surplus, s^o, were to exceed the cost of research, R. Since only half of s^o, i.e. π, accrues to the patent-holder, one would expect that some worthwhile inventions will not be created, even when there is patent protection. Patents are therefore an imperfect method of fostering invention, both because they lead to monopoly distortions of consumer choice, and because they fail to foster all worthwhile inventions. This latter point will be made more clearly if we now consider multiple inventions and bring the choice of the level of invention explicitly into the analysis.

Multiple inventions in a single country

The case of multiple inventions will be most tractable if we consider a continuum of them and hence abstract from the indivisibility of individual inventions and the discontinuities that this would imply. As long as the actual number of inventions is large, this simplification will not matter appreciably for the results.

Suppose then that inventions are indexed by non-negative real numbers, z. Let $a(z)$, $b(z)$, $c(z)$ and $R(z)$ be the demand and cost parameters for invention z, as in the analysis above. Then let $s^o(z)$ be the optimal consumer surplus corresponding to invention z, as in (4), but normalized to be expressed per unit of research cost. That is,

$$(11)\qquad s^o(z) = \frac{n}{2}\frac{[a(z)-c(z)]^2}{b(z)}\Big/ R(z).$$

Without loss of generality, let inventions be ordered so that

$$(12) \qquad z_1 > z_2 \quad \Rightarrow \quad s^o(z_1) \leq s^o(z_2).$$

Because of the assumed linearity of demand and cost, this ordering of inventions by optimal consumer surplus will also be the ordering by monopoly profit, and therefore the inventions that will be undertaken will always be those with the lowest indices, z, up to some cutoff point.

I will measure the level of invention by its research cost. Hence if all inventions from $z = 0$ to some $z = \hat{z}$ are invented, then the total cost of invention, I, will be

$$(13) \qquad I(\hat{z}) = \int_0^{\hat{z}} R(z)\, \mathrm{d}z.$$

Since $\mathrm{d}I(\hat{z})/\mathrm{d}\hat{z} = R(\hat{z}) > 0$, the function $I(\cdot)$ is monotonic and can be inverted. I therefore re-express the optimal consumer surplus of the marginal invention in terms of I, the total cost of invention:

$$(14) \qquad s^o(I) = s^o[I^{-1}(I)].$$

From (12) and (13), $s^o(I)$ is also weakly monotonically decreasing in I. What it represents is the optimal consumer surplus per dollar of research obtainable from the marginal dollar of research, given that I dollars have already been spent on all inventions yielding a greater surplus per dollar.

From the earlier analysis of a single invention, it follows that various properties of a monopoly equilibrium can also be calculated from $s^o(I)$. In particular,

$$(15) \qquad \pi^m(I) = \tfrac{1}{2} s^o(I)$$

is the monopoly profit, per dollar of research, from the marginal invention, and

$$(16) \qquad s^m(I) = \tfrac{1}{4} s^o(I)$$

is the consumer surplus, per dollar of research, from the marginal invention, given that production is monopolized.

From their derivation, it is clear that these functions ought actually to be step functions, declining discontinuously at each level of investment that completes the full research cost, $R(z)$, of the marginal invention. For simplicity, however, I will assume that the number of inventions is large, so that these functions can be approximated as continuous. Further, and much more restrictively, I will assume that these functions are linear, represented by

$$(17) \qquad s^o(I) = n(f - gI),$$

where $f, g > 0$ are parameters of this linear function and n, as before, is the number of consumers in the country.

Population is included here explicitly in order to facilitate analysis of the two-country case below. It appears multiplicatively because of its role in (4). Note, therefore, that $f - gI$ is the optimal consumer surplus per dollar of research for a representative consumer and that, from (4), $f = [a(z) - c(z)]^2/2b(z)$ for $z = 0$, highest-priority invention. The slope parameter g indicates the rapidity with which diminishing returns to invention set in. A particular level of invention, $\bar{I} = f/g$, represents the total research cost of all available inventions whose products would be demanded if competitively priced and thus provides an upper bound on the level of invention that will actually take place.

Competitive invention. I can now examine the equilibrium levels of invention and welfare under various scenarios. The competitive case is simplest, because nothing happens. Without patent protection, the level of invention will be zero in this model, since there will be no way for any inventor to recover the cost of research. Levels of total consumer surplus, S^c, and monopoly profit, Π^c, will also be zero:

$$(18) \qquad I^c = S^c = \Pi^c = 0.$$

Optimal invention. The optimal level of invention, I^o, will include all inventions that yield an optimal consumer surplus greater than their cost of research, and hence whose optimal consumer surplus per dollar is greater than 1. Thus, from (17),

$$(19) \qquad I^o = s^{o^{-1}}(1) = \frac{nf-1}{ng}.$$

Since the optimal consumer surplus is obtainable only if products are competitively priced, the monopoly profits corresponding to this optimal level of invention must be zero:

$$(20) \qquad \Pi^o = 0.$$

The total consumer surplus obtained in this optimal situation will then be found by adding across all inventions the optimal consumer surplus per dollar, multiplied by the research cost of each invention. With the assumed continuity of the surplus function, s^o, this addition is accomplished by integration:

$$(21) \qquad S^o = \int_0^{I^o} s^o(I)\,\mathrm{d}I = \int_0^{(nf-1)/ng} n(f-gI)\,\mathrm{d}I = \frac{(nf)^2-1}{2ng}.$$

Finally, the net gain to society from this optimal level of invention is the sum of the consumer and producer gains (the latter being zero in this case) minus the research cost, I^o, of the inventions:

$$(22) \qquad N^o = S^o + \Pi^o - I^o = \frac{(nf)^2-1}{2ng} - \frac{nf-1}{ng} = \frac{(nf-1)^2}{2ng}.$$

Monopolized invention. If inventors are protected with patents, then production will take place under conditions of monopoly, as discussed above. The level of invention will be that which equates the monopoly profit from the marginal invention to its research cost, or in other words which equates the monopoly profit per dollar to unity. Thus,

$$(23) \qquad I^m = s^{m^{-1}}(1) = s^{o^{-1}}(2) = \frac{nf-2}{ng}.$$

The level of monopoly profit is obtained by integrating the profit function from (15) and (17), i.e.

$$(24) \qquad \Pi^m = \int_0^{I^m} \tfrac{1}{2}s^o(I)\,\mathrm{d}I = \int_0^{(nf-2)/ng} \tfrac{1}{2}n(f-gI)\,\mathrm{d}I = \frac{(nf)^2-4}{4ng},$$

while the level of consumer surplus is obtained by integrating (16):

$$(25)\qquad S^m = \int_0^{I^m} \tfrac{1}{4}s^o(I)\,\mathrm{d}I = \int_0^{(nf-2)/ng} \tfrac{1}{4}n(f-gI)\,\mathrm{d}I = \frac{(nf)^2-4}{8ng}.$$

Summing (24) and (25) and subtracting (23), the net gain to society from invention in the patent-protected monopoly situation is

$$(26)\qquad N^m = S^m + \Pi^m - I^m$$

$$= \frac{(nf)^2-4}{8ng} + \frac{(nf)^2-4}{4ng} - \frac{nf-2}{ng} = \frac{(nf-2)(3nf-2)}{8ng}.$$

These results are illustrated in Figure 2. The uppermost curve represents the optimal consumer surplus per dollar cost of research, and is drawn as the straight line $n(f-gI)$. Its intersection with the horizontal line at 1 indicates the socially optimal level of invention, so long as goods once invented are also produced optimally. The total consumer surplus generated by this level of invention is the area under the $s^o(I)$ curve between $I=0$ and $I=I^o$. The net gain to society, however, is smaller by the cost of research, and is therefore given by the area of the triangle under $s^o(I)$ and above 1.

As was found from the analysis of a single invention, the monopoly profits, π^m, and the consumer surplus in the presence of monopoly, s^m, are one-half and one-quarter, respectively, of s^o. These are therefore also drawn in Figure 2 as straight lines, starting from correspondingly lower intercepts and ending at the same level of invention $\bar{I}$. Since monopolists earn only π^m per dollar of research, patent rights will foster invention only up to the point where these

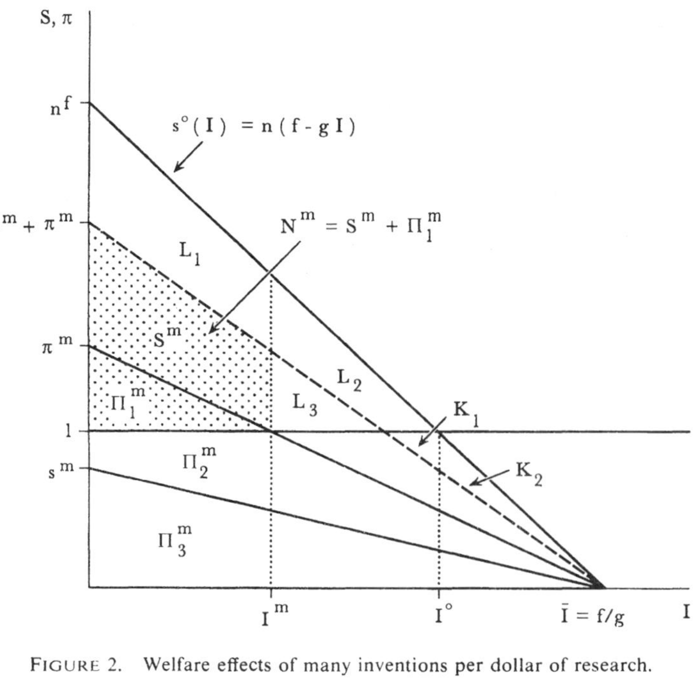

FIGURE 2. Welfare effects of many inventions per dollar of research.

monopoly profits equal one dollar. Thus, the level of invention with patent protection is shown as I^m.

With this construction, the total profits from all inventions up to I^m are given by the area under π^m, shown in Figure 2 as the sum of areas Π_1^m, Π_2^m and Π_3^m. Consumer surplus is the area under s^m between 0 and I^m, which is equal to Π_3^m, but is shown separately by first adding together π^m and s^m in the line $s^m + \pi^m = (3/4)s^o$. Consumer surplus is then the area S^m, below this line and above π^m. The total net benefit to society due to inventions up to I^m is the sum of consumer surplus and profit, minus the cost of research. Since the latter is the area of the rectangle under the horizontal line at 1, this net benefit is simply the shaded area, $S^m + \Pi_1^m$.

Comparing this with the larger triangle of optimal social benefit from invention, there is a deadweight loss of areas $L_1 + L_2 + L_3$. Area L_1 represents the loss of consumer surplus arising from the monopoly pricing of products that are invented. Area $L_2 + L_3$, on the other hand, represents the consumer surplus that is forgone because less than the optimal amount of invention takes place, even when inventors are granted monopoly patent rights. The total deadweight loss is calculated from (22) and (26) as[5]

$$(27) \qquad N^o - N^m = \frac{(nf-1)^2}{2ng} - \frac{(nf-2)(3nf-2)}{8ng} = \frac{nf^2}{8g}.$$

Multiple inventions in two countries

Suppose now that there are two countries, A and B. All invention takes place in country A, but once a good has been invented the technology is known and it can be produced in either country, subject of course to any limitations imposed legally by patent rights. Consumers in the two countries have identical individual demand functions for all goods. Populations (numbers of consumers) in the two countries are n^A and n^B respectively. It will be convenient to define

$$(28) \qquad n = n^A + n^B$$

and to express results in terms of n and the fraction of the world's population that is in country A:

$$(29) \qquad \gamma = \frac{n^a}{n}.$$

As before, let (1) represent the common individual inverse demand functions for a particular good, so that the market inverse demand functions in the two countries are

$$(30) \qquad p^J = a - (b/n^J)q^J, \qquad J = A, B.$$

With marginal cost, c, of producing the good common to both countries, the optimal consumer surplus for the good in country J is

$$(31) \qquad s^{oJ} = \frac{n^J}{2}\frac{(a-c)^2}{b} = n^J\tilde{s},$$

where $\tilde{s}$ is the optimal *per capita* consumer surplus for the good.

As before, let inventions be ordered by decreasing values of $\tilde{s}/R$, and assume that these values can be expressed as a linear function of I. That is,

(32) $\tilde{s}(I)=f-gI$

is the optimal *per capita* consumer surplus per dollar of research for the marginal invention, given that I dollars have been spent inventing all goods of equal or greater $\tilde{s}/R$. The relevant values of consumer surplus and monopoly profits for the two countries can then also be expressed in terms of this linear function. First, multiplying the *per capita* consumer surplus in (32) by population,

(33) $s^{oJ}(I)=n^J(f-gI), \qquad J=A, B,$

is the total optimal consumer surplus per research dollar in country $J=A, B$ owing to the marginal invention at level of invention I (and would be received by consumers in country J if the good were competitively priced there). From this, again exploiting the linearity of demand, properties of the monopoly equilibria can be found as well:

(34) $\pi^J(I)=\frac{1}{2}s^{oJ}(I)=\frac{1}{2}n^J(f-gI), \qquad J=A, B,$

is the monopoly profit per dollar of research to be obtained by selling the product of the marginal invention in country J at the monopoly price. Similarly,

(35) $s^{mJ}(I)=\frac{1}{4}s^{oJ}(I)=\frac{1}{4}n^J(f-gI), \qquad J=A, B,$

is the consumer surplus per dollar received by consumers in country J from the marginal invention if they pay the monopoly price.

It is now possible to calculate the totals of consumer surplus and monopoly profit for different patent protection regimes by first using (34) to identify the level of invention that will take place, and then integrating these various functions. The two regimes that I will consider are 'restricted patent protection', in which patent protection is provided only in country A, and 'extended patent protection', in which protection is extended to country B as well.

Restricted patent protection. With patent protection only in country A, monopoly profits will be earned only there, and invention will take place up to the point where

(36) $\pi^A(I^r)=1.$

Using (34) and (29), it follows that

(37) $$I^r=\frac{\gamma nf-2}{\gamma ng}.$$

Integrating (35) up to this level of invention and using (29), the level of total consumer surplus in country A may be found as

(38) $$S^{rA}=\int_0^{I^r}\frac{1}{4}n^A(f-gI)\,\mathrm{d}I=\frac{\gamma^2n^2f^2-4}{8\gamma ng}.$$

Monopoly profits are made only in country A, and thus may be found by integrating (34) for country A alone. Since (34) is just twice (35), profits are found immediately as twice (38):

(39) $$\Pi^r=\Pi^{rA}=\frac{\gamma^2n^2f^2-4}{4\gamma ng}.$$

Finally, because patent protection is limited to country A, consumers in country B have access to a competitive supply of all invented goods. Their total consumer surplus is therefore obtained by integrating (33) for country B:

$$S^{rB}=\int_0^{I^r} n^B(f-gI)\,\mathrm{d}I=\frac{(1-\gamma)(\gamma^2n^2f^2-4)}{2\gamma^2ng}. \tag{40}$$

The net gain to all residents of country A, including their monopoly inventors, is their consumer surplus plus their monopoly profit, minus the cost of invention. Using (37), (38) and (39),

$$N^{rA}=S^{rA}+\Pi^r-I^r=\frac{(\gamma nf-2)(3\gamma nf-2)}{8\gamma ng}. \tag{41}$$

The net gain to all residents of country B includes only their consumer surplus, $N^{rB}=S^{rB}$, in (40). Together, these give the net gain for the world as a whole as

$$N^{rW}=N^{rA}+N^{rB}=\frac{(\gamma nf-2)[\gamma(3\gamma nf-2)+4(1-\gamma)(\gamma nf+2)]}{8\gamma^2ng}. \tag{42}$$

All of this is illustrated in Figure 3, which replicates Figure 2 for country A in the top panel and for country B, upside down, in the bottom panel. With monpoly profits earned only in country A, invention takes place up to I^r, where the marginal per-dollar profit in country A, π^A, intersects the horizontal line at 1. Gross profits are then the area under π^A, or $u_1+u_2+u_3$. Consumer surplus in country A is area u_1. Since the cost of invention, I^r, is the area u_1+u_2, the net gain for country A is u_1+u_3.

Meanwhile, consumers in country B get a free ride, receiving the optimal, or competitive, consumer surplus equal to area $v_1+v_2+v_3$.

Extended patent protection. If patent protection is now extended to country B as well as country A, then an invention once patented in country A will also entitle the inventor to monopoly profits in country B.[6] With potential investors knowing this, invention in country A will take place up to the point where the total profits from the two sources from the marginal invention just covers the cost of research. Thus,

$$\pi^A(I^e)+\pi^B(I^e)=1. \tag{43}$$

Using (34), this can be solved to yield

$$I^e=\frac{nf-2}{ng}. \tag{44}$$

As before, the totals of consumer surplus and monopoly profits in the two countries can be found by integrating (34) and (35) up to I^e. In country A this gives

$$S^{eA}=\int_0^{I^e}\frac{1}{4}n^A(f-gI)\,\mathrm{d}I=\frac{\gamma(n^2f^2-4)}{8ng} \tag{45}$$

and

$$\Pi^{eA}=\int_0^{I^e}\frac{1}{2}n^A(f-gI)\,\mathrm{d}I=\frac{\gamma(n^2f^2-4)}{4ng}, \tag{46}$$

where Π^{eA} is now only a portion of the total profits.

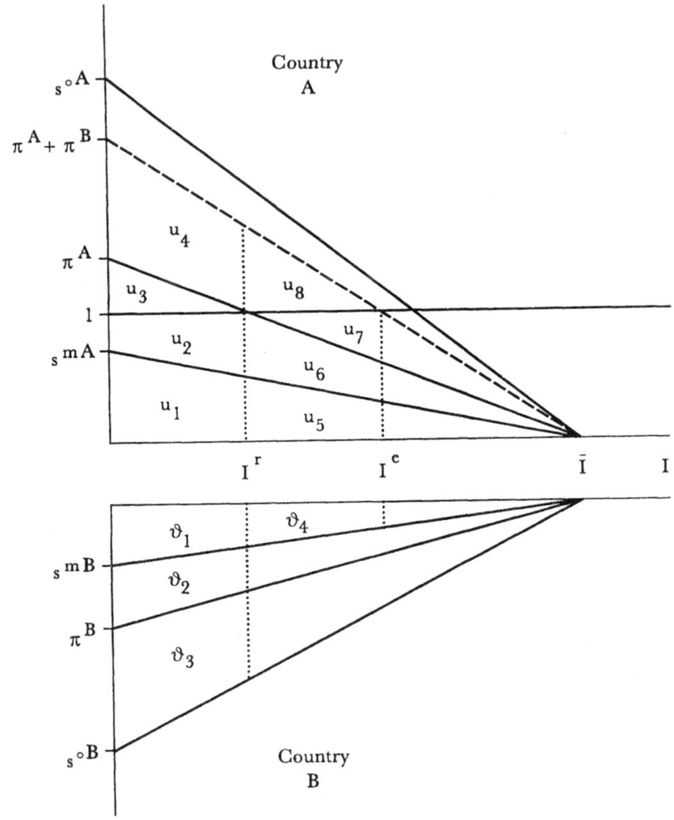

FIGURE 3. Welfare effects in two countries of inventions in one, with restricted and extended patent protection.

In country B the inventors from country A also earn monopoly profits equal to

$$\Pi^{eB} = \int_0^{I^e} \frac{1}{2} n^B (f - gI)\, \mathrm{d}I = \frac{(1-\gamma)(n^2 f^2 - 4)}{4ng}. \tag{47}$$

Consumers in country B now get only the reduced consumer surplus of the monopoly case:

$$S^{eB} = \int_0^{I^e} \frac{1}{4} n^B (f - gI)\, \mathrm{d}I = \frac{(1-\gamma)(n^2 f^2 - 4)}{8ng}. \tag{48}$$

Total profit is

$$\Pi^e = \Pi^{eA} + \Pi^{eB} = \frac{n^2 f^2 - 4}{4ng}, \tag{49}$$

which is the same expression found in the single-country case in (24), since the monopolist inventors are now treating the world as essentially a single market. The net gain to country A is found from (44), (45) and (49):

$$N^{eA} = S^{eA} + \Pi^e - I^e = \frac{nf-2}{8ng}[(2+\gamma)(nf+2)-8]. \tag{50}$$

Finally, the net gain to country B is again just its gain in consumer surplus,

$$N^{eB} = S^{eB}. \tag{51}$$

The net benefit to the world is therefore

$$N^{eW} = N^{eA} + N^{eB} = \frac{(3nf-2)(nf-2)}{8ng}. \tag{52}$$

To illustrate these results in Figure 3, the marginal profit earned in country B, π^B, is first added to π^A in the top panel. The level of invention with extended patent protection, I^e, is then found where this new line crosses the horizontal line at 1. In country A, consumer surplus expands to include u_5, while profits now include $u_5 + u_6$ earned on sales in country A as well as $u_4 + u_7 + u_8$ on sales to country B. Deducting the research cost, I^e, the net benefit to country A is $u_1 + u_3 + u_4 + u_5 + u_8$.

Consumers in country B now earn only the monopoly consumer surplus under s^{mB} for all goods up to I^e. Thus their total benefit is now $v_1 + v_4$.

Comparison of restricted and extended regimes. It is clear from Figure 3 that residents of country A gain unambiguously from extending patent protection to country B. Consumers in A get consumer surplus from the additional goods that are invented, as shown by the area u_5. The monopolist inventors in country A also gain the even larger area u_4, which is the monopoly profit on sales to country B of goods they would have invented anyway, plus u_8, the excess monopoly profits in both markets on the additional inventions. Formally, the gain to country A from extending patent protection is found from (41) and (50) to be

$$N^{eA} - N^{rA} = \frac{2(1-\gamma)}{8\gamma ng}[\gamma n^2 f^2 - 2(1-\gamma)]. \tag{53}$$

As long as

$$\gamma nf = n^A f > 2, \tag{54}$$

so that I^r in (37) is positive, (53) is also positive, verifying the gain to country A.

Residents of country B, on the other hand, are likely to lose. The monopoly pricing of the goods they were previously getting competitively causes them to lose three-quarters of the optimal consumer surplus on those goods. In Figure 3 this loss is area $v_2 + v_3$. In return for this they do get consumer surplus on the new goods whose invention is stimulated by the extended protection, but even on these they only get the monopoly consumer surplus, shown as v_4 in Figure 3. If $v_2 + v_3$ is greater than v_4, as drawn in the figure, they lose.

Formally, the change in welfare for country B is found from (40) and (48) to be

$$N^{eB} - N^{rB} = -\frac{1-\gamma}{8\gamma^2 ng}[3\gamma^2 n^2 f^2 + 4(\gamma^2 - 4)]. \tag{55}$$

If γnf is only slightly greater than required in (54), this will be negative regardless of the value of γ alone. That is,

$$\gamma nf = n^A f > \sqrt{\frac{16}{3}} = 2.31 \quad (56)$$

is sufficient for (55) to be negative. Alternatively, as long as the fraction of the world's population that is located in the innovating country, γ, is sufficiently large, then country B will lose. If

$$\gamma^2 > \sqrt{\frac{16}{4+3n^2f^2}}, \quad (57)$$

then (55) will also be negative.

Clearly, much depends on the size of the two populations, together with the parameter f. The latter represents the intercept of the optimal consumer surplus function, and hence the per capita consumer surplus optimally obtainable from the highest priority invention, per dollar cost of research needed for that invention. Condition (54) merely requires that this highest-priority invention yield a total benefit to the population of country A that is twice its cost. Likewise, condition (55) implies that, if the per dollar benefit from the highest-priority invention for the world, nf, is, say, ten times its cost ($nf = 10$), then country B will be hurt by extending patent protection if the share of world population in country A is greater than only $16/304 = 5{\cdot}3$ per cent. Thus, it seems quite likely that (55) will indeed be negative under plausible circumstances.

Turning finally to effects on the world as a whole, these can be observed in Figure 3 by first noting that areas u_4 and v_3 are equal, so that part of the gain to country A cancels directly with part of the loss to country B. This leaves the net effect on the two countries together as $u_5 + u_8 + v_4 - v_2$. As drawn in Figure 3, it appears that the three areas of gain are together larger than the single area of loss, v_2, and that the world gains here from extending patent protection.

This is not inevitable, however, as Figure 4 shows. There, the relevant portions of Figure 3 are reproduced, but the proportions are changed. As a result, the three areas of gain from extended patent protection, shown as the shaded areas u_5, u_8 and v_4, are much smaller than in Figure 3, while the area of loss, the cross-hatched area v_3, is larger. As drawn, the latter area is larger than the former, and the case drawn is therefore one in which extended patent protection lowers welfare of the world as a whole.

How do Figures 3 and 4 differ? In drawing Figure 4, I attempted to capture what would happen if population were shifted from country B to country A, thus expanding all of the amounts of surplus and profit in country A and contracting them in country B. By doing this, the level of invention in the restricted protection equilibrium is made larger, since inventors in A have a larger protected market, and at the same time the scope for expanding invention still further by extending protection is reduced.

To check that this is a correct interpretation, consider the more formal expression for the gain to the world from extending protection. From (42) and (52),

$$N^{eW} - N^{rW} = \frac{1-\gamma}{8\gamma^2 ng}(16 - 4\gamma - n^2f^2\gamma^2). \quad (58)$$

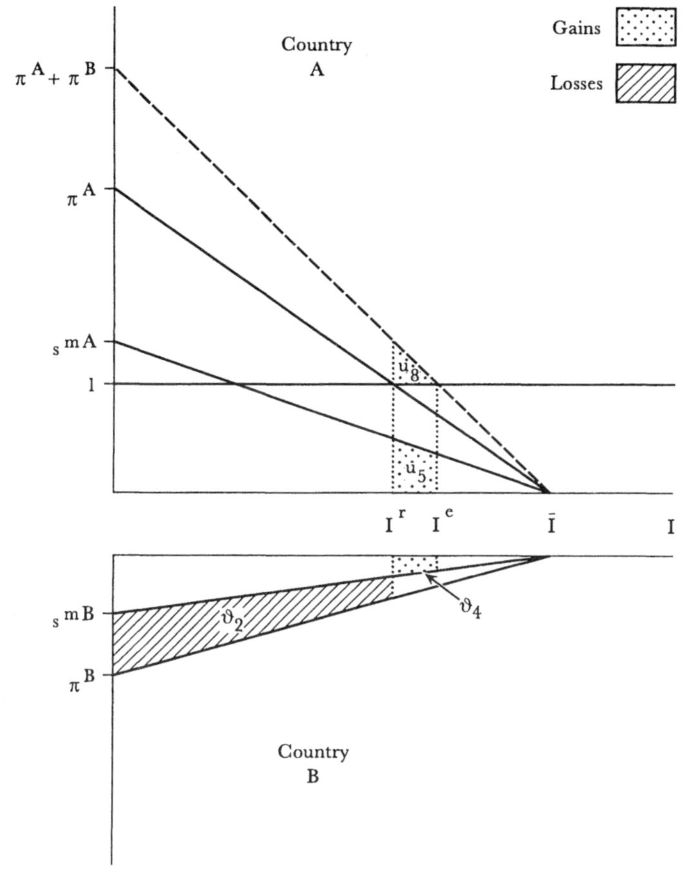

FIGURE 4. World welfare effects of extending patent protection to a relatively small country.

The sign of this depends on the expression in parentheses. Setting that expression equal to zero for $\gamma = 1$, it follows that if

(59) $nf > \sqrt{12} = 3{\cdot}46,$

then (58) will be negative for γ sufficiently close to 1. I will assume from here on that (59) is indeed satisfied, that is, that the most desirable invention would yield a surplus for world consumers at least three-and-a-half times its cost.

Under that assumption, then, the world as a whole loses from extended patent protection once the portion of the world already covered by patent protection is sufficiently large. In particular, it cannot be optimal from a world welfare standpoint for patent protection to be extended to the entire world.

II. Conclusions and Qualifications

I have now shown what I set out to show: that under specified circumstances it is not optimal to extend patent protection to all countries of the world. The reason for this result is implicit in the analysis. Patent protection has the offsetting effects of, on the one hand, permitting inventors to earn monopoly profits on their inventions and thus stimulating inventive activity and, on the other hand, distorting consumer choice by monopoly pricing. If all innovation originates in one part of the world, then extending patent protection to a broader and broader area does have these two effects, but there are diminishing returns to the first of them. That is, as more and more of the world is already covered by patent protection, the extra market that can be covered, and hence the extra invention that can be stimulated by extending patent protection still further, becomes smaller. Thus, at some point the costs due to extending monopoly pricing to existing inventions come to outweigh the benefits of generating new ones.

Many assumptions are explicit, and others implicit, in this analysis, and the results depend to varying degrees upon all of them. Let me conclude by suggesting my own judgements as to the importance of some of these assumptions for the main result.

Location of invention

First, it is not crucial to world welfare, though it may be to the individual countries, that no invention take place in country B. If inventors in both countries had a chance of creating the inventions of the model and of patenting them wherever patent protection is available, then some of the monopoly profits that I have modelled as accruing to country A would accrue instead to inventors in country B. With free trade, however, the same levels of invention would take place in equilibrium, and levels of world welfare would be the same.

Identical demands

On the other hand, it is crucial that *per capita* demands for invented goods be the same, or at least similar, in both countries. If they are not—if some inventions would be demanded more in country B than in country A—then an important benefit to extending patent protection to B is missing from the model. Patent protection in country B will stimulate precisely those inventions that are of particular importance to B's population, and thus will yield a greater benefit to B than to A. This possibility would therefore increase the net gain, both to country B and to the world as a whole, of extended patent protection.

Linearity

The analysis here has been greatly facilitated by assuming that demands for goods were linear and that the function relating optimal surplus to the level of invention was linear as well. Linearity of demands seems of comparatively minor importance: what really matters is that there be some welfare loss arising from monopoly pricing, and this would be the case for a wide variety of demand functions.

Linearity of the surplus function is a bit more critical, as is seen in Figure 3, for example. If the curves were not linear, there would be the possibility that they would, say, turn sharply downward just to the right of I^r. In that case, there would be very little additional invention stimulated by extending patent protection, and the case against it would be strengthened. In contrast, if the curves were to flatten out just to the right of I^r, then I^e might be pushed to a much higher level, and the benefits to extending patent protection would be increased. Thus, the cases for and against extending protection can be materially altered by the curvature and position of these curves. On the other hand, in the absence of any information about what these curves do in fact look like, the linear case seems to be about as neutral as one could hope for.

Transmission of information

I have assumed here that, once an invention is discovered, the information about how to produce it is freely available worldwide. This is important, since otherwise production could not take place at all in country B in the absence of patent protection, and the main source of loss arising from extending protection, both for country B and for the world as a whole, would be removed. It is of course true that information about many new inventions is not costlessly transmitted abroad, and that extending patent protection may therefore be beneficial to the extent that it stimulates the transfer of technology. On the other hand, the demands for protection on the part of innovating firms in the United States and other advanced countries make it clear that, in at least some industries, information about new products is diffusing without patent protection much more readily than the innovating firms would like.

I am sure that many other objections to this model can and will be raised as discussion proceeds. It may well be that extending patent protection to a larger part of the world is in fact in the interest of the world as a whole, and perhaps even in the interests of some of the developing countries who may resist such a change. All I have tried to establish is the intellectual legitimacy of the position that worldwide patent protection may not be desirable. I am inclined to believe, on the basis of this model and other considerations discussed in Deardorff (1990), that at least the very poorest of countries should be exempted from any new agreement that is made to extend patent protection under the GATT.

ACKNOWLEDGMENTS

I have received helpful suggestions from many people, including John H. Jackson, Jim Levinsohn, Jeff Mackie-Mason and Robert M. Stern, as well as from participants in The University of Michigan Law School seminar that Professor Jackson and I taught together in winter 1989 on the subject of intellectual property protection. Helpful comments were also made by participants at the Western Ontario-Michigan conference on TRIPs and TRIMs in Washington, D.C. in April 1989 and by participants in the Research Seminar in International Economics at The University of Michigan. I received partial support in writing this paper from a Ford Foundation to the Institute of Public Policy Studies of The University of Michigan for a program of research on trade policy.

NOTES

1. Trademarks, on the other hand, seem to play a distinctly different role from patents and copyrights, and I would not extend the argument to them.
2. See Nordhaus (1969) and Scherer (1980).
3. A first-best policy would eliminate the monopoly distortion and somehow subsidize invention more directly. However, given the difficulty of measuring the value of inventive activity for this purpose, this may not be feasible.
4. Chin and Grossman (1990) have also made this point elegantly in the context of a somewhat different model of process innovation. They too found the possibility of a welfare loss for the world as a whole as a result of extending patent protection, though they did not relate it to the portion of the world that is covered.

5. It is intriguing—though not at all important, as far as I can see—that this expression turns out to be so simple. Noting that nf and f/g are the vertical and horizontal intercepts of the s^o line in Figure 2, this expression for net loss is exactly one-quarter of the area of the triangle formed by s^o and the two axes. Since $s^m + \pi^m = (3/4)s^o$, this means that the awkwardly shaped area $L_1 + L_2 + L_3$ is actually equal to the triangle between $s^m + \pi^m$ and s^o. This implies that the area L_3 is equal to the area $K_1 + K_2$, a result that can also be shown using the traditional tools of plane geometry. The proof, which I leave to interested readers or their highschool-age children, uses the fact that the vertical line above I^m is broken into four equal segments by the lines that cross it.
6. It is not necessary, of course, that the inventor also be the producer in country B. The inventor can license someone else to produce there and can extract the monopoly profit by setting the licence fee at an appropriate level.

REFERENCES

CHIN, JUDITH C. and GROSSMAN, GENE M. (1990). Intellectual property rights and North-South trade. In Ronald W. Jones and Anne O. Krueger (eds.), *The Political Economy of International Trade: Essays in Honor of Robert E. Baldwin.* Cambridge, Mass.: Basil Blackwell, pp. 90-107.

DEARDORFF, ALAN V. (1990). Should patent protection be extended to all developing countries? *The World Economy*, **13**, 497-507.

NORDHAUS, W. D. (1969). *Invention, Growth, and Welfare: A Theoretical Treatment of Technological Change*, Cambridge, Mass.: MIT Press.

SCHERER, F. M. (1980). The economics of the patent system. Chapter 16 in *Industrial Market Structure and Economic Performance.* Boston: Houghton Mifflin, pp. 439-58.

CHAPTER 29

Trade and Welfare Implications of Networks[†]

Alan V. Deardorff[*]

The University of Michigan

ABSTRACT

This paper examines the effects on welfare and on patterns of trade of a reduction in costs of trading, such as might be the result of newly formed networks among residents of different countries with common culture or other ties. It argues that such a reduction in trade costs, even when it applies only to a particular bilateral trade route and may cause imports to be diverted from one source to another, must in the absence of distortions be welfare improving in the aggregate. On the other hand, such a change can indeed alter trade patterns distinctly, and they may also lower the welfare of particular countries. Examples are provided in which falling trade costs cause reversals of a country's pattern of trade, and in which a country that becomes part of a trade-cost-reducing network that alters its trade loses as a result.

Keywords: Gains from trade
Trade costs
Networks

JEL Subject Code: F1 Trade

Correspondence:

Alan V. Deardorff
Department of Economics
University of Michigan
Ann Arbor, MI 48109-1220

Tel. 734-764-6817
Fax. 734-763-9181
E-mail: alandear@umich.ed
http://www.econ.lsa.umich.edu/~alandear/

* I have obviously benefited from reading the work of Jim Rauch in preparing this paper. I am also indebted to Peter Debaere, for prompting me to explore these issues, and to others who participated in the Murray S. Johnson Conference at Texas.

† Paper prepared for the Murray S. Johnson, Conference on International Economics, University of Texas, April 28–29, 2001.

I. Introduction

Recent research has begun to explore the roles of business and social networks in international trade. Rauch (1999) has surveyed much of that literature, as well as contributing importantly to it himself in a number of other papers, including Rauch and Casella (1998). The message of this work is that these networks matter for trade. The incentive for trade no doubt lies in the international differences in relative costs that have preoccupied trade theory since Ricardo, but to respond to these incentives requires effort and knowledge of their existence. It therefore matters "who you know." Firms that have connections in other countries, formal or informal, are better placed to learn about trading opportunities and to take advantage of them. Therefore, networks can play an important role in determining which firms and which countries succeed in penetrating a particular foreign market.

To the best of my knowledge, this literature has focused, understandably, on making the case that networks exist and that they do indeed matter. In this paper, I will take their existence and importance as given, and move on to ask some of the other questions that trade theorists routinely ask about phenomena that are newly identified: What effects do networks have on the welfare of particular countries and of the world as a whole? And granted that networks can stimulate trade along particular routes and in particular industries, how may this matter more broadly for international patterns of trade? In particular, is it possible that network effects could undermine the law of comparative advantage, causing trade to flow in directions that traditional trade theory would view as perverse?

To address these questions, I will simplify – probably oversimplify – the network literature by focusing on what strikes me as its most important feature for these purposes: that networks reduce the costs of trade. If international trade could take place as freely and easily as we often assume in our theoretical models, then there would be no place for networks. If a small difference in price of a good between two countries led automatically to a sufficient flow of the good from the low-price to the high-price country so as to equalize their prices, then the opportunities for trade would be gone before a network could exploit them. And the same would be true even if there were transportation costs that would prevent the full equalization of prices. For networks to play any role at all, then, it must be the case that there are other costs associated with this process, costs that prevent prices from converging to the level of observable transport costs. The form that these trade costs take is important for some purposes, no doubt, but not for others. For my purposes here, it is enough to assume that networks work by reducing these costs.

What my paper is about, then, is really the implications of reductions in trade costs. To the extent that this does indeed capture an important feature of networks, then what I say is applicable to networks as well. But the results are also more general, applying to reductions in trade costs – including transport costs, if you like – regardless of the source of those reductions.

It is therefore somewhat surprising to me that these questions have not already been answered, or at least that they have not been answered in literature that I am aware of. I will no doubt get, and will welcome, direction to the works of others that have addressed these issues. But as far as I know right now, trade theorists have paid remarkably little attention to trade costs and to changes in them. It is true that they are a bit messy to deal with, which may account for this neglect. But I think the more important reason is that we have not thought them to be important. Economics has often taken its lead from the field of mechanics, within physics, where great success was achieved by assuming away friction as an unimportant complication. We have done the same with trade costs.

Recent evidence suggests, however, that this may have been a mistake. The world does not trade nearly as much as our models say that it should if there were no costs to trade. Focusing on the factor content of trade, Trefler (1995) noted this with his Mystery of the Missing Trade. Obstfeld and Rogoff (2000) point to possible trade costs to explain all of their "Six Puzzles." And if trade costs are substantial, then we need to understand their role, not just in explaining such mysteries and puzzles, but in the more mundane task of exploring how they matter for things like the patterns of trade and the gains from trade that we thought we understood from our frictionless models.

There are really just two such questions that I will address in this paper: First, what are the welfare implications of a drop in trade costs? Can the world lose? Can particular countries lose? And if so, which countries, and under what circumstances? Second, how do trade costs, or changes in them, matter for trade patterns? Does the Law of Comparative Advantage still hold in their presence? And can trade costs cause particular goods to be exported that would otherwise have been imported, or vice versa?

For both of these purposes, I will be most interested in changes in trade costs that do *not* occur across the board, for example to a country's trade with all of its potential trading partners. Motivated by the role of networks in reducing trade costs, I will be particularly interested in trade costs that are reduced only over particular trading routes, such as between a pair of countries that have acquired a common population through migration.

II. Welfare Implications

Can a fall in trade costs reduce welfare? In general, of course, anything is possible, so the answer to this must be yes. But a more instructive answer might identify conditions under which the answer is no, plus particular departures from those conditions that make it yes. That is what I will examine here.

I suspect that no one would doubt, for example, that if trade costs exist on all trade flows, and if these costs were to be reduced by the same proportion on all of these flows, then this would be beneficial for the world. This is true, as I will show below, and it closely resembles a result due to Bruno (1972) from tariff theory: a proportional reduction in all *ad valorem* tariffs is welfare improving. It also suggests that a non-proportional reduction in trade costs could reduce welfare. Indeed, we know that this is true of tariffs, where a preferential tariff reduction, such as in a free trade area, can reduce welfare due to its possible trade diverting effects. Can the same be true of trade costs?

In the conclusion of his paper, Rauch (1999) conjectures that it can, and says that "a transnational network can have an effect analogous to harmful trade diversion if it links the 'wrong' countries." However, the analogy may be misplaced. Trade diversion due to a preferential tariff reduction lowers welfare because the reduced tariff induces buyers to substitute toward a good that truly costs more than what they bought before, and only seems to cost less because it is subject to a lower tariff. But if real trade costs fall on imports from one country and not another, such substitution is toward goods that really do cost less, once one takes into account the real costs of accomplishing the trade. It is not obvious, therefore, that reduced trade costs (due to a network or any other cause) with a trading partner whose production costs are high can be welfare worsening. And I will argue next that, under otherwise ideal conditions, such a reduction will not lower aggregate welfare. The key is that trade costs are real costs, using up real resources, whereas tariffs are not. Tariffs therefore distort behavior by artificially altering the price signals that guide behavior. But trade costs enter into prices in ways that *should* guide behavior, since the costs are real.

I will argue that in an undistorted world economy, any meaningful reduction in real trade costs will increase world welfare. By "meaningful," I mean a reduction that actually matters, in that it changes some behavior, thus excluding only those reductions that leave welfare unchanged. The argument is simple. Because real trade costs use real resources, a reduction in these costs permits the world economy to do exactly what it did before and have some resources left over. A competitive economy will then use these released resources to produce more, yielding a world output that is worth more, at the new equilibrium prices, than the outputs previously produced. With a suitable redistribution of this income, every consumer can be made capable of consuming what they did before, while some consumer or consumers can get more. Thus world welfare is increased.

Note that, as usual in the welfare propositions of trade theory, this one assumes costless redistribution of income. World welfare is defined as increasing, here, only if the gainers could compensate the losers and remain better off, and thus we must allow for such potential income redistribution. It is *not* the case, as I will discuss below, that a reduction in trade costs necessarily benefits everybody in the absence of such redistribution.

To make the argument slightly more formal, consider an ideal world in which perfectly competitive producers of G goods in C countries produce these goods and trade them with consumers in all countries. There are no tariffs or other artificial barriers to this trade, but the trade itself may be costly in that it uses real resources. To capture this, I define X_{gci} as the quantity of good g delivered by country c to country i, or collected at country i if negative. Thus the X_{gci} include both domestic production (i=c), exports ($i \neq c$, $X_{gci} > 0$), and imports ($i \neq c$, $X_{gci} < 0$) of country c. I let each country have a production set, $F_c = \{X_{gci}, g = 1,...,G; i = 1,...,C\}$, that incorporates both the usual constraints of production technology and factor endowments, plus also the constraints of the resources needed for trade itself. Of these sets, I assume only that they are (weakly) convex, and that trade costs are nonnegative, in the sense that[1]

$$X^0 \in F_c \Rightarrow X^1 \in F_c \tag{2.1}$$

where $X^1_{gcc} = X^0_{gcc} + \sum_{i \neq c} X^0_{gci}$

$$X^1_{gci} = 0, \quad i \neq c$$

[1] See Deardorff (1980).

A competitive equilibrium in this world economy will consist of a matrix of prices, $p^e = \{p^e_{gc}\}$, of each good in each country, and matrices of output and trade, $X^e_c = \{X^e_{gci}\}$, such that equal quantities of each good are supplied and demanded. On the supply side, we need only that the activities chosen (production and trade) maximize their value at these prices:

$$\sum_g \sum_i p^e_{gi} X^e_{gci} \geq \sum_g \sum_i p^e_{gi} X_{gci} \quad \forall X_c \in F_c, \; c = 1,\ldots,C. \tag{2.2}$$

On the demand side, this same bundle of goods must be demanded at these prices and at incomes that are earned from production. In order to allow for the income redistribution that will be needed later, let Y_c be income of country c and require only that world income, Y^e_w be earned:

$$Y^e_w = \sum_c Y^e_c = \sum_c \sum_g \sum_i p^e_{gi} X^e_{gci} \tag{2.3}$$

Letting preferences be represented by demand functions $D_c(p,Y)$, equilibrium therefore requires that

$$D_{gc}(p^e_{1c},\ldots,p^e_{Gc},Y^e_c) = D^e_{gc} = \sum_i X^e_{gic}, \text{ for } g = 1,\ldots,G;\; c = 1,\ldots,C. \tag{2.4}$$

Now suppose that we start from an initial equilibrium, $e1$, with an initial technology, and that technology then changes to capture reduced real costs of trade. This will appear as an expansion of one or more of the production sets, F_c, to become F_c'.

Since everything that was possible before is still possible, it must be true that the new sets contain the old ones:

$$F_c' \subset F_c, \text{ for } c = 1,\ldots,C. \tag{2.5}$$

Consider any new equilibrium, *e*2. Since (2.2) must hold for this new equilibrium, and since the original quantities were elements of F_c and therefore, by (2.5), of F_c', it follows that

$$\sum_g \sum_i p_{gi}^{e2} X_{gci}^{e2} \geq \sum_g \sum_i p_{gi}^{e2} X_{gci}^{e1} \quad , \text{ for } c = 1,\ldots,C. \tag{2.6}$$

Summing over all countries, *c*, this tells us that world income in the new equilibrium is at least large enough for world consumers to purchase the same goods that they did before, and assuming that the expansion of the production sets was "meaningful," as defined above, income will be more than enough for this purpose. That is,

$$Y_w^{e2} > \sum_g \sum_c p_{gc}^{e2} D_{gc}^{e1} \tag{2.7}$$

Thus it is possible for world income to be distributed such that each country can afford the same goods that it consumed in the old equilibrium and some country can afford more. Therefore the world has gained from this reduction in trade costs, in the same sense that the world gains from trade.

Redistribution is necessary, here, because there is no guarantee that each country will gain without it. This is not because of trade diversion, but because of terms-of-trade effects. It is easy to construct an example when a single country loses from a fall in trade costs, but its loss is more than made up for by a larger gain to someone else.

For example, suppose that one country is the world's sole supplier of an essential and tradable good, the only substitute for which is a second good that is extremely costly to transport and that is produced in abundance but only by a single, second country. If the cost of transporting this second good were to fall, the price of the first good would also fall and the first country would suffer a worsening of its terms of trade. Of course, the world as a whole would benefit from the cheaper availability of both goods, and the second country would benefit especially from its new access to the world market. But the first country would lose. Thus individual countries can certainly lose from a fall in trade costs, even though the world as a whole must gain, even when there are no distortions.

Furthermore, if there are distortions, then even the world may lose from a fall in trade costs, for reasons that should be familiar from the theory of the second best. For example, suppose that trade costs fall for a good that is already oversupplied, from a social perspective, due to a global negative externality associated with its production. Then the expansion in its output that will occur when trade costs fall will worsen that externality, and the costs of this may outweigh the benefits found above.

III. Trade Implications

A fall in trade costs, due to networks or any other source, and especially a fall that affects only some trade flows and not others, can easily alter the pattern of trade. In Deardorff (1979) I showed how sensitive trade patterns could be to tariffs, either when goods are used as intermediate inputs into production or when trade involves multiple countries. In either case, a change in a tariff can cause a good that was imported by a country to become exported and another good that was exported to become imported. Real trade costs are different from tariffs, as noted above, but in this respect they are the same. All that was needed for those reversals of trade patterns was that tariffs drive a wedge between domestic and foreign prices, and real trade costs do this as well as tariffs. Therefore, we know immediately that changing trade costs, whatever their cause, can potentially alter not just the size but even the direction of trade flows.

For example, suppose the United States has a comparative advantage in agriculture, and an even stronger comparative advantage in assembling cars, but a comparative disadvantage in producing the steel that it needs as input to making cars. If the cost of transporting steel is too large for it to be traded, the U.S may be uncompetitive in producing cars and find itself importing them, paying for them with exports of agricultural products. But if the cost of transporting steel goes down sufficiently for it to import steel, then it will export cars instead, perhaps even importing agricultural products as well as steel.

Or, in an example involving networks, suppose that Indonesia has an abundance of timber, and also a comparative advantage in turning logs into plywood and other processed forms. But it lacks the knowledge of developed country markets to enable it to move its processed goods to market. It therefore exports only logs, in spite of its seeming comparative advantage in plywood, because the cost, for it, of exporting plywood is too high. But now if a community of Indonesian emigrants establishes itself in some developed country, that community may provide the connections needed to facilitate this trade, and Indonesia will be able to export the processed good. Depending on the extent of its resources of both timber and labor, these connections may ultimately lead it to switch from exporting to importing logs in order to serve its processing industry.

These examples may suggest that comparative advantage no longer plays a role in determining trade, once trade costs are involved. But that is not the case. All of these examples fit within the framework of a general model of comparative advantage, for which I showed in Deardorff (1980) that the Law of Comparative Advantage holds in the weak form of various correlations. That is, while it is indeed true that the direction of trade of any particular good may be sensitive to trade costs (both real and artificial), it is also true that, on average across all goods, net trade is positively correlated with comparative advantage. This is true both for individual countries relative to the world and for the world as a whole.

Of course, the Law of Comparative Advantage in this form is extremely weak, telling us very little about what to expect of a country's trade. It is far from vacuous, essentially cutting in half the number of possibilities that one may see in the world, but that is much less than we might hope for from a theory of trade.[2] To finish this discussion, therefore, I would like to suggest a somewhat more useful interpretation that I have been working on recently, within which trade costs and therefore networks could play an important explanatory role.[3]

The idea is that a country's trade depends not so much on its comparative advantage relative to the world as a whole (except under perfectly free and frictionless

[2] The Law cuts possibilities in half, in the sense that it rules out all vectors of trade that would yield correlations of the wrong sign. While this may not sound like much, this is really all that a two-good, two-country model does also: of the two possible trade patterns, it rules out one.
[3] See Deardorff (2001).

trade), but rather on its comparative advantage relative to the countries that are "closest" to it in the sense of having the lowest trade costs. If trade costs happen to depend only on geographical distance, and if they are large, then comparative advantage will be a local phenomenon, each country's trade pattern depending on its comparative advantages relative to its nearest neighbors. If and as trade costs come down over time, we can expect trade patterns to change, as the relevant measure of comparative advantage broadens to include ever more distant countries.

Of course, one of the messages of the network literature is that trade costs may *not* depend just on distance, but also on the connections that happen to exist between even distant countries that share significant cross-border networks. For a theory of local comparative advantage to make sense, it may be necessary to treat such network-connected trading partners as neighbors, even though they are geographically separated.

I will illustrate the role of trade costs in comparative advantage with two examples. The first illustrates the point just made that when trade costs are high it is local, not global comparative advantage that matters. And the second shows how something that lowers trade costs between a pair of countries can alter local comparative advantage.

To keep things simple, both examples use a partial equilibrium model of trade in which several countries, $c=1,\ldots,C$, each provides a net supply of a good that depends on its price, p_c, relative to their autarky price, a_c, as follows:

$$S_c(p_c) = p_c - a_c \tag{3.1}$$

If trade were free and frictionless, then equilibrium in this model would consist of a single world price, p_w, prevailing in every country, such that the world market would clear:

$$\sum_c S_c(p_w) = \sum_c (p_w - a_c) = Cp_w - \sum_c a_c = 0 \tag{3.2}$$

Thus the world price is just the simple average of the autarky prices, $p_w = \bar{a} = \sum_c a_c / C$, and each country exports or imports the good depending on whether its own autarky price is below or above this average. This, in a sense, is global comparative advantage at work, to the extent that one can make such a statement in a partial equilibrium model.

Now suppose that these countries are arranged geographically around a circle, along which any trade must flow, with the cost of trading this good proportional to distance along the circle. Then for any cost of trade per unit distance, we can work out what the prices in each country must be, and the trade (if any) between them, in order to clear the markets. Letting d_{ij} be the distance along the circle between countries i and j, and letting t be the cost of trading a unit of the good one unit of this distance, then equilibrium consists of prices p_c^e in each country and quantities of exports x_{ij} from country i to country j such that each country's net supply equals its exports minus its imports

$$S_c(p_c^e) = p_c^e - a_c = \sum_i x_{ci} - \sum_i x_{ic} \tag{3.3}$$

and also that prices differ in adjacent countries by at most the trade cost between them, equaling that trade cost if trade actually takes place:

$$\left.\begin{array}{l} x_{ij}\left[(p_j^e - p_i^e) - td_{ij}\right] = 0 \\ x_{ij} \ge 0 \\ (p_j^e - p_i^e) \le td_{ij} \end{array}\right\} \quad \text{for all } i, j = 1, \ldots, C \qquad (3.3)$$

Example 1:

My two examples, within this framework, both include four countries, with considerable symmetry to make them easy to follow. The parameters of the first example are shown in Figure 1, where four countries, *A*, *B*, *C*, and *D*, are arranged around a circle (not shown) at the distances indicated. Their autarky prices for the good, a_c, are also shown.

From a global perspective, countries *A* and *B* have lower autarky prices than *C* and *D*, and therefore comparative advantage in the good. If trade were free and frictionless, the world price would be 25, and *A* and *B* both would export it. However, countries *A* and *B* are much closer to each other than they are to countries *C* and *D*, and compared to their closer neighbors the comparative advantages of *A* and *C* are different than they are globally. *A* has a local comparative disadvantage in this good, while *C* has a local comparative advantage. Indeed, if we try different values for the unit trade cost, *t*, we see that both local and global comparative advantage matter at different levels for this trade cost. Table 1 shows the relevant variables for several arbitrary values of the trade cost.

If the cost of trade, *t*, is 10 or more per unit, then there is no trade, since the differences between adjacent autarky prices are everywhere at least this large. When the trade cost drops to 8, then trade between neighbors *A* and *B* becomes possible, since the trade cost is 8 and the autarky price difference is 10. Trade also occurs between *C* and *D*, for the same reason, but not between the two groups of countries. Because of the larger difference between the groups (4), the cost of trade is 32, which is too large to be overcome. Instead, each country's price adjusts towards that of its neighbor and they trade with each other. As the trade cost falls still further, to 6, this local trade increases and trade between the groups remains zero.

However, when the trade cost reaches 5 (not shown in the table), the cost of trading across groups becomes equal to their price difference (between *A* and *D*, for example), and from there on, trade between the groups becomes possible. The next stop in Table 1 is t=4, at which the cost of trading between *A* and *D*, for example, (16) becomes less than the price difference that would exist between them if they did not trade (20). As a result, the two together become net exporters of the good, pulling its price up in *A* and *B* and down in *C* and *D*. At this point too, the pattern of bilateral trade becomes indeterminate, since the excess supply from country *B* can equally well travel clockwise through *A* or counterclockwise through *C* to reach the excess demand in *D*. This indeterminacy is reflected in the ranges of values shown for the bilateral exports in the last four columns of Table 1.

As the trade cost continues to fall toward zero, the prices in, say, *A* and *B*, not only come closer together, but they also rise absolutely, since it becomes increasingly possible for the two countries both to be net suppliers to countries *C* and *D*. And of course, when the trade cost reaches zero, then we have a single world price of 25, as explained above.

The important message from this example is how sensitive trade patterns can be to trade costs. Country *A* is a net importer of the good when trade costs are relatively high, but it becomes a net exporter when they are low, and country *C* does the reverse. Correspondingly, as the trade cost falls monotonically, the prices in these two countries change, first in one direction and then the other.

Does this mean that comparative advantage is not working? Hardly. The overall correlation of trade with comparative advantage holds throughout, but the correlation leaves open a great many possible trade patterns that are consistent with it, and we are seeing different ones of them arise as trade costs fall. Also, the gains from trade are present throughout this exercise, and in fact they become larger – in worldwide aggregate – as trade costs fall. What the example shows, then, is not a failure of comparative advantage but rather a refinement, in which a slightly more precise definition of comparative advantage, relative to the trading partners that are accessible with given trade costs, determines more fully the pattern of trade.

Example 2:

My second example appears in Figure 2 and Table 2. Here again I have four countries arranged at various intervals around a circular world, but I have altered the autarky prices to suit my needs. In particular, the patterns of local and global comparative advantage are now the same, with countries *B* and *C* both having lower autarky prices for the good both compared to their neighbors and compared to the ultimate world single-market price (which in this case is 47.5). My purpose here is to show how the trade pattern can change if trade cost falls substantially over a particular trade route, perhaps due to a network between two countries that forms and facilitates trade. In my example, I reduce the trade costs only between countries *A* and *D*, and I reduce them to zero by the expedient of changing the "distance" between *A* and *D* from 4 to zero.

The results appear in Table 2. In the initial equilibrium I set the trade cost at 20, large enough that countries trade only with their close neighbors. That is, country *A* imports the good from its neighbor, *B*, while country *D* likewise imports from *C*. There is no trade between the more distant groups.

Now the trade cost between *A* and *D* disappears. Prices in *A* and *D* must therefore become the same, and it turns out that equilibrium is found at a price in both of 55, which is higher than the autarky price in *A*. Thus country *A*, due to this (network-facilitated) drop in trade costs has become a net exporter of the good, rather than the net importer that it was before. It is an even larger gross exporter, since country *B* exports even more than before, all of which flows through country *A* and on to *D*. As it happens, price in *D* falls enough that exports from *C* are no longer viable. Therefore another effect of this drop in trade costs along one trade route is that another country drops out of trade altogether.

At the start of this paper I noted the concern expressed by Rauch (1999) that falling trade costs between certain pairs of countries could have "trade diverting" effects, and that is exactly what has happened here. Furthermore, country *D*'s imports have been diverted from a lower cost supplier *C* (autarky price 45) to a higher cost supplier *A* (autarky price 50). How then can it not be that the world has suffered a loss?

The answer, of course, is that to buy from *C*, country *D* must incur the additional real cost of 20 per unit imported, while to buy from *A* it does not. And unlike a tariff, this is a cost in real resources somewhere, not a transfer to someone else or to its own government. Just as a check that I have not contradicted the welfare result of the previous section, Table 3 shows the welfare effects on each of the four countries – and therefore the world as a whole – of this reduction in trade costs, calculated from the usual changes in producer/consumer surplus.

The calculation confirms that the world as a whole gains substantially from this fall in trade costs, even though it may seem to have "distorted" the pattern of trade. Not surprisingly, countries *B* and *D* gain substantially from the change, since they were the countries with the most extreme comparative advantage and disadvantage to be exploited by trade. Also not surprisingly, country *C* is hurt, for the change has deprived it completely of the gains from trade in this product.

What may be surprising, however, is that country *A*, which one may have thought of as initiating the change by creating a network, happens to lose. The network permitted it to switch from importing the good to exporting it, and a mercantilist would be confident that this makes it better off. But in fact, when this happens its gives up all the gains from trade that it had as an importer, and since in this example it then exports only a smaller quantity than it previously imported, its new gains from exporting are outweighed by the lost gains from importing. Of course there is no reason to think that this is a generally likely result, but it points to an outcome that could be quite unexpected.

IV. Conclusion

My conclusion from this is twofold. First, at least if I am correct in my interpretation of networks as being primarily about ways of reducing costs of trade, then we do not need to worry (if anybody ever did) that the presence of networks may undermine what we thought we knew about trade. And, whether we knew it or not, the overall effect of reducing trade costs due to networks (or any other cause) is likely to be beneficial for the world as a whole. I say "likely," rather than "sure to be," only because there is always the possibility in an imperfect world that distortions will interact with trade costs in a way that could undermine this result. But in general, the presence of unknown and (therefore?) random distortions should not be expected to interfere with this result or any other proposition from trade theory.

However, the presence of networks also draws our attention to the likely fact that the total costs of trade are much larger than just more obvious costs of transportation. Theory tells us that trade costs can matter a great deal for patterns of trade as well as for the gains from trade of individual countries. It is therefore important that we learn as much as we can about what trade costs actually are and about how they may be affected by networks and other aspects of the trading environment.

References

Bruno, Michael 1972 "Market Distortions and Gradual Reform," *Review of Economic Studies* 39 (July), pp. 373-383.

Deardorff, Alan V. 1980 "The General Validity of the Law of Comparative Advantage," *Journal of Political Economy* 88, (October), pp. 941-957.

Deardorff, Alan V. 2001 "Local Comparative Advantage: Trade Costs and the Pattern of Trade," Research Seminar in International Economics, University of Michigan, Discussion Paper No. 471, July.

Obstfeld, Maurice and Kenneth Rogoff 2000 "The Six Major Puzzles in International Macroeconomics: Is There a Common Cause?" *NBER Macroeconomics Annual 2000.*

Rauch, James E. 1999 "Business and Social Networks in International Trade," *Journal of Economic Literature*, forthcoming.

Rauch, James E. and Alessandra Casella. 1998 "Overcoming Informational Barriers to International Resource Allocation: Prices and Group Ties," National Bureau of Economic Research, Working Paper No. 6628, June.

Trefler, Daniel 1995 "The Case of the Missing Trade and Other Mysteries," *American Economic Review* 85, (December), pp. 1029-1046.

Table 1
Prices and trade for various trade costs, *t*, in Example 1

	A		*B*		*C*		*D*		x_{AB}	x_{BC}	x_{CD}	x_{DA}
t	p_A	S_A	p_B	S_B	p_C	S_C	p_D	S_D	$(-x_{BA})$	$(-x_{CB})$	$(-x_{DC})$	$(-x_{AD})$
10	20	0	10	0	30	0	40	0	0	0	0	0
8	19	−1	11	1	31	1	39	−1	−1	0	1	0
6	18	−2	12	2	32	2	38	−2	−2	0	2	0
4	19	−1	15	5	31	1	35	−5	−1,−5	4,0	5,1	0,−4
2	22	2	20	10	28	−2	30	−10	0,−8	10,2	8,0	−2,−10
0	25	5	25	15	25	−5	25	−15	0,−10	15,5	10,0	−5,−15

Table 2
Prices and trade in Example 2, with trade cost *t*=20 and varying "distance" between *A* and *D*.

	A		*B*		*C*		*D*		x_{AB}	x_{BC}	x_{CD}	x_{DA}
d_{AD}	p_A	S_A	p_B	S_B	p_C	S_C	p_D	S_D	$(-x_{BA})$	$(-x_{CB})$	$(-x_{DC})$	$(-x_{AD})$
4	40	−10	20	10	55	10	75	−10	−10	0	10	0
0	55	5	35	25	45	0	55	−30	−25	0	0	−30

Table 3
Welfare effects of reducing "distance" d_{AD} from 4 to 0 in Example 2.

Country *A*	−37.5
Country *B*	+262.5
Country *C*	−50
Country *D*	+400
World	+575

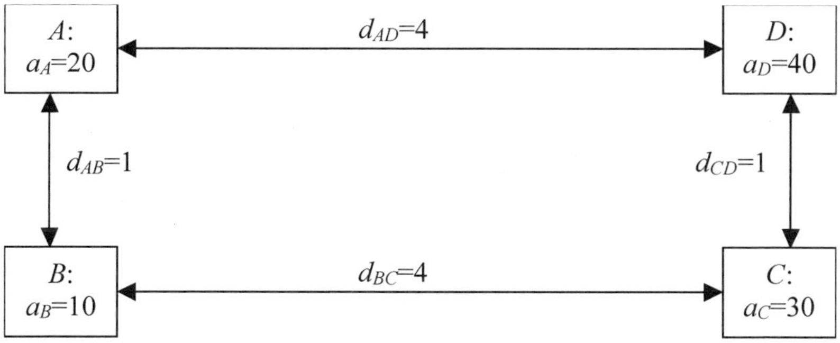

Figure 1

Example 1: Four countries, local and global comparative advantage disagree

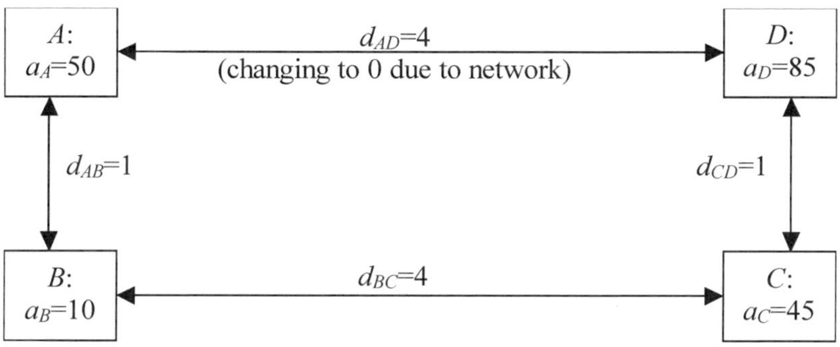

Figure 2

Example 2: Four countries, local and global comparative advantage agree

CHAPTER 30

What Might Globalisation's Critics Believe?

Alan V. Deardorff

1. INTRODUCTION

IN anticipation of preparing this talk, and as a project for the sabbatical that I began in September of last year, I decided to read a good deal more than I had before of the writings of what we have loosely called the anti-globalists. I read a number of books, ranging from William Greider's (1997) *One World, Ready or Not: The Manic Logic of Global Capitalism* and Naomi Klein's (2000) *No Logo*, both of which were quite informative for me but which surpass in passion their economic logic, to Joe Stiglitz's (2002) *Globalization and Its Discontents*, which, despite its title,[1] is mostly a strong critique of IMF policy with very little on other aspects of globalisation. I also read a large number of items from the World Wide Web, again ranging from ill-informed diatribes that I won't mention, to the very thoughtful and balanced white paper by the Oxfam (2000) non-governmental organisation (NGO).

My original intention, as signalled in the tentative title that I gave David Greenaway for this lecture, was simply to find out what the complaints of the anti-globalists really were, and I assembled quite a long list of these as I read. Some of them were complaints that I agreed with, as I will indicate below. Others were ones that I disagreed with, but that could nonetheless be easily understood within a typical economist's view of the world. For example, we all know and understand that free trade and other aspects of globalisation cause harm to some

ALAN V. DEARDORFF is from the University of Michigan. This paper was conceived while he was visiting at the Institute for International Economic Studies, Stockholm University, during the fall of 2002, during which time he benefited from financial support from Tore Browaldh's Research Foundation. He also benefited from discussions of these ideas with Jim Anderson, Harry Flam, David Greenaway, Henrik Horn, Bob Staiger, Ulrika Stavlöt, and from members of the audience at *The World Economy* Annual Lecture at the Leverhulme Centre, University of Nottingham, where it was presented. In this case, more than most, they may all choose to disavow these conversations.

[1] The misleading title, which echoes several other prior books of the same name, has made Stiglitz a champion of the anti-globalists, even though parts of his message this author would interpret as saying that globalisation has not gone far enough. This is especially true in the trade dimension, where he criticises developed-country trade barriers.

groups in society, at the same time that they benefit others, and we know that, according to our models, trade increases the total of economic welfare that could potentially be achieved through redistribution. Although I may favour such redistribution, I recognise that it seldom occurs, and I nonetheless make the value judgment that the overall gain from trade is worth having even when some will be hurt. Some anti-globalists see the world in the same way, but make the opposite value judgment, viewing the harm that is done, often to the poorest in society, as unacceptable, and therefore viewing globalisation as harmful unless the terms are somehow altered to share the gains more equitably. I may disagree with that conclusion, but I do not disagree with the view of the world from which it emerges.

Still other complaints about globalisation, however, seem to emerge from a different world than I am familiar with, and it is here that I wish to devote most of my attention today. Some of the alleged effects of globalisation simply make no sense to me within the context of the neoclassical economic model on which I and my colleagues base most of our teaching and research. Our response to that fact is usually simply to say this – that the criticisms make no sense – and expect others to see the light. What I want to do here, instead, is to try to identify some alternative frameworks, or views of the world, within which the criticisms may make sense. That is, I will suggest several models of the world economy that seem to be implicit in some of the anti-globalists' writings.

In fact, I will suggest three such models, two of which are sufficiently straightforward modifications of standard economic models that I think their implications should also be straightforward. One, as I will elaborate further shortly, is a model in which capitalists seek, not to benefit themselves, so much as to hurt labour – what I will call the anti-labour model. The second will be a model in which all of the world's capitalists collude for their own collective benefit at the expense of the labour that they employ – what I will call the labour-monopsony model. The third framework will actually be a class of models that I am not prepared to spell out in any detail, in which private-sector actors use political tools to influence not just tariffs, as in conventional political economy of trade models, but also other trade policies including export policies, and, even more important, seek also to influence the international negotiations that set the rules for international economic institutions such as NAFTA and the WTO.

In all of this, my ultimate aim is not even close to being achieved in this paper. It is to extract implications from these models that might distinguish them from our conventional economic model and from each other. Then, somewhere down the road, if the anti-globalists agree that one or more of these alternative models is what they have in mind, then it might be possible to test for which model's implications come closest to being confirmed empirically.

Of course, I will not get that far today. I will just sketch the three sorts of model I have just mentioned and suggest what seem to be a few of their implications. I then invite critics of globalisation to respond, either by confirming that one of these models captures their view of the world or, if that is not the case, by explaining their views in a way that might be susceptible to such modelling. My hope is that, at a minimum, this exercise will allow us to communicate more effectively across the divide that currently seems to separate most of the advocates and opponents of globalisation. And perhaps, some day, some of us or some of them will be persuaded to modify their views.

As the three models I've just outlined indicate, my focus will be almost entirely on the role of 'capitalists' in the world economy. This reflects my view that, while anti-globalists have a large number and variety of complaints, their most common theme is that they object to the power held and used by large corporations, the corporations that they identify as 'transnational,' or TNCs. Some would narrow this to American transnational corporations, while others would then broaden this to Americans more generally, but I think these are a minority. Anti-globalisation is not primarily anti-Americanism, but primarily anti-corporate.

Another focus of anti-globalisation 'discontent' is of course the international (or transnational) institutions: the IMF, World Bank and WTO. But here too I believe that the reason for popular distrust of these organisations is not the belief that they are themselves intrinsically harmful, but rather that they are dominated by, or primarily influenced by, corporate interests. This is certainly the view expressed forcefully by Stiglitz (2002).

Finally, one more important theme of some anti-globalists within the developed countries is their perception that their own incomes and wages are being undermined by competition with low-wage labour in developing countries (and also, in a similar way, by labour-saving changes in technology). Here you might think that the focus of their complaints would be against the developing countries or their workers, but in fact it is not. Again, they blame corporations for taking the jobs to those countries, not the countries themselves for attracting them.[2] On the contrary, the critics have a remarkable ability to perceive this process as hurting both rich-country workers and poor-country workers, the former through lost wages and lost jobs, and the latter by exploiting workers with substandard wages and working conditions. So here too, it is the corporations that are the villains.

What about the 'market'? Don't they object to it, as well? Yes, and there are plenty of complaints about impersonal market forces that alter the lives of people without regard to their wishes or well-being. But while a few of the protesters may in fact see the market as an economist would – the collective result of a multitude of atomistic agents, and therefore, indeed, truly impersonal – I would

[2] An example of this is nicely documented in Cowie (1999), which describes the repeated shifts in production of televisions by the RCA company from New Jersey, first to Indiana, then to Tennessee, and finally to Mexico. At each stage, movement was in response to high wages and strong unionisation in the old location and low wages and weak unionisation in the new, but the workers in an old location virtually never blamed the workers in the new locations for their lost jobs, only the company itself.

bet that most of them see the market too as a creature of the big corporations. The market is impersonal, not because no person controls it, but because the persons that do, in the form of corporate owners and managers, are heartless, greedy, profit-seeking monsters. Or perhaps, somewhat less viciously, the market really is an impersonal force, but it is the corporations that give it importance by caring only about its dictates rather than about human values.

A byproduct of this is that critics see the harm done by open international markets, in both trade and capital flows, as being done by corporations and other 'capitalists' to the rest of society, and not as the collective expression of the world's supplies and demands as an economist would see it.

That may seem trivial. Corporations, after all, are primarily about making money, not about doing good, so isn't it natural to see them as inherently bad? Perhaps it is, but of course that is not exactly the view of economists. We agree that profit-seeking firms, if given too much power, will at least be suboptimal if not actually undesirable. But we also tend to believe in the power of competition among such firms to render their greed harmless and in fact to turn it into an engine for making people better off. We have this model, you see, in which competition among firms leads in a perfect world to economic efficiency. And while the world is obviously imperfect in many ways, we still tend to believe that this force for good usually plays the dominant role.

We are so sure of this that some of us, at least, automatically discount both the views of those who disagree with us, and the evidence that they present. We have built our academic careers on the foundation of this model, and it has served us well, so we believe that evidence of its failure is either anomalous or insufficient to negate the main message: that markets are good. When confronted with those who disagree with us, we almost always can find elements of their arguments that are contrary to fact – or if not to fact, then to theory – and we marshal our own arguments in the comfortable context of our theory without really hearing what others are saying.

So, as I've said, what I want to do is to try to listen more carefully to what the anti-globalists are saying. I want not only to understand their arguments, but also to try to comprehend the world that they think we live in. Instead of seeing their objections within the context of my standard economist's model, where I already know that many of them do not make sense, let me try to formulate the model that they have in mind. Ideally, if I can do this, then their model or models will have different implications than ours, perhaps even testable implications that could ultimately be used to differentiate between them.

a. What to Call Them

First, let me confront an issue that always gets in the way of this discussion: what should I call the group of anti-globalists. The term I've mostly used so far, anti-globalists, is familiar and relatively easy, but it would be rejected by a fair fraction of those it is supposed to describe. At most, many of these people would say that they are opposed to globalisation in its current form, not to globalisation in general. And indeed, as many on both sides of the debate have pointed out, these people, whoever they are, have themselves made great use of globalised communications and often also globalised commerce in pressing their point of view, as why should they not? As I've already said, what they really oppose, more than globalisation, is the power of transnational corporations, but it would be incorrect as well simply to identify them as anti-corporate. I don't think that most of them want to destroy the corporate world. They only want to change it too for the better, either by changing how corporations themselves behave or by having government play a larger role with respect to them.

An alternative term for this group is 'globalisation sceptics.' That seems much better, since it does not presuppose a desire to eliminate globalisation, but it is too weak. They do not just remain to be convinced of the benefits of globalisation; they are downright sure that many aspects of it are awful. The term that I will favour, therefore, is also the one settled on by a previous paper that confronted this issue, 'globalisation critics.'[3] They do indeed criticise globalisation and are often very sure in their criticism. But like critics in other realms, their criticism is not necessarily unmixed with praise, and many of them are quite capable of imagining changes in the global economy that would leave it global, and perhaps even in the hands of corporations, but that they would then be able to accept.

b. Where We Agree

First, let me identify the ways in which I too am a critic of globalisation. There are several criticisms of globalisation, and specifically of the policies of governments and international institutions that are part of globalisation, that I wholeheartedly agree with. There are still others for which I have varying amounts of sympathy, whether or not I agree completely.

Most of these tend to be areas in which, in a sense, globalisation has not gone far enough, rather than where it has gone too far.[4] That is, like most economists, I strongly condemn the trade barriers that developed countries continue to impose on exports from developing countries. This is most obvious in the labour-intensive industries producing textiles and apparel, where developing countries would be most likely to find their comparative advantage were they permitted to export freely. But it is also the case in other mature industries where rich countries have repeatedly used administrative protection – anti-dumping duties and other forms

[3] See Elliot et al. (2002).
[4] See Rodrik (1997).

– to limit imports from multiple sources including developing countries. This behaviour is not what I would call a part of globalisation but rather a counter to it or resistance to it, but be that as it may, it is certainly a fact of current globalised life, and it confirms the impression of some in developing countries that the powers of globalisation are stacked against them.

Similarly, and again like most economists, I condemn the subsidies that Europe especially, but also the United States, continue to provide in agriculture. Here too is an industry in many parts of which developing countries often have a plausible comparative advantage, and yet they are unable to compete against the rich country subsidies. As a trade economist, I am fond of pointing out that in the aggregate such subsidies hurt the country whose government pays them and actually benefit the rest of the world. And if the subsidies were in fact delivering affordable food to the world's hungry, I would not mind them at all, as long as they could be depended on to continue. But in fact, as I understand it, most of the hungry in developing countries are in rural areas where, instead of benefiting from this cheap food, they have to compete with it for a livelihood. In the long run, that may or may not be the best use of their labour, but in the short run these subsidies are simply driving small developing country farmers further into poverty. That is inexcusable.

A third issue on which I criticise the current stance of globalisation is intellectual property (IP). Here the issue is one of balance, since a certain amount of intellectual property protection is certainly necessary to provide the incentive for innovation and creativity, so long as these are left in the hands of the private sector. But IP protection creates costs as well as benefits, those costs arising from the monopoly power of, and the monopoly prices charged by, the IP owners. This is not only economically inefficient; it also causes redistribution of income from consumers broadly to the producers of IP. This mostly means redistribution away from developing countries toward corporate owners in developed countries. Just where the balance should be struck between protecting rich country IP producers at the expense of poor country IP consumers cannot be answered objectively, but my own impression is that the TRIPs agreement of the WTO goes way too far in favour of the producers. Whether redressing this balance would be a move toward more globalisation or less, I do not know, but I think it should be done.

Finally, there is one issue area where it appears that less globalisation and even less freedom of markets would be desirable: short-term capital flows. Changes in technology have accompanied changes in policy during the last thirty years or so to permit financial capital to flow among countries at speeds and in quantities that are almost impossible to comprehend. If markets were static and came at all close to the ideal of fully informed, perfect competition, then the case could easily be made that these markets enhance efficiency, transferring capital from those who have it to those who need it, to the benefit of all. But if ever there were markets that were not static, these are them. And the assumption that there is full information in these markets is laughable. Instead, the large swings in fashion and expectations that cause short-term capital to flow into and then out of vulnerable countries seem most unlikely to be beneficial for the world, and they certainly are not beneficial to the countries that become their victims. I am far from alone, even among economists, in believing that this just has to stop.

These are the major issues on which my own criticisms of current policies and institutions are most clear: developed country trade barriers, especially in textiles and apparel; administered protection in both developed and developing countries, especially anti-dumping duties; developed country subsidies in agriculture; the extreme coverage and discipline of the WTO TRIPs agreement; and the volatility of short-term capital movements. There are also several other issues on which I certainly sympathise with the globalisation critics, even though I may not be prepared to agree with them fully:

- Although I reject the claim that the WTO would be more democratic if it included a voice for non-governmental organisations (NGOs), I do agree that WTO decision making seems to be unduly dominated by the rich countries, and some more formal means of representing developing country interests should be devised.
- Likewise, although I see the danger inherent in opening WTO dispute settlement to public view, on balance I think the benefits outweigh the costs.
- I have little patience with the view that the IMF and World Bank are motivated by ill will in their prescriptions for policy changes in developing countries, but I do believe that some of their advice has turned out to be unfortunately misguided and destructive. I hope and believe that they will learn from that experience and pursue their aims of truly helping developing countries in the future more successfully.

2. THE CRITICS' MODELS

In reading what the critics have to say about globalisation, I came across hints of several views about why it is that globalisation has such perceived harmful effects. What I want to suggest here are a few models that may capture pieces of what the critics may be thinking. All of these models focus on the behaviour of 'capital,' which I take to stand for the managers of large firms rather than necessarily their owners. I will call these people 'capitalists' for want of a better term.

a. The Anti-labour Model

One idea is simply that the capitalists share, in one respect, the point of view of the globalisation critics: they believe that they are engaged in a struggle in opposition to labour, and that, in order to win, they must reduce as far as possible the economic benefits that accrue to labour. That is, they see labour as in some sense the enemy, and victory for them requires defeat for labour. Thus, whenever capital has the opportunity to reduce what it pays to labour, either per hour or in total, it will do so.

Now that statement cannot, in itself, provide a workable model, since on its face it predicts that all use of labour would simply stop, and that the economy would shut down completely unless the capitalists can find a way to produce with machines alone. The view here may well be that this is the ideal, but since it is not (yet?) possible, we must modify the model somewhat to have it make any sense at all. My thought would be, then, to assume that capitalists take advantage of any opportunity they can to reduce payments to labour, so long as doing so does not actually cause their firm to make a loss. Thus they do not seek to maximise profits, necessarily, but rather to minimise payments to labour subject to the constraint of zero (or perhaps 'normal') profits.

Please don't ask me the question of why they would do this, since I cannot answer it. But it does seem to me that some of the more extreme globalisation critics have in mind exactly such an adversarial view of capital and labour, and that they believe this to be the case. If capitalists shared this view of the world, then perhaps they would in fact behave this way.

What does this 'model' imply? If we interpret it together with all the other usual assumptions of perfect competition, then it actually does not generate any implications that are different from the standard model. With free entry and exit of firms, and with common knowledge of available technology, we may expect profits to be driven to zero. These anti-labour capitalists will then have no room to exercise their supposed preference for hurting labour. In order to avoid making a loss, they will have to do all the things that a profit-maximising capitalist would do, including hire labour up to the point that the value of its marginal product equals its wage. Failure to do so will induce entry by other capitalists who are willing to operate even marginally closer to this condition, and drive those who fail to observe it out of business.

Admittedly, the assumption of free entry fits uneasily with the assumption that capitalists seek to hurt labour, so perhaps a better assumption would be that capital in an industry is fixed and that positive profits are possible. And even with free entry, other market imperfections such as patents or trade secrets that secure a technology for a single firm may lead to positive profits. And it is here, with positive profits, that this model generates implications that are different from the conventional model.

With the potential for positive profits, the anti-labour model predicts that, given a wage, firms will hire less labour than would maximise profits, sacrificing this profit in order to hurt labour. And if firms also have some market power over the wage, so that they need not take the wage as given, they will also seek to depress wages below the levels that would maximise profits. I will start with the first case, a potentially profitable firm that is a perfect competitor in the labour market.

Such a firm may or may not have market power in its product market. If it does not – if it takes the price of its output as well as the wage and other prices of inputs as given – then rather than hiring labour up to the point that the value (at these prices) of the marginal product of labour equals the wage, it will hire less labour than this. Thus in its anti-labour equilibrium, the value of labour's marginal product will be greater than its wage. In principle this might provide us a way of distinguishing the behaviour of anti-labour capitalists from normal profit-maximising ones: if price-taking firms display a value of marginal product of labour that is greater than the wage, then this would be evidence of such antipathy toward labour.

Thus, if we could learn how much output a firm could achieve by employing an additional unit of labour, and if we believed the firm to be a price taker in its output market, then we could just multiply this price times the extra output and compare to the wage in order to infer whether it is deliberately trying to hurt labour even at the expense of its own profits. If an additional hour of labour in a shoe factory, for example, could produce one additional shoe with a value of, say, $20, then evidence that the firm pays less than a $20 wage would support this model of capitalist motivation.

Unfortunately, however, things are not this simple if firms have market power over the price of their output. Indeed, this same condition would also necessarily be violated by profit-maximising firms if they have such product market power. With product market power, firms expand output only to the point that marginal cost equals marginal revenue, not price, and this too implies that the value of labour's marginal product is greater than its wage. The condition for equilibrium here is, instead, that the marginal-revenue product of labour should be equal to the wage. Calculation of this requires knowledge not just of the marginal product and the price, but also of the level and the elasticity of demand for the product. This is therefore a much more demanding condition to check. For the hypothetical shoe manufacturer above, we would need to know how much the price of shoes would have to fall in order to expand demand by one shoe, and what this would do therefore to the revenue from all sales of shoes together. In principle, I suppose, this could be ascertained, but the calculation would be so sensitive to the data used that I doubt much confidence could be placed in the results. Some other implication of the model might therefore be more useful.

Such an implication is not hard to find. This anti-labour model not only implies, in the case of profitable firms, that they will hire less labour than would be optimal for profits. It also implies that they will produce less than the profit-maximising output, keeping output down precisely in order to avoid benefiting the hated labour. Thus we can ignore labour altogether and simply ask whether the firm could be making a larger profit than it is, if only it were to produce and sell more product. Thus, those who wish to provide evidence for this sort of anti-labour behaviour need only show that firms could be making more profits if they were to produce more output and sell it for a lower price.

I do not doubt that, if such evidence were to be found, defenders of capitalism would respond by finding explanations for it other than a desire to hurt labour, and some of these defences need to be accounted for in any sensible test. Thus, for example, the true demand for a branded shoe may depend in rather unconventional ways on both its price and on the quantities being sold, as signals of its quality and/or its level of market cachet. Thus the usual estimation of market demand curves may not be appropriate for evaluating such a market. But regardless of how one diagnoses the problem faced by the firm, the objective of defenders of this anti-labour model of capitalists should be to show that capitalists are sacrificing profit in a way that hurts labour.

Another implication of this model that distinguishes it from the profit-maximising model can be found in the response to a technological improvement. Suppose an improvement occurs that increases output for each level of labour input in an industry for which demand is elastic. If firms were to hold employment constant, industry output would rise and price would fall while still increasing revenues and thus profit. Since the improvement would increase the marginal product of labour, profit-maximising firms would increase their demand for labour and expand. But labour-minimising firms would see the increase in profit as an opportunity to reduce employment, and they would do so. If the industry faces an upward sloping supply of labour, then the wage will also rise in the first case and fall in the second. But even without that we find employment in the industry expanding under profit-maximising firms and contracting under labour-minimising firms. Thus the response of such an industry to an exogenous improvement in labour productivity provides another possible way of distinguishing conventional models from this anti-labour model.

b. The Labour Monopsony Model

Consider now a model in which capitalists are after all quite rational, seeking simply to maximise their own well-being and not directly concerned about that of labour, positively or negatively. This is the assumption that we economists are most comfortable with, but unlike our usual models in which self-interested capitalists lack market power, assume now that they are somehow able to collaborate and act in their collective self-interest. That is, capital is managed as a monopoly, the purpose of which is to maximise the total returns to capital. Thus, capitalists exercise monopsony power in the labour market. This is a sort of conspiracy theory of factor markets, and it also I gather has a Marxian flavour.

Within a closed economy, these monopsonists would pay lower wages and employ less labour than perfect competitors, in ways that I will explore in a moment. International trade alone will not lessen that market power, but international capital mobility will, if the conspiracy is at the national level and yet foreign capitalists, not part of the conspiracy, are permitted to employ domestic workers. Since that seems to be the essence of the much vilified transnational corporation, the assumption of collaboration only at the national level will not get us very far. Instead, this view on the part of the critics would seem to require that the monopsony be global. That is, the capitalists of the world are united in collectively exploiting labour as best they can, given labour's behaviour as suppliers.

Countervailing against this, one could assume that labour too is able to act collectively, though this seems unlikely on a global basis, and in any case it is not the model of the critics. I assume therefore that labour acts competitively, individual workers supplying labour in passive response to whatever wage the capitalists collectively choose to set. This wage will then depend on the nature of this labour supply curve in each country.

Of course, if labour supply were perfectly elastic at some wage, then the monopsony power would be meaningless: the capitalists would be wage takers in spite of their ability to collaborate. If on the other hand labour supply were everywhere perfectly inelastic, then the capitalists would simply reduce the wage to zero, making the assumption of inelasticity untenable. We must therefore assume an upward sloping labour supply curve, one that is presumably quite elastic at the subsistence level where workers' effectiveness is compromised by poor nutrition, but that becomes less elastic at wages above this.

The standard model of monopsony then tells us what to expect. Whereas competitive labour demanders would present a demand for labour that is the value of its marginal product, monopsony demanders will hire less than this, setting a level of employment that equates the value of labour's marginal product not to the wage, but rather to the marginal wage bill. They then set the wage to elicit that amount of labour. The result is, as in the previous model, a wage that is less than the value of labour's marginal product. Thus the observation that labour is paid less than its marginal product would be consistent not only with the previous model of capitalists that irrationally seek to hurt labour, but also with this monopsony model. On the other hand, the monopsony model shares the property of the competitive model that a technological improvement in an elastically-demanded industry will cause that industry to expand, in contrast to the implication that we saw above for labour-minimising firms.

c. International Political Economy

While the most standard economic models of international trade have focused solely on economic processes and economic actors, there has long been an interest also in political processes, usually for the purpose of trying to understand why governments so often restrict trade. What has not, to my knowledge, gotten much attention is the interaction between private and public sectors beyond the realm of simple protection and especially into the realm of international economic rule making. And yet much of the rhetoric of globalisation's critics suggests that they believe that the rules of the international economy have been tailored to the interests of large corporations. This, to me, suggests the need for a model in which capitalists attempt to influence political actors, but where this influence extends far beyond the setting of tariffs into other aspects of international economic policy, and especially into the setting of the rules of the international trading system.

For example, suppose that we take an existing model of the political economy of protection and expand it to allow, as a policy option, export subsidies. Since these have much the same effect on profits in an export industry as do tariffs in an import competing industry, we should expect that political processes would promote their use just as they do protection. That is, political actors will be motivated to strike a compromise between the general interests of the electorate, which presumably favour free trade in both export and import-competing industries, and the special interests of lobbying firms in these industries. If corporate profits are the main driver of trade policy, then we should see export subsidies in exporting industries, just as we see import tariffs in import-competing industries. Of course, both of these policies may be constrained by international agreements such as the GATT, raising the separate question of how these institutions and their rules are influenced by political pressures. But the constraints themselves, and perhaps various efforts to circumvent them, may be taken as evidence of the power of capital to capture the political process and secure these policies.

In contrast, an alternative model might place power to influence the political process in the hands of labour rather than capital. Labour is employed in both exporting and import-competing industries, so it might be thought that it would lobby for the same policies as capital. But whereas tariffs benefit existing workers by preventing their industries from contracting, export subsidies primarily benefit workers who will be added to an industry as it expands, and neither they nor their union may know who they are in advance. Such a model therefore suggests that the political power of labour, if it exists, will primarily generate import protection, while that of capital will generate both import protection and export subsidies.

It is tempting, therefore, to counter the critics by observing that the GATT prohibits export subsidies but actually permits import tariffs, constraining the latter only by prohibiting their increase beyond bound levels. Can we take that as evidence that trade policies favour labour more than capital? Perhaps. But in fact export subsidies are far from non-existent, in spite of their supposed prohibition under the GATT. In agriculture they have been explicitly permitted, and getting rid of them today is proving to be extremely hard. Even in manufacturing, although industry-specific export subsidies do seem to be effectively curtailed, programmes like the United States Foreign Sales Corporation, which the WTO has now judged to be an export subsidy and which the United States is finding it politically very difficult to abandon, suggest that export subsidies have never yet been eliminated.

Adding export subsidies to the menu of policies in a political-economy model only begins to capture the role that political forces, and thus corporate capital, might play in international trade policy. Although formal modelling of these effects might be too cumbersome to pursue, it is surely plausible to imagine that one country's exporters may play an active role in inducing its government to press another country to reduce its trade barriers. These may be simple tariffs and quotas, or they may involve much more subtle regulations and practices that the exporters perceive as interfering with their 'market access.' Indeed, the exporters have an incentive to allege the existence of such invisible barriers whether or not they exist, since they will benefit from efforts to offset them in either case. Thus, policies of 'voluntary import expansion,' such as were urged upon Japan by United States policy in the 1980s, could be taken as evidence of lobbying by capital especially if the Japanese barriers to imports were in fact imagined. Not that such lobbying needs to be inferred indirectly; it was done quite openly and was alleged to be based on the principles of free trade.

If such barriers are explicit or otherwise demonstrably exist, then I suppose the standard model would be that enlightened governments negotiate with others to pursue free trade simply because they recognise the compelling intellectual case for it, passed along to them by academics. But surely as plausible a model is that these governments are actually responding to political inducements offered them by export interests. And export interests, as noted above, are more plausibly those of capital rather than labour.

What about the making not of trade policies themselves, but of the rules that countries accept as constraining those policies? Are these subject to political processes, and do they respond to the interests of capital and/or labour? It seems obvious that they do, even though I know of no formal models that try to capture this effect. Models of the GATT, for example, such as Bagwell and Staiger (1999), focus mostly on the process of negotiations under the GATT and WTO, and not on the rules of these two institutions. Indeed, I am not sure that the original structure of the GATT – as it was drafted in the mid-1940s amid the idealism of the anticipated post-war recovery and the fear of a renewed Great Depression – requires a conventional political-economy explanation. Also, at that time the process of international institution building was new and uncertain enough that I doubt that private sector interests, including corporations, were yet aware of the potential to gain advantage by influencing the rules. But over subsequent decades of GATT and other international negotiations, they surely learned. The forces of economic self-interest expressed through politics seem to be written all over the more recent expansion of the GATT as embodied in the WTO, and also in other international trade arrangements that have been negotiated or contemplated especially during the 1990s.

The Canada-US Free Trade Agreement of 1989 may have been the last agreement to be relatively free of political-economic influence. It seems to have arisen primarily out of Canada's frustration with US application of administered protection, together with a new US willingness to negotiate bilaterally when multilateral negotiations seemed to be bogged down. But the FTA may have awakened corporate interests in both countries to what could be accomplished through trade agreements, and they became active players in the subsequent negotiation of the NAFTA. Ross Perot, with his 'great sucking sound,' greatly exaggerated the role that the NAFTA would play in permitting industry to migrate into Mexico, but he was quite correct that many US corporations supported the NAFTA and participated in drafting its rules because they hoped to take advantage of its provisions.

During the NAFTA debate, critics made much of the fact that the agreement occupied such a large document, including far more complicated provisions than one might have thought were necessary if the aim were simple free trade. On the one hand, this criticism was unfair, in part because it covered so much more than free trade. Also, as a free trade agreement – unlike a customs union with a common external tariff – NAFTA intrinsically requires rules of origin that necessarily are somewhat complicated to spell out. But on the other hand, the NAFTA rules of origin are well known to be far more complicated than would be necessary, with details that reflected both the fine points of sector-specific negotiations and also the influence of industry representatives who were involved in the negotiating process. The NAFTA agreement grew to the size it did in part because, like an omnibus legislative act that tries to cater to a wide variety of interests in Congress, it incorporated numerous provisions designed to satisfy special interests in each of the negotiating countries and especially in the most powerful country, the United States.

Did those interests include both capital and labour? I don't know, and I think a study of the NAFTA text to ascertain the contributions of the various interests involved would be worthwhile. But judging both from the fact that it was negotiated by a Republican administration in the US and from the perceived need by the Democrats who then took power for a separate side agreement on labour issues, I am sure that the original NAFTA agreement reflected the interests of capital far more than those of labour.

One might argue that any free trade agreement will seem to favour capital over labour, without capital necessarily participating in the negotiating process, and this may be true. But there are features of the NAFTA that seem especially to favour capital. The rules of origin in the automobile industry, for example, are explicitly designed to favour US-owned companies compared to their Japanese-owned rivals, without any similar tilt that I know of toward US workers. The rules for the trucking industry, in another example that I happen to favour, are very much for the benefits of the industry's corporate customers, and they have been so resisted by the US truckers themselves that they have still not, as far as I know, been implemented. Finally, and most egregiously, consider the now notorious NAFTA Chapter 11, which gives foreign direct investors a private right of action against host country governments. This can only have been inserted into the NAFTA in the interests of capital, since it gives corporations a level of recourse against governments that they have been unable to obtain under domestic laws, even in the United States. To me, with only very partial knowledge of what the NAFTA includes in its lengthy agreement, all this suggests that the rules of NAFTA were indeed drafted for the benefit of corporations. It is also very plausible that they should have been. The incentive for drafting rules in their corporate interests seems easily as clear as the incentive to seek tariff protection. Furthermore, government negotiators were eager to seek their participation in the negotiations, both in order to lighten the workload and to smooth the way toward passage of the agreement once it was completed.[5]

At the same time that the NAFTA was being negotiated, the Uruguay Round was also plodding along, and it too had extensive participation by corporate interests. Not everything that found its way into the resulting agreement can be attributed to this, by any means, but some of the major components of the resulting World Trade Organisation, both good and bad in my view, seem clearly to have been the creation of capitalists. Exceptions include the strengthening of anti-dumping rules, which seem to reflect the interests of both labour and capital in import-competing industries, and the scheduled termination of the Multi-Fibre Arrangement, which actually goes against certain corporate and labour interests in developed countries in favour of the developing world.[6]

The latter, however, was viewed as a price that the developed world and a larger corporate constituency was willing to pay in return for the TRIPs agreement, which strikes me as the best evidence yet of the role that corporate interests have been able to play in the setting of the international rules of trade policy. The TRIPs agreement was sought by a subset of corporate interests who perceived that they were losing profits from unauthorised use of their intellectual property (IP) – patents, copyrights, and trademarks – in countries with weaker or more laxly enforced intellectual property rights regimes than exist in most industrialised countries. They lobbied aggressively, first to include IP in the Uruguay Round negotiations under the heading of Trade Related Intellectual Property Rights (TRIPs), but then expanding the coverage of these negotiations well

[5] See Deardorff and Hall (1998) who stress the role of lobbyists in the United States in helping with the workload of legislators.

[6] I don't know, however, what role corporate importers such as WalMart may have played.

beyond what could plausibly be called trade related to include the entire domestic IP regimes of all member countries. The result was to require that all WTO members implement and enforce IP regimes comparable to those in the developed countries.

IP protection is certainly not a bad idea economically, even though the obvious beneficiaries are the owners of IP rights, most often corporations. Without IP protection, the incentive to produce IP – to invent, write, or otherwise create – is weak or non-existent. IP protection grants to owners of IP monopoly rights over their creations, thus providing that incentive. But the monopoly power distorts market signals, leading to an equilibrium that is inefficient. And worse, it distributes income toward the owner of the IP and away from its consumers. In the case of the products most affected by the TRIPs agreement, this means that they are provided at inefficiently low levels and that, compared to the regime in which IP protection was absent from developing countries, income has been redistributed away from them and toward the corporate owners of IP in the rich countries.

From the point of view of the corporations that operate most successfully in international markets, the TRIPs agreement seemed like a natural extension of other aspects of the GATT, in that it extended their market access into developing countries. But from the perspective of the economic case for free markets and free trade, it did not fit in at all. It is no accident that within the GATT 'protection' is viewed as a negative, while within TRIPs the same word has a positive connotation. The GATT is about making markets freer, while TRIPs is about making them less free, albeit with the admirable purpose of promoting innovation and creativity. Thus the fact that TRIPs became part of the WTO is surely evidence of the growing role of corporate interests and a move away from freedom of markets as a guiding principle. IP protection, like tariff protection, distorts markets at the expense of consumers for the benefit of a subset of producers.

The corporate role also seems to have been decisive in creating the other new component of the WTO, the General Agreement on Trade in Services, GATS. Here, as in the role of corporations in pushing for reduced barriers to exports, I see this role in a largely positive light. The fact that the GATT did not cover services from the start was due to the administrative difficulty of addressing them, and not to any intrinsic reason why trade in services should be less free than trade in goods.[7] However, it was certainly not the intellectual case for free trade in services that put them onto the agenda of the Uruguay Round negotiators, but rather the active influence of large international corporate service providers, who lobbied governments especially in the United States to bring them on board. Indeed, it was only after corporate pressure set the agenda for services

[7] See Deardorff (1985).

trade liberalisation that academics like myself thought to look at the economics of the issue. Again, therefore, as in the case of TRIPs but here with more unambiguously positive effects, it was the corporate capitalists who were responsible for this entirely new initiative in international trade law.

Since the completion of the Uruguay Round and the formation of the WTO, international rule making has moved out of the spotlight. Within the WTO, further negotiations have reached new agreements in the areas of financial services and basic telecommunications, both of which consisted primarily of balancing the corporate interests from different countries.

The only other new initiative of which I am aware prior to the current Doha Round has been the negotiations within the OECD of a proposed Multilateral Agreement on Investment, MAI. As I understand it, this was intended to do for international investors worldwide much of what the NAFTA had done for them within North America, and as was the case there, the initiative came from corporations. The case for relatively free international movements of real capital, in the form of FDI, is similar to the case for free trade, and therefore this initiative might well be expected to be beneficial. But because it was focused almost exclusively on the rights of investors, rather than on the benefits that their investment might provide to consumers, it also may well have included bias in favour of corporate interests.

In fact, I do not know a great deal about the MAI, which attracted the attention of globalisation critics well before it attracted mine. The critics today take credit for having derailed this initiative, though I am told that this failure, like that of the WTO in Seattle, had more to do with conflicting interests among the negotiating countries than with pressure from NGOs. In any case, the MAI does not today seem to have much chance of being revived. My sense is that its demise may have marked an important change in the international rule-making environment. Corporate interests may have been the first to recognise the potential for gain from influencing international rules, and they exploited this leverage on world affairs quietly and effectively during the NAFTA negotiations and with the creation of the WTO. But today many other interests have been alerted, and they have shown their presence, if not their influence, in the fight against the MAI.

I conclude that a political-economy model of international rule-making is still what is needed to understand events. However, while the model of the 1990s may have been one in which corporations alone wielded power related to their positions in international markets, the model from now on will include competing players. Corporations will continue to be an important influence, but now they must contend with countervailing forces from more organised labour, as well as from NGOs representing the environment, human rights, and other issues. Furthermore, while in the 1990s the corporate lobbyists only had to deal with government of the industrialised countries, today the developing countries are increasingly recognising also the importance of advancing their own interests. With all of these other forces to contend with, it remains to be seen whether corporations will continue to wield the power that they may have in the past.

3. CONCLUSION

In preparing for this talk, I read more than I ever had before of the writings of globalisation critics, including several books and numerous items on the web. My intention, as I have said, was not only to find out what their criticisms were, but also to infer, if I could, something about the worldview that underlay their criticisms. There are of course plenty of faults in the world trading system that I can identify and deplore within my own worldview. But many of their other criticisms simply make no sense within the traditional neoclassical, neoliberal model of a perfectly competitive world economy that, like most economists, I take as my starting point for understanding the world. Nor do many of these criticisms make much more sense if one relaxes the assumption of perfect competition and allows various market distortions to enter the picture. Therefore, what I have sought to find were alternative models, ones that I would not necessarily even begin to believe myself nor expect other economists to subscribe to, but that might capture important features of how at least some of the globalisation critics view the world.

My purpose in doing this has most definitely *not* been then to take issue with these alternative assumptions, by saying for example that it is implausible that the world's capitalists are so cohesive that they are able to coordinate in collusive behaviour toward labour. The assumptions of the neoclassical model are no doubt very implausible as well. Rather, my ultimate objective is to find testable implications of such alternative models, implications that differ from those of the neoclassical model and that might provide an opportunity to differentiate between it and them, or among them. I have not achieved this objective in this paper, but have only suggested several such alternative models that, I hope, others will want to develop further and explore.

I will not recapitulate here the three alternative models that I have suggested above. Rather, I'd like to close by reporting how my own attitudes toward globalisation have changed during the course of this exercise of reading and writing.

As I mentioned to colleagues along the way, I sometimes felt that I was brainwashing myself by reading the works of globalisation critics. Particularly, perhaps, because I was determined to keep an open mind to their point of view rather than constantly marshalling my economist's presumptions against them, I found as I read that I too sometimes became appalled at the state of the world that they described. I too sometimes easily accepted that it was globalisation that had in some manner contributed to this situation.

In the end, what I realised was that my previous defensive posture towards the critics of globalisation had perhaps prevented me from giving proper weight to the flaws in the world system that even defenders of globalisation have long deplored. I tended, before this, to dismiss those flaws as exceptional and to focus instead on the much broader good that I thought globalisation could do and had done. The latter, I still think, was appropriate, but the flaws deserve attention too. Some of these flaws, like textile protection and agricultural subsidies, can properly be seen as globalisation not going far enough, failures that deprive a large part of the world from enjoying the benefits of globalisation that are rightfully theirs. But others, like TRIPs and short-term capital flows, do genuinely reflect globalisation going too far, and the reason for them seems easy to identify in the strong political role played by powerful corporations.

Perhaps more than most economists, I am personally predisposed to see corporations as beneficial to society.[8] It seems obvious to me that corporations have made possible a level of well-being throughout most of the world that far exceeds what could have been achieved without them. The invisible hand of the market only partly accounts for this, since large corporations clearly have far more power over markets than we assume in our competitive models. But as long as these large corporations are forced to compete with one another and also with small new entrants that may at any moment emerge – a level of competition that requires the active vigilance and sometimes enforcement by government competition authorities – I have no doubt but that they do far more good than harm for the vast majority of the world's population. And indeed, within the markets in which they operate, corporations are much more vulnerable to public opinion and therefore powerless than is often thought. (This, incidentally, was one of the surprising messages that I got from reading Naomi Klein's 2000 book, *No Logo*, though probably not the message that she intended.)

But it is also true that much that is wrong with the world trading system reflects the influence of private-sector actors on the public sector, including especially some of the international rules and the actions of international organisations. Such influence has been wielded to some extent by the labour movement and by NGOs, but at least until recently I think it is clear that it has been wielded far more by corporations. For all of these groups, the influence is sometimes good and sometimes bad, but because it by definition reflects special interests, not general interests, one cannot count on it being beneficial.

So the result of my reading is now that I am much more attuned than I was before to the role that special interests, including but not limited to corporations,

[8] This is not because of any personal corporate connections. Neither I, nor any of my forebears that I know of, have owned any capital to speak of, except perhaps for my pension holding in TIAA-CREF. Nor have we worked in any capacity for corporations. I really don't know why I take this view.

play in the setting of international economic policies and in the writing of the international rules under which such policies are conducted. I suggest that others like myself should become similarly attuned.

REFERENCES

Bagwell, K. and R. W. Staiger (1999), 'An Economic Theory of GATT,' *American Economic Review*, **89**, 215–48.

Cowie, J. (1999), *Capital Moves: RCA's Seventy-Year Quest for Cheap Labor* (New York: The New Press).

Deardorff, A. V. (1985), 'Comparative Advantage and International Trade and Investment in Services,' in R. M. Stern (ed.), *Trade and Investment in Services: Canada/US Perspectives* (Toronto: Ontario Economic Council), 39–71.

Deardorff, A. V. (1990), 'Should Patent Protection Be Extended to All Developing Countries?' *The World Economy*, **13**, 4, 497–507.

Deardorff, A. V. (1992), 'Welfare Effects of Global Patent Protection,' *Economica*, **59**, 35–51.

Deardorff, A. V. and R. L. Hall (1998), 'Explaining the Role of Interest Groups in United States Trade Policy,' *Social Sciences Electronic Library* (Social Science Electronic Publishing, Inc.).

Elliot, K. A., D. Kar and J. D. Richardson (2002), 'Assessing Globalization's Critics: "Talkers Are No Good Doers???"' (Washington, DC: Institute for International Economics).

Greider, W. (1997), *One World, Ready or Not: The Manic Logic of Global Capitalism* (New York: Simon & Schuster).

Klein, N. (2000), *No Logo* (London: Flamingo).

Oxfam (2000), 'Globalization,' Submission to the UK Government's White Paper on Globalization, May (http://www.oxfam.org.uk/policy/papers/global/global1a.htm).

Rodrik, D. (1997), *Has Globalization Gone Too Far*? (Washington, DC: Institute for International Economics).

Stiglitz, J. (2002), *Globalization and its Discontents* (London: Penguin).

World Development Vol. 34, No. 8, pp. 1419–1429, 2006

0305-750X/$ - see front matter

ELSEVIER
www.elsevier.com/locate/worlddev

doi:10.1016/j.worlddev.2005.10.012

Globalization's Bystanders: Does Trade Liberalization Hurt Countries That Do Not Participate?

ROBERT M. STERN and ALAN V. DEARDORFF *
University of Michigan, Ann Arbor, USA

Summary. — This paper uses trade theory to examine the effects of trade liberalization on countries that do not participate in it. These include both countries that fail to participate in multilateral trade negotiations, and also countries that lie outside of preferential trading arrangements such as free trade areas. The analysis suggests that, while it is theoretically possible for excluded countries to gain from trade liberalization through improved terms of trade, several reasons suggest that they are more likely to lose.

Key words — globalization, trade liberalization, free trade, preferential trade, tariffs, participation

1. INTRODUCTION

Globalization has many meanings, and many effects. Here we will focus on only one of each: globalization as the reduction in barriers to international trade, and its effect on the countries that, for whatever reason, do not themselves participate in that process. It is often observed by proponents of globalization that, while not all countries have prospered during the recent upsurge in global integration, most of the countries that have failed to prosper, especially in Africa, have been distinctive in the extent to which they have remained relatively closed off from world markets. The supposed implications are that these countries, had they embraced trade liberalization, would have done better, and that, while trade liberalization by others has perhaps not helped these countries due to their own reluctance to participate, it has not hurt them either. They have only hurt themselves.

In this paper, we use the tools of international trade theory to examine especially the second of these implications. How has trade liberalization by the larger part of the world's economy affected those countries that have not participated? Have they, perhaps, benefited from trade liberalization in spite of their outsider status, as free riders? Or have they instead been harmed by trade liberalization, made worse off than if trade liberalization had not occurred?

For the sake of argument, we will divide the world's countries into just two types: the "included" countries and the "excluded." The included countries are those that have substantially lowered their barriers to international trade, perhaps as part of the trade liberalization fostered by the General Agreement on Tariffs and Trade (GATT) and now the World Trade Organization (WTO), and/or perhaps through preferential trading arrangements (PTAs) such as the European Union (EU) and the North American Free Trade Agreement (NAFTA). The excluded countries are those that have stayed out of PTAs and have either failed to join the GATT/WTO or who have joined but have taken such advantage of the provision for "special and differential treatment" that their trade barriers have remained high. For the most part, these excluded countries have remained in that category through their own choice (their governments', that is) and not because the included countries would not have welcomed their participation in trade liberalization.

In principle, presumably, a country could cut itself off completely from world markets, and thus achieve an extreme form of this excluded

* Final revision accepted: October 20, 2005.

status. From the perspective of the analysis here, such a country could not be hurt by globalization, since it would not be aware of it, except perhaps through non-economic mechanisms that we will not examine, such as trans-border pollution. Instead, the excluded countries that we will consider are engaged to some extent with world markets, exporting and importing at a moderate rate that is subject to trade barriers that are high, but that are not all prohibitive. It is the fact that they trade at all that makes them vulnerable to the effects of trade liberalization by others, since it may change their terms of this trade. Indeed, it is the effect of trade liberalization on an excluded country's terms of trade that will be the sole concern of this paper, and we will examine this effect through several quite standard theoretical models of international trade. There are, of course, other ways that a country could potentially be affected by another country's trade liberalization, other than through the terms of trade. But these other mechanisms are less well understood both theoretically and empirically, so we will only say a few words about them, in the concluding section of the paper.

In Section 2, we take our first two passes at the question by using one of the oldest tools of international trade theory: the offer curve. From this we will see first how an excluded country might easily be expected to benefit, not lose, from trade liberalization by other countries. But on more careful inspection, the same tool will suggest that such a benefit is conditional on the relative extent of liberalization by two subsets of the other countries: those who export the same good as the excluded country, and those who import it. Indeed, much depends on the degree to which the included countries reduce their tariffs on the good or goods of export interest to the excluded country.

In Section 3, instead of simply taking as given the tariff cuts of included countries, we then ask in which sectors these tariff cuts are likely to occur. A simple "political economy" model suggests that tariffs are not likely to be cut on the products that excluded countries happen to export, thus making it more likely that they will lose from trade liberalization by other countries. This theoretical result is of course motivated by the common observation that developing countries today face higher tariffs than developed countries, a fact that, on this interpretation, can be attributed to the developing countries' own collective choice to exclude themselves from trade liberalization.

In both of Sections 2 and 3, we assume that, when included countries do lower their tariffs on particular goods, they do it on imports from all other countries, even the excluded ones. That is, this trade liberalization is done, in the WTO's language, on an MFN (most favored country) basis. This is of course required by the WTO for imports from any countries that are themselves members of the WTO, and in fact, although it is not required, it seems to be fairly commonly done even for most excluded countries that are not members. The United States, for example, gives MFN status to almost every country in the world, even though it does not have to do this under WTO rules. [1] The results in Sections 2 and 3, therefore, show that excluded countries may be hurt by trade liberalization of other countries, even though they remain subject to the same tariffs as everybody else.

In fact, however, they do not. Increasingly in recent years, countries who wish to participate in trade liberalization have done so not just through the MFN liberalization of the WTO, but also through PTAs negotiated among pairs or small groups of countries. In Section 4, therefore, we examine the additional harm that is likely to be done to excluded countries if a significant part of trade liberalization takes this form.

In Section 5, we conclude by trying to extract some policy implications from all of this. Since nothing in our analysis contradicts the traditional presumption from trade theory that trade liberalization is beneficial for the world as a whole, we certainly would not conclude that this aspect of globalization should be stopped, or even slowed down. But the harm that it may do to excluded countries needs to be recognized, and greater efforts need to be made to deal with it. The most obvious way to do that, of course, would simply be to include these countries more fully in trade liberalization.

2. WHEN CAN A COUNTRY FREE RIDE?

The simplest analysis of the effect of one country's liberalization on another is provided by offer curves. Suppose there are two countries, A and E, where E will be the "excluded country" throughout the analysis in this section. Both countries produce and trade two goods, X and Y. If E exports good X, then its

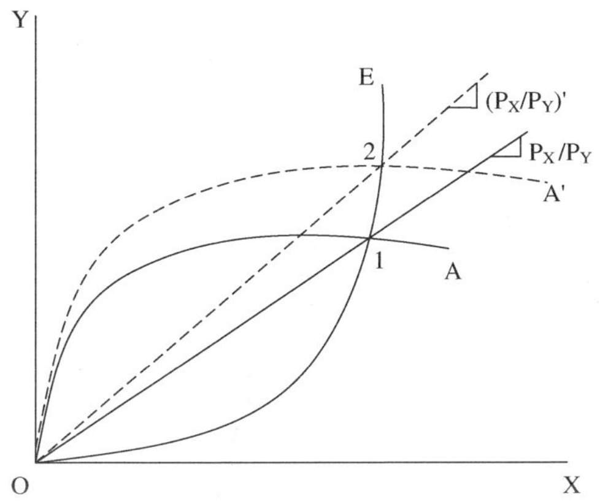

Figure 1. *The excluded country, E, gains when the rest of the world, A, liberalizes.*

offer curve is something like *OE* in Figure 1, showing the quantities of *X* that it is willing to export in exchange for various quantities imported of good *Y*. The slope of any line from the origin to the curve is the relative price of good *X*. The curve *OE* indicates that country *E* will import more of good *Y* only if it gets a higher relative price for its export of good *X*, or equivalently, if it pays a lower relative price for its import of good *Y*. The curve also suggests that a higher relative price of *X* will elicit more exports from country *E*, although from the curvature it is possible that beyond some point a further increase in price will cause exports to fall. The reason is that a rise in the relative price of *X* is an improvement in country *E*'s terms of trade, implying that its real income rises, and it may choose to use this income to consume more of both goods, thus possibly exporting less. In any case, it is this improvement in the terms of trade that we will be looking for, to see whether country *E* may benefit from liberalization elsewhere.

If *E* were itself engaged in free trade, then we could easily use trade indifference curves [2] to indicate the level of welfare within country *E*, since these would be tangent to any price line from the origin where it crosses the offer curve. However, since our interest is in a country that certainly does not have zero tariffs, this cannot be done. Nonetheless, because a tariff reduces a country's imports below what would be optimal, a rise in its terms of trade that permits it to import more will always improve its welfare. Therefore, it will be enough, in order to infer effects on country *E*'s welfare, to see what happens to its terms of trade.

In Figure 1, country *E* engages in trade with a single other country, *A*, which is an exporter of the other good, *Y*. Initially country *A*, like *E*, has a tariff on its imports of good *X*. Then, for whatever reason (perhaps because it newly recognizes the gains from trade), it reduces that tariff. The effect, familiar from offer-curve analysis, is to shift *A*'s offer curve outward, away from the origin, as shown, to *OA'*. Equilibrium moves from point 1 to point 2 in the figure, and the terms of trade of the excluded country *E* improve. Thus the excluded country benefits from country *A*'s liberalization.

Of course, if the world really contained only these two countries, then one might wonder whether country *A* would really liberalize to this extent, since the improvement in *E*'s terms of trade is a worsening of *A*'s. For this reason, country *A*, if it were sensible, might not reduce its tariff to zero, since doing so would cause it to forego some of the benefits of levying a monopoly tariff, which, given country *E*'s continuing protection, there is no reason for it not to use. But if *A* previously had a tariff above the monopoly level, then it could gain by a tariff reduction, and country *E*, as shown, would gain along with it. In any case, as we now consider a world with a larger number of countries, such monopoly-tariff considerations become less relevant.

For the two-country case it is hardly what we want to see. In practice, our excluded country confronts a large world of a great many countries, all of whom may be liberalizing. If we can think of the foreign offer curve, *OA*, as representing the aggregate of all those countries, then Figure 1 suggests a much more relevant gain for the excluded country *E* as a free rider on global liberalization. It must of course be true that, since *E* is an exporter of good *X*, the rest of the world must in aggregate be a net importer of good *X*, and therefore the world's offer curve does indeed look something like *OA*. Since trade liberalization by any country must cause its offer curve to expand outward, Figure 1 may seem to guarantee that, in fact, excluded countries can only gain from the rest of the world's liberalization.

That is not the case, however. While it is true that individual country offer curves expand with their liberalization, and it is also true that any group of countries may be represented by an aggregate offer curve that is, in effect, their sum, it is *not* true that trade liberalization by those countries necessarily expands the aggregate offer curve outward. Suppose, for example, that the rest of the world consists of just two countries, one that exports *Y* and the other that imports it. If the latter imports less than the former exports, the offer curve of the two together will look like *OA* in Figure 1. But if now only the second of these two countries were to lower its tariff (on *Y*, since that is what it imports), it would import more *Y* and thus reduce, not expand, the amount that the two together export. The aggregate offer curve would shift inward.

To correctly identify the effect of liberalization on world markets, then, we need to separate countries with different trade patterns. This is done in Figure 2, where for convenience we now take the excluded country *E* to be very small compared to others, as suggested by drawing its offer curve, *OE*, 100 times its actual size. The rest of the world then consists of two countries, *A* that exports *Y* and *B* that exports *X*. In the initial equilibrium at point 1, world prices are determined (since country *E* is negligibly small) by the offer curves *OA* and *OB*. Now, as *A* and *B* both reduce their tariffs, both offer curves expand outward by some amounts, perhaps to *OA′* and *OB′*, and the new equilibrium is at point 2. As drawn, the terms of trade of country *E* worsens. It is hurt by the rest of the world's liberalization. [3]

What determines this result? Most simply, country *E* (as an exporter of *X*) will be hurt

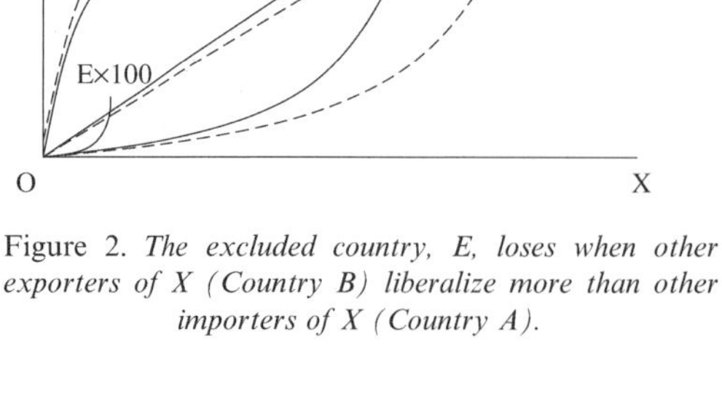

Figure 2. *The excluded country, E, loses when other exporters of X (Country B) liberalize more than other importers of X (Country A).*

if, at initial prices, those countries that are also net exporters of *X* expand their trade more than those countries that are net importers of *X*. This in turn depends, though only in part, on the sizes of the two groups of countries' tariff reductions. If the *X*-exporters, whose relevant tariffs are on *Y*, reduce their tariffs more than the *Y*-exporters, whose relevant tariffs are on *X*, then other things equal we may expect country *E* to lose. Conversely, in order for country *E* to free ride on others' liberalization, it needs greater reductions in tariffs on what it exports than on what it imports. This is not exactly right, even in this simple two-good case, since countries may differ for various reasons in the extent to which their quantities of trade respond to tariff reductions. But as a first approximation in ignorance of these other determinants of trade, what matters is these two sets of tariff reductions.

It is obvious why the excluded country gains from others' reductions in their tariffs on its exports. These cause increases in demand for its export good on world markets and thus increase its world price. But why do other countries' tariff cuts on its imports matter at all? The answer is that these tariff cuts cause world prices of the imports to rise, reducing what the excluded country can get in exchange for its exports. In a two good model, there really is no difference between a rise in export prices and fall in import prices, and the same is true with many goods if one looks at appropriate indexes of the prices of both. However, in the real world, people seldom do look at such indexes, and the public and political perception of the effects of export prices and import prices may be quite different. We will look next at a model that allows for this.

3. WHICH TARIFFS WILL FALL WITH MULTILATERAL LIBERALIZATION?

The aim of this section is to argue what may seem obvious: that countries that do not themselves participate in tariff liberalization are likely to find that other countries do not reduce tariffs on their exports. Obvious or not, this does not follow easily from the simple welfare economics of tariffs, which says that the gain to importing countries from lowering their own tariffs does not depend on whether other countries do. Except for terms-of-trade motivations in large countries—which some, though not all, regard as implausible motivators for trade policies—the rest-of-world will always benefit from lowering its tariffs on a country's products, even if that country keeps its own tariffs high. Of course, the same reasoning implies that we should already see tariffs close to zero in most of the world, which we do not, and which we certainly did not see prior to the liberalizations undertaken under the GATT/WTO.

To answer this question, then, we must have some sort of model of the political economy of trade policy. Such models have been built and increasingly refined in the trade literature, with early efforts by Findlay and Wellisz (1982), Mayer (1984), and Hillman (1989), whose approaches were then integrated successfully by Grossman and Helpman (1994). For the purpose here, however, a much simpler framework will suffice, one that could perhaps be viewed as a simplification of the Grossman and Helpman model.

The true welfare effects of a tariff reduction include the following, as a simple partial equilibrium model would suggest: a gain to domestic consumers; a loss (of tariff revenue) to the domestic government; a loss to import-competing domestic producers; and—if the size of the importing country is large enough for the tariff cut to raise the world price of the good—a gain to foreign producers and a loss to foreign consumers. In a world where the tariff was the only prior distortion, it is well known that the sum of these effects must be positive—that is, the world as a whole gains from a tariff cut. The importing country alone also gains if it is small enough such that the world price is unaffected, but it may not gain if the worsening of its terms of trade outweighs the efficiency gain.

All of this may be beside the point, however, if political forces favor some constituencies over others, as seems to be the case given that virtually all countries, and especially many small ones, have had positive and often quite high tariffs throughout history. The political economy literature explains this by allowing producers to exert special influence on trade policy, by one means or another. Grossman and Helpman, in particular, model producers as contributing financially to incumbent politicians in return for their providing or maintaining tariff protection. The politicians, in turn take account of both the contributions that they receive and also broad economic welfare in making their policy decisions.

Here, however, we will assume instead that policy makers in most countries are concerned *only* about producer welfare, ignoring completely any gains or losses to consumers and, in most cases, ignoring also any effects of tariff revenues. This could perhaps be justified along the lines of Grossman and Helpman as an extreme case of putting all weight on the contributions that politicians receive. However it could also be motivated less cynically by observing that the gains and losses to producers, very much including their employees, are much easier to see than the gains and losses to consumers. Also, because they tend to be concentrated on small groups in the population, the severity of effects on producers is evident, while the effects on individual consumers may be dismissed as too small to worry about. As for also ignoring tariff revenues, that would be a dubious assumption in a country where tariffs provide the bulk of government revenues, and we will bring it back into the analysis for such countries below. But in advanced countries with many other (and more efficient) revenue generating opportunities, it seems plausible that these revenues might also play only a negligible role.

In order to incorporate this simple assumption into a correspondingly simple model, we follow Grossman and Helpman in assuming that preferences are "quasi-linear" so that, except in a numeraire sector in which we always assume free trade, demand in each country for each good depends only on its price relative to the numeraire. And we go even further than Grossman and Helpman on the production side. They assumed specific factors in each sector, with labor being mobile among sectors. We assume that *all* factors are specific, so that output in each sector in each country is simply fixed. We also follow Grossman and Helpman in assuming that all goods are only final goods, so that there are no imported intermediate inputs. That is an important limiting assumption, as we will note.

Suppose, then, that there are C countries, $c = 1, \ldots, C$, and $G + 1$ goods, $g = 0, 1, \ldots, G$, with good zero the aforementioned numeraire. All countries share the same demand functions for the non-numeraire goods, $D_{gc} = 1 - p_{gc}$, $g = 1, \ldots, G$, so that trade patterns depend only on differences across countries in exogenous production levels. These take either of the two values, a low value $\underline{X}_g$ in countries that will be importing the good, and a high value $\overline{X}_g$ in countries that will be exporting it.

Although we will assume there is some trade, even before any liberalization, it is worth noting the autarky prices that would follow from these production levels and demands: Countries with low production have a high autarky price, denoted $\tilde{p}_g = 1 - \overline{X}_g$, while countries with high production have a low autarky price, $\tilde{\tilde{p}}_g = 1 - \overline{\overline{X}}_g < \tilde{p}_g$. Let $\overline{S}^C_g = \{c|X_{gc} = \overline{X}_g\}$ be the set of all countries with low production of good g and $\overline{N}^C_g = \left(\sum_{c\in\overline{S}^C_g} 1\right)$ be the number of those countries; define $\overline{\overline{S}}^C_g$, $\overline{\overline{N}}^C_g$ analogously. And let $\overline{S}^G_c = \{g|X_{gc} = \overline{X}_g\}$ be the set of all goods that country c produces in small quantity; $\overline{N}^G_c$ the number of those goods; and $\overline{\overline{S}}^G_c$, $\overline{\overline{N}}^G_C$ analogously.

Initially, we let all countries have the same *ad valorem* tariff on a good, t^0_g, which is assumed small enough to permit trade: $t^0_g < (\tilde{p}_g - \tilde{\tilde{p}}_g)/\tilde{\tilde{p}}_g$. In the initial equilibrium denoted as "0", exporters receive a world price p^{W0}_g while importers pay a higher importer's price, $p^{M0}_g = (1 + t^0_g)p^{W0}_g$, both of which are determined by the requirement that demands, at these prices, add up to production:

$$\overline{\overline{N}}^C_g(1 - p^{W0}_g) + \overline{N}^C_g(1 - (1 + t^0_g)p^{W0}_g) = \overline{\overline{N}}^C_g\overline{\overline{X}}_g + \overline{N}^C_g\overline{X}_g, \quad (1)$$

from which

$$p^{W0}_g = \frac{\overline{\overline{N}}^C_g\tilde{\tilde{p}}_g + \overline{N}^C_g\tilde{p}_g}{C + t^0_g\overline{N}^C_g}. \quad (2)$$

Now consider the possibility of all countries moving to free trade, denoted "F", in all sectors. The world price—given by (2) but with t^0_g replaced by zero—is then simply the average of the two autarky prices with weights equal to the fraction of countries with each. Relevant to the choice—of whether or not to make this move to free trade—is the change in producer welfare. Since production is fixed, this is simply

$$\Delta\pi^F_{gc} = (p^{WF}_g - p^0_{gc})X_{gc}, \quad (3)$$

where p^0_{gc} and X_{gc} are to be replaced by p^{W0}_g and $\overline{\overline{X}}_g$ for an exporter and by p^{M0}_g and $\overline{X}_g$ for an importer. Letting

$$\delta_{gc} = \begin{cases} 1 & \text{if } c \in \overline{S}^C_g, \\ 0 & \text{if } c \in \overline{\overline{S}}^C_g \end{cases} \quad (4)$$

indicate that country c imports good g, it turns out that

$$\Delta\pi^F_{gc} = \frac{p^{WF}_g X^0_{gc} t^0_g}{C + t^0_g\overline{N}^C_g}\left(\overline{N}^C_g - \delta_{gc}C\right). \quad (5)$$

Thus, as one would expect, looking only at producers' welfare, the move to free trade in one sector causes exporters to gain and importers to lose. [4] It is easily confirmed, however, that the sum of these changes across all countries is positive, simply because individual exporters produce more than individual import-competitors. Summing (5) across all countries yields:

$$\sum_c \Delta\pi^F_{gc} = \frac{p^{WF}_g t^0_g \overline{N}^C_g \overline{\overline{N}}^C_g}{C + t^0_g\overline{N}^C_g}(\overline{\overline{X}}_g - \overline{X}_g) > 0. \quad (6)$$

Thus even from the perspective of producers alone, the world as a whole benefits from a move to free trade.

Individual countries may not gain in this sense, however. Certainly they lose in particular sectors if they are importers and a positive tariff is reduced, since that hurts their competing producers. It is true that if positive tariffs are reduced by all countries in all sectors, then a country is likely to have export-sector producers who gain at the same time that import-competing producers lose. But there is no guarantee that the gain to the former is larger, for a given country, than the loss to the latter. In an extreme case, a country could be an importer of every good other than the numeraire, in which case it would have no producers who gain. And even if we require a plausible mix of export and import sectors outside the numeraire, if a country happens to export only in sectors with a large number of other exporting countries, then its exporters will gain little from the liberalization. Thus there may well be countries that stand to lose, from this producers-only perspective, from a multilateral move to free trade. Such countries would presumably not participate in such a move. [5]

Thus an actual liberalization, if it occurs in this framework, is likely to include only a subset of the world's countries: a group of countries for whom MFN [6] tariff reductions benefit their export-sector producers more than they harm their import-competing producers. Of course, by not including tariff reductions by countries outside that group, the gains to the former are likely to be smaller than if all countries had moved together to free trade. But this may be offset by the included group simply not reducing tariffs on products that its members do not export.

Note that in this framework, a country would never unilaterally reduce its tariffs. [7] To do so would provide no benefit at all to its exporters, and only harm its import competitors. So for MFN liberalization to occur, countries must find others who are willing to reduce their tariffs as well, so as to create benefits for their exporters. Whether such willing participants can be found is uncertain. It depends on the patterns of comparative advantage across countries.

Suppose, to take a simple example where limited liberalization can succeed, that there are two or more goods that importing countries do not produce at all. Then a group of countries who export different ones of these goods will necessarily benefit, as producers, if they agree to reduce tariffs on these goods alone, since the export-sector producers in each will gain from the others' tariff reductions, and they will not have any import-competing producers who will lose. Thus we know that there may exist a group of countries that will willingly reduce their tariffs on a set of goods. On the other hand, suppose that all countries but one are importers of all goods except the numeraire, on which by assumption all have zero tariffs. Then there will not exist any group of countries willing to reduce tariffs at all.

The important point, however, is the following. Suppose that there does exist a set of countries, S^C, that would be willing to reduce tariffs on a set of goods, S^G. And suppose that any good within S^G is exported only by countries not in S^C. Then producers in the countries of S^C will gain at least as much by excluding that good from S^G as by including it, and they will gain strictly more if any of them produce this good. Thus in this model we should not expect multilateral liberalization by a subset of the world's countries, if it occurs, to include goods that are exported only by countries outside that group. Again, of course, this would not be the case if consumer welfare were to be taken fully into account. [8]

If the outside countries export goods that are also exported by some of the inside countries, then producers in the latter would lose if these goods were removed from S^G. Their governments might still accept this exclusion, however, if they have other export producers who gain sufficiently.

The conclusion from this section, then, is that excluded countries are *not* likely to benefit from MFN liberalization by other countries, simply because these other countries are not likely to reduce tariffs on the goods of greatest export interest to the excluded countries. Somewhat ironically, this would not be the case if a particular excluded country were very similar, in its pattern of trade, to the countries that are liberalizing. But it is certain to be true if the excluded countries are distinctly different from the included ones, as perhaps by being less economically developed.

One might wonder how large these adverse effects may be. Unfortunately we are not in a position to answer that question for the countries where it is most relevant, where a detailed study of their particular exports and imports would be needed, together with estimates of the effects of liberalization on corresponding prices. A hint of what might be found, however, can be obtained from studies of trade liberalization using computable general equilibrium (CGE) models. In Brown, Deardorff, and Stern (2003), for example, we calculated the effects of the Uruguay Round tariff reductions on the terms of trade of some twenty countries and groups of countries. We found that while the terms of trade improved for most developed parts of the world, terms of trade worsened in most of the developing world, including declines of about 1% in India, Sri Lanka, the Rest of South Asia, and the Philippines.

4. PREFERENTIAL TRADE LIBERALIZATION

So far we have considered only MFN liberalization. But an increasing amount of trade liberalization in recent years has taken the form of PTAs. In these arrangements, as required by the WTO, the liberalization is typically more extreme, with tariffs reduced further and on more goods than may be covered in a multilateral WTO agreement. They are, however, discriminatory. Countries that are not part of a particular PTA continue to be subject to what are still called the MFN tariffs of the PTA countries, although the MFN name is now insidiously misleading. Countries outside a PTA are not being treated as well as the "most favored country" at all, but instead have their exports to countries within the PTA taxed at a higher rate than is applied to exports from other member countries.

The literature on PTAs, starting with Viner's (1950) analysis of customs unions and continuing today, emphasizes the positive and negative effects that arise from "trade creation" and "trade diversion." This seems to suggest that if the former somehow outweighs the latter, then the PTA is beneficial. That may be true for the countries inside the PTA, and perhaps even for the world as a whole. But it is very unlikely to be true for the countries that remain outside the PTA. For them trade creation is largely irrelevant, while trade diversion represents a loss. That is, when a PTA causes a member country to import from a partner rather than from an outside country, that constitutes a fall in demand for the product of the outside country. If the affected trade flow is large enough to matter at all, then this will cause a fall in the world price of the imported good and a worsening of the terms of trade of the outside country.

This does not have to happen. PTAs can take several forms, in particular with regard to the tariffs that the countries levy on trade from outside. If these tariffs are low enough, then the countries of the PTA may continue to trade with the rest of the world as much as they did before. Kemp and Wan (1976), for example, showed that a customs union could set a common external tariff that would keep net imports of every good from the rest of the world unchanged, thus assuring no impact at all on the well being of the rest of the world. [9] However, if external tariffs are not changed when the PTA is formed, as is usually the case in a free trade area (FTA), then the fact that the preferences favor trade with partners over trade with outside countries suggests that trade with the rest of the world is likely to fall.

If that happens, then the effect on the excluded countries is exactly like Figure 1 in reverse. That is, the collective offer curve of the countries of the FTA before it is formed is OA', and formation of the FTA shifts it inward to OA, causing a worsening of the excluded country's terms of trade.

Even with an FTA and unchanged external tariffs, this is not a necessary outcome, although it seems far more likely than the alternative. For example, in a two-good model, suppose that the FTA includes countries A and B which import goods X and Y respectively, over positive tariffs. When they eliminate these tariffs on trade with each other, at the initial world price each will import from the other instead of from the outside world, as long as each can supply all of the other's needs at a price differing from the world price by less than the tariff. If this is the case, then whatever may have been the two-countries' combined trade with the world before the FTA, this trade shrinks to zero in its presence. Only if the countries differ in size by enough such that one of them cannot meet the other's demands at such a price, will the two together continue to trade with the world at the initial price. And even then it is likely that their combined net trade will shrink. [10,11]

Thus, while exceptions do seem to be possible, on the whole it appears that preferential liberalization is even more likely to be harmful than multilateral liberalization to those countries that do not participate in it. Note that this does not require that trade diversion somehow outweigh trade diversion, but only that it occurs at all. The same conclusion can also be obtained by different means in different models. Brown, Kiyota, and Stern (2005), for example, used a CGE model to calculate the effects of a Free Trade Agreement of the Americas and found that the elimination of tariffs on manufactures in such an FTA would improve the welfare of all the participating countries and regions but lower welfare in all but two of the 16 non-participating countries and regions that were included in their model. Using a different economic mechanism, Chang and Winters (2002) argue (and support empirically, with data from MERCOSUR) that preferential liberalization favoring one of two Bertrand competitors will cause the unfavored firm to lower its export price. No doubt there are many other mechanisms that could work as well.

5. CONCLUSION

This analysis suggests that, although it is not inevitable, it is strongly likely that excluded countries will be hurt by trade liberalization undertaken by other countries. It may be true that, if tariff reductions are MFN on products that are selected at random, then an excluded country has as good a chance of gaining from them as of losing. But MFN tariff reductions have not in practice been in randomly selected sectors, but rather in sectors in which the tariff-reducing countries stand most to gain as exporters. Thus MFN tariffs are unlikely to be cut on products that are primarily exported by the excluded countries. Furthermore, much of the trade liberalization that has occurred in recent years has been preferential, not MFN. While preferential liberalization usually covers (almost) all products, its discriminatory nature means that it tends to divert trade away from excluded countries and thereby makes them worse off by moving their terms of trade against them.

The models here have focused only on these terms-of-trade effects because these are well understood and amenable to static analysis. There may well be other, perhaps more important, effects than these that should be considered, but it seems likely that they would act in the same direction. Consider for example the "dynamic gains from trade" that are often mentioned as augmenting the benefits from trade as in Baldwin (1992). One such source of dynamic gains might arise from economies of scale that allow some industries' costs to fall over time as they expand production. To the extent that other countries' trade liberalization reduces demand for an excluded country's exports, this will undermine not only its terms of trade but also its ability to take advantage of such dynamic scale economies in export industries. Or consider the alternative possibility that technology flows follow trade flows, permitting countries to tap into the technological advances that are occurring in other countries, as in Coe and Helpman (1995). Here too, if excluded countries find their trade with such countries reduced, they may suffer an ever widening gap between their technologies and those at the frontier. No doubt other mechanisms could be suggested as well that lie outside the simple models looked at here, but it seems likely that all would build on sources of gain from trade that are lost when excluded countries have their volumes of trade reduced.

Note that these losses from trade liberalization occur only because the excluded countries do in fact trade. The effects analyzed here all work through the terms of trade, and a country would be immune from them if it did not trade at all. But this is no reason not to trade, for these losses all represent a reduction of their gains from trade, not a reduction of welfare to below what it would have been in autarky. Thus the excluded countries would be ill-advised to exclude themselves even further from world markets as a means of avoiding these losses. It will not work.

Nor is it a reason for trade liberalization itself to be restrained, at least not in its MFN manifestation. As should be clear from this analysis, the reason that excluded countries may lose from trade liberalization is that the liberalization does not go far enough, not that it goes too far. It is the exclusion of some sectors and/or some exporting countries from the benefits of tariff cuts that creates a bias against excluded countries.

Thus the best chance of avoiding these losses to excluded countries is simply not to exclude them. Or, if they cannot be persuaded to participate, we need to find a mechanism for cutting tariffs that will work across all sectors instead of favoring only the export sectors of the participating countries.

The current multilateral trade negotiations of the Doha Development Agenda show promising signs of doing exactly this. Developing countries are playing a more active role than ever before, at least in pressing the developed countries to reduce trade barriers in sectors that are of export interest to them. At the same time, developed countries are insisting that the developing countries also participate more than they have before by reducing their own tariffs. If both of these outcomes can be achieved, developing countries—at least those who participate—will stand to gain substantially. Even those countries that remain outside the WTO may gain from this, to the extent that tariffs are reduced on their exports as well.

Preferential liberalization, in the form of proliferating FTAs, poses a more difficult problem. If this proliferation does not abate, there are only two ways that an excluded country may hope to avoid being harmed by it. One is to join in and negotiate FTAs of its own with as many partners as it can. Unfortunately, the poorer a country is, the less likely it is that others will have any interest in negotiating with it. And even if FTAs were to be formed including all possible pairings or groupings of countries, the administrative complications of conforming to all of their rules would put the poorest countries at a disadvantage.

The other route toward lessening the harm from preferential liberalization, as it affects excluded countries, is for nondiscriminatory liberalization to render preferences meaningless. If MFN tariffs were all zero, then any FTA would be both unnecessary and ineffective. Thus the best cure for the side effects of preferential trade liberalization is nondiscriminatory trade liberalization.

NOTES

1. There are only two or three exceptions, including Cuba and North Korea. MFN status for China was of course a matter of annual controversy before China joined the WTO, but in practice, in spite of threats to withdraw it, China regularly had its MFN status renewed.

2. See Meade (1952).

3. If country *E* were not small, then its supply and demand in the international market would have to be taken into account in determining the new equilibrium world price. This would not change the conclusion, however, since this would only reduce the size of the change in price, not reverse its direction.

4. If we allowed for traded intermediate inputs, it would not be this simple. A local producer could benefit from a tariff cut on its input.

5. In addition, the assumption here that governments care only about producers, and not even about their own revenues, is particularly questionable in poor countries where tariff revenues may bulk large in government budgets. Such countries, even if their export-sector producers would gain more from liberalization than their import-competitors would lose, might opt out of liberalization for that reason.

6. We will look at preferential agreements in the next section.

7. Again, this need not be the case if there are traded intermediate inputs. Indeed, a tariff on any input that is only imported and not produced domestically would be eliminated based on the interests of producers that use it.

8. On the other hand, allowing the government to care about tariff revenues would only make the point stronger.

9. Panagariya and Krishna (2000) showed a similar result for free trade areas.

10. However, this does not seem to be inevitable. In analysis not included here, it appears to be possible to construct a case where opposite income effects in the two FTA countries cause an increase in their net trade with the world.

11. Another case would have both of the FTA members importing the same good from the world. If their tariffs are the same, then the FTA has no effect on this trade. But if their tariffs are different, then as pointed out by Richardson (1995), the high-tariff country will import as much as possible from the low-tariff country, which will expand its imports to replace those of the high-tariff country. In this case, too, net trade of the two may expand since, in effect, the tariff of the high-tariff country is rendered irrelevant.

REFERENCES

Baldwin, R. E. (1992). Measurable dynamic gains from trade. *Journal of Political Economy, 100*, 162–174.

Brown, D. K., Deardorff, A. V., & Stern, R. M. (2003). Computational analysis of multilateral trade liberalization in the Uruguay Round and Doha development round. In A. Mattoo, & R. M. Stern (Eds.). *India and the WTO* (pp. 13–46). Washington, DC: World Bank and Oxford University Press.

Brown, D. K., Kiyota, K., & Stern, R. M. (2005). Computational analysis of the free trade area of the Americas (FTAA). *North American Journal of Economics and Finance, 16*(August), 153–185.

Chang, W., & Winters, L. A. (2002). How regional blocs affect excluded countries: The price effects of MERCOSUR. *American Economic Review, 92*(4), 889–904.

Coe, D. T., & Helpman, E. (1995). International R&D spillovers. *European Economic Review, 39*(May), 859–887.

Findlay, R., & Wellisz, S. (1982). Endogenous tariffs, the political economy of trade restrictions, and welfare. In J. Bhagwati (Ed.). *Import competition and response*. Chicago: University of Chicago Press.

Grossman, G. M., & Helpman, E. (1994). Protection for sale. *American Economic Review, 84*(September), 833–850.

Hillman, A. L. (1989). *The political economy of protection*. London: Harwood.

Kemp, M. C., & Wan, H. Y. Jr., (1976). An elementary proposition concerning the formation of customs unions. In M. Kemp (Ed.). *Three topics in the theory of international trade: Distribution, welfare, and uncertainty*. Amsterdam: North Holland.

Mayer, W. (1984). Endogenous tariff formation. *American Economic Review, 74*, 970–985.

Meade, J. E. (1952). *A geometry of international trade*. London: Unwin.

Panagariya, A., & Krishna, P. (2000). On necessarily welfare-enhancing free trade areas. *Journal of International Economics, 57*, 353–367.

Richardson, M. (1995). Tariff revenue competition in a free trade area. *European Economic Review, 39*, 1429–1437.

Viner, J. (1950). *The customs union issue*. New York: Carnegie Endowment for International Peace.

CHAPTER 32

Who Makes the Rules of Globalization? Corporate Influence in Global and Regional Trade Agreements†

Alan V. Deardorff*
The University of Michigan

ABSTRACT

In this paper I argue that profit maximizing firms, even though they contribute to social welfare when they compete in the market, may not do so when they influence the political process. In particular, I suggest, through several examples from both the real world and from economic theory, that corporations have played a significant role in the formulation of the rules of the international trading system. They did this in the formation of the WTO, where they were responsible for the expansion to cover both intellectual property and services. And they do this in preferential trading arrangements such as the NAFTA, where they inserted the notorious Chapter 11 and specified rules of origin for automotive products. All of this is quite consistent with economic theory, including the literature on the political economy of trade policy. I also use a simple duopoly model to illustrate a domestic firm's interest in setting rules of origin. The corporate influence on rules need not be bad, but there is no reason why it should be good either, as these examples illustrate.

Keywords: Political economy of trade
Trade institutions

JEL Subject Code: F13 Commercial Policy

Correspondence:

Alan V. Deardorff
Department of Economics
University of Michigan
Ann Arbor, MI 48109-1220

Tel. 734-764-6817
Fax. 734-763-9181
E-mail: alandear@umich.edu
http://www-personal.umich.edu/~alandear/

† Paper presented at CESifo, Venice Summer Institute 2004, Globalization Workshop, July 21–22, 2004. A revision of the paper was published in Elias Dinopoulos, Pravin Krishna, Arvind Panagariya, and Kar-yiu Wong, eds., Trade Globalization and Poverty, Routledge, 2008, pp. 173–186.
* I have benefited especially from the comments of participants at the CESifo conference in Venice.

I. Introduction

When economists think of globalization, most of us think first of free trade and therefore the gains from trade that we have been studying and teaching for two centuries. But actual globalization takes many forms, including not only trade but also foreign direct investment (FDI), financial capital flows, and sometimes even migration of labor. More importantly, even the liberalization of trade has not been the simple move to zero trade barriers that we understand from our models, but has taken the form of trade liberalization that was only partial. Some of this is multilateral, but with barriers only partially eliminated. And increasingly it is minilateral, with barriers removed more completely but only between pairs or among small groups of countries in free trade areas (FTAs) and the like.

Furthermore, in both of these cases the liberalization of trade typically is attached to a variety of other measures that may or may not generate the same sorts of benefits as reducing tariffs. Multilaterally, the World Trade Organization (WTO) has expanded beyond the General Agreement on Tariffs and Trade (GATT) to include services and intellectual property, as well as to address policies relevant to trade other than trade barriers. Minilaterally, FTAs routinely address issues other than trade, including not only investment but also labor standards and environment, the effects of which may be very different from tariffs. And even for trade, because FTAs are only partial liberalization, they have features that may reduce or even reverse the beneficial effects of free trade. The importance of all of this is that, while we have a solid understanding from economic theory and experience of the benefits of multilateral free trade, these actual modes of globalization are something else.

Many of those who oppose or are skeptical of globalization – who tend not to be economists – base their doubts fundamentally on suspicion of corporations. Free trade increases the ability for large corporations to operate across national borders, thus – the skeptics would say – increasing their power over the economy and over peoples and governments around the world. Because corporations pursue only their self interest and not the social good, they exploit the world for their own profit. Thus Globalization ≡ Corporate Power ≡ Everybody Else Loses!

As economists we take issue with the second of these identities, and perhaps also with the first. Economic theory tells us, since Adam Smith, that firms, pursuing their self interest but competing with one another, lead, under ideal conditions at least, to maximizing well being for society as a whole. And indeed their competition among themselves reduces and, again under ideal conditions, even eliminates their own profits. So the fact that corporations are controlling economic activity does not, as long as they compete with each other or with smaller firms, mean that society loses. On the contrary, it is society that gains, and the corporations themselves find their profits competed away. Indeed, by this argument globalization itself may reduce corporate power by forcing large firms to compete with each other across borders, rather than allowing each to enjoy market power behind its home country's trade barriers.

This would be fine if in fact globalization did entail simply the move to free trade. But as I have said, actual globalization includes both more and less than free trade. One implication of this is that the welfare theorems of trade theory need not apply, since their conditions are not met. This is the meaning of the Theorem of the Second Best, where partial moves toward free trade may be welfare reducing if other markets remain distorted. I am not too worried about that, however, except perhaps in cases where the importance of particular distortions and their implications for gains from trade are well established. I certainly would not in general want to reject partial trade liberalization based on just the vague fear that it may not be welfare improving. Distortions, after all, not only undermine the benefits of some moves toward liberalization; they also increase the benefits of others.[i]

My greater concern is that the particular ways that the world has embraced globalization have been selected for it not by obviously unbiased and high-minded academics, but rather by governments acting under the influence of special interests – often corporate interests. That is, governments have negotiated both multilateral trade treaties and minilateral preferential arrangements in response to, and in the presence of, pressures brought to bear upon them by domestic interests. These interests could take a variety of forms, and in principle they could represent very broad constituencies. But in practice it seems clear that corporate interests have so far dominated. And while economic theory is reassuring about the effects of the profit motive when it drives behavior in the marketplace, there is no such reason to trust its effects in the political arena. In short, my concern in this paper is that the influence of producers, especially of large corporations, has dominated the drafting of the texts of international economic agreements and has done so, understandably, so as to promote the interests of those producers.[ii] Their interests are not necessarily harmful to society, but they are not necessarily beneficial either. And there is no reason to expect an invisible hand to guide governments that are under corporate influence toward desirable outcomes.

In the remainder of this paper I will first, in section II, elaborate on some particular examples of corporate influence that are suggested by casual observation. Most of these are ones that I mentioned when I first began to worry about this issue in Deardorff (2003). I will then turn, in section III, to looking at what economic theory can suggest about this process in the context specifically of FTAs. I will first review the implications for this issue of some of the existing literature, then provide my own simple example of how producer interests might seek to determine rules of origin.

II. Episodes of Corporate Influence

The "rules" of globalization might be thought to take many forms at many levels, including import tariffs and the procedures for collecting them, the nontariff barriers that still restrict trade in many sectors, and the national laws that specify these restrictions. However I will focus here only on the rules that are embodied in international trade agreements, and specifically on the WTO and the North American Free Trade Agreement (NAFTA).

TRIPs

I will start with what to me is the most egregious example of corporate influence on international rulemaking: the Uruguay Round Agreement on Trade Related Intellectual Property Rights (TRIPs). When issues of intellectual property rights (IPRs) first began to be discussed as part of the Uruguay Round, the claim was that any new rules would be confined to their "trade related" aspects. That presumably referred to the entry of IPR-violating goods into international trade, especially the export of such goods into a country where the IPR was established and enforced. It is not clear that new rules were needed for that, but in any case the negotiations soon left that narrow problem behind. The resulting TRIPs agreement requires that all WTO member countries enact and enforce IPR laws that are roughly comparable to those in the developed countries. The effect of this, since most IPRs are owned by developed-country firms, has been to force developing countries to protect the IPRs of individuals and firms in the developed countries. And this, aside from any stimulus it might provide to the creation of intellectual property of particular use to developing countries, is a change that can only benefit rich-country owners of IPRs and harm poor-country consumers. A case can of course be made for IPR protection as a second-best means of simulating innovation. But I have argued in Deardorff (1990, 1992) that, even on efficiency grounds, extending IPR protection to the whole world is going too far. And developing countries – notably India – resisted this effort to bring IPRs into the rules of the world trading system.

So why did this effort succeed? Clearly because of corporate influence. A group of very large corporations especially in the pharmaceutical industry were the initiators of the push for TRIPs in these negotiations, and they played an active role in moving the negotiations along. It was they, after all, who depended most heavily on the defense of IPRs, since their products, once developed, can be imitated at very low cost. It was in their interest of course to prevent the importation into the U.S. and Europe of unlicensed generic drugs that might be manufactured in, say, India. But once they entered the international rule-making arena, the advocates of IPRs did not stop there. They pushed to have the international trading system override the decision that many developing countries had made, that the short-term health of their populations was more important than the profits of the big drug companies. I say "short-term" here because in making this choice they were almost certainly giving up the chance for new drugs to be developed of particular interest to those same populations. Whether they understood that cost or not, I don't know, but it was the choice they had made. And the drug companies sought to rule that choice essentially illegal.

My point here is not that the TRIPs agreement is harmful, even though I may believe that it is. My point is that the TRIPs agreement was negotiated for reasons that had nothing to do with whether it was harmful or not, but only to do with whether it would increase the profits of some powerful corporations. And I am not saying either that these corporations were behaving badly. I happen to think that pharmaceutical companies have made a huge contribution to the well-being of modern society, and I do not generally begrudge them the large profits that they earn when one of their discoveries is a success. Their pursuit of profit through research and development as well as marketing has, I am quite willing to believe, made the world a better place.

The problem is that they were permitted to pursue profit not just in their industry but also by influencing international negotiations on the rules that they themselves would follow and benefit from. And not surprisingly, they used their power to design those rules to their own maximum advantage. They could hardly have been expected not to. The error was in letting them influence the negotiations in the first place. In their particular case, it would not have been hard to prevent this, since the relevance of their concerns for trade negotiations was always suspect. They could have been told to take their case to the World Intellectual Property Organization, rather than to GATT and the WTO.

GATS

I claim that there is no reason to expect corporate influence on rule making to be beneficial. But there is also no reason to expect it to be harmful. My second example, I believe, demonstrates this. Prior to the Uruguay Round, the GATT covered only trade in goods. Indeed, international transactions in services were not even regarded as trade. Since they typically required some sort of producer presence in the country consuming the service, they were considered to be part of FDI, and so were subject to much weaker disciplines on restrictive policies than the rules governing trade policy under the GATT.

At some point during the 1980s, participants in certain service industries got the idea of arguing that what they did was trade after all, and that it should be covered under GATT. They made this case to the U.S. government, which in turn placed services on the agenda of the Uruguay Round. The end result was not, of course, to include services in the GATT *per se*, which continues to be the central pillar of the WTO, but instead to negotiate a new General Agreement on Trade in Services (GATS) to provide its own discipline to service transactions.

This made good sense, in two respects. First, many have argued that the gains from international service transactions are just as real as the gains from trade in goods, and indeed the economic causes and effects are very much the same. I made this case myself early on, in Deardorff (1985).

On the other hand, the policies that are applied to services are quite different from the policies that are applied to trade in goods, and they do not even include anything that is exactly comparable to the tariffs that were the original focus of the GATT. So the same rules could not apply directly, and it made sense to negotiate a new agreement to cover services.

The GATS itself did not accomplish much liberalization, if any, although some has come in subsequent agreements. And there are disagreements about how liberalization in these markets ought to proceed. But my point here is simply to note that these issues might never have been addressed had it not been for the influence of American corporate executives in the service industries who saw an opportunity and pressed their case. They did it, I presume, primarily to benefit themselves and their firms, but in this case economics is very much on their side and I think the world as a whole stands to benefit.

Not all would agree with this, of course. Precisely because services are interlinked with FDI, imports of services can be seen as even more threatening to a country's domestic interests than imports of goods. And furthermore, the perception that many service industries were dominated by large corporations from rich countries created the fear that, in these industries, developing countries stood only to lose from freer trade.

Of course this second concern is exactly what trade following comparative advantage is all about, and while competing industries may lose, their countries gain from services that are supplied to them more efficiently. Indeed, one can argue that the gains from trade are even larger here than in many goods industries, because so many services provide essential inputs, including infrastructure, for other industries. Access to world-class service providers might well allow some developing-country manufacturing industries to exploit a comparative advantage that would otherwise be undermined by the need to use expensive and low quality local services.

NAFTA Chapter 11

The NAFTA agreement was a massive document, and those of us who tried to analyze the likely effects of NAFTA tended to focus on those few aspects of it that we best understood. Not surprisingly, there were pieces of it that we neglected, some that we failed even to know about. One of these that later drew a good deal of public attention was Chapter 11, on investment. Motivated by concern that a government might expropriate the property of a foreign direct investor, Chapter 11 requires that any such expropriation, direct or indirect, be accompanied by appropriate compensation. Furthermore, it entitles the victim of such expropriation to bring a case before a NAFTA tribunal against the national government of the country where the expropriation took place.

This, it turns out, may provide a powerful tool for corporations in one NAFTA country to use against governments (including state and local) in another NAFTA country, whenever a government uses a policy or regulation that reduces the corporation's profit. Or so it seems, at least from the cases that have been brought. All three NAFTA governments have been named in such cases. Opponents of NAFTA point especially to attempts at environmental regulation that have been challenged under Chapter 11 on the grounds that they reduce the profit of a foreign NAFTA firm. The most visible such case has been against the US by the Canadian Methanex Corporation, seeking compensation for a California prohibition against a fuel additive that they supplied and that had been judged to be toxic.

This particular case is still pending, so it is too soon to know how it will be decided. Of the 22 other cases that have been brought under Chapter 11, only five have led to decisions – three of them positive – while others have been settled or withdrawn. I find it hard to judge the merits of these cases, since many who write about this issue do not even pretend to be unbiased. But my impression is that the panels deciding these cases have been far less expansive than the NAFTA opponents feared.

However, my point here is not to argue the merits of Chapter 11 and the way it has been administered. Rather what I want to stress is the unprecedented nature of the agreement itself, in two respects. First, as I said above, Chapter 11 covers not just direct expropriation – as when a government takes over ownership of foreign firm's property – but also indirect. What that actually means remains to be determined by the cases as they are brought and decided, but as the Methanex case suggests, some would argue that indirect expropriation includes policy changes that reduce the value of a foreign investment. If that interpretation stands, it could turn out to be an expansion of property rights beyond what most countries, including the United States, include in domestic law.

Second, and perhaps more importantly, Chapter 11 allows an unprecedented right of private action against the government of another country to be decided by an international tribunal. Prior to NAFTA – in the US-Canada FTA for example, and also in the GATT – such tribunals were available in trade law only for disputes between governments. But NAFTA does not require that an aggrieved private party go through its own government; it files the case directly against the government of another country.

So why did NAFTA come to include such an unusually strong facility for private action? Consider who gains from Chapter 11. On the one hand, companies from NAFTA countries that invest in other NAFTA countries gain, acquiring either leverage over policies that might harm them or substantial compensation, if their cases succeed or induce a settlement in their favor. On the other hand, the countries themselves may gain from a higher level of direct investment, as foreign investors are reassured by Chapter 11 against the risk of adverse policy decisions. But if the latter was the dominant factor in motivating Chapter 11, one has to wonder why governments eager to attract FDI could not have provided such reassurance more directly with their own laws. The likelihood therefore seems high that Chapter 11 was written expressly for the companies that stood to benefit from it. And the impression that this was the case seems heightened by the fact that nobody spoke of Chapter 11 when the NAFTA agreement was being debated.

So regardless of the merits of Chapter 11, its existence strikes me as fairly strong evidence, once again, of the power of corporate interests in setting the rules of the international trading system.

NAFTA Rules of Origin

Because it is a free trade area rather than a customs union, thus leaving external tariffs unchanged and usually different for imports of the same good into different member countries, the NAFTA must include rules of origin. That is, for a good to cross from one NAFTA country to another free of tariff, it must be regarded as having "originated" within NAFTA, and the word "originated" must be defined. What this definition should be is not obvious, and it can matter a great deal as I will illustrate in section III below. Economists have examined the effects of various rules of origin, without any consensus emerging as to what they should be.[iii]

Two plausible candidates would base origin on either the percentage of domestic value added or on changes in tariff classification between inputs and outputs. The NAFTA Chapter 4, on rules of origin, uses both of these criteria and more, in an elaborate series of provisions that I suspect only a team of lawyers and accountants together could understand. The complexity of these rules must itself discourage some producers from attempting to take advantage of the tariff preferences that NAFTA provides. I have no idea whether the complexity is a deliberate attempt to discourage trade, or is only the natural outcome of compensating the drafters of the agreement in proportion to the time they spend on it.

But there is one aspect of the NAFTA rules of origin whose purpose seems more explicit. The fourth article of Chapter 4 deals exclusively with Automotive Goods, spelling out rules of origin for these that are even more explicit, detailed, and (to me) opaque than for other goods. Are these more restrictive than the rest of NAFTA's rules of origin? I certainly cannot tell from reading the text. But I do happen to know that this text was drafted by a group that included at least one economist who was an employee of a U.S. auto company. And that person's purpose was to draft rules that would permit his or her company to export tariff free from Mexico to the U.S. while preventing its Japanese competitors from doing the same. In Section III I will give an example of how this might be possible, in case it is not obvious.

So it appears that, by having American firms at the table in drafting rules of origin, at least in the automotive sector, the NAFTA was explicitly designed to benefit certain US corporations. Was this the intent of the U.S. government? Perhaps, but not necessarily. For all I know there may be a good reason why the automotive sector cannot be handled by the same rules as others, and, if so, then the expertise to write the rules would certainly not lie in USTR, whose staff should be experts on trade, not automobiles. To whom should they turn to assist them if not experts from the auto industry, with US auto companies being the natural choice? But once in the room, those experts can hardly be expected to represent the interests of Japanese or European firms.

Other?

These four examples of the role that corporate influence has apparently played, two in the WTO and two in NAFTA, are just the examples that I happen to know about and think I understand. Given the extreme complexity of both of these agreements and the fact that corporate representatives certainly were involved during their negotiations, if not as parties to the negotiations then as advisors to the negotiators, I have to believe that there are many other perhaps smaller ways that corporate interests have been represented. It is of course not in their interest to draw attention to these.

III. What Theory Says

Political Economy of Trade Policy

Trade economists have been led to look at political forces mainly by the otherwise inexplicable reluctance of governments to take our advice. After all, we have been very consistent for two centuries in advising all who will listen that governments should not interfere with trade. There are exceptions to our case for free trade, but we have always found credible counter-arguments to them. In the end, even those of us who have been most creative in constructing cases where protection might be beneficial have ultimately agreed that the economic interests of countries are best served by eliminating tariffs and other barriers to trade.[iv] Yet hardly any government in history seems to have listened. Given the choice between believing that we were wrong, or that they were pursuing something other than their economic interests, we naturally chose the latter.

Hence the theories of political economy of trade have focused on explaining why import tariffs were positive. This literature, which has been surveyed frequently,[v] seems to have converged on the model of Grossman and Helpman (1994) as the standard. In this model, a specific factor in each industry benefits from a tariff on its output, and the owners of specific factors are thus motivated to contribute toward the election of incumbent politicians in return for protection. Politicians in turn maximize a combination of social welfare and these contributions, with the result that they provide positive protection.

The Grossman-Helpman model says rather directly that owners of capital (as a specific factor) exert influence on international trade policy through political contributions. The model has also received some empirical support from Goldberg and Maggi (1999), although with a higher weight on social welfare than many might have expected. It does not, however, address the making of the rules of trade policy, but only the setting of tariffs within rules that have already been made.

However, a subsequent application of the Grossman-Helpman model comes closer to addressing rule making. In Grossman and Helpman (1995), they use the same model to examine the formation of FTAs. And after applying their framework in the first part of the paper just to the binary problem of whether to agree on an FTA with a given partner or not, they then turn to the question of exclusions. That is, actual FTAs do not always eliminate tariffs on absolutely every sector of the economy, and instead may exempt certain "sensitive" sectors. What are those sectors likely to be sensitive to? Politics, of course. Grossman and Helpman show how the selection of exempted sectors will depend, as do tariffs in their first application, on contributions from specific factors in exempted industries. These in turn depend on the extra returns that these specific factors stand to gain (or avoid losing) by being exempted. This, then, is an example of corporate influence over the rules of an FTA, if we equate corporate profits with returns to specific factors.

Another example is provided by Krishna (1998). He uses a model of imperfect competition and political economy to examine how the political process might favor one choice of FTA partner over another, and how both might compare to an alternative of multilateral liberalization. What he finds is that, the more likely is an FTA to be trade diverting and therefore welfare reducing, the more likely it is to be selected by the political process, over other potential FTAs and over multilateral liberalization. Thus, again, the rules of trade policy in the form of FTAs are influenced by the profits of those sectors that stand to gain. It should be said, however, that political-economy models of issues like this do not necessarily rest on the influence of owners of capital. Levy (1997), for example, examines how FTAs influence the choice of multilateral liberalization, but in a median voter model.

Rules of Origin – A Theoretical Example

I turn now to a theoretical example that is focused more explicitly on the determination of one of the rules of international trade – specifically, a rule of origin in an FTA. I will show a simple model in which a domestic firm stands to increase its profit by setting a rule of origin that favors it over its foreign competitor, thus giving it the incentive to influence the formulation of that rule in whatever way it can. As will be clear, the model attempts to formalize what seems to have been going on in the NAFTA rules of origin in automotive goods, as discussed above. I do not model the political process, which I presume could be similar to that of Grossman and Helpman, although I will conclude with a brief discussion of an alternative mechanism that might more plausibly have the same effect.

Consider a simple model of Bertrand duopoly. That is, there are two firms that are the only suppliers of a single differentiated product to the market in country U, which is segmented from other countries' markets. One of the firms is based in country U and the other in another country, J. Production requires an intermediate input that each can produce only in its own country, due to a specialized factor, perhaps expertise, that is available only there and that is needed to sustain the final product's differentiated characteristics. Their costs for this input are constants, b^U and b^J respectively, for the quantity needed to produce one unit of the final good. The input can then be assembled at constant cost in either country U or country J, and also in another country, M, which will become the partner in an FTA with country U. These per-unit costs of assembly are the same for both firms, but differ across countries: c^U, c^J, and c^M, of which I will assume $c^U = c^J > c^M$. The firms face demand functions in country U, $D^U = D^U(p^U, p^J)$ and $D^J = D^J(p^J, p^U)$ respectively, where p^i is the price of firm *i*'s product in country U. The demand functions are linear, as I will specify below. Countries U and M levy specific tariffs on imports of the unassembled good, t^{Uu} and t^{Mu} respectively, which may but need not be different. Initially, country U also levies a specific tariff, t^{Uf}, on imports of the final good from either other country. I assume that this tariff is larger than the cost saving that either firm could secure by assembling in country M rather than country U, $t^{Uf} > \max\left[(c^U - c^M), (t^{Uu} - t^{Mu} + c^U - c^M)\right]$, so that both firms do assembly in country U.[vi] Later I will have country U form an FTA with country M, eliminating this tariff on imports from there but subject to a rule of origin.

Formally, then, the model has two firms, A and B, each with constant unit costs of production $k^i, i = A, B$. They face demands for their products given by

$$D^i = a^i - p^i + sp^j, \quad i \neq j = A, B \tag{1}$$

where $a^i > 0$, $0 < s < 1$ are parameters.[vii] That is, demand for each is downward sloping in its own price, but increases in the price of its competitor. Each firm's profit is therefore

$$\pi^i = (p^i - k^i)(a^i - p^i + sp^j) \tag{2}$$

With Bertrand competition, each firm selects its price to maximize this profit given the price of the other. First order conditions for this maximization imply their reaction functions,

$$p^i = (a^i + k^i + sp^j)/2 \tag{3}$$

which together yield equilibrium prices

$$p^i = \Omega\left(A^i + 2k^i + sk^j\right) \tag{4}$$

where

$$\Omega = 1/(4 - s^2), \quad A^i = 2a^i + sa^j \tag{5}$$

Profits in equilibrium turn out to be

$$\pi^i = \Omega^2\left(A^i - (2 - s^2)k^i + sk^j\right)^2 \tag{6}$$

Applying this result to the firms U and J, before the FTA we have their input costs as b^U and $b^J + t^{Uu}$ respectively, but a common assembly cost in country U, c^U. Thus, in the notation of the model, $k^U = b^U + c^U$ and $k^J = b^J + t^{Uu} + c^U$. Using (6), their pre-FTA profits are

$$\begin{aligned} \pi^U &= \Omega^2\left(A^U - (2-s^2)(b^U + c^U) + s(b^J + t^{Uu} + c^U)\right)^2 \\ \pi^J &= \Omega^2\left(A^J - (2-s^2)(b^J + t^{Uu} + c^U) + s(b^U + c^U)\right)^2 \end{aligned} \tag{7}$$

After the FTA, firm U can do assembly in the cheaper country M, since its exports from M back to U will easily satisfy any rule of origin, having been produced entirely in U and M. Thus, letting "~" denote the FTA, k^U becomes $\tilde{k}^U = b^U + c^M < k^U$. Firm J, on the other hand, since its input comes from outside the FTA, if it were to assemble in country M would fail to satisfy any rule of origin that, say, requires content from within the FTA countries of more than $c^M/(b^J + t^{Mu} + c^M)$ percent. Assuming this is the case, then firm J continues to assemble in U and its cost continues to be $\tilde{k}^J = k^J = b^J + t^{Uu} + c^U$. Applying these costs to (6), we find the FTA profits of the firms to be

$$\begin{aligned} \tilde{\pi}^U &= \Omega^2\left(A^U - (2-s^2)(b^U + c^M) + s(b^J + t^{Uu} + c^U)\right)^2 \\ \tilde{\pi}^J &= \Omega^2\left(A^J - (2-s^2)(b^J + t^{Uu} + c^U) + s(b^U + c^M)\right)^2 \end{aligned} \tag{8}$$

Comparing (8) with (7),

$$\begin{aligned} \tilde{\pi}^U &= \left(\sqrt{\pi^U} + \Omega(2-s^2)(c^U - c^M)\right)^2 > \pi^U \\ \tilde{\pi}^J &= \left(\sqrt{\pi^J} - \Omega s(c^U - c^M)\right)^2 < \pi^J \end{aligned} \tag{9}$$

Thus, a rule of origin, which can prevent firm J from taking advantage of the lower cost assembly in country M while firm U avails itself of it through the FTA, both raises the profit of firm U and lowers the profit of firm J. This is hardly surprising, and in the example here it can be achieved very simply: just specify as a rule of origin that imports from M to U will be duty free only if they have content from among the FTA countries of more than $\Gamma = c^M / (b^J + t^{Mu} + c^M)$ percent. That would easily be satisfied by an FTA content requirement of 100%, but since that might be too blatantly protectionist, the firm may be expected instead to use its knowledge of the industry to seek content requirement that is lower, but that is high enough to achieve the same purpose, just more than Γ.

I have not attempted here to model the means by which a firm in this situation might influence the writing of the rule of origin. The Grossman-Helpman story, I suppose, would be that the firm would offer a financial contribution of some sort to incumbent politicians in return for their setting a content requirement in this industry of more than Γ. Whether this would succeed or not would depend on how the politician weights the financial contribution (which is limited by the gain in profit that is implicit in (9)) against the loss in economic welfare for the country as a whole. Realistically it would also depend on whether the politician can manage to influence the negotiations on the FTA at the level that would make this possible.

A more plausible story for political influence in this context is suggested by Hall (2001).[viii] In his description of lobbying, private interests do not in any sense pay money to politicians. Rather, they help them. That is, recognizing the limited time and resources that legislators have with which to accomplish their many objectives, only one of which is being re-elected, they welcome assistance from lobbyists who assist them by doing research and drafting legal texts on issues of their common interest. Hall points out first that a great deal of lobbying takes place, not between lobbyists and the politicians whose minds they wish to change, but between lobbyists and politician who are already their friends – the politicians who because of ideology or their constituencies already wish to achieve the same objectives as the lobbyists. Such behavior makes no sense from the perspective of other models of political economy. For example, in Grossman and Helpman's story, a firm would never pay a politician to vote for a tariff that he or she already favored on grounds of social welfare. But it does make sense if by helping the politician the lobbyist can help to make progress toward their common objective. The result of this is that lobbyists and their staff members play an active role in formulating policy.

Hall's theory is intended to explain the interaction between lobbyists and legislators, but the idea seems to extend easily to the executive branch. The office of U.S. Trade Representative, in particular, is surprisingly small in proportion to the size of its mission, and I would guess that it needs all the help it can get. In addition, the negotiations that it undertakes necessarily involve the intricacies of many individual industries, and even a much larger USTR staff would be unlikely to possess the expertise needed to deal with these. Therefore it is natural for trade negotiators to enlist the assistance of willing participants from domestic industries who have this expertise. And that gives the industries access to the drafting of trade agreements. It is through this mechanism, it seems, that trade rules negotiated by the U.S. government come to represent the interests of domestic industries.

IV. Conclusion

In this paper I have argued that profit maximizing firms, even though they contribute to social welfare when they compete in the market, may not do so when they influence the political process. In particular, I have suggested, through several examples from both the real world and from economic theory, that corporations have played a significant role in the formulation of the rules of the modern international trading system. They do this both in the multilateral system overseen by the WTO, and within regional trade agreements such as NAFTA. Their influence on rules need not be bad, but there is no reason why it should be good either. We therefore need to give more thought to constraining not just trade policy, but also the making of the rules of trade, to try to assure that this process moves us to a better world.

References

Deardorff, Alan V. 1985 "Comparative Advantage and International Trade and Investment in Services," in Robert M. Stern, (ed.), *Trade and Investment in Services: Canada/US Perspectives*, Toronto: Ontario Economic Council, pp. 39 71.

Deardorff, Alan V. 1990 "Should Patent Protection Be Extended to All Developing Countries," *The World Economy* 13, (December), pp. 497-507.

Deardorff, Alan V. 1992 "Welfare Effects of Global Patent Protection," *Economica* 59, (February), pp. 35-51.

Deardorff, Alan V. 2003 "What Might Globalization's Critics Believe?" *The World Economy* 26, (May), pp. 639-658.

Deardorff, Alan V. and Richard L. Hall 1997 "Explaining the Role of Interest Groups in United States Trade Policy," Research Seminar in International Economics Discussion Paper No. 415, University of Michigan.

Goldberg, Pinelopi Koujianou and Giovanni Maggi 1999 "Protection for Sale: An Empirical Investigation," *American Economic Review* 89, (December), pp. 1135-1155.

Grossman, Gene M. and Elhanan Helpman 1994 "Protection for Sale," *American Economic Review* 84, (September), pp. 833-850.

Grossman, Gene M. and Elhanan Helpman 1995 "The Politics of Free-Trade Agreements," *American Economic Review* 85(4), (September), pp. 667-690.

Hall, Richard L 2001 "Lobbying as Legislative Subsidy," paper presented at the annual meetings of the American Political Science Association.

Helpman, Elhanan 1999 "Politics and Trade Policy," in Richard Baldwin et al. eds., *Market Integration, Regionalism, and the Global Economy*, Cambridge: Cambridge University Press, pp. 86-112.

Krishna, Kala. 2004 "Understanding Rules of Origin," in process, February 11.

Krishna, Pravin 1998 "Regionalism and Multilateralism: A Political Economy Approach," *Quarterly Journal of Economics* 113, (February), pp. 227-251.

Krugman, Paul R. 1987 "Is Free Trade Passé?" *Journal of Economic Perspectives* 1, (Fall), pp. 131-144.

Levy, Philip I. 1997 "A Political-Economic Analysis of Free-Trade Agreements," *American Economic Review* 87, (September), pp. 50-519.

Rodrik, Dani 1995 "Political Economy of Trade Policy," in G. Grossman and K. Rogoff, eds., *Handbook of International Economics*, Vol. III, Amsterdam: North-Holland.

Notes

[i] For example, suppose we know that a domestic industry provides a positive externality that somehow cannot be internalized through a first-best production subsidy. Then while this means that a tariff may be beneficial if the industry competes with imports, it also means that a tariff (on another good) is even more harmful than usual if this industry exports.

[ii] It is, of course, not only corporations who influence policy, and that is true of the rules as much as of individual policy actions. Producers are also represented by labor unions and by producer organizations, including agricultural ones. Interests other than those of producers are also articulated by various nongovernmental organizations. Even consumers play a role, although many so-called consumer organizations seem to argue for protection that will raise prices to consumers. My focus here is on corporations because they seem to have played the greatest role in influencing rules of the WTO and NAFTA.

[iii] See Krishna (2004) for a recent survey of this literature.

[iv] See, for example, Krugman (1987).

[v] See Rodrik (1995), Helpman (1999).

[vi] I do not require, though I permit, that U and M have different size tariffs on the unassembled good, even though that would be the normal justification for having a rule of origin at all.

[vii] The upper bound on s, $s<1$, is only to assure the plausible property that equal increases in both prices reduce demand, but only $s<2$ turns out to be needed for the model to be well behaved.

[viii] See also Deardorff and Hall (1997).

PART V

COMPUTATIONAL MODELING AND TRADE POLICY ANALYSIS

CHAPTER 33

Alan Deardorff's Contributions to Computational Analysis of International Trade

Thomas W. Hertel

Purdue University

The general equilibrium analysis of gains from international trade is necessarily a high-dimensioned and complex undertaking. While the workhorse 2 × 2 × 2 model so elegantly developed by Ron Jones and others offers many insights, when it comes to the matter of offering policy advice, it is impossible to avoid moving to higher dimensions. Whether this involves disaggregating the "rest of world" to permit analysis of bilateral trade agreements, capturing differential tariff treatment of intermediate inputs employed in export industries, or disaggregating factors of production to discern the distributional impacts of trade policy reform, policy-oriented economists are inevitably called upon to move beyond the dimensions that are tractable in purely analytical models. This has spawned a growth industry in the supply of computational analyses for international trade policy.

However, computational partial and general equilibrium (CPE and CGE) analyses of trade are often discounted by the academic community. Such models are referred to disparagingly as "black boxes," papers based on computational models are often discounted out of hand, and they are rarely published in the leading journals of international economics. Indeed, I expect that the majority of presenters in this symposium today would discourage their students from doing computational work during their graduate studies. It is a sad state of affairs when economic policy advisors are demanding more computational analysis even as the best and brightest in our community are supplying less of this very same product, leaving the bulk of computational work to be done by others — largely those outside of academia.

Fortunately, there are a few academic trade economists who have swum against this tide of intellectual purity, striving to link rigorous theory with computational analysis of important policy questions. Alan Deardorff is one of these few, and I am extremely honored to have the opportunity to celebrate his contributions to the computational analysis of trade policy.

THE PLANNING-FEEDBACK APPROACH TO COMPUTATIONAL TRADE MODELING

In the two Deardorff–Stern (1986, 1990) books documenting the first two decades of the development of the Michigan trade model and some of its major applications, the authors describe "the curious and cumbersome process of informed trial and error by which we have used numerical models to grope toward an understanding of both theory and reality." They divide this process into two distinct parts, *the planning phase* and *the feedback phase.* Here, a quotation from the 1986 volume is in order:

> Only the first of these phases, which we shall call the planning phase, shows up clearly in the finished product. Yet it is the second phase, the feedback phase, that yields most of the insights that we shall discuss..... It is their interaction that we have found fascinating and informative over the years of working with the model, much more so than the ultimate numerical answers to the particular problems we set out to solve (Deardorff and Stern, 1986, p. 220).

In my own reading of Alan Deardorff's contributions to computational trade analysis, I have found these discoveries, motivated by the feedback process, to be especially intriguing and worthy of note by theorists and applied trade economists alike. I believe both groups could benefit from being "more like Alan" in their attention to this feedback phase of model development. Therefore, permit me to consider three such examples. (I'm sure there are more, but these are three salient illustrations that I was able to discern from a distance.)

The factor content of trade: The first example of highly productive feedback from computational analysis of practical policy issues to theoretical trade insights is offered by Robert Staiger, a former student of Deardorff's, now on the faculty at Stanford University. (I took the liberty of contacting a number of Alan's former students while preparing this paper.) Staiger's work came to my attention because he appeared as an author on two papers in 1988: one, a computational paper in *The Review of Economics and Statistics*, and one a theoretical paper in the *Journal of International Economics.* Both papers seek to answer the question of whether we can infer something useful about the effects of trade on relative factor prices from our knowledge of the factor content of trade. Based on my personal correspondence with Professor Staiger, the computational paper came first. Indeed, it was the presentation of an early version of this paper on the factor content of trade at an NBER conference which precipitated both publications.

According to Staiger, at the NBER workshop, Gene Grossman raised the question of whether one could make inferences about the impact of trade on factor prices from the factor content of trade. Staiger and Deardorff returned to Michigan and started with a blank sheet of paper and a simple theoretical model aimed at proving this link. This gave rise to the *JIE* paper in which Deardorff and Staiger establish a positive correlation between relative changes in the factor content of trade and proportional changes in factor prices. Indeed, under a more restrictive set of assumptions about production and utility functions, the factor content of trade provides an accurate measure of the relative effects of trade on *individual* factor returns. Meanwhile, the *RESTAT* paper, which developed in parallel to the theory paper, brought these theoretical insights to bear in an analysis of the relative impact of Japanese and US tariffs on factor markets in those two countries (Staiger, Deardorff and

Stern, 1988). Without the interplay between theory and computational analysis, these two papers would not have been published.

The love of variety: With the advent of the Spence–Dixit–Stiglitz CES, the love of variety utility function, and its introduction in the trade context by Paul Krugman, this formulation of consumer demand has become pervasive in the trade literature. However, this specification also puts a great burden on the constant elasticity of substitution in that function, for it must determine both the price elasticity of demand — and hence the optimal markup — as well as consumers' love of variety (LoV) — and therefore the gains from product proliferation. While it was initially introduced into consumer demand, Ethier (1984) suggested using this specification for modeling firms' derived demands, and the cost reductions from added variety became a key element of the gains from trade liberalization (Romer, 1994). Thus the incorporation of scale economies and the love of variety became a natural extension of the Michigan model (Brown, Deardorff and Stern, 1992a,b).

However, there was a problem. When confronted with real world data, in which the vast majority of trade is in intermediate inputs, the standard CES love of variety cost function led to extreme model instability. Consider the case of a reduction in tariffs on intermediate inputs utilized in a domestic industry. In the absence of love of variety, this leads to a cost reduction and expansion of the industry, but this expansion is curtailed by rising factor prices and the model finds a new equilibrium at a higher level of output. However, product differentiation by firm and love of variety is added to this picture, and the reduction in costs also leads to firm entry. When such entry occurs in input-supplying industries, this expanded product variety contributes to further cost reductions, additional entry and so on. For this reason, CGE models with the CES LoV specification are prone to far greater specialization than observed in reality (Brown, Deardorff and Stern, 1995).

This problem was first confronted by Drusilla Brown (personal communication) when working on the application of the Michigan model to an analysis of trade reforms in Tunisia. She was unable to get the model to solve and called Alan Deardorff to vent her frustrations. Alan responded by proposing a modification of the standard Spence–Dixit–Stiglitz CES specification, in which another parameter explicitly governing agents' LoV is introduced. This parameter, let's call it β, is bounded between zero and one and produces both the Krugman-style trade model ($\beta = 1$) and the Armington model (no love of variety) ($\beta = 0$) as special cases. When Drusilla asked Alan for a suggestion on the value to assign this parameter, he suggested 0.5. (As we will see in a moment, this turns out to be a remarkably prescient choice!) This indeed solved Brown's convergence problem, and she was able to complete the project successfully. Meanwhile, this new LoV parameter became embedded in the Michigan model.[1]

[1] It should be noted that Benassy (1996) published a paper at about the same time, exploring the implications of deviations from the CES-LoV specification for the optimal number of varieties in an economy. It appears that these developments were fully independent discoveries.

A few years later, I was attempting a large-scale, disaggregated application of the CES-LoV model within the GTAP modeling framework at Purdue University, and ran across the same problem of model instability. After scratching my head for a while, I contacted Drusilla to inquire about her experience, whereupon she related to me Alan's suggested model revision. It worked like a charm! Of course, this left open the question of what the appropriate value of the LoV parameter might be, which brings us to the remarkable conclusion of this tale of the "feedback" phase of model development.

In 2003, Adina Ardelean, a student of David Hummels's (another Deardorff/Michigan connection in this story), took my graduate class in computational trade modeling at Purdue University. Her work on CGE analysis of trade policy in this course got her interested in Deardorff's modified LoV specification and she developed this into her doctoral dissertation. In addition to working out the theoretical properties of this model, she came up with an innovative approach to estimating the LoV parameter (Ardelean, 2009). I recommend this paper to you. For the purposes at hand, suffice it to say that Adina's global trade-weighted mean estimate of the LoV parameter is 0.54 (with a standard deviation of 0.13) — remarkably close to Alan's initial intuitive estimate of $\beta = 0.5$. I find this to be an excellent example of the feedback phase in which computational analysis is iterated with theoretical (and econometric) work to produce an improved model of the way international trade really works.

Protection and real wages: One of the oldest questions in international trade pertains to the impact of trade liberalization on real wages. The Stolper–Samuelson theorem represents a milestone in this literature, stating that a tariff cut would decrease the real wage of a country's scarce factor of production. In the 1990s, the question of the likely wage impacts of trade policy reform loomed large in the NAFTA debate — a policy debate in which the Michigan model played an important role. In the context of this debate, it was assumed that real wages in the U.S. — a labor-scarce country — would likely fall in the face of tariff cuts. However, the Michigan model results for NAFTA produced the opposite result: real wages rose (Brown, Deardorff and Stern, 1992a,b). In a subsequent paper, Brown, Deardorff and Stern (1992c) explain how this phenomenon can arise. In so doing, they extend the Stopler–Samuelson theorem to an environment with scale economies, imperfect competition, and product differentiation. In this context, increased scale of production, reduced markups, and varietal gains can all work against the traditional Stopler–Samuelson effect, giving rise to an outcome where real wages of the scarce factor of production rise with tariff reductions.

This last example nicely illustrates a further discussion of the feedback phase of model development from Deardorff and Stern (1986):

> What typically happened when we solved the model was that we found something unexpected in the results. Sometimes the results were just nonsense and we had to go back and find out why. More often the results were plausible overall but contained one or two features that we did not expect in terms of either direction or size of the effect. (*e.g.*, the real wage impacts of NAFTA.) The feedback phase of model construction

consists of examining the assumptions of the model carefully until such surprises can be explained, and then either modifying the model or modifying our ideas of what to expect so that the results are no longer surprising. Either way, something can be learned in the process (p. 221).

OTHER IMPORTANT CONTRIBUTIONS

While there is not sufficient space to develop all of Alan Deardorff's contributions to CGE analysis of trade policy (and I need to leave some material for my fellow panelists), I would like to highlight a few more things which are important and notable about the Deardorff–Stern work. Their focus on short-run labor market impacts provided policy makers with highly relevant information about the likely impacts of trade reform on employment by industry. They also were ahead of their time in seeking to come to grips with non-tariff barriers as well as trade in services, both of which have now (two decades later) moved front and center in the global trade policy landscape.

As his career progressed, the focus of Alan Deardorff's computational work shifted increasingly to developing country impacts of trade policy. Of special note is his long-term collaboration with Rajesh Chadha and Sanjib Pohit, as well as Robert Stern, on the CGE analysis of domestic policy reforms in India. The ensuing model, documented in Chadha *et al.* (1998) represented an innovative approach to CGE modeling of an economy with significant elements of state monopoly and administered pricing.

As a direct result of his willingness to engage with policy makers in the messy world of computational trade policy analysis, Alan Deardorff has also become a much sought after advisor on issues relating to the multilateral trading system, undertaking numerous projects with the U.S. government, the United Nations agencies, the World Bank, and others.

FUTURE DIRECTIONS FOR COMPUTATIONAL ANALYSIS OF INTERNATIONAL TRADE

Alan Deardorff was a pioneer in the computational analysis of international trade. As was the case with other pioneers in this field, he had to be a jack of all trades. In addition to writing down the theory of the model, he also wrote the FORTRAN code necessary for its numerical implementation. Implementation of the Michigan model required him to develop clever techniques for partitioning the numerical model and solution strategies that permitted him to solve models that were exceptionally large, by the standards of the time. He and Bob Stern were also required to develop globally consistent data sets, and had to worry about obtaining sensible parameters for their model. In short, this was a lot of ground to cover before actually getting to the point where results could be generated. Fortunately for those coming later to this field, there have been some important institutional advances which have lowered the entry barriers to this field, while simultaneously enhancing the credibility of such work in policy circles.

More specifically, the advent of the publicly available, regularly updated Global Trade Analysis Project (GTAP) database has removed one of the biggest barriers to CGE analysis of trade policy. And as the community of CGE modelers has grown, so too has the software industry servicing the computational needs of this group. The GAMS and GEMPACK software packages have greatly enhanced the efficiency of computational modelers, while also making it much easier to replicate the work of others. Indeed, as the CGE (and CPE) analysis of trade policies moves forward, the availability of libraries of alternative models and policy analyses will prove increasingly important. The only way to overcome the black-box critique of these models is to permit others to readily replicate, critique, and extend published work. I encourage everyone serving as a reviewer on a CGE or CPE journal submission to require such submissions to be accompanied by an archive permitting the reviewer and/or future readers to easily replicate all of the findings in the paper. Without such replication, computational studies will remain little more than one-off exercises with limited potential for longer-term, scientific impact.

As with the efforts by Deardorff and Stern to bring to bear elements of the Krugman model of international trade within their computational framework, future research in this field must be on the lookout for promising new theoretical innovations. Prime among such innovations currently available are the Melitz-style models of producer heterogeneity (Melitz, 2003; the appearance of Marc Melitz at this point provides yet another Deardorff/Michigan connection in this story). Early attempts to incorporate heterogeneous firms into a global CGE model (*e.g.*, Zhai, 2008) suggest that this captures an element of trade policy reform long held by practitioners to be important — namely the impact on industry total factor productivity. CGE models with heterogeneous producers also open the way for incorporation of additional empirical characteristics of specific industries which are amenable to measurement — namely the distribution of firm-level productivities in a given industry. Indeed, some CGE analyses suggest that these productivity distribution parameters may be more important than the time-worn elasticities of substitution in trade which have hitherto governed the overall size of trade gains.

The revolution in empirical trade which has occurred over the past two decades also offers a great opportunity for computational analysis. This econometric work, coupled with systematic sensitivity analysis with respect to the estimated parameter distributions, gives CGE modelers the opportunity for the first time to put serious confidence intervals on their findings (*e.g.*, Hertel *et al.*, 2007). And recent estimates of the relative importance of the extensive and intensive margins of trade expansion (Hummels and Klenow, 2005) have proven critical for calibrating new CGE models of international trade (Zhai, 2008). There is also scope for statistically testing competing models of international trade for specific industries (Villoria, 2009). Despite all the noise to the contrary, econometricians studying international trade and computational modelers are natural partners. The latter are typically addressing critical policy issues, but are challenged as to the validity of their models. Meanwhile, the former are often congratulated on the quality of their estimates, but they are faced at the end of the day with the question: Who cares? Greater cross-fertilization between these two groups can yield significant gains from trade.

In closing, I would like to call attention to the increasing role for trade economists in the debate over global environmental policy. The national impacts of climate change will hinge critically on the capability of a smoothly functioning global trading system to even out the differential regional impacts of climate change. Meanwhile, the policies aimed at mitigating climate change are likely to significantly alter the global pattern of comparative advantage, thereby creating new pressures for protectionism, as well as new potential gains from trade. In some cases, national environmental policies — specifically U.S. renewable fuel mandates — are being written in such a way that their impacts through the global trading system must also be taken into account. Even more so than for trade policy, the world of global environmental policy relies heavily on computational models. Indeed the Intergovernmental Panel on Climate Change maintains a library of results from 22 Global Circulation Models (the CMIP3 project), upon which scientists regularly draw to publish scholarly works. If trade economists wish to have an impact on these important deliberations, they will have to "get their hands dirty" in the world of computational modeling. As Alan Deardorff has shown over the past three decades, there is great scope for trade theorists, working in conjunction with computational modelers, to contribute — both to the policy dialogue, as well as to the further development of economic theory.

REFERENCES

Ardelean, Adina, 2009, How strong is the love of variety?, unpublished manuscript, Santa Clara University.

Benassy, Jean-Pascal, 1996, Taste for variety and optimum production patterns in monopolistic competition, *Economics Letters* 52, 41–47.

Brown, Drusilla K., Alan V. Deardorff, and Robert M. Stern, 1992a, A North American Free Trade Agreement: Analytical issues and a computational assessment, *The World Economy* 15, 11–29.

Brown, Drusilla K., Alan V. Deardorff, and Robert M. Stern, 1992b, A U.S.-Mexico-Canada Free Trade Agreement: Sectoral employment effects and regional/occupational employment realignments in the United States, National Commission for Employment Policy (October).

Brown, Drusilla K., Alan V. Deardorff, and Robert M. Stern, 1992c, Protection and real wages: Old and new trade theories and their empirical counterparts, Research Seminar in International Economics, Post-Print Paper No. 6, University of Michigan.

Brown, Drusilla K., Alan V. Deardorff, and Robert M. Stern, 1995, Modeling multilateral trade liberalization in services, *Asia-Pacific Economic Review* 2, 21–34.

Chadha, R., A. Deardorff and R. Stern, 1998, The Impact of Trade and Domestic Policy Reforms in India: A CGE Modelling Approach (University of Michigan Press, Ann Arbor).

Deardorff, Alan V. and Robert W. Staiger, 1988, An interpretation of the factor content of trade, *Journal of International Economics* 24, 93–107.

Deardorff, Alan V. and Robert M. Stern, 1986, The Michigan Model of World Production and Trade, (MIT Press, Cambridge, MA).

Deardorff, Alan V. and Robert M. Stern, 1990, Computational Analysis of Global Trading Arrangements (University of Michigan Press, Ann Arbor).

Dixit, Avinash and Joseph E. Stiglitz, 1977, Monopolistic competition and optimum product diversity, *American Economic Review* 76, 297–308.

Ethier, Wilfred J., 1984, Higher dimensional issues in trade theory, in Ronald W. Jones and Peter B. Kenen, eds., Handbook of International Economics, Volume 1 (North-Holland, Amsterdam), pp. 131–184.

Hertel, T.W., D. Hummels, M. Ivanic, and R. Keeney, 2007, How confident can we be in CGE-based analysis of free trade agreements?, *Economic Modelling* 24, 611–635.

Hummels, David and Peter J. Klenow, 2005, The variety and quality of a nation's exports, *American Economic Review* 95(3), 704–723.

Krugman, Paul R., 1980, Scale economies, product differentiation, and the pattern of trade, *American Economic Review* 70, 950–959.

Melitz, Marc J., 2003, The impact of trade on intra-industry reallocations and aggregate industry productivity, *Econometrica* 71, 1695–1725.

Romer, Paul M., 1994, New goods, old theory, and the welfare costs of trade restrictions, *Journal of Development Economics* 43, 5–38.

Staiger, Robert W., Alan V. Deardorff, and Robert M. Stern, 1988, The effects of protection on the factor content of Japanese and American foreign trade, *Review of Economics and Statistics* 70, 475–483.

Villoria, Nelson, 2009, Three essays on the geography of international trade, unpublished Ph.D. dissertation, Purdue University.

Zhai, Fan, 2008, Armington meets Melitz: Introducing firm heterogeneity in a global CGE model of trade, *Journal of Economic Integration* 23(3), 575–604.

CHAPTER 34

The Third Way: Applied General-Equilibrium Modeling as a Complement to Analytical Theory and Econometrics

James R. Markusen

University of Colorado, Boulder University College, Dublin

THE THIRD WAY

Congratulations to Alan Deardorff on a long and distinguished research career that has shown great breadth as well as depth. It is a pleasure to be here and participate in these events. I am honored to be invited given that I have never worked with Alan and that our research interests have been rather different. Yet, in spite of the latter, I have great admiration for the things Alan has done and accomplished.

I have been asked to offer some thoughts on Alan's work on applied general-equilibrium modeling and indeed this is an area where our interests have a different focus. Alan and the Michigan group used the computer and computational tools for policy simulations, working through the horrible task of calibrating these models to real data. I have used simulations more as an extension of my theoretical tool kit, attacking problems that have too many dimensions, too many non-linearities, or too many inequality constraints to be tractable with our traditional analytical techniques. To be honest, my knowledge of the difficulties involved in data work and calibration programs was in good measure why I did not go the same route. But that indeed makes the Michigan group's accomplishments much appreciated by myself.

The basic theme of my comments is that applied general-equilibrium (AGE) modeling represents a "third way" of doing economics, complementing the more traditional methods of analytical theory and econometrics. Most of us at this conference were schooled only in the latter two methodologies and, worryingly, that limitation generally persists to this day. This is in spite of the fact that analytical theory, "pencil and paper" theory if you like, and econometrics have limitations that prevent us from analyzing or even asking certain important questions. I shall argue a bit later that in fact some traditional theorists and econometricians have been hostile to calibrated modeling and simulations and make that clear to their graduate students. I have never understood this point of view, and see simulation modeling as an excellent complement to our other techniques.

I am going to offer some praise and support for simulation modeling in the comments that follow, and also offer some criticism of the critics. When I do this, please keep in mind that this is not really my field at all: I don't want to be dismissed as merely touting my own research agenda. Most of my 37-year career has been as a pencil-and-paper theorist, and more recently I have also been a co-author with competent econometricians. My own publications constructing and using calibrated models with real data amount to three papers.

LIMITATIONS OF TRADITIONAL ANALYTICAL THEORY

As I just noted, I have spent the bulk of my career doing analytical theory; I continue to work primarily in this direction and place great value on the discipline of this approach and on the value of its insights. But I believe that this approach has sharp boundaries and limitations, and that the computer is an excellent research tool to push back these boundaries.

A first limitation of the analytical approach to theory is that it generally offers no quantitative estimates; *e.g.*, with respect to comparative statics experiments. I remember learning in graduate school about the optimal tariff. Well, it turns out it is not an optimal tariff *number*, it is an optimal tariff *formula*. It is a very complicated general-equilibrium effect even in the very simple $2 \times 2 \times 2$ Heckscher–Ohlin model, where it involves elasticities of substitution in both production sectors and in consumption, country sizes and so forth. No one has a clue what its *numerical* magnitude might be, and analytical theory cannot even solve for it in terms of underlying numerical magnitudes of structural parameters.

A second example is gains from trade liberalization. Analytical theory gives us a gains-from-trade theorem for moving from autarky to free (or restricted) trade, but little else, and even in the case of autarky to free trade there is of course no quantitative estimate of what the size of gains might be. In realistic cases of second-best liberalization scenarios, trade theory has virtually nothing to say. But gains from trade is in fact a crucial question that policy makers need estimates about. I have long observed a tendency for trade economists to invariably assure policy makers and journalists that trade liberalization is always and everywhere a good thing. In fact, our theory says no such thing.

To put this on a more general level, analytical methods have no ability to analyze complex comparative statics, generally not even with respect to qualitative properties except in extremely special cases. There are several different problems, often coming together in bundles. The first is dimensionality: large numbers of equations and unknowns often defy analytical methods. The second difficulty is that the equations are typically non-linear in our theories, and, thirdly, there is often complex simultaneity (meaning no simple recursive structure for example).

The next difficulty is that in most reasonable general-equilibrium situations, the "true" model is actually a set of non-linear inequalities instead of equations. The actual model we would like to solve includes the possibility of many corner solutions and slack activities. These models are termed non-linear complementarity problems in mathematical programming terminology: each non-linear inequality has an associated or complementary non-negative variable. The classic simple supply and demand problem has in fact three possible equilibria in two unknowns, price and quantity: (1) There is an interior equilibrium with both variables positive, (2) supply can lie entirely above demand so the equilibrium quantity is zero (production is unprofitable), and (3) supply can lie entirely to the right of demand so that the price is zero (it is a free good). Traditional methods have difficulty even with this very simple case.

The traditional way around this is to simplify the problem down to the point in which it is analytically tractable. In my probably unpopular view, this often leads to extremely unrealistic assumptions that "throw the baby out with the bathwater." The interesting features of the problem are assumed away! I have heard or read many presentations in which I find a very odd assumption or two. When I then try to figure out the reason for this oddity, I often as not find that without the offending assumption the entire paper falls apart, meaning that the results don't hold or that the model can no longer be solved analytically.

Let me give three quick examples of over-used constructions in trade theory, chosen for analytical convenience despite generally counter-empirical predictions: (1) The $2 \times 2 \times 2$ Heckscher–Ohlin model, generally inconsistent with stylized facts about political economy. (2) The large-group monopolistic-competition model, inconsistent with growing firm size and falling markups as the world economy grows and liberalizes. (3) Quasi-linear preference and the reliance on an "outside" good so common in the industrial-organization approach to trade theory, inconsistent with the high income elasticities of demand for the goods in question.

There is nothing wrong with starting in these places; the sin is in finishing there. As I will propose later, start with a simple analytical case for insight and then simulate the model you really believe in. One of my favorite quotes along these lines is the following:

> Many branches of both pure and applied mathematics are in great need of computing instruments to break the present stalemate created by the failure of the purely analytical approach to nonlinear problems (John von Neumann, 1945).

Yup, 1945, and yet there is still considerable resistance in our field to this very basic observation and truth 64 years later.

DISCONNECT BETWEEN AGE MODELING AND ECONOMETRICS

I have virtually no expertise in this area and thus I will try to be brief and not discredit myself. My view is that calibrated AGE modeling (calibrators) and econometrics (estimators) have different objectives, and critical comments made by one camp or the other are sometimes irrelevant and miss the point. Estimators doing trade are interested in estimating the parameters involved in important relationships suggested by theory. To continue my Heckscher–Ohlin example, an estimator may restrict the parameter space by imposing the HO assumptions that countries have identical technologies, identical, homothetic preferences, and no domestic distortions and then estimate the contribution of endowment differences across countries to trade. Results give an "average" response of trade to endowment changes. There are positive degrees of freedom, standard errors, and measures of how good the HO model fits the data.

Calibrators are interested in the counter-factuals and have no reason to believe the HO model is "true": countries surely have different technologies, tastes, endowments, and domestic distortions. Their assumption is that the observed data (once made micro-consistent) represent an equilibrium, and the (endogenous) parameter space is expanded until the data fits the model exactly. So, for example, countries are allowed to have Hicks-neutral differences in technology which "soak up" the error terms in the estimator's equations. There are no standard errors or degrees of freedom by assumption. Obviously, estimators point to the lack of standard errors and degrees of freedom with enthusiasm, and I think calibrators are well aware of these issues. But I surely don't want to get into this debate here.

As in the case of analytical methods, it seems to me that traditional econometrics has difficulties in assessing complex general-equilibrium counter-factuals. One of the areas where this is most obvious and most worrying is in providing quantitative *ex ante* estimates of the gains from complex regional trade agreements. A few years ago, I heard a prominent empirical trade economist give an excellent survey on all of the recent empirical work on international trade issues. When he finished, a questioner asked, "What about gains from trade?" The answer was that econometricians don't do that, and that it is the province of applied general-equilibrium modelers. But as mentioned above, this is surely one of the crucial things that policy makers want to know about before going into complex and lengthy negotiations. In the case of NAFTA negotiations, econometric findings based on past multilateral liberalization (and at which time Mexico was a very small economy) were not very useful or appropriate in assessing this counter-factual.

To be more constructive, I think applied general-equilibrium models are useful for complementing both the theoretical and empirical branches of economic science. Models calibrated to real data for use in policy simulations pick up where econometrics leaves off, and econometrics has a crucial role in estimating elasticities and other parameters that go into the models. I have never seen a conflict here and have had a hard time understanding the negative attitude of some traditionalists.

Simulation of theory models with too many dimensions, two many non-linearities, and/or too many inequalities to permit analytical solutions is surely a very worthwhile practice. Again, I am in no way criticizing the use of analytical models simple enough to solve; that would, after all, be trashing my own career. I just don't want to stop there as I have indicated above. In short, I strongly believe that simulation modeling is a complement to traditional theory and empirical methods, and we should embrace that complementarity in our own work and in our graduate teaching.

ACKNOWLEDGMENT OF EARLY CONTRIBUTORS TO THE DEVELOPMENT OF SIMULATION MODELING

Going back starting a couple of decades ago, the Stroh's/Labatt's region, as we used to call it, was a world leader in the development of applied general-equilibrium modeling. Over on the Michigan side (Stroh's) we had the Michigan model with Brown, Deardorff, and Stern. Over on the Ontario side (Labatt's), we had John Whalley and assistants and graduate students that the rest of us at UWO referred to as "Whalley World," and we had Richard Harris at Queen's.

Not doing this type of large-scale calibrated modeling, I am in no position to comment in detail about the many developments that are credited to the Michigan group, but I know they were path-breaking and hope that my colleagues in this session will comment in more detail. I do believe that the Michigan group, along with Richard Harris, were pioneers in incorporating industrial-organization features into AGE models. Based on being a colleague of John Whalley's for 15 years, I can tell you that I have immense respect for what these early modelers went through in the late 1970s and 1980. Many a day we saw John with bags under his eyes, having spent most of the night in the computer center where he would book out the VAX for six or so hours at a time in order to do a couple of runs of a 167-sector model.

I am certain that Alan and the Michigan group did the same and I have great admiration for that sort of dedication. I suspect that Alan was the theory guru of the group, but collectively they took on a difficult task: bad data, bad computers, and bad to non-existent software. Again, I don't know the details of the Michigan model, but most of these early modelers wrote their own computer code, generally in FORTRAN. I actually started sitting in on John Whalley's course for a few weeks before I quit after trying to code up an algorithm in FORTRAN. I got lost somewhere between Newton steps and Lemke pivots. This is nuts, I thought.

NATTERING NABOBS OF NEGATIVITY[1]

Over the years, I have heard a lot of criticism and negativity from both theorists and econometricians about calibrated simulation modeling; beware, your graduate students talk. I suppose what bothers me most is that these individuals generally had essentially nothing else to offer on the important counter-factual questions, such as the income and distributional consequences of NAFTA as I just indicated. Why the nattering?

Perhaps the most puzzling objection to me is the analytical theorist's "black box" criticism used to dismiss simulation modeling and, once you dismiss it, there is of course no need to actually learn anything about it. The black-box criticism essentially says that we do not know what is going on inside the computer program and thus we can dismiss and ignore it. In fact, I have generally felt that GE modeling is quite transparent (given lots of dimensions): the structure of the models (equation and unknowns) are clear, the functional forms are described in detail, the choice of exogenous versus calibrated parameters are clear, and the solution algorithm is understood.

---

[1] The title of this section is from an infamous speech by then U.S. Vice President Spiro T. Agnew in 1970. The speech and phrase were however written by speechwriter William Safire, not Spiro.

A strong and convincing feature of applied general-equilibrium models that I think should calm the critics is the "replication check." If we begin with a micro-consistent data set, then the program must be able to reproduce the input data as an equilibrium. Not until the model passes the replication check will any respectable modeler proceed to actually use the model. No way, no exceptions. After the replication check, modelers often give their models questions to which we know the answer and make sure that the right answer comes back as a further version of the replication check. I certainly do that in my theory simulations. For example, if I make two countries identical, I better get a symmetric solution or I know something is wrong. While I do not write the FORTRAN or C code myself, I certainly do understand exactly what Newton steps and Lemke pivots are and how they work.

I don't think that econometricians typically use the black-box argument; they have other objections as noted above. Nevertheless, I cannot resist speculating that they have little or no knowledge of how their canned programs work. Most never write the code for their estimations and don't have an idea of how the code works. I have been told in discussing this with applied econometricians that there are well-known examples of tests where the same data are submitted to different econometrics packages or attempts are made to replicate published papers and the results can come back different. To the best of my knowledge, there is no equivalent of the replication check in econometrics, and thus many errors are harder to find than they are in AGE modeling.

I regret that there is not a seat at the table for applied general-equilibrium modeling in most graduate programs. At this time, the AGE crowd is fairly disjoint from mainstream economics but everyone should understand that it is now a very large crowd indeed. The Global Trade Analysis Project (GTAP), the home professional society for modelers, now has 7769 registered members representing 157 different countries. Governments take this seriously, many corporations or industry groups take this seriously (*e.g.*, the electric power industry is a big client of private-sector consulting companies doing GE modeling).

WAYS FORWARD?

To the extent I could make an appeal to fellow theorists, I would simply ask that they recognize the limitations of analytical theory. If you have to make assumptions that throw out the interesting part of the question or if the results are extremely fragile to the assumptions you choose, then there is a problem. Once again, I am a strong supporter of the traditional methods of analytical theory and continue to do much of my work in this vein. I am simply suggesting that we do not stop there. What I have often done is to make a model of the model: a simplified analytical version of the problem I really want to work on. An example of a model of the model is a partial-equilibrium version of a question which can be solved analytically, and surely the author and reader gain some insights from such an exercise. Then I attack the real GE model via general-equilibrium simulations.

I just don't have enough expertise to comment much on trying to find common ground between econometrics and calibrated modeling. Clearly, there is great need for econometrics in estimating parameters that go into applied general-equilibrium models.

Engineering data are valuable as well as has been demonstrated in energy modeling; for example, how unprofitable is wind or solar energy at today's prices? Technologies that are not currently in use, like inactive trade links, pose a particular challenge to econometrics.

I do know that there are a number of current papers that could be interpreted as pointing in the direction that suggests there is far more overlap between structural econometrics and calibrated general-equilibrium modeling than is currently realized. In a number of recent papers, authors are estimating the structural response parameters (*e.g.*, elasticities) by running regressions subject to the full GE simulation model. The regressions cannot be inconsistent with the GE, and the parameter estimates are those that minimize the sum of squared errors in the econometric objective. This class of problems is called a mathematical program with equilibrium constraints (MPEC). That is, optimize something subject to the general equilibrium defined by the constraint set, typically a complementarity problem of inequalities with complementary non-negative variables (*e.g.*, zero-profit conditions for activities, market-clearing conditions for commodities and factors, and so forth).

Traditionally, MPECs have been used to find an optimal set of policy instruments (optimal tax policy), but this numeric method is now being used to estimate structural parameters. This method allows us the opportunity to move the benchmark replication up to the second order. This is found in Balistreri and Hillberry (2007, 2008). Working separately, Su and Judd (2008) advance the MPEC as a general method for direct structural estimation. Again, it is beyond my competence to evaluate this idea in detail, but I hope that it proves to be a fruitful avenue for getting the estimators and calibrators to work together.

CONCLUSIONS

I want to conclude by saying "well done" to Alan and others in the Michigan group, Brown and Stern in particular.[2] I would go on about Alan's many important contributions in analytical theory which I know more about, but I was asked to comment more narrowly on the simulation work which I have now said several times I know less about. I want to thank Brown, Stern, and Deardorff for persisting in the face of huge technical problems and limitations as well as in the face of the intellectual resistance I discussed earlier. I am sure that Von Neumann would be proud of you, though apparently he was not the great human being that everyone knows Alan is.

Thanks for the invitation and my very best wishes.

REFERENCES

Balistreri, Edward J. and Russell H. Hillberry, 2007, Structural estimation and the border puzzle, *Journal of International Economics* 72, 451–463.

[2] Alan Fox and others should surely be included.

Balistreri, Edward J. and Russell H. Hillberry, 2008, The gravity model: An illustration of structural estimation as calibration, *Economic Inquiry* 46, 511–527.

Deardorff, Alan V. and Robert M. Stern, 1986, The Michigan Model of World Production and Trade: Theory and Applications (MIT Press, Cambridge, MA).

Deardorff, Alan V. and Robert M. Stern, 1990, Computational Analysis of Global Trading Arrangements (University of Michigan Press, Ann Arbor).

Deardorff, Alan V. and Robert M. Stern, 1998, Measurement of Nontariff Barriers (University of Michigan Press, Ann Arbor).

Harrison, Glen W., Richard Jones, Lawrance J. Kimbell, and Randall Wigle, 1993, How robust is applied general-equilibrium analysis?, *Journal of Policy Modeling* 15, 99–115.

Judd, Kenneth L., 1997, Computational economics and economic theory: Substitutes or Complements?, *Journal of Economic Dynamics and Control*, 907–942.

Markusen, James R. and Randall Wigle, 1989, Nash equilibrium tariffs for the U.S. and Canada: The roles of country size, scale economies, and capital mobility, *Journal of Political Economy* 97, 368–386.

Markusen, James R., 2002, Multinational Firms and the Theory of International Trade (MIT Press, Cambridge, MA).

Rutherford, Thomas F., 1999, Extension of GAMS for complementarity problems arising in applied economic analysis, *Journal of Economic Dynamics and Control* 19, 1299–1995.

Su, Che-Lin and Kenneth L. Judd, 2008, Constrained optimization approaches to estimation of structural models, Discussion Papers 1460, Northwestern University, Center for Mathematical Studies in Economics and Management.

CHAPTER 35

Computational Modeling and Trade Policy Analysis: Some Key Contributions of Alan Deardorff

Will Martin

The World Bank

It's a pleasure to have the opportunity to comment on Alan's work on computational modeling and trade policy analysis. Alan came to this field from highbrow economic theory, where he made particularly important contributions on esoteric theoretical issues such as cones of diversification. From this background, he and his collaborators made major practical contributions to helping build support for some of the most important and far-reaching agreements — including the Tokyo Round of the GATT; the Uruguay Round of the GATT/WTO, and the North American Free Trade Agreement. Alan's applied studies took into account many of the mind-numbing details of these agreements, and incorporated new developments — such as services — where the data were poor and even the theoretical basis for analysis needed to be developed from scratch. This contribution by a leading theorist to influential analyses of applied policies is very unusual, and deserves high praise.

Some of the key themes and interests in Alan's long and productive career have been

1. Highbrow economic theory,
2. Computational analysis of trade negotiations,
3. Trade in services,
4. Trade and labor, and
5. Globalization and intellectual property.

Here, I'll focus on Alan's contributions to the computational analysis of trade negotiations.

Alan was, along with Bob Stern, a pioneer in the use of quantitative economic models for the analysis of trade negotiations. Beginning in 1973–4, they developed the Michigan model of global production, consumption, and trade, and employed it in pioneering analyses of the implications of the Tokyo Round (Deardorff and Stern, 1979). This study, produced as a report to the Committee on Finance for the United States Senate, calculates the reductions in average tariffs implied by the tariff-cutting formula (the famous Swiss formula) and the exceptions from this formula allowed during the negotiating process. It then proceeds to calculate the impacts on economic welfare, exchange rates, outputs, sectoral employment, and other key economic variables.

The Michigan model used simpler, linear solution methods than many other models, with the advantage that this allowed solution of larger models, and hence more detailed information on the sectoral impacts of reforms — information of great interest to many policy makers. In an era where modelers needed to be jacks of all trades, this model was originally solved using FORTRAN code written from scratch by Alan. In an era before the large-scale collection and harmonization of input-output, trade, and protection data under the GTAP project (Hertel, 1997), Alan and Bob found it necessary to make the striking assumption that the structure of numerous developing countries could be approximated using the available input-output table for Brazil.

A key element of the Michigan model project was careful documentation of the model, and its applications, in volumes such as Deardorff and Stern (1986). Alan and Bob sought, and sometimes obtained unsolicited, comments and advice on their model and its results. A key feature of their work — and a model for subsequent scholars — was the way they built careful responses to these comments into subsequent versions of their models.

The Michigan model was part of the pioneering wave of models that showed the importance of taking general-equilibrium effects into account when evaluating trade agreements. Taking into account cross-price effects, input-market linkages, and market access implications is particularly important when considering the effects of thousands of simultaneous tariff changes. Yet most of the studies of the Tokyo Round used much simpler techniques that omitted these important linkages. A key feature of this modeling effort was the attention paid by Alan and Bob to surveying the econometric literature — and estimating directly where necessary — the key parameters on which the reliability of their results depended.

The Michigan model was regularly updated and developed through the 1980s as new software became available, and theoretical developments provided new opportunities for enhancement. Pioneering work with Drusilla Brown resulted in a new model, the Brown–Deardorff–Stern model, that included key insights from the "new" trade theory, particularly the welfare implications of the new trade theory where consumers have a preference for variety. Because it included preference for variety only amongst manufactures, this model emphasized the importance of liberalizing manufactures, relative to agriculture, and was particularly suited to the analysis of liberalization of services trade.

Another key area of interest for Alan has been the liberalization of trade in services. When this was first incorporated into international agreements, economists had to rush to catch up. At first, the best that could be done was to classify — a process which generated the classification into four modes of supply which lives to this day in the General Agreement on Trade in Services. However, Brown, Deardorff, Fox, and Stern (1996) quickly moved to fill the analytical gap, providing measures of the consequences of liberalizing trade in services. To do this, they relied heavily on the measures of the extent of liberalization of services trade developed by Alan's and Bob's former student, Bernard Hoekman (1996).

Alan's long and distinguished career and his important contributions to policy analysis provide some important lessons for those seeking a brilliant career in analysis and policy. The first lesson is the importance of keeping policy work well grounded in — and motivated and guided by — economic theory. The second is the importance of ensuring that the relevant measures of economic distortions are estimated using sound conceptual and empirical measures. The third is to carefully examine the features of any agreements under analysis — as the devil can be thoroughly embedded in the details. The fourth is surely the desirability of having a great seminar series like the Michigan research seminar in international economics. The fifth is to have great graduate students like the many presenting in this seminar. The sixth lesson is surely the desirability of seeking feedback and criticism, and taking it on board in subsequent phases of project work. The final, and most important, lesson is surely the importance of being a delightful, humorous, and slightly eccentric colleague and friend to all.

Of course, our hypothetical scholar also has the opportunity to stand on the shoulders of Alan and his cohort. Anyone seeking to follow Alan in using computable general equilibrium analysis has many advantages. Perhaps foremost is the development of the GTAP database (Hertel, 1997) that frees the researcher from the need to become a master of the intricacies of input-output databases, and their concordance with databases on trade and protection. Another advantage is the availability of software suites such as GAMS and GEMPACK specifically designed for solving large-scale models. Protection databases such as MAcMAPs have also advanced in leaps and bounds, allowing us to capture the intricacies of preferential trade regimes. And new aggregation schemes (Bach and Martin, 2001; Anderson, 2009; Laborde, Martin, and van der Mensbrugghe, 2011) allow us to avoid the errors inherent in using crude trade-weighted averages. A key challenge of the moment is to include the insights of the new new trade theory (Melitz, 2003) where the implications of heterogeneity in firms and other actors are taken into account, and extensive-margin adjustments to the range of products traded (Hummels and Klenow, 2005) are taken into account.

REFERENCES

Anderson, J.E., 2009, Consistent trade policy aggregation, *International Economic Review* 50(3), 903–927.

Bach, C. and W. Martin, 2001, Would the right tariff aggregator for policy analysis please stand up?, *Journal of Policy Modeling* 23(6), 621–635.

Brown, D., A.V. Deardorff, A.K. Fox, and R.M. Stern, 1996, The liberalization of services trade: Potential impacts in the aftermath of the Uruguay Round, in W. Martin, and L.A. Winters, eds., The Uruguay Round and the Developing Countries (Cambridge University Press, Cambridge).

Deardorff, A. and R. Stern, 1979, An economic analysis of the effects of the Tokyo Round of Multilateral Trade Negotiations on the United States and the other major industrialized countries, MTN Studies 5, Committee on Finance, United States Senate.

Deardorff, A. and R. Stern, 1986, The Michigan Model of World Production and Trade (MIT Press, Cambridge, MA).

Hertel, T., 1997, Global Economic Analysis: Modeling and Applications (Cambridge University Press, New York).

Hoekman, B., 1996, Assessing the Uruguay Round agreement on services, in W. Martin and L.A. Winters, eds., The Uruguay Round and the Developing Countries (Cambridge University Press, Cambridge).

Hummels, D. and P. Klenow, 2005, The variety and quality of a nation's exports, *American Economic Review* 95(3), 704–723.

Laborde, D., W. Martin, and D. van der Mensbrugghe, 2011, Measuring the benefits of global trade reform with optimal aggregators of distortions, World Bank Policy Research Working Paper, forthcoming.

Melitz, M., 2003, The Impact of trade on intra-industry reallocations and aggregate industry productivity, *Econometrica* 71(6), 1695–1725.

CHAPTER 36†

The Michigan Model of World Production and Trade

Alan V. Deardorff and Robert M. Stern

2 Theoretical Structure of the Model

We begin this chapter with a pictorial overview of one version of the model and a discussion of some of its relevant features that may be helpful in understanding how it works. We then present the detailed equations, including the notation for the endogenous and exogenous variables. Thereafter, we discuss how the supply and demand functions of consumers and firms are modeled, the substitution between imports and domestic goods, and the treatment of nontariff barriers, import licensing, rest-of-world net supply, and economic welfare. As an aid to understanding the significance of many of these features of the model, the last portion of the chapter provides a pair of simple theoretical models that illustrate how the more elaborate computational model works. The first of these simple models is a microeconomic, partial-equilibrium model, while the second is a simple Keynesian macroeconomic model. The latter also allows us to discuss briefly the issue of macroeconomic closure and how it is resolved in the Michigan model. The chapter closes with a short comparison of the Michigan model with others in the literature.

Overview of the Model[1]

The model is best thought of as composed of two parts: the country system and the world system. The country system is depicted in figure 2.1. It contains separate blocks of equations for each country, each one of which takes the form shown in the figure. The world system, sketched in figure 2.2, contains a single set of equations for the world as a whole. The country blocks are used first to determine each country's supplies and demands for goods and currencies on world markets as functions of exogenous variables and of world prices and exchange rates. These functions for each country are then combined to provide the input to the world system in figure 2.2, which permits world prices and exchange rates to be determined. These variables

† This chapter is taken with permission from Alan V. Deardorff and Robert M. Stern, 1986, The Michigan Model of World Production and Trade: Theory and Applications (MIT Press, Cambridge, MA), Chapter 2, pp. 9–36 and Chapter 10, pp. 219–233, along with the respective Notes, pp. 249–250 and 260–261, and References, pp. 263–268.

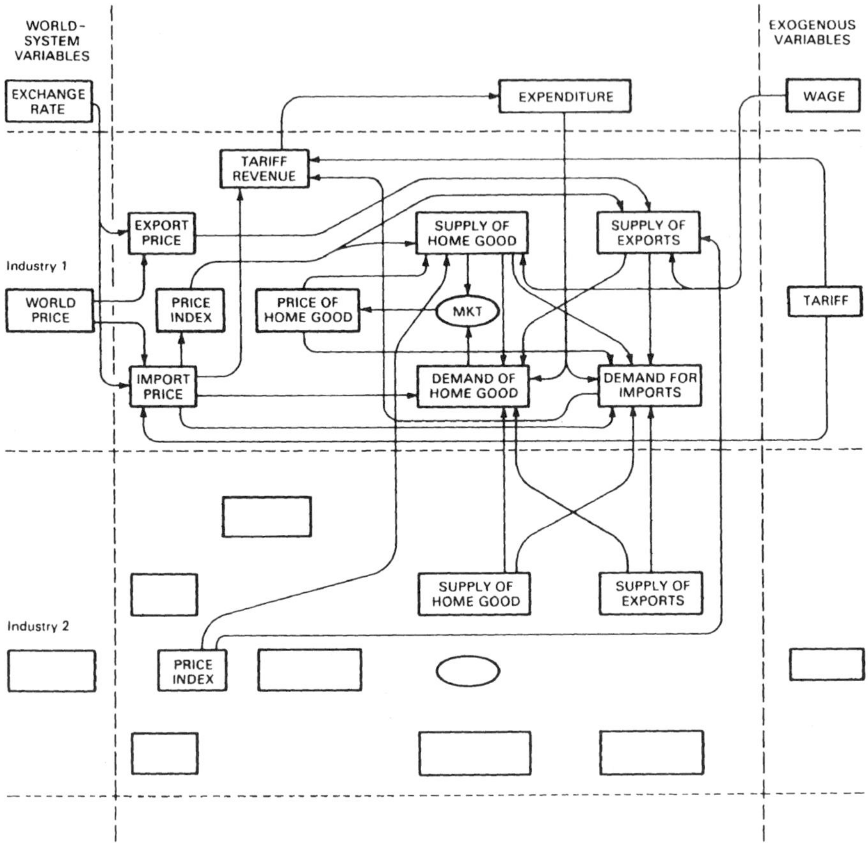

Figure 2.1
Country system.

are finally entered back into the separate country blocks to obtain values for other country-specific variables.

The most complicated economic interactions that are incorporated in the model are contained in the country blocks depicted in figure 2.1. The figure is divided into a number of parts, both horizontally and vertically. The horizontal divisions (finely dashed lines) separate industries, with those variables that pertain to the country as a whole listed across the top. As will be noted, each country included in the model has 29 industries. But since these industries are assumed to be identical in structure, we include only two of them in figure 2.1, with complete labels and arrows only in the first. The reader should thus imagine figure 2.1 extending a considerable distance beyond the page, with additional horizontal blocks for each of the remaining industries.

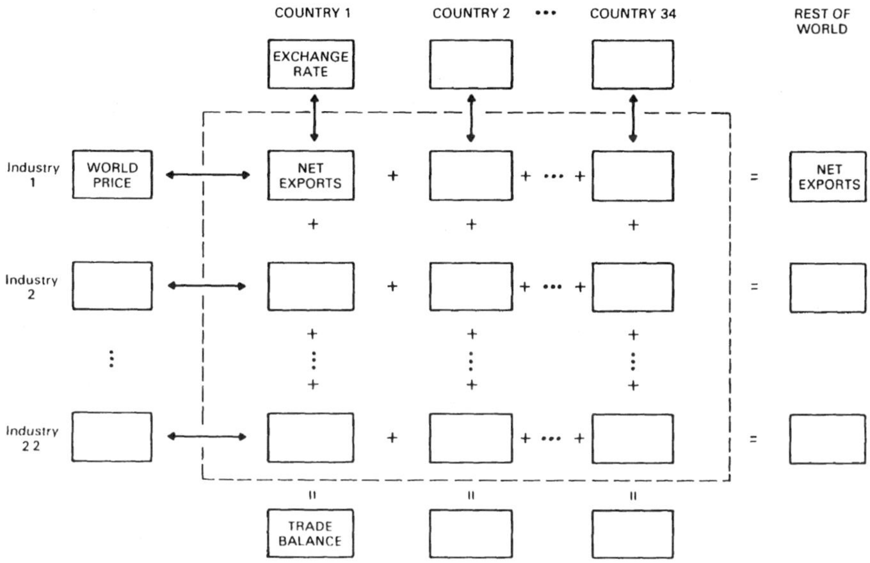

Figure 2.2
World system.

The vertical divisions in figure 2.1 (broadly dashed lines) separate exogenous variables on the right, country-specific endogenous variables in the middle, and variables to be determined in the world on the left. For illustrative purposes we include in the right-hand column only two exogenous variables: the country's tariff in each industry and its money wage, which we take here to be common to all industries. Other exogenous variables included in the model will be noted. The left-hand column contains the country's exchange rate and the world price for each industry. The variables in the center column reflect the complex demand and supply interactions of the consumers and firms represented in the model.

The world system in figure 2.2 is much simpler than the country system. We start with the export-supply and import-demand functions from the country equations, which depend on both world prices and exchange rates. To get world prices we simply add these supplies and demands for all countries (along rows in the figure) and set the difference equal to net demand from the rest of the world. To get exchange rates, when these are flexible, we likewise add the values of these excess supplies for a given country for all industries (along columns in the figure) and equate the resulting trade balances to exogenously given net capital flows. As mentioned, once we obtain the world prices for each traded-good industry and the exchange rate for each country, we can enter them into the separate country blocks in order to determine the rest of the relevant country-specific variables.

Figures 2.1 and 2.2 should provide the reader with some feel for the model. Let us now examine the structure of the model more formally and in greater detail.

Equations of the Model[2]

What we have described so far is a simple version of our model, without many of the complicating features, most of them optional, that we have built in over the years. The complete model, though without functional forms, is presented as equations (2.1)–(2.17)[3] (square brackets indicate variables that appear only with Cobb-Douglas specification of technology); functional forms appear in the technical appendix at the end of the book:

Country-system equations

Supply functions of products for export:

$$S_{ij}^{X} = S_{ij}^{X}(p_{ij}^{X}, p_{i1}^{H}, \ldots, p_{in'}^{H}, p_{i1}^{M}, \ldots, p_{in}^{M}, w_{ij}, K_{ij}^{X}), \quad i = 1, \ldots, m, \quad j = 1, \ldots, n. \tag{2.1}$$

Supply functions of products for home use:

$$S_{ij}^{H} = S_{ij}^{H}(t_{ij}^{H}\, p_{ij}^{H}, p_{i1}^{H}, \ldots, p_{in'}^{H}, p_{i1}^{M}, \ldots, p_{in}^{M}, w_{ij}, K_{ij}^{H}), \quad i = 1, \ldots, m, \quad j = 1, \ldots, n'. \tag{2.2}$$

Demand functions for imported goods:

$$\begin{aligned} D_{ij}^{M} = D_{ij}^{M}(&p_{ij}^{M}, p_{ij}^{H}, E_i, [p_{i1}^{H}]\, S_{i1}^{H}, \ldots, [p_{in'}^{H}]\, S_{in'}^{H}, \\ &[p_{i1}^{X}]S_{i1}^{X}, \ldots, [p_{in}^{X}]S_{in}^{X}, G_{ij}), \\ &i = 1, \ldots, m, \quad j = 1, \ldots, n. \end{aligned} \tag{2.3}$$

Demand functions for home-produced goods:

Tradables:

$$\begin{aligned} D_{ij}^{H} = D_{ij}^{H}(&p_{ij}^{H}, p_{ij}^{M}, E_i, [p_{i1}^{H}]S_{i1}^{H}, \ldots, [p_{in'}^{H}]S_{in'}^{H}, \\ &[p_{i1}^{X}]S_{i1}^{X}, \ldots, [p_{in}^{X}]S_{in}^{X}, G_{ij}), \\ &i = 1, \ldots, m, \quad j = 1, \ldots, n. \end{aligned} \tag{2.4a}$$

Nontradables:

$$\begin{aligned} D_{ij}^{H} = D_{ij}^{H}(&p_{ij}^{H}, E_i, [p_{i1}^{H}]S_{i1}^{H}, \ldots, [p_{in'}^{H}]S_{in'}^{H}, \\ &[p_{i1}^{X}]S_{i1}^{X}, \ldots, [p_{in}^{X}]S_{in}^{X}), \\ &i = 1, \ldots, m, \quad j = n + 1, \ldots, n'. \end{aligned} \tag{2.4b}$$

Export prices:

$$p_{ij}^{X} = t_{ij}^{Xeq} R_i p_j^{W}, \qquad i = 1, \ldots, m, \quad j = 1, \ldots, n. \tag{2.5}$$

Import prices:

$$p_{ij}^{M} = t_{ij}^{Meq} R_i p_j^{W}, \qquad i = 1, \ldots, m, \quad j = 1, \ldots, n. \tag{2.6}$$

Consumer expenditure and tariff revenue:

With exogenous expenditure component:

$$E_i = E_i^0 + \sum_{j=1}^{n} (t_{ij}^{Meq} - 1) R_i p_j^W D_{ij}^M + \sum_{j=1}^{n} (1 - t_{ij}^{Xeq}) R_i p_j^W S_{ij}^X + \sum_{j=1}^{n'} (1 - t_{ij}^{H}) p_{ij}^{H} S_{ij}^{H}, \qquad i = 1, \ldots, m. \tag{2.7a}$$

Endogenous to hold employment constant:

$$\sum_{j=1}^{n'} D_{ij}^{L} = S_i^{L0}, \qquad i = 1, \ldots, m. \tag{2.7b}$$

Market equilibrium for home goods:

$$S_{ij}^{H} = D_{ij}^{H}, \qquad i = 1, \ldots, m, \quad j = 1, \ldots, n'. \tag{2.8}$$

Tariff equivalents:

To reflect quantitative restrictions:

$$t_{ij}^{Meq} = t_{ij}^{Meq}(t_{ij}^{M}, D_{ij}^{M}, Q_{ij}^{M}), \qquad i = 1, \ldots, m, \quad j = 1, \ldots, n. \tag{2.9a}$$

To reflect import licensing:

$$D_{ij}^{M} = L_{ij}\left(\sum_{k=1}^{n} p_k^W S_{ik}^X + B_i^{K0} \right), \qquad i = 1, \ldots, m, \quad j = 1, \ldots, n. \tag{2.9b}$$

To determine exogenous imports:

$$D_{ij}^{M} = D_{ij}^{M0}, \qquad i = 1, \ldots, m, \quad j = 1, \ldots, n. \tag{2.9c}$$

Export tax equivalents:

To reflect quantitative restrictions:

$$t_{ij}^{Xeq} = t_{ij}^{Xeq}(t_{ij}^{X}, S_{ij}^{X}, Q_{ij}^{X}), \qquad i = 1,\ldots,m, \quad j = 1,\ldots,n. \tag{2.10a}$$

To determine exogenous exports:

$$S_{ij}^{X} = S_{ij}^{X0}, \qquad i = 1,\ldots,m, \quad j = 1,\ldots,n. \tag{2.10b}$$

Demand for labor by industry:

Tradables:

$$D_{ij}^{L} = D_{ij}^{L}([w_{ij}], [p_{ij}^{X}], [p_{ij}^{H}], S_{ij}^{X}, S_{ij}^{H}, K_{ij}^{X}, K_{ij}^{H}), \qquad i = 1,\ldots,m, \quad j = 1,\ldots,n. \tag{2.11a}$$

Nontradables:

$$D_{ij}^{L} = D_{ij}^{L}([w_{ij}], [p_{ij}^{H}], S_{ij}^{H}, K_{ij}^{H}), \qquad i = 1,\ldots,m, \quad j = n+1,\ldots,n'. \tag{2.11b}$$

Labour markets:

Exogenous wages:

$$w_{ij} = w_i^0, \qquad i = 1,\ldots,m, \quad j = 1,\ldots,n'. \tag{2.12a}$$

Country-wide labor market:

$$\sum_{j=1}^{n'} D_{ij}^{L} = S_i^{L0}, \qquad w_{ij} = w_{ik}, \qquad i = 1,\ldots,m, \quad j \neq k = 1,\ldots,n'. \tag{2.12b}$$

Industry labor market:

$$D_{ij}^{L} = S_{ij}^{L0}, \qquad i = 1,\ldots,m, \quad j = 1,\ldots,n'. \tag{2.12c}$$

Net exports:

$$N_{ij}^{X} = S_{ij}^{X} - D_{ij}^{M}, \qquad i = 1,\ldots,m, \quad j = 1,\ldots,n. \tag{2.13}$$

World-system equations

Market equilibrium for traded goods:

$$\sum_{i=1}^{m} N_{ij}^{X} + N_{j}^{row} = 0, \qquad j = 1, \ldots, n. \tag{2.14}$$

Trade balances:

$$B_i^T = \sum_{j=1}^{n} p_j^W N_{ij}^X, \qquad i = 1, \ldots, m. \tag{2.15}$$

Rest-of-world net supply:

$$N_j^{row} = N_j^{row}(p_1^W, \ldots, p_n^W, R_1, \ldots, R_m), \qquad j = 1, \ldots, n. \tag{2.16}$$

Exchange rates:

Fixed rates:

$$R_i = \prod_{j \neq i} R_j^{\theta_{ij}^R} R_i^0, \qquad i = 1, \ldots, m. \tag{2.17a}$$

Flexible rates:

$$B_i^T + B_i^{K0} = 0, \qquad R_m = R_m^0, \qquad i = 1, \ldots, m-1. \tag{2.17b}$$

Notation (m = number of countries; n = number of tradable goods; n' = number of goods total)

Endogenous variables:

S_{ij}^X, S_{ij}^H = supply of good j by country i, export and home sectors, respectively,

D_{ij}^M, D_{ij}^H = demand for good j in country i, imported and home-produced, respectively,

p_{ij}^X, p_{ij}^M = domestic price of good j in country i, exported and imported, respectively,

p_{ij}^H = home-sector price of good j in country i,

p_j^W = world price of good j,

E_i = consumer expenditure in country i,

B_i^T = balance of trade of country i,

R_i = exchange rate of country i, (domestic currency per unit of world currency),

D_{ij}^L = demand for labor in industry j in country i,

w_{ij} = wage of labor in industry j in country i,

$t_{ij}^{Xeq}, t_{ij}^{Meq}$ = export tax and tariff equivalents in industry j in country i, respectively,

N_{ij}^{X} = net exports of industry j in country i,

N_{j}^{row} = rest-of-world net supply in industry j.

Exogenous variables:

K_{ij}^{X}, K_{ij}^{H} = capital stock of industry j in country i, export and home sectors, respectively,

w_{i}^{0} = money wage in country i, if exogenous,

t_{ij}^{M} = 1 plus the ad valorem tariff on imports of good j into country i,

t_{ij}^{X}, t_{ij}^{H} = 1 minus the ad valorem tax on exports and home production, respectively, in industry j of country i,

G_{ij} = shift parameter representing government procurement in industry j in country i,

E_{i}^{0} = exogenous component of expenditure in country i,

R_{i}^{0} = exogenous exchange rate,

B_{i}^{K0} = exogenous capital inflow in country i,

Q_{ij}^{X}, Q_{ij}^{M} = shift parameter for quantitative restrictions on exports and imports, respectively, in industry j in country i,

D_{ij}^{M0}, S_{ij}^{X0} = imports and exports respectively, of industry j in country i, if exogenous,

S_{i}^{L0}, S_{ij}^{L0} = country i and industry j supplies of labor,

θ_{ij}^{R} = weight used in pegging currency of country i to that of country j.

The model includes m countries, $i = 1, \ldots, m$, producing and trading n goods, $j = 1, \ldots, n$, and producing an additional $(n' - n)$ nontradable goods, $j = n + 1, \ldots, n'$. A distinguishing characteristic of our model, however, is that both producers and consumers distinguish, within tradable industries, between home goods, which are produced and used domestically, and those that are either exported or imported. As a result there are really $2n$ goods produced by the n tradable industries, since each has both a home-market and an export product. Also, the number of markets for these goods is even greater than $2n$, since each country has its own home market in each industry.

Thus, within each country and tradable industry, producers are separated into a home sector and an export sector. Each has its own supply function, reflecting certain fixed factors of production that cannot easily be transferred between the sectors. This nontransferability may result from locational requirements or from the need to tailor products to national markets, though these features are not explicit in our model.

Demanders, too, differentiate between home-produced and imported products of a given tradable industry. Consumers and government, as well as producers who demand intermediate inputs and investment goods, are assumed to regard home-produced and imported goods as imperfect substitutes, but imports from various foreign countries as perfect substitutes.[4] The same elasticity of substitution is assumed to apply to all of these groups of demanders. Thus, demands for imports and home-produced goods are separate, but depend on the prices of both. On the other hand, a unit elasticity of substitution in final demand is assumed across industries, so that there are no direct cross-price effects in the demand functions of equations (2.3) and (2.4) except when there is a Cobb-Douglas specification of intermediate input technology.

Three separate prices obtain in each country, i, for each tradable industry, $j = 1, \ldots, n$. First, a home price, p_{ij}^H, is paid by users and received by producers in the home sector.[5] It is determined by the equality of home-sector supply and demand in equation (2.8). The second and third prices are those received for exports, p_{ij}^X, and those paid for imports, p_{ij}^M. All countries face a common world price, p_j^W, in each tradable industry, and it is determined in a world market to be described. Export and import prices are obtained from this in equations (2.5) and (2.6) by using exchange rates, R_i, and export tax and tariff-equivalent variables to be explained.

Equations (2.1)–(2.4), then, present supply and demand functions in terms of these prices, plus wages, expenditure levels, and various exogenous shift parameters. Supplies depend on all home and import prices, and demands depend on all supplies, both to reflect the use of intermediate inputs to production.

The aggregate behavior of the model depends crucially on the assumption made about aggregate expenditure, E_i. Our model is intended to focus on microeconomic and intersectoral issues, and we therefore wanted as neutral a characterization of macroeconomic policy as possible, one that would leave aggregates largely unaffected.[6] With this in mind we have, at various times, employed the two alternative assumptions shown in equations (2.7a) and (2.7b). In (2.7a) aggregate nominal expenditure is essentially exogenous. However, all tax and tariff revenue is assumed to be redistributed to consumers and spent, so that expenditure in (2.7a) equals this revenue plus an exogenous component. Alternatively, in (2.7b) we let aggregate expenditure vary endogenously so as to hold aggregate employment constant. One might think of the latter as assuming that macroeconomic policy is somehow successfully undertaken so as to stabilize the economy.

The remaining equations for each country, (2.9)–(2.13), determine tariff and export-tax equivalents, labor demands and wages, and net exports. The first of these include several cases to be explained. There are also three different assumptions made about labor markets, but these should be self-explanatory from the list of equations and variables. Net exports in each industry are just the difference between export supplies and import demands, and it is these that feed into the world-system equations (2.14)–(2.17), where world prices and exchange rates, if flexible, are determined.

Focusing on the world-system equations, note first that equilibrium in world markets for traded goods is required in equation (2.14), where the sum of these net exports plus net supply from the rest of the world is set equal to zero. This determines world prices, p_j^W. Next, the values of net exports are added over industries to form each country's balance of trade in equation (2.15). Rest-of-world net supply in each industry is determined in equation (2.16) as a simple and rather ad hoc function of world prices and exchange rates.

Finally, the exchange rates are determined in equations (2.17), with separate cases for fixed and flexible exchange-rate regimes. For any country with a pegged exchange rate, equation (2.17a) sets it equal to an index of other-country rates. Depending on the weights in this index, the peg may either be to a basket of currencies or to a particular currency. For any country with a flexible exchange rate, on the other hand, (2.17b) determines it by the requirement that its balance of trade plus an exogenous capital inflow be equal to zero.

Only $m - 1$ markets need to be cleared explicitly, due to Walras's law.[7] However, to determine absolute prices and exchange rates, we must then specify a numeraire. This is done in the last of equations (2.17b), where we fix the exchange rate of country m.

Since exogenous capital flows are specified in units of the numeraire, the selection of m is not trivial. In applying the model, we have chosen the U.S. dollar as the numeraire, with means that the dollar values of capital flows are assumed to be constant.

Supply and Demand Functions

We derived explicit supply and demand functions from utility and profit maximization of consumers and firms, assuming explicit utility and production functions. Details of these derivations are contained in Deardorff, Stern, and Baum (1976). Here we merely report the assumptions that were made, and the results themselves are listed in the appendix.

Since both producers and consumers demand goods, and since each tradable industry has both imported and home-produced goods available, we first characterized the choice between the two. This was done, for each industry, with functions that aggregate the services of home and imported goods. These then enter as arguments in both utility and production functions. To permit choice of the degree of substitution between home and imported goods, these aggregation functions were specified as Constant Elasticity of Substitution (CES) functions. The substitution elasticities for each industry were then inferred from published econometric estimates of import-demand elasticities.[8]

To obtain consumer demand functions, we used a Cobb-Douglas utility function. Its arguments were nontradable consumption levels plus these aggregates of home and imported tradable goods. By maximizing this utility function for a given level of expenditure, we obtained consumer demand functions for each industry.

It will be noted that the demands depend only on expenditure and on home and import prices of the own industry. Prices from other industries do not appear, since Cobb-Douglas utility forces cross elasticities of demand to be zero.

For firms, we assumed production functions whose arguments were again these home-import aggregates for each industry plus an aggregate of primary factors as well. The aggregate function for primary factors (labor and capital) was also specified as CES.[9] These aggregates were related by fixed coefficients in the primary version of the model, though we have also used a Cobb-Douglas technology, which permits more substitution among the inputs. The model can accommodate different input-output data for each country. However, we have so far been unable to gather and process that much data. Instead, we have used tables for only the United States, Japan, EEC member countries, and Brazil. The US table has been applied to the remaining 8 industrial countries and the Brazilian table to the other 13 developing countries included in the model.

By solving profit-maximization problems for firms, given their production technologies and capital stocks, we obtained supply functions for the export and home sectors, demand functions for home and imported intermediate inputs, and demand functions for labor. Unlike consumer demand functions, the firm-supply functions depend on prices in all industries, since all may provide intermediate inputs. Also, while firm-demand functions do not directly involve cross-price effects, they do have such effects indirectly, since they depend on supplies, which in turn depend on all prices.

The main difference between the two specifications of technology is that input-demand functions for Cobb-Douglas technology depend directly on output price and, for labor, on the wage. With fixed coefficients, output alone determines the demand for all inputs except for the division between home goods and imports. But with substitution allowed, the prices of inputs relative to output matter for input demands, even once the level of output is known.

A further difference is also worth noting. Own-price elasticities of supply and demand are all somewhat larger with Cobb-Douglas technology than with fixed coefficients, as one would expect with increased substitution.

The supply and demand functions of firms and consumers have been aggregated to get the explicit versions of equations (2.1)–(2.4) and (2.11) that appear as (A.4.1)–(A.4.4) and (A.4.11) in the appendix.

The Armington Assumption

In common with other empirically based trade models, we found early on that the traditional trade-theoretic assumption of perfect substitutability between domestic and foreign goods was not workable. On the one hand, such perfect substitutability is inconsistent with the empirical fact that countries have both exports and imports in any given industry. While such "cross hauling" may be dismissed as an artificial result of aggregation, an empirical model is necessarily aggregative and must be designed to be consistent with the data. Even more important, as we shall discuss further in chapter 10, perfect substitutability between domestic and foreign goods is inconsistent with the empirically observed elasticities that seem to prevail in international trade. It is difficult, if not impossible, to specify the parameters of behavior in such a way as to generate these observed elasticities and still maintain the assumption of perfect substitutability.

However, the size of our model in terms of countries has until recently made it impractical to implement fully the Armington (1969) assumption that goods are differentiated completely on the basis of country of origin. To implement the Armington assumption requires simultaneous solution for equilibrium in some 748 world markets (22 tradable goods times 34 countries). Such a task has been completed in Brown (1984), and it will be interesting in subsequent research to determine what differences may emerge between our model and Brown's. Some differences will be noted later. In any event, the assumptions that we have made instead—which separate production for export from production for the domestic market and which permit demanders to differentiate only between home-produced goods and imports—together enable us to represent the essence of the Armington assumption. That is, we have "home" markets for each tradable good, and in these home markets prices can vary independently of the prices of both exports and imports.

Although, as mentioned, it is now possible using Brown's model to implement the full Armington differentiation of imports by place of production, the model that accomplishes this is still very expensive to solve and therefore not practical for many of our purposes here, which require that multiple solutions be carried out. In addition, the Armington assumption as it is usually implemented dampens not only the substitution between a country's own goods and imports, but also the substitution in third-country markets between a country's exports and exports of its competitors. We remain unconvinced that this is necessarily the best assumption that can be made, and therefore believe that our own approach, even though it was originally motivated for computational reasons, has much to recommend it.

Nonetheless, the two alternative assumptions do have different implications for some of our results. For example, Brown (1985) has compared her results for the Tokyo Round with ours and has found a notable difference between the results of the two models in terms of which countries tend to benefit from multilateral tariff reductions. Thus, while the total effects of the Tokyo Round are very small in both models, the distribution of those effects across countries is different in the two. In our model, where efficiency effects seem to dominate the welfare calculations, those countries that reduce tariffs the most tend to gain the most from the Tokyo Round. In contrast, in Brown's model with the full Armington assumption, there are stronger terms of trade effects because of each country's greater influence over its own export prices. As a result, Brown's analysis of the Tokyo Round finds the greatest gainers to be those countries that reduce tariffs the least, including especially the LDCs (Less Developed Countries) that were not included in the negotiations.

Nontariff Barriers

We modeled the presence of quantitative restrictions (QRs) on imports by using tariff equivalents, t_{ij}^{Meq}, that vary endogenously to dampen the quantitative response of imports to changes in other variables. We also include a similar facility for handling QRs on exports, through an export-tax-equivalent variable, t_{ij}^{Xeq}, though we have not yet had much occasion to use this.

The tariff equivalent is defined as a weighted average of the nominal tariff variable, t_{ij}^{M}, and a second implicit tariff variable, t_{ij}^{QM}, that would reflect binding QRs for the entire industry. The weights are given by the fraction of the industry in which QRs are binding. The implicit tariff is defined as one that would, in a typical import demand equation, keep the quantity demanded equal to an exogenous value, Q_{ij}^{M}, set by a quota. The result, as shown in the appendix, is a simple expression relating the tariff equivalent to the nominal tariff and to the difference between the quota and import demand.

A rise in the quantity of permitted imports lowers the tariff equivalent and does in fact stimulate imports. On the other hand, changes (such as a fall in the world price) that would normally increase demand for imports will cause the tariff equivalent to rise and so cause the change in quantity to be smaller than it would otherwise be. Similar remarks apply to the export-tax equivalent, where it should be remembered that t_{ij}^{Xeq} is actually *one minus* the export-tax equivalent, which therefore varies inversely with t_{ij}^{Xeq}.

This formulation permits us to analyze problems other than nontariff barriers (NTBs) under the realistic and important assumption that NTBs are present and restrict the responsiveness of trade. This is accomplished by merely making the fractions θ_{ij}^{QM} and θ_{ij}^{QX} nonzero in industries where this is appropriate. In addition, by using the exogenous variables, Q_{ij}^{M} and Q_{ij}^{X}, we have been able to analyze the effect of changing a QR, so long as we know the volume of trade that is being released from a binding constraint. This is how we have treated the changes in agricultural quotas in our analysis of the Tokyo Round.

Import Licensing

A new feature of the model that we felt necessary with the addition of developing countries is the treatment of import licensing. Many of these countries have pegged exchange rates, but they are often unable to finance all of the imports that would be desired at that (or perhaps any) exchange rate and so resort to more direct regulation of import behavior.

We have modeled this again through the tariff-equivalent variable, t_{ij}^{Meq}. For countries where licensing is in effect, we suppress equation (2.9a) and assume instead that t_{ij}^{Meq} incorporates the shadow price of scarce foreign exchange to a particular sector. The government is assumed to allocate the foreign exchange that is earned from exports and capital inflows among importers in proportion to some base level of imports that is established. As a result, each sector's imports depend on the total value of exports and capital inflow as shown in the licensing function L_{ij} of equation (2.9b). What this specification does is to assure approximate balance-of-payments equilibrium even though the exchange rate is pegged.

Along with import licensing, we also modeled a subsidy to exports equal to the export sector's payment of any tariff equivalent on imported inputs. This was done to prevent import licensing from adversely affecting exports through its effect on input prices. Essentially, we are saying that exporters are exempt from licensing when what they import will contribute to production for export.[10]

Rest-of-World Net Supply

With the addition of 16 developing countries to our model, the importance of the sector representing the rest of the world is correspondingly reduced. In the past, we have experimented with several ways of specifying rest-of-world behavior, but for present purposes we have used only one.

We assume that rest-of-world exports in each industry respond positively to the world price with an elasticity, ε_j^r, that is typical of the included countries. Rest-of-world imports are assumed to be subject to import licensing and so are fixed at a constant fraction of the value of rest-of-world exports. Exchange rates in the rest of the world are assumed to be pegged to a basket of currencies of the included countries, with weights that depend primarily on their importance in trade. As a result, rest-of-world net exports in any particular industry depend upon all world prices and exchange rates.

There is one exception to this, however, that concerns the supply, and pricing, of oil. The major oil-producing countries are not part of our model, except as part of the aggregated rest-of-world. Normally this rest-of-world sector is modeled as pegging its exchange rate to a basket of currencies only about 60% of which is the US dollar. To reflect the fact that oil is priced in US dollars, however, we have made rest-of-world supply in the oil industry respond directly to the US dollar price. Since the elasticity of supply in this sector is quite large, this has the effect of essentially fixing that price.

Departures from General Equilibrium

We have already noted that ours is not a full general-equilibrium model. For example, because of our interest in effects on sectoral unemployment in the relatively short run, we do not ordinarily assume equilibrium in labor markets. This same motivation also accounts for our assumption of fixed sectoral stocks of capital. In the case of labor markets we implement our disequilibrium assumption in a rather Keynesian fashion by specifying money wages as fixed.

The model also departs from full general equilibrium in another fundamental way. The system is not "closed" in the sense of having the level of expenditure related directly to the level of earned income. Instead, as noted, we usually take aggregate expenditure to be essentially exogenous, except for a minor modification to permit tax and tariff revenues to be redistributed and spent by consumers. Or, alternatively, we sometimes allow aggregate expenditure to vary endogenously so as to hold aggregate employment constant.

Our treatment of money wages and expenditure together explains the role that exchange rates play in the model. If all nominal values were variable, presumably an exchange rate would play only a nominal role in the model. A devaluation, for example, would simply raise all wages and prices by the same percentage and leave real variables unchanged. With nominally fixed wages and expenditure, however, the exchange rate alters the values of these variables in one country relative to others. Thus, for example, a devaluation reduces the ratio of domestic to foreign wages and has real effects working through relative costs.

It is also important to note that our model is linearized in the neighborhood of an initial equilibrium, and thus yields only an approximation to comparative static changes in the neighborhood of that equilibrium, rather than old and new equilibria themselves. As a result of this linearization, solution of the model does not require any special algorithm. The advantage of this simplicity of solution is that we can include in the model somewhat more industries and countries than are typically present in computable general-equilibrium models, though not as many as have sometimes been included in partial equilibrium estimates of tariff effects.[11] The price we pay for this ability to deal with a large system is that our results are only approximate, and are good approximations depending on whether the changes we consider are relatively small.

Economic Welfare

Although our model provides information on changes in prices and changes in production, consumption, and trade, it does not readily lend itself conceptually to analysis of changes in economic welfare. We decided nonetheless to develop some ad hoc procedures for welfare calculations, and the ones we report in later chapters are based on the static, partial-equilibrium measures commonly used in the literature to calculate changes in consumer and producer surplus.

Theoretical Illustrations of the Model

As a further aid to the reader in understanding the model and how it works, it may be helpful to provide two simplified theoretical models that illustrate certain assumptions and behavior of the model. The first of these is based on conventional supply and demand analysis and is intended to illuminate the microeconomic workings of the Michigan model. The second simple model is based on a Keynesian framework and illustrates the macroeconomic assumptions that are implicit in the Michigan model.

The first of these simple models is shown in figure 2.3 and illustrates the case of a unilateral 50% tariff reduction in a small country with a fixed exchange rate and fixed level of expenditure. To simplify the illustration, suppose that there is only one industry in the economy, and that initial supplies and demands are as shown by the solid curves in the figure.

The world price of the good is p_W yielding an export price in domestic currency of $p_X = Rp_W$, where R is the exchange rate. The tariff, t, implies the somewhat higher import price, p_M^0. In figure 2.3a the home sector of this industry is shown, with supply and demand curves that both depend not only on the home-sector price, p_H, but on the import price, p_M^0, as well. The reasons are that demanders can substitute between home and imported goods, while suppliers rely partly on imported inputs. Together these supply and demand curves determine the equilibrium price, p_H^0, in the home sector.

Similarly, the supply of exports and the demand for imports depend, in figure 2.3b, not only on their respective own prices, p_X and p_M^0, but also on the home sector price p_H^0. Given p_H^0 these curves are determined and lead to quantities traded Q_M^0 and Q_X^0. Since this is the only industry, we have drawn these two quantities as equal, showing initially balanced trade.

Imagine now that the tariff is cut in half. This reduces the import price to p_M, which is easily determined since we assume that both R and p_W are fixed in this illustration. The lower import price shifts both curves in figure 2.3a as shown. The demand curve shifts down by the same proportion as p_M, since essentially only relative prices matter for demand. The supply curve shifts down by less than this, since imports constitute only a fraction of total costs. The result is a drop in both price and quantity in the home sector.

The fall in p_H in turn causes similar shifts in figure 2.3b. That is, both supply of imports and demand for imports are shifted vertically downward

Chapter 2 26

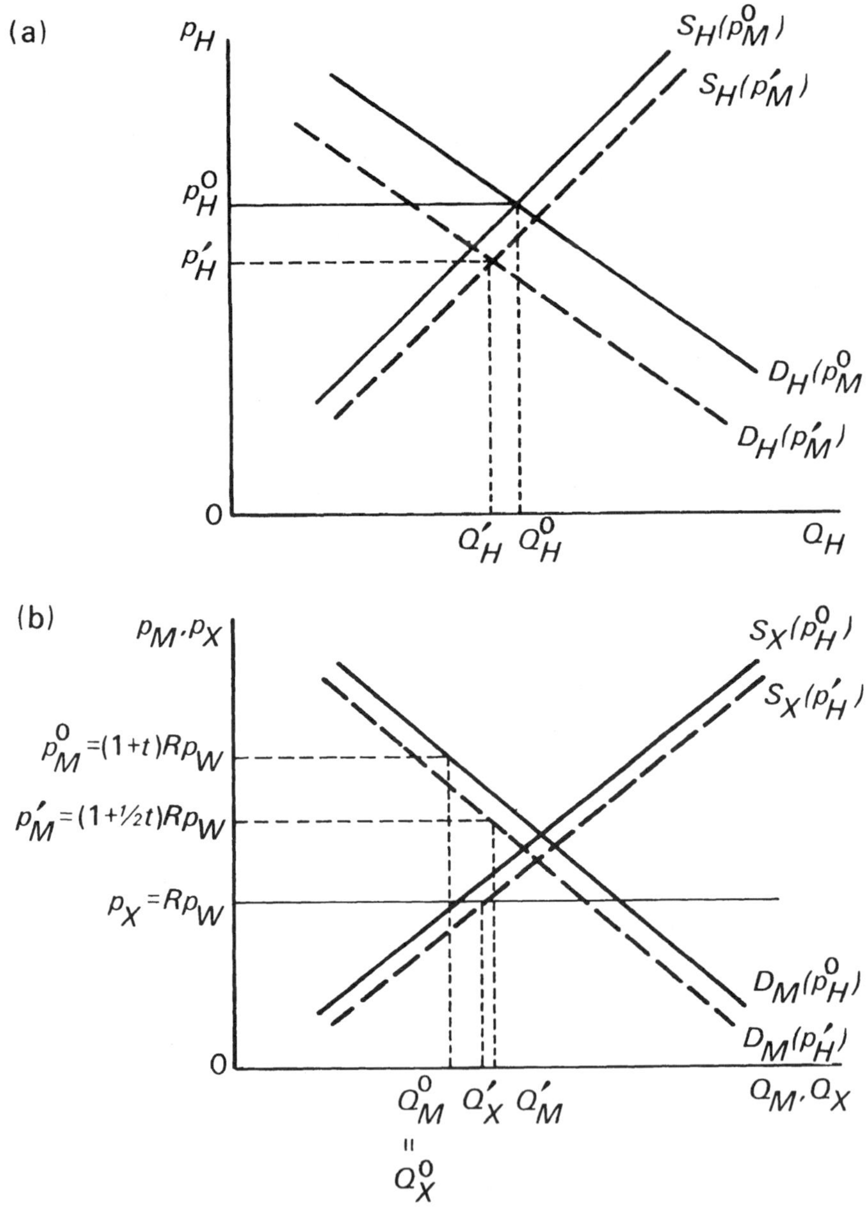

Figure 2.3
Microeconomic effects of a 50% tariff reduction: (a) home sector; (b) exports and imports.

by a small amount. Thus the new quantities traded are found at Q'_H and Q'_M, both above their initial levels. Exports have increased due to a reduction in their costs as input prices have fallen. Imports have increased as a more direct result of the tariff reduction, but the increase has been partially offset by the reduction in the price of home sector goods with which imports compete.

This is as far as the simple analysis of figure 2.3 can take us, but we can use it to sketch briefly some of the additional adjustments that take place in the model. First, we note that quantities produced have fallen in the home sector and risen in the export sector, entailing a movement of labor from the former to the latter. In the event that export expansion is insufficient to absorb all of the labor released from the home sector, then either there will be additional aggregate unemployment or total expenditure will have to be increased, expanding demand in both sectors. Similarly, it is likely as shown in figure 2.3 that a unilateral tariff reduction will expand imports more than exports, worsening the balance of trade. If the exchange rate is flexible, R will rise and both p_X and p_M will increase until trade balance is restored. Finally, if the tariff cut is multilateral, there will be tariff cuts abroad as well as at home, which will cause excess demand on the world market. Thus p_W will also rise somewhat, again causing further adjustments of domestic supplies and demands. Indeed the rise in p_W may eliminate or even reverse the need, in some countries, for the adjustments in expenditure and exchange rates just described.

We turn now to the second of our simple models, which is shown in figure 2.4 and is essentially the standard Keynesian model of income determination and the trade balance, such as may be found, for example, in Dornbusch (1980, chapter 3). The macroeconomic features of the Michigan model have been deliberately kept simple, with the intent of focusing attention more on microeconomic effects such as those we just discussed. Still, in a model where certain nominal values such as wages are held fixed, it is inevitable that some macroeconomic assumptions are being made, and it is as well to understand what they are.

If we imagine aggregating all of the domestic sectors of a country into one, then the Michigan model has the structure of an extremely simple Keynesian model. In goods-market equilibrium, income in a country must be equal to the country's expenditure plus its trade balance,

$$Y = E + (X - M),$$

and income will adjust to bring this about. The top panel of figure 2.4 describes how income is determined in this fashion, equating $(Y - E)$ and $(X - M)$.

Chapter 2 28

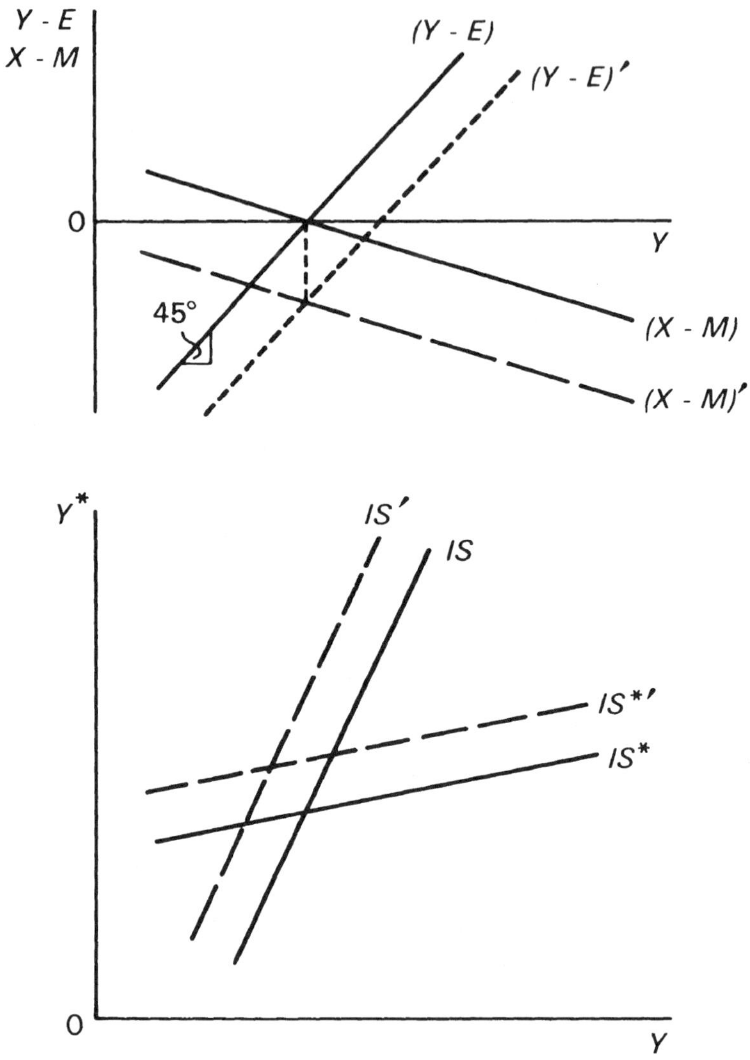

Figure 2.4
Macroeconomic effects of a tariff reduction and exchange-rate appreciation.

If expenditure (which includes all categories of final demand) is held fixed independently of income, as it is in one version of our model, then income net of expenditure ($Y - E$) will be an upward sloping 45° line as shown.[12] The other curve in the top panel is the trade balance, ($X - M$), which is downward sloping under the usual assumption of constant exports and a positive propensity to import. In the Michigan model, while exports are determined by domestic export suppliers rather than directly by foreign demand, it is still true that they depend on variables other than domestic income and can be taken as constant in this kind of analysis. The positive propensity to import is also a feature of the Michigan model, even when expenditure is held fixed, since imports are demanded as intermediate inputs to domestic production.

For a given country, then, income is determined by the intersection of these two curves, which depend in turn on a number of variables, such as aggregate expenditure, foreign income (which affects exports through world prices), and the exchange rate. Incomes in different countries are in turn interrelated, as shown in the bottom panel of figure 2.4 for a simple case of only two countries.

Let Y and Y^* be domestic and foreign incomes, respectively. Suppose first that foreign income, Y^*, falls. The foreign country will then demand fewer imports, causing prices to fall on world markets and inducing domestic firms to export less. This fall in X causes a downward shift in the ($X - M$) curve in the top panel, lowering equilibrium domestic income, Y. Thus a fall in foreign income causes a fall in domestic income, tracing out something like the curve IS in the bottom panel. By similar reasoning, changes in domestic income also lead to changes in foreign income, along a curve such as IS^*, and the two incomes together are determined by the intersection of these curves.

We are now in a position to examine how incomes in the countries, singly and together, are affected by various policy changes under various of the assumptions that we customarily make in the Michigan model. Consider first a unilateral tariff reduction by the domestic country, such as we considered above in figure 2.3. Such a tariff reduction will stimulate the country's imports, raising M and shifting the ($X - M$) curve down. If nothing else happens,[13] this will show up also as a shift of the IS curve in the lower panel to the left to IS'. In addition, the rise in imports will raise world prices of our imported goods, stimulating exports of the foreign country, and thus shifting the IS^* curve also to the left to $IS^{*\prime}$. Together these changes lead to a fall in domestic income and a rise in foreign income, as shown.[14]

However, as we normally use the Michigan model, it is not true that nothing else happens. First, in examining tariff reductions we customarily assume that aggregate expenditure is adjusted endogenously to maintain constant aggregate employment. In this simple model with only one good being produced, this is essentially the same as stabilizing national income.[15] Thus in the analysis of a unilateral tariff reduction, the $(Y - E)$ curve will also shift as this endogenous stabilization policy takes place. That is, while the tariff reduction shifts the $(X - M)$ curve down as shown, it also leads to a rise in expenditure, E, that shifts the $(Y - E)$ curve down as well by just enough to keep equilibrium income constant. This exacerbates the trade imbalance caused by the tariff cut. But if the stabilization policy is pursued in both countries, then it leaves both of the *IS* curves in the lower panel unchanged and thus prevents any change in either country's income. It is in this sense that we have used the assumption of endogenous stabilization policy to neutralize at least some of the aggregate effects of tariff reductions.

Another feature of the model for some countries, and one that reduces the need for this endogenous stabilization policy, is the flexibility of the exchange rate. If the exchange rate is flexible, then the increased trade deficit that would result from a tariff cut will lead instead to a depreciation. This will shift the $(X - M)$ curve back to its initial position without any need for E to change. Thus again, the tariff cut has no effect on equilibrium incomes in either country.

Finally, there may not even be a need for exchange-rate adjustment if the tariff cuts are multilateral rather than unilateral. If tariffs both at home and abroad are reduced, then both exports and imports will rise. Depending on the relative sizes of the tariff reductions and on various elasticities of supply and demand, $(X - M)$ may rise, fall, or remain unchanged. In any case, the need for induced changes in exchange rates and/or expenditure will be considerably reduced.

Thus for tariff reductions the assumptions that we make in applying the Michigan model do have important macroeconomic implications, but they are such as to neutralize, for the most part, the macroeconomic effects of the changes in tariffs.

In contrast, when we analyze exogenous exchange-rate changes in later chapters, we do allow more room for macroeconomic effects. Obviously, in order to examine such changes, we must assume that exchange rates are fixed, and thus one of the mechanisms just mentioned for neutralizing macroeconomic effects is absent. Aggregate expenditure could still be endogenous, of course, but we have preferred to follow the more Keynesian course of keeping it fixed in our analyses of exchange-rate changes. Thus we treat an exchange-rate change as altering not only relative wages across countries (since money wages are fixed), but also relative levels of expenditure.

The simple macroeconomic effects of an exchange rate change can also be seen in figure 2.4. An appreciation of the home country's currency, for example, leads to both a fall in exports and a rise in imports that together reduce $(X - M)$.[16] The downward shift in $(X - M)$, and its analogue abroad, again cause *IS* and *IS** in the lower panel to shift to the left, and once again we find a fall in domestic income and a rise in foreign income. These changes in turn translate into changes in aggregate employment in the two countries as a result of the appreciation.

Thus when we analyze exchange rate changes, we do allow them to have the familiar Keynesian multiplier effects on national incomes. It should be noted, however, that by holding expenditure constant rather than allowing it to rise with income, these multiplier effects are made smaller than would be the case in standard simple Keynesian models where the multiplier is made large by a marginal propensity to consume that is positive. We do not view this as a drawback of our model, however, since more elaborate Keynesian models include a number of features, not present in ours, that would dampen these multipliers considerably. For example, an IS-LM model includes feedback through money and interest rates that can reduce the multiplier even below unity. Short of building a complete macroeconomic model that would include these effects and others not present in the simple multiplier analysis, we feel it is better that the multiplier in the Michigan model is kept fairly small by the assumption of constant expenditure.

These macroeconomic results are not at all profound. Our purpose in presenting them here is to make the reader aware of what is being assumed in the Michigan model, as we go on in later chapters to analyze what it says for the effects of various policy changes. It is important to understand the model at this crude level, in order not to be misled into thinking that the macroeconomic results it generates are any more subtle or complicated than could be found in a much simpler model such as this.

The Closure Issue

There has been considerable discussion and confusion in the literature on computable general-equilibrium models concerning the issue of macroeconomic closure. From the simple macroeconomic model that we just presented, it should be clear what assumptions about closure are being used in the Michigan model, but it may be helpful to relate these to the alternatives that have been described in the closure literature.

The closure issue, as we would describe it, concerns the means that is chosen to determine aggregate expenditure in a general-equilibrium model. It derives its name from the method that is used in Walrasian general-equilibrium models, where expenditure is set equal to the total of factor incomes in the economy. This rule may be said to "close the loop," since factor incomes already equal the value of output from the supply side of the economy, and this rule assures that this same value of output will be demanded. This Walrasian closure rule serves a number of purposes, among which is to make disequilibrium in only one market of the economy impossible, since supply and demand are identically equal in the aggregate.

The Walrasian closure rule is unsatisfactory for a number of reasons, one of which is this strong association with equilibrium in all markets. If one wishes to allow at times for involuntary unemployment of labor, then the Walrasian closure rule is an awkward choice, since it means that one must explain not only why labor markets fail to clear (due perhaps to rigidity of wages in some form), but also why excess demand in some other market is allowed to persist.

The Walrasian closure rule is also unsatisfactory for another reason, however, even if one does not wish to allow for labor-market disequilibrium. The notion that all income should be spent is compelling only in a model that includes explicitly all of the things that income might be spent on, including not only financial assets but also demands for goods at all times. In a static model such as ours, which covers only the markets for goods (and perhaps factors), and which has no explicit time dimension but is directed implicitly at the short run, it seems quite inappropriate to assume that all income is spent. Therefore we have never tried to close the Michigan model in Walrasian fashion.

Alternatives to the Walrasian closure rule have been nicely described by Lysy (1983). In addition to the Walrasian, or neoclassical, closure rule, Lysy discusses three others. Of interest here are what he calls the Keynesian closure and the Johansen closure.[17]

The Keynesian closure is quite familiar, and consists of dropping the requirement of full employment and using instead an independent aggregate consumption function which permits desired expenditure to differ from income. In this sense our assumption of constant aggregate expenditure, which we use in some applications of the Michigan model, including our analyses of exchange-rate changes, constitutes a Keynesian closure. We differ from Keynes only in the form that we choose for our consumption function.

The Johansen closure is less familiar and consists, as Lysy describes it, of

Table 2.1
Summary of model characteristics of trade models

		Demand side		Production side	
Model	Country(ies)	Demand functions	Disaggregation	Production functions	Disaggregation
Multicountry models					
Cunning, Carrin, and Waelbroeck (with Burniaux and Mercenier) (1982)	11 groups of less developed countries and the rest of the world	Demand for CES import-export composite goods modeled as Extended Linear Expenditure System (ELES) for each consumer group	2 consumer groups (rural, urban) for each region, plus a rudimentary rest of the world	CES value-added functions plus fixed coefficient intermediate use of composite goods in the urban sectors; linear production functions in the rural sectors	6 production sectors (2 rural, 4 urban) in each regional model
Deardroff and Stern (1981)	18 major industralized countries, 16 major developing countries, and the rest of the world	Cobb-Douglas utility functions; CES between home and imported goods in the same industry	34 countries plus the rest of the world	CES value-added functions; fixed coefficient intermediate use of CES composites of home and imported goods[a]	22 tradable and 7 nontradable industries for each of the 34 countries plus a residual rest of the world
Manne and Preckel (1983)	3 regions: industrialized countries, oil-exporting developing countries, oil importing developing countries	Demand for energy and nonenergy imports derived from CES production functions	3 regions: industrialized countries, oil-exporting developing countries, oil-importing developing countries	Nested CES	Energy and aggregated nonenergy commodities for each region
Miller and Spencer (1977)	4 "countries": UK, (6-member) EEC, Australia and New Zealand, rest of the world	Derived from 2-stage CES utility functions	4 "countries": UK, (6-member) EEC, Australia and New Zealand, rest of the world	Cobb-Douglas	2 commodities per country (agriculture and nonagriculture)

Table 2.1 (continued)

Model	Country(ies)	Demand side: Demand functions	Demand side: Disaggregation	Production side: Production functions	Production side: Disaggregation
Whalley (1982)	EEC, US, Japan, rest of the world	Derived from nested CES utility functions	41 consuming groups comprising households, government, investment (stratified by income in US and Japan and by region in EEC)	CES value-added functions; fixed coefficient intermediate use of CES domestic-import composites	33 commodities in each of 4 regions
Whalley (1984)	7 trade blocs: US, EEC, Japan, other developed countries, OPEC, newly industrialized countries, less developed countries	Derived from nested CES-LES utility functions	7 trade blocs	Nested CES value-added functions; fixed coefficient intermediate use of composite inputs	6 commodities in each of 7 trade blocs
Single-country models					
Boadway and Treddenick (1978)	Canada	Domestic final demand for each CES composite good is unit price and income elastic; import supply and export demand own price dependent only (constant elasticity)	Domestic demand for final goods, world demand for domestic exports	3 alternative specifications: fixed intermediate coefficients with Cobb-Douglas functions for labor and capital, fixed intermediate coefficients with CES functions for labor and capital, and variable coefficients Cobb-Douglas functions	2 alternate aggregations of industries: 1. 16 groups; 2. 56 groups

Dervis, de Melo, and Robinson (1982)	Turkey	Constant expenditure proportions for import-export composite goods	One aggregate household[b]	2-level CES production functions; fixed coefficient use of intermediate goods	19 industries, 3 labor types
Dixon, Parmenter, Sutton, and Vincent (1982)	Australia	Derived from Klein-Rubin utility functions with CES aggregration of comparable imported and domestic goods	Effectively one household	4-level input functions 1-Leontief between inputs of composite products 2-CES between imported and domestic products 3-CRESH between primary factors 4-CRESH between labor inputs CRESH output functions	114 commodities (112 industries)

a. Alternative assumptions are also used in other versions of this model.

b. In chapter 13 of this reference, the model is disaggregated to include 7 socioeconomic household groups in order to study income distribution effects.

Source: Shoven and Whalley (1984, pp. 1036–37).

keeping the requirement of full employment while dropping the consumption function. This means that consumption can be thought of as adjusting endogenously to assure full employment. Since in the Michigan model we do not distinguish consumption from other forms of final demand, our assumption that expenditure adjusts to maintain full employment may be thought of as analogous to this Johansen closure rule.

Thus the Michigan model handles the closure issue by rejecting, with cause, the Walrasian closure and using instead either the Keynesian closure or the Johansen closure, depending on the policy issue being addressed.

Comparison with Other Computational Models

Now that the details of the Michigan model have been laid out, it may be useful to compare them with several other models that have been constructed and used for a variety of purposes. Relevant details are summarized in table 2.1, which has been adapted from Shoven and Whalley (1984). It is evident that the models noted differ essentially based upon whether they are multicountry or single-country in character and the kinds of issues they are designed to analyze. The demand and production functions used in the various models apparently share many features, which is not surprising since the functional forms involved have many characteristics that make them tractable and convenient for computational work. Finally, the models differ noticeably in terms of the types and details of the disaggregation scheme used on the demand and production sides.

As we noted in chapter 1, the models can be further distinguished according to whether they are linearized and solved for approximations to comparative static equilibrium or whether they are fully general equilibrium in terms of their structure and solution. The former, in the Johansen (1960) tradition, include the Michigan model as well as the Boadway and Treddenick (1978) model of Canada and the Dixon et al. (1982) model of Australia.[18] The latter, which we shall refer to as Walrasian-type systems, include the others listed in table 2.1.

There is considerable debate, needless to say, about the advantages and limitations of these alternative approaches to computational modeling.[19] We have already mentioned that our choice of a Johansen-type model was dictated initially in large part by an interest in analyzing the employment and related effects of trade liberalization in a multicountry, multisector setting such as the Tokyo Round negotiations. This range of issues can also be analyzed using a Walrasian-type model, as Whalley (1982) has done, but the particular effects on employment, prices, and so forth, that we get in the Michigan model do not appear in the full Walrasian general equilibrium.

10 Experience from the Michigan Model and Implications for Research

In the previous chapters, we have set forth the structure of our model of world production and trade and then considered a variety of applications of the model, including changes in tariffs and NTBs, domestic taxes and subsidies, exchange rates, and the effects of trade on employment. It is time now to step back from all of this and ask what we have learned from our efforts and what are the most promising directions for future research.

Lessons from Computer Modeling of Trade[1]

In 1973–1974 the present authors embarked on what has turned out to be a lengthy and time-consuming project, namely, the construction and use of a large computable model of world production and trade. Our object originally was to devise a means of estimating the disaggregated employment effects of a round of multilateral tariff reductions, such as the Tokyo Round, which was then in progress. Analysis of tariff changes has continued to be a major focus of our work with this model, although we have also applied it to a variety of other problems. In the course of this research we have learned a great deal in quantitative terms about these different problems, and we would hope that we have contributed to the level of economic understanding that now informs the conduct of trade policy in the United States and elsewhere. Our quantitative results have already been discussed extensively in earlier chapters of this book. In addition, through the process of building and revising the model, we have also learned some things about trade *theory*, and its relation to empirical reality. Because of the more practical and policy orientation of many of our papers we did not develop these theoretical insights in any detail. Yet it is precisely these insights that have made the whole process of computer modeling worthwhile from the conceptual point of view. In this section we would like to explain how this process has worked—how the building of an empirically based computable model can lead one to learn things about theoretical relations or their importance—and also to lay out what a few of these lessons have been.

We should say immediately that while these lessons were new, or newly appreciated, by ourselves, they are not necessarily new to others. Large computable models never tell one anything about theory that could not have been learned as well or better from a small theoretical model. Indeed, one would not believe a result of a large model if it could not also be understood in simpler terms. Thus we may merely be exposing our ignorance of matters that others more knowledgeable than us have always understood. However, we shall present these lessons as though they were new, for the benefit of others who may have shared our ignorance.

We shall begin by describing our methodology: the curious and cumbersome process of informed trial and error by which we have used numerical models to grope toward an understanding of both theory and reality. We shall then describe several particular problems that we encountered with the model, the ways we dealt with them, and the insights we derived about them from this process. We shall deal with these matters more or less in the order that they arose for us in the decade or so that we have been working with the model.

The first issue to be addressed is the empirical inadequacy of the usual trade-theoretic assumptions that foreign and domestic goods are perfect substitutes in perfectly competitive markets. The second concerns the importance of another familiar trade-theoretic assumption: that tariff revenues are redistributed to consumers. Third, we shall explain why we were led to model import licensing in developing countries and the problems that arose when we did. Finally, we shall pull together briefly several of the general results that we have obtained regarding the effects of tariffs, which were after all the original object of our research.

Methodology

The process of developing our model has included two distinct parts, or phases, which are probably typical of empirical modeling in general. Only the first of these phases, which we shall call the planning phase, shows up clearly in the finished product. Yet it is the second phase, the feedback phase, that yields most of the insights that we shall discuss. These two phases alternated back and forth as the model was being developed, extended, and refined. It is their interaction that we have found fascinating and informative over the years of working with the model, much more so than the ultimate numerical answers to the particular problems we set out to solve.

The planning phase is the aspect of model construction that is most straightforward. We started with a problem we wished to solve: in our case the effect of multilateral tariff reductions on employment. Next we used standard theoretical relations, where these could be found, to specify equations that, if quantified and solved, could solve this problem. If received theory were not sufficient for this purpose, some original theorizing would be needed here, but this was not a problem for the relatively straightforward and familiar problems we have dealt with in our model. Next, the equations had to be quantified. One approach would be to use econometric techniques to estimate various parameters of the equations. In our case, far too many relations were involved for this to be feasible. Instead, we used standard functional forms in our behavioral assumptions (regarding production and utility functions), and derived our equations with parameters that could either be obtained from point estimates of things like trade and factor shares, or inferred from published estimates of behavioral elasticities. Once quantified, the equations were programmed into the computer and solved to yield answers to the questions originally being addressed. This ended the planning phase of the modeling effort, and would seem, on the face of it, to be the end of the process completely.

However it is not the end, for the following reason. What typically happened when we solved the model was that we found something unexpected in the results. Sometimes the results were just nonsense and we had to go back and find out why. More often the results were plausible overall but contained one or two features that we did not expect in terms of either direction or size of an effect. The feedback phase of model construction consists of examining the assumptions of the model carefully until such surprises can be explained, and then either modifying the model or modifying our ideas of what to expect so that the results are no longer surprising. Either way something can be learned in the process.

Thus, in our view, the modeling effort is not complete until it yields only *expected* results—in general terms, of course, since we do not require that specific numerical answers be altogether predictable. To some this may seem to make the whole exercise either pointless or illegitimate. If we keep fiddling with the model until it gives us the answers we want, then what confidence can one have in these answers? Or if we trust our intuition as to what is reasonable, why not bypass the modeling entirely and just let us pull the answers out of our heads? One answer to these questions is that our expectations are only general. We could not predict specific numerical results, such as the effect of the Tokyo Round on employment in the Belgian glass industry, even if we wanted to, and many users of our results do seem to be interested in this kind of detail. But the better answer, from the standpoint of trade theory, is that the feedback phase of modeling is as often as much a process of revising expectations as it is of revising the model itself. And even when we have revised the model, what we have learned about the viability of certain assumptions has been important in itself.

When feedback led us to change our assumptions, then the planning phase began once again. Often we found it necessary to bring into the model new aspects of economic behavior, and these too had to be modeled by finding acceptable assumptions that could generate quantifiable and solvable equations. This led to a new version of the model whose results, once obtained, had also to be evaluated for reasonableness in yet another feedback phase. Thus the development of the model proceeded in a succession of alternating planning and feedback phases until a final set of results was obtained that was no longer surprising. Furthermore, the process began anew each time we extended the model by adding new data or the capability of dealing with new problems.

To some extent this process of continually revising the model was necessary only because we failed initially to understand the world as well as we ultimately had the need to do. A more accomplished theorist, one might argue, would already know and appreciate the importance of all of the issues that we shall describe. Such a theorist would succeed in building the "right" model the first time out, and would go through the planning phase only once. This may be true in part. But it is also true that even the most enlightened thinker may not be able to assess a priori the empirical importance of all the assumptions that might be made, and therefore might not be able to choose among assumptions until their numerical implications have been worked out. This too is a part of the process. Sometimes the feedback phase merely tells us that an aspect of behavior that we knew about, but thought we could ignore, is too important quantitatively to be left out of the analysis.

The Armington Assumption

When we first began our efforts to quantify the effects of multilateral tariff reductions, our analysis paralleled that most commonly found in the textbooks on international trade. In particular, we modeled the demand for imports of a particular product and the supply of exports as excess demands and supplies from the domestic market. This implicitly meant that imported and domestically produced goods were assumed to be perfect substitutes in demand. Our contribution in Deardorff and Stern (1974) was merely to recognize that all of these excess supplies and demands interact on world markets and thus that the tariffs of all countries must be taken into account simultaneously in determining trade and employment in each.

Our procedure for doing this in our 1974 paper was to assume simple functional forms for production and utility functions, use these to derive market supply and demand—and therefore excess supply and demand—functions for each country, and then put these together with tariffs into a single world-market-clearing equation for each good. These were solved to determine the effects of multilateral tariff changes in each industry and country.

As we began to explore this model further, and in particular as we began to use it to look at the trade balance in order to model flexible exchange rates, we found aspects of its behavior unacceptable. Specifically, we found tariff reductions to have a much larger effect on trade and the trade balance than seemed reasonable given what had been found especially in more aggregated studies of trade. Looking at our model more carefully, we found that our assumptions about demand implied elasticities of demand for imports that were much larger than any that had been found in the numerous econometric estimates of import demand equations that appeared in the literature.

This problem has by now become a familiar one in empirical studies of trade such as ours, and may be seen quite simply. If import demand is the excess of domestic demand over supply, then the price elasticity of import demand, η_M, is related to the elasticities of domestic supply, ε, and demand, η, as follows:

$$\eta_M = \frac{1}{\theta_M}\eta + \frac{(1-\theta_M)}{\theta_M}\varepsilon,$$

where θ_M is the share of demand satisfied by imports. In a country like the United States, where these import shares average only 10% this means that import demand elasticities will on the average be at least 10 times as large as domestic demand elasticities, even if domestic supplies are completely inelastic, and considerably larger if not. According to Stern, Francis, and Schumacher (1976), the "best" econometric estimates of import demand elasticities for the United States range around 2, thus implying implausibly small values for elasticities of domestic demand.

Of the several possible ways of resolving this seeming inconsistency, the one we chose, and the one that has been adopted most frequently in empirical trade models, is to assume that imports and domestic goods are not perfect substitutes.[2] Most commonly, following Armington (1969), it is assumed that goods are differentiated by country of origin. While in our model for technical reasons a slightly different assumption is made, the effect is essentially the same as for the Armington assumption.[3]

This, then, is a good example of a case in which our first try at model building led us to implausible results, causing us to reconsider the assumptions on which the model was based. We had ignored the phenomenon of differentiated products initially, assuming, as has traditionally been done in applying economic theory to international trade, that departures from perfect substitution would not be sufficiently pervasive or important to invalidate the results. In practice we found, as have others, that at least for the problem we were dealing with this was not the case. We therefore modified the model in a way that would make it more consistent with empirical appearance.

The use of the Armington assumption has in turn led to other patterns in our results that would not have been predictable from simple traditional theory with its assumption of perfect substitutability, though these patterns are no longer surprising once imperfect substitution is recognized. First, and in rather general terms, imperfect substitution tends to insulate economies from changes abroad. Changes in world prices and/or tariffs cause a country's import prices to change, of course, but this no longer causes domestic prices of otherwise comparable goods to change by the same amount, as they would if they were perfect substitutes for imports. Thus imperfect substitution dampens the changes in the domestic economy compared with what they would otherwise be.

One implication of this insulation that has been a constant theme of our work analyzing the Tokyo Round and other tariff cutting exercises is that such changes have really tiny effects on employment and welfare. While there are several reasons that contribute to this result, the assumption of imperfect substitution is definitely significant.[4]

A second implication, which we noted in chapter 5, concerns effective protection. The simple measure of effective protection derived by Corden (1966) can be generalized and calculated within our model in terms of changes in per unit value added. However, when this is done, the fact that domestic prices are dampened in their response to tariff changes means that the true effective protection provided by a tariff structure is much smaller, by an order of magnitude, than would be calculated from the simple Corden formula.

Tariff Revenue Redistribution

When trade theorists analyze tariffs in a general-equilibrium context, they routinely grapple with the problem of specifying how the tariff revenue is spent. Without that, a general-equilibrium model is indeterminate, since income and expenditure are not equal. A standard solution to this problem that avoids the need to describe government behavior is to assume that tariff revenue is redistributed in some nondistorting fashion to consumers, to be spent like any other income.

When we built our model initially, for reasons discussed in chapter 2, we chose deliberately not to specify it as a full general-equilibrium model. Instead, in part because we wished to analyze effects of tariffs on unemployment in the short run, we allowed disequilibrium in labor markets. Furthermore, because we do not view the Walrasian closure of a general-equilibrium model as necessarily appropriate in this situation, we did not relate expenditure to factor incomes, but instead made it exogenous in nominal terms. Together with a fixed money wage, this left employment and therefore factor incomes to be determined at the disaggregated level by the way that exogenous expenditure found its way into domestic and foreign markets. At the same time, because we did not directly relate income and expenditure, it did not occur to us to do anything special with the tariff revenue. We ignored it, implicitly assuming that it went into government savings.

What we did not anticipate was that this implicit treatment of tariff revenues would bias our results for aggregate employment. When we solved this version of the model for the effects of tariff reductions, we found that aggregate employment went up noticeably in most countries, regardless of the exact nature of the tariff cuts or other assumptions made, for example, about the exchange-rate regime. This was at first a pleasant surprise, since it reinforced our theoretical presumption in favor of free trade, and we were tempted to attribute it to gains in efficiency. But on reflection we realized that this was not the case, that however much allocative efficiency might improve, there was no reason for this improvement to increase employment. Instead what was happening was a direct result of our treatment of tariff revenues.

Given a constant money wage and a constant level of nominal expenditure, employment is determined roughly by the amount of labor that can be paid out of that expenditure, allowing also for a share that must go to capital. However, if taxes are levied and their revenues not redistributed, it is after-tax expenditure that determines employment. Now this is also true in the world economy, and tariffs act as taxes that divert a fraction of expenditure from ever becoming available to pay primary factors. Thus any reduction in these tariffs tends to increase aggregate employment in the world as a whole.

Recognizing this, we then modified our model to require that tariff revenues (as well as the revenues from other kinds of taxes, when these are included) be calculated and added to the otherwise exogenous level of nominal expenditure in each country. This eliminates the bias in our aggregate employment results, and leaves employment to be determined by the composition of demand among supplying countries and among labor- versus capital-intensive industries.

The point of relating this little episode is twofold. First, the treatment of tariff revenues can have economic implications, analogous to taxes, that are usually neglected in trade theory, where the issue is typically only one of model consistency. Second, this provides another example of a case where the feedback phase of model construction mentioned previously led us to change an assumption of the model and at the same time drew our attention to an economic relation we would otherwise have neglected.

Import Licensing

For the first several years during which we used our model, it included only the 18 most industrialized countries of the world. Among these countries we modeled exchange rate relations as either all fixed rates or all flexible rates, depending on which seemed most appropriate for the issue at hand. We did not make any effort to characterize exchange regimes more accurately than this, and since most of these industrialized countries did in fact allow their currencies to float during much of the 1970s, this seemed appropriate.

Beginning in about 1979, however, we undertook to expand the model, incorporating data on production, trade, and employment for an additional 16 developing countries. Because most of these countries peg their currencies to some degree, it no longer seemed appropriate to assume either that all exchange rates were pegged or that all were flexible. Instead, as we expanded the model to include the additional countries, we also included a facility for specifying exchange regimes on a country-by-country basis. Each currency could be set either to float or to be pegged, and, if pegged, it could be pegged either to a particular other currency in the model or to a prespecified basket of currencies. Then when we solved the model, we set each country's exchange regime in accordance with what had been reported to the International Monetary Fund.

When we solved this expanded model, we once again got a surprising result. Even though we had specified the US dollar as one of the floating currencies, the US balance of trade was far from constant in the face of tariff reductions. Part of the reason for this was obvious. Because the dollar was the numeraire in our model, the exchange market equilibrium condition that appeared for other floating currencies was not in fact used for the dollar. But the question remained as to why the market for the dollar had apparently not cleared automatically, as one would expect from Walras's law.[5]

The real reason for the problem turned out to be the following. Exchange rates for the newly added developing countries were mostly pegged, and therefore there was no requirement that trade for these countries be balanced. Furthermore, we had always modeled the financing of trade imbalances as taking place in US dollars. Thus equilibrium required that the US trade balance be the mirror image of the aggregate of those elsewhere. In this case, it meant that the US trade balance would reflect the changing trade imbalances of the pegging LDCs (less developed countries). And this would be true, incidentally, regardless of whether these countries pegged to the dollar itself or to some other currency or currencies.

This was an aspect of economic behavior that we had certainly not anticipated, but that our model had inadvertently brought to light. On reflection it seemed a valid phenomenon. Given the role of the dollar as a vehicle and reserve currency, it is quite correct that the US balance of trade is a reflection of conditions and policies elsewhere. We saw no reason to modify this particular feature of the model.

On the other hand, it did seem implausible for US trade to depend so much on the relatively small and otherwise economically unimportant developing countries. The problem, we decided, was not that US payments depended on theirs, but that theirs were being allowed to vary so widely. Having assumed pegged exchange rates for these developing countries, we naturally found their balances of trade to vary when tariff changes altered conditions in world markets. But was it really reasonable to expect such changes in developing country trade balances? We had noticed the problem as reflected in US trade, but the real anomaly was the result that developing country trade balances would be allowed to worsen or improve substantially.

All of this led us to model what was, if you like, a third kind of exchange regime for these countries. In our model, we do peg their exchange rates to one or more of those in the developed world, but we also model a system of import licensing as controlling trade. Specifically, we calculate each country's earnings of foreign exchange from exports. Imports are then regulated (through endogenous industry-specific tariff equivalents) to just exhaust this foreign exchange. Thus when tariffs in the industrialized countries fall and they import more both from among themselves and from the developing countries, the exchange constraint in the latter is relaxed, tariff equivalents fall, and imports rise. In this way the need for a substantial change in the US trade balance is removed, and at the same time, the modeling of trade in the developing countries is made more realistic in an important and interesting way.

Thus once again, what we learned in the feedback phase of using our model led us to alter the model at the same time that it taught us something—about the operation of the international monetary system—that we had not fully appreciated before. However, this time the process was not yet over. For when we rebuilt the model to include import licensing and solved it, we found yet another surprise.

This time something appeared to have gone terribly wrong. When we solved, as before, for the effect of tariff reductions by the industrialized countries, and looked at the effects on the newly added developing countries, we no longer found the effects to be small, as had always been the case before. Instead, in a handful of the developing countries, we found changes that were much larger than in the industrialized countries. Worse still, in one country, India, results were not only large in size but opposite in sign to those elsewhere. Thus when prices on world markets rose somewhat due to industrialized-country tariff reductions, one expected exports of the developing countries to rise in response. In most of them this happened, but in a few the increases were much larger than could be accounted for by the price changes themselves, given the supply elasticities for exports that we knew were in the model. And most perversely, in India exports fell and by large amounts.

What was happening here was not hard to guess, since this is precisely the pattern of response one expects in comparative static analysis when markets are dynamically unstable or nearly so. In the elasticities approach to the foreign exchange market, for example, when the Marshall-Lerner condition is only barely satisfied, a small shift in supply or demand will cause the equilibrium exchange rate to change in the expected direction but by a much larger amount than if elasticities were comfortably large. If the market is actually unstable, the Marshall-Lerner condition being violated, then the same shifts will cause the equilibrium rate to move in the wrong direction. This, of course, together with the doubt it casts on the usefulness of results of the latter sort, is just the lesson of Samuelson's Correspondence Principle.

In our case, what had happened then was this: By modeling import licensing in what we thought was a simple and straightforward manner, we had come up with a system that could be unstable, and appeared in fact to be so in the case of India. It is easiest to see this instability by example. Suppose that world prices rise, stimulating a country's exports. The addition to export revenue permits the rationing of imports to be relaxed. Thus the shadow prices, or tariff equivalents, on imports are reduced and the prices of both imports and their domestic substitutes both fall. But production for export requires inputs from other sectors, and as prices of imports and domestic goods both fall, this will stimulate production for export, and export revenue, still further. That exports might rise considerably more than can be accounted for by simple export supply elasticities is clear. And one can imagine that this process might fail to converge. If it does not converge, then equilibrium would have to be found in the other direction. A rise in world prices would require tighter rationing of foreign exchange so as to reduce both exports and imports rather than increase them.

Once we recognized the problem, we were even more dismayed. It did seem that we had hit upon what could be a serious problem in the real world. The error seemed to lie with the institution of import licensing itself, rather than with our modeling of it. However, in an equilibrium, comparative-static model like ours, one could not legitimately proceed if the equilibria one was studying were unstable. In view of the relative economic unimportance of the developing countries in our model, it would not be too much of an error, perhaps, to retain the results for countries that appeared stable, and simply dismiss those for India as anomalies. But even the near instability in several other LDCs made us uncomfortable.

At about this time we were fortunate to be visited at Michigan by T. N. Srinivasan, with whom we discussed this problem. He too felt that this source of instability might be a real problem. But with his help we realized that a sensible import-licensing scheme would be run somewhat differently than we had modeled it, and so possibly avoid this instability. Given the importance placed on exports, one would expect those who allocate scarce foreign exchange to favor exporters who require imported inputs in order to produce. Thus foreign exchange would not be allocated among importers solely in proportion to, say, existing imports as we modeled it, but preference would instead be given to producers for export who would be able to buy all they needed at the market rate. In terms of our model, imported inputs to the export sectors would be exempted from the tariff equivalents that were used to regulate other imports.

So once again we embarked on a revision of the model. This time we added a rebate facility, whereby producers in export sectors had any tariff equivalents that they paid returned to them. Decisions to produce in these sectors were therefore responsive directly to world prices and exchange rates, but not to the state of the balance of payments. The new model was run, and indeed the apparent instability did disappear, as did most of the cases in which developing countries appeared to be overresponsive to export prices.

The potential for instability, by the way, is still present. Even though exporters are no longer rationed in the model, they must still purchase inputs that are produced domestically and the prices of these are also raised by the rationing of scarce foreign exchange. It is still possible, therefore, that import licensing might worsen the balance of trade rather than improve it, through its effects on domestic prices and costs. Based on our rather crude data for some developing countries, this does not appear to be the case empirically, but there is some evidence of a tendency in this direction in certain countries.[6]

Tariffs

We have focused thus far on some lessons we have learned essentially by accident, as by-products of our efforts to model the effects of tariffs and trade. Lest the reader be left with the impression that these were the only things we learned from our model, we shall conclude by mentioning a few things we have learned about the effects of tariffs, since this, after all, was what we set out to study in the first place.

We have already mentioned the conclusion that permeates our results regarding the overall magnitude of the effects of tariff reductions. We have consistently found, as have other investigators, that tariff reductions such as those of the Tokyo Round will have effects on trade, employment, and welfare that are so small as to be negligible among all the other changes that continually occur in the world. A major reason for this, technically, is the Armington assumption that domestic and foreign goods are imperfect substitutes, but the ultimate justification for both the assumption and the conclusion lies in the relatively low elasticities of import demand that have been estimated repeatedly by many authors.

Our model is intended not only to calculate the overall effects of tariff changes, but even more so the disaggregated effects among industries. Here another pattern has consistently emerged and provides a second theme throughout our work on tariff reductions. Tariff reductions tend to stimulate output and employment worldwide in those industries where tariffs are reduced, at the expense of those industries where they are not. Since the latter include primarily the nontraded sectors, this means that trade liberalization generally shifts resources away from nontraded goods and toward traded goods. The reason for this result is that tariffs, viewed from the perspective of the world rather than of any particular country, constitute simply a tax on traded goods. When tariffs are reduced multilaterally, this tax falls and the prices of traded goods facing consumers fall relative to those of nontraded goods. They therefore substitute toward the goods with the lower prices. There are numerous exceptions to this pattern, of course, for nontraded goods that interact heavily with traded goods and for traded goods that are exempt from tariff reductions or are insulated from them by NTBs. But the overall pattern stands out clearly.

Finally, we can mention a possibility that arises in our model, and that is not surprising in context, but is not what one normally expects. Unilateral tariff reduction or elimination may, particularly in small countries, cause an improvement in their balance of trade. We found this to be the case for the Netherlands when we examined the structure of protection, as in chapter 5. The reason for this possibility is similar to the problem noted earlier for import licensing, and arises only in a model where interindustry flows are important. Tariff reduction reduces the domestic prices of imported inputs to the export sectors. If export producers depend heavily on imported inputs, as they must in a very small country, then exports may be stimulated more than imports. Again this possibility would be precluded if exporters were exempt from paying tariffs, but this is probably not generally the case.

Directions for Future Research

It should be evident from the preceding discussion that our modeling efforts have evolved in a variety of interesting ways. We are currently pursuing several new directions for research, and it may be useful therefore to conclude this volume by discussing briefly our agenda for future research. This agenda includes (1) development and implementation of a model in which traded goods are distinguished by country of origin, (2) more accurate measurement and representation of NTBs, (3) incorporation of macroeconomic relations and development of alternative methods for macroeconomic closure of the model, (4) further disaggregation, and (5) incorporation of trade in services.

As mentioned previously, we allowed for imperfect substitution between imports and home goods and separated production for export from production for the home market. This enabled us to capture the essence of the Armington assumption and at the same time to solve simultaneously for equilibrium in as many world markets as there are goods. The complete implementation of the Armington assumption requires that goods be differentiated by country of origin. In terms of the present country and commodity coverage of our model, this would mean 748 separate world markets since we have 34 countries and 22 tradable goods. A revised version of our model that incorporates the full Armington assumption has been completed by Brown (1984). The data and parameter requirements of Brown's model are clearly much greater than our model in its present form, and the solution is more costly because there are so many more markets being considered. Nonetheless, this new model will be useful because it will permit analysis of changes in bilateral trade and commercial policies. This is something that we have not been able to do with the current model because it has world markets that treat goods homogeneously no matter where produced. Brown's model can thus be used to analyze a variety of changes in preferential arrangements such as, for example, the impact of the Tokyo Round negotiations on the EEC and the effects of GSP (generalized system of preferences).

We described earlier the representation of NTBs in our model in terms of the fraction of trade in individual sectors subject to NTBs of any kind. This is a rather crude way to capture the effects of NTBs. We are now engaged accordingly in research that is designed to measure the effects of different kinds of NTBs directly in terms of their impact on the price and/or the volume of imports in the individual countries in our model. Once these measures of NTBs are complete, they will be incorporated into the model. This will permit calculations to be made of the effects of reducing or removing NTBs by sector and country, which is something that cannot be done with the present version of our model. Such analysis is especially important in light of the increased use of NTBs in the advanced industrialized countries especially as existing nominal tariffs have been lowered or removed in the course of the Tokyo Round and previous multilateral negotiations.

We purposely abstracted from macroeconomic relations and policies in our model in order to concentrate attention on the intersectoral effects on production, trade, and employment of changes in tariffs and other variables involving relative prices. By severing the link between expenditure and income, the model is thus not closed satisfactorily from the macroeconomic standpoint. We plan therefore to address these macroeconomic deficiencies in order to design more appropriate rules for closure of the model. Once accomplished, this will enable us to analyze more fully the micro-macro effects of changes in a variety of variables, including exchange rates, domestic taxes/subsidies, and monetary and fiscal policies.

In choosing the sectoral coverage of our model, we were constrained by the availability of data for individual sectors across all the countries included in the model. As mentioned, the most feasible disaggregation was to the 3-digit ISIC level for tradable goods in agriculture and manufacturing and the 1-digit level for private sector and government services. This has the drawback that we cannot readily analyze changes that affect more detailed industry categories. It is with this point in mind that we plan to explore the development of an input-output submodel for the United States that will be tied into our present multilateral model with its more highly aggregated sectors. This does not appear to present any unusual conceptual difficulties, though it does involve a potentially large increase in data requirements. A detailed submodel will nonetheless be useful because it will enable us to break down the effects of changes in different variables for many additional sectors beyond what can be done at present.

Finally, our model covers only merchandise trade and not trade in services. There is considerable interest especially in the United States in assessing the importance of trade in services and the various barriers that serve as impediments to this trade. We plan accordingly to make an effort to incorporate services into our model. This will involve estimating the portions of existing trade flows that may be attributed to services of various kinds as well as taking into account services trade not included currently in our trade measures. It will further require estimates of the barriers to trade in services as well as a more careful elaboration of how trade in services is represented in our industry categories in national input-output tables. It will no doubt be difficult to expand our model to include trade in services, but the effort may be worthwhile in terms of the computational assessments of service-related issues that will be made possible.

Notes

Chapter 2

1. Adapted from Deardorff and Stern (1979b, pp. 19–23).

2. This section and those following are adapted from Deardorff and Stern (1981, pp. 128–137; 1984c).

3. As will become clear, the microeconomic focus of our model distinguishes it from the macro-oriented world-linkage systems typified by the LINK, DESMOS, METEOR, and Federal Reserve Multicountry models. These latter models are also highly aggregated in terms of their sectoral coverage within countries.

4. This approximation to the Armington (1969) assumption will be discussed further.

5. Actually, if the tax on home production $(1 - t_{ij}^{H})$ is not zero, producers receive only $t_{ij}^{H} p_{ij}^{H}$.

6. Given that we normally assume fixed money wages, the model would behave in the aggregate in a very simple Keynesian fashion were we to make expenditure a function of income. This would also enable us to "close" the model.

7. For consistency we specify the total value of rest-of-world net supplies as equal to the sum of exogenous capital inflows. If then follows from equations (2.14)–(2.17) that $B_{m}^{T} + B_{m}^{KO} = 0$. This means, as Walras's law would suggest, that equilibrium in all but the mth currency market implies equilibrium in it as well.

8. These elasticities are surveyed in Stern, Francis, and Schumacher (1976). To infer elasticities of substitution from these estimates, we first used our model to derive import-demand elasticities in terms of substitution elasticities and measurable parameters such as import shares. The result was then solved for the substitution elasticities. Details are contained in Deardorff, Stern, and Baum (1976).

9. Elasticities of substitution between capital and labor were taken from Zarembka and Chernicoff (1971). Shares of value-added and intermediate inputs were obtained from the various national input-output tables.

10. See Dervis, de Melo, and Robinson (1981) for a more extensive analysis of alternative adjustment mechanisms of payments imbalances in developing countries.

11. As, for example, Baldwin (1976) and Cline et al. (1978).

12. If expenditure were positively related to income, as is more conventional in Keynesian models, then this curve would be flatter than a 45° line. Still, the qualitative properties of the model are the same in either case. The main implication of holding expenditure constant is that the Keynesian multiplier is smaller than one normally expects.

13. As noted earlier in this chapter, we never exactly hold expenditure fixed, but instead allow for redistributed tariff revenue, and it might be thought that this should show up in figure 2.4 as a drop in expenditure when tariffs are reduced. In fact, however, the relevant relation in the figure is between real income and real expenditure. When tariff reductions occur, import prices fall and some reduction in nominal expenditure is needed to hold real expenditure constant. Redistributing tariff revenue may not serve exactly to hold real expenditure constant, but it does do so approximately.

14. As usual in models of this sort, it is not difficult to show that the relative slopes of the *IS* and *IS** curves are as drawn, and that their intersection moves up and to the left with a tariff cut.

15. With the many sectors of the Michigan model, on the other hand, income and employment are not uniquely related and some change in national income can occur. This will happen, for example, if tariff reductions shift the composition of national output in favor of less labor-intensive goods. Then a given level of employment will support a larger quantity of output, and national income will rise somewhat.

16. Elasticities of import demand are large enough in the model that the Marshall-Lerner condition is satisfied, so that this is in fact the direction of change that occurs.

17. He also mentions a closure rule associated with Kaldor, which we shall not discuss.

18. The Johansen approach has also been applied by Brown (1984).

19. In this connection see Scarf and Shoven (1984), Shoven and Whalley (1984), and Whalley and Srinivasan (1985).

Chapter 10

1. The material in this section is adapted from Deardorff (1982).

2. An alternative approach, which can actually be complementary to the differentiated products assumption, is that markets are monopolistically, rather than perfectly, competitive. See Harris and Cox (1984) for an effort to incorporate such a departure from perfect competition into a computable, empirically based model.

3. We assume that demanders differentiate between domestic and imported goods, but that all imports are perfect substitutes. We also assume that producers cannot shift freely between production for the home market and production for export. Together these two assumptions mimic the effects of the full Armington assumption, but permit us to solve simultaneously for equilibrium in only as many world markets as there are goods, rather than having a world market for each good-and-country combination.

4. Other reasons for the small effects of tariff cuts are detailed in chapter 4. They include the small size of the tariffs themselves, the fact that tariffs are generally reduced in many countries at once and may be partly offset by exchange rate changes, and the off-setting effects of tariffs on prices of outputs and inputs.

5. In the earlier 18-country version of the model when all exchange rates were flexible, Walras's law had been seen to be valid for combined world goods and exchange markets, and indeed we had successfully used the US trade balance as a ready indicator of whether our solution program was working correctly.

6. As noted in chapter 4, for example, we found such a tendency especially in Chile, where the effects of the Tokyo Round cuts in tariffs and selected NTBs were found to be an order of magnitude larger than in other developing countries.

References

Armington, P. S. (1969). "A Theory of Demand for Products Distinguished by Place of Production," *IMF Staff Papers* 16.

Balassa, B. (1979). "The Changing International Division of Labor in Manufactured Goods," Banca Nazionale del Lavoro, *Quarterly Review* 130.

Baldwin, R. E. (1976). "Trade and Employment Effects in the United States of Multilateral Tariff Reductions," *American Economic Review* (Papers and Proceedings) 66.

Baldwin, R. E. (1981). *The Political Economy of U.S. Import Policy*, in process.

Baldwin, R. E., J. H. Mutti, and J. D. Richardson (1980). "Welfare Effects on the United States of a Significant Multilateral Tariff Reduction," *Journal of International Economics* 10.

Belton, T., S. H. Hymans, and C. Lown (1981). "The Dynamics of the Michigan Quarterly Econometric Model of the U.S. Economy," Research Seminar in Quantitative Economics, The University of Michigan, R-108.81, December.

Boadway, R. W., and J. M. Treddenick (1978). "A General Equilibrium Computation of the Effects of the Canadian Tariff Structure," *Canadian Journal of Economics* 11.

Brown, D. K. (1984). "The Economic Effects of the Tokyo Round, Using a Computational Model with Bilateral Trade Flows and Commercial Policies," Ph.D. Dissertation, The University of Michigan.

Brown, D. K. (1985). "A Theoretical and Computational Evaluation of Commercial Policies in a Model in Which Imports Are Disaggregated by Place of Production," in process.

Brown, F., and J. Whalley (1980). "General Equilibrium Evaluations of Tariff-Cutting Proposals in the Tokyo Round and Comparisons to More Extensive Liberalization of Trade," *Economic Journal* 90.

Cline, W. R. (1984). *Exports of Manufactures from Developing Countries: Performance and Prospects for Market Access.* Washington: The Brookings Institution.

Cline, W. R., N. Kawanabe, T. O. M. Kronso, and T. Williams (1978). *Trade Negotiations in the Tokyo Round: A Quantitative Assessment.* Washington: The Brookings Institution.

References 264

Corden, W. M. (1966). "The Structure of a Tariff System and the Effective Protective Rate," *Journal of Political Economy* 74.

Corden, W. M. (1971). *The Theory of Protection.* London: Oxford University Press.

Deardorff, A. V. (1982). "Lessons from Computer Modeling of Trade," presented at Summer Institute in International Studies, National Bureau of Economic Research, Cambridge, MA, August.

Deardorff, A. V. (1984). "Essential Features of the Harris and Keyzer Models," in Whalley and Srinivasan (1985).

Deardorff, A. V., and R. M. Stern (1974). "Partial Equilibrium Estimation of the Effects of Trade Liberalization," presented at the Winter Meeting of the Econometric Society, San Francisco, December.

Deardorff, A. V., and R. M. Stern (1978). "The Terms-of-Trade Effect on Expenditure: Some Evidence from Econometric Models," *Journal of International Economics* 8.

Deardorff, A. V., and R. M. Stern (1979a). "American Labor's Stake in International Trade," in Institute for Contemporary Studies, *Tariffs, Quotas, and Trade: The Politics of Protectionism.* San Francisco: Institute for Contemporary Studies.

Deardorff, A. V., and R. M. Stern (1979b). *An Economic Analysis of the Effects of the Tokyo Round of Multilateral Trade Negotiations on the United States and the Other Major Industrialized Countries.* MTN Studies 5. Washington: U.S. Government Printing Office.

Deardorff, A. V., and R. M. Stern (1981). "A Disaggregated Model of World Production and Trade: An Estimate of the Impact of the Tokyo Round," *Journal of Policy Modeling* 3.

Deardorff, A. V., and R. M. Stern (1982a). "The Effects of Exchange-Rate Changes on Domestic Prices, Trade, and Employment in the U.S., European Community, and Japan," International Economic Association Conference, "Structural Adjustment in Trade Dependent Advanced Economies," Yxtaholm, Sweden, August, in process.

Deardorff, A. V., and R. M. Stern (1982b). "The Role of Exchange Rates in the Michigan Computational Model of World Production and Trade," *Tijdschrift voor Economie en Management* 27.

Deardorff, A. V., and R. M. Stern (1982c). "The Sectoral Impact of the Recent Appreciation of the U.S. Dollar," a report to the Office of the U.S. Trade Representative, unpublished.

Deardorff, A. V., and R. M. Stern (1983a). "Changes in Trade and Employment in the Major Industrialized Countries, 1970–76," in B. Weisbrod and H. Hughes (eds.), *The Problems of Developed Countries and the International Economy.* London: Macmillan Press.

Deardorff, A. V., and R. M. Stern (1983b). "Economic Effects of the Tokyo Round," *Southern Economic Journal* 49. [Reprinted in *PORTFOLIO: International Economic Perspectives* 10 (1984).]

Deardorff, A. V., and R. M. Stern (1983c). "Tariff and Exchange-Rate Protection under Fixed and Flexible Exchange Rates in the Major Industrialized Countries," in J. S. Bhandari and B. P. Putnam (eds.), *Economic Interdependence and Flexible Exchange Rates*. Cambridge: MIT Press.

Deardorff, A. V., and R. M. Stern (1983d). "The Economic Effects of Complete Elimination of Post-Tokyo Round Tariffs on the Major Industrialized and Developing Countries," in W. R. Cline (ed.), *Trade Policy in the 1980s*. Washington: Institute for International Economics.

Deardorff, A. V., and R. M. Stern (1983e). "The Effects of Domestic Tax/Subsidies and Import Tariffs on the Structure of Protection in the United States, United Kingdom, and Japan," in J. Black and A. L. Winters (eds.), *Policy and Performance in International Trade*. London: Macmillan Press.

Deardorff, A. V., and R. M. Stern (1984a). "Input-Output Technologies and the Effects of Tariff Reductions," *Journal of Policy Modeling*, forthcoming.

Deardorff, A. V., and R. M. Stern (1984b). "The Effects of the Tokyo Round on the Structure of Protection," in R. E. Baldwin and A. O. Krueger (eds.), *The Structure and Evolution of Recent U.S. Trade Policy*. Chicago: University of Chicago Press for the National Bureau of Economic Research.

Deardorff, A. V., and R. M. Stern (1984c). "The Structure and Sample Results of the Michigan Computational Model of World Production and Trade," in Whalley and Srinivasan (1985).

Deardorff, A. V., and R. M. Stern (1984d). "The Structure of Tariff Protection: Effects of Foreign Tariffs and Existing NTBs," *Review of Economics and Statistics*, forthcoming.

Deardorff, A. V., and R. M. Stern (1985). "Neighborhood Effects of Developing Country Protection," *Journal of Development Economics*, forthcoming.

Deardorff, A. V., R. M. Stern, and C. F. Baum (1976). "A Simulation Model of World Production and Trade," unpublished manuscript.

Deardorff, A. V., R. M. Stern, and C. F. Baum (1977). "A Multi-Country Simulation of the Employment and Exchange-Rate Effects of Post-Kennedy Round Tariff Reductions," in N. Akrasanee et al. (eds.), *Trade and Employment in Asia and the Pacific*. Honolulu: University Press of Hawaii.

Deardorff, A. V., R. M. Stern, and M. N. Greene (1979a). "The Implications of Alternative Trade Strategies for the United States," in D. B. H. Denoon (ed.), *The New International Economic Order: A U.S. Response*. New York: New York University Press. [Original-unrevised version reprinted in *The 1978 Midyear Review of the Economy*, Hearings before the Joint Economic Committee, 95th Congress, Second Session, Part 2, Washington: U.S. Government Printing Office.]

Deardorff, A. V., R. M. Stern, and M. N. Greene (1979b). "The Sensitivity of Industrial Output and Employment to Exchange-Rate Changes in the Major Industrialized Countries," in J. P. Martin and M. A. M. Smith (eds.), *Trade and Payments Adjustment under Flexible Exchange Rates*. London: Macmillan Press.

de Melo, J. (1978). "Protection and Resource Allocation in a Walrasian Trade Model," *International Economic Review* 19.

de Melo, J. (1980). "Tariffs and Resource Allocation in Partial and in General Equilibrium," *Weltwirtschaftliches Archiv* 116.

de Melo, J., and S. Robinson (1981). "Trade Policy and Resource Allocation in the Presence of Product Differentiation," *Review of Economics and Statistics* 63.

de Melo, J., and S. Robinson (1982). "Trade Adjustment Policies and Income Distribution in Three Archetype Developing Economies," *Journal of Development Economics* 10.

Dervis, K., J. de Melo, and S. Robinson (1981). "A General Equilibrium Analysis of Foreign Exchange Shortages in a Developing Economy," *Economic Journal* 91.

Dervis, K., J. de Melo, and S. Robinson (1982). *General Equilibrium Models for Development Policy*. New York: Cambridge University Press.

Dhrymes, P. (1969). "A Model of Short-Run Labor Adjustment," in J. Duesenberry et al. (eds.), *The Brookings Model: Some Further Results*. Chicago: Rand McNally.

Dixon, P. B., B. R. Parmenter, J. Sutton, and D. P. Vincent (1982). *ORANI: A Multisectoral Model of the Australian Economy*. Amsterdam: North-Holland.

Dornbusch, R. (1980). *Open Economy Macroeconomics*. New York: Basic Books.

Frenkel, J. A. (1981). "Flexible Exchange Rates, Prices, and the Role of 'News': Lessons from the 1970s," *Journal of Political Economy* 89.

GATT (General Agreement on Tariffs and Trade) (1974). *Basic Documentation for the Tariff Study*. Geneva: GATT.

Ginsburgh, V., and J. Waelbroeck (1981). *Activity Analysis and General Equilibrium Modeling*. Amsterdam: North-Holland.

Gunning, J. W., G. Carrin, and J. Waelbroeck (1982). "Growth and Trade of Developing Countries: A General Equilibrium Analysis," Discussion Paper 8210, Centre d'Economie Mathématique et d'Econometrie, Université Libre de Bruxelles.

Hamermesh, D. S. (1976). "Econometric Studies of Labor Demand and Their Application to Policy Analysis," *Journal of Human Resources* 11.

Harberger, A. C. (1950). "Currency Depreciation, Income and the Balance of Trade," *Journal of Political Economy* 58.

Harris, R. G., and D. Cox (1984). *Trade, Industrial Policy, and Canadian Manufacturing*. Toronto: Ontario Economic Council.

Hooper, P. (1982). "Estimated Impacts of Recent Movements in the Dollar Based on Simulations with the MCM," Quantitative Studies Section, U.S. Federal Reserve Board, Washington D.C., February, mimeo.

Johansen, L. (1960). *A Multi-Sectoral Study of Economic Growth*. Amsterdam: North-Holland.

Kreinin, M. E., and L. H. Officer (1979). "Tariff Reductions under the Tokyo Round: A Review of Their Effects on Trade Flows, Employment, and Welfare," *Weltwirtschaftliches Archiv* 115.

Laursen, S., and L. A. Metzler (1950). "Flexible Exchange Rates and the Theory of Employment," *Review of Economics and Statistics* 32.

Leamer, E. E., R. M. Stern, and C. F. Baum (1977). "An Empirical Analysis of the Composition of Manufacturing Employment in the Industrialized Countries," *European Economic Review* 17.

Lysy, F. J. (1983). "The Character of General Equilibrium Models under Alternative Closures," in process.

Manne, A. S., and P. Preckel (1983). "A Three-Region Intertemporal Model of Energy, International Trade, and Capital Flows," Operations Research, Stanford University.

Melvin, J. R. (1979). "Short-Run Price Effects of the Corporate Income Tax and Implications for International Trade," *American Economic Review* 69.

Miller, M. H., and J. E. Spencer (1977). "The Static Economic Effects of the U.K. Joining the EEC: A General Equilibrium Approach," *Review of Economic Studies* 44.

Murray, T., and I. Walter (1978). "Special and Differential Liberalization of Quantitative Restrictions on Imports from Developing Countries," in L. Perez (ed.), *Trade Policies toward Developing Countries: The Multilateral Trade Negotiations.* Washington: Agency for International Development.

Neumann, G. R. (1979). "Adjustment Assistance for Trade-Displaced Workers," in D. B. H. Denoon (ed.), *The New International Economic Order: A U.S. Response.* New York: New York University Press.

OECD (Organization for Economic Cooperation and Development) (1979). "The Impact of the Newly Industrialized Countries on Production and Trade in Manufactures," Report by the Secretary-General, Paris.

Piggott, J. R., and J. Whalley (1981). *Economic Effects of U.K. Tax-Subsidy Policies: A General Equilibrium Appraisal,* in process.

Scarf, H. E. (1967). "On the Computation of Equilibrium Prices," in W. J. Fellner (ed.), *Ten Economic Studies in the Tradition of Irving Fisher.* New York: Wiley.

Scarf, H. E., and J. F. Shoven (1984). *Applied General Equilibrium Analysis.* New York: Cambridge University Press.

Shoven, J. B., and J. Whalley (1984). "Applied General Equilibrium Models of Taxation and International Trade: An Introduction and Survey," *Journal of Economic Literature* 22.

Srinivasan, T. N., and J. Whalley, eds. (1986). *General Equilibrium Trade Policy Modeling*. Cambridge: MIT Press.

Staiger, R. W., A. V. Deardorff, and R. M. Stern (1985a). "An Evaluation of Factor Endowments and Protection as Determinants of Japanese and American Foreign Trade," in process.

Staiger, R. W., A. V. Deardorff, and R. M. Stern (1985b). "The Effects of Protection on the Factor Content of Japanese and American Foreign Trade," in process.

Stern, R. M. (1979). "Evaluating the Consequences of Alternative Policies for Trade Liberalization in the MTN," in G. and V. Curzon (eds.), *Commercial Policy Issues 3,4: Evaluating the Effects of Trade Liberalization*. Leiden: Sijthoff.

Stern, R. M., J. F. Francis, and B. F. Schumacher (1976). *Price Elasticities in International Trade: An Annotated Bibliography*. London: Macmillan Press.

Taylor, L., and S. L. Black (1974). "Practical General Equilibrium Estimation of Resource Pulls under Trade Liberalization," *Journal of International Economics* 4.

Whalley, J. (1980). "Discriminatory Features of Domestic Factor Tax Systems in a Good Mobile-Factors Immobile Trade Model: An Empirical General Equilibrium Approach," *Journal of Political Economy* 88.

Whalley, J. (1982). "An Evaluation of the Tokyo Round Agreement Using General Equilibrium Computational Methods," *Journal of Policy Modeling* 4.

Whalley, J. (1984). *Trade Liberalization among Major World Trading Areas*. Cambridge: MIT Press.

Zarembka, P., and H. B. Chernicoff (1971). "Further Results on the Empirical Relevance of the CES Production Function," *Review of Economics and Statistics* 53.

CHAPTER 37†

10 The Effects of the Tokyo Round on the Structure of Protection

Alan V. Deardorff and Robert M. Stern

In this paper, we use the Michigan Model of World Production and Trade to analyze the structure of protection in the United States and abroad as it was altered by reductions in tariffs and selected nontariff barriers (NTBs) negotiated in the Tokyo Round. We employ a methodology developed in Deardorff and Stern (1983b) which accounts for the protective effects of trade barriers in many countries simultaneously, both directly and indirectly through the exchange rate changes that these barriers may induce. In addition to calculating the effects of the Tokyo Round on the structure of protection, we also examine how our measures of protection correspond to alternative specifications of our data inputs and assumed technology, and to a number of economic variables and other characteristics of our model, including the resource flows that are calculated directly by the model.

The paper is organized as follows. We describe the Michigan Model briefly in section 10.1, our methodology in section 10.2, and data and results in sections 10.3 and 10.4. Some concluding remarks are given in section 10.5.

10.1 Description of the Model

The Michigan Model is a disaggregated, microeconomic model that we have developed in the past several years to analyze the effects of changes

Alan V. Deardorff and Robert M. Stern are associated with the Department of Economics and the Institute of Public Policy Studies, the University of Michigan.

The authors would especially like to thank Robert Baldwin for his valuable comments on various versions of this paper. Useful comments were also received from other participants in the NBER conference and in seminars at the University of Michigan, Georgetown University, and the University of Colorado.

† This chapter is taken with permission from Robert E. Baldwin and Anne O. Krueger, 1984, The Structure and Evolution of Recent U.S. Trade Policy (University of Chicago Press, Chicago and London), Chapter 10, pp. 361–388.

in tariffs and NTBs and a variety of other important variables.[1] The equations of the model are listed in the appendix. While a full description of the model is given in Deardorff and Stern (1981), some brief comments describing the model may nonetheless be useful here for those not familiar with our previous work.

The model incorporates supply and demand functions and market-clearing conditions for twenty-two tradable and seven nontradable industries in thirty-four countries.[2] There is also an aggregated sector representing the rest of the world. Exchange rates are assumed to be flexible in all the industrialized countries except New Zealand and pegged in most developing countries.

Supply and demand functions interact on both national and world markets to determine equilibrium prices, quantities traded and produced, plus the flexible exchange rates. Labor demand functions also determine employment in each industry and country. We abstract from such macroeconomic determinants of aggregate employment as levels of government spending, taxes, and the money stock. Instead, aggregate expenditure is adjusted endogenously to hold aggregate employment constant in each country.

Supply and demand functions were derived from maximization of profit and utility functions. These in turn were selected to permit a rich variety of behavior, but also to have parameters that could be either readily observed from available data or inferred from published econometric estimates. The current version of the model uses a base of 1976 data on trade, production, and employment for all thirty-four countries, plus tariffs in the industrialized countries. To describe technology, we use the 1972 input-output table for the United States and the 1970 national tables for the individual EEC-member countries and for Japan. The U.S. table is applied to the remaining industrialized countries. We use the 1970 input-output table for Brazil and apply this table to the other developing countries. Estimates of import demand elasticities and elasticities of substitution between capital and labor were obtained from the literature.

For want of a better measure, we represent existing NTBs in developed countries in terms of the fractions of 1976 trade that were covered by any kind of NTB in particular sectors and countries. We then model these sectors as less sensitive to tariff changes than would otherwise be the case. Specifically, the model includes, for each industry and country, an endogenous tariff-equivalent variable that reduces changes in imports to a fraction of what they would be without NTBs. That fraction is taken to be the fraction of trade not covered by NTBs in 1976. In addition, the model also includes several shift parameters in supply and demand functions that can be used to represent aggregate negotiated changes in NTBs as described below.

For developing countries, we have data on trade, production, and employment but no data on tariffs and NTBs. This is not serious since they will make few, if any, changes in policies as a result of the Tokyo Round. We do, however, capture elements of their existing NTBs by modeling a system of import licensing in most of these countries.

10.2 Conceptual Framework

Our conceptual framework[3] derives from the theory of effective protection, which is defined by Corden (1966, 22) as "the percentage increase in value added made possible by the tariff structure." Since our model treats prices as endogenous, it is well suited to the measurement of value added. But, more importantly, our model incorporates general equilibrium relations and takes into account the rather moderate degree of substitution between imports and home-produced goods that characterizes behavior in international trade.[4] We can thus provide a more realistic indication of the degree to which industries are protected than is possible using the simple partial equilibrium formula that was so popular in early studies of effective protection. Further, because of the multilateral and flexible exchange rate features of the model, we can capture the protective effects of both domestic and foreign tariffs, as well as the effects of changes in exchange rates.

To proceed more formally, let us define the value added per unit of an activity which produces a good j as:

$$(1) \qquad v_j = p_j^O - \sum_{i=1}^{n} a_{ij} p_i^I ,$$

where v_j is value added per unit in production of good j, p_j^O is the price that producers receive for their output of good j, p_i^I is the price they must pay for intermediate inputs of good i, and a_{ij} is the number of units of good i used in producing one unit of good j. Our objective is to calculate the "change in per unit value added" (CPVA) that will result from the implementation or change of some measure of protection. From equation (1), in proportional terms, this is

$$(2) \qquad \text{CPVA}_j \equiv \frac{\Delta v_j}{v_j} = \left(\frac{1}{1 - \sum_{i=1}^{n} b_{ij}} \right) \left[\frac{\Delta p_j^O}{p_j^O} - \sum_{i=1}^{n} b_{ij} \frac{\Delta p_i^I}{p_i^I} \right] ,$$

where

$$(3) \qquad b_{ij} = \frac{p_i^I a_{ij}}{p_j^O}$$

is the share of input i in the value of production of a unit of good j. The changes (Δs) in equation (2) can refer to the results of any protective policy one wishes to examine. Most often, they refer to the results of implementing an entire structure of tariffs, starting from a base of free trade. But they could just as easily be used to measure the effects of changing particular tariffs or groups of tariffs, or installing or removing a system of nontariff barriers.

Calculation of all of the price changes that appear on the right-hand side of equation (2) would normally be very difficult, though, of course, that is what our computational model is designed to do. In most previous studies of the structure of protection, however, the problem has been considerably simplified by assuming that all traded goods are infinitely elastically supplied at given world prices p_i^W. It follows, for imported goods, that the domestic prices p_i^D of both outputs and inputs are given by the world price plus the tariff. For ad valorem tariffs t_i, this gives us

(4) $$p_i^D = (1 + t_i)p_i^W.$$

The price changes that result when these tariffs are levied, starting from tariffs of zero, are just the tariffs themselves, since the world prices are constant. Equation (2) then provides the following simpler measure of protection:

(5) $$\mathrm{ERP}_j \equiv \frac{\Delta v_j}{v_j} = \frac{t_j - \sum_{i=1}^{n} b_{ij} t_i}{1 - \sum_{i=1}^{n} b_{ij}}.$$

This is the formula used by Corden (1966) and many others to measure the protection due to a tariff structure. For convenience, we shall use the term, "effective rate of protection," to refer only to this simple calculation, and reserve the term "change in per unit value added," or CPVA, for the more accurate measure of protection defined in equation (2).[5]

As our derivation of (5) indicates, and as Corden himself acknowledges, the validity and usefulness of (5) depend on a number of assumptions, of which the following three will be of particular interest to us here:[6]

1. Goods are infinitely elastically supplied or demanded on world markets, so that tariff-exclusive prices are independent of the tariffs themselves.
2. Exchange rates are held constant.
3. Foreign tariffs are either constant or irrelevant.

Each of these assumptions plays in identifiable role in causing differences between ERP and CPVA. These differences were explained and verified using our model in Deardorff and Stern (1983b). Since they are important for interpreting the results in this paper, we shall review them here as well.

10.2.1 Exogeneity of Tariff-Exclusive Prices

For this to be true, two further assumptions are necessary. First, the country must be sufficiently small, as a participant in world markets, so that its changes in supply and demand do not affect world prices. For some countries this may be approximately true, but for the United States it most certainly is not. Thus, if the United States were to levy tariffs and consequently reduce its demand for imports, the world prices in affected sectors would fall and the U.S. domestic price would not rise by the full amount of the tariff. The precise implication of this phenomenon for calculation of protection in equation (2) depends on how the country's importance to world markets is distributed among outputs and inputs. But we would expect, in general, that by dampening the domestic price changes that occur, country size would tend to reduce somewhat the levels of protection.

The second assumption needed for price exogeneity is that domestic and foreign goods are perfect substitutes. If they are not, then even if the price of an import rises by the full amount of the tariff, the price of a corresponding domestic good will not. Thus imperfect substitutability will further dampen the price changes in equation (2) and reduce levels of protection below what would be calculated by the ERP.

Imperfect substitutability is also what warrants the distinction we made in equations (1) and (2) between input and output prices. Outputs are, by definition, domestically produced, while inputs will in general come from both imported and domestic sources. If the two are imperfect substitutes, with the prices of domestic goods varying by less than the price of imports as just suggested, then the prices of outputs will also vary by less than the prices of inputs. When, as we impose a structure of tariffs, all are tending to rise, this means that the positive term in (2) is dampened by more than the negative terms, and the level of effective protection is reduced algebraically compared to (5).

All prices are endogenous in our computational model. World prices are determined simultaneously by the interaction of all countries together, and no country is assumed ex ante to be small. Further, domestic and traded goods are distinct, with finite elasticities of substitution between them based on empirically estimated import elasticities. Thus from what we have said so far, we would expect our calculations of CPVA based on equation (2) to be both smaller in absolute value and more often negative than the effective rate of protection based on the Corden formula (5). This was confirmed by our numerical results in Deardorff and Stern (1983b).

10.2.2 Exogeneity of Exchange Rates

While Corden defined effective protection under the assumption of a fixed exchange rate, he recognized the inevitability of an eventual exchange rate change in response to the imposition or elimination of a complete structure of tariffs. He thus suggested a simple adjustment of all effective rates to take this into account. Such an ad hoc procedure is not necessary for us here, since our computational model can be solved for endogenous exchange rates along with everything else. Nor need the effect of the exchange rate change be quite so trivial as it was for Corden, since different sectors can be affected differently by exchange rates in our model.[7]

In general terms, both we and Corden expect exchange rate adjustment to alter the protection calculation as follows. When a country imposes tariffs in most industries, its trade balance is expected to improve. If the exchange rate is flexible, its currency will appreciate to restore equilibrium, and this will reduce the domestic prices of both imports and exports, leading to negative protection in those sectors which were least protected by the tariffs themselves. Thus, exchange rate flexibility reduces and makes more negative our measures of CPVA based on equation (2) as compared to analogous rates based on fixed currency values. Naturally, the opposite is true of the CPVA due to a general tariff reduction rather than an increase.

10.2.3 Exogeneity of Foreign Tariffs

Nothing in the concept of effective protection limits it to a country's own tariffs, though these are obviously the only policies that can be taken into account in the simplified formula (5). Industries also experience protective and antiprotective effects from the tariffs levied by other countries, and one might want to include them with a country's own tariffs in a complete analysis of the structure of protection worldwide. Whether to do so is largely a matter of choice, depending less on economic reasoning than on the question one wishes to answer. For our purpose here of analyzing the effects of the Tokyo Round of multilateral trade negotiations, the world view is clearly the most appropriate.

Presumably a country's own tariffs tend to protect its industries and foreign tariffs tend to play the opposite role. Therefore, we expect levels of protection to be even smaller and more negative when allowance is made for foreign tariffs. It thus appears that the modifications of the simple analysis that we have discussed here—endogenizing prices and exchange rates and allowing for foreign tariffs—all tend to reduce, either absolutely or algebraically, the levels of protection that we should expect.

10.2.4 Traded versus Nontraded Goods

The treatment of nontraded goods has always been a source of difficulty in calculations of effective protection. The problem is that the prices of nontraded goods are not pegged to any world prices as in equation (4). Corden (1966) describes two alternative procedures for handling them, neither of which is wholly satisfactory. One alternative is to include them with the traded inputs in both summations of equation (5), letting their tariffs in the numerator be zero. This would be valid only if the nontraded goods were themselves infinitely elastically supplied, so that their prices would be unaffected by the tariffs on traded goods. Since this is manifestly implausible, especially if the nontraded goods are themselves produced with traded inputs, Corden prefers the second alternative of including nontraded goods with value added, and thus excluding them from both summations in (5). This second alternative, which differs from the first only in the denominator, leaves us with no clear idea of which sectors are actually being protected by the levels of effective protection that we measure.

An important advantage of using our computational model to estimate protection via equation (2) instead of (5) is that none of this difficulty arises. From the model we have estimates of how all prices are affected by tariffs, and these include the prices of nontraded goods. Thus, we can include nontraded with traded goods in calculating (2), and the results refer clearly to the protection of value added actually employed directly in each sector. Protection of value added in nontraded sectors is handled in the same way.

Using the simple formula (5) to estimate effective protection of nontraded sectors, one would of course find their levels of protection to be negative. This results from the rise in the prices of traded inputs that are used in the nontraded sectors. In a general equilibrium context, however, this can be reversed. Tariffs on most tradable goods, especially if levied by all countries at once, tend to act like a consumption tax on tradables, raising their prices relative to nontradables. As demanders substitute toward nontradables their prices also tend to rise, and since the output price in (2) gets a larger weight than even the combined prices of the inputs, the nontradables in general may be protected positively. This phenomenon, that tariffs may afford positive protection to nontradable industries, is an important implication of a general equilibrium model that deserves to be studied further.

10.3 Data

The Tokyo Round of Multilateral Trade Negotiations (MTN) was concluded in April 1979. It marked the seventh round of multilateral reductions in trade barriers negotiated under the auspices of the General Agreement on Tariffs and Trade (GATT) since World War II. Tariffs on industrial products had last been reduced on a major scale in the Kennedy Round, which was concluded in 1967 and implemented over the subsequent five years. The Tokyo Round tariff reductions began in 1980 and will be phased in over a seven-year period. An even more noteworthy accomplishment of the Tokyo Round is the negotiation of a series of codes covering such NTBs as customs valuation, government procurement, import-licensing procedures, subsidies and countervailing duties, and product standards.

In Deardorff and Stern (1983a), we used our model to analyze the effects of the Tokyo Round negotiations on trade, employment, economic welfare, exchange rates, and domestic prices for the thirty-four countries and twenty-nine sectors covered by the model. To obtain the tariffs for use in the model, we began at the line-item level of the Brussels Tariff Nomenclature and aggregated by ISIC sector in each country, using own-country imports as weights for each of the twenty-two tradable sectors. This was done for both the pre-Tokyo Round tariff rates and the offer rates that were negotiated. The differences between these rates thus represent the negotiated changes in tariffs.

As mentioned above, because of the lack of information, we were unable to represent most existing NTBs in our model in an explicit manner to capture their protective effects. What we did was to calculate the fraction of trade covered by any kind of NTB in particular sectors and countries and to model these sectors as less sensitive to tariff changes than would otherwise be the case. This may not be too great a drawback for present purposes. Except for certain bilateral agricultural concessions and the liberalization of government procurement, whose effects we did model explicitly together with the tariff reductions,[8] the NTB codes that were negotiated do not lend themselves readily to quantification. Moreover, most of the existing NTBs affecting trade in agricultural products, textiles and clothing, footwear, iron and steel products, consumer electronic products, automobiles, and shipbuilding were exempted from the negotiations.

10.4 Results

The weighted average nominal tariffs by sector for pre- and post-Tokyo Round are shown in columns (1) and (4) of tables 10.1–10.3 for the United States, EEC, and Japan.[9] The rank order by sector is shown in parentheses. Thus, the sectors with the highest nominal tariffs in the United States were wearing apparel, textiles, leather products, nonmetallic mineral products, and glass and glass products. In the EEC, the highest nominal tariffs were in wearing apparel, food products, footwear, chemicals, and transport equipment. In Japan, the highest nominal tariffs were in food products, agriculture, footwear, wearing apparel, and nonelectric machinery.

Levels of the effective rate of protection based on formula (5) for pre- and post-Tokyo Round are shown in columns (2) and (5) of tables 10.1–10.3, together with the sector rankings.[10] We used here the first of Corden's alternatives for handling nontraded goods mentioned above. That is, they are included in both summations in (5) but with zero tariffs. These simplified effective rates are noticeably higher than the nominal rates, especially in the United States and the EEC, although in Japan several of the effective rates were negative. Further, the nontraded sectors all have negative effective rates.

In columns (3) and (6) of tables 10.1–10.3, we report the "change in per unit value added" (CPVA) for pre- and post-Tokyo Round based on our model, using equation (2) above. These calculations were obtained by reducing the tariffs from their given levels to zero and then using the negative of the resulting price changes in equation (2) to calculate the CPVAs by sector. The calculations in column (6) reflect as well the agricultural concessions and liberalization of government procurement. Since the results in columns (3) and (6) are based on a full model solution, they take into account all of the interactions both within and among all thirty-four countries in the model.

The most noticeable feature of these results, which was also noted in Deardorff and Stern (1983b), is that our model calculations of CPVA are an order of magnitude smaller than the nominal tariffs and the simple effective tariffs based on the Corden formula. Also, there are many more sectors with negative protection in our calculations. We discussed earlier several reasons why we expect smaller and more negative values for our measure of protection than have traditionally been calculated. The most important of these reasons, based on our model, appears to be the imperfect substitutability between domestic and foreign goods.[11]

Given the importance of imperfect substitutability, some further explanation of how it works may be useful. When tariffs are increased, they raise the prices of imports. If domestic goods were perfect substitutes for imports, their prices also would rise by the same amount. But if substitution is imperfect, an equal rise in domestic prices would leave demand unchanged while increasing supply. Equilibrium requires instead that domestic prices rise by less than import prices to stimulate both supply and demand by equal amounts. This smaller rise in domestic prices means that protection, as calculated from equation (2), is reduced from what it would be if substitution were perfect.

Note further that domestic prices are only part of what appears in the numerator of (2). Import prices also enter, but negatively, to the extent that imports are used as inputs. Thus, imperfect substitution reduces substantially the protective effect of tariffs on output prices, but does not reduce by nearly as much the antiprotective effect of tariffs on input prices. Together these two mechanisms can account for much of the reduction in measures of protection going from columns (2) to (3) and (5) to (6) in the tables.

A related phenomenon, not mentioned so far, is the effect of tariffs on exports. If domestic and foreign goods were perfect substitutes, then a given industry could not both export and import. But with imperfect substitution such two-way trade can and does take place. Now, producers for export enjoy no increase at all in their output price when tariffs are

Table 10.1 **Protection Measures in the United States (Percent levels and changes in protection. Numbers in parentheses are column ranks.)**

		Pre-Tokyo Round			Post-Tokyo Round			Change due to Tokyo Round		
	ISIC	Nominal Tariffs (1)	Effective Rate of Protection (Corden) (2)	CPVA (Change Per Unit Value Added) (3)	Nominal Tariffs (4)	Effective Rate of Protection (Corden) (5)	CPVA (Change Per Unit Value Added) (6)	Nominal Tariffs (7)	Effective Rate of Protection (Corden) (8)	CPVA (Change Per Unit Value Added) (9)
Traded goods:										
Agr., for., & fish.	(1)	2.20(18)	2.09(18)	−1.96(29)	1.80(17)	1.91(18)	−0.21(27)	−0.40(4)	−0.18(12)	1.74(1)
Food., bev., & tob.	(310)	6.30(10)	13.41(5)	−0.01(20)	4.70(7)	10.16(4)	−0.05(24)	−1.60(12)	−3.26(22)	−0.04(23)
Textiles	(321)	14.40(2)	28.33(2)	0.12(5)	9.20(2)	18.02(2)	0.16(3)	−5.20(22)	−10.31(29)	0.04(7)
Wearing apparel	(322)	27.80(1)	50.63(1)	0.14(4)	22.70(1)	43.30(1)	0.12(5)	−5.10(21)	−7.33(28)	−0.02(21)
Leather products	(323)	5.60(11)	5.62(14)	0.11(6)	4.20(9)	4.95(12)	0.30(1)	−1.40(10)	−0.67(16)	0.19(2)
Footwear	(324)	8.80(5)	13.14(6)	0.06(9)	8.80(3)	15.37(3)	0.07(7)	0.0 (1)	2.23(1)	0.01(13)
Wood products	(331)	3.60(16)	4.58(15)	0.10(7)	1.70(18)	1.72(19)	0.05(9)	−1.90(14)	−2.86(20)	−0.05(26)
Furniture & fixt.	(332)	8.10(6)	12.33(8)	0.02(14)	4.10(11)	5.52(11)	−0.01(22)	−4.00(19)	−6.81(26)	−0.04(22)
Paper & paper prod.	(341)	0.50(22)	−1.14(28)	−0.02(23)	0.20(22)	−0.86(28)	0.00(14)	−0.30(3)	0.27(4)	0.03(9)
Printing & publ.	(342)	1.10(21)	1.32(20)	−0.00(18)	0.70(21)	0.90(20)	0.00(15)	−0.40(5)	−0.43(14)	0.00(15)
Chemicals	(35A)	3.80(14)	5.76(13)	−0.24(26)	2.40(16)	3.66(15)	−0.12(26)	−1.40(11)	−2.11(18)	0.12(4)

Pet. & rel. prod.	(35B)	1.40(19)	4.27(16)	−0.02(22)	1.40(19)	4.69(13)	−0.00(20)	0.0 (2)	0.42(3)	0.02(11)
Rubber products	(355)	3.60(15)	2.37(17)	0.15(3)	2.50(14)	1.95(16)	0.15(4)	−1.10(9)	−0.42(13)	0.00(16)
Nonmet. min. prod.	(36A)	9.10(4)	15.93(4)	0.31(2)	5.30(5)	9.23(6)	0.18(2)	−3.80(18)	−6.70(25)	−0.13(28)
Glass & glass prod.	(362)	10.70(3)	16.87(3)	0.08(8)	6.20(4)	9.77(5)	0.03(11)	−4.50(20)	−7.10(27)	−0.04(24)
Iron & steel	(371)	4.70(13)	7.81(11)	0.04(12)	3.60(12)	6.18(9)	0.05(10)	−1.10(8)	−1.63(17)	0.01(14)
Nonferrous metals	(372)	1.20(20)	1.03(21)	0.03(13)	0.70(20)	0.50(21)	0.05(8)	−0.50(6)	−0.53(15)	0.02(10)
Metal products	(381)	7.50(8)	12.70(7)	−0.02(21)	4.80(6)	7.86(7)	−0.01(21)	−2.70(16)	−4.84(23)	0.01(12)
Nonelec. machinery	(382)	5.00(12)	6.25(12)	−0.16(25)	3.30(13)	4.06(14)	−0.08(25)	−1.70(13)	−2.20(19)	0.08(6)
Elec. machinery	(383)	6.60(9)	9.38(10)	−0.26(27)	4.40(8)	6.34(8)	−0.22(28)	−2.20(15)	−3.04(21)	0.03(8)
Transport equip.	(384)	3.30(17)	1.80(19)	−0.43(28)	2.50(15)	1.94(17)	−0.28(29)	−0.80(7)	0.14(8)	0.15(3)
Misc. manufact.	(38A)	7.80(7)	11.11(9)	0.34(1)	4.20(10)	5.79(10)	0.11(6)	−3.60(17)	−5.32(24)	−0.23(29)
Nontraded goods:										
Mining & Quarrying	(2)		−0.70(26)	−0.09(24)		−0.47(26)	0.02(12)		0.23(5)	0.10(5)
Elec., gas, & water	(4)		−0.20(23)	0.05(10)		−0.16(23)	0.01(13)		0.04(11)	−0.05(25)
Construction	(5)		−4.69(29)	−0.01(19)		−2.88(29)	−0.02(23)		1.81(2)	−0.01(17)
Wh. & ret. trade	(6)		−0.77(27)	0.02(15)		−0.55(27)	0.00(16)		0.21(6)	−0.02(20)
Transp., stor., & comm.	(7)		−0.52(25)	0.01(16)		−0.35(25)	−0.00(18)		0.17(7)	−0.02(19)
Fin., ins., & real est.	(8)		−0.14(22)	0.05(11)		−0.09(22)	−0.00(19)		0.05(10)	−0.05(27)
Com., soc., pers. serv.	(9)		−0.41(24)	0.01(17)		−0.28(24)	−0.00(17)		0.13(9)	−0.01(18)

Table 10.2 **Protection Measures in the European Community (Percent levels and changes in protection. Numbers in parentheses are column ranks.)**

		Pre-Tokyo Round			Post-Tokyo Round			Change due to Tokyo Round		
	ISIC	Nominal Tariffs (1)	Effective Rate of Protection (Corden) (2)	CPVA (Change Per Unit Value Added) (3)	Nominal Tariffs (4)	Effective Rate of Protection (Corden) (5)	CPVA (Change Per Unit Value Added) (6)	Nominal Tariffs (7)	Effective Rate of Protection (Corden) (8)	CPVA (Change Per Unit Value Added) (9)
Traded goods:										
Agr., for., & fish.	(1)	7.10(13)	6.18(17)	−0.44(18)	4.86(12)	4.10(17)	−0.53(22)	−2.24(14)	−2.08(14)	−0.09(23)
Food, bev., & tob.	(310)	12.44(2)	20.96(2)	−0.20(14)	10.06(3)	17.83(3)	−0.07(13)	−2.38(16)	−3.13(21)	0.13(8)
Textiles	(321)	9.78(8)	11.42(11)	−1.52(28)	7.17(8)	8.79(10)	−1.14(29)	−2.62(18)	−2.63(17)	0.38(3)
Wearing apparel	(322)	16.77(1)	23.49(1)	−0.50(19)	13.37(1)	19.26(2)	−0.41(19)	−3.40(21)	−4.23(26)	0.09(11)
Leather products	(323)	3.65(18)	1.35(21)	−0.70(22)	2.01(21)	−2.19(28)	−1.07(28)	−1.63(8)	−3.54(23)	−0.37(28)
Footwear	(324)	11.67(3)	17.90(4)	−0.74(23)	11.63(2)	20.08(1)	−0.64(24)	−0.04(2)	2.17(1)	0.10(10)
Wood products	(331)	3.31(19)	2.00(20)	0.38(3)	2.51(18)	1.68(20)	0.11(6)	−0.79(4)	−0.32(10)	−0.27(27)
Furniture & fixt.	(332)	8.50(9)	18.20(3)	−0.83(24)	5.60(9)	11.30(8)	−0.52(21)	−2.90(19)	−6.90(29)	0.31(5)
Paper & paper prod.	(341)	7.32(12)	11.13(12)	0.54(1)	5.37(11)	8.29(12)	0.11(7)	−1.95(10)	−2.85(20)	−0.43(29)
Printing & publ.	(342)	3.23(20)	−0.64(22)	0.07(11)	2.06(20)	−1.03(26)	0.09(10)	−1.17(5)	−0.39(11)	0.02(15)
Chemicals	(35A)	11.49(4)	17.00(5)	−0.88(25)	7.95(5)	11.71(6)	−0.67(25)	−3.55(22)	−5.29(27)	0.20(7)

Pet. & rel. prod.	(35B)	1.16(22)	3.11(19)	0.37(4)	1.16(22)	3.39(18)	0.11(8)	0.0 (1)	0.28(4)	−0.26(26)
Rubber products	(355)	5.28(16)	3.76(18)	−0.63(20)	3.54(17)	2.29(19)	−0.52(20)	−1.74(9)	−1.47(12)	0.10(9)
Nonmet. min. prod.	(36A)	5.19(17)	8.95(15)	0.03(12)	3.66(16)	6.52(15)	0.02(11)	−1.53(6)	−2.43(16)	−0.01(16)
Glass & glass prod.	(362)	9.89(7)	15.30(7)	−0.29(17)	7.70(7)	12.16(5)	−0.20(17)	−2.19(13)	−3.14(22)	0.09(12)
Iron & steel	(371)	6.21(15)	15.43(6)	−0.25(15)	4.67(14)	11.59(7)	−0.18(15)	−1.54(7)	−3.84(25)	0.08(13)
Nonferrous metals	(372)	2.56(21)	9.92(14)	0.07(10)	2.13(19)	8.29(11)	−0.04(12)	−0.43(3)	−1.63(13)	−0.11(24)
Metal products	(381)	7.88(10)	10.75(13)	−0.26(16)	5.46(10)	7.07(13)	−0.19(16)	−2.42(17)	−3.68(24)	0.07(14)
Nonelec. machinery	(382)	6.45(14)	7.35(16)	−0.88(26)	4.37(15)	4.71(16)	−0.57(23)	−2.07(12)	−2.64(18)	0.31(4)
Elec. machinery	(383)	9.92(6)	13.51(9)	−0.66(21)	7.89(6)	10.79(9)	−0.40(18)	−2.03(11)	−2.72(19)	0.26(6)
Transport equip.	(384)	10.23(5)	14.65(8)	−1.38(27)	7.95(4)	12.31(4)	−0.99(26)	−2.27(15)	−2.34(15)	0.39(2)
Misc. manufact.	(38A)	7.70(11)	12.13(10)	−1.88(29)	4.67(13)	6.55(14)	−1.02(27)	−3.03(20)	−5.58(28)	0.86(1)
Nontraded goods:										
Mining & quarrying	(2)		−0.72(24)	−0.10(13)		−0.51(22)	−0.14(14)		0.22(5)	−0.04(18)
Elec., gas, & water	(4)		−0.80(25)	0.20(7)		−0.61(23)	0.14(4)		0.19(9)	−0.05(21)
Construction	(5)		−4.10(29)	0.21(6)		−2.96(29)	0.17(3)		1.14(2)	−0.04(20)
Wh. & ret. trade	(6)		−1.76(28)	0.26(5)		−1.37(27)	0.20(2)		0.39(3)	−0.06(22)
Transp., stor., & comm.	(7)		−0.94(27)	0.12(9)		−0.74(25)	0.09(9)		0.20(7)	−0.03(17)
Fin., ins., & real est.	(8)		−0.66(23)	0.45(2)		−0.46(21)	0.34(1)		0.19(8)	−0.11(25)
Comm., soc., pers. serv.	(9)		−0.83(26)	0.18(8)		−0.61(24)	0.13(5)		0.21(6)	−0.04(19)

Table 10.3 Protection Measures in Japan (Percent levels and changes in protection. Numbers in parentheses are column ranks.)

		Pre-Tokyo Round			Post-Tokyo Round			Change due to Tokyo Round		
	ISIC	Nominal Tariffs (1)	Effective Rate of Protection (Corden) (2)	CPVA (Change Per Unit Value Added) (3)	Nominal Tariffs (4)	Effective Rate of Protection (Corden) (5)	CPVA (Change Per Unit Value Added) (6)	Nominal Tariffs (7)	Effective Rate of Protection (Corden) (8)	CPVA (Change Per Unit Value Added) (9)
Traded goods:										
Agr., for., & fish.	(1)	18.40(2)	21.17(4)	0.86(1)	18.40(2)	21.40(4)	0.77(1)	0.0 (1)	0.23(14)	−0.08(26)
Food, bev., & tob.	(310)	25.40(1)	49.80(2)	−0.18(20)	25.40(1)	50.31(1)	−0.14(20)	0.0 (2)	0.51(7)	0.03(10)
Textiles	(321)	3.30(14)	−3.55(24)	−0.37(24)	3.30(12)	−2.41(24)	−0.39(24)	0.0 (3)	1.14(2)	−0.02(18)
Wearing apparel	(322)	13.80(4)	41.62(3)	−0.13(18)	13.80(4)	42.20(3)	−0.09(16)	0.0 (4)	0.58(4)	0.04(9)
Leather products	(323)	3.00(15)	−15.56(28)	−0.05(16)	3.00(13)	−14.75(28)	−0.12(19)	0.0 (5)	0.81(3)	−0.07(24)
Footwear	(324)	16.40(3)	51.99(1)	0.06(4)	15.70(3)	50.02(2)	−0.02(13)	−0.70(14)	−1.98(21)	−0.08(27)
Wood products	(331)	0.30(21)	−30.94(29)	−0.32(22)	0.30(21)	−30.59(29)	−0.27(22)	0.0 (6)	0.35(11)	0.05(8)
Furniture & fixt.	(332)	7.80(6)	16.45(5)	0.03(8)	5.10(7)	10.26(5)	0.00(10)	−2.70(19)	−6.18(27)	−0.02(20)
Paper & paper prod.	(341)	2.10(17)	1.22(15)	−0.04(14)	2.10(16)	1.75(14)	−0.05(14)	0.0 (7)	0.53(6)	−0.00(14)
Printing & publ.	(342)	0.20(22)	−1.58(23)	−0.01(12)	0.10(22)	−1.51(23)	−0.01(12)	−0.10(9)	0.07(17)	0.01(11)
Chemicals	(35A)	6.20(10)	8.69(11)	−0.04(13)	4.80(8)	6.39(11)	−0.11(17)	−1.40(15)	−2.31(22)	−0.07(25)

Pet. & rel. prod.	(35B)	2.80(16)	5.21(13)	0.51(2)	2.20(15)	4.14(13)	0.17(2)	−0.60(13)	−1.08(20)	−0.34(29)
Rubber products	(355)	1.50(18)	−5.17(27)	−0.78(26)	1.10(18)	−4.99(27)	−0.60(25)	−0.40(11)	0.18(16)	0.18(3)
Nonmet. min. prod.	(36A)	0.60(20)	−0.92(19)	−0.16(19)	0.50(20)	−0.54(19)	−0.11(18)	−0.10(10)	0.38(10)	0.05(7)
Glass & glass prod.	(362)	7.50(7)	12.02(9)	−0.05(15)	5.10(6)	8.10(7)	−0.07(15)	−2.40(18)	−3.92(25)	−0.02(19)
Iron & steel	(371)	3.30(13)	4.77(14)	−0.48(25)	2.80(14)	4.34(12)	−0.65(27)	−0.50(12)	−0.43(19)	−0.17(28)
Nonferrous metals	(372)	1.10(19)	1.18(16)	−0.08(17)	1.10(19)	1.73(15)	0.09(4)	0.0 (8)	0.55(5)	0.17(4)
Metal products	(381)	6.90(9)	12.52(7)	−0.33(23)	5.20(5)	9.23(6)	−0.23(21)	−1.70(17)	−3.29(24)	0.10(6)
Nonelec. machinery	(382)	9.10(5)	15.57(6)	−0.23(21)	4.40(10)	6.74(9)	−0.27(23)	−4.70(22)	−8.83(29)	−0.04(22)
Elec. machinery	(383)	7.40(8)	12.49(8)	−1.10(28)	4.30(11)	6.73(10)	−0.86(28)	−3.10(20)	−5.76(26)	0.24(2)
Transport equip.	(384)	6.00(12)	8.42(12)	−1.73(29)	1.50(17)	0.03(16)	−1.58(29)	−4.50(21)	−8.39(28)	0.15(5)
Misc. manufact.	(38A)	6.00(11)	10.00(10)	−0.87(27)	4.60(9)	7.30(8)	−0.62(26)	−1.40(16)	−2.70(23)	0.25(1)
Nontraded goods:										
Mining & quarrying	(2)		−1.49(22)	0.06(5)		−0.99(22)	0.01(9)		0.50(9)	−0.05(23)
Elec., gas, & water	(4)		−1.11(21)	−0.00(11)		−0.79(21)	−0.00(11)		0.33(12)	−0.00(15)
Construction	(5)		−5.07(26)	0.06(6)		−3.64(25)	0.06(5)		1.43(1)	0.00(12)
Wh. & ret. trade	(6)		−0.59(18)	0.04(7)		−0.39(18)	0.03(6)		0.21(15)	−0.00(17)
Transp., stor., & comm.	(7)		−1.04(20)	0.02(10)		−0.54(20)	0.02(7)		0.50(8)	0.00(13)
Fin., ins., & real est.	(8)		−0.21(17)	0.16(3)		−0.16(17)	0.14(3)		0.05(18)	−0.03(21)
Com., soc., pers. serv.	(9)		−3.96(25)	0.02(9)		−3.69(26)	0.02(8)		0.27(13)	−0.00(16)

raised and, if anything, suffer a fall in price if world markets weaken. Thus, producers for export experience only antiprotective effects of tariffs. When they are averaged in with producers for domestic markets, as they are in the calculations we report, they account still further for the smallness of our measures of CPVA.

Regarding nontraded goods, we find that in most cases they are protected positively rather than negatively in a general equilibrium model.

Finally, in columns (7) to (9) of tables 10.1–10.3, we report the *changes* due to the Tokyo Round in nominal tariffs, simple effective tariffs based on equation (5), and our model calculations of CPVA based on equation (2). The calculations in column (9) are of most immediate interest since they provide an indication of which sectors will tend to expand or contract relatively in response to the tariff reductions and NTB concessions that were negotiated among the major industrialized countries.

Thus, in the United States, the largest percentage increases in value added due to the Tokyo Round were recorded in agriculture, leather products, transport equipment, chemicals, and mining and quarrying; while the largest percentage declines were in miscellaneous manufactures, nonmetallic minerals, finance, insurance, and real estate, wood products, and electricity, gas, and water. For the EEC, the largest percentage increases in value added due to the Tokyo Round were in miscellaneous manufactures, transport equipment, textiles, nonelectric machinery, and furniture and fixtures; and the largest declines were in paper and paper products, leather products, wood products, petroleum and related products, and finance, insurance, and real estate. For Japan, the largest increases were in miscellaneous manufactures, electrical machinery, rubber products, nonferrous metals, and transport equipment; and the largest declines were in petroleum and related products, iron and steel, footwear, agriculture, and chemicals.

To make comparisons involving the columns in these tables, we calculated both simple and rank correlations for each pair of columns in each table. Based on these correlations (which are not reported here but are available on request), it does not seem to matter very much whether one uses nominal tariffs or effective tariffs to measure protection. The two are highly correlated for each group of columns. On the other hand, our measure of CPVA is generally not significantly correlated with either of the other two measures of protection. Thus, one needs something like the approach based on our model to evaluate correctly the positions of individual sectors due to protection or changes therein. Otherwise, the effects of general equilibrium and imperfect substitution are not taken into account. Corden's simple formula does not even provide a poor approximation for this purpose.

The similarity of pre- and post-Tokyo Round structures of protection also is apparent from the correlations, regardless of how protection is measured. This can be seen by comparing columns (1) and (4), (2) and (5), and (3) and (6). Likewise, the change in protection due to the Tokyo Round is for the most part strongly negatively correlated with the levels of protection, again regardless of how both are measured. This is evident by comparing columns (1) and (4) with (7), (2) and (5) with (8), and (3) and (6) with (9). Thus, the effects of the Tokyo Round were in the direction of undoing the protection that previously existed, but were not strong enough to cause the overall pattern of protection to change significantly.

Besides calculating the effects of the Tokyo Round as just noted, we made several additional calculations of interest. These involved alternative measures of CPVA, correlation analysis designed to explain the nature of tariff reductions in the Tokyo Round, evaluation of indicators of resource pull, some further comparisons of the structures of protection in pre- and post-Tokyo Round, and the effects of the Tokyo Round on the developing countries. Let us consider each of these in turn.

10.4.1 Alternative Measures of CPVA

Our basic measure of the CPVA due to the Tokyo Round is calculated from our model assuming simultaneous changes in both tariffs and quantifiable NTBs in all (developed) countries at once. Also, our basic solution assumes a technology of fixed coefficients among intermediate inputs. To investigate the importance of these assumptions, we conducted alternative runs of the model in which we calculated CPVA for tariff changes only, for own-country tariff and NTB changes only, and for a version of the model with a Cobb-Douglas technology. The results were as follows.

For most developed countries, it made little difference whether the tariff and NTB changes for all countries were accounted for or only the own-country effects were calculated. This may be a surprise, since one might expect the effects of foreign tariff reductions to be quite different from one's own. The reason that this is not the case is that the patterns of tariff reduction were quite similar in most countries. This means that foreign tariff reductions do tend to offset the effects of domestic ones, but in the same industries, thus merely dampening their effects and not changing their pattern very much.[12] This pattern of correlated tariff reductions may bear out earlier observations of previous negotiations, namely, that trade liberalization has usually been balanced, presumably to avoid major industry dislocation.

Further, it does not seem to matter very much for the structure of protection whether negotiated changes in NTBs are or are not included in calculating the effects of the Tokyo Round. All correlations between the two sets of results are large and quite significant except for Norway and Sweden, where correlations are negative, and to a lesser extent Finland,

Switzerland, and Mexico. These are all countries where NTB concessions were substantial, especially compared to country size.

Finally, the introduction of a Cobb-Douglas technology into the model in place of fixed coefficients made virtually no difference for the results, especially in the major industrialized countries.[13] Both simple and rank correlations were above 0.90 and highly significant for CPVA measures from the two runs, except in a few developing countries.

10.4.2 Explanations of the Pattern of Changes in Tariffs and Protection

We correlated both nominal tariff changes and CPVA with a number of variables that we thought might help to explain *why* tariffs were reduced as they were in the Tokyo Round. The ideas here stem from the recent interest in the political economy of protection. Ideally, policymakers and their constituents understand the economy well enough so that it is the actual *effects* of protection that guide their lobbying and policy choices. These effects are what we try to capture in our CPVA measure. However, if either our measure is inaccurate or, more likely, if policymakers are unable to perceive where true economic interest lies, then they may view nominal tariffs as the more appropriate indicator of protection, and it is this that will be correlated with the variables explaining protection.

One problem here is that the variables we look at are likely to influence both the level of protection and its change. Thus, for example, import penetration seems a likely source of protectionist pressure, and this could show up as small Tokyo Round tariff reductions and hence a large protective effect of the Tokyo Round. On the other hand, this same import penetration would also account for high pre-Tokyo Round tariffs and, if in general tariffs are reduced by some across-the-board proportion, it would also show up as large tariff reductions and a small or negative protective effect. Therefore, we do not know a priori whether a determinant of protection will show up in our results as a large or as a small protective effect due to the Tokyo Round. Our results are important in indicating the pattern of changes that are likely to have occurred, but they do not tell us anything about the validity or otherwise of various political theories of protection.

A final problem with the interpretation of these correlations concerns the mechanism of causation. The CPVA is calculated endogenously in our model and depends on everything in it. It is not at all an exogenous indicator of the results of the Tokyo Round negotiations. Thus it may be, as we have found before, that virtually *any* pattern of tariff reductions will tend to benefit traded sectors at the expense of nontraded ones, and thus give us a positive correlation between CPVA and import or export shares independently of whether the negotiations in fact favored sectors with large trade shares. Again, our results telling who has benefited are valid.

But whether this benefit was the deliberate outcome of the political process or instead a built-in economic effect of the way an economy responds to trade liberalization, we cannot say.

With these remarks as caveats, let us turn now to our findings. The patterns we report are based on correlations that were run between pairs of variables, both for individual countries and industries, across groups of countries and industries, and overall.

Initial Tariffs. As just explained, an across-the-board tariff reduction would reduce large tariffs the most, and a harmonization formula (e.g., the Swiss formula) should have this effect to an even greater extent. When we correlated nominal tariff changes with initial (pre-Tokyo Round) nominal tariff levels, this was confirmed. That is, the correlation between the two was negative and significant, although not terribly large. Thus, tariffs in the Tokyo Round were in fact reduced the most in those sectors where they were initially highest.[14] Interestingly, this relationship does *not* carry over to the estimated effects of the Tokyo Round as measured by the CPVA. Here the only significant correlations are positive, but these are few enough to be not particularly meaningful. Thus, it appears that initial tariffs are a poor guide to the protective effects that actually occurred as the general equilibrium implications of the Tokyo Round worked themselves out.

Initial Protection. When we correlated CPVA due to the Tokyo Round with the CPVA due to initial tariffs, we did find a strong relationship. The simple correlation is negative and significant (−0.61). Previously protected sectors appear therefore to be the greatest losers from the Tokyo Round. It may well be that this result is the automatic bias in favor of traded goods that we normally observe for trade liberalization. Presumably those sectors that were initially the most protected were also rather lightly involved with trade as a result.

Trade Shares. We correlated both tariff changes and CPVA due to the Tokyo Round with various import and export shares. Since trade shares are zero for nontraded sectors, and since tariff changes were zero for the developing countries, the only meaningful correlations here are those for the traded sectors of the developed countries. We looked first at each sector's share of its country's imports and exports. We found nothing significant for import shares, yet small but significant correlations with export shares. The latter were negative for tariff changes, but positive for CPVA. This indicates that tariffs tended to be reduced in most sectors with large export shares, but that these sectors were also the most likely to benefit from reductions overall. This suggests that it is not really the country's own tariff reductions that are providing the benefit here, but rather those of its trading partners. We have already seen how the tariff changes tend to be correlated across countries, so this makes some sense. The failure of the import shares to show a significant correlation is somewhat surprising, given our expectation of benefits from relying on trade. Indeed, when nontraded sectors arc included, the correlation does become positive and significant, making it clear that traded sectors benefit more than nontraded ones, but within the traded sector group we find no such relationship.

Looking at countries' shares of *world* exports and imports by sector, similar results were found. No significant correlations appeared for import shares, but significant correlations were noted for export shares of world markets. Again though, they are small and of opposite sign for tariff changes and CPVA. These indicate that tariff reductions were largest where they were also presumably the least meaningful, that is, in those sectors and countries with the most dominant export positions in world markets. Furthermore, since the benefits of general trade liberalization go substantially to exporters, it is the dominant export sectors and countries that benefit the most.

Net Exports. We also looked for correlations with net export positions and found results that parallel those for exports above.

Final Demand Shares. In light of the observation that tariffs are highest on final goods and lowest on primary and semiprocessed goods, we might then expect some relationship between our results and the shares of final demand in total demand by industry. However, we did not find anything significant here either, except for a slight tendency for tariffs to be reduced most in sectors with large final demand shares. Thus, we find no evidence that protection has become any more or less cascaded against imports of final goods as the result of the Tokyo Round.

Labor Shares. To see whether the Tokyo Round favored labor-intensive industries, we correlated tariff changes and CPVA with shares of labor in both value added and gross output. Nothing meaningful was found.

Employment. As another check on the connection between protection and labor, we correlated our results with employment, both levels and shares. While nothing much significant was found, the results had one odd feature. Simple correlations were not significant, but in several instances rank correlations, though small, were. These rank correlations show some evidence, admittedly weak, that tariffs were reduced most in those sectors where both employment levels and shares were large, while at the same time the Tokyo Round had its most beneficial effects, measured by CPVA, in these same sectors.

NTBs. We correlated CPVA with our data on quantitative restrictions on trade and found nothing significant.

10.4.3 Indicators of Resource Pull Effects of Protection

Corden's formula in equation (5) for the effective rate of protection was intended to provide a better indicator of the effect of protection on resource allocation than was provided by nominal tariffs. Our measure of CPVA is intended to be even better. To check that the various measures do in fact perform this way, we correlated them with estimates calculated from the model of changes in employment, changes in outputs, and changes in the returns to capital by sector and country. The results of these correlations demonstrate clearly the superiority of our measure of CPVA over both nominal and effective tariffs in determining resource flows.[15]

Looking first at employment changes, in percentage terms, we found a strong positive relationship between these and our CPVA measure. The rank correlation across developed country traded sectors was 0.97 and was almost as high when developing countries and nontraded goods were included. Simple correlations were smaller, but still significant at the 99 percent level. Corden's effective tariff changes showed no significant correlation with employment changes in developed country traded sectors. Nominal tariff changes did even worse, since they showed a small but significant *negative* correlation with employment changes, even for developed country traded goods. The reason, again, is the similarity of tariff reductions among the developed countries, which leads employment to expand in precisely those sectors where tariffs are being reduced the most. Here, presumably, it is the fact that our measure of protection captures worldwide tariff changes that makes it work so well.

Output changes, again in percentage terms by sector and country, were similarly well explained by our CPVA measure and not at all by nominal and effective tariff changes. The only difference in comparison with the employment change results just noted is that nominal tariffs no longer showed any significant correlation of any sign.

Finally, we calculated the change in the return to capital by sector and country due to the Tokyo Round as an indicator of the incentives for long-run resource movement. This was calculated as the change in value added net of wages, as a percent of the (fixed) value of the capital stock. From this definition it may not be surprising that the CPVA will be related to it, since their definitions overlap. However, the relationship is not at all trivial, since changes in employment change the wage bill in a direction that could conceivably cancel out improvements in the return to capital. Nonetheless, our correlations showed the strongest connection yet between CPVA and changes in the return to capital, both simple and rank correlations being close to unity wherever we measured them. Once again, both nominal and effective tariffs failed to show any significant correlations with this variable worth noting.

We conclude therefore that our measure provides a vastly superior indicator of resource flows than the alternatives. Given that our basis for comparison is the pattern of resource flows calculated by our own model, the success of our measure may not be surprising. But the failure of even the Corden measure to correspond at all with these calculated flows is surprising indeed, since the Corden formula is intended to yield an approximation to the same economic magnitude of the change in per unit value added. Nonetheless, the Corden measure seems to provide no guidance at all, and nominal tariffs are actually misleading as to the pattern of resource flows as we have calculated them.

10.4.4 Further Comparison of the Pre- and Post-Tokyo Round Structure of Protection

We have already noted that changes in protection were negatively correlated with their levels prior to the Tokyo Round. This was also true for the structure of protection remaining after completion of the Tokyo Round. Both of these results are consistent with the view that the Tokyo Round tended to reduce tariffs across the board, without much effect on the cross-industry and cross-country pattern of protection. This was verified even more strongly when we correlated the structures of protection for the pre- and post-Tokyo Round with each other. Here both simple and rank correlations were in the 90 percent range throughout and highly significant.

It was also of interest to examine whether the efforts to "harmonize" the tariff reductions using the Swiss formula had the desired effect of making structures of protection more uniform. To check this we calculated coefficients of variation of our CPVA measures of pre- and post-Tokyo Round protection across industries, across countries, and overall. These turned out to have remained roughly the same before and after the Tokyo Round, suggesting that if levels of protection are indeed more uniform, it is only because they are closer to zero. This is in marked contrast, incidentally, to the pattern of nominal tariffs. The coefficients of variation for these fell consistently due to the Tokyo Round for all countries, almost all industries, and overall. Thus, while the general adherence to the Swiss formula resulted in some harmonization of nominal tariffs, this may not be particularly meaningful in terms of harmonizing levels of protection.[16]

10.4.5 The Terms of Trade of the Major Developing Countries

Our final concern was to investigate whether the structure of changes in tariffs and NTBs in the Tokyo Round was biased in favor of, or against, the major developing countries. As an indicator of this, we correlated the changes in world prices that our model ascribes to the Tokyo Round with various measures of trade performance of the developing countries. These measures were import shares, export shares, and trade balances. None of the results was significant, with some minor exceptions. This suggests that the effects of the Tokyo Round were *not* significantly biased either for or against the major developing countries as far as changes in world prices are concerned.[17]

10.5 Conclusion

In this paper we have analyzed the protective effects of the changes in tariffs and NTBs that were negotiated in the Tokyo Round, using the Michigan Model of World Production and Trade. Since prices are endogenous in the model, we are able to calculate the changes in value added by sector for all the major industrialized and developing countries that participated in the Tokyo Round negotiations. We take into account the direct effects of changes in both domestic and foreign tariffs and NTBs, as well as the direct effects of exchange rate changes that may result from trade liberalization.

Clearly a general equilibrium model like ours is needed to analyze how individual sectors may be affected by trade liberalization. It will not be very helpful in this regard to look at changes in nominal tariffs or even effective rates of protection calculated under simplified conditions. As our results show, calculations from the model of changes in value added by sector are very good indicators of the sectoral resource shifts that tend to take place within a general equilibrium model.

Among the many findings noted in the paper, the following are especially noteworthy:

1. As just mentioned, the change in per unit value added (CPVA) as calculated using our model, provided substantially different information about the structure of protection than is available from either nominal or effective tariffs. This information is also superior in that it is closely related to the flows of resources that changes in protection bring about, while other measures are not very useful in this respect.

2. The Tokyo Round reduced protection most in those sectors that were previously most protected. Nonetheless, the pattern of protection remains substantially unaltered from what it was before.

3. The greatest benefits of the Tokyo Round will tend to be felt in those sectors with the greatest export interests. This is true even though these are also the sectors in which nominal tariffs tended to be reduced the most, and this reflects the fact that the pattern of tariff reductions was quite similar across most countries.

4. We found no evidence that levels of protection have become more uniform as a result of the Tokyo Round. Nor did we find, within the constraints of our model and the level of aggregation of our data, any significant evidence that protection is becoming any more or less cascaded against imports of final goods, or that the Tokyo Round has been biased against the exports of the major developing countries.

Appendix *Equations of the Model*

Country System Equations

Supply functions for export (X) and home (H) markets:

(A1) $S^I_{ij} = S^I_{ij}(p^I_{ij}, p^H_{i1}, \ldots, p^H_{in'}, p^M_{i1}, \ldots, p^M_{in'}, \bar{w}_i, \bar{K}^I_{ij})$; $I = X, H$;
$i = 1, \ldots, m$; $j = 1, \ldots, n$ or n'.

Demand functions for imported (M) and home-produced (H) goods;

(A2) $D^I_{ij} = D^I_{ij}(p^J_{ij}, [p^I_{ij}], E_i, S^H_{i1}, \ldots, S^H_{in'}, S^X_{i1}, \ldots, S^X_{in}, \bar{G}_{ij})$; I,
$J = M, H$; $i = 1, \ldots, m$; $j = 1, \ldots, n$ or n'; [] if $j \leq n$.

Export and import prices:

(A3) $p^I_{ij} = [t^{Meq}_{ij}]R_i p^W_j$; $I = X, M$; $i = 1, \ldots, m$; $j = 1, \ldots, n$; []
if $I = M$.

Consumer expenditure and tariff revenue:

(A4) $E_i = \bar{E}^0_i + \sum_{j=1}^{n} (t^{Meq}_{ij} - 1)R_i p^W_j D^M_{ij}$;
$i = 1, \ldots, m$.

Market equilibrium for home goods:

(A5) $S^H_{ij} = D^H_{ij}$;
$i = 1, \ldots, m$; $j = 1, \ldots, n'$.

Tariff equivalents (a: quotas; or b: import licensing):

(A6a) $t^{Meq}_{ij} = t^{Meq}_{ij}(\bar{t}^M_{ij}, D^M_{ij}, \bar{Q}^M_{ij})$;
$i = 1, \ldots, m$; $j = 1, \ldots, n$.

(A6b) $D^M_{ij} = L_{ij}\left(\sum_{k=1}^{n} p^W_k S^X_{ik} + \bar{B}^K_i\right)$;
$i = 1, \ldots, m$; $j = 1, \ldots, n$.

Employment by industry:

(A7) $D^L_{ij} = D^L_{ij}([S^X_{ij}], S^H_{ij}, [\bar{K}^X_{ij}], \bar{K}^H_{ij})$;
$i = 1, \ldots, m$; $j = 1, \ldots, n$ or n'; [] if $j \leq n$.

Net exports:

(A8) $N^X_{ij} = S^X_{ij} - D^M_{ij}$;
$i = 1, \ldots, m$; $j = 1, \ldots, n$.

World System Equations

Market equilibrium for traded goods:

(A9) $\sum_{i=1}^{m} N_{ij}^{X} + N_{j}^{row}(p_1^W, \ldots, p_n^W, R_1, \ldots, R_m) = 0;$

$j = 1, \ldots, n.$

Trade balances:

(A10) $B_i^T = \sum_{j=1}^{n} p_j^W N_{ij}^X;$

$i = 1, \ldots, m.$

Exchange rates (a: fixed; or b: flexible):

(A11a) $R_i = \prod_{j \neq i} (R_j)^{\theta_{ij}^R} \bar{R}_{ij}^O \; i = 1, \ldots, m.$

(A11b) $B_i^T + \bar{B}_i^K = 0, \; (R_m = \bar{R}_m^O);$

$i = 1, \ldots, m-1.$

Notation (m = number of countries; n = number of tradable goods; n' = number of goods total)

Endogenous Variables:

S_{ij}^I = supply of good j by country i, sector $I = X, H$.

D_{ij}^I = demand for good j in country i from sector $I = M, H$.

$P_{[i]}^I$ = price of good j on world market ($I = W$) [or, in country i, price of export ($I = X$), import ($I = M$), or home sector ($I = H$)].

E_i = final expenditure in country i.

B_i^T = balance of trade of country i.

R_i = exchange rate of country i (price of world currency).

D_{ij}^L = demand for labor by industry j in country i.

t_{ij}^{Meq} = tariff equivalent on good j in country i.

$N_{[i]j}^I$ = net exports of good j by the rest of world (I = row) [or by country i ($I = X$)].

Exogenous Variables:

$\bar{K}_{ij}^I$ = capital stock of industry j, country i, sector $I = X, H$.

$\bar{w}_i$ = money wage in counry i.

$\bar{t}_{ij}^M$ = one plus tariff on good j in country i.

$\bar{G}_{ij}$ = government procurement parameter in industry j, country i.

$\bar{E}_i^O$ = exogenous component of expenditure in country i.
$\bar{R}_i^O$ = exogenous exchange rate of country i.
$\bar{B}_i^K$ = capital inflow into country i.
$\bar{Q}_{ij}^M$ = quota parameter for good j, country i.
θ_{ij}^R = pegged exchange rate weight.

Explanation of Functions and Regimes

(A1): Supplies, $S_{ij}^I(\cdot)$, depend on price of output, prices of all home and imported inputs, an exogenous country-wide wage, and exogenous capital stocks that are specific to the home and export sectors of each industry.

(A2): Demands, $D_{ij}^I(\cdot)$, depend on home and import prices, aggregate expenditure, outputs in all sectors (reflecting demands for inputs), and a shift parameter for government procurement.

(A6a): With quotas covering part of an industry, the tariff equivalent, $t_{ij}^{Meq}(\cdot)$, depends on the nominal tariff, other determinants of import demand, and a shift parameter representing the quota.

(A6b): With import licensing, tariff equivalents are determined implicitly to hold import demands at licensed levels. The licensing function, $L_{ij}(\cdot)$, allocates changes in net foreign exchange earnings, from exports and capital flows, to imports in proportion to their existing levels.

(A7): Employment equals labor demand, $D_{ij}^L(\cdot)$, and depends on output and sector-specific capital.

(A9): The rest of world contributes net supplies to world markets, $N_j^{\text{row}}(\cdot)$, that depend on world prices and exchange rates, the latter reflecting pegging by the rest of world to currencies in the model.

(A11a): Some currencies in the model are pegged, either to particular currencies or to baskets of currencies expressed as geometric weighted averages.

(A11b): Other currencies are flexible and determined so as to maintain zero balance of payments. One currency (the mth, usually the U.S. dollar) is numéraire and its value is exogenous.

Functional Forms

The behavioral functions in (A1), (A2), (A6), (A7), and (A9) are expressed as log-linear functions of the changes in the variables involved. They were derived from the first-order conditions for utility and profit maximation. The assumed utility and production functions were nested composites of the Cobb-Douglas, CES, and fixed-coefficient functional forms. Coefficients are calculated from data on production, trade, employment, and input-output transactions, plus published estimates of demand and substitution elasticities. Details are contained in Deardorff and Stern (1981).

Notes

1. In our early applications of the model, we examined proposed Tokyo Round tariff reductions in Deardorff, Stern, and Baum (1977) and the effects of exchange rate changes in Deardorff, Stern, and Greene (1979).

2. The industries are identified by names and International Standard Industrial Classification (ISIC) number in the accompanying tables. The model originally covered the eighteen major industrialized countries: Australia, Austria, Canada, the members of the European Economic Community, Finland, Japan, New Zealand, Norway, Sweden, Switzerland, and the United States. We have since added sixteen major developing countries: Argentina, Brazil, Chile, Colombia, Greece, Hong Kong, India, Israel, South Korea, Mexico, Portugal, Singapore, Spain, Taiwan, Turkey, and Yugoslavia.

3. This section is based in large measure on Deardorff and Stern (1983b).

4. The role of imperfect substitutability in trade modeling has been addressed also in de Melo and Robinson (1981).

5. Corden (1971) has gone well beyond the simple formula of equation (5) in considering many of the general equilibrium complications that our model is designed to incorporate. We will associate the simple formula with his name only for ease of reference.

6. It is also common to assume fixed production coefficients. Our model is capable of handling either fixed or variable coefficients, and, as will be noted below, we have done the calculations both ways.

7. We have explored the sectoral impact of exchange rate changes in several papers, beginning with Deardorff, Stern, and Greene (1979).

8. The bilateral agricultural concessions were modeled as a relaxation of import quotas in each of the countries. For government procurement, we had information on the amounts of nondefense procurement that governments had tentatively agreed to open to foreign bidding. We assumed these amounts would be spent in proportion to the sector breakdown of each government's expenditures. Estimated government imports by sector were then determined by applying import shares from the private sector. This procedure will tend somewhat to overestimate the effects of procurement liberalization since, due to data limitations, no allowance has been made for existing government imports.

9. To make the reporting of our results somewhat less burdensome, we decided to concentrate only on the United States, EEC, and Japan. For this purpose, the EEC member countries have been combined using weighted averages for the particular measures noted. It should be noted, however, that all of our calculations have been done using the full thirty-four-country model and that detailed results are available for each country.

10. In calculating these effective rates, we did not attempt to make any adjustments in the input-output coefficients to correct for any biases in using actual rather than free trade conditions.

11. In Deardorff and Stern (1983b), we examined the effects of country size, exchange rate flexibility, and foreign tariffs, all of which had relatively much smaller effects than imperfect substitutability.

12. It is noteworthy that this is not the case in Japan, where the correlation between own-country and all-country protection measures is not significant, and New Zealand, where the correlation is negative. In correlations run between pairs of developed country vectors of tariff reductions, these two countries stand out as unusual.

13. It should be noted that our model is not able currently to incorporate differences between the capital-to-intermediate good elasticity, on the one hand, and the labor-to-

intermediate good elasticity, on the other. Our experiment using Cobb-Douglas technology should thus be interpreted with this limitation in mind.

14. This finding was least true for Japan, where neither simple nor rank correlations, though negative, were significant. Since our data on tariff offers reflected the unilateral tariff reductions made by Japan prior to the conclusion of the Tokyo Round negotiations, our comparisons for Japan may not reflect accurately the forces involved there.

15. De Melo and Robinson showed that across-the-board tariff changes are likely to have different effects on resource allocation than tariffs changed individually by sector. Our results, which involve comparisons of across-the-board tariff changes for the individual measures noted, are in agreement with their conclusion but show it to be the case even more strongly.

16. With only twenty-two tradable industries in our model, it is certainly possible that harmonization did occur but is obscured by our level of aggregation. Since we did find evidence of harmonization of nominal tariffs, however, such harmonization of true protection must have been relatively weak.

17. As we point out in Deardorff and Stern (1983a), the Tokyo Round tariff reductions will be beneficial to some developing countries involved currently in the exports of manufactures. But since many existing NTBs affecting a variety of manufactured exports from developing countries were left intact (e.g., textiles and apparel, footwear, etc.), the Tokyo Round may be of limited consequence for these countries.

References

Corden, W. M. 1966. The structure of a tariff system and the effective protective rate. *Journal of Political Economy* 74:221–37.

———. 1971. *The theory of protection*. Oxford: Oxford University Press.

Deardorff, A. V., and R. M. Stern. 1981. A disaggregated model of world production and trade. *Journal of Policy Modeling* 3:127–52.

———. 1983a. Economic effects of the Tokyo Round. *Southern Economic Journal*, 49:605–24.

———. 1983b. Tariff and exchange rate protection under fixed and flexible exchange rates in the major industrialized countries. In *Economic Interdependence and flexible rates*, ed. J. Bhandari and B. Putnam. Cambridge: MIT Press.

Deardorff, A. V., R. M. Stern, and C. F. Baum. 1977. A multi-country simulation of the employment and exchange-rate effects of post-Kennedy Round tariff reductions. In *Trade and employment in Asia and the Pacific*, ed. N. Akrasanee et al. Honolulu: University Press of Hawaii.

Deardorff, A. V., R. M. Stern, and M. N. Greene. 1979. The sensitivity of industrial output and employment to exchange-rate changes in the major industrialized countries. In *Trade and Payments Adjustment Under Flexible Exchange Rates*, ed. J. P. Martin and M. A. M. Smith. London: Macmillan.

De Melo, J., and S. Robinson. 1981. Trade policy and resource allocation in the presence of product differentiation. *Review of Economics and Statistics* 63:169–77.

CHAPTER 38

Journal of International Economics 24 (1988) 93–107. North-Holland

AN INTERPRETATION OF THE FACTOR CONTENT OF TRADE

Alan V. DEARDORFF

The University of Michigan, Ann Arbor, MI 48109-1220, USA

Robert W. STAIGER*

Stanford University, Stanford, CA 94305, USA

Received December 1986, revised version received May 1987

This paper shows that the factor content of trade can be used to indicate effects of trade on relative factor prices. Factor prices in two trading equilibria can be compared by comparing instead their two 'equivalent autarky equilibria' constructed by changing factor endowments by the factor content of trade. Using relationships between autarky factor prices and factor endowments, several relationships are derived between factor prices with trade and its factor content. The most general result is a positive correlation between relative changes in the factor content of trade, appropriately normalized, and proportional changes in factor prices.

1. Introduction

The factor content of trade is well known to be useful as a way of formulating versions of the Heckscher–Ohlin Theorem that will be valid even under circumstances in which the commodity composition of trade is indeterminate.[1] This in turn has led to measurement of the factor content of trade as a means of applying and testing the Theorem empirically.[2] We argue in this paper that the factor content of trade is also useful as an indicator of the effects of trade on relative factor prices. Thus, for example, measurement of the factor content of trade can be used as an indicator of which factors of production have gained the most from trade relative to autarky, making it unnecessary actually to observe an autarky equilibrium in order to answer this question.

To show this, we note first in section 2 that, under fairly general conditions, a trading equilibrium has the same factor prices as an equivalent

*This paper was written with partial support from the Ford Foundation. We would like to thank Bob Stern and two anonymous referees for their helpful comments on an earlier draft.

[1]See Melvin (1968) and Vanek (1968).

[2]Leontief (1954) actually measured the factor content of trade in obtaining his famous Paradox, which Stern and Maskus (1981) have re-evaluated as suggested by Leamer (1980). Factor content has also been used more recently as the basis for tests of the Heckscher–Ohlin Theorem by Harkness (1983), Bowen, Leamer and Sveikauskas (1987), and Staiger (1987).

autarky equilibrium that can be constructed by changing factor endowments by the amounts of the factor content of trade. Thus, factor prices in two trading equilibria can be compared by comparing instead their two equivalent autarky equilibria. Since factor prices in autarky are related to factor endowments, it follows that factor prices with trade are related to its factor content.[3]

To derive a formal statement of this result, we first examine in section 3 a model in which all preferences and production functions are Cobb–Douglas. In this model, the unitary elasticities of substitution that prevail in all activities imply a very strong relationship between autarky factor prices and endowments. This in turn gives us a similarly strong relationship involving the factor content of trade.

In sections 4 and 5, then, we turn to the much weaker relationship that exists more generally between autarky factor prices and endowments: the fact, as shown for example by Dixit and Norman (1980), that the two are negatively correlated. In section 4, we use this result to derive a similar relationship involving the factor content of trade and the effects of trade on factor prices. We then use this relationship in section 5 to obtain several corollaries that establish correlations between these two variables. In our most general result, proved as corollary 3.4 in section 5, we establish a positive correlation between relative changes in the factor content of trade, appropriately normalized, and the proportional changes in the corresponding factor prices.

Section 6 concludes by noting certain limitations of this result.

2. Equivalent autarky equilibria

Consider an economy capable of producing n goods, $X_1,\ldots,X_n$, using m primary factors, $L_1,\ldots,L_m$. Let technology be non-joint and linearly homogeneous, so that techniques of production can be characterized by $m\times n$ matrices $A=\{a_{ij}\}$, whose elements are the quantities of factor i used in producing one unit of good j. Let F be the set of all such matrices of techniques that can be used.

A competitive production equilibrium for this economy can be defined for any given endowments of the factors, $L^0=(L_1^0,\ldots,L_m^0)'$ and prices of the goods, $p^0=(p_1^0,\ldots,p_n^0)'$. Such an equilibrium will consist of a vector of factor

[3]The relationship between post-trade factor prices and the factor content of trade has been explored by several authors. Helpman (1984) derives a relationship between bilateral post-trade factor price differentials and the factor content of bilateral trade. Neary and Schweinberger (1986) derive a relationship between *changes* in the factor content of a country's trade and the factor price vector in the *original* equilibrium. We focus here on the relationship between *changes* in the factor content of a country's trade and *changes* in its factor prices. Hence, in contrast to previous work, our results allow inferences to be made concerning the effects of trade on relative factor prices.

prices, w^0, a vector of outputs, $X^0 \geqq 0$, and a matrix of techniques $A^0 \in F$ such that

$$A^0 X^0 \leqq L^0, \tag{2.1}$$

$$p^{0\prime} X^0 - w^{0\prime} A^0 X^0 \geqq p^{0\prime} X - w^{0\prime} AX, \quad \text{for all} \quad X \geqq 0, A \in F. \tag{2.2}$$

That is, (2.1) says that X^0 is feasible given the factor endowments L^0 and (2.2) says that it yields at least as great a profit as any other vector of outputs that competitive producers might attempt to produce. Since a strictly positive profit in any activity could always be improved upon simply by expanding output, while a negative profit could be eliminated by contracting output to zero, (2.2) implies the following:

$$w^{0\prime} A^0 \geqq p^0, \tag{2.3}$$

$$p^{0\prime} X^0 = w^{0\prime} A^0 X^0, \tag{2.4}$$

so that unit cost equals price for each good that is produced and total profit is zero.

Now suppose that the economy is in a trading situation, and that a vector of goods C^0 is being demanded. The difference between production and demand, $T^0 = X^0 - C^0$, is the net trade vector. We do not necessarily assume that trade is either balanced or free. Nor need we assume anything special about the properties of the rest of the world, e.g. that technologies are internationally identical.

Define the factor content of trade, S^0, as the vector of factors needed to produce what is exported, less the factors needed to produce replacements for what is imported:

$$S^0 = A^0 T^0. \tag{2.5}$$

Note that (2.5) measures the economy's factor content of trade according to its *own* matrix of techniques, A^0.[4]

Define an equivalent autarky equilibrium as an equilibrium that would arise if the original economy's factor endowments were changed by the amounts in S^0, net factor exports being removed and net factor imports

[4]This is therefore not the same measure of factor content that was used in Deardorff (1982) to generalize various versions of the Heckscher–Ohlin Theorem. There, factor content was defined in terms of the factors actually used in producing traded goods in the exporting country. Our use of home-country techniques here has the advantage of being easier to apply, and indeed this is the definition implicitly used in Leontief's (1954) classic study. It should be noted, however, that the factor content of trade as defined here need not add up to zero across countries.

being added, and the economy were not allowed to trade. We show, under one additional assumption, that an equivalent autarky equilibrium exists in which outputs equal C^0 and prices of both goods and factors are the same as prevailed in the original trading equilibrium. The additional assumption is that the economy is initially incompletely specialized, in the sense that it produces a positive amount of each good that it consumes. Since goods that are not consumed at all are not very interesting, we will simply assume that all outputs are strictly positive:

$$X^0 >> 0. \tag{2.6}$$

Proposition 1. If factor endowments in the economy are $B^0 = L^0 - S^0$, then with the same goods prices, p^0, as prevailed in the trading equilibrium, a competitive production equilibrium exists in which outputs are C^0, factor prices are w^0 and techniques are A^0.

Proof. We need only establish that relationships analogous to (2.1) and (2.2) hold in the new equilibrium. These are established as follows:

$$\begin{aligned} A^0C^0 &= A^0[X^0 - (X^0 - C^0)] \\ &\leqq L^0 - A^0T^0 \\ &= L^0 - S^0 = B^0, \end{aligned} \tag{2.7}$$

where the inequality follows from (2.1). Thus with the new endowments it is feasible to produce the bundle of goods, C^0. To see that such production also maximizes profits, note that (2.6) together with (2.3) and (2.4) imply that price equals average cost in all industries:

$$p^0 = w^{0\prime}A^0, \tag{2.8}$$

and thus that production of C^0 with techniques A^0 yields zero profit, which is the best that one can do when facing p^0 and w^0:

$$\begin{aligned} p^{0\prime}C^0 - w^{0\prime}A^0C^0 &= 0 \\ &= p^{0\prime}X^0 - w^{0\prime}A^0X^0 \\ &\geqq p^{0\prime}X - w^{0\prime}AX, \quad \text{for all} \quad X \geqq 0, A \in F, \end{aligned} \tag{2.9}$$

where the last inequality follows from (2.2) Q.E.D.

Proposition 1 deals only with the production side of the economy. However, since the same bundle of goods is demanded in this new equilibrium as in the initial trading equilibrium, and the same domestic prices prevail, it is an equilibrium for demand as well.[5]

The intuition behind this result may be appreciated by noting in (2.7) that, with full employment of all factors, B^0 is the factor content of consumption, A^0C^0. Thus, the equivalent autarky equilibrium merely endows the economy with the factors needed to produce what it consumes, and thus obviates the need for trade at prevailing prices of goods and factors.

The significance of this result should also be explained. It means that factor prices in any non-specialized trading equilibrium can be inferred from an equivalent autarky equilibrium based on factor endowment $L-S$, where L is the endowment in the trading equilibrium and S is the factor content of trade in the trading equilibrium measured with the techniques of production used by the home country in the trading equilibrium. Since factor prices can be somewhat easier to specify theoretically in autarky than in trade, this result can be very useful. In the following sections we use it to relate factor prices to the factor content of trade.

3. Strong results with a Cobb–Douglas model

Now consider an economy with the very strong property that all preferences and production functions are Cobb–Douglas. This assumption allows us to derive autarky factor prices explicitly as functions of factor endowments, and thus use the result of section 2 to get a strong relationship between factor prices and the factor content of trade.

Cobb–Douglas production functions imply that each factor earns a constant share of the revenue in each industry. Cobb–Douglas preferences imply similarly that consumers spend a constant fraction of their total expenditure, E, on each good. In autarky, where consumer expenditure on a good equals the revenue of the industry producing that good, the two together imply that each factor's total income (from employment in all industries together) is a constant fraction of consumer expenditure. Letting that constant for factor i be c_i, we have:

$$w_i L_i = c_i E. \tag{3.1}$$

[5]One also needs to check that there is still income sufficient to purchase the goods. If in the initial equilibrium producers and consumers were faced with the same prices, p^0, then factor income in the equivalent autarky equilibrium would exactly equal $p^{0\prime}C^0$. Notice that any tariff revenue in the trading equilibrium can be safely ignored here, since direct production of the consumption bundle C^0 generates earned income sufficient to purchase it, even if that was not the case with trade. On the other hand, if domestic taxes in the initial trading equilibrium caused producer and consumer prices to diverge, then appropriate transfers may be necessary.

Were we to divide through by L_i, we would have immediately that autarky factor prices are inversely related to factor endowments.

Now consider for this economy two equilibria, numbered 1 and 2, that may involve trade. With trade, (3.1) does not apply directly. However, we can use the result of section 2 to express factor prices with trade in terms of what they would be without trade in an equivalent autarky equilibrium, the factor endowments of which are $B=L-S$. Thus, letting L^0 be the actual factor endowments, assumed the same in both trading equilibria, the price of factor i can be expressed as:

$$w_i^h = c_i E^h/(L_i^0 - S_i^h), \quad h=1,2. \tag{3.2}$$

If we now compare factor prices in the two equilibria, we have:

$$\frac{w_i^2}{w_i^1} = \frac{E^2(L_i^0 - S_i^1)}{E^1(L_i^0 - S_i^2)}. \tag{3.3}$$

Thus, factor prices depend positively on levels of expenditure and inversely on endowments net of the factor content of trade. The result can be simplified if we normalize prices in both equilibria so that total expenditure is unity. Then the expenditure ratio in (3.3) drops out, and we can express the relative change in factor prices between the two equilibria in terms of the change in the factor content of trade relative to the factor content of consumption:

Proposition 2. If a country's preferences and technologies are Cobb–Douglas and identical in two trading equilibria for which factor endowments are also identical, then if prices are normalized to equate total expenditure to unity in both equilibria,

$$\frac{w_i^2 - w_i^1}{w_i^1} = \frac{S_i^2 - S_i^1}{B_i^2} \tag{3.4}$$

for every factor i.

Finally, instead of comparing two trading equilibria, we can compare a single trading equilibrium with the autarky equilibrium that would have obtained with the same endowments. Letting $1=t$ be the trading equilibrium and $2=a$ be the autarky equilibrium, and noting that trade and its factor content are zero in autarky, we get the following very simple relationship:

Corollary 2.1. Under the assumptions of Proposition 2, if one of the equilibria is itself an autarky equilibrium, then for any factor i:

$$\frac{w_i^t - w_i^a}{w_i^t} = \frac{S_i^t}{L_i^0}. \tag{3.5}$$

Thus, if we consider the move from autarky to any trading equilibrium for this Cobb–Douglas country, the factor content of trade as a fraction of each factor endowment is an exact measure of the fraction of each factor price that can be attributed to that trade.

These are very strong results, but they are not quite as strong as they may at first appear. They do not indicate in any absolute or real sense what the effects of trade and changes in trade will be on factor prices. Instead, they indicate only the effects on factor prices *relative* to one another. That is, if (3.5) is negative, for example, this does not necessarily mean that the price of factor i has fallen in real terms or in any relevant nominal terms. It does, however, mean that the price of factor i has fallen relative to the prices of other factors which are determined by (3.5) to have increased.

What the factor prices here represent can be seen more clearly by considering the particular normalization we have chosen. By equating nominal aggregate expenditure, E, in the two equilibria being compared, we make factor prices reflect the shares of aggregate expenditure earned by a unit of each factor. If prices and aggregate expenditure happened to be such as to yield a constant level of aggregate welfare, then these factor prices would indeed measure welfare. But in general aggregate welfare does change between the two equilibria and this interpretation is generally not possible.

For example, in the comparison of autarky and trade in (3.5), it is normally the case that aggregate welfare rises with trade. Thus, the effects on welfare of individual factors include both the effects on their shares of aggregate welfare described by (3.5), plus their shares of the usual gains from trade. It follows that, while we can be sure that factors for which (3.5) is positive do gain from trade, other factors for which (3.5) is negative may gain from trade as well, if the aggregate gain from trade is large enough to offset the relative loss indicated by (3.5). That a net loss is nonetheless possible, however, is well known from the Stolper–Samuelson Theorem.

4. Weak results with a more general model

Without a strong assumption such as Cobb–Douglas preferences and production functions, there does not exist in general a relationship between factor endowments and autarky factor prices that is strong enough to hold for each and every factor. Variations of complementarity and substitutability among goods and factors – which are ruled out by the Cobb–Douglas assumption – can cause prices of particular factors to move in ways that contradict the changes in their own factor endowments. A factor that is closely substitutable for another factor, for example, may rise in price even though its endowment rises, if the endowment of its close substitute shrinks sufficiently. These problems with relating factor prices and endowments in autarky also make it difficult to derive any generally valid strong relationship between factor prices and the factor content of trade that holds for every factor of production.

However, a general result is possible if we look for a relationship that holds on average across all factors. In a model like that of section 3 but without the Cobb–Douglas restriction, Dixit and Norman (1980, p. 99) derived the following simple relationship between autarky factor prices and factor endowments:

$$(w^1-w^2)'(L^1-L^2)\leqq 0, \tag{4.1}$$

where factor prices, w^1 and w^2, are those that correspond to endowments, L^1 and L^2, respectively, in autarky. For this result they required only that preferences be homothetic, that production functions be linearly homogeneous and non-joint, and that prices of goods be normalized so that aggregate nominal expenditure is the same in both equilibria, just as we did in section 3.

Dixit and Norman interpret (4.1) as showing that 'autarky factor price differences are negatively correlated with endowment differences'. This is not strictly correct, but it is true that (4.1) imposes an important restriction on the relationship between endowments and autarky factor prices that is related to a correlation.[6]

If we now draw on the result of section 2, we can compare factor prices in trading equilibria in terms of their equivalent autarky equilibria.

Proposition 3. Let w^i be the vector of factor prices in a non-specialized trading equilibrium in which the factor endowments are L^0 and the factor content of trade is S^i, for $i=1,2$. Then

$$(w^1-w^2)'(S^1-S^2)\geqq 0. \tag{4.2}$$

[6]The inequality in (4.1) directly implies the sign of a correlation if either of the two vectors in the inner product has zero mean. See Deardorff (1980). In this case factor endowments could easily all move in the same direction, while the normalization on goods prices prevents us from imposing a similar normalization on factor prices. It remains to be seen what sort of true correlation results can be derived from (4.1).

Proof. From section 2, factor prices, w^i are the same as would obtain in an autarky equilibrium with factor endowments $L^0 - S^i$, and we can therefore replace the factor endowments in (4.1) with these expressions,

$$(w^1 - w^2)'[(L^0 - S^1) - (L^0 - S^2)] \leqq 0, \tag{4.3}$$

and (4.2) then follows. Q.E.D.

This is the basic general result of this paper. It establishes a simple correlation-like relationship between changes in factor prices and changes in the factor content of trade. If, between two trading equilibria, the factor content of trade rises for some factors and falls for others, this says that the prices of the former will tend to rise relative to the prices of the latter.

As in section 2, it is also possible to compare a trading equilibrium with autarky. Letting $1 = t$ and $2 = a$ in (4.2), and noting that the factor content of trade is zero in autarky, we have:

Corollary 3.1.

$$(w^t - w^a)'S^t \geqq 0. \tag{4.4}$$

Thus, the effect of trade relative to autarky is to tend to raise the returns to those factors which are exported in factor content terms relative to those which are imported.

5. Corollaries involving true correlations

The simple results just derived, as already noted, are not the same as true correlations. Further assumptions and further work are needed to derive true correlations from them, and to determine therefore whether the results tell us anything meaningful about the models from which they derive.

Such correlations are particularly easy to derive if it happens to be the case that there exist factor prices subject to which the factor content of trade is balanced. Thus, we have:

Corollary 3.2. If the factor content of trade is balanced when valued at some vector of factor prices, w^0, then there is a non-negative correlation between changes in the value of the factor content of trade at these factor prices and the changes in the factor prices themselves relative also to w^0:

$$\mathrm{Cor}\left[\frac{(w_i^1 - w_i^2)}{w_i^0}, w_i^0(S_i^1 - S_i^2)\right] \geqq 0. \tag{5.1}$$

Also, comparing a trade equilibrium with autarky,

$$\mathrm{Cor}\left[\frac{(w_i^t - w_i^a)}{w_i^0}, w_i^0 S_i^t\right] \geqq 0. \tag{5.2}$$

These results follow immediately from the assumption of balanced factor trade, since it implies that the sums of the second arguments in these correlations are zero and thus have zero means.[7]

These results would be most useful only in cases where the factor content of trade actually is balanced at one of the prevailing sets of factor prices. Unfortunately, only with free trade is this likely to be the case:

Corollary 3.3. If commodity trade is free and balanced at world prices, p^w, then

$$\mathrm{Cor}\left[\frac{(w_i^f - w_i^a)}{w_i^f}, w_i^f S_i^f\right] \geqq 0 \tag{5.3}$$

where w^f and S^f are the vectors of factor prices and the factor content of trade that exist with free trade.

Proof. With incomplete specialization, so that (2.3) holds with equality, we have

$$w^{f\prime} S^f = w^{f\prime} A^f T^f = p^{f\prime} T^f = 0, \tag{5.4}$$

so that factor trade is balanced at free-trade factor prices and we can apply Corollary 3.2. Q.E.D.

This is a useful result for the theoretical world of free and balanced trade, but unfortunately it does not apply to the more relevant world of impediments to trade. And in the latter world, there is in general no reason to expect factor trade to be balanced even when goods trade is. Tariffs, for example, permit countries to consume bundles of goods that are worth more, at domestic prices, than what they produce, and this in general causes the factor content of their trade valued at domestic factor prices to appear to be in deficit.

Indeed, it is possible in general for the factor content of trade to be negative for all factors, and it is possible similarly for changes in the factor content of trade to be in the same direction for all factors. In such cases the above corollaries, which rely at a minimum on trade in at least some factors going in opposite directions, are of little use. What is needed is a relationship

[7]See Deardorff (1980).

between factor prices and factor trade that focuses instead on the *relative* magnitudes.

One such result can be obtained by comparing the value of the change in factor content of trade to what it would be if all factor contents were to change in the same proportion to factor consumption. That is, let

$$B^1 = L^0 - S^1 \tag{5.5}$$

be the factor content of consumption in the initial equilibrium. As a measure of the relative change in the factor content of trade for each factor, i, we then define:

$$\Delta_i = w_i^1(S_i^2 - S_i^1) - \left[\frac{w_i^1 B_i^1}{w^{1\prime}B^1}\right][w^{1\prime}(S^2 - S^1)]. \tag{5.6}$$

From this, Δ_i is positive if the value of the change in factor-i trade is greater than its 'share' of the value of the total change over all factors, where its share [in large brackets in (5.6)] is the expenditure share on factor i in equilibrium 1. Note also that, from its definition, it follows immediately that

$$\sum_i \Delta_i = 0. \tag{5.7}$$

With this definition of the change in the relative factor content of trade at our disposal, we can now state the most general correlation result of the paper.

Corollary 3.4. If factor prices are normalized on the vector of factor content of consumption in equilibrium 2, then there is a nonnegative correlation between changes in relative factor prices and relative changes in the factor content of trade as defined in (5.6):

$$\mathrm{Cor}\left[\frac{(w_i^2 - w_i^1)}{w_i^1}, \Delta_i\right] \geqq 0. \tag{5.8}$$

Proof. In addition to the two equilibria, 1 and 2, being compared, consider a third equilibrium for this economy, numbered 3, with the property that the factor content of consumption is proportional to that in equilibrium 1 but equal in value, at factor prices w^1, to that in equilibrium 2. That is, define a vector S^3 such that

$$L^0 - S^3 = B^3 = \lambda B^1 \tag{5.9}$$

and

$$w^{1\prime}(L^0-S^3)=w^{1\prime}B^3=w^{1\prime}B^2. \tag{5.10}$$

Substituting (5.9) into (5.10), λ can be determined as

$$\lambda=\frac{w^{1\prime}B^2}{w^{1\prime}B^1} \tag{5.11}$$

and thus

$$\begin{aligned}
S^3&=L^0-\lambda B^1\\
&=L^0-B^1+(1-\lambda)B^1\\
&=S^1+\frac{w^{1\prime}B^1-w^{1\prime}B^2}{w^{1\prime}B^1}B^1\\
&=S^1+\frac{w^{1\prime}(S^2-S^1)}{w^{1\prime}B^1}B^1\\
&=S^1+\Gamma B^1,
\end{aligned} \tag{5.12}$$

where Γ is defined as

$$\Gamma=\frac{w^{1\prime}(S^2-S^1)}{w^{1\prime}B^1}. \tag{5.13}$$

Using the assumed homogeneity of technology and homotheticity of preferences, (5.9) implies that this new equilibrium has the same prices of both goods and factors as equilibrium 1,

$$w^3=w^1, \qquad p^3=p^1, \tag{5.14}$$

and that consumption is proportional to that in equilibrium 1,

$$C^3=\lambda C^1. \tag{5.15}$$

Suppose now that the vector of factor content of consumption in equilibrium 2 is used as numeraire. That is, factor prices are normalized so that

$$w^{2\prime}B^2=w^{1\prime}B^2. \tag{5.16}$$

It follows that

$$\begin{aligned} p^{3\prime}C^3 &= p^{1\prime}\lambda C^1 \\ &= \lambda w^{1\prime}A^1C^1 \\ &= \lambda w^{1\prime}B^1 \\ &= \frac{w^{1\prime}B^2}{w^{1\prime}B^1}w^{1\prime}B^1 \\ &= w^{1\prime}B^2 \\ &= w^{2\prime}B^2 \\ &= w^{2\prime}A^2C^2 \\ &= p^{2\prime}C^2. \end{aligned} \tag{5.17}$$

Thus, we can apply Proposition 3 to a comparison of equilibria 2 and 3:

$$(w^3 - w^2)'(S^3 - S^2) \geqq 0. \tag{5.18}$$

Writing this inner product as a summation, using (5.12) and (5.14), this becomes:

$$\begin{aligned} 0 &\leqq \sum_i (w_i^3 - w_i^2)(S_i^3 - S_i^2) \\ &= \sum_i (w_i^1 - w_i^2)(S_i^1 - S_i^2 + \Gamma B_i^1) \\ &= \sum_i \left[\frac{w_i^2 - w_i^1}{w_i^1}\right][w_i^1(S_i^2 - S_i^1) - \Gamma w_i^1 B_i^1] \\ &= \sum_i \frac{w_i^2 - w_i^1}{w_i^1}\Delta_i. \end{aligned} \tag{5.19}$$

From (5.7) and the definition of a correlation, (5.8) then follows.[8] Q.E.D.

6. Conclusion

We have already mentioned the fact that our results relate only to relative factor prices, and should not be viewed as indicating which factor prices go

[8]See Deardorff (1980).

up and down absolutely or in real terms. This qualification needs to be repeated and stressed, since there will inevitably be a strong temptation to regard a positive or negative factor content of trade as automatically associated with an absolute gain or loss from trade. But this could be quite misleading.

An example of why it may be misleading arose in another paper [Staiger, Deardorff and Stern (1988)], where we used the Michigan Computational Model of World Production and Trade to calculate changes in trade due to trade barriers and then computed the corresponding changes in the factor content of that trade. In one instance we found the factor content of a country's trade to rise for all factors when another country raised tariffs. This was true even though we required balanced trade in our calculations, and it seemed to suggest that all of the country's factors had gained from the foreign tariff. This is not the case, however.

What happened, as we have already suggested in section 5, was that the foreign tariff had caused a worsening of the country's terms of trade – a fall in the prices of its exports relative to its imports – requiring a rise in the quantities of exports and/or a fall in the quantities of imports in order to keep trade balanced. Thus, the factor content of trade increased. But this clearly does not imply a gain for all factor owners, since the worsening of the terms of trade implies that the country as a whole has suffered a loss.

However, this calculation also illustrates the usefulness of the result put forward in this paper. It is much easier to measure the factor content of trade, and even to estimate how the factor content of trade will change in response to policy, than it is to estimate empirically the complete effects of trade on factor markets. Thus, the factor content of trade can be used as a manageable indicator of what the effects of trade and trade policy may be on factor rewards. Even though the effects that are captured are only relative, this can still be a very useful piece of information.

Just how complete this information is depends, clearly, on the nature of preferences and production functions. As section 3 indicates, if a country is well approximated by Cobb–Douglas preferences and technologies, then the factor content of trade provides an accurate measure of relative effects on factor prices that holds for each individual factor. On the other hand, if variations in substitutability among factors are important, then only the average relationships of sections 4 and 5 can be established.

References

Bowen, H.P., E.E. Leamer and L. Sveikauskas, 1987, Multicountry, multifactor tests of the factor abundance theory, American Economic Review 77, 791–809.

Deardorff, A.V., 1980, The general validity of the law of comparative advantage, Journal of Political Economy 88, 941–957.

Deardorff, A.V., 1982, The general validity of the Heckscher–Ohlin theorem, American Economic Review 72, 683–694.

Dixit, A.K. and V. Norman, 1980, Theory of international trade (Cambridge University Press, London).

Harkness, J.P., 1983, The factor-proportions model with many nations, goods and factors: Theory and evidence, Review of Economics and Statistics 65, 298–305.

Helpman, E., 1984, The factor content of foreign trade, The Economic Journal 94, 89–94.

Leamer, E., 1980, The Leontief paradox, reconsidered, Journal of Political Economy 88, 495–503.

Leontief, W., 1954, Domestic production and foreign trade: The American capital position reexamined, Economia Internazionale 7.

Melvin, J.R., 1968, Production and trade with two factors and three goods, American Economic Review 58, 1248–1268.

Neary, J.P. and A.G. Schweinberger, 1986, Factor content functions and the theory of international trade, The Review of Economic Studies 53, 421–432.

Staiger, R.W., 1987, A specification test of the Heckscher–Ohlin theory, Journal of International Economics, forthcoming.

Staiger, R.W., A.V. Deardorff and R.M. Stern, 1988, The effects of protection on the factor content of Japanese and American foreign trade, Review of Economics and Statistics, forthcoming.

Stern, R.M. and K.E. Maskus, 1981, Determinants of the structure of U.S. foreign trade, Journal of International Economics 11, 207–224.

Vanek, J., 1968, The factors proportions theory: The n-factor case, Kyklos 4, 749–756.

CHAPTER 39

THE EFFECTS OF PROTECTION ON THE FACTOR CONTENT OF JAPANESE AND AMERICAN FOREIGN TRADE

Robert W. Staiger, Alan V. Deardorff, and Robert M. Stern*

Abstract—Data on pre-Tokyo Round tariffs and ad valorem approximations of nontariff barriers are used in the Michigan Computational Model of World Production and Trade to calculate changes in commodity trade attributable to protection in Japan and the United States. Data on factor requirements in production are then used to calculate the factor contents of these computed changes in trade. Results indicate that Japanese protection is more distortionary of factor markets in Japan and the United States than is American protection, and that U.S. manufacturing labor would be the least likely to gain from trade liberalization in Japan and/or the United States.

I. Introduction

THIS paper examines the effects of protection on the factor content of Japanese and American foreign trade. Using the Michigan Model of World Production and Trade, we calculate the effects of the hypothetical removal by the United States and Japan individually and jointly of the actual pre-Tokyo Round (1976) tariffs and constructed approximations of the ad valorem equivalents of nontariff barriers (NTBs) covering the period from 1973 to the early 1980s. In each case, the model is solved for changes in trade, employment, and other variables of interest. We then calculate the changes implied for the factor content of trade, and assess the degree to which protection has been used to distort the "normal" pattern of international trade.

We begin in section II by describing briefly the general structure of the Michigan Model and the data used for computational purposes. Section III presents a description of the various protection scenarios to be explored and the solution procedure used to generate the experimental results. In section IV we discuss why we focus on the factor content of trade and consider measurement issues that arise in a world where techniques of production differ internationally. Our results are presented in section V and conclusions in section VI.

Throughout the paper we use the term "factor trade" to mean the factor content of commodity trade. We do not allow in our analysis for any direct trade in factors themselves, such as international direct investment or migration.

II. Description of the Model and Data

The Michigan Model of World Production and Trade was developed originally to analyze the economic effects of the Tokyo Round, and it has been used as well to analyze a variety of other issues. Since space does not permit us to present the model, we refer the reader to Deardorff and Stern (1986) for details on the structure, implementation, and applications of the model. Some brief comments on the measurement of tariffs and NTBs to be used in the analysis may be useful however.

Our data on tariffs come from the GATT Secretariat and are based on pre-Tokyo Round (1976) rates. These were available at the line-item level of the Brussels Tariff Nomenclature (BTN) and were aggregated using own-country total imports as weights for each of our 22 tradable industries in each industrialized country in the model. The detailed tariff rates are available on request.

In the basic version of the model, existing NTBs in industrialized countries are represented by the fractions of 1976 trade in each sector and country that were covered by any kind of NTB. However, this representation of NTBs does not enable us to capture the economic effects that would be experienced if the NTBs themselves were reduced or removed. It is necessary for this purpose to have

Received for publication October 8, 1985. Revision accepted for publication December 16, 1987.

* Stanford University; University of Michigan; and University of Michigan and Brandeis University, respectively.

The research underlying this paper was assisted by grants from the Joint Committee on Japanese Studies of the American Council of Learned Societies and the Social Science Research Council and from the Ford Foundation. Helpful comments on earlier versions of this paper were received from Gary Saxonhouse, participants in the NBER International Studies Program Meeting, "Empirical Studies of the Structure and Impact of International Trade," New York, June 21, 1985, and two anonymous referees. We are grateful to Deborah Laren for computational assistance and Gary Saxonhouse for assistance with the data for Japan.

direct estimates of the price or quantity effects associated with particular NTBs by sector. Such estimates are very difficult to obtain, however, for a variety of reasons that are discussed at length in Deardorff and Stern (1985). In the absence of accurate and reliable estimates, we have constructed "high" and "low" approximations of the ad valorem equivalents of selected NTBs by major sector for the U.S. and Japan, ranging from 1973 to the early 1980s. These high and low approximations, which are presented in Staiger, Deardorff, and Stern (1987) and are also available on request, were constructed using price differentials between domestic and foreign goods drawn from a variety of sources and some rough guesses using the component weights of the NTB trade coverage indexes reported in Deardorff and Stern (1986).[1] While our various approximations of NTB ad valorem equivalents cover a span of years, and although some of the NTBs were not applicable in all years, we assumed that they were representative of the late 1970s.

As explained in Deardorff and Stern (1986), the Michigan Model permits a variety of assumptions to be implemented as regards exchange rates, flexibility of wages, and the determination of aggregate expenditure. The assumptions used in the present paper should be spelled out before we proceed. For the scenarios to be reported below, we have modelled each country with an exchange regime roughly paralleling what actually prevailed in the base year (1976) for our calculations. This means in particular that the Japanese yen is flexible and that the U.S. dollar, too, is floating against most major currencies. Nominal wages of labor in all countries are taken as fixed. This by itself would leave scope for changes in aggregate employment. However, as we have done in other studies of the effects of trade barriers, we neutralize such aggregate effects by having aggregate expenditure adjust endogenously to stabilize aggregate employment. Thus, we assume the existence of a successful policy of macroeconomic stabilization in each country.

TABLE 1.—DESCRIPTION OF TRADE LIBERALIZATION SCENARIOS

Scenario Number	Description
1	Japan Tariffs and NTBs Removed
2	U.S. Tariffs and NTBs Removed
3	Japan Tariffs Removed
4	U.S. Tariffs Removed
5	Japan NTBs Removed
6	U.S. NTBs Removed
7	Japan and U.S. Tariffs and NTBs Removed

III. Model Scenarios and Solution Procedure

Our choice of model scenarios was dictated by the desire to explore several different aspects of the effects of protection on Japanese and U.S. trade. In particular, we wish to examine the extent to which Japanese and American trade may be distorted by the commercial policies of these two countries, as well as to explore the implications of the mix of tariff and nontariff barriers. Thus, we have solved the model using seven different scenarios that are distinguished from one another by the country or countries whose tariffs and NTBs are to be altered. These scenarios are listed in table 1.[2]

To explore the relative distortions brought about by the commercial policy of each country, we reduced to zero Japanese and American tariffs and NTBs (scenarios 1 and 2, respectively) and then

[1] As noted in Deardorff and Stern (1985), the use of price differentials may overstate the price effects of existing NTBs especially because of differences in product quality. Instead of using price differentials, Morici and Megna (1983) calculate NTBs by sector for the United States, based on the estimated price effects of specific types of NTBs that were susceptible to measurement. These estimates are much lower than ours and may themselves be understated because they do not reflect all existing NTBs for the United States. Petri (1984, p. 138) presents estimates of ad valorem tariffs and tariff equivalents of quantitative restrictions for the United States and Japan covering twelve sectors for 1960, 1970, and 1980. Petri's estimates are based on work by Turner (1981) and, with the exception of textiles and apparel for Japan in 1980, are considerably lower than most of our approximations. These differences may reflect the fact that Turner focused only on quantitative restrictions and, further, some of his estimates apparently refer to bilateral trade between the United States and Japan.

[2] Petri (1984) presents a variety of calculations of the effects of existing protection and hypothetical scenarios of protection based upon a multisectoral computational general equilibrium model that includes the United States, Japan, and rest-of-world. He also calculates the factor content of U.S. and Japanese trade for 1980, based only on labor and physical capital, using the traditional Leontief method and also with reference to assumed appreciation of each country's currency. Although there is some overlap, our work can be distinguished from Petri's because we use a more detailed breakdown of factors and focus explicitly on how these factors may be affected by protection.

solved the model for the resulting changes in trade (and other endogenous variables). The effects of each country's tariffs were disentangled from the effects of NTBs by running several further experiments, which involved reducing to zero Japanese and American tariffs (scenarios 3 and 4, respectively) while leaving NTBs intact, and reducing to zero Japanese and American NTBs (scenarios 5 and 6, respectively) while maintaining tariff barriers.[3] Finally, scenario 7 explores the joint effects of the commercial policies of the two countries taken together.[4]

TABLE 2.—DESCRIPTION OF FACTOR CATEGORIES

Factor Category
1. Professional, Technical, Managerial, Administrative
2. Sales workers, Clerical
3. Craftsmen
4. Operatives
5. Laborers, except farm
6. Farm workers
7. Scientists, Engineers
8. Service workers
9. Capital

IV. The Factor Content of Trade

Solution of the model under a particular scenario provides us with changes in the commodity trade pattern associated with the stated liberalization program. While a direct examination of the changes in commodity trade, employment, and real incomes resulting from liberalization would be of interest in evaluating the effects of protection, we have chosen for several reasons to focus on changes in the factor content of trade.[5]

First, a focus on changes in the factor content of trade associated with trade liberalization is appealing because it follows an established tradition of characterizing trade patterns by their factor content that began with the pioneering work of Leontief (1953, 1956). As such, it provides a convenient and familiar summary measure of the positive implications of protection for the pattern of trade. Second, as a means of gauging the relative magnitude of the distortions introduced by American and Japanese trade policy, the factor content of trade avoids ambiguities associated with the pattern of commodity trade.[6] Finally, interpreting our experimental results as approximations of the full-employment general equilibrium effects of trade liberalization, changes in the factor content of trade allow a useful normative evaluation of the effects of protection. In particular, we have shown elsewhere (see Deardorff and Staiger (1988)) under strong assumptions concerning technology and tastes that relative changes in the factor content of trade as a fraction of endowment represent an exact measure of relative percentage changes in factor incomes.[7] Under weaker assumptions, the relationship becomes an average association between relative changes in factor trade (divided by endowments) and relative percentage changes in factor income. Hence, we can appeal to these theoretical results and characterize the relative

[3] In fact we will report below results for only scenarios 5 and 6, since scenarios 3 and 4 are implied by 1 and 5 and by 2 and 6, respectively, due to the linearity of the model.

[4] We make no effort in our choice of scenarios to account for adjustments in the international structure of protection that might be initiated in response to the unilateral liberalization of Japanese or American trade policy. Instead, our scenarios explore the degree to which, within the existing global structure of protection, Japanese and/or American trade policy might be considered distortionary.

[5] See Staiger, Deardorff, and Stern (1987) for an exploration of the industry and aggregate employment effects of Japanese and American protection. As mentioned, it would also be interesting if we could analyze directly changes in real incomes due to protection. In this connection, the Michigan model has a facility for wages to adjust by industry and to calculate changes in prices, but only under the restrictive assumption that relative wages for the various labor skill groups remain unchanged. Moreover, we do not have information on consumption patterns by skill groups so that it is not possible to determine changes in real incomes. If we were to explore these issues, it would require different assumptions than we have used in the present paper and, in effect, would constitute a separate undertaking in its own right. We plan to pursue these issues in further work and trust for now that the analysis based on the factor content of trade is interesting and robust.

[6] An examination of the changes in commodity trade that come about as a result of protection can suffer from a number of ambiguities. For example, in a Heckscher-Ohlin world with more goods than factors and factor price equalization, the free-trade pattern of commodity trade is indeterminant. Hence, it is unclear from which free-trade commodity trade pattern one should measure the distortions introduced by protection. The factor content of commodity trade, however, remains unambiguous, and avoids this conceptual problem.

[7] These strong assumptions are that both utility and production functions are Cobb-Douglas. Thus, this exact relationship obtains in a model that is essentially the same as that of Hartigan and Tower (1986), who derived a formula comparing income distributions in autarky and trade. They did not, however, relate their formula to the factor content of trade, nor did they generalize their result to a more general model as is done in Deardorff and Staiger (1988).

gains and losses from changes in protection using our calculated changes in factor trade.

To calculate the factor content of trade, data on the gross (direct plus indirect) factor content of production in Japan and the United States have been generated for labor of eight skill groups, and physical capital.[8] Table 2 lists the nine factor categories. Several approximations were necessary to calculate the sector-by-sector gross factor requirement and aggregate endowment data for Japan and the United States for 1976. A detailed description of the steps involved in generating these data is available from the authors on request.

As might be expected, production techniques employed in the United States as represented by gross factor requirements for unit production differ from those employed in Japan. Based on our data, these differences can sometimes be substantial. This raises the important empirical question of how to construct a measure of the factor content of international trade. One possibility would be to calculate the "actual" factor content of trade by examining each country's gross exports and imports separately and then applying factor requirements data on a country-of-origin basis. However, our interest in the importance of commercial policy for national factor markets leads us to focus on the "domestic" factor content of trade, calculated by applying the factor requirements data of each country to its own net trade. As shown in Deardorff and Staiger (1988), it is this measure, based on the techniques of production used domestically, that is relevant for evaluating the effects on national factor markets of changes in a country's net trade.

One other feature of the factor content of trade should be mentioned, since otherwise some of the results we report below may appear surprising and be misinterpreted. Whenever there is a change in a country's terms of trade, balanced trade requires an adjustment of the average quantities of exports and imports in opposite directions. For example, if the terms of trade improve, the increased *value* of existing exports relative to imports requires that either the *quantities* of imports expand or of exports contract to restore trade balance. These changes in quantities of trade in turn imply analogous changes in the factor content of trade, so that it is possible, even with balanced trade in goods, for the factor content of trade to appear quite unbalanced. This shows up most apparently in the factor content of one country's trade in response to trade liberalization by the other. Since the terms of trade of the former are likely to improve, one may find that the factor content of its exports contracts while the factor content of its imports expands for all or almost all factors. This in fact is what we find in some of the results reported below.

For this reason, while we report the changes in factor content of trade for individual factors, the average levels of these numbers tend to reflect only such terms-of-trade effects. The relative performance of the factors, and therefore the extent to which trade patterns have been distorted, can be understood only by comparing the effects for individual factors to one another. Thus we will direct attention to the range of values that arise across factors, since this indicates the maximum amount that one factor's content has risen or fallen relative to another. This too is consistent with the results in Deardorff and Staiger (1988) in which the factor content of trade is indicative only of the relative gainers and losers among factors.

V. The Effects of Protection

In this section we examine the distortions brought about by Japanese and American commercial policy as reflected in each nation's pre-Tokyo Round tariffs and our constructed approximations of NTBs. We attempt to answer two questions. First, how do the magnitudes of gains or losses experienced in the United States by one factor relative to another compare to those in Japan? This provides some sense of how substantial the distortions are in each of the two countries as a result of their commercial policies. Second, with respect to these policies, which factors are likely to be the relative losers and gainers in each country?

In what follows, we will speak of one factor "gaining" relative to another from protection if

[8] In an earlier version of this paper, we included two additional factor categories: mineral resources and agriculture, forest, and fishery resources. However, the difficulties of interpreting the natural resource endowment data for Japan and the United States using available input-output data sources led us to question the value of including these additional factors in our analysis, and we have since eliminated the natural resource categories altogether.

TABLE 3.—CHANGE IN FACTOR CONTENT OF NET EXPORTS AS A PERCENTAGE OF NATIONAL ENDOWMENT RESULTING FROM THE REMOVAL OF JAPANESE AND U.S. TARIFFS AND NTBS (Scenarios 1 and 2)

Factor Category	Effects of Removal of Japanese Tariffs and NTBs		Effects of Removal of U.S. Tariffs and NTBs	
	Japanese Net Exports (1)	U.S. Net Exports (2)	U.S. Net Exports (3)	Japanese Net Exports (4)
Prof., Tech., Manag., Adm.	1.0%	−0.0%	−0.0%	−0.1%
Sales workers, Clerical	1.8	−0.1	−0.1	−0.1
Craftsmen	2.5	−0.2	−0.1	−0.2
Operatives	5.0	−0.3	−0.8	−0.4
Laborers, except farm	1.1	−0.1	−0.0	−0.1
Farm workers	−9.5	1.6	−0.0	−0.2
Scientists, Engineers	2.1	−0.1	0.1	−0.2
Service workers	0.7	−0.0	−0.0	−0.1
Capital	2.0	−0.0	0.1	−0.3
Range (Percentage points)	14.5	1.9	0.9	0.3

the removal of that protection would, according to our calculations, result in a decrease in net factor exports as a fraction of factor endowments. While this way of identifying the relative gainers from protection conforms to intuition, we can, as noted above, attach a more formal rationale to our terminology by appealing to the results of Deardorff and Staiger (1988).

We begin by comparing the magnitude of the distortions in Japan brought about by protection with those in the United States. For purposes of calculation, we have used the pre-Tokyo Round (1976) nominal tariffs and the high values of the ad valorem equivalents of NTBs mentioned above. The results of model solutions under scenarios 1 and 2, in which tariffs and NTBs are removed in Japan and in the United States, respectively, are presented in table 3. Though the results are presented factor by factor, the main focus is on the range over factors of the changes in factor trade, presented in percentage points in the last row of the table. An entry in this row corresponds to the relative change in factor trade (as a fraction of endowment) between the biggest relative gainer in the economy and the biggest relative loser. Thus, a larger (smaller) entry in this row is associated with a greater (lesser) differential impact of protection across a country's factors, and hence a greater (lesser) degree of distortion associated with protection.[9]

Comparing the entries in the last row of columns (1) and (3) illustrates clearly the greater distortionary impact on home factor markets of Japanese as compared to American commercial policy. In particular, column (1) shows that the removal of existing Japanese protection would decrease the net factor exports of farm workers in Japan by an amount equal to 9.5% of endowment and increase the net factor exports of operatives by an amount equal to 5.0% of endowment. The differential impact of Japan's protection on its biggest relative gainer (farm workers) and its biggest relative loser (operatives) from that protection is given in the last row of column (1) as 14.5 percentage points. The impact of American commercial policy on American factor exports is shown in column (3), and provides quite a different picture. The differential in the effects of American protection for the biggest relative gainer (operatives) and biggest relative loser (capital) is given

[9] Under strong assumptions which include those of Cobb-Douglas preferences and technologies, an entry in the bottom row of table 3 would measure in percentage points the amount by which the factor income of the biggest relative gainer in the country increases over that of the biggest relative loser as a result of existing protection (see Deardorff and Staiger (1988)). It should also be noted that the theoretically appropriate measure of factor endowments for use in these calculations is the endowments of a hypothetical "autarky equivalent economy," which reduces to the domestic factor content of a country's observed consumption. The calculations we report in this paper are based on changes in factor trade as a fraction of *actual* factor endowments, a concept that has some intuitive appeal in addition to being linked closely with the theory. We have also calculated changes in factor trade as a fraction of factor consumption, and although we do not report these calculations, they provide an essentially identical characterization of the distortions brought about by Japanese and American trade policy.

TABLE 4.—FRACTION OF THE CHANGE IN FACTOR CONTENT OF NET EXPORTS AS A PERCENTAGE OF NATIONAL ENDOWMENT ATTRIBUTABLE TO JAPANESE AND AMERICAN NTBS (Scenarios 5 and 6)

	Fraction Attributable to Japanese NTBs		Fraction Attributable to U.S. NTBs	
Factor Category	Japanese Net Exports (1)	U.S. Net Exports (2)	U.S. Net Exports (3)	Japanese Net Exports (4)
Prof., Tech., Manag., Adm.	0.93	0.90	0.45	0.95
Sales workers, Clerical	0.94	0.90	0.63	0.92
Craftsmen	0.93	0.90	0.56	0.87
Operatives	0.93	0.89	0.71	0.79
Laborers, except farm	0.92	0.84	0.28	0.99
Farm workers	0.89	0.90	0.65	0.79
Scientists, Engineers	0.93	0.97	0.99	0.97
Service workers	0.93	0.90	0.70	0.87
Capital	0.95	0.91	0.68	0.84
Range	0.90	0.90	0.71	0.76

in the last row of column (3) as 0.9 percentage points. Thus, the distortionary homemarket effects of protection appear to be much more pronounced in Japan than in the United States.

This conclusion is qualified but not undone when cross-market effects of Japanese and American protection are considered, as noted in columns (2) and (4) of table 3. The biggest relative loser in American markets from Japanese protection is the American farm worker, while the biggest relative gainer is the American operative. The differential impact on factor trade as a percentage of endowment between the two is given in the last row of column (2) as 1.9 percentage points. The biggest relative loser in Japanese markets as a result of American protection is the service worker, while the biggest relative gainer is the Japanese operative. Here the differential impact on factor trade as a percentage of endowment between the two is given in the last row of column (4) as 0.3 percentage points. Hence, while the cross-market effect of protection in each country is clearly smaller than the home-market effect, the relatively more pronounced distortionary impact of Japanese as compared to American policy remains. Moreover, comparing the last rows of columns (2) and (3), our calculations suggest that Japanese commercial policy introduces a greater degree of distortion into American factor markets than does American commercial policy itself. The last row of columns (1) and (4) show that this is definitely not the case for Japanese factors. That is, the distortions in Japanese factor markets resulting from Japanese commercial policy are much greater than those associated with American commercial policy.

In an attempt to characterize the relative mix of tariffs and NTBs, we also examined the effects of each separately in scenarios 3–6. To facilitate comparison, results are expressed as the fraction of the total distortion in the factor content of net exports as a percentage of endowment associated with national commercial policy that can be attributed to either tariffs or NTBs.[10] Since the fractions add to one, we report only the effects attributable to NTBs (scenarios 5 and 6) in table 4. Thus, each entry in table 4 gives that fraction of the corresponding entry in table 3 which is attributable to a country's NTBs. Consistent with our discussion of the implications of table 3, we report our results factor by factor, but focus on the entries in the last row of each column of table 4.[11]

As can be seen in columns (1) and (2) in table 4, the distortions in Japanese and American factor trade associated with Japan's commercial policy can largely be attributed to its NTBs. That is,

[10] While distortions associated with Japanese tariffs and NTBs are of the same sign, factor by factor, the effects of American tariffs on a particular factor occasionally differ in sign from those of American NTBs. We calculate total distortion here as the sum of the absolute values of the distortions associated with tariffs and NTBs.

[11] To calculate the "range" entries in the last row of table 4, we first use table 3 to identify the biggest relative gainers and losers in each country as a result of each country's combined tariffs and NTBs. We then calculate the differential impact on these two factors of NTBs alone, and divide this by the differential impact of tariffs and NTBs together (the range entries in table 3) to arrive at the entries in the last row of table 4. Hence the entries in the last row of table 4 can be interpreted as that fraction of the difference between the biggest relative gainers and losers from tariffs and NTBs together that is attributable to NTBs alone.

TABLE 5.—RANKING OF RELATIVE GAINERS IN JAPAN AND THE U.S. FROM PRE-TOKYO ROUND TARIFFS AND APPROXIMATIONS OF NTBs (SCENARIO 7)

Ranking	Japanese Factors (1)	U.S. Factors (2)
1	Farm workers	Operatives
2	Service workers	Craftsmen
3	Prof., Tech., Manag., Adm.	Sales workers, Clerical
4	Laborers, except farm	Laborers, except farm
5	Sales workers, Clerical	Prof., Tech., Manag., Adm.
6	Capital	Service workers
7	Scientists, Engineers	Scientists, Engineers
8	Craftsmen	Capital
9	Operatives	Farm workers

based on our constructed NTB ad valorem approximations, the last row of columns (1) and (2) indicates that 90% of the differential in the effects of Japanese protection between the biggest relative gainers and losers in Japan and the United States is accounted for by Japan's NTBs. Japanese tariffs appear accordingly to have a relatively minor distortionary impact on Japanese and American factor markets.

The relative mix of American commercial policy presents a somewhat different picture. As can be seen from the entries in the last row of columns (3) and (4), NTBs also play a dominant role in the distortionary effects of American commercial policy in the factor markets of Japan and the United States. However, these entries indicate that roughly three quarters of the differential in the effects of American protection between the biggest relative gainers and losers in Japan and the United States are accounted for by America's NTBs. Hence, while relying more heavily on NTBs than tariffs, American commercial policy appears to be less dominated by its NTBs than is the commercial policy of Japan.

Finally, we provide a rough ranking of relative gainers and losers from our measures of the structure of Japanese and American protection, based on the factor content of trade (as a percentage of endowment) that can be attributed to that protection. Our interpretation of the results is not that they reflect an exact ordering of relative gainers and losers, but that they provide general guidance as to which factors might benefit most in a relative sense from protection. The elimination of all Japanese and American tariffs and NTBs (scenario 7) underlies the results, which are presented in table 5.[12] Column (1) provides the ranking for Japanese factors while column (2) refers to factors in the United States. Factors are ordered from relative gainers to relative losers with respect to our measures of pre-Tokyo Round tariffs and constructed approximations of NTBs. The results suggest that Japanese farm workers and service workers may be the biggest relative gainers from the structure of Japanese and American protection, and would stand to lose the most if this protection were removed. Japanese operatives and craftsmen appear to be the biggest relative losers from protection, and would consequently gain the most under liberalization. The results for the United States are quite the opposite, with American operatives and craftsmen the biggest relative gainers from protection, while American farm workers and capital interests would stand to gain the most from liberalization.

Though these results must be viewed as tentative and descriptive, their implications are nonetheless suggestive. That is, based on our measures of protection, it appears that operatives and craftsmen—the major components of labor in the U.S. manufacturing sector—may well be the greatest relative beneficiaries of the commercial policies of the United States and Japan. Thus, rather than helping the American manufacturing labor force, the liberalization of Japanese (or Japanese and American) trade policy could well work against the interests of these factors in the United States.

[12] While the rankings in table 5 reflect the results of scenario 7, the qualitative nature of our normative conclusions remains under each of the seven trade-liberalization scenarios listed in table 1.

By the same token American capital and farm workers might benefit the most from liberalization.

We mentioned earlier that we constructed high and low approximations of the ad valorem equivalents of NTBs in view of the uncertainties of what the appropriate price differentials might be. Having used the high values in the experiments reported in tables 3–5, the question arises as to how sensitive our results may be to the values chosen. To determine this, we conducted a series of further experiments using the low NTB ad valorem equivalents and various combinations of high and low values. While the results of these sensitivity experiments are too detailed to report here, they tended to support the findings described above.

VI. Conclusion

Japan is often alleged to embrace a commercial policy which distorts to a substantial degree its pattern of international trade. Our computational results suggest that, as of the mid-to-late 1970s, there is some basis for this allegation. Using our measures of protection, it appears that Japan's commercial policy may distort its trading pattern and its factor markets to a much greater extent than the distortions introduced into American trade and factor markets by American commercial policy. Moreover, it appears from our calculations that Japan's commercial policy has an inordinately large effect on factor markets in the United States. That is, our results suggest that the distortionary impact of Japanese commercial policy is more important for American factor markets than is American commercial policy itself. In contrast, the distortions introduced into Japan's factor markets by American commercial policy are small compared to those resulting from Japan's own protective policies.

Using our measures of tariffs and NTBs to characterize each country's commercial policy, our results also suggest that both countries rely relatively more on NTBs than on tariffs. The magnitude of the effects of each country's NTBs on home and foreign factor markets would appear to overwhelm any accompanying tariff effects. Nevertheless, with respect to both own-country and cross-country effects of commercial policy, Japan's reliance on NTBs appears greater than that of the United States.

Finally, our results suggest that labor in the United States manufacturing sector would be the least likely and capital and farm workers in the United States the most likely to gain from trade liberalization in Japan and/or the United States.[13]

It would be interesting, of course, to determine if these findings would be altered materially if more accurate measures of NTBs were available. The constructed high and low ad valorem approximations that we have used are based on a variety of methods which are not altogether comparable conceptually and which may apply to different years in the span from 1973 to the early 1980s. But unless we have misrepresented the sectoral pattern of NTBs in a systematic fashion, our conclusions should be robust.

It would also be interesting to consider how our results might be affected if we had information on tariffs and NTBs for earlier periods and for the mid-1980s. Casual empiricism suggests that the United States has introduced some important restrictions in recent years affecting exports from Japan, in particular automobiles until 1985 and steel currently, whereas Japan has liberalized some of its existing NTBs. By the same token, tariffs on industrial products have been reduced in both the United States and Japan as the result of the implementation of the Tokyo Round agreements. While the increased use of NTBs by the United States may well have narrowed the relative effects of Japan's NTBs, it seems likely that these changes would not reverse our findings concerning the effects of protection on the factor content of trade.

[13] This conclusion is further supported by results in Staiger, Deardorff, Stern (1987), where we focus on employment effects of Japanese and American protection as opposed to the effects, through the factor content of trade, on relative factor incomes.

REFERENCES

Deardorff, Alan V., and Robert W. Staiger, "An Interpretation of the Factor Content of Trade," *Journal of International Economics* 24 (Feb. 1988), 93–107.

Deardorff, Alan V., and Robert M. Stern, "Methods of Measurement of Nontariff Barriers," United Nations Conference on Trade and Development, UNCTAD/ST/MD/28, United Nations, Geneva, January 1985.

______, *The Michigan Model of World Production and Trade: Theory and Applications* (Cambridge: MIT Press, 1986).

Hartigan, John C., and Edward Tower, "The Leontief Question: A Cobb-Douglas Approach to Simulating the U.S. Income Distribution in Autarky," *Welwirtschaftliches Archiv*, Band 122, heft 4 (1986), 677–688.

Leontief, Wassily, "Domestic Production and Foreign Trade; The American Capital Position Reexamined," *Proceedings of the American Philosophical Society* 97 (Sept. 1953), 332–349.

______, "Factor Proportions and the Structure of American Trade: Further Theoretical and Empirical Analysis," this REVIEW 38 (Nov. 1956), 386–407.

Morici, Peter, and Laura L. Megna, *U.S. Economic Policies Affecting Industrial Trade: A Quantitative Assessment*, NPA Report #200 (Washington, D.C.: National Planning Association, 1983).

Petri, Peter A., *Modeling Japanese-American Foreign Trade: A Study of Asymmetric Interdependence* (Cambridge: Harvard University Press, 1984).

Staiger, Robert W., Alan V. Deardorff, and Robert M. Stern, "The Employment Effects of Japanese and American Protection," in Dominick Salvatore (ed.), *The New Protectionist Threat to World Welfare* (Amsterdam: North-Holland, 1987), 164–180.

Turner, Charlie G., "Quantitative Restrictions on the International Trade of the United States and Japan," Ph.D. Dissertation, Harvard University; 1981.

CHAPTER 40

A North American Free Trade Agreement: Analytical Issues and a Computational Assessment

Drusilla K. Brown, Alan V. Deardorff and Robert M. Stern

1. INTRODUCTION

THE successful pursuit of North American economic integration, beginning with the Autopact between the United States and Canada, has been under way for more than 25 years. The motivations for seeking agreement have varied with each stage, ranging from an initial desire to settle the US-Canadian dispute over automobile industry market shares to the sweeping economic development ambitions of the current Mexican government. Concerns raised by the fear of economic dislocation associated with trade liberalisation mirror the ambitions of the negotiating parties. An observer cannot avoid being struck by the intense political discussions in the United States over the proposed addition of Mexico to a North American Free Trade Area (NAFTA), as compared to the near US indifference to the 1987 US-Canada agreement. This was the case despite the considerably smaller trade flows involved between the United States and Mexico.

There are a number of issues raised by the addition of Mexico to the NAFTA that quite appropriately concern Canadians and Americans, such as the implication of an agreement for wages and employment of unskilled labour and

---

DRUSILLA K. BROWN is from Tufts University. ALAN V. DEARDORFF and ROBERT M. STERN are from the University of Michigan. This paper was presented at 'North American Free Trade: Economic and Political Implications,' A Conference of the Fraser Institute, Center for Strategic and International Studies, University of Toronto Centre for International Studies, and the Stanford University Americas Program, Washington, DC., June 27-28, 1991. Financial assistance was provided in part by the Fraser Institute and by a grant from the Ford Foundation in support of a program for research on trade policy in the Institute of Public Policy Studies at the University of Michigan. The authors would like to thank John Alfaro, Sundari Baru, and Seong-Hun Yun for assistance with the data and the computations, Judith Jackson for editorial and typing assistance, Andy Parks for assistance with data and concordances and Tracy Murray for data on Maquiladora and GSP trade.

12 DRUSILLA BROWN, ALAN DEARDORFF AND ROBERT STERN

the international allocation of capital. Similarly, for Mexico, the expected benefits of economic liberalisation may not be sufficient to compensate for the accompanying cost of economic dislocation. While these concerns are undoubtedly important from an analytical point of view, the likely quantitative dimensions of the employment problems due to a trade agreement are not clear. Our purpose in this paper is to identify some of the important issues in analysing the economic impact of a NAFTA and to provide some quantitative estimates of the effects of the elimination or reduction of trilateral tariffs, nontariff barriers (NTBs), and investment restrictions between Mexico, Canada, and the United States that might be implemented following the negotiation and legislative approval of an agreement.

We begin in Section 2 by identifying several issues that arise in undertaking an analysis of a NAFTA. In Section 3, we present an overview of the computable general equilibrium model that we have developed to assess the possible economic effects of a NAFTA. Our computational results are presented in Section 4, and our conclusions are summarised in Section 5.

2. ISSUES IN ANALYSING THE ECONOMIC IMPACT OF THE NAFTA

Perhaps the overriding motivation for Canada in pursuing a US-Canada free trade agreement was a concern on the part of some government officials and academic economists that a high level of import protection had insulated some imperfectly competitive domestic industries from the competitive pressures associated with an open trading regime. The end result was that Canadian firms were foregoing economies of scale in production in order to provide a wide variety of products to the Canadian market. The United States, on the other hand, turned to the bilateral-liberalisation option partly out of frustration with the multilateral negotiations, but it was also certainly aware of the potential political benefits of trade liberalisation within the hemisphere. The subsequent negotiations between the United States and Canada proceeded relatively uneventfully, in part due to the fact that the US and Canadian economies are broadly similar in terms of factor endowments, quality of labour force, and standard of living.

The Mexican government's objectives in entering into the US-Canada FTA are considerably more ambitious, concomitantly raising many more difficult and controversial issues. Following the generally failed attempt at industrial policy during the 1970s, Mexico is now seeking to develop through a program of internal goods and factors markets deregulation along with a more liberal international trade policy. That is, Mexico seeks to grow economically by increasing the degree of international specialisation in production.

Since Mexico is the relatively labour abundant country, we expect that trade liberalisation will stimulate production of the labour-intensive sectors in Mexico and shift labour into the capital-intensive sectors in the United States and Canada. To the extent that intersectoral labour reallocation is substantial, the subsequent fall in wages in the United States, particularly of unskilled labour, is likely to aggravate the already growing income disparity between skilled and unskilled workers. In addition, concern has been expressed that capital may relocate to Mexico in order to take advantage of lower Mexican wages and more lax labour and environmental standards.

Despite concerns with the loss in economic welfare associated with the sometimes difficult movement of resources from one sector to another, we can nonetheless expect welfare in all three countries to rise as a consequence of a free trade agreement. First, there is a strong presumption that an agreement will improve the international allocation of production as each country specialises in the sectors in which it has a comparative advantage. We know, of course, from the theory of the second best that welfare gains from preferential liberalisation are not assured. The NAFTA will eliminate any tariff-induced consumption distortions between domestic goods and imports from NAFTA partners, but a new consumption distortion between imports from NAFTA partners and non-NAFTA trade partners is introduced.

However, in the case of both Canada and Mexico, a very large fraction of trade already occurs within North America. Therefore, the volume of trade that could be potentially diverted is relatively small. This is much less the case, though, for the United States, which has sizable trade with both Europe and Asia. However, US tariffs are already quite low so that, again, the introduced consumption distortion is likely to be small.

Second, the transition costs once an agreement is in place are not expected to be large, particularly for the United States. The Mexican economy is so much smaller than the US economy, including sensitive sectors such as wearing apparel, that it is unlikely that even a substantial percentage increase in Mexican exports would noticeably alter US production levels in most sectors.

A trade agreement could be considerably more disruptive to the Mexican economy. As the smaller partner, Mexico will tend to specialise production in a narrower range of labour-intensive goods. However, the cost of transferring labour to the sectors in which Mexico has a comparative advantage must be weighed against the enormous burden that government regulations have imposed by limiting Mexico's economic growth. In addition, the Mexican government has indicated its intention to liberalise rules on foreign direct investment as part of its overall deregulation of markets. The capital inflow will reduce the difference in factor endowments in Mexico relative to its trade partners and, therefore, diminish the degree to which Mexico will specialise in the production of labour-intensive goods.

Third, all three countries in the NAFTA may experience an improvement in their terms of trade with the excluded countries, further raising economic welfare. Conventional general equilibrium theory of customs unions leads us to expect that the included countries will enjoy a terms-of-trade gain at the expense of the excluded countries. This result follows from the fact that the countries in the FTA will increase intra-NAFTA trade, thereby reducing supply to and demand from the rest of the world. Rest-of-world terms of trade tend to deteriorate as a result.

Fourth, international specialisation is expected to narrow the wage gap between the United States and Mexico, thus reducing immigration pressure on the United States. In principle, it is possible that a narrowing of the wage gap will come about by lowering wages for US workers, but this outcome is not inevitable. We expect the marginal physical product of US labour to fall as production in the capital intensive sectors expands. However, the value of US labour's marginal product may still increase due to the rise in the price of US goods on the world market. Thus, both US labour and capital may gain from the agreement.

Finally, the expected realisation of economies of scale due to a more competitive environment within the NAFTA could potentially raise the real return to both capital and labour in all three countries.[1] Normally, the Stolper-Samuelson Theorem would lead us to expect that trade liberalisation would lower the real return to at least one factor of production. However, in the case of increasing returns to scale, as firms move down their average total cost curves, the average product of both factors could rise. Thus, while the relative return of one factor may fall, the real return to both factors may rise.

3. THE COMPUTATIONAL MODEL

For the purpose of analysis, we have constructed a large scale computable general equilibrium model that is capable of evaluating the comparative static effects of changes in trade policy on factor prices, economic welfare, the intersectoral allocation of resources, and the international allocation of production. An overview of the model is provided below. For those readers interested in the technical details, the equations and variables of the model are available upon request.

---

[1] A profit maximising firm will hire each factor up to the point where the wage equals the marginal revenue product, which is given by

$$w^i = \text{MR} \times \text{MP}^i = \text{P}[1 - \frac{1}{e}] \times \text{MP}^i$$

for an imperfectly competitive firm, where w^i is the return to factor i, MR is marginal revenue for the firm, MP^i is the marginal product of factor i, and e>0 is the firm's perceived elasticity of demand. Trade liberalisation tends to push down the return to the scarce factor by lowering its marginal product. However, if trade liberalisation also leads each firm to perceive a more elastic demand curve, then the real return to each factor measured by w^i/P may rise even if factor i's marginal physical product falls.

Countries in the model are aggregated into three broad groups. Each of the NAFTA members (the United States, Canada, and Mexico) is modelled individually, a group of 31 other major trading countries are aggregated to create a fourth country,[2] and the remaining countries are consigned to residual rest-of-world supply and demand equations. The countries of the model produce, consume, and trade 23 tradable aggregate products. In addition, there are six nontraded goods. The market structure in each sector is either perfectly competitive or monopolistically competitive, depending on the degree of scale economies in production. Product categories and market structure assignments are listed in Table 1.

TABLE 1
Industry Structure

Sector	*Market Structure*	*Entry*
Agriculture	Perfect Competition	Free
Food	Monopolistic Competition	Free
Textiles	Monopolistic Competition	Free
Clothing	Monopolistic Competition	Free
Leather Products	Monopolistic Competition	Free
Footwear	Monopolistic Competition	Free
Wood Products	Monopolistic Competition	Free
Furniture, Fixtures	Monopolistic Competition	Free
Paper Products	Monopolistic Competition	Free
Printing, Publishing	Monopolistic Competition	Free
Chemicals	Monopolistic Competition	Free
Petroleum Products	Monopolistic Competition	Free
Rubber Products	Monopolistic Competition	Free
Nonmetal Min. Prod.	Monopolistic Competition	Free
Glass Products	Monopolistic Competition	Free
Iron, Steel	Monopolistic Competition	Free
Nonferrous Metals	Monopolistic Competition	Free
Metal Products	Monopolistic Competition	Free
Nonelec. Machinery	Monopolistic Competition	Free
Electrical Machinery	Monopolistic Competition	Free
Transport Equipment	Monopolistic Competition	Free
Misc. Mfrs.	Monopolistic Competition	Free
Mining, Quarrying	Monopolistic Competition	Free
Utilities	Perfect Competition	Free
Construction	Perfect Competition	Free
Wholesale Trade	Perfect Competition	Free
Transportation	Perfect Competition	Free
Financial Services	Perfect Competition	Free
Personal Services	Perfect Competition	Free

[2] The 31 other countries include 16 industrialised countries — Australia, Austria, Belgium-Luxembourg, Denmark, Federal Republic of Germany, Finland, France, Ireland, Italy, Japan, the Netherlands, New Zealand, Norway, Sweden, Switzerland, and the United Kingdom — and 15 newly industrialising countries — Argentina, Brazil, Chile, Colombia, Greece, Hong Kong, India, Israel, Portugal, Singapore, South Korea, Spain, Taiwan, Turkey, and Yugoslavia.

16 DRUSILLA BROWN, ALAN DEARDORFF AND ROBERT STERN

Final demand equations in each country are obtained assuming a representative consumer who maximises utility subject to a budget constraint,[3] and intermediate demands are derived from the profit maximisation decisions of representative firms in each sector. Products in both the perfectly competitive and monopolistically competitive industries are assumed to be characterised by some degree of product differentiation. In the case where markets are taken to be perfectly competitive, products are differentiated by country, while in the monopolistically competitive industries products are differentiated by firm.[4]

Turning to the factor markets, the variable input requirements are taken to be the same for the two market structures. Primary and intermediate input aggregates are required in fixed proportion to output.[5] In the monopolistically competitive industries, additional fixed inputs of capital and labour are required.[6] Capital and labour are assumed to be perfectly mobile between sectors and the returns to capital and labour are determined to equate factor demand to an exogenous supply of each factor.

Perfectly competitive firms set price equal to marginal cost, while monopolistically competitive firms maximise profits by setting price as an optimal mark-up over marginal cost. The number of firms in each industry is determined by the condition that there are zero profits.

International trade in goods is assumed to be subject to tariffs and nontariff barriers (NTBs). NTBs are incorporated by endogenously solving for the ad valorem tariff rate that will hold imports within each product category covered by NTBs at a predetermined level. An ad valorem tariff variable in each product category is an average of the NTB tariff-equivalent rate and the nominal tariff rate, using the NTB coverage ratio to weight the NTB tariff equivalent.[7]

The bilateral trade-weighted tariff rates are reported in the last two columns of Tables 2, 3, and 4 for the United States, Canada, and Mexico, respectively.

---

[3] Household income underlying the final demand equations is set at the level that will hold the trade balance equal to its level in the base data set. This procedure is, in principle, equivalent to setting income equal to factor payments plus tariff revenue.

[4] In both cases, we adopt a modified version of the approach to product differentiation suggested by Dixit and Stiglitz (1977) and Spence (1976). Consumers and producers are assumed to use a two-stage procedure to allocate expenditure across differentiated products. At the first stage, expenditure is allocated across goods, without regard for the country of origin or the producing firm. At this stage the utility function is taken to be Cobb-Douglas, and the production function requires inputs in fixed proportion. In the second stage, expenditure on each monopolistically competitive good is allocated across competing firms without regard to place of production. However, in the case of perfectly competitive goods, individual firm supply is indeterminant. Therefore, expenditure on each good must be allocated across individual countries. The aggregation function in the second stage is CES.

[5] Expenditure on primary inputs is allocated between capital and labour, assuming that a CES function is used to form the primary input aggregate.

[6] It is assumed that fixed capital and labour are used in the same proportion as variable capital and labour so that the production function is homogeneous.

[7] For additional details, see Deardorff and Stern (1990, pp. 23-24).

TABLE 2
Parameters of the Model: United States

ISIC Sector	*Demand Elasticity*	*Variable K Share of Total K*	*Variable Input Cost Share*	*Labour Share of Primary Input Cost*	*Tariff on Canada Exports*	*Tariff on Mexico Exports*
1 Agriculture	–2.9	1.00	1.00	0.24	1.6	4.0
310 Food	–3.0	0.12	0.75	0.47	3.8	2.6
321 Textiles	–2.9	0.11	0.73	0.71	7.2	2.8
322 Clothing	–3.0	0.12	0.66	0.79	18.4	6.2
323 Leather Products	–2.9	0.13	0.66	0.69	2.5	4.8
324 Footwear	–3.0	0.21	0.66	0.81	9.0	3.5
331 Wood Products	–3.0	0.11	0.66	0.59	0.2	1.3
332 Furniture, Fixtures	–3.0	0.19	0.66	0.76	4.6	1.4
341 Paper Products	–3.0	0.08	0.66	0.62	0.0	2.5
342 Printing, Publishing	–3.0	0.29	0.66	0.71	0.3	0.2
35A Chemicals	–2.9	0.02	0.66	0.54	0.6	1.2
35B Petroleum Products	–3.0	0.30	0.90	0.36	0.0	0.1
355 Rubber Products	–2.9	0.26	0.66	0.67	3.2	0.1
36A Nonmetal Min. Prod.	–3.0	0.24	0.66	0.62	0.3	1.0
362 Glass Products	–2.9	0.35	0.66	0.74	5.7	5.9
371 Iron, Steel	–3.0	0.07	0.66	0.81	2.7	1.6
372 Nonferrous Metals	–3.0	0.14	0.78	0.65	0.5	1.6
381 Metal Products	–3.0	0.21	0.66	0.68	4.0	2.2
382 Nonelec. Machinery	–2.9	0.27	0.66	0.69	2.2	0.9
383 Electrical Machinery	–3.0	0.28	0.66	0.76	4.5	2.3
384 Transport Equipment	–3.0	0.10	0.70	0.75	0.0	1.4
38A Misc. Mfrs.	–2.9	0.44	0.66	0.36	0.9	1.2
2 Mining, Quarrying	–3.0	0.48	0.66	0.25	0.0	0.1
4 Utilities		1.00	1.00	0.26		
5 Construction		1.00	1.00	0.81		
6 Wholesale Trade		1.00	1.00	0.60		
7 Transportation		1.00	1.00	0.62		
8 Financial Services		1.00	1.00	0.28		
9 Personal Services		1.00	1.00	0.86		

TABLE 3
Parameters of the Model: Canada

ISIC Sector	*Demand Elasticity*	*Variable K Share of Total K*	*Variable Input Cost Share*	*Labour Share of Primary Input Cost*	*Tariff on US Exports*	*Tariff on Mexico Exports*
1 Agriculture	–2.7	1.00	1.00	0.24	2.2	1.8
310 Food	–2.8	0.13	0.77	0.60	5.4	5.4
321 Textiles	–2.8	0.04	0.64	0.76	16.9	9.1
322 Clothing	–2.9	0.20	0.66	0.80	23.7	19.8
323 Leather Products	–2.9	0.08	0.66	0.83	4.0	16.8
324 Footwear	–2.9	0.19	0.66	0.86	21.5	22.5
331 Wood Products	–2.9	0.10	0.65	0.76	2.5	8.3
332 Furniture, Fixtures	–2.9	0.23	0.66	0.79	14.3	13.6
341 Paper Products	–2.9	0.14	0.65	0.63	6.6	9.9
342 Printing, Publishing	–2.9	0.36	0.65	0.71	1.1	3.9
35A Chemicals	–2.8	0.03	0.65	0.58	7.9	8.4
35B Petroleum Products	–2.8	0.33	0.91	0.36	0.4	0.0
355 Rubber Products	–2.9	0.19	0.66	0.78	7.3	0.0
36A Nonmetal Min. Prod.	–2.7	0.27	0.63	0.58	4.4	1.8
362 Glass Products	–2.9	0.34	0.65	0.66	6.9	4.2
371 Iron, Steel	–2.7	0.12	0.74	0.76	5.1	0.0
372 Nonferrous Metals	–2.7	0.16	0.80	0.77	3.3	0.0
381 Metal Products	–2.9	0.19	0.65	0.70	8.6	10.1
382 Nonelec. Machinery	–2.9	0.11	0.72	0.69	4.6	1.4
383 Electrical Machinery	–2.8	0.15	0.79	0.57	7.5	4.9
384 Transport Equipment	–2.8	0.15	0.79	0.70	0.0	0.9
38A Misc. Mfrs.	–2.9	0.11	0.65	0.69	5.0	8.3
2 Mining, Quarrying	–2.8	0.50	0.64	0.21	0.4	0.0
4 Utilities		1.00	1.00	0.32		
5 Construction		1.00	1.00	0.64		
6 Wholesale Trade		1.00	1.00	0.67		
7 Transportation		1.00	1.00	0.66		
8 Financial Services		1.00	1.00	0.34		
9 Personal Services		1.00	1.00	0.61		

TABLE 4
Parameters of the Model: Mexico

ISIC Sector	*Demand Elasticity*	*Variable K Share of Total K*	*Variable Input Cost Share*	*Labour Share of Primary Input Cost*	*Tariff on US Exports*	*Tariff on Canada Exports*
1 Agriculture	−1.5	1.00	1.00	0.26	2.0	1.1
310 Food	−2.8	0.10	0.69	0.25	9.3	1.6
321 Textiles	−2.8	0.23	0.64	0.33	11.6	11.7
322 Clothing	−2.9	0.26	0.66	0.27	19.8	19.4
323 Leather Products	−3.0	0.23	0.66	0.40	12.3	8.8
324 Footwear	−2.9	0.32	0.66	0.56	19.7	19.3
331 Wood Products	−2.9	0.21	0.66	0.34	13.6	15.0
332 Furniture, Fixtures	−2.9	0.32	0.66	0.26	14.7	14.2
341 Paper Products	−2.6	0.08	0.61	0.29	3.0	2.9
342 Printing, Publishing	−2.8	0.32	0.65	0.39	8.2	6.3
35A Chemicals	−2.8	0.17	0.64	0.35	7.1	9.8
35B Petroleum Products	−2.7	0.14	0.78	0.46	3.4	13.0
355 Rubber Products	−2.9	0.34	0.66	0.38	12.3	9.0
36A Nonmetal Min. Prod.	−2.9	0.42	0.66	0.24	14.6	14.7
362 Glass Products	−2.9	0.40	0.65	0.37	15.1	19.7
371 Iron, Steel	−2.9	0.01	0.66	0.38	7.5	3.8
372 Nonferrous Metals	−2.9	0.14	0.66	0.27	7.9	4.2
381 Metal Products	−2.8	0.27	0.65	0.40	9.6	8.3
382 Nonelec. Machinery	−2.9	0.33	0.66	0.37	12.7	12.1
383 Electrical Machinery	−3.0	0.29	0.66	0.43	14.2	13.9
384 Transport Equipment	−2.8	0.06	0.64	0.41	13.7	11.0
38A Misc. Mfrs.	−3.0	0.34	0.66	0.28	14.0	11.9
2 Mining, Quarrying	−2.7	0.51	0.63	0.21	3.7	3.6
4 Utilities		1.00	1.00	0.54		
5 Construction		1.00	1.00	0.64		
6 Wholesale Trade		1.00	1.00	0.19		
7 Transportation		1.00	1.00	0.35		
8 Financial Services		1.00	1.00	0.18		
9 Personal Services		1.00	1.00	0.82		

20 DRUSILLA BROWN, ALAN DEARDORFF AND ROBERT STERN

Tariffs in each case are aggregated up from the line-item level using bilateral trade as weights. US tariffs applying to imports from Mexico are then scaled down by a factor that reflects the value added applied to US exports to Maquiladora plants in Mexico.

Equilibrium prices are determined in world markets. In the perfectly competitive industries, total demand for each national variety must equal national output. For monopolistically competitive industries, total demand for the variety produced by each firm must equal supply by that firm. The ad valorem tariff variable discussed above then links equilibrium prices determined in the world system to prices paid by consumers in the country system.

The model is linear in form and thus can be solved by matrix inversion. The base year is 1989 for data on production, employment, and trade. Input-output coefficients for the production function were derived from the US input-output table for 1977, the Mexican table for 1980, and the Canadian table for 1976.

Some of the key parameters of the model are reported in Tables 2 to 4, for the United States, Canada, and Mexico. For the monopolistically competitive industries, the elasticity of demand, share of primary factors that are fixed, variable cost share of total cost, and the mark-up of price over marginal cost are all derivable from the theoretical structure of the model. Details are given in Brown and Stern (1989). The only data required are labour-share of primary input cost and primary input share of total cost, which were obtained from the input-out tables, and an indicator of the elasticity of substitution among different varieties of each good. The elasticity of substitution between all varieties of each good has been set equal to three.

4. COMPUTATIONAL RESULTS

The negotiations to form a NAFTA are currently at a very early stage. Therefore, the specific aspects of an agreement are yet to emerge. Our purpose here is to explore computationally the economic implications of some likely liberalisation scenarios. The model described above has been used to evaluate five experiments. These are: (A) removal of tariffs on trade among the United States, Canada, and Mexico, and expansion of US import quotas applied to Mexican exports of agriculture, food, textiles, and clothing by 25 per cent; (B) same as experiment (A) plus Mexico is assumed to relax capital import restrictions, resulting in a capital inflow from outside of the NAFTA that expands Mexico's capital stock by 10 per cent; (C) removal of tariffs on trade between the United States and Mexico, and expansion of US import quotas applied to Mexican exports of agriculture, food, textiles, and clothing by 25 per cent; (D) same as experiment (C) plus Mexico is assumed to relax capital import restrictions, resulting in a capital inflow from outside of the NAFTA that expands Mexico's capital stock by 10 per cent; and for purposes of comparison (E) removal of post-Tokyo Round tariffs on trade between the United States and Canada.

A summary of results for these five experiments is detailed in Table 5. The changes in the quantity of imports and exports measured in base period US dollars are reported in columns two and three and the per cent changes in the terms of trade are reported in column four. Note first, countries that enjoy an improvement in the terms of trade also tend to increase imports relative to exports. This outcome is simply a result of the fact that an increase in the price of exportables raises the volume of imports affordable without violating the balanced trade constraint.

However, the impact of a NAFTA on trade volumes is particularly lopsided for Mexico and the other 31 countries in scenarios (B) and (D). For example, under scenario (B) the quantity of Mexico's imports rise by $2.2 billion whereas exports rise by $12.4 billion. A deterioration in Mexico's terms of trade by 2.5 per cent is playing a small role in the rise in exports relative to imports, but the imbalance is caused primarily by the capital flows assumed to occur in this scenario. In scenarios (B) and (D), Other 31 is assumed to install capital in Mexico, generating interest payments from Mexico to Other 31 of approximately $9.5 billion each year. The remittance of interest payments by Mexico must be offset by a surplus on the trade balance if the current account balance is to remain at the level prevailing in the base period. The opposite is the case for Other 31, which increases imports by $6.7 billion but reduces exports by $4.1 billion under scenario (B).

A second interesting point to note about the second, third, and fourth columns of Table 5 is that the formation of the NAFTA generally reduces the volume of trade between the NAFTA countries and the Other 31 countries in the model. The formation of the NAFTA reduces the demand for imports from and the supply of exports to the excluded countries, thereby lowering external trade and worsening the terms of trade of the Other 31.

The exceptions to this rule again occur in scenarios (B) and (D) in which Other 31 is assumed to relocate capital in Mexico. Recall that the change in Mexico's capital stock must also generate a surplus on Mexico's trade balance. The world goods market will be willing to absorb the increased supply of goods from Mexico only if the price of Mexico's goods falls on the world market. The opposite is the case for goods produced by the Other 31. Hence, Mexico's terms of trade tend to deteriorate substantially while Other's terms of trade improve. For example, under scenario (B) Mexico's terms of trade deteriorate by 2.5 per cent, but Other's terms of trade improve by 0.2 per cent.

The welfare effects of the various liberalisation scenarios are reported in columns five and six of Table 5. Here we use the equivalent variation to measure

22 DRUSILLA BROWN, ALAN DEARDORFF AND ROBERT STERN

TABLE 5
Summary Results of a North America Free Trade Area*:
Changes in Country Imports, Exports, Terms of Trade, Welfare, and Return to Labour and Capital
(Trade and Welfare in Millions of US Dollars)

Country	Imports*	Exports*	Terms of Trade Per Cent Change	Equivalent Variation Per Cent	Equivalent Variation Millions	Wage Rate Per Cent Change	Rental Rate Per Cent Change
A. North American Free Trade: Tariffs and NTBs							
United States	9374.8	8595.8	0.2	0.1	6449.1	0.2	0.2
Other	–830.0	–475.8	–0.0	–0.0	–15.3	–0.1	–0.1
Canada	5537.9	6107.7	–0.5	0.7	3508.4	0.4	0.4
Mexico	2951.7	2984.2	–0.1	1.6	1977.2	0.7	0.6
B. North American Free Trade: Tariffs, NTBs, and Foreign Direct Investment							
United States	10451.6	10287.5	–0.0	0.3	13226.6	0.2	0.2
Other	6749.2	–4132.9	0.2	–0.0	–2081.2	–0.0	0.2
Canada	5579.2	6203.5	–0.5	0.7	3662.9	0.5	0.5
Mexico	2201.4	12353.0	–2.5	5.0	6298.5	9.3	3.3
C. US-Mexico Free Trade: Tariffs and NTBs							
United States	3116.5	2936.7	0.0	0.1	3664.5	0.0	0.1
Other	–286.7	–124.0	–0.0	0.0	96.8	–0.0	–0.0
Canada	–5.6	28.5	–0.0	0.0	78.2	–0.1	–0.1
Mexico	2900.9	2933.7	–0.1	1.5	1922.7	0.7	0.6
D. US-Mexico Free Trade: Tariffs, NTBs, and Foreign Direct Investment							
United States	4193.7	4628.7	–0.1	0.2	10654.1	0.1	0.1
Other	7293.6	–3780.1	0.2	–0.0	–1947.6	0.0	0.2
Canada	35.9	124.4	–0.1	0.0	234.2	0.1	0.1
Mexico	2151.2	12302.8	–2.5	4.9	6255.3	9.3	3.3
E. US-Canada Free Trade: Tariffs Only							
United States	6266.2	5651.8	0.1	0.1	2867.8	0.1	0.1
Other	–522.2	–326.4	–0.0	–0.0	–107.3	–0.1	–0.0
Canada	5491.6	6036.7	–0.5	0.6	3356.4	0.4	0.4
Mexico	3.7	8.6	–0.0	0.0	35.8	–0.1	–0.1

* Five experiments have been performed. These are:
A. Removal of tariffs on trade among the United States, Canada, and Mexico, plus a 25 per cent expansion of US import quotas imposed on Mexican exports of agriculture, food, textiles and clothing;
B. Same as experiment (A) plus relaxation of Mexico's capital import controls that results in a 10 per cent increase in the capital stock in Mexico;
C. Removal of tariffs on trade between the United States and Mexico, plus a 25 per cent expansion of US import quotas imposed on Mexican exports of agriculture, food, textiles, and clothing;
D. Same as experiment (C) plus relaxation of Mexico's capital import controls that results in a 10 per cent increase in the capital stock in Mexico; and
E. Removal of tariffs on trade between the United States and Canada.
*Exports and imports valued in US dollar base period prices.

welfare and express this value both nominally and as a per cent of GDP.[8] Clearly, a NAFTA would be welfare improving for all three countries, but will have the largest impact on the Mexican economy. Mexican welfare rises by 1.6 per cent of GDP under scenario (A) and, when capital flows are incorporated under scenario (B), Mexican welfare rises by 5 per cent of GDP. Welfare gains for the United States and Canada are considerably smaller but not inconsequential.

It is worth pointing out that relaxing capital import restrictions by Mexico will not only ease the transition to the new NAFTA equilibrium but also dramatically enhances the static welfare benefits of trade liberalisation. The capital inflow into Mexico substantially raises the equilibrium scale of production in Mexico, so that Mexican firms are led to realise economies of scale. The end result is to substantially raise the real return to both capital and labour. The per cent changes in factor returns deflated by a consumer price index are reported in the last two columns of Table 5. The capital inflow into Mexico has the expected effect of raising the return to labour relative to the return to capital by six per cent. But note that the rise in the wage-rent ratio occurs even though the return to capital rises by 3.3 per cent. The rise in the return to both factors is made possible by increases in output per firm in Mexico, which, thus, tends to raise the average product of both factors.

These results also suggest that it is in Canada's interest to participate in the US-Mexican negotiations, though the gain to Canada of doing so is very small. The formation of a NAFTA raises Canada's welfare by $3.5 billion. In comparison, a US-Canada agreement combined with a US-Mexico agreement would raise Canada's welfare by a slightly smaller $3.4 billion. Canada, of course, has other political reasons for participating in the negotiations, such as taking the opportunity to impose restrictions on further accession to the NAFTA by other countries in central and South America.

Two other conclusions can be drawn by examining the last two columns of Table 5. First, the formation of a NAFTA has the expected effect of narrowing the wage gap between US and Mexican workers. In scenario (B), the wage paid to Mexican workers relative to US workers rises by over nine per cent. Thus, the pressure for illegal immigration may be reduced.

However, the narrowing of the wage gap is not accomplished at the expense of US workers. Real wages rise in the US by 0.2 per cent. This is partly a consequence of the improvement in the US terms of trade which raises the value of workers' marginal product on the world market and partly a consequence of the increase in the scale of production as a result of liberalisation, the benefits of which accrue to both US workers and capital owners.

Sectoral results for the United States, Canada, and Mexico are reported in Tables 6, 7, and 8 respectively, for liberalisation scenario A. The sectoral results

[8] The equivalent variation is the change in income valued at base period prices that yields the same change in welfare that occurs with the assumed liberalisation.

TABLE 6
Sectoral Effects on the United States of North American Free Trade: Tariffs and NTBs
Per Cent Change

ISIC Sector	Exports	Imports	Bilateral Imports Canada	Bilateral Imports Mexico	Output	No. Firms	Elasticity	Capital	Employment
1 Agriculture	0.07	2.03	4.28	10.81	–0.03	0.00	0.00	–0.03	–0.02
310 Food	1.87	1.71	9.98	12.22	0.11	–0.03	0.00	–0.03	0.00
321 Textiles	7.73	0.23	15.54	14.10	1.11	0.64	0.00	0.67	0.70
322 Clothing	10.01	1.47	46.59	24.90	0.65	0.12	0.00	0.15	0.20
323 Leather Products	1.16	1.93	11.75	14.47	0.04	–0.18	0.00	–0.21	–0.13
324 Footwear	11.16	2.52	29.17	10.53	0.24	–0.02	0.00	0.00	0.04
331 Wood Products	1.92	0.86	1.20	0.67	0.14	–0.01	0.00	0.00	0.02
332 Furniture, Fixtures	9.80	3.58	12.99	8.94	0.34	0.12	0.00	0.15	0.17
341 Paper Products	2.35	0.09	–0.00	5.12	0.21	0.05	0.00	0.04	0.08
342 Printing, Publishing	1.70	0.17	–0.37	–2.20	0.11	0.02	0.00	0.03	0.05
35A Chemicals	3.73	–0.48	–1.44	–3.76	0.62	0.43	0.00	0.42	0.44
35B Petroleum Products	–0.05	0.52	1.27	–4.73	0.02	–0.03	–0.00	–0.02	–0.00
355 Rubber Products	6.15	0.54	9.85	–9.26	0.63	0.38	0.00	0.43	0.45
36A Nonmetal Min. Prod.	4.83	0.73	2.52	–0.12	0.14	0.05	0.00	0.05	0.08
362 Glass Products	–1.91	57.64	173.47	19.10	–11.45	–11.63	0.00	–11.58	–11.56
371 Iron, Steel	6.49	1.51	10.48	–4.84	0.28	0.14	0.00	0.14	0.16
372 Nonferrous Metals	–0.89	5.32	12.11	27.60	–1.01	–1.02	–0.00	–1.05	–1.01
381 Metal Products	6.02	2.71	13.25	2.25	0.29	0.14	0.00	0.16	0.18
382 Nonelec. Machinery	3.94	0.01	2.62	–24.56	0.72	0.54	0.00	0.58	0.59
383 Electrical Machinery	1.86	9.97	14.03	102.18	–0.80	–0.93	0.00	–0.90	–0.89
384 Transport Equipment	–0.18	2.13	7.47	–9.00	–0.17	–0.37	–0.00	–0.37	–0.34
38A Misc. Mfrs.	4.05	–0.76	–1.80	–7.92	0.87	0.73	0.00	0.77	0.81
2 Mining, Quarrying	–0.21	0.53	1.25	–1.76	–0.18	–0.23	–0.00	–0.22	–0.17
4 Utilities					–0.02			–0.02	0.01
5 Construction					0.05			0.04	0.06
6 Wholesale Trade					0.02			–0.00	0.03
7 Transportation					0.02			0.01	0.03
8 Financial Services					–0.00			–0.01	0.02
9 Personal Services					0.01			–0.01	0.01

TABLE 7
Sectoral Effects on Canada of North American Free Trade: Tariffs and NTBs
Per Cent Change

ISIC Sector	*Exports*	*Imports*	*Bilateral Imports US*	*Bilateral Imports Mexico*	*Output*	*No. Firms*	*Elasticity*	*Capital*	*Employment*
1 Agriculture	0.38	3.23	4.74	3.65	–0.15	0.00	0.00	–0.15	–0.14
310 Food	4.99	4.61	12.35	15.12	0.26	–0.32	–0.00	–0.26	–0.23
321 Textiles	5.80	20.62	43.76	23.32	–3.80	–4.45	0.00	–4.44	–4.42
322 Clothing	31.01	11.27	56.59	25.52	0.66	–0.05	0.03	0.08	0.09
323 Leather Products	8.35	0.89	7.45	40.01	3.87	3.01	0.05	3.07	3.08
324 Footwear	26.80	7.51	45.33	45.97	3.04	1.69	0.05	1.94	1.96
331 Wood Products	0.95	4.41	6.33	18.88	0.44	–0.22	0.00	–0.16	–0.15
332 Furniture, Fixtures	11.38	21.00	35.70	38.93	–0.46	–1.31	0.02	–1.13	–1.11
341 Paper Products	–0.09	11.98	18.16	24.30	–0.29	–0.84	–0.00	–0.78	–0.75
342 Printing, Publishing	–0.51	2.67	3.33	8.34	–1.19	–1.40	–0.04	–1.33	–1.32
35A Chemicals	–1.68	12.83	21.36	15.07	–3.37	–4.01	–0.01	–4.00	–3.98
35B Petroleum Products	1.12	0.08	0.52	–5.73	0.70	0.11	0.01	0.30	0.32
355 Rubber Products	8.15	7.43	18.64	–11.61	0.92	0.21	0.06	0.33	0.35
36A Nonmetal Min. Prod.	2.48	4.45	11.67	1.27	0.99	0.22	0.05	0.42	0.44
362 Glass Products	159.80	–2.90	–1.86	8.77	157.93	156.45	–0.03	156.94	156.96
371 Iron, Steel	8.12	5.35	12.09	–10.36	2.71	1.49	0.16	1.62	1.64
372 Nonferrous Metals	9.58	–1.62	0.58	14.66	7.60	5.55	0.09	5.87	5.88
381 Metal Products	10.15	12.92	19.94	19.74	0.06	–1.45	0.02	–1.18	–1.16
382 Nonelec. Machinery	1.43	7.69	10.50	–25.74	–3.98	–4.83	0.02	–4.74	–4.73
383 Electrical Machinery	10.10	10.21	16.39	108.81	–0.16	–1.48	0.06	–1.28	–1.27
384 Transport Equipment	7.01	–2.92	–3.05	–12.65	5.41	3.82	0.05	4.06	4.06
38A Misc. Mfrs.	–2.06	7.42	11.75	8.47	–5.08	–6.07	0.02	–5.98	–5.96
2 Mining, Quarrying	0.94	0.57	0.90	–2.19	1.08	0.69	0.03	0.88	0.90
4 Utilities					0.17			0.16	0.20
5 Construction					0.13			0.12	0.13
6 Wholesale Trade					–0.21			–0.23	–0.20
7 Transportation					0.12			0.11	0.13
8 Financial Services					–0.14			–0.14	–0.12
9 Personal Services					–0.33			–0.34	–0.33

TABLE 8
Sectoral Effects on Mexico of North American Free Trade: Tariffs and NTBs
Per Cent Change

ISIC Sector	Exports	Imports	Bilateral Imports US	Bilateral Imports Canada	Output	No. Firms	Elasticity	Capital	Employment
1 Agriculture	6.60	3.21	3.36	2.04	0.17	0.00	0.00	0.18	0.15
310 Food	7.39	12.11	20.45	4.27	–0.25	–0.62	0.01	–0.56	–0.67
321 Textiles	5.57	22.54	32.77	28.03	0.13	–0.15	0.03	–0.06	–0.13
322 Clothing	22.90	25.40	45.64	44.56	4.24	3.54	0.12	3.75	3.63
323 Leather Products	13.46	15.44	31.66	27.59	1.57	0.98	0.02	1.19	1.00
324 Footwear	10.53	38.33	48.90	52.62	0.84	0.05	0.01	0.32	0.28
331 Wood Products	0.58	29.56	36.68	40.79	–1.97	–2.25	0.02	–2.18	–2.23
332 Furniture, Fixtures	9.48	15.58	35.39	34.43	5.95	5.33	0.10	5.63	5.23
341 Paper Products	4.63	8.23	9.49	9.26	–1.14	–1.41	–0.02	–1.35	–1.47
342 Printing, Publishing	–1.74	10.63	23.29	17.08	–2.26	–2.67	–0.03	–2.52	–2.56
35A Chemicals	–4.74	15.83	21.59	24.87	–5.31	–5.28	–0.02	–5.27	–5.30
35B Petroleum Products	–4.72	4.60	4.74	14.73	–3.42	–2.73	–0.18	–2.63	–3.06
355 Rubber Products	–8.85	26.03	35.56	28.20	–7.40	–7.34	–0.02	–7.34	–7.39
36A Nonmetal Min. Prod.	–0.32	27.40	39.21	41.02	–1.85	–2.02	0.00	–1.92	–2.03
362 Glass Products	14.67	13.42	21.07	202.75	6.31	5.37	0.04	5.77	5.71
371 Iron, Steel	–5.39	13.10	23.20	16.69	–7.69	–7.42	–0.02	–7.40	–7.45
372 Nonferrous Metals	23.76	4.25	9.69	11.40	21.31	19.74	0.12	19.98	19.89
381 Metal Products	1.91	18.22	25.97	24.86	–3.21	–3.82	0.04	–3.64	–3.69
382 Nonelec. Machinery	–23.08	19.19	32.00	27.05	–27.13	–27.98	–0.00	–27.68	–27.73
383 Electrical Machinery	100.17	–18.69	–2.30	–0.68	92.37	87.60	0.15	89.01	88.99
384 Transport Equipment	–8.63	18.56	22.91	23.66	–11.09	–10.67	–0.12	–10.69	–10.70
38A Misc. Mfrs.	–7.80	14.14	26.12	16.40	–10.95	–11.62	0.02	–11.37	–11.46
2 Mining, Quarrying	–1.98	5.43	6.13	6.59	–0.92	–0.93	–0.05	–0.89	–1.06
4 Utilities					–0.45			–0.44	–0.46
5 Construction					–0.33			–0.30	–0.34
6 Wholesale Trade					–0.22			–0.19	–0.37
7 Transportation					–0.40			–0.36	–0.49
8 Financial Services					–0.34			–0.27	–0.66
9 Personal Services					–0.47			–0.45	–0.47

for the other scenarios are available from the authors on request. The per cent changes in bilateral imports with each NAFTA trade partner are reported in columns four and five of each table. The bilateral trade changes between the United States and Canada exhibit a strong indication of increased intra-industry trade. Both the United States and Canada generally increase imports from each other in most product categories. The broad similarity between the US and Canadian economies in terms of factor endowments, labour force quality, and per capita income suggest that the benefits of liberalised US-Canada trade stem primarily from increased product variety rather than intersectoral specialisation. Our use here of a model that combines both the roles of factor endowments and product variety in determining the pattern of trade allows this result to emerge.

In contrast, while Mexican imports from its two trade partners rise in every product category, Mexico's exports are heavily concentrated in a small range of sectors. For example, the United States reduces imports from Mexico in a wide range of industrial products. The notable exceptions are glass products (19.1%), nonferrous metals (27.6%), metal products (2.2%), and electrical machinery (102.2%). These results suggest a much stronger pattern of intersectoral specialisation for Mexico which would be expected given Mexico's very different factor abundance as compared to the United States and Canada.

These results also suggest that Canada's fear that a US-Mexico agreement may seriously erode the position of Canadian firms in the US market is unfounded. There is not a single product category in which US imports from Mexico are displacing Canadian exports. Rather the opposite appears to be the case. Canadian exports to the United States of petroleum products, rubber products, non-metallic mineral products, iron and steel, non-electrical machinery, transport equipment, and mining and quarrying all rise while Mexican exports in these product categories fall. Gains by Mexican exporters to the United States appear to be primarily concentrated in agriculture, the semi-manufactured sectors, and some heavy industry. However, Canadian firms also expand exports to the United States in these product categories. Similarly, US producers displace Mexican producers in five different Canadian sectors, whereas the opposite occurs in only one (glass products), as can be seen in Table 7.

Mexico's increased exports to the US market are quite substantial in several product categories, such as clothing (24.9%), glass products (19.1%), nonferrous metals (27.6%), and electrical machinery (102.2%). The increases in US imports from Mexico in agriculture (10.8%), food (12.2%), and textiles (14.1%) are also substantial due to the assumed relaxation of US NTBs in these three product categories. However, the impact on total US imports is quite small due to Mexico's small share of the US market, as can be seen from column three of Table 6. The per cent changes in total US imports of agriculture, food, textiles, and clothing under scenario (A) are only 2.0, 1.7, 0.2, and 1.5 per cent, respectively.

Columns six and seven of Tables 6, 7, and 8 report the per cent change in industry output and number of firms for each country. These results can also be used to calculate the per cent change in firm output by taking the difference between these two columns. It is especially worth noting that firm output rises in the United States and Canada in every industry. The only exceptions in Mexico are chemicals, petroleum products, rubber products, and iron and steel, and in all four cases the decline in firm output is trivially small. This is the case despite the fact that firm perceived elasticity of demand falls in many sectors, as reported in column eight of each table.

The rationalisation effect is sufficiently distinct that there are some sectors in Canada in which total industry production rises but employment of both capital and labour declines. For example, production of metal products rises by 0.1 per cent in Canada even though capital and labour employment each fall by 1.2 per cent (reported in the last two columns of Table 8). The industry expansion is possible due to the exit of 1.4 per cent of the sector's firms, thus releasing fixed capital and labour for employment by the surviving firms.

Despite the distinctive increase in intra-industry trade, inter-sectoral specialisation also emerges, particularly in Mexico. For example, employment of labour declines in 21 of the 29 industries in Mexico, shifting primarily toward the labour-intensive sectors: agriculture (0.2%), clothing (3.6%), leather products (1.0%), footwear (0.3%), furniture and fixtures (5.2%) and glass products (5.7%). However, the largest percentage changes in employment are in some of the industrial sectors, such as nonferrous metals (19.9%) and electrical machinery (89.0%).

Employment effects in the United States are more diffuse and are generally small, with per cent employment declines generally less than one per cent in each sector. The only exception is the glass products sector in which US employment declines by 11.6 per cent. Note also that despite the sizable increase in US import quotas applied to Mexican exports of food, textiles, and clothing, US employment in these sectors still rises in order to satisfy the increase in Canadian demand for US produced goods. US exports to Canada rise in food (12.4%), textiles (43.8%), and clothing (56.6%) due to the removal of Canada's relatively high tariffs in these product categories.

5. CONCLUSIONS

We have attempted to identify some important issues arising in the analysis of a NAFTA and to provide a computational assessment of some of the economic effects involved. While the various experiments that we have conducted are not exhaustive of all the possible changes that might be negotiated in connection with a NAFTA, they are nonetheless indicative of the order of magnitude on trade, output, number of firms, factor returns, and employment that could result from trilateral trade liberalisation and increased investment.

Overall, our results suggest that the formation of a NAFTA will have positive benefits for all countries involved on several accounts, as follows:

1. The participating countries all enjoy an increase in aggregate welfare.
2. Although the inclusion of Mexico erodes some of Canada's benefits under the US-Canada FTA, the effect is minuscule.
3. The wage gap between the United States and Mexico will narrow, thereby reducing the incentive for illegal immigration. However, the real wage in the United States still rises as a result of trade liberalisation.
4. A NAFTA will have beneficial scale effects in all three countries.
5. A reduction in barriers against foreign direct investment in Mexico will stimulate new capital formation, which has the beneficial effects of alleviating poverty in Mexico by raising the marginal product of labour and raising the average product of both capital and labour by increasing the scale of production in Mexico.
6. The inflow of capital into Mexico may come primarily from outside the NAFTA, not from the United States, suggesting the fear that US firms will relocate production in Mexico may be largely unfounded.
7. There appears to be relatively little intersectoral factor reallocation in the United States especially, so that the associated relocation costs are likely to be small.
8. While there are negative effects on the rest of the world, they appear to be relatively small.

REFERENCES

Brown, D. K., A. V. Deardorff and R. M. Stern (1991), 'Some Estimates of a North American Free Trade Agreement,' *Federal Reserve Bank of Minneapolis Quarterly Review* (Winter).

Brown, D. K. and R. M. Stern (1989), 'US-Canada Bilateral Tariff Elimination: The Role of Product Differentiation and Market Structure,' in R. C. Feenstra (ed.) *Trade Policies for International Competitiveness* (Chicago: University of Chicago Press).

Deardorff, A. V. and R. M. Stern (1990), *Computational Analysis of Global Trading Arrangements* (Ann Arbor: University of Michigan Press).

Dixit, A. and J. E. Stiglitz (1977), 'Monopolistic Competition and Optimum Product Diversity,' *American Economic Review* 76, 297-308.

Hinojosa-Ojeda, R. and S. Robinson (1991), 'Alternative Scenarios of US-Mexico Integration: A Computable General Equilibrium Approach,' Working Paper No. 609 (Department of Agricultural and Resource Economics, University of California, Berkeley).

KPMG Peat Marwick/Policy Economics Group (1991), 'Analysis of Economic Effects of a Free Trade Area Between the United States and Mexico: Executive Summary' (Washington, DC: US Council of the Mexico-US Business Committee).

Spence, M. E. (1976), 'Product Selection, Fixed Costs, and Monopolistic Competition,' *Review of Economic Studies* 43, 217-36.

CHAPTER 41

RESEARCH SEMINAR IN INTERNATIONAL ECONOMICS

Gerald R. Ford School of Public Policy
The University of Michigan
Ann Arbor, Michigan 48109-1220

Post-Print Paper No. 6

Protection and Real Wages: Old and New Trade Theories and Their Empirical Counterparts*,†

Drusilla K. Brown
Tufts University

Alan V. Deardorff
University of Michigan

Robert M. Stern
University of Michigan

May 18, 1993

---

* The authors are Associate Professors at Tufts University (Brown) and Professors at the University of Michigan (Deardorff and Stern). Financial support in writing this paper was provided in part by a grant from the Ford Foundation.

† Paper prepared for the CEPR/CESPRI Conference, "New Trade Theories: A Look at the Empirical Evidence" Milan, 27-28 May 1993, Bocconi University.

I. Introduction

Our purpose in this paper is to examine the issue of how tariffs, or their removal, affect wages. This is an old issue, of course, dating back in the theoretical literature of international trade to the Stolper-Samuelson Theorem and beyond. The Stolper-Samuelson Theorem, based on the assumptions of the standard Heckscher-Ohlin (H-O) Model of international trade, stated that a tariff would increase the real wage of a country's scarce factor of production. In the context of a presumed labor-scarce country like the United States, this suggests that a move closer to free trade, such as is being negotiated in the North American Free Trade Agreement (NAFTA), would reduce the real wage of labor. Since several computational models of the NAFTA, including our own Michigan Model of the NAFTA (Brown, Deardorff, and Stem, 1992a,b), provide the opposite result, our purpose in this paper will be to explain why.

The reason, of course, is to be found in various departures of the Michigan NAFTA Model from the H-O assumptions. In particular, the Michigan NAFTA Model incorporates several of the assumptions of the New Trade Theory, including particular forms of increasing returns to scale, product differentiation, and imperfect competition, none of which is permitted in the H-O Model. Our procedure here will be first to rederive the effect of a tariff on the real wage from a framework that includes these features alongside more traditional H-O linkages. From the theoretical expression we derive, it will be possible both to understand intuitively, and then to relate quantitatively, the roles that both the old and the new assumptions play in the result. In particular, we will show how the New Trade Theory assumptions serve to alter the effects of a tariff on the real wage in ways that are separate from, and often counter to, the Stolper-Samuelson Theorem. This point has been made previously by Helpman and Krugman (1985, pp.190-195), who argued that the gains from increasing returns to scale could accrue to all factors and thus permit the scarce factor to gain from trade.[1] We make the same point, but we also note that scale effects, if they arise asymmetrically in different industries, will also be shared unevenly across factors for reasons analogous to the uneven Stolper-Samuelson effects of relative price changes.

Our final step will be to use the results of a Michigan NAFTA Model scenario to quantify these several effects. This will provide some, albeit very limited, empirical perspective on the problem. Like any computable general equilibrium (CGE) model, the Michigan NAFTA Model is really a theoretical model that has only been benchmarked with real-world data and estimates of elasticities. Therefore, when we use that model to quantify the components of the effects of tariffs on the real wage, we are falling considerably short of identifying the effects themselves from the data.

The Michigan NAFTA Model is also limited in its allowance for only a single type of labor and thus a single real wage. In contrast to our analysis, Leamer (1992) uses an H-O framework in which there are two types of labor (skilled and unskilled) and physical capital in order to determine how real wages in the United States and Mexico may be affected by a free trade agreement. In his empirical analysis, he relies on factor

[1] Actually, while they argued on the basis of the benefits of increased scale, Helpman and Krugman looked formally only at a simple case in which output per firm did not rise with trade, and in which the additional gains from trade were due to variety, not reduction in cost. We allow for both of these channels for gain, as well as increased competition, in our discussion below.

endowment and trade data for the OECD countries for 1972 and 1985. He then uses his regression estimates combined with measures of Mexican factor endowments under different assumptions that allow for the relative scarcity of capital in Mexico compared to the OECD countries in order to calculate hypothetical levels of Mexican output. His results suggest that Mexico could supply sufficiently large amounts of exports of a number of products to the United States so that the real wages of U.S. workers might be adversely affected. Aside from the differences in including one versus two types of labor, our analysis differs from Leamer's insofar as we include a variety of effects that are part of the New Trade Theory. Since Leamer relies on an H-O framework, it is difficult to determine therefore the extent to which these effects may be reflected in his empirical estimates or how important these effects may be in their own right in relation to the endowment measures that he considers.

There have been some other studies in recent years – see for example Borjas, Freeman, and Katz (1991) and Revenga (1992) – that have used time series data for the United States for the 1970s and 1980s and have concluded that changes in U.S. trade may have led to reductions in the real wages of unskilled as compared to skilled workers. We may also note that Johnson and Stafford (1992) have analyzed the relation between changes in trade and real wages using a theoretical framework in which the United States is presumed to have lost its technological dominance and thus experienced lower real wages as the result of increased imports. These studies would suggest accordingly that the expansion of U.S. trade with Mexico could result in a decline in U.S. real wages of unskilled workers. However, one cannot be certain that this will occur because these studies do not allow explicitly for the role that scale and other effects associated with the New Trade Theory might play in the particular context of the trade liberalization associated with the NAFTA. In any case, since the effects of the NAFTA on the real wage that we have reported in our research depend on a variety of effects incorporated in both the Old and the New Trade Theory, it is desirable to know in more detail how they have come about.

II. A Theoretical Framework

We will examine the effect of a tariff on the real wage in the context of a theoretical framework that incorporates both H-O and New Trade Theory assumptions. The framework is not quite a fully specified model, in that effects on several variables are left unspecified. This will enable us to decompose the tariff-real wage linkage in ways that are common to any of several more complete specific models. For example, the framework is consistent with forms of imperfect competition that include monopolistic competition, oligopoly (with any of a variety of assumptions about strategic behavior), and monopoly, as well as perfect competition. It is also consistent with various forms of product differentiation, both by country (the Armington Assumption) and by firm (monopolistic competition). This amount of generality is bought at the cost of not being able to solve explicitly for effects of the tariff on such important variables as output per firm, number of firms, and the markup of price over marginal cost. These variables will therefore be calculated instead from the Michigan NAFTA Model, where the assumptions about these behaviors are more explicit.

We do not, on the other hand, strive for such generality in all respects. In the theoretical framework (though not, again, in the Michigan NAFTA Model) we allow for only two goods and two factors, so that the strong and familiar Stolper-Samuelson conclusion holds in the absence of New Trade Theory considerations. That is, we do not explore whether departures from Stolper-Samuelson in the CGE literature may result from the fact that they typically include more than two goods and sometimes factors.[2] In addition, while we do allow for departures from perfect competition in goods markets, we assume perfect competition in factor markets. Finally, in common with Stolper-Samuelson, we also assume (both here and in the Michigan NAFTA Model) that both factors are perfectly mobile between sectors. Therefore we are not allowing for the kinds of short-run departures from Stolper-Samuelson that are familiar in the specific factors model.[3]

Following the Jones (1965) explication of the Stolper-Samuelson Theorem, we start with cost-minimizing unit variable factor requirements, a_{ij}, for goods j=1,2 and factors i=L,K, that depend on the ratio of the wage of labor, w, to the rental on capital, r. However, to allow for possible increasing returns to scale, we assume that the a_{ij} include only variable factors and that there may be additional fixed factors required that do not vary with output. Also, we allow these cost-minimizing unit variable factor requirements themselves to depend on an output variable, x_j, though in a manner that does not change optimal variable input proportions. If variable returns were external to the firm, then x_j would be the output of the industry within the country or the world, depending on the reach of the externality. However, for most of our discussion we will interpret x_j as output per firm. Thus

$$a_{ij} = a_{ij}(w/r, x_j) \qquad i = L, K;\ j = 1,2 \tag{1}$$

Using the familiar notation from Jones (1965), we let θ_{ij} be the factor shares of marginal variable cost. To measure scale effects on variable cost, we define

$$\eta_j \equiv -\frac{\partial a_{ij}}{\partial x_j}\frac{x_j}{a_{ij}} \qquad i = 1,2;\ j = L, K \tag{2}$$

which is therefore zero for constant returns to scale and positive for increasing returns to scale in the variable inputs.

With this notation, letting c_j be marginal cost in industry j,

$$c_j = a_{Lj}w + a_{Kj}r \qquad j = 1,2 \tag{3}$$

the usual "hat algebra" of Jones (1965) yields

$$\hat{c}_j = \theta_{Lj}\hat{w} + \theta_{Kj}\hat{r} - \eta_j\hat{x}_j \qquad j = 1,2 \tag{4}$$

---

[2] See Ethier (1984) for discussion of extension of the Stolper-Samuelson Theorem to higher dimensions.

[3] See Jones and Neary (1984) for a survey of this literature.

From this system of equations for the two industries, the changes in both the wage and the rental can be solved. Since we are concerned here only with the wage, we obtain

$$\hat{w} = \varepsilon_{L1}(\hat{c}_1 + \eta_1\hat{x}_1) - (\varepsilon_{L1} - 1)(\hat{c}_2 + \eta_2\hat{x}_2) \tag{5}$$

where

$$\varepsilon_{L1} \equiv \frac{1-\theta_{L2}}{\theta_{L1} - \theta_{L2}} > 1 \tag{6}$$

is the "Stolper-Samuelson elasticity." Under H-O assumptions, such that $p_j = c_j$, this gives the effect of a rise in the price of good 1 on the wage, holding the price of good 2 constant as numeraire. It is positive and greater than one if, as we assume, good 1 is relatively labor intensive. Thus, if a tariff raises the domestic relative price of good 1, under H-O assumptions it will raise the nominal wage more than the price.

The remainder of our assumptions here, departing from H-O, allow for divergences between marginal cost and price, as well as divergences among various prices. Let p_j be prices of domestically produced goods, p_j^* be domestic prices of foreign goods, and p_j^w be world prices of foreign goods. Also, let p_j^I be an hedonic index of foreign and domestic prices in industry *j*, taking into account, as noted below, any preference for variety that may be present. We then make the following assumptions:

Markup Pricing

Letting price be a multiple, m_j, of marginal cost, we have

$$\hat{p}_j = \hat{m}_j + \hat{c}_j \qquad j = 1,2 \tag{7}$$

Product Differentiation

If domestically produced goods are not perfect substitutes for foreign goods, either because consumers differentiate on the basis of country of origin (the Armington Assumption) or because individual firms at home and abroad produce differentiated products, then prices of both domestically produced goods may depend partially on the domestic prices of foreign goods. Letting φ_j be one minus the elasticity of p_j with respect to p_j^* (so that φ_j is zero if the two are perfect substitutes) and φ_j^+ be the elasticity of p_j with respect to p_i^* we write

$$\hat{p}_j = (1-\varphi_j)\hat{p}_j^* + \varphi_j^+\hat{p}_i^* \qquad j = 1,2; i \neq j \tag{8}$$

Tariffs

Letting t_j be one plus the tariff on good *j*, domestic prices of foreign goods are related to world prices by

$$\hat{p}_j^* = \hat{t}_j + \hat{p}_j^w \qquad j = 1,2 \tag{9}$$

Since we will take good 2 as numeraire and only consider a tariff on good 1, we will have $\hat{t}_2 = \hat{p}_2^* = \hat{p}_2^w = 0$.

Country Size

If the country is small, then p_j^w are unaffected by the tariff. However, if the country is large, then that is not the case. Again taking good 1 as numeraire, we capture this with

$$\hat{p}_1^w = -\Omega \hat{t}_1 \tag{10}$$

Thus Ω is a measure of country size.

Real Wages, Price Indices, and Love of Variety

We assume that the utility function of the representative worker is

$$U = \alpha_1 \log\left[\sum_{i=1}^{n_1} (x_{i1})^{\rho_1} + \sum_{i=1}^{n_1^*} (x_{i1}^*)^{\rho_1}\right] + \alpha_2 \log\left[\sum_{i=1}^{n_2} (x_{i2})^{\rho_2} + \sum_{i=1}^{n_2^*} (x_{i2}^*)^{\rho_2}\right] \tag{11}$$

where

$$\rho_j = 1 - \frac{1}{\sigma_j} \qquad j = 1,2 \tag{12}$$

and $\sigma_j > 1$ are the elasticities of substitution among varieties of good *j*. The utility of the worker then depends on a real wage defined in terms of an hedonic price index that takes account of the preference for variety that is implicit in (11) when σ_j is less than infinite:

$$\hat{p}_j^I = (1 - \delta_j)\left(\hat{p}_j - \frac{\hat{n}_j}{\sigma_j - 1}\right) + \delta_j\left(\hat{p}_j^* - \frac{\hat{n}_j^*}{\sigma_j - 1}\right) \qquad j = 1,2 \tag{13}$$

where δ_j is the import share of good *j*, and n_j, n_j^* are the numbers of varieties of (firms producing) domestic and imported versions of good *j*.

The real wage, ω, is then

$$\hat{\omega} = \hat{w} - \alpha_1 \hat{p}_1^I - \alpha_2 \hat{p}_2^I \tag{14}$$

Solutions

By substituting into (14), first (5) and (13), and then substituting $\hat{c}_j$ from (7), this becomes

$$\hat{\omega} = \varepsilon_{L1}(\hat{p}_1 - \hat{m}_1 + \eta_1\hat{x}_1) - (\varepsilon_{L1} - 1)(\hat{p}_2 - \hat{m}_2 + \eta_2\hat{x}_2)$$
$$- \alpha_1\left[(1-\delta_1)\left(\hat{p}_1 - \frac{\hat{n}_1}{\sigma_1 - 1}\right) + \delta_1\left(\hat{p}_1^* - \frac{\hat{n}_1^*}{\sigma_1 - 1}\right)\right] \tag{15}$$
$$- \alpha_2\left[(1-\delta_2)\left(\hat{p}_2 - \frac{\hat{n}_2}{\sigma_2 - 1}\right) + \delta_2\left(\hat{p}_2^* - \frac{\hat{n}_2^*}{\sigma_2 - 1}\right)\right]$$

This is our basic result. It breaks down the effects of a tariff on the real wage into a variety of components that we will discuss and quantify as we go along. These include, in the first term of the first line, the basic Stolper-Samuelson result of a magnified effect of the price on the wage. But they also include, in the first line, various effects that may occur through changing markups, changes in output per firm, and changes in the domestic price of the other good. Finally, in the second and third lines, they include effects on the real value of a given nominal wage, both through the prices of domestic and imported goods in both sectors, and through changes in the numbers of goods available.

For purposes of discussion of these effects, some further manipulation and sorting of the effects in (15) is useful, taking into account the effects among different prices that were assumed above, as well as the effects of a tariff on the non-price variables in (15). For the latter, and again in order to encompass a variety of more specific assumptions about market and industry structure, we simply assume that the variables depend on the relative domestic prices of the two foreign-produced goods, p_1^*/p_2^*, and hence, since we fix p_2^* as numeraire, on p_1^* alone:

$$\hat{m}_j = \mu_j \hat{p}_1^* \qquad j = 1,2 \tag{16}$$

$$\hat{x}_j = \chi_j \hat{p}_1^* \qquad j = 1,2 \tag{17}$$

$$(\hat{n}_j, \hat{n}_j^*) = (\nu_j, \nu_j^*)\hat{p}_1^* \qquad j = 1,2 \tag{18}$$

The signs of these parameters will be discussed shortly as we examine the specific effects.

If we now substitute (8) and (16-18) into (15) and let $\hat{p}_2^* = 0$ as numeraire, we get the real wage in terms only of p_1^*. Using (9) and (10), the latter can be expressed in terms of the tariff change. With some combining and rearranging of terms, the result is as follows:

$$\hat{\omega} = \Delta(1 - \Omega)\hat{t}_1 \tag{19}$$

where

$$
\begin{aligned}
&(a)\ \Delta = \varepsilon_{L1} - \alpha_1 \\
&(b)\qquad -(\varepsilon_{L1} - \alpha_1)\varphi_1 - \alpha_1\delta_1\varphi_1 \\
&(c)\qquad -\left[(\varepsilon_{L1} - 1)\varphi_2^{+} + \alpha_2(1-\delta_2)\varphi_2^{+}\right] \\
&(d)\qquad +\left[-\varepsilon_{L1}\mu_1 + (\varepsilon_{L1} - 1)\mu_2\right] \\
&(e)\qquad +\left[\varepsilon_{L1}\eta_1\chi_1 - (\varepsilon_{L1} - 1)\eta_2\chi_2\right] \\
&(f)\qquad +\left[\alpha_1\frac{(1-\delta_1)v_1 + \delta_1 v_1^{*}}{\sigma_1 - 1} + \alpha_2\frac{(1-\delta_2)v_2 + \delta_2 v_2^{*}}{\sigma_2 - 1}\right]
\end{aligned}
\tag{20}
$$

III. Economic Linkages between Tariffs and Real Wages

At this point it is useful to review in intuitive terms the various mechanisms by which a tariff may affect the real wage. For this purpose, we will first run through the logic of the Stolper-Samuelson Theorem itself, then identify the various modifications in this logic that arise when elements of the New Trade Theory are included.

The Logic of the Stolper-Samuelson Theorem

Under the usual assumptions of the H-O model, the Stolper-Samuelson story can be told as follows. Suppose that a country increases a tariff on its (labor-intensive) import good. A number of logical implications follow, each of which is stated below.

1. In a small country, a tariff will raise the price of the imported good by the amount of the tariff.
2. With homogeneous goods, the rise in price of the import good will be matched by an equal rise in price of the import-competing good.
3. This rise in the relative price of the import-competing good will cause the economy's resources to shift towards it and away from export goods.
4. From the Heckscher-Ohlin Theorem, import competing goods will make intensive use of the scarce factor. Therefore, this shift of resources will raise demand for, and hence the price of, the scarce factor relative to the abundant factor.
5. With free entry into the import-competing sector, zero profit requires that the average prices of all factors employed there rise (relative to the price of the export good) by the same amount as the price of the import-competing good.
6. If the scarce factor is not the only factor employed there, this, together with the rise in its price relative to other factors, requires that the scarce factor rise in price also relative to the price of the import-competing good.
7. Since the prices of imports and import-competing goods are equal and have both risen relative to all other prices, this rise in the scarce factor price is therefore an increase in real terms.

That is all that is needed to confirm the Stolper-Samuelson Theorem under the usual assumptions. Now consider how various alternative assumptions might or might not interfere with this chain of logic:

Terms of Trade Effects

Under the usual assumption of homogeneous products, the above logic is correct in assuming that there are no terms of trade effects. World prices are given for both imports and exports, and these cannot be changed by a tariff. Terms of trade effects do arise, however, either if there is product differentiation or if the country is not small. Terms of trade effects do not, of themselves, interfere with Stolper-Samuelson, as we will note. But they are important for the broader issue of the effect of the NAFTA, since they matter for the effect of the Mexican tariff on the United States.

Terms of Trade Effects of Product Differentiation, Small Country

With product differentiation and a small country, the tariff still raises the domestic price of, and reduces the demand for, imports. The price of the imports themselves on the world market will not change, however, because the country is small. If the country's export goods are differentiated from the goods with which they compete abroad though (either by country of origin or by firm), then their prices can change. The shift in demand away from the now tariff-encumbered imports toward domestic goods will raise their price, causing the price of the country's exports to rise relative to its imports. Thus the tariff improves the terms of trade, even for a small country, when there is product differentiation.

This improvement in the terms of trade to some extent undermines the Stolper-Samuelson logic above, since it means that domestic goods rise in price relative to the numeraire world export-competing goods. This rise in price lowers both the nominal and the real values of the factor price increase. These effects are illustrated in (20) in line (c), where φ_2^+ measures the extent to which substitution from imported good 1 to domestic good 2 causes the price of the latter to rise. This increase both reduces the extent to which the relative price of good 1 rises on the domestic market (the first term in (c)), and increases the cost of consuming the domestic good (the second term in (c)). Since this rise in price only occurs because of the increased domestic price of imports, it cannot be as large as that increase, and the increased real factor return must survive. Product differentiation may, as noted below, have a more direct effect in undermining the Stolper-Samuelson logic, but it does not do so through terms of trade effects.

Terms of Trade Effects for a Large Country, Homogeneous Products

If the country is not small, there can also be terms of trade effects of the more usual sort. However, with homogeneous products these effects again cannot interfere with the Stolper-Samuelson logic, except under the extreme conditions of the Metzler paradox. For a large country, the tariff will now fail to raise the price of imports by the full amount of the tariff. This is indicated above by $\Omega > 0$. Indeed, following Metzler, if enough of the tariff revenue is spent on the export good (more than the private sector would have spent), there can be such a fall in demand for imports that their world price falls by more than the tariff ($\Omega > 1$), causing the domestic (tariff-inclusive) price of imports to fall too.

If that happens, then the above chain of causation starts out in the opposite direction, and leads to completely reverse effects on everything, including factor prices.

However, failing that, the improvement in the terms of trade will mean that the domestic price of imports will not rise by as much as the tariff, but it will still rise. Since the Stolper-Samuelson argument depends only on the sign, not the size, of this rise in price, the rest of the logic continues to hold.

Direct Effects of Product Differentiation

Now consider how product differentiation can interfere with the Stolper-Samuelson logic more directly. The argument depended in part on a tariff raising the domestic price of import-competing goods by the same amount as the imports themselves. With product differentiation this will not occur. Instead, the increased price of the imports will cause substitution toward domestic goods and raise their price, but the substitution will not be perfect and the price rise will be less than that of the imports.

At the end of the argument, then, where it is shown that the scarce factor will rise in price relative to the import-competing good, this is no longer sufficient to assure that this is a real increase. It may seem unlikely, but the possibility exists that owners of the scarce factor spend such a large fraction of their income on the import (not the import-competing) good that its still higher price relative to their factor price will make them worse off. Thus we have one mechanism whereby product differentiation can lead a tariff to lower the real price of the scarce factor.

This is seen in the two terms of line (b) of (20). In the first term, product differentiation ($\varphi_1 > 0$) reduces the size of the increase in p_1 and therefore reduces the positive Stolper-Samuelson effect on the real wage. At the same time, in the second term of line (b), by leaving the price of the imported version of good 1 above that of the domestically produced version, it reduces the purchasing power of a given wage in proportion to the share of those imports in consumption ($\alpha_1\delta_1$).

Imperfect Competition

Imperfect competition can also lead to this result, through a different channel, if there are profits made in an industry. In that case, there is no need for cost to equal price, and therefore for average factor prices to rise by as much as the price of the import-competing good. If the tariff somehow increases market power in the import-competing sector, so that the markup of price over cost rises, then average factor prices in that sector will rise by less than the goods price. It then follows that even though the price of the scarce factor rises relative to other factors, it need not rise relative to the good itself. If the good is heavily demanded by the scarce factor owners, then the tariff may lower their real return.

These effects appear in line (d) of (20), where μ_1 represents the effect of the tariff on the markup in domestic industry 1. To the extent that a tariff makes this industry less competitive, this markup will rise and reduce the real wage effects of the tariff. The markup in industry 2, on the other hand, has the opposite effect. Were it to rise as a result of the tariff (as seems unlikely), then factor costs in industry 2 would have to fall relative to industry 1, increasing the needed rise in the relative wage. If, as seems more likely, the tariff in industry 1 increases competition in industry 2 and lowers the markup there ($\mu_2 < 0$), then this further offsets the Stolper-Samuelson effect.

Increasing Returns to Scale

Whether increasing returns to scale strengthen or weaken the Stolper-Samuelson argument depends on what the tariff does to output per firm (or to industry or world output if the increasing returns are external to the firm). This in turn depends on details of the industry that are not explicit in our framework. For example, if there were no entry of firms so that the number of firms was fixed, then a tariff might expand demand for domestically produced goods and output per firm would rise. Alternatively, if there is free entry, a tariff might attract more firms but the output of each might decline.[4] If firm output does rise in the import-competing sector, then costs there will fall for given factor prices, and the restoration of a given markup will require an even larger increase in average factor prices.[5] Therefore the real return to the scarce factor will rise even more. If on the other hand the tariff lowers firm outputs in the import-competing sector and raises costs, then the opposite will occur. Similarly, if the tariff in sector 1 changes output per firm in sector 2, then analogous effects arise there as well, though there a reduction in costs hurts the real wage, since it reduces the relative cost increase of the import sector that must be accommodated by changing factor prices.

To better understand these effects of scale on factor prices, consider an increase in firm output in sector 1, while holding prices and mark-ups constant. The increase in x_1 reduces marginal cost in sector 1, thereby raising the mark-up of price over marginal cost. In order to restore the original mark-up in sector 1 without changing goods prices or disturbing sector 2, we must manipulate factor prices so as to raise marginal cost in sector 1 without changing marginal cost in sector 2. This, in a manner that is completely analogous to the Stolper-Samuelson response to a relative price change, is accomplished by raising the return to the factor used intensively in sector 1, labor, and lowering the return to the other factor.

Therefore, an increase in firm output raises the return to the factor used intensively in that sector and lowers the return to the other factor. Note however, from equation (15), that if scale were to rise in both sectors and if the scale elasticities were the same, then the returns to both factors would rise. (This result is analogous to the fact that an equiproportionate rise in the prices of both goods will also raise the return to both factors of production.)

In line (e) of (20), all of these effects are represented by the changes in output per firm in the two sectors caused by the tariff, χ_1 and χ_2, together with the extent of scale economies in each, η_1 and η_2.

Variety

The final consideration is product variety, which is likely to be inherently ambiguous in its effects on real wages. A tariff seems likely to lead to entry of firms and products in the domestic import-competing industry, but cause exit and a reduction in products by foreigners in that industry and by both domestic and foreign firms in the export sector. Thus, unless there is a relatively strong preference for variety in the import sector compared to the export sector, together with a preference for domestic instead of foreign

---

[4] The direction of change in firm output depends, in some circumstances at least, on how the elasticity of demand for firm output varies with price.

[5] If the markup changes, then that is handled by the effect already discussed above.

varieties, the presumption will be that the tariff will lower welfare and thus the real wage still further on this account.

These effects appear in line (f) of (20), where four different changes in numbers of firms all appear with positive coefficients.

We turn now to use the Michigan NAFTA Model to evaluate some likely effects of the NAFTA for wages in Mexico, Canada, and the United States.

IV. Description of the Michigan NAFTA Model

Thus far, we have set out a somewhat general, though simplified, theoretical framework designed to decompose the linkages between a tariff and the real wage, and we have provided some intuition about these linkages that may be present in both the Old and the New Trade Theories. We wish now to quantify the different linkages, using our multi-country, multi-sectoral Michigan NAFTA CGE Model. The equations, variables, and parameters of the model are set out in detail in the appendix below. In what follows we will describe briefly some of the main features of the model.[6]

The Michigan NAFTA Model is a large scale computable general equilibrium model that is capable of evaluating the comparative static effects of changes in trade policy on factor prices, economic welfare, the intersectoral allocation of resources, and the international allocation of production. Countries of the model are aggregated into three broad groups. Each of the NAFTA members (the United States, Canada, and Mexico) is modeled individually; another 31 major trading countries are aggregated to create a fourth country;[7] and the remaining countries of the world are consigned to residual rest-of-world supply and demand equations. The countries of the model produce, consume, and trade 23 tradable aggregate products. In addition, there are six nontraded goods. The market structure in each sector is either perfectly competitive or monopolistically competitive, depending on the degree of scale economies in production.[8]

Final demand equations in each country are obtained assuming a representative consumer who maximizes utility subject to a budget constraint,[9] and intermediate demands are derived from the profit maximization decisions of representative firms in each sector. Products in both the perfectly competitive and monopolistically competitive industries are assumed to be characterized by some degree of product differentiation. In the cases where markets are taken to be perfectly competitive, products are differentiated

[6] The remainder of this section is adapted from Brown, Deardorff and Stern (1992a).

[7] The 31 other countries include 16 industrialized countries – Australia, Austria, Belgium-Luxembourg, Denmark, Germany, Finland, France, Ireland, Italy, Japan, the Netherlands, New Zealand, Norway, Sweden, Switzerland, and the United Kingdom – and 15 newly industrializing countries – Argentina, Brazil, Chile, Colombia, Greece, Hong Kong, India, Israel, Portugal, Singapore, South Korea, Spain, Taiwan, Turkey, and Yugoslavia.

[8] The six nontraded sectors, which are ISIC one-digit industries 4-9, are assumed to be perfectly competitive, as is the first tradable sector, agriculture. The remaining tradable sectors – 21 3-digit ISIC manufacturing industries plus ISIC 2, Mining and Quarrying – are assumed to be monopolistically competitive.

[9] Household income underlying the final demand equations is set at the level that will hold the trade balance equal to its level in the base data set. This procedure is, in principle, equivalent to setting income equal to factor payments plus tariff revenue.

by country, while in the monopolistically competitive industries products are differentiated by firm.[10]

Turning to the factor markets, the variable input requirements are taken to be the same for the two market structures. Primary and intermediate input aggregates are required in fixed proportion to output.[11] In the monopolistically competitive industries, additional fixed inputs of capital and labor are required.[12] Capital and labor are assumed to be perfectly mobile between sectors and the returns to capital and labor are determined to equate factor demand to an exogenous supply of each factor.

Perfectly competitive firms set price equal to marginal cost, while monopolistically competitive firms maximize profits by setting price as an optimal markup over marginal cost. The number of firms in each industry is determined by the condition that there are zero profits.

International trade in goods is assumed to be subject to tariffs and nontariff barriers (NTBs). NTBs are incorporated by endogenously solving for the *ad valorem* tariff-equivalent rate that would hold imports within each product category covered by NTBs at a predetermined level. An *ad valorem* tariff variable in each product category is then an average of this NTB tariff-equivalent rate and the nominal tariff rate, using the NTB coverage ratio to weight the NTB tariff equivalent.[13]

The bilateral tariff rates are aggregated up from the line-item level using bilateral trade as weights. U.S. tariffs applying to imports from Mexico are then scaled down by factors that reflect the proportions of value in each sector accounted for by U.S. exports to Maquiladora plants in Mexico.

Equilibrium prices are determined in world markets. In the perfectly competitive industries, total demand for each national variety must equal national output. For monopolistically competitive industries, total demand for the variety produced by each firm must equal production by the firm. The *ad valorem* tariff variable discussed above then links equilibrium prices determined in the world system to prices paid by consumers in the country system.

The model is linear in form and thus can be solved by substitution and matrix inversion. The base year is 1989 for data on production, employment, and trade. Input-output coefficients for the production functions were derived from the U.S. input-output table for 1977, the Mexican table for 1980, and the Canadian table for 1976.

For more detail on the values of the key parameters of the model, see Brown, Deardorff and Stem (1992a).

---

[10] In both cases, we adopt a modified version of the approach to product differentiation suggested by Dixit and Stiglitz (1977) and Spence (1976). Consumers and producers are assumed to use a two-stage procedure to allocate expenditure across differentiated products. At the first stage, expenditure is allocated across goods, without regard for the country of origin or the producing firm. At this stage the utility function is taken to be Cobb-Douglas, and the production function requires inputs in fixed proportion. In the second stage, expenditure on each monopolistically competitive good is allocated across competing firms without regard to place of production. However, in the case of perfectly competitive goods, individual firm supply is indeterminate. Therefore, expenditure on each good must be allocated across individual countries. The aggregation function in the second case is CES.

[11] Expenditure on primary inputs is allocated between capital and labor, assuming that a CES function is used to form the primary input aggregate.

[12] It is assumed that fixed capital and labor are used in the same proportion as variable capital and labor so that the production function is homothetic.

[13] For additional details, see Deardorff and Stern (1990, pp. 23-24).

V. Adaptation of the Theory to the Michigan NAFTA Model

In order to adapt the theoretical framework discussed in Section II to the Michigan NAFTA Model, we need only to incorporate the zero-profits condition into equation (15). Here, we assume that costs can be decomposed into fixed cost plus variable cost, the latter of which is taken to be proportional to output. Therefore, zero profits implies that

$$\hat{p}_j = \hat{c}_j - \frac{(m_j - 1)}{m_j}\hat{x}_j \tag{21}$$

Comparing this zero-profits equation (21) with mark-up equation (7), we can see that

$$\hat{m}_j = -\frac{(m_j - 1)}{m_j}\hat{x}_j\,. \tag{22}$$

Substituting (22) and (9) into (15), and taking note of the fact that the scale elasticity of marginal cost is zero in the Michigan NAFTA Model (increasing returns enters only through the presence of fixed cost), gives

$$\begin{aligned}\hat{\omega} = {} & \varepsilon_{L1}\left[\hat{p}_1 + \frac{(m_1-1)}{m_1}\hat{x}_1\right] - (\varepsilon_{L1}-1)\left[\hat{p}_2 + \frac{(m_2-1)}{m_2}\hat{x}_2\right] \\ & - \alpha_1\left[(1-\delta_1)\left(\hat{p}_1 - \frac{\hat{n}_1}{\sigma_1 - 1}\right) + \delta_1\left(\hat{p}_1^w + \hat{t}_1 - \frac{\hat{n}_1^*}{\sigma_1 - 1}\right)\right] \\ & - \alpha_2\left[(1-\delta_2)\left(\hat{p}_2 - \frac{\hat{n}_2}{\sigma_2 - 1}\right) + \delta_2\left(\hat{p}_2^w + \hat{t}_2 - \frac{\hat{n}_2^*}{\sigma_2 - 1}\right)\right]\end{aligned} \quad . \tag{15'}$$

Using (15') we can decompose the change in wages under the NAFTA into five components: (a) The Stolper-Samuelson effect captures the change in the wage due to the reallocation of resources between sectors accompanying a change in relative prices within an economy. (b) The terms of trade effect captures the increase in the real wage due to a rise in the price of domestic varieties relative to imports. A rise in the price of domestic varieties relative to foreign varieties raises the value of the marginal product of labor in terms of imported goods. (c) The scale effect captures the rise in the real wage due to the realization of economies of scale. (d) The tariff effect captures the increase in the real wage due to the removal of the consumption tax on imports. (e) The product variety effect captures the rise in the real wage due to the increased number of differentiated products available.

Rearranging equation (15'), $\hat{\omega}$ is then the sum of the following five terms:

$$\begin{aligned}
&(a)\ \textit{Stolper-Samuelson} && (\varepsilon_{L1}-\alpha_1)\hat{p}_1-(\varepsilon_{L1}-1+\alpha_2)\hat{p}_2 \\
&(b)\ \textit{terms of trade} && \alpha_1\delta_1(\hat{p}_1-\hat{p}_1^w)+\alpha_2\delta_2(\hat{p}_2-\hat{p}_2^w) \\
&(c)\ \textit{economies of scale} && \varepsilon_{L1}\frac{(m_1-1)}{m_1}\hat{x}_1-(\varepsilon_{L1}-1)\frac{(m_2-1)}{m_2}\hat{x}_2 \qquad (23) \\
&(d)\ \textit{tariff change} && -\alpha_1\delta_1\hat{t}_1-\alpha_2\delta_2\hat{t}_2 \\
&(e)\ \textit{product variety} && \frac{\alpha_1}{\sigma_1-1}\left[\delta_1\hat{n}_1^*+(1-\delta_1)\hat{n}_1\right]+\frac{\alpha_2}{\sigma_2-1}\left[(1-\delta_2)\hat{n}_2+\delta_2\hat{n}_2^*\right]
\end{aligned}$$

VI. Real Wage Effects in NAFTA Scenarios

The real wage decomposition of equation (23) has been applied to two NAFTA scenarios analyzed using the Michigan Model. Scenario A examines the effect of trilateral tariff elimination. Scenario B additionally allows for a capital inflow into Mexico from the rest of the world that raises Mexico's capital stock by ten percent.

It is straightforward to calculate the terms-of-trade, tariff, and variety effects from the data and model results. The combined Stolper-Samuelson and scale effects are then found as a residual from the effect on the real wage calculated from the model. Results are reported in Table 1.

Tariff Elimination Only

Consider first, Scenario A: NAFTA Tariff Elimination. The "Total" column, indicating percent change in the real wage, is just the sum across the preceding four columns. Note, for example, that the real wage in Mexico rises by 0.46 percent. The tariff component (0.41 %) is of the expected sign. A tariff reduction lowers the consumer price index in Mexico, thereby raising the purchasing power of a worker's wages.

The terms-of-trade effect (-0.06) is negative. For Mexico, import prices rose relative to domestic goods, measured in world prices, offsetting some of the gain associated with the tariff reduction. Mexico's terms-of-trade loss is a byproduct of the fact that its current average tariffs are higher than for other members of the NAFTA.

The variety effect (-0.16%) is also negative for Mexico. Trade liberalization has the effect on Mexico of reducing the number of firms while raising the output of those firms who survive. The associated realization of economies of scale is therefore to some extent offset by the negative effect of reducing the variety of goods available for consumption. Mexican workers are hurt particularly by this loss of variety, because of the important role that Mexican goods play in their consumption bundle prior to free trade.

Finally, as expected, the change in relative prices and the realization of economies of scale also pull up the Mexican real wage by about 0.27 percent. Liberalization was expected to raise the real return to Mexico's abundant factor of production, via the normal Stolper-Samuelson reasoning. But since scale and relative price effects are combined here, we cannot determine from this result whether the Stolper-Samuelson effect is being augmented or offset by a scale effect, although we would expect that both would be contributing to the positive change in the real wage.[14]

Notice also that the combined scale and relative price effects are pulling up the U.S. wage as well. We have previously reported that the NAFTA will increase the real wage in the United States, but we were uncertain what the source of this result might be. Here we see that we still have a positive effect on the real wage after removing the several effects of terms of trade, variety, and the direct effect of tariffs on the price of imports. To the extent that Stolper-Samuelson considerations were to dominate what is left, we would have normally expected that liberalization would lower the real return to labor, but this is not what we find. Evidently scale effects are dominating any Stolper-Samuelson effects that may be present, and raising the real wage in the United States at the same time that wages rise in Mexico.

There are two possible explanations for this result. First, scale gains may have been "tilted" in favor of labor; that is, they may have been most pronounced in the import-competing, labor-intensive sectors of the United States. In models with monopolistic competition, liberalization tends to have its strongest pro-competitive effects in sectors that are most heavily protected. As discussed above, if imports are labor-intensive, then the wage-rent ratio will tend to rise under such circumstances.

However, it is also possible that scale gains were uniformly positive across sectors. In this case, it would be the level, not the tilt, of the scale effects that would matter, and all factors of production would tend to benefit from economies of scale. We will look in a moment at the industry breakdown of these effects to determine whether the level effect or the tilt effect dominates.

Tariff Elimination with Investment

Turn now to scenario B. Here we consider a combination of trilateral tariff removal and a ten percent increase in Mexico's capital stock coming from outside the NAFTA countries. From Table 1 it is clear that the rise in the capital stock has its most pronounced effect on product variety. Note that Mexican labor now gains 0.67% due to increased variety. The capital inflow seems to have increased the overall size of the Mexican economy. In this scenario, Mexico now produces both more output and more variety.

The scale-cum-Stolper Samuelson effects in this scenario are also quite pronounced. Mexican labor experiences a 5.47 percent increase in the real wage. The other effects on the other countries are not noticeably different from Scenario A, however, suggesting that, for labor at least, the inflow of investment into Mexico should not be a major concern.

Decomposition by Industry

At this point we are unable to go much further than the results reported in Table 1. We had hoped to be able to further decompose the wage effects of the NAFTA so as to separate the Stolper-Samuelson and scale effects. We have as yet, however, been unable to do this. The simple two-sector theoretical framework explored above makes this decomposition appear more straightforward than it really is. In a model of many sectors,

[14] See below, however, where we find some evidence to suggest the opposite.

such as the Michigan NAFTA model, the counterpart of the relative price and scale effect in equation (23) is unfortunately not obvious.

We can nonetheless attempt to gain some insight into the relative importance of these scale and price effects for wages by performing our decomposition for each industry individually. In Tables 2-5, we report for each industry the percent changes in producer prices, $\hat{p}_j$ and the markup-adjusted percent changes in firm outputs, $[(m_j - 1)/m_j]\hat{x}_j$, that together with the Stolper-Samuelson elasticities comprise the Stolper-Samuelson and economies-of-scale effects that we identified in equation (23). Tables 2 and 3 report these changes for the United States and Mexico, respectively, under the tariff-only liberalization Scenario A. Similar calculations are reported in Tables 4 and 5 for the tariffs-with-investment scenario. In all of these tables, the industries are ranked according to labor's share in primary input cost, which is also reported. A final column in each table reports the sum of the price and scale effects, essentially the same as the bracketed expressions in the first line of equation (15'), but for each industry individually.

Corresponding to each of Tables 2-5, we have also graphed the results in Figures 1-4. In each case, the purpose is to identify visually whether these price and scale effects tend to rise or fall with labor intensity. As explained above, to the extent that the price changes vary systematically with labor intensity, then they will lead to Stolper-Samuelson effects on wages. A "tilt" in favor of labor intensive sectors will raise the real wage, a tilt against them lower it. Similarly, if changes in scale vary systematically with labor intensity, then these too will have Stolper-Samuelson-like effects on real wages. If scale changes are tilted in favor of the industries with high labor share, then this will tend to raise real wages and lower rents, and if scale changes are tilted against high labor shares, the opposite will occur.

However, unlike the effects of prices, uniform scale changes also have an effect. Whereas a uniform increase in all prices in the same proportion would not alter the real wage (merely changing the numeraire), a similarly uniform increase in scale in all sectors would raise both factor prices by the same proportion. All of this should be evident from equation (23).

The graphs, then, are intended to show whether the price and scale changes are tilted in this way for or against labor intensive sectors, and, in the case of scale effect, also to indicate these "level effects" of uniform scale expansions. It is, however, somewhat difficult to draw strong conclusions from the diagrams. At this point we offer only the visual impression that we think we can see there, and we leave it to the reader to agree or disagree.

In Figure 1, for the United States, it does seem to be the case that the scale changes are tilted slightly upward, so that the scale effect is positively correlated with labor's cost share. As one might expect, tariff liberalization may have had its strongest pro-competitive effects on the labor-intensive sectors in the United States. Consequently, Stolper-Samuelson-like effects associated with increased scale of production in the labor-intensive sectors may have played a role in raising the U.S. wage.

Price effects for the United States also conform to expectations, in that they appear to be tilted downward in Figure 1, though the trend is even less pronounced. As a labor-scarce country, the labor-intensive sectors in the United States are the most heavily protected. Therefore, producer-price changes following liberalization ought to be negatively correlated with labor cost share, and this appears to be the case in Figure 1.

Note, however, that the price component clearly dominates scale. One wonders, then, whether the Stolper-Samuelson type effects associated with the positive correlation between scale and labor-cost share is sufficient to explain the rise in the U.S. wage under the NAFTA. It is perhaps more likely that the overall rise in scale in the United States is drawing up the wage; that is, that the level effect of scale is more important that the combined tilt effects of price and scale together.

These patterns are less evident for Mexico, as shown in Figure 2, although it appears again that scale is positively correlated and price is negatively correlated with labor-cost share. Two industries seem to be most responsible for the observed results: nonferrous metals, which has a labor-cost share of 0.27 in Mexico, and electrical machinery, which has a labor cost share of 0.43.

This is somewhat surprising since Mexico, as the capital-scarce country, might normally be expected to protect its capital-intensive industries. Thus, liberalization should have *lowered* scale and *raised* price in the labor-intensive sectors. However, the opposite appears to be the case. The two most heavily tariff-protected industries in Mexico are wearing apparel and footwear. Therefore, intra-industry specialization, rather than inter-industry specialization, may characterize the NAFTA.

Similar results emerge under scenario B in which capital inflows accompany tariff removal. Price and scale effects are reported in Tables 4 and 5 and depicted in Figures 3 and 4 for the United States and Mexico, respectively. For both countries, scale appears to be positively correlated and producer-price to be negatively correlated with labor-cost share. Scale effects are positive or zero in every single industry in both countries, with the lone exception of nonferrous metals in the United States. Despite this fact, scale still appears to be dominated by price changes.

VII. Conclusion

As we have seen in this paper, the innovations of the New Trade Theory can certainly have important implications for the effects of protection on real wages. By introducing increasing returns to scale, imperfect competition, and product differentiation into a loosely general equilibrium model, we add significantly to the number of linkages between a tariff and the real wage, well beyond the effect traditionally taken into account in the Stolper-Samuelson Theorem. These effects can easily, in theory at least, more than offset the Stolper-Samuelson prediction and lead, for example, to a negative effect of the imposition of a tariff on the real wage of the scarce factor. Some of the channels for this effect that we have identified are reductions in scale, reductions in competition as evidenced by increases in markups, relative price effects that become possible when domestic and foreign goods are imperfect substitutes, and changes in the variety of goods available to consumers. These channels would work in the opposite direction for removal of a tariff.

We have also made a preliminary attempt to quantify some of these effects in the context of the Michigan NAFTA Model, where our earlier work had indicated that the freer trade of the NAFTA would raise real wages in both the United States and Mexico, the former being a surprising result in terms of the Stolper-Samuelson Theorem. Since the Michigan NAFTA Model incorporates a number of features of the New Trade

Theory, we undertook to decompose this effect on the real wage into various components embodying these innovations.

To some extent we were successful. Our Table 1 is able to distinguish several of these effects. However, it leaves two of the most important – the Stolper-Samuelson relative price effect and the effect of increasing returns to scale – intertwined. The combined effect of scale and relative price, it turns out, is enough to generate a rise in the real wage in all three NAFTA countries. Thus the other effects reported there – terms of trade, tariff change, and variety – do not account for the violations of Stolper-Samuelson that we observed.

In an effort to disentangle the scale and price effects of the NAFTA, therefore, we also reported and graphed them for individual industries, ranked by labor shares. Here, although our conclusions are based only on visual inspection of these data and graphs, we conclude the following:

1. Positive scale effects are present in almost all industries in both the United States and Mexico, and the "level effect" of these, we know theoretically, works to raise real wages.

2. Scale effects seem also to be positively correlated with labor intensity, especially in the United States. This asymmetric incidence, or "tilt," of the scale effects would, by itself, tend to raise real wages still further, through a mechanism analogous to the Stolper-Samuelson Theorem but acting through cost rather than price.

3. Scale effects are, however, negatively correlated with price effects, and when they disagree in sign the latter are almost uniformly larger. Therefore, the apparent negative correlation between price effects and labor shares in the United States is likely to dominate the tilt effects of scale, leaving the net effect of the asymmetric incidence of both being negative for the real wage.

4. Thus it appears that the tilt of the scale effects only partially offsets the tilt of the price effects on the real wage. It is instead the overall level of the scale effects that turns the net effect on the real wage positive.

5. In Mexico, we also find, surprisingly, a negative correlation between price changes and labor share. Thus even though Mexico is presumably capital scarce in comparison with the United States, it appears that Mexican tariff protection has tended to favor labor-intensive sectors instead. Thus the rise in the real wage in Mexico due to the NAFTA is also perhaps better attributed to the effects of scale, together with other innovations of the New Trade Theory, than to the more traditional Stolper-Samuelson mechanism.

References

Borjas, George J., Richard B. Freeman, and Lawrence F. Katz. 1991. "On the Labor Market Effects of Immigration and Trade," Working Paper No. 3761, National Bureau of Economic Research, Working Paper Series.

Brown, Drusilla K., Alan V. Deardorff, and Robert M. Stem 1992a "A North American Free Trade Agreement: Analytical Issues and a Computational Assessment," *The World Economy* (January), pp. 11-29.

Brown, Drusilla K., Alan V. Deardorff, and Robert M. Stem 1992b "A U .S.-Mexico-Canada Free Trade Agreement: Sectoral Employment Effects and Regional/Occupational Employment Realignments in the United States," National Commission for Employment Policy, (October).

Deardorff, Alan V. and Robert M. Stem 1990 *"Computational Analysis of Global Trading Arrangements,* Ann Arbor: University of Michigan Press.

Dixit, Avinash, and Joseph E. Stiglitz 1977 "Monopolistic Competition and Optimum Product Diversity," *American Economic Review* 76, pp. 297-308.

Ethier, Wilfred J. 1984 "Higher Dimensional Issues in Trade Theory," in Ronald W. Jones and Peter B. Kenen, eds., *Handbook of International Economics, Volume 1*, Amsterdam: North- Holland, pp. 131-184.

Helpman, Elhanan, and Paul R. Krugman 1985 *Market Structure and Foreign Trade: Increasing Returns, Imperfect Competition, and the International Economy,* Cambridge, MA: MIT Press.

Johnson, George E. and Frank P. Stafford. 1992. "Models of Real Wages and International Competition," Discussion Paper No. 314, Research Forum on International Economics, Institute of Public Policy Studies/Department of Economics, University of Michigan.

Jones, Ronald W. 1965 "The Structure of Simple General Equilibrium Models," *Journal of Political Economy* (December), pp. 557-572.

Jones, Ronald W. and J. Peter Neary 1984 "The Positive Theory of International Trade," in Ronald W. Jones and Peter B. Kenen, eds., *Handbook of International Economics, Volume 1*, Amsterdam: North-Holland, pp. 1-62.

Leamer, Edward E. 1992. "Wage Effects of a U.S.-Mexican Free Trade Agreement," Working Paper No. 3991, National Bureau of Economic Research, Working Paper Series.

Revenga, Ana L. 1992. "Exporting Jobs: The Impact of Import Competition on Employment and Wages in U.S. Manufacturing," *Quarterly Journal of Economics* 107, pp. 255-284.

Spence, Michael E. 1976 "Product Selection, Fixed Costs, and Monopolistic Competition," *Review of Economic Studies* 43, pp. 217-236.

Table 1

North American Free Trade
Decomposition of the Effects on the Real Wage

	Percent Changes in the Real Wage Due to				
	Scale and Relative Price	Terms of Trade	Tariff Change	Variety	Total
Scenario A: NAFTA Tariff Elimination					
United States	0.05	0.01	0.01	0.00	0.07
Canada	0.36	-0.06	0.14	0.03	0.47
Mexico	0.27	-0.06	0.41	-0.16	0.46
Scenario B: NAFTA Tariff Elimination Plus Capital Inflow into Mexico					
United States	0.06	0.00	0.01	0.02	0.09
Canada	0.36	-0.06	0.14	0.02	0.48
Mexico	5.47	-0.32	0.41	0.67	6.23

Table 2: NAFTA Only, United States

Price and Scale Effects, Ranked by Labor Share

Product		Labor Share	Price Change	Scale Change	Sum
1	Agriculture	0.24	0.15	0.00	0.15
2	Mining, Quarrying	0.25	0.18	0.01	0.19
4	Utilities	0.26	0.21	0.00	0.21
8	Financial Services	0.28	0.21	0.00	0.21
35B	Petroleum Products	0.36	0.19	0.01	0.20
38A	Misc. Mfrs.	0.36	0.11	0.04	0.15
310	Food	0.47	0.10	0.04	0.14
35A	Chemicals	0.54	0.05	0.06	0.11
331	Wood Products	0.59	0.09	0.04	0.13
6	Wholesale Trade	0.60	0.20	0.00	0.20
36A	Nonmetal Min. Prod.	0.62	0.15	0.02	0.17
341	Paper Products	0.62	0.06	0.05	0.11
7	Transportation	0.62	0.21	0.00	0.21
372	Nonferrous Metals	0.65	0.32	-0.03	0.29
355	Rubber Products	0.67	0.00	0.08	0.08
381	Metal Products	0.68	0.14	0.03	0.17
382	Nonelec. Machinery	0.69	0.10	0.04	0.14
323	Leather Products	0.69	0.01	0.07	0.08
321	Textiles	0.71	-0.22	0.15	-0.07
342	Printing, Publishing	0.71	0.12	0.03	0.15
362	Glass Products	0.74	0.09	0.05	0.14
384	Transport Equipment	0.75	0.12	0.03	0.15
332	Furniture, Fixtures	0.76	0.03	0.07	0.10
383	Electrical Machinery	0.76	0.14	0.03	0.17
322	Clothing	0.79	-0.28	0.17	-0.11
324	Footwear	0.81	-0.02	0.08	0.06
371	Iron, Steel	0.81	0.14	0.03	0.17
5	Construction	0.81	0.16	0.00	0.16
9	Personal Services	0.86	0.20	0.00	0.20

Table 3: NAFTA Only, Mexico

Price and Scale Effects, Ranked by Labor Share

Product		Labor Share	Price Change	Scale Change	Price Plus Scale
8	Financial Services	0.18	0.35	0.00	0.35
6	Wholesale Trade	0.19	0.32	0.00	0.32
2	Mining, Quarrying	0.21	-0.35	0.36	0.01
36A	Nonmetal Min. Prod.	0.24	-0.26	0.23	-0.03
310	Food	0.25	0.01	0.13	0.14
332	Furniture, Fixtures	0.26	-0.25	0.26	0.01
1	Agriculture	0.26	0.22	0.00	0.22
322	Clothing	0.27	0.07	0.11	0.18
372	Nonferrous Metals	0.27	-2.65	1.12	-1.53
38A	Misc. Mfrs.	0.28	-0.87	0.44	-0.43
341	Paper Products	0.29	-0.13	0.20	0.07
321	Textiles	0.33	0.04	0.11	0.15
331	Wood Products	0.34	0.04	0.13	0.17
7	Transportation	0.35	0.26	0.00	0.26
35A	Chemicals	0.35	-0.54	0.32	-0.22
382	Nonelec. Machinery	0.37	-0.85	0.42	-0.43
362	Glass Products	0.37	-0.91	0.46	-0.45
355	Rubber Products	0.38	0.04	0.11	0.15
371	Iron, Steel	0.38	-0.32	0.23	-0.09
342	Printing, Publishing	0.39	-0.30	0.23	-0.07
323	Leather Products	0.40	-0.29	0.23	-0.06
381	Metal Products	0.40	-0.73	0.40	-0.33
384	Transport Equipment	0.41	0.21	0.02	0.23
383	Electrical Machinery	0.43	-4.02	1.57	-2.45
35B	Petroleum Products	0.46	-1.31	0.62	-0.69
4	Utilities	0.54	-0.47	0.00	-0.47
324	Footwear	0.56	-0.52	0.30	-0.22
5	Construction	0.64	-0.32	0.00	-0.32
9	Personal Services	0.82	0.07	0.00	0.07

Table 4: NAFTA with Investment, United States

Price and Scale Effects, Ranked by Labor Share

Product		Labor Share	Price Change	Scale Change	Price Plus Scale
1	Agriculture	0.24	-0.15	0.00	-0.15
2	Mining, Quarrying	0.25	-0.12	0.01	-0.11
4	Utilities	0.26	-0.10	0.00	-0.10
8	Financial Services	0.28	-0.09	0.00	-0.09
35B	Petroleum Products	0.36	-0.12	0.01	-0.11
38A	Misc. Mfrs.	0.36	-0.19	0.04	-0.15
310	Food	0.47	-0.20	0.04	-0.16
35A	Chemicals	0.54	-0.26	0.06	-0.20
331	Wood Products	0.59	-0.23	0.05	-0.18
6	Wholesale Trade	0.60	-0.10	0.00	-0.10
36A	Nonmetal Min. Prod.	0.62	-0.15	0.03	-0.12
341	Paper Products	0.62	-0.26	0.06	-0.20
7	Transportation	0.62	-0.09	0.00	-0.09
372	Nonferrous Metals	0.65	0.25	-0.11	0.14
355	Rubber Products	0.67	-0.33	0.09	-0.24
381	Metal Products	0.68	-0.08	0.00	-0.08
382	Nonelec. Machinery	0.69	-0.16	0.03	-0.13
323	Leather Products	0.69	-0.33	0.09	-0.24
321	Textiles	0.71	-0.59	0.18	-0.41
342	Printing, Publishing	0.71	-0.19	0.04	-0.15
362	Glass Products	0.74	-0.23	0.06	-0.17
384	Transport Equipment	0.75	-0.16	0.03	-0.13
332	Furniture, Fixtures	0.76	-0.29	0.07	-0.22
383	Electrical Machinery	0.76	-0.10	0.01	-0.09
322	Clothing	0.79	-0.67	0.20	-0.47
324	Footwear	0.81	-0.39	0.11	-0.28
371	Iron, Steel	0.81	-0.13	0.02	-0.11
5	Construction	0.81	-0.13	0.00	-0.13
9	Personal Services	0.86	-0.10	0.00	-0.10

Table 5: NAFTA with Investment, Mexico

Price and Scale Effects, Ranked by Labor Share

Product		Labor Share	Price Change	Scale Change	Price Plus Scale
8	Financial Services	0.18	2.04	0.00	2.04
6	Wholesale Trade	0.19	1.86	0.00	1.86
2	Mining, Quarrying	0.21	-2.89	2.57	-0.32
36A	Nonmetal Min. Prod.	0.24	-2.26	1.64	-0.62
310	Food	0.25	0.25	0.84	1.09
332	Furniture, Fixtures	0.26	-0.68	1.15	0.47
1	Agriculture	0.26	1.36	0.00	1.36
322	Clothing	0.27	-0.83	1.19	0.36
372	Nonferrous Metals	0.27	-15.10	6.40	-8.70
38A	Misc. Mfrs.	0.28	-4.71	2.51	-2.20
341	Paper Products	0.29	-3.32	2.49	-0.83
321	Textiles	0.33	-1.21	1.46	0.25
331	Wood Products	0.34	0.75	0.78	1.53
7	Transportation	0.35	1.17	0.00	1.17
35A	Chemicals	0.35	-5.21	2.95	-2.26
382	Nonelec. Machinery	0.37	-6.01	3.09	-2.92
362	Glass Products	0.37	-2.58	1.98	-0.60
355	Rubber Products	0.38	-1.36	1.52	0.16
371	Iron, Steel	0.38	-9.61	4.31	-5.30
342	Printing, Publishing	0.39	-2.71	2.08	-0.63
323	Leather Products	0.40	-0.99	1.41	0.42
381	Metal Products	0.40	-7.20	3.72	-3.48
384	Transport Equipment	0.41	-4.89	2.90	-1.99
383	Electrical Machinery	0.43	-11.11	5.03	-6.08
35B	Petroleum Products	0.46	-10.71	5.75	-4.96
4	Utilities	0.54	-1.89	0.00	-1.89
324	Footwear	0.56	-0.24	1.42	1.18
5	Construction	0.64	-1.56	0.00	-1.56
9	Personal Services	0.82	3.26	0.00	3.26

Figure 1: NAFTA Only, United States

Price, Scale Effects, vs. Labor Share

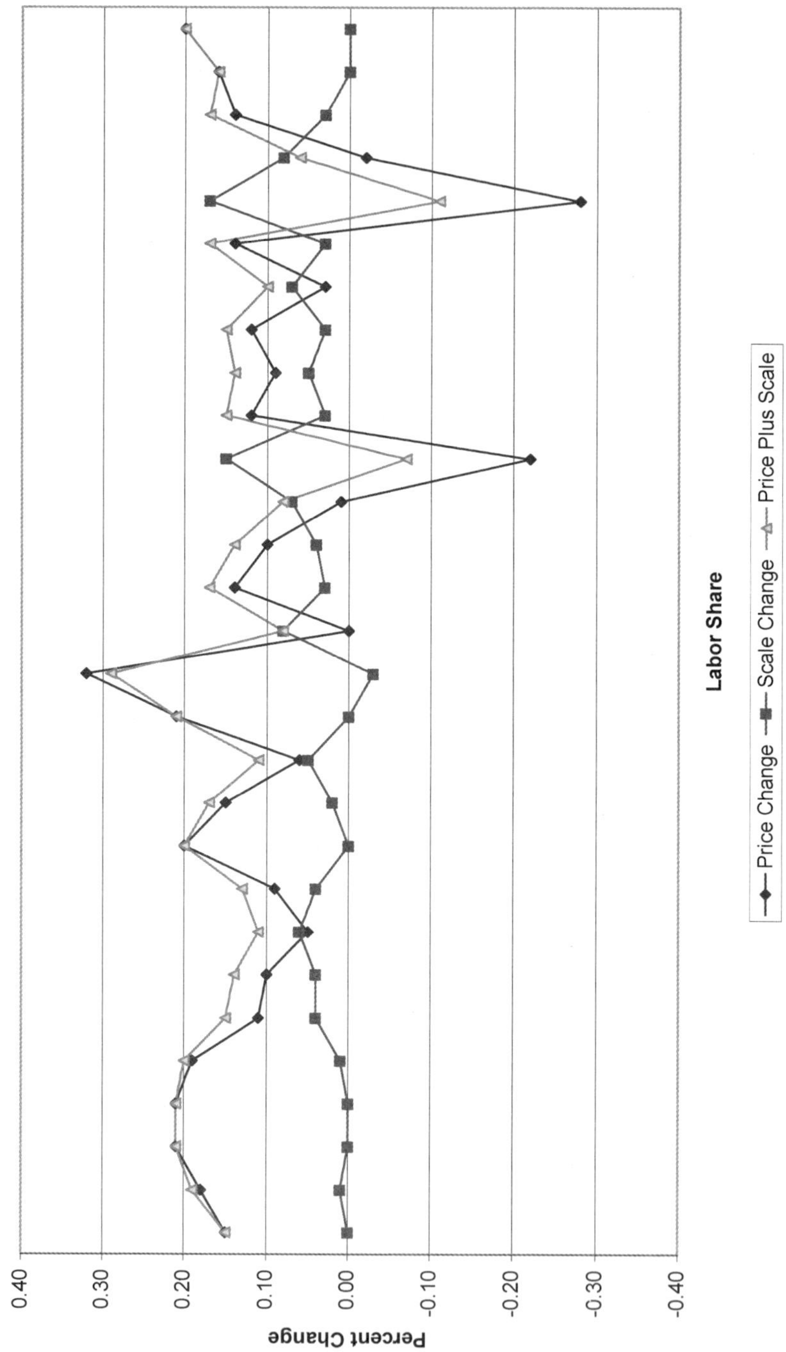

Figure 2: NAFTA Only, Mexico

Price, Scale Effects, vs. Labor Share

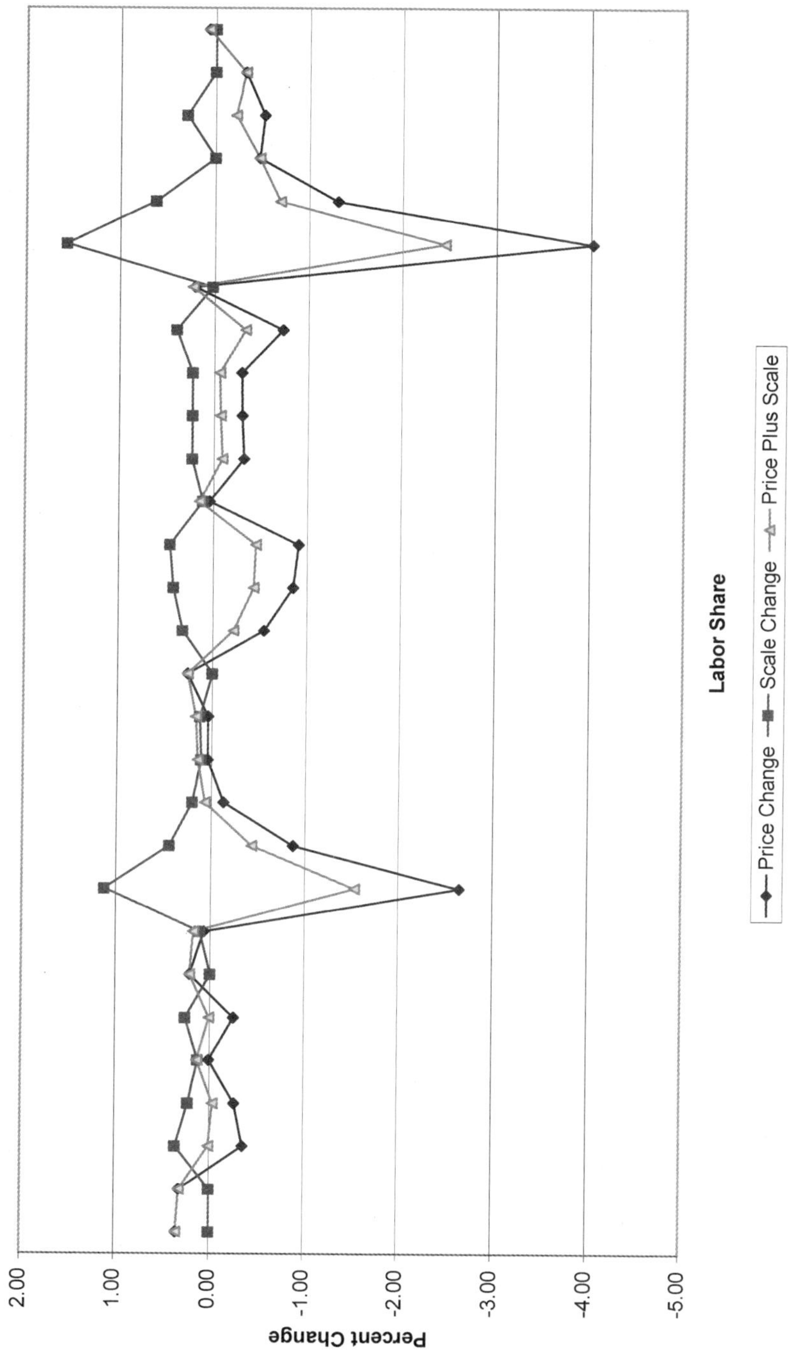

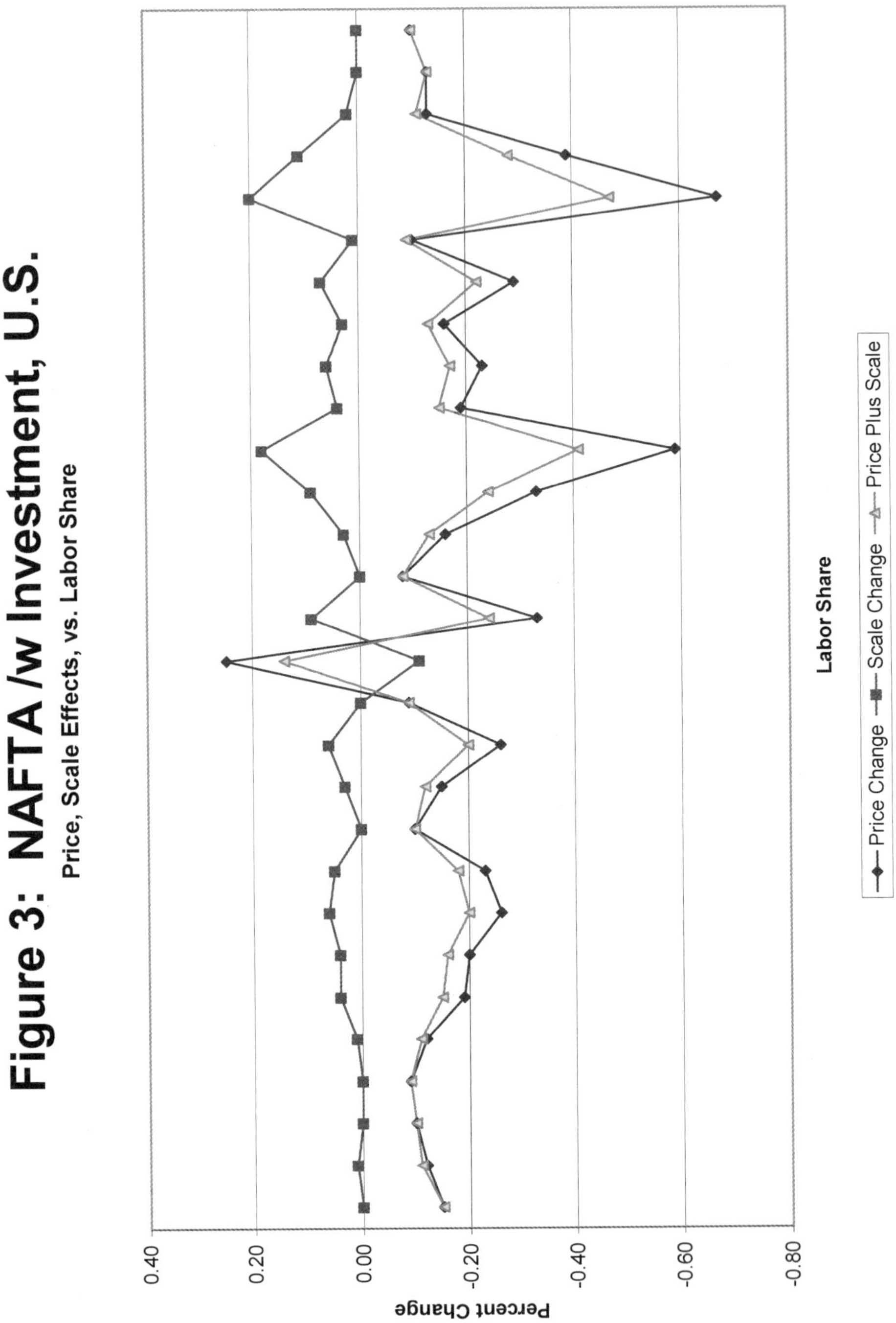
Figure 3: NAFTA /w Investment, U.S.
Price, Scale Effects, vs. Labor Share
Percent Change
0.40
0.20
0.00
-0.20
-0.40
-0.60
-0.80
Labor Share
Price Change
Scale Change
Price Plus Scale

Figure 4: NAFTA /w Investment, Mexico

Price, Scale Effects, vs. Labor Share

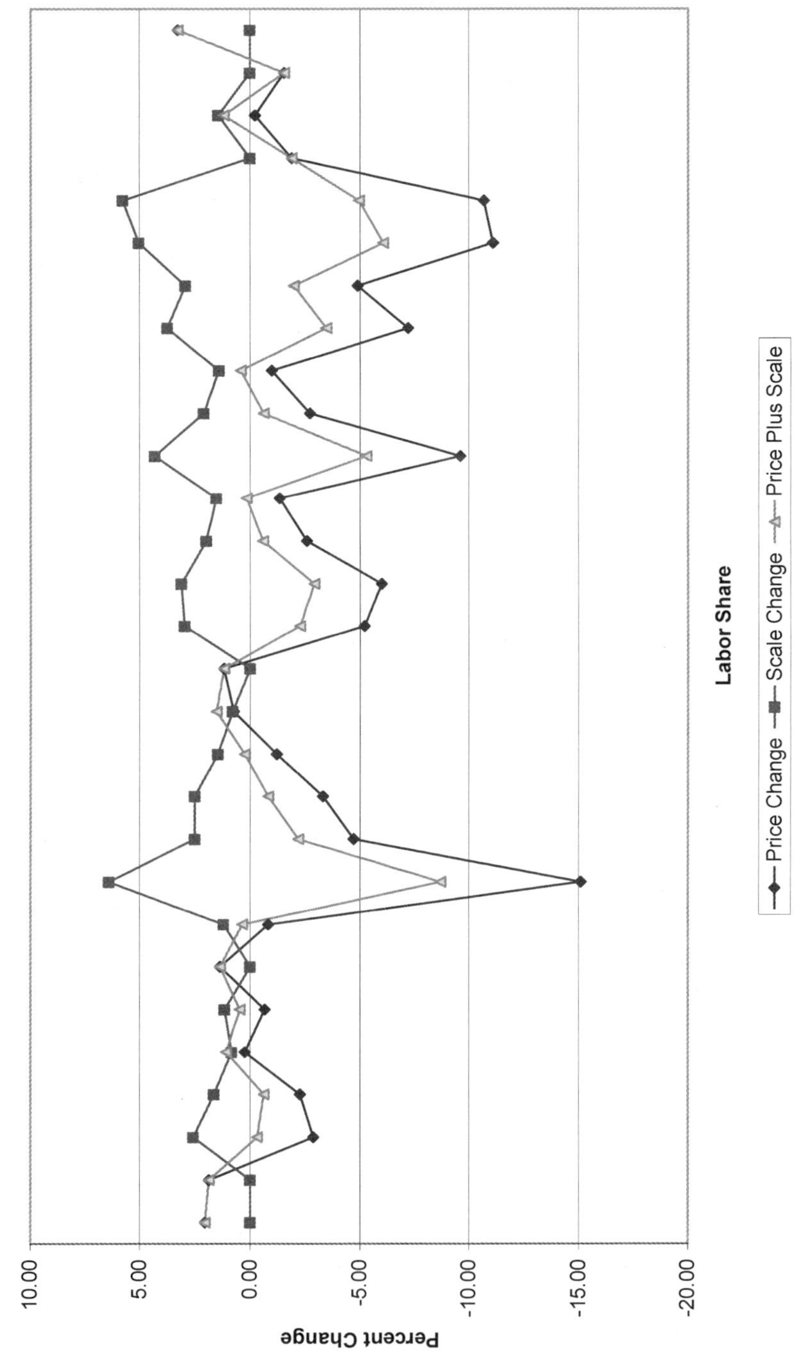

APPENDIX

The Michigan NAFTA Model: Equation, Notation, and Explanation

COUNTRY EQUATIONS ($i = 1,\ldots,m$)

A. Final Demand

(1) $\hat{C}_{ij}^{T} = \hat{E}_{i} - \hat{P}_{ij}^{T}$ $\quad j = 1,\ldots,n$

(2) $\hat{C}_{ij}^{N} = \hat{E}_{i} - \hat{P}_{ij}^{N}$ $\quad j = n+1,\ldots,n'$

B. Intermediate Demand

(3) $\hat{Z}_{ijk}^{T} = \hat{S}_{ik}$ $\quad j = 1,\ldots,n;\ k = 1,\ldots,n'$

(4) $\hat{Z}_{ijk}^{N} = \hat{S}_{ik}$ $\quad j = n+1,\ldots,n';\ k = 1,\ldots,n'$

C. Total Demand

(5) $\hat{D}_{ij}^{T} = v_{ij0}\hat{C}_{ij}^{T} + \sum_{k=1}^{n'} v_{ijk}\hat{Z}_{ijk}^{T}$ $\quad j = 1,\ldots,n$

(6) $\hat{D}_{ij}^{N} = v_{ij0}\hat{C}_{ij}^{N} + \sum_{k=1}^{n'} v_{ijk}\hat{Z}_{ijk}^{N}$ $\quad j = n+1,\ldots,n'$

D. Product Demand

(7) $\hat{D}_{ij}^{M} = \hat{D}_{ij}^{T} + \sigma_{ij}\theta_{ij}^{i}\left(\hat{P}_{ij}^{*} - \hat{P}_{ij}^{M}\right) - \frac{\sigma_{ij}\theta_{ij}^{i}}{\sigma_{ij} - 1}\hat{n}_{ij}$ $\quad j = 1,\ldots,n$

(8) $\hat{D}_{ij}^{r} = \hat{D}_{ij}^{M} + \sigma_{ij}\left(\hat{P}_{ij}^{M} - \hat{P}_{ij}^{r}\right)$ $\quad j = 1,\ldots,n;\ r \neq i;\ r = 1,\ldots,m$

(9) $\hat{D}_{ij}^{E} = \hat{D}_{ij}^{M} + \sigma_{ij}\left(\hat{P}_{ij}^{M} - \hat{P}_{ij}^{E}\right)$ $\quad j = 1,\ldots,n$

(10) $\hat{D}_{ij}^{i} = \hat{D}_{ij}^{T} + \sigma_{ij}\theta_{ij}^{M}\left(\hat{P}_{ij}^{M} - \hat{P}_{ij}^{*}\right) - \frac{\sigma_{ij}\theta_{ij}^{i}}{\sigma_{ij} - 1}\hat{n}_{ij}$ $\quad j = 1,\ldots,n$

E. Prices

(11) $\hat{P}_{ij}^{T} = \theta_{ij}^{i}\hat{P}_{ij}^{*} + \theta_{ij}^{M}\hat{P}_{ij}^{M} - \frac{\theta_{ij}^{i}}{\sigma_{ij}-1}\hat{n}_{ij}$ $\quad j = 1,\ldots,n$

(12) $\hat{P}_{ij}^{M} = \sum_{r=1}^{m+1}\theta_{ij}^{rM}\hat{P}_{ij}^{r} - \sum_{r=1}^{m}\frac{\theta_{ij}^{r}}{\sigma_{ij}-1}\hat{n}_{rj}$ $\quad j = 1,\ldots,n$

(13) $\hat{P}_{ij}^{r} = \hat{P}_{wj}^{r} + \hat{t}_{ij}^{rMeq}$ $\quad j = 1,\ldots,n;\ r \neq i;\ r = 1,\ldots,m+1$

(14) $\hat{P}_{ij}^{*} = \hat{P}_{wj}^{i}$ $\quad j = 1,\ldots,n$

(15) $\hat{P}_{ij}^{N} = M\hat{C}_{ij}$ $\quad j = n+1,\ldots,n'$

(16) $\hat{P}_{ij}^{*} = \theta_{ij}^{MC}M\hat{C}_{ij} + \theta_{ij}^{FC}\left[\hat{P}_{ij}^{V} + \hat{n}_{ij} - \hat{S}_{ij}\right]$ $\quad j = 1,\ldots,n$

(17) $\hat{P}_{ij}^{*} = M\hat{C}_{ij} + \frac{\hat{\eta}_{ij}}{\eta_{ij}+1}$ $\quad j = 1,\ldots,n$

(18) $\hat{P}_{ij}^{V} = \theta_{ij}^{L}\hat{w}_{i} + \theta_{ij}^{K}\hat{r}_{ij}$ $\quad j = 1,\ldots,n'$

F. Marginal Cost

(19) $M\hat{C}_{ij} = b_{ij0}\frac{\theta_{ij}^{VK}}{\theta_{ij}^{MC}}\hat{P}_{ij}^{V} + \sum_{k=1}^{n'}\frac{b_{ikj}}{\theta_{ij}^{MC}}\hat{P}_{ik}$ $\quad j = 1,\ldots,n'$

G. Demand for Primary Inputs

(20) $\hat{V}_{ij} = \hat{S}_{ij} - \hat{n}_{ij}$ $\quad j = 1,\ldots,n'$

(21) $\hat{L}_{ij} = \theta_{ij}^{VK}\hat{V}_{ij} - \overline{\sigma}_{ij}\theta_{ij}^{K}(\hat{w}_{ij} - \hat{r}_{ij}) + \hat{n}_{ij}$ $\quad j = 1,\ldots,n'$

(22) $\hat{K}_{ij} = \theta_{ij}^{VK}\hat{V}_{ij} + \overline{\sigma}_{ij}\theta_{ij}^{L}(\hat{w}_{ij} - \hat{r}_{ij}) + \hat{n}_{ij}$ $\quad j = 1,\ldots,n'$

H. Nontradable Goods Market Equilibrium

(23) $\hat{S}_{ij}^{N} = \hat{D}_{ij}^{N}$ $\quad j = n+1,\ldots,n'$

I. Demand Elasticities

$$(24)\quad \hat{\eta}^{i}_{rj} = \frac{(\sigma_{ij}-1)\theta^{r}_{ij}}{\eta^{i}_{rj}n_{rj}}\left[\hat{P}^{r}_{ij} + \hat{D}^{r}_{ij} - \hat{P}^{T}_{ij} - \hat{D}^{T}_{ij}\right] \qquad j=1,\ldots,n;\ r \neq i;\ r=1,\ldots,m$$

$$(25)\quad \hat{\eta}^{i}_{ij} = \frac{(\sigma_{ij}-1)\theta^{i}_{ij}}{\eta^{i}_{ij}n_{ij}}\left[\hat{P}^{*}_{ij} + \hat{D}^{i}_{ij} - \hat{P}^{T}_{ij} - \hat{D}^{T}_{ij}\right] \qquad j=1,\ldots,n$$

$$(26)\quad \hat{\eta}_{ij} = \sum_{r=1}^{m}\delta^{r}_{ij}\frac{\eta^{i}_{rj}}{\eta_{ij}}\hat{\eta}^{i}_{rj} \qquad j=1,\ldots,n$$

J. Primary Factors Market Equilibrium

$$(27)\quad \sum_{j=1}^{n'} h^{K}_{ij}\hat{K}_{ij} = \hat{K}^{0}_{i}$$

$$(28)\quad \sum_{j=1}^{n'} h^{L}_{ij}\hat{L}_{ij} = \hat{L}^{0}_{i}$$

K. National Income Determination

$$(29)\quad dB^{T}_{i} = dB^{T}_{i0}$$

L. Nontariff Barriers

$$(30)\quad \hat{t}^{rMeq}_{ij} = \hat{t}^{r}_{ij} + \left(\hat{D}^{r}_{ij} - \hat{Q}^{r}_{ij} + \hat{n}_{rj}\right)\frac{\theta^{rQ}_{ij}}{\sigma_{ij}\left(1-\theta^{rQ}_{ij}\right)} \qquad j=1,\ldots,n;\ r \neq i;\ r=1,\ldots,m$$

WORLD EQUATIONS

A. Trade Balance

(31)
$$dB_i^T = \sum_{j=1}^{n}\left[X_{ij}\hat{P}_{wj}^i + \sum_{r\neq i}^{m} X_{ij}^r\left(\hat{D}_{rj}^i + \hat{n}_{ij}\right) + X_{ij}^E L_E\right] - \sum_{j=1}^{n}\left[M_{ij}^E\left(\hat{P}_{wj}^E + \hat{D}_{ij}^E\right) + \sum_{r\neq i}^{m}\left(\hat{P}_{wj}^r + \hat{D}_{ij}^r + \hat{n}_{rj}\right)\right] \qquad i = 1,\ldots,m$$

B. Tradable Goods Market Equilibrium

(32)
$$S_{ij}^T \hat{S}_{ij}^T = D_{Ej}^i L_E + \sum_{r=1}^{m} D_{rj}^i\left(\hat{D}_{rj}^i + \hat{n}_{ij}\right) \qquad j = 1,\ldots,n;\ i = 1,\ldots,m$$

(33)
$$dS_j^E = \sum_{i=1}^{m} D_{ij}^E \hat{D}_{ij}^E \qquad j = 1,\ldots,n$$

(34)
$$dS_j^E = S_j^E \varepsilon_j^E \hat{P}_{wj}^E \qquad j = 1,\ldots,n$$

B. ROW Import Licensing

(35)
$$0 = \sum_{j=1}^{n}\left[\left(dS_j^E + S_j^E \hat{P}_{wj}^E\right) - M_j^E L_E - \sum_{i=1}^{m} M_{Ej}^i \hat{P}_{wj}^i\right]$$

Variables

C_{ij}^T, C_{ij}^N	Final demand for tradable and nontradable goods *j* in country *i*.
E_i	Household income in country *i*.
P_{ij}^T, P_{ij}^N	Price index of tradable and nontradable goods *j* in country *i*.
Z_{ijk}^T, Z_{ijk}^N	Intermediate demand for tradable and nontradable goods *j* by industry *k* in country *i*.
S_{ik}	Production of good *k* in country *i*.
D_{ij}^T, D_{ij}^N	Total demand for tradable and nontradable goods *j* in country *i*.
D_{ij}^M	Total demand for imports of good *j* in *i*.
P_{ij}^M	Price index of import good *j* in country *i*.
P_{ij}^*	Price of domestic good produced by a representative firm in industry *j* in country *i*.
n_{ij}	Number of firms in industry *j* in country *i*.
D_{ij}^r	Demand in country *i* for the good produced by a representative firm in industry *j* in country *r*.
t_{ij}^{rMeq}	Tariff equivalent imposed by country *i* on imports of good *j* from country *r*.
P_{wj}^i	World price of good *j* produced in country *i*.
MC_{ij}	Marginal cost of a representative firm in country *i* in industry *j*.
P_{ij}^V	Price index of primary input aggregate in industry *j* in country *i*.
η_{ij}	Perceived elasticity of demand by a representative firm in industry *j*, country *i*.
η_{rj}^i	Perceived elasticity of demand by a firm in industry *j*, country *i* on its sales to country *r*.
w_i	Wage paid to labor in country *i*.
r_i	Return to capital in country *i*.
V_{ij}	Primary input aggregate demanded by a representative firm in industry *j* in country *i*.
L_{ij}	Demand for labor in industry *j* in country *i*.
K_{ij}	Demand for capital in industry *j* in country *i*.
B_i^T	Country *i*'s trade balance.
Q_{ij}^r	Quota restriction on imports of good *j* from country *r* by country *i*.
L_E	Import licensing variable for ROW.

Parameters

v_{ij0} Final consumption share of total purchases of good j in country i.

v_{ijk} Intermediate demand for good j by industry k share of purchases of good j in country i.

σ_{ij} Elasticity of substitution between different varieties of good j in country i.

θ_{ij}^{M} Fraction of expenditure on good j in country i devoted to imports.

θ_{ij}^{r} Fraction of expenditure on good j in country i devoted to goods produced in country r.

θ_{ij}^{MC} Variable input share of total cost in industry j in country i.

θ_{ij}^{FC} Fixed cost share of total cost in industry j in country i.

θ_{ij}^{L} Labor's share of expenditure on primary inputs in industry j in country i.

θ_{ij}^{K} Capital's share of expenditure on primary inputs in industry j in country i.

θ_{ij}^{VK} Variable capital's share of total capital employed in industry j in country i.

b_{ij0} Primary input share of total cost in industry j in country i.

b_{ijk} Intermediate input k's share of total cost of production in industry j, country i.

$\overline{\sigma}_{ij}$ Elasticity of substitution between capital and labor in industry j in country i.

δ_{ij}^{r} Fraction of sales by a representative firm in industry j in country i that go to country r.

h_{ij}^{K} Fraction of capital in country i employed in industry j.

h_{ij}^{L} Fraction of labor in country i employed in industry j.

K_{i}^{0} Capital stock in country i.

L_{i}^{0} Labor supply in country i.

B_{i0}^{T} Trade balance of country i.

t_{ij}^{r} Tariff imposed by country i on imports of good j from country r.

θ_{ij}^{rQ} Fraction of imports of good j by country i from country r that are subject to quantitative restrictions.

X_{ij} Country i's exports of good j.

X_{ij}^{r} Country i's exports of good j to country r.

M_{ij}^{r} Country i's imports of good j from country r.

S_{j}^{E} ROW supply of good j.

ε_{j}^{E} ROW supply of good j price elasticity.

Explanation of Equations

Notes: Circumflex denotes percent change
"d" denotes a level change
"T'" refers to tradable goods, indexed j=1,…,n
"N" refers to nontradable goods, indexed j=n+1,...,n'

Country Equations

A. Final demand is derived assuming that all households share a common Cobb-Douglas utility function. The percent change in the demand for tradables (j=1,...,n)and nontradables (j=n+1,...,n') is therefore the difference between the percent changes in income and prices.

B. Intermediate demand is derived assuming that all tradable and nontradable goods are required in fixed proportion to production. The demand for each tradable good as an intermediate input is thus proportional to the change in production.

C. Total demand for each good is obtained by summing over final and intermediate demands.

D. Product demand allocates demand for each industry across individual suppliers in all countries, assuming total demand is a CES function of demands from individual suppliers. Allocation is made to all imports (equation 7) and individual domestic suppliers (equation 10), and then expenditure on imports is allocated to individual foreign suppliers (equation 8) and the rest of world (equation 9). In each case, demand depends on relative prices and the number of competing firms.

E. The tradable price index (equation 11) is a weighted average of import prices and prices from individual domestic suppliers. The import price index (equation 12) is a weighted average of all individual foreign firms. All landed prices are related to the world prices, adjusted for tariffs and import quotas (equation 13), except for the price of the domestically produced varieties (equation 14) to which tariffs do not apply.

All nontradable goods markets are taken to be perfectly competitive (equation 15). However, the tradable goods industries are taken to be monopolistically competitive, and firms must incur a fixed cost that is independent of output. The price of tradable goods must therefore cover both marginal cost and average fixed cost (equation 16) and is an optimal markup of price over marginal cost, where the markup is determined by the firm's perceived elasticity of demand (equation 17).

The price of the primary input aggregate (equation 18) is a weighted average of the returns to primary inputs, capital and labor.

F. Marginal cost is the fraction of primary and intermediate inputs that are variable.

G. The primary input aggregate (equation 20), which is a CES aggregate of capital and labor, is required in fixed proportion to firm production. The allocation between labor (equation 21) and capital (equation 22) depends on the wage-rent ratio.

H. The market clearing condition for the nontradable goods sectors requires that supply be equal to demand (equation 23), but that price be equal to marginal cost (equation 15).

I. The firms' perceived elasticity of demand is derived from each firm's demand curve. Firms first calculate the elasticity of demand for their good in each market (equations 24 and 25) and then take a weighted average across all markets.

J. Primary factor market clearing requires that the demand for each factor, summed over all industries, must equal the supply of each factor.

K. National income is equal to the sum of factor payments plus redistributed tariff revenue. This is, according to Walras's Law, equivalent to imposing a balanced trade condition.

L. The import tariff equivalent that connects world prices to landed prices is an average of the *ad valorem* import tariff and the tariff equivalent of any quantitative import restrictions that may apply.

World Equations

A. The trade balance is calculated as the difference between the value of exports and the value of imports.

B. The tradable goods market clearing condition requires that the supply by each firm be equal to its demand summed over all country markets. Rest-of-world supply (equation 34) is an ad hoc supply equation applying a supply elasticity to world price.

C. The rest-of-world is assumed to use an import licensing scheme which holds the value of total demand equal to export revenue.

CHAPTER 42†

10 The liberalization of services trade: potential impacts in the aftermath of the Uruguay Round

Drusilla K. Brown, Alan V. Deardorff, Alan K. Fox, and Robert M. Stern

This study was designed originally to examine the effects of the liberalization in services trade to be achieved under the Uruguay Round. But the general consensus is that little or no actual liberalization was achieved, and that the services-trade negotiations merely established the institutional structure for negotiating liberalization in the future. The focus of this study thus shifted to the more hypothetical one of examining what the effects of services liberalization might be when it finally occurs. For this purpose, we used Hoekman's (1995) "guesstimates" of the size of trade barriers in services and calculated the effects of an assumed 25 percent reduction in these barriers, which is a reduction that we believe represents a plausible order of magnitude that may eventually be achieved. To provide a benchmark for comparison, we have also calculated the effects of the liberalization in tariffs for industrial products that actually was negotiated. Our focus is on the world's major trading countries/regions which account for the largest part of trade in services and merchandise. Several results emerge from our analysis.

First, the effects of liberalization in services trade are of the same order of magnitude as for liberalization in industrial products. Despite the fact that trade in services is smaller than trade in industrial products, the size of the services sectors, and thus the size of their trade barriers, is large. Because liberalization in services trade is just starting on a process that in the goods sectors began fifty years ago and is now almost complete, it has substantial scope for expanding trade and welfare in the world's economies. The decision to include services in the Uruguay Round negotiations was thus not misplaced.

Second, by including services trade in our model simulations, we were able for the first time to examine the effects of goods-market trade liberalization on trade in services. This relationship yielded a mix of effects; services trade would expand in some countries and sectors and contract in others. We also found that these effects on services trade did not change the

292

† This chapter is taken with permission from Will Martin and L. Alan Winters, eds., 1996, The Uruguay Round and the Developing Countries (Cambridge University Press, New York), Chapter 10, pp. 292–315.

results of our analysis that trade liberalization in goods, because it acts as a tax cut in these sectors, would tend to reduce employment in services.

Third, we found that the sectoral effects of services trade liberalization would be substantial in the service sectors themselves. This result holds true despite the fact that services trade is small compared with its outputs, which is again due to the size of the barriers that are assumed to be reduced. Services liberalization also has some notable effects on trade in goods, although whether the two are substitutable or complementary varies across countries.

A description of the analytical model

To estimate the potential economic impacts of the tariff reductions for industrial products negotiated in the Uruguay Round and the gains that might be realized from service sector liberalization in the post-Round period, we use a specially constructed version of the Michigan Brown–Deardorff–Stern CGE model of world production and trade. The model simulates the effects of three liberalization (tariff-reduction scenarios) on trade, economic welfare, and real returns to labor and capital for individual countries and regions.

The model is an extension of the CGE model first constructed by Brown and Stern (1989) to analyze the economic impacts of the Canada–US Trade Agreement, and later for analyses of NAFTA, the extension of NAFTA to some major trading countries in South America, and the formation of an East Asian trading bloc (Brown, Deardorff, and Stern 1992a and b and 1996; Brown, Deardoff, Hummels, and Stern 1994). For the analysis in this chapter, we grouped the thirty-four countries in our data base into eight major countries/regions: the United States, Canada, Mexico, Europe, Japan, the newly industrial economies of Asia, Australia/New Zealand, and a group of other major trading nations.[1] We closed the model by assigning remaining countries to a residual rest-of-world. In each country or region, the model covers twenty-nine sectors; twenty-three are "tradable" (import–export) product categories covering agriculture and manufacturing, and six are "tradable" categories covering services and government.[2]

Assumptions underlying the model

The model assumes that the agricultural sector is perfectly competitive, and that the manufacturing and services sectors are monopolistically competitive, with free entry.[3] Agricultural products are differentiated by country of production. Manufacturing and service-sector products are differentiated by firm to correspond to an imperfectly competitive market structure.[4] The reference year for the data base of the model is 1990. The input–output relationships used in the model refer to various years, depending on the availability of national input–output tables.[5] The data base and documentation, as well as a full statement and description of the equations and parameters of the model, are available from the authors on request.[6]

The model is also built on five assumptions that are important to interpreting our simulation results.

Full employment

The aggregate, or economywide, level of employment is held constant in each country. The simulated effects of the Uruguay Round thus do not change any country's overall rates of employment or unemployment. This assumption is made because overall employment is determined by macroeconomic forces and policies that are not included in a negotiated agreement and thus not contained in the model. The model captures the composition of employment across sectors as determined by the microeconomic interactions between supply and demand due to the Uruguay Round and the liberalization of goods and services trade in the future.

Balanced trade

The model assumes that each country maintains balanced trade (or, more accurately, that any initial trade imbalance remains constant) as trade barriers change. This assumption reflects the prevalence of flexible exchange rates among the countries involved. And as with the full employment assumption, it is an appropriate way to abstract from the macroeconomic forces and policies that are the main determinants of trade balances.

Rents and revenues

Revenue from tariffs is assumed to be redistributed to consumers in the tariff-levying country and spent like any other income. Similarly, the rents from nontariff barriers (and the tariff equivalents of the services barriers discussed in this chapter) are also assumed to remain within the importing country and to be spent like other income. When tariffs and tariff equivalents are reduced, the income available for purchasing imports falls along with the prices of those imports, without exerting any overall bias on expansion or contraction in demand.

Fixed relative wages

While the model adjusts the economywide wage in each country so as to maintain the assumption of full employment, it keeps wages across sectors constant. This feature allows the analysis to focus on the labor-market adjustments that might be required, independently of any wage changes that may induce those adjustments.[7]

Fixed labor supply

The model assumes that total labor supply in each country is fixed, and that cross-border movement of labor does not exist. This assumption does not imply that labor supply will not change as the Uruguay Round liberalization is phased in, but only that the Round will not induce such changes.

Our model also does not account for changes in FDI and the cross-border movement of workers that might occur as the rate of return on capital and real wages change. Nor does the model make any allowance for dynamic efficiency changes and economic growth. We are aware that the Uruguay Round involved much more than negotiated reductions and/or the removal of tariffs and nontariff barriers. It involved numerous changes and clarifications of existing agreements covering antidumping and subsidy/countervailing duty procedures; new agreements covering TRIPS and TRIMs; and the creation of the WTO, in part to strengthen dispute settlement procedures. While these various features of the Uruguay Round may be important, quantifying the roles they will play is difficult. Thus, by assessing only the liberalization of trade in industrial products and services and by abstracting from dynamic changes in efficiency and economic growth, we have provided "incomplete" calculations of the consequences of the Uruguay Round.

Policy input data: comments on reductions in tariffs and tariff equivalents

The policy inputs into the model are the pre- and post-Uruguay Round tariffs for industrial and agricultural products and "guesstimated" tariff equivalents for services (table 10.1). In the analyses, we apply each to the bilateral trade of the countries or regions being modeled.[8] Because our model is static, we assume that the reduction or removal of tariffs and tariff equivalents takes place at one time, rather than in stages. When the policy changes are introduced into the model, the method of solution yields percentage changes in the variables of interest for each country/region. Multiplying the percentage changes by the actual (1990) levels given in the data base yields the absolute changes, positive or negative, that might be the result of liberalization.

Before proceeding with the simulations and analyses, we provide some remarks on these various rates.

Table 10.1 *Weighted average tariffs on industrial and agricultural products and "guesstimated" tariff equivalents on services in the major trading countries/regions (percent)*

Country/region	Industrial products			Agricultural products			Services
	Pre-UR	Post-UR	Percentage reduction	Pre-UR	Post-UR	Percentage reduction	Post-UR
United States	4.9	3.4	30.0	14.9	14.0	6.0	67.5
Canada	7.7	4.5	42.2	2.6	2.3	14.9	57.2
Mexico	11.9	11.9	0.1	35.3	35.3	0.0	76.9
Europe	6.9	4.8	30.4	13.2	11.7	11.1	79.2
Japan	6.0	3.9	36.2	60.9	35.1	42.4	61.2
Newly industrial economies of Asia	0.9	0.7	17.2	12.7	7.9	37.3	46.0
Australia–New Zealand	13.8	9.1	34.3	0.8	0.4	44.8	105.9
Other trading nations	28.9	21.0	27.2	18.6	17.6	5.3	107.4

Sources: industrial products: World Bank Uruguay Round data base; agricultural products: Ingco 1995; and services: Hoekman 1995.

Tariff rates on industrial products

As noted in Martin (1994a), estimates of tariff reductions for industrial products should be based on differences between the Uruguay Round base rate and the Uruguay Round final offer rate as contained in the GATT IDB, which is the primary source of tariff data used in the Uruguay Round negotiations.[9] For industrial countries, the base rate is generally the rate that has been notified officially to the GATT as being legally bound as of 1986; the measure of liberalization to be used is thus the difference between the offer rate and the base rate as long as this difference is negative. If the difference is zero or positive, the tariff liberalization measure is set at zero. This procedure, in effect, excludes any changes in applied rates that industrial countries may have implemented after 1986.

The calculation is more complicated for many developing countries, insofar as they may have been using applied rates that were not previously bound. As noted in Martin (1994b) and Martin and Francois (1994), developing countries participated much more actively in the Uruguay Round than in previous rounds, with the result that the percentage of their industrial tariff lines that became bound increased from 22 to 72 percent. It can be argued that these bound tariffs represent trade liberalization – even if the applied rates have not changed or the rates are bound above the applied rate, since the binding will obviate any future increase in tariffs beyond the bound rate.

As a practical matter, however, the choice for developing countries is to define liberalization as either the difference between the newly bound and the applied rates or, alternatively, the difference between these rates only when the bound rates is below the initial applied rate, and nonexistent (or zero) otherwise. The first measure is misleading, since it would imply an increase in protection if the bound rate were above the applied rate. The second measure avoids this problem of misrepresenting restrictiveness and is thus the one that has been used for our purposes.

Tariff rates on agricultural products

One of the accomplishments of the Uruguay Round was to convert all existing forms of agricultural protection into tariffs. The GATT IDB, however, does not calculate these agricultural tariffs; rather, they were constructed by Ingco (1995) based on information in the country schedules for agricultural and related products. We aggregated these tariffs to correspond to our sectors for agriculture (ISIC 1) and food and related products (ISIC 310). Following Martin (1994a), we used the average pre-Uruguay Round tariff rate for a particular agricultural product category as the base rate, and measured agricultural liberalization as the difference between the base rate and the lower final offer rate. If the final offer tariff rate exceeded the base rate, we set the liberalization measure at zero.[10]

Services-trade barriers

Compared with trade barriers in goods, it is difficult to obtain systematic information on services-trade barriers (appendix A describes how we developed data on "tradable" services). We followed Hoekman (1995) by constructing "guesstimates" of comparative trade restrictiveness across countries, on the assumption that each country "revealed" its policy stance with its commitments in the Uruguay Round GATS.

Hoekman's procedure classifies each country's GATS commitments for each of 155 possible services sectors and each of four modes of supply in terms of the extent to which they indicated restrictions on market access.[11] Values are assigned to each of these 620 (4 × 155) cells for each of ninety-seven countries: 1.0 for the absence of restrictions under the commitments; 0.5 for the presence of restrictions under the commitments; and 0.0 for "unbound," or the absence of commitments. The major two-digit ISIC services sectors are then assigned an index of trade coverage restrictiveness equal to $1 - x/y$, where x is the sum of these values in the cells corresponding to the two-digit sector and y is the number of such cells. The resulting numbers range from "0" to "1" – or from "free access" (no restrictions), to "no access," in the sense that each supply mode in each subsector is "unbound."

Tariff-equivalent benchmarks are then assigned to each two-digit sector under assumptions about the restrictiveness of market access for each country. A benchmark of 200 percent is assigned to sectors in which market access tends to be prohibitive in most countries and which do not appear in most offers (for example, maritime, cabotage, air transport, postal services, voice telecommunications, and life insurance). The remaining sectors are assigned tariff-equivalent benchmarks that range from 20 to 50 percent. Each coverage index (the $1-x/y$ measure) is then multiplied by the tariff-equivalent benchmark guesstimate to obtain a country/sector-specific tariff equivalent. (For example, in Australia construction services (ISIC 5) have a coverage rate of 0.3, and the tariff equivalent for this sector is set at 40 percent. In this case, then, Australia is assigned a tariff equivalent of 12 percent: $0.3 \times .40 \times 100 = 12$ percent.) Values for the two-digit ISIC sectors are then aggregated to obtain the one-digit guesstimates in table 10.1. Hoekman's tariff-equivalent guesstimates for ISIC 5 and 6 (construction and wholesale and retail trade) tend to be relatively low; those for ISIC sector 7 (transportation) tend to be relatively high; and those for ISIC sectors 8 and 9 (financial services and personal services) tend to fall in between. The detailed two-digit ISIC guesstimates are available in annex 2 of Hoekman (1995).

Hoekman is aware of the limitations of these judgmental estimates, since it is not clear what the benchmark tariff vector for the "most restrictive" sector(s) should be, and the assumption that the coverage ratios of country offers are correlated with actual policy stances is quite heroic. More research in this area is urgently required. It is unfortunate that efforts in this domain were not initiated during the negotiations. As it stands, the GATS schedules are thus the only source of cross-country information on services-trade policy regimes. Given the arbitrariness of Hoekman's procedure, we emphasize that our main objective here is to get a sense of the comparative importance of trade barriers in services, and the types of interactions that may emerge between the goods and services sectors under the assumption that services are tradable, and that countries open their services markets to foreign competition. In this light, the results we report in this chapter are indicative at best.

How do we use these guesstimates, arbitrary as they may appear? Hoekman has concluded that trade was not liberalized in the Uruguay Round, so that any benefits from liberalization will come in the post-Uruguay Round period. We thus compare the effects of the liberalization associated with the reductions in tariff rates on industrial products under the Uruguay Round with comparable reductions in tariff equivalents for services to be undertaken in the future. This is the strategy that we have followed in implementing our liberalization simulations.

Model simulations

How should we simulate the reduction or elimination of nontariff barriers on industrial products negotiated during the Uruguay Round? Consonant with the spirit of the Uruguay Round negotiations, the most desirable way to handle nontariff barriers would be to convert them into tariff equivalents and then assume that they would be reduced to zero.[12] Unfortunately, we have been unable to obtain sufficient data for measuring nontariff barriers as tariff equivalents. Also at issue is whether or not many of the existing nontariff barriers will in fact be eliminated over whatever period may have been specified in the negotiations. That is, it is conceivable that countries may find ways to continue to impose their nontariff barrier restrictions either in their present form or in some alternative form yet to be determined. In this case, the tariff equivalents of nontariff barriers would be only partially reduced and the quantitative restrictions would remain in place, thus diminishing the effects of the reduction or elimination of tariffs in these sectors. Moreover, as already mentioned in our discussion of services, services barriers were not liberalized in the Uruguay Round, and they thus remain a post-Uruguay Round negotiating option.

Trade coverage ratios are used to represent pre-Uruguay Round nontariff barriers in the data base of our model. If tariffs are reduced or removed and nontariff barriers are assumed to stay in place, the effects of tariff liberalization would be dampened. Alternatively, we could set our nontariff barrier coverage ratios at zero, thus assuming that tariff liberalization would not be dampened. Taking the Uruguay Round commitment to eliminate nontariff barriers at face value, it is this strategy that we have followed in our various computational scenarios:

Simulation 1

Reductions in Uruguay Round tariff rates on industrial products only, with nontariff barrier trade coverage ratios set at zero. (This simulation excludes the effects of the elimination of the MFA.)

Simulation 2

Assumed 25 percent reduction in post-Uruguay Round services-sector *ad valorem* tariff equivalents, with nontariff barrier coverage ratios in the agricultural and manufacturing sectors set at zero.

Simulation 3

Reductions in Uruguay Round tariff rates on industrial products combined with a 25 percent reduction in post-Uruguay Round services-sector *ad valorem* tariff equivalents, with nontariff barrier trade coverage ratios set at zero.

We use our CGE model to analyze both the aggregate impacts of the Uruguay Round under the three liberalization scenarios and the sector-specific impacts of the Round under the three scenarios for the United States and Europe individually as well as in combination. As discussed in the preceding section, we have data on pre- and post-Uruguay Round nominal tariff rates for industrial and agricultural sectors as well as guesstimates of post-Uruguay Round *ad valorem* tariff equivalents of services barriers.

Aggregate impacts of the three liberalization scenarios

The aggregate results measure the impacts of liberalization on the terms of trade, welfare, and factor payments for our eight countries/regions (table 10.2). Of greatest interest is the impact on economic welfare – that is, the "equivalent variation" measure of the change in real GDP.

Table 10.2 *Summary results of the Uruguay Round: changes in terms of trade, welfare, and real return to labor and capital (percentage change)*

Country	Terms of trade (1)	Equivalent variation (2)	Real wage rate (3)	Real return to capital (4)
Simulation 1: industrial products trade liberalization				
United States	−0.1	0.3	0.1	0.3
Canada	−0.2	0.4	0.2	0.3
Mexico	0.1	0.1	0.0	0.2
Europe	−0.1	0.3	0.1	0.3
Japan	0.1	0.6	0.3	−0.1
Asian newly industrial countries	0.9	2.4	1.3	−0.9
Australia–New Zealand	−1.0	1.2	0.3	1.0
Other trading nations	−1.6	0.0	0.2	1.7
Simulation 2: services trade liberalization				
United States	0.2	0.7	0.2	−0.1
Canada	−0.1	1.6	0.5	0.1
Mexico	−0.2	2.7	0.4	0.3
Europe	0.1	0.6	0.1	0.0
Japan	−0.5	0.8	0.2	0.4
Asian newly industrial countries	0.1	1.1	0.7	0.3
Australia–New Zealand	−0.4	2.8	0.3	0.5
Other trading nations	−0.3	1.0	0.3	0.4
Simulation 3: industrial products and services liberalization				
United States	0.2	0.9	0.3	0.2
Canada	−0.3	2.0	0.7	0.4
Mexico	−0.1	2.8	0.4	0.5
Europe	0.0	0.9	0.3	0.3
Japan	−0.4	1.4	0.5	0.3
Asian newly industrial countries	1.0	3.6	2.1	−0.6
Australia–New Zealand	−1.4	3.9	0.6	1.6
Other trading nations	−1.9	1.0	0.5	2.1

Economic welfare

Under simulation 1, economic welfare in all the countries and regions would rise. The largest welfare gains would accrue to Europe (US $20.7 billion, or 0.3 percent of GDP); Japan (US $16.6 billion, or 0.6 percent of GDP); the United States (US $14.5 billion, or 0.3 percent of GDP); and the newly industrial economies of Asia (US $12.2 billion, or 2.4 percent of GDP).[13] Under simulation 2, which assesses what the effects might be in post-Uruguay Round negotiations if services barriers were reduced, economic welfare in Europe would rise by 0.6 percent of GDP (US $39.3 billion), in the United States by 0.7 percent of GDP (US $36.1 billion), and in Japan by 0.8 percent of GDP (US $23.7 billion). Welfare would also increase in all other countries and regions shown.[14]

Under simulation 3, which combines simulations 1 and 2, the welfare gains from a reduction in industrial tariffs and services-trade barriers would reach 0.9 percent of GDP (US $60.1 billion) in Europe, 0.9 percent of GDP (US $50.6 billion) in the United States, 1.4 percent of GDP (US $40.4 billion) in Japan, 3.6 percent of GDP in the newly industrializing economies of Asia, and 2.0 percent GDP (US $11.5 billion) in Canada. To the extent that Hoekman's guesstimates of *ad valorem* tariff equivalents for services provide an indication of services barriers, our results suggest that reducing these barriers in post-Uruguay Round negotiations offers considerable scope for welfare gains.

In interpreting these results, one should note that positive welfare gains are not inevitable when trade is liberalized. Consumers will of course gain as the removal of tariffs will lower prices and as countries begin to specialize in the range of goods in which they have a comparative advantage. But trade liberalization could either increase or worsen a country's terms of trade; if import prices rose and export prices fell, welfare gains from specialization and exchange could be reversed. Each of our simulations shows several instances of negative terms-of-trade effects (see table 10.2). But these effects tend to be relatively small.

Our models also include the effects of economies of scale, which can either raise or lower welfare (results not shown). In industries that exhibit significant economies of scale and thus declining average costs, firms that charge a lower price may also have to increase output in order to break even. As firms lower their average total cost curve, the inputs they require to produce a unit of output will decline on average. If competition pressures force many of the firms in a country to economize on inputs in this way, then the country will be able to produce more under liberalization using the same inputs and technology. The gains from the realization of economies of scale will enhance the more traditional gains from specialization and exchange. It is also possible that scale effects could be negative, which we discuss in more detail later.[15]

Real wages and return to capital

Having established the welfare effects of the three liberalization simulations, we are now interested in which factors of production are likely to gain or lose – specifically the percentage changes in wages and the return to capital that are common to all sectors due to intersectoral labor and capital mobility. Under simulation 1, the real returns to both factors rise by relatively small percentages in the United States, Canada, Mexico, Europe, Australia/New Zealand, and the other trading nations (see table 10.2). In Japan and the newly industrial economies of Asia, real wages rise and the return to capital falls.

Increases in returns to both labor and capital may seem inconsistent with the Stolper–Samuelson theorem, which suggests that trade liberalization will increase the return to the more abundant factor in each country while making the other factor worse off. But in the context of a differentiated products model with IRTS, such as the one we are using, other forces at work may be undermining Stolper–Samuelson-type mechanics (Brown, Deardorff, and Stern 1993). That is, scale effects work much like the relative price effects articulated in the Stolper–Samuelson theorem to determine the implications of trade liberalization for factor prices. Scale effects, as with price effects, tend to accrue only to one factor. For example, an increase in output per firm in an industry will increase the real return to the factor used intensively in that industry and will lower the return to the other factor. But price and scale effects differ in one important respect. If scale effects emerge across the board in nearly all industries, then both factors may gain – a result that emerged several times in our model. But this result is by no means universal, since, as noted, the models yielded several cases in which the changes in factor returns have the opposite sign.

Sector-specific impacts of the three liberalization scenarios

Table 10.3 reports sector-specific results for employment in all countries/regions in simulation 1, reflecting trade liberalization in industrial products only. For simulation 2, reflecting the results of hypothetical liberalization in services, we report more detailed results for the United States, Europe, and Japan (tables 10.4 to 10.6).

Simulation 1

Considering first the sectoral employment results for industrial products trade liberalization, it can be seen in table 10.3 that the Uruguay Round will cause relatively small percentage shifts of employment among sectors, with some sectors gaining employment and others losing, as indicated.[16] In the United States, for example, the largest percentage reductions in employment are reported for clothing and iron and steel and the largest percentage increases are in footwear and leather products. The declines are never

Table 10.3 *Simulation 1: industrial products; sectoral employment effects of the Uruguay Round (percentage change)*

Sector	United States (1)	Canada (2)	Mexico (3)	European Union (4)	Japan (5)	Newly industrial economies of Asia (6)	Australia and New Zealand (7)	Other major trading nations (8)
1 Agriculture	0.3	0.6	0.0	0.1	−0.2	−1.5	0.9	0.2
310 Food	0.2	0.2	−0.0	0.0	−0.4	−3.0	0.9	0.0
321 Textiles	−0.3	−1.8	0.2	0.2	−0.1	2.0	−3.9	1.6
322 Clothing	−0.9	−2.9	0.1	−0.3	−2.2	5.2	−2.7	3.5
323 Leather products	1.0	−4.2	−0.3	0.1	−0.2	−3.7	0.9	1.5
324 Footwear	2.1	−4.2	0.0	0.4	0.0	−5.6	−3.2	0.5
331 Wood products	0.0	1.3	−0.1	−0.0	−0.3	1.6	−0.2	0.2
332 Furniture, fixtures	−0.4	−1.0	0.0	0.2	−0.4	8.7	−1.4	−0.5
341 Paper products	−0.1	2.9	−0.1	−0.1	−0.1	−0.3	−1.7	−0.1
342 Printing, publishing	0.0	−0.2	−0.2	0.0	0.0	−0.4	0.0	−0.3
35A Chemicals	0.3	0.6	−0.0	0.3	−0.1	−0.0	−2.7	−1.1
35B Petroleum products	0.0	0.0	0.1	0.1	−0.3	−0.5	0.6	−0.2
355 Rubber products	0.1	0.0	−0.1	0.1	−0.1	−1.5	0.2	−0.5
36A Nonmetal min. prod.	−0.1	−1.2	0.0	0.2	−0.1	0.0	−0.3	−0.6
362 Glass products	−0.1	−0.1	−0.1	0.2	0.1	1.8	−0.2	−0.8
371 Iron, steel	−0.8	−1.5	0.1	0.5	0.4	0.8	−1.2	−1.8
372 Nonferrous metals	0.0	3.1	−0.3	−0.0	−0.6	2.4	1.8	−0.1
381 Metal products	−0.0	−0.4	−0.1	0.0	0.0	0.8	−0.5	−0.5
382 Nonelec. machinery	−0.0	−0.6	−0.7	0.6	0.3	−1.7	−2.7	−3.4
383 Electrical machinery	0.3	−1.6	−0.9	−0.7	0.8	6.9	−3.8	−3.2
384 Transport equipment	0.2	−0.4	−0.4	0.1	−0.3	−2.7	−1.3	−1.2

38A Misc. mfrs.	−0.1	2.6	−0.1	−0.2	0.4	1.1	6.7	−2.2
2 Mining, quarrying	−0.3	0.8	0.7	−0.1	−2.2	−9.0	2.0	4.6
4 Utilities	0.0	0.3	0.0	0.0	0.0	0.4	0.1	−0.2
5 Construction	−0.1	−0.1	−0.0	−0.1	−0.0	−0.2	−0.2	−0.6
6 Wholesale trade	0.0	−0.0	−0.0	−0.0	0.0	0.1	0.1	−0.3
7 Transportation	0.1	0.2	0.0	0.0	0.0	−2.7	0.8	0.4
8 Financial services	−0.0	0.1	−0.0	−0.0	0.1	0.5	0.2	−0.4
9 Personal services	−0.0	−0.1	0.0	−0.0	−0.0	−0.4	−0.2	−0.5
Total	0.0	0.0	0.0	0.0	0.0	0.0	0.0	0.0

Note: Europe includes the fifteen members of the European Union plus Norway and Switzerland; the newly industrial economies of Asia include Hong Kong, South Korea, Singapore, and Taiwan (China); and the other major trading nations include Argentina, Brazil, Chile, Colombia, India, Israel, Turkey, and Venezuela. Sector 35A comprises industrial chemicals (351) and other chemical products (352); Sector 35B comprises petroleum refineries (353) and miscellaneous products of petroleum and coal (354); Sector 36A comprises pottery, china, and earthenware (361) and other nonmetallic mineral products (369); Sector 38A comprises plastic products not elsewhere classified (356), professional photographic goods, etc. (385), and other manufacturing industries (390).

Table 10.4 *Simulation 2: services; sectoral effects on the United States of the Uruguay Round (percentage change)*

Sector	Exports (1)	Imports (2)	Output (3)	No. firms (4)	Change in employment Percent (5)	Change in employment 1,000s (6)
1 Agriculture	−0.3	0.4	−0.1	0.0	−0.1	−2.7
310 Food	−0.4	0.5	0.0	−0.1	−0.1	−2.3
321 Textiles	−0.4	0.3	0.0	−0.1	−0.1	−1.2
322 Clothing	−0.3	−1.0	0.2	0.1	0.1	0.7
323 Leather products	−0.3	0.6	0.0	−0.2	−0.2	−0.1
324 Footwear	−0.1	−0.7	0.2	0.1	0.2	0.1
331 Wood products	−0.6	0.0	0.0	−0.2	−0.1	−0.9
332 Furniture, fixtures	−0.2	−0.1	0.0	−0.2	−0.1	−0.7
341 Paper products	−0.3	0.1	0.0	−0.2	−0.2	−1.2
342 Printing, publishing	−0.2	0.5	0.1	−0.1	−0.1	−1.3
35A Chemicals	−0.6	0.7	−0.1	−0.3	−0.3	−2.8
35B Petroleum products	−0.3	0.6	0.1	−0.1	0.0	0.0
355 Rubber products	−0.4	1.1	−0.1	−0.2	−0.2	−0.5
36A Nonmetal min. prod.	−0.2	0.5	0.0	−0.2	−0.1	−0.7
362 Glass products	−0.4	0.6	−0.1	−0.3	−0.2	−0.3
371 Iron, steel	−0.6	0.9	−0.2	−0.4	−0.4	−1.8
372 Nonferrous metals	−0.6	0.4	−0.2	−0.4	−0.3	−1.0
381 Metal products	−0.5	0.6	−0.1	−0.2	−0.2	−2.7
382 Nonelec. machinery	−0.7	1.1	−0.2	−0.3	−0.3	−7.1
383 Electrical machinery	−1.0	1.0	−0.5	−0.6	−0.5	−10.0
384 Transport equipment	−0.8	1.7	−0.3	−0.4	−0.4	−9.2
38A Misc. mfrs.	−0.8	0.7	−0.2	−0.3	−0.3	−6.7
2 Mining, quarrying	−0.5	0.8	−0.1	−0.2	−0.2	−1.3
4 Utilities	0.5	−0.4	0.0	−0.1	−0.1	−1.2
5 Construction	4.5	4.3	0.1	−0.1	−0.0	3.2
6 Wholesale trade	6.1	3.6	0.0	−0.1	−0.0	−2.7
7 Transportation	40.4	34.9	1.0	0.7	0.8	53.9
8 Financial services	14.2	13.5	0.1	0.0	0.1	7.3
9 Personal services	16.9	18.5	0.0	0.0	−0.0	−0.4
Total	4.2	3.9	0.0	−0.2	0.0	0.0

Note: see Table 10.3.

Table 10.5. *Simulation 2: services; sectoral effects on Europe of the Uruguay Round (percentage change)*

					Change in employment	
Sector	Exports (1)	Imports (2)	Output (3)	No. firms (4)	Percent (5)	1,000s (6)
1 Agriculture	−0.1	0.3	0.0	0.0	−0.0	−1.2
310 Food	−0.1	0.3	0.0	−0.1	−0.1	−2.9
321 Textiles	−0.2	0.3	0.0	−0.1	−0.1	−1.5
322 Clothing	0.0	−0.6	0.1	0.0	0.0	0.0
323 Leather products	0.0	0.6	0.0	−0.1	−0.1	−0.1
324 Footwear	0.1	−0.7	0.1	0.0	0.0	0.0
331 Wood products	−0.1	0.0	0.1	−0.1	−0.1	−0.4
332 Furniture, fixtures	0.0	−0.1	0.0	−0.1	−0.1	−0.5
341 Paper products	−0.1	0.1	0.0	−0.1	−0.1	−0.9
342 Printing, publishing	−0.2	0.1	0.1	−0.1	−0.0	−0.6
35A Chemicals	−0.2	0.3	0.0	−0.1	−0.1	−3.3
35B Petroleum products	0.1	0.2	0.1	0.0	0.0	0.0
355 Rubber products	−0.1	0.7	0.0	−0.1	−0.1	−0.3
36A Nonmetal min. prod.	−0.1	0.4	0.1	−0.1	−0.1	−0.9
362 Glass products	−0.2	0.4	0.0	−0.1	−0.1	−0.2
371 Iron, steel	−0.1	0.4	0.0	−0.1	−0.1	−1.7
372 Nonferrous metals	−0.2	0.5	0.0	−0.2	−0.1	−0.7
381 Metal products	−0.1	0.2	0.0	−0.1	−0.1	−1.7
382 Nonelec. machinery	−0.2	0.5	0.0	−0.1	−0.1	−4.4
383 Electrical machinery	−0.2	0.3	0.0	−0.1	−0.1	−3.7
384 Transport equipment	−0.2	0.6	0.0	−0.1	−0.1	−4.6
38A Misc. mfrs.	−0.2	0.2	−0.1	−0.1	−0.1	−2.3
2 Mining, quarrying	−0.2	0.3	−0.1	−0.1	−0.1	−1.0
4 Utilities	0.6	0.4	0.0	−0.1	−0.1	−0.7
5 Construction	3.3	7.6	0.1	−0.1	−0.0	−4.4
6 Wholesale trade	6.1	6.7	0.0	0.0	−0.0	−2.7
7 Transportation	36.8	38.5	0.4	0.2	0.3	24.4
8 Financial services	7.9	15.8	0.0	0.0	−0.0	−0.5
9 Personal services	17.2	14.7	0.1	0.0	0.0	16.9
Total	3.2	3.3	0.0	−0.1	0.0	0.0

Note: see Table 10.3.

Table 10.6 *Simulation 2: services; sectoral effects on Japan of the Uruguay Round (percentage change)*

					Change in employment	
Sector	Exports (1)	Imports (2)	Output (3)	No. firms (4)	Percent (5)	1,000s (6)
1 Agriculture	1.1	−0.8	0.1	0.0	0.2	7.3
310 Food	1.2	−1.1	0.0	−0.1	−0.0	−0.4
321 Textiles	1.2	−1.6	0.4	0.2	0.2	1.8
322 Clothing	2.5	−2.7	0.7	0.4	0.5	3.1
323 Leather products	1.6	−1.3	0.4	0.2	0.3	0.2
324 Footwear	2.5	−2.5	0.6	0.4	0.4	0.2
331 Wood products	1.4	−1.1	0.4	0.2	0.3	1.1
332 Furniture, fixtures	1.6	−1.7	0.4	0.2	0.2	0.5
341 Paper products	1.4	−1.2	0.4	0.2	0.2	0.8
342 Printing, publishing	1.2	−1.2	0.1	−0.1	−0.0	−0.1
35A Chemicals	1.2	−1.4	0.4	0.2	0.3	1.4
35B Petroleum products	1.1	−0.5	0.2	0.2	0.2	0.1
355 Rubber products	1.3	−1.4	0.5	0.2	0.3	0.6
36A Nonmetal min. prod.	1.2	−0.9	0.2	0.0	0.0	0.1
362 Glass products	1.3	−1.4	0.4	0.2	0.3	0.3
371 Iron, steel	1.2	−1.4	0.5	0.3	0.4	1.7
372 Nonferrous metals	1.8	−0.6	0.8	0.6	0.7	1.1
381 Metal products	1.3	−1.5	0.2	0.0	0.1	1.0
382 Nonelec. machinery	1.6	−1.8	0.6	0.3	0.3	6.0
383 Electrical machinery	2.3	−2.6	0.9	0.7	0.7	17.5
384 Transport equipment	1.7	−2.0	0.6	0.3	0.3	3.5
38A Misc. mfrs.	2.1	−1.7	0.8	0.5	0.6	7.1
2 Mining, quarrying	2.3	−0.4	1.5	1.3	1.4	0.8
4 Utilities	0.7	−0.5	0.2	0.1	0.1	0.4
5 Construction	4.7	2.5	0.1	−0.2	−0.1	−5.7
6 Wholesale trade	6.2	2.1	0.1	−0.1	0.0	2.4
7 Transportation	33.8	34.5	−0.7	−1.0	−0.9	−33.2
8 Financial services	10.3	15.5	−0.1	−0.2	−0.1	−4.8
9 Personal services	15.0	17.0	−0.1	−0.2	−0.1	−14.6
Total	4.2	4.2	0.2	0.2	0.0	0.0

Note: see Table 10.3.

more than 1 percent, however. The largest absolute reductions in US sectoral employment (not reported in the table) are in personal, community and social services (−12,500), clothing (−8,500), iron and steel products (−3,800), and textiles (−3,500), while the absolute largest increases are in agriculture (9,600), transportation services (8,100), transportation equipment (5,700), electrical machinery (4,700), and food and related products (3,900).

Because of the size of the United States and its relatively low initial tariffs, these percentage changes are as small as those reported for any of the other countries/regions, but similar results appear especially for Europe and Japan. Somewhat larger changes are reported for the small industrialized countries/regions of Canada, where employment in leather and footwear both decline by more than 4 percent, and Australia/New Zealand, where employment levels in textiles and electrical machinery both decline by almost 4 percent and employment in miscellaneous manufactures increases by almost 4 percent. The largest percentage employment changes are found in the Asian newly industrial economies and the group of developing other trading nations, but even here the percentage changes in sectoral employment remain in the single digits. Recalling that the results of the Uruguay Round are to be phased in over a period of up to ten years, these employment changes suggest only minimal disruption to domestic labor markets.

One pattern that emerges in the results for simulation 1 is that employment would decline in most of the services sectors in most countries. This result arises naturally in the simulation, since it holds services-trade barriers constant while reducing tariffs throughout most of the rest of the economy. We have observed this result in previous models that did not include "tradable" services. The presence of tariffs on industrial goods in most countries of the world acts much as a tax would in a closed economy, and the reduction in these tariffs is thus similar to a cut in production taxes. Not surprisingly, resources are drawn into these sectors – in this case, industrial products – and away from the sectors in which liberalization has not occurred. Exceptions do of course emerge, but it is interesting that this phenomenon appears in our results even in the presence of trade in services.

Simulation 2

Turning now to the results of hypothetical liberalization of trade in services in simulation 2, sectoral results are reported for the United States, Europe, and Japan in tables 10.4 to 10.6. For each country/region, the percentage changes in total exports and imports are reported in columns 1 and 2. The percentage changes in sectoral output and number of firms are listed in columns 3 and 4. One can determine the change in output per firm, and thus the extent to which economies of scale have been realized, by subtracting column 4 from column 3. The percent and absolute changes in employment are listed in columns 5 and 6. The sectoral results for the remaining countries/regions and for simulation 3 are available from the authors on request.[17]

This simulation assumes a 25 percent reduction in the "guesstimated" *ad valorem* tariff equivalents for the services sectors, ISIC 5–9. Recall that the transportation sector (ISIC 7) had the greatest level of protection, that construction (ISIC 5) and wholesale and retail trade (ISIC 6) had the lowest levels of protection, and that financial services (ISIC 8) and personal, community, and social services (ISIC 9) had levels of protection that fell in between. In the United States, total exports would decline in the goods sectors by relatively small percentages, but would increase significantly in the services sectors (table 10.4).[18] Total imports would rise in almost all sectors. Employment would increase in the transportation services sector (53,900) and in financial services (7,300); it would fall in almost all other sectors.

Very similar results are shown for Europe in table 10.5. Again it is the transportation sector, with its high assumed level of protection, that experiences by far the greatest expansion of both trade and employment. Trade again expands substantially in both financial services and personal services, but in Europe it is the personal services sector that expands substantially in absolute terms rather than financial services. As in the United States, services liberalization causes the industrial sectors to experience small percentage declines in both exports and employment, while imports in these sectors expand slightly.

The story is somewhat different in Japan (table 10.6). Here too both exports and imports expand significantly in all of the services sectors, but in industrial products Japan's exports also expand and imports contract. The reason for this may be inferred from the changes in output and employment, both of which contract in most of Japan's services sectors. Evidently Japan's comparative advantage is not in services.

The results for the United States (and the other countries and regions) suggest that services-trade liberalization would expand output and trade in the services sectors. What is more surprising, however, is that employment in many of these sectors would contract. The reason is that increases in output per firm would accompany the expansion in trade, and thus that fewer workers would be able to produce greater output.

Services trade and goods trade also show relationships, although not consistent, across countries. In the United States, Europe, and the newly industrial economies of Asia, the expansion in services trade would reduce the export of goods, but would expand the export of goods in all of the other countries and regions. Services trade can thus substitute for goods trade or it can complement it, depending, presumably, on the roles that services play as inputs into the production of goods. (Input variables for the model come from the various national input–output tables.)

Simulation 3

This simulation combines the results of the liberalization of industrial products and services that were derived under simulations 1 and 2. Their joint effects can be determined by simple addition. Tables for the results of simulation 3 are available from the authors on request.

Appendix A Developing data on "tradable" services

As already mentioned, we are applying our Michigan CGE model to tradable services for the first time, having previously treated services as nontradable. To do so, we sought to develop a set of 35×35 matrixes of bilateral trade in the services sectors, ISIC 5–9, for the thirty-four model countries (plus rest of world) with a 1990 base year.[19] This was a problem because of the unavailability of sufficiently disaggregated data. That is, while there is published information for 1990 for the global services trade for all the countries of the model, the data available bilaterally and by sector are seriously deficient.

In order to construct the five bilateral services trade matrixes that we needed for modeling purposes, we first assembled a set of thirty-five-element vectors of total exports and imports for each of the five services sectors. We used these vectors as row and column totals of our target bilateral vectors and applied the rAs method to scale an underlying reference matrix to match.[20] For this purpose, we used our 35×35 data for 1990 bilateral merchandise trade as the underlying matrix that serves as the initial estimate of bilateral flows.[21] This yielded a set of 35×35 matrixes of bilateral trade flows for each of the five services sectors.

The next step was to take advantage of more detailed bilateral services-trade data where available. Here, we had data assembled by the European Community's Statistical Office for intra-EC services trade and EC trade with the EFTA countries, the United States, and Japan. The EC merchandise trade data gave us total exports and imports for each EC member with one another. This allowed us to apply the rAs method to the smaller EC matrix separately and then to overlay the larger matrix with the result.[22] Likewise, EC merchandise trade with the EFTA countries, the United States, and Japan allowed us to scale those trade flows properly. We also included in the final matrix some bilateral services-trade data for the United States that were published in the *U.S. Survey of Current Business*. The five ISIC sectoral 35×35 bilateral services-trade matrixes, as well as additional technical details on their construction, are available from the authors on request.

Notes

1. Europe includes the fifteen members of the European Union plus Norway and Switzerland; the newly industrial economies of Asia include Hong Kong, South Korea, Singapore, and Taiwan (China); and the other major trading nations include Argentina, Brazil, Chile, Colombia, India, Israel, Turkey, and Venezuela.
2. This is the first time that we have treated all twenty-nine model sectors as tradable; doing so enables us to analyze the effects and interaction of the liberalization of both merchandise trade and trade in services.
3. Brown and Stern (1989) discuss issues pertaining to modeling market structure, in using different imperfectly competitive market structures to analyze the economic effects of the Canada–United States Trade Agreement. The model in this chapter uses a structure of monopolistic competition for all manufacturing and service sectors, based on Helpman and Krugman (1985). Firms do not face entry barriers, and each produces a different variety of a good/service at a fixed cost and constant marginal cost for primary and intermediate inputs. In his conference commentary, Sherman Robinson pointed out that our treatment of monopolistic competition may not be appropriate for all sectors and may thus exaggerate the importance of the effects of scale and variety. In principle, we could allow for different market structures in the sectors for our model countries/regions. But doing so would require considerable empirical detail that is not readily available.
4. We use a Dixit–Stiglitz (1977) aggregation function to enter varieties into both utility and production functions, with the implication that greater variety reduces cost and increases utility. As discussed in Brown, Deardorff, and Stern (1996), this structure introduces potential market instability, since the expansion of an industry with the entry of a firm adds varieties and thus makes the product of the industry more desirable as a whole. To avoid this instability, we have introduced a damping parameter that reduces the beneficial effects of variety by 50 percent from the original Dixit–Stiglitz formulation.
5. Using completely up-to-date input–output tables is problematic, given ongoing changes in technology and productivity that would alter the input–output coefficients for particular sectors. Our CGE model, however, relies primarily on the intermediate input-value shares and the shares of primary factors as data. These shares tend to be more stable over time than physical input requirements. For more discussion of this point, see Deardorff and Stern (1990).
6. The sectoral data for merchandise trade, production, and employment come primarily from United Nations sources and to a lesser extent from national sources. The model parameters are constructed from the trade and input–output data for the countries included in the model and from published studies of trade and capital/labor substitution elasticities. More details on the data on agricultural and industrial tariffs and trade and trade barriers for services are provided in the following section. (See also Deardorff and Stern 1990.)

7. In effect, then, we do not distinguish among workers according to their skill characteristics, and, as such, we do not assess how Uruguay Round liberalization will affect the wages and employment of different skill groups.
8. In the absence of tariff equivalents, we model nontariff barriers as percentage of trade subject to those barriers, based primarily on the nontariff barrier inventory data assembled by the UNCTAD. The model uses the nontariff barrier coverage ratios to dampen the effects of tariff reductions undertaken when the nontariff barriers are assumed to remain in place. It is important to emphasize that these measures of nontariff barrier trade coverage are *not* the same as the tariff equivalents of the nontariff barriers. Deardorff and Stern (1990, pp. 23–25) provide a more detailed discussion of this issue.
9. The GATT IDB provides detailed, line-item information for the pre- and post-Uruguay Round tariff rates based on the HS tariff classification. Since we have twenty-three tradable-goods sectors for each country and region in our model, we aggregated the detailed tariff lines using own-country imports as weights, based on a concordance between the HS and our sectoral classification derived from the ISIC codes. We recognize that own-country import weights introduce a downward bias into the aggregate measures since higher tariffs will induce less trade, but we have not corrected for this bias. (The sectoral tariff rates used in our computational analysis are available upon request.)
10. In addition to the tariffication of agricultural protection, the Uruguay Round calls for a 36 percent reduction in export subsidies by industrial countries and a 24 percent reduction by developing countries, as well as a 20 percent reduction in input subsidies by industrial countries and a 13 percent reduction by developing countries.
11. The four modes of supply are cross-border delivery; consumption abroad; commercial presence (FDI); and the temporary entry of persons (professional, technical, sales personnel, and so on).
12. When nontariff barriers remain in place during other trade liberalization, their presence is felt as a quantitative restriction that reduces the response of trade to price changes. When nontariff barriers are removed, this can best be modeled as the elimination of a tariff of equivalent size, capturing the restrictiveness of the nontariff barrier, but in the absence of any restraint on quantitative responses. That is, elimination of the nontariff barriers mimics what is actually being attempted in agriculture: the conversion of import quotas and of the restrictions into tariff equivalents, which are then removed.
13. Details on the absolute dollar changes in welfare for the individual scenarios are available on request.
14. We also ran a simulation for agricultural liberalization. We had expected that reductions in agricultural tariff equivalents would increase the economic welfare of agricultural exporting countries. But the simulation indicated that welfare would decline in the United States and Australia/New Zealand; although output and employment in the agricultural sector would increase significantly in these countries, output and employment in practically all the manufacturing and services sectors would decline. Because the contraction in

output in manufacturing and services would exceed the decline in the number of firms, negative scale effects would occur, thus reducing economic welfare. In Japan and the newly industrial economies of Asia, where an apparently sizable reduction in agricultural tariff rates occurred, output and employment in agriculture would decline, but would increase in all other sectors. Our model is thus rather sensitive to specialization and scale effects when large changes in protection occur in such important sectors as agriculture. This issue will be addressed in our future research. (The results of our agriculture simulation, not reported in this chapter, are available from the authors on request.)

15. Our agricultural liberalization simulation suggested this result for the United States and Australia/New Zealand.
16. Recall that total employment is assumed constant in each country in these simulations.
17. As are the results for variables other than employment for simulation 1.
18. Due to space limitations, we do not report the results for the other countries and regions. They are available on request.
19. We thus have services data for 1990 for these ISIC sectors covering both gross output and employment as well as exports and imports. The ratios of services trade to gross output are relatively small, reflecting the fact that most services sector output is confined to domestic markets.
20. Technical details relating to the rAs method can be found in Bacharach (1970).
21. It should be pointed out that bilateral goods and services flows may not correspond well in cases in which countries are relatively more specialized in one or the other.
22. We overlaid the larger matrix with these figures, rather than scaling them to better match the results of the larger rAs procedure, for two reasons. First, we had much more confidence in the quality of the selective bilateral trade data from the European Union and other sources than we had in the total overall trade flows that came primarily from balance-of-payments sources. Therefore we were unwilling to scale the bilateral flows to make them consistent with the total flows. In addition, we understood that the bilateral trade measurements in many cases included types of services trade that are relatively new and that are likely to be absent from the balance-of-payments-based data. Because we believe that these new types of trade are likely to be concentrated among the industrial countries, we also chose not to scale the other bilateral flows (up) to include them. Instead, therefore, we simply used the bilateral flows directly whenever they were available and used the (partial) results of applying the rAs procedure to the total flows whenever they were not.

References

Bacharach, Michael 1970. *Biproportional Matrices and Input–Output Change*. Cambridge: Cambridge University Press.

Brown, Drusilla K., and Robert M. Stern 1989. "Computable General Equilibrium Estimates of the Gains from U.S.–Canadian Trade Liberalization." In Thomas Hyclak, and Robert J. Thornton, eds., *Economic Aspects of Regional Trading Arrangements*. London: Harvester Wheatsheaf.

Brown, Drusilla K., Alan V. Deardorff, and Robert M. Stern. 1992a. "A North American Free Trade Agreement: Analytical Issues and a Computational Assessment." *The World Economy* 15: 15–29.

1992b. "North American Economic Integration." *Economic Journal* 102: 1507–18.

1993. "Protection and Real Wages: Old and New Trade Theories and their Empirical Counterparts." Discussion Paper 331, Research Forum on International Economics, University of Michigan, May.

1996. "Computational Analysis of the Economic Effects of an East Asian Preferential Trading Bloc," *Journal of the Japanese and International Economies* 10.

Brown, Drusilla K., Alan V. Deardorff, David L. Hummels, and Robert M. Stern 1994. "An Assessment of Extending NAFTA to Other Major Trading Countries in South America." Ann Arbor: University of Michigan, mimeo.

Deardorff, Alan V., and Robert M. Stern 1990. *Computational Analysis of Global Trading Arrangements*. Ann Arbor: University of Michigan Press.

Dixit, Avinash K., and Joseph E. Stiglitz 1977. "Monopolistic Competition and Optimum Product Diversity." *American Economic Review* 67: 297–308.

Helpman, Elhanan, and Paul R. Krugman 1985. *Market Structure and Foreign Trade: Increasing Returns, Imperfect Competition, and the International Economy*. Cambridge, Mass.: MIT Press.

Hoekman, Bernard 1995. "Tentative First Steps: An Assessment of the Uruguay Round Agreement on Services." In W. Martin and L. A. Winters, eds., *The Uruguay Round and the Developing Economies*. World Bank Discussion Paper 307. Washington, DC: World Bank.

Ingco, Merlinda 1995. "Agricultural Trade Liberalization in the Uruguay Round: One Step Forward, One Step Back?" Supplemental Paper to the World Bank Uruguay Round Conference, January 26–27.

Martin, Will 1994a. "Draft Notes on Tariff Bindings as Trade Liberalization." Mimeo (May).

1994b. "Methodology for Evaluating Tariff Reductions in the Round." Mimeo (August).

Martin, Will, and Joseph Francois 1994. "Bindings and Rules as Trade Liberalization." Presented at the Festschrift Conference, "Quiet Pioneering: Robert M. Stern and his International Economic Legacy," University of Michigan, Ann Arbor, November 18–20.

CHAPTER 43†

Methods of Measurement of Nontariff Barriers

Alan V. Deardorff
and Robert M. Stern

In order to quantify the particular occurrence of an NTB, it is probably best to look at the specific details of the implementation of that NTB. For example, a quota usually permits an announced quantity of imports of a certain type, so that an analysis of the quota should begin with direct information pertaining to that quantity. Or to take another example, a variable levy is defined in terms of a specified price of an imported good, and that price provides the most direct information about what the levy entails. In these and other cases a good deal of additional work may be required, however, to translate this direct information into a useful form that can be understood and compared to other forms of trade intervention. Nonetheless this direct information still provides the most obvious starting point for an empirical analysis.

There are serious disadvantages to this direct approach, however, especially when one is looking for a broad measure of NTBs in general and not just of a specific type. First, the direct approach only captures those NTBs that have been identified. If a country or industry makes use of a particular form of NTB that the investigator does not take into account or include in the analysis, then trade may appear much freer than it actually is. Second, even for those NTBs that are included, it is extremely difficult to process the diverse direct information that is available on each NTB in a way that will be comparable across NTBs and thus permit them to be added up to obtain a total measure of trade interference. Third, if more than one NTB is present in a given industry, it is conceivable that the presence of one reduces the effects of another, so that an analysis of each of them separately may lead to an overstatement of their total effects. More generally, in evaluating overall levels of protection by NTBs, general equilibrium effects are bound to matter, such as the effects of barriers in one sector on trade in another, and the effects of all together on exchange rates. Thus even though direct information about NTBs is likely to be the most accurate available, it does not necessarily provide a good starting point for a general analysis.

Fortunately there exist a variety of more general approaches that can bypass some of these difficulties, though admittedly while introducing new ones. The various general methods that have been used or attempted for measuring NTBs can be classified as follows: *frequency-type measures* based upon inventory listings of observed NTBs that apply to particular countries, sectors, or categories of trade; *price-comparison measures* calculated in terms of tariff

† This chapter is taken with permission from Alan V. Deardorff and Robert M. Stern, 1998, Measurement of Nontariff Barriers (University of Michigan Press, USA), Chapter 3, pp. 11–45; Notes, pp. 82–87; and Appendix 3, pp. 105–122.

equivalents or price relatives; ***quantity-impact measures*** based upon econometric estimates of models of trade flows; and measures of ***equivalent nominal rates of assistance***. We shall discuss each of these in turn. Thereafter, we consider some special purpose methods that may be useful in assessing some of the characteristics of NTBs that were identified in the preceding chapter. We shall then return to NTB-specific methods when we discuss several types of NTBs themselves. Finally, we discuss briefly issues arising in measurement of the *effects* of NTBs in which case measurement of the size of NTBs is a key input.

An issue that arises in common for all of these methods is how to aggregate the measurements once they have been obtained for disaggregated product categories. Most common, but also in many ways least satisfactory, is to use own-country imports as weights in calculating weighted averages of the NTBs in a larger product group. The obvious drawback is that the most restrictive NTBs reduce imports to zero, and therefore do not show up at all in the aggregate. Own-country production levels avoid this problem, but are subject to the opposite bias in that protective NTBs stimulate domestic production above the levels that would otherwise obtain. Preferable for many purposes, but also requiring data that may not be available, is to use world production levels or world trade as weights.

General Methods for Measuring the Presence or Size of NTBs

Frequency-Type Measures

In appendix 1, as already mentioned, we provide a list and brief description of the major types of existing NTBs and related policies. Since the detailed information collected especially by UNCTAD for its database on trade control measures is commodity/sector and country specific,[17] it is possible to construct a variety of measures that indicate the frequency of occurrence of NTBs.[18] Such measures may be unweighted, or they may be weighted by imports or by production. Examples are provided in tables 3.1 and 3.2 for the United States, the 12-member European Union (EU), Japan, and Canada for 1988 and 1993.[19]

Table 3.1 contains Frequency Ratios and Import Coverage Ratios for: "All" NTBs and "Hard core" NTBs;[20] Quantitative Restrictions (QRs), including export restraints, non-automatic licensing, and other QRs; and Price Control Measures (PCMs), including variable charges, antidumping/countervailing duties (AD/CVDs) and voluntary export price restraints (VEPRs), and other PCMs. The frequencies are calculated first for applicable Harmonized System (HS) commodity categories that were subject to some identifiable NTB in 1988 and 1993. The number of product categories subject to NTBs is then expressed as a percentage of the total number of product categories in each HS group. This is referred to as the Frequency Ratio (F). The

TABLE 3.1. Pervasiveness of Different Types of NTBs in OECD Countries in 1988 and 1993: the "Quad" (Percent)

	United States				EU-12				Japan				Canada			
	Frequency Ratio (F)		Import Coverage Ratio (IC)		Frequency Ratio (F)		Import Coverage Ratio (IC)		Frequency Ratio (F)		Import Coverage Ratio (IC)		Frequency Ratio (F)		Import Coverage Ratio (IC)	
NTB Categories	1988	1993	1988	1993	1988	1993	1988	1993	1988	1993	1988	1993	1988	1993	1988	1993
All NTBs	25.5	22.9	16.7	17.0	26.6	23.7	13.2	11.1	8.3	7.7	8.5	8.0	11.1	11.0	5.7	4.5
"Hard core" NTBs	25.5	22.9	16.6	17.0	25.2	21.8	10.9	9.0	7.6	7.0	7.2	3.6	8.9	8.2	4.1	2.5
Quantitative Restrictions (QRs)	20.4	18.1	13.7	10.2	19.5	17.2	7.8	7.1	7.3	6.7	6.5	2.8	6.6	6.8	3.0	1.7
Export Restraints	19.5	13.1	12.9	10.1	15.5	13.9	6.2	5.6	0.3	0.3	0.2	0.2	4.8	5.8	1.2	1.4
Non-automatic licensing	0.0	0.0	0.0	0.0	4.4	3.5	2.2	1.7	5.7	5.7	1.0	1.0	2.6	0.2	0.7	0.0
Other QRs	6.6	5.6	1.1	0.2	0.2	0.2	0.1	0.0	1.6	1.0	5.5	1.8	0.8	0.8	1.1	0.3
Price Control Measures (PCMs)	17.8	10.8	3.6	7.3	12.4	8.4	6.0	3.5	0.3	0.3	0.7	0.8	2.4	1.4	1.1	0.8
Variable charges	0.1	0.0	0.1	0.0	6.3	5.4	1.8	1.5	0.3	0.3	0.7	0.8	0.0	0.0	0.0	0.0
AD/CVs and VEPRs	17.8	10.8	3.4	7.3	2.6	1.9	2.2	1.3	0.0	0.0	0.0	0.0	2.4	1.4	1.1	0.8
Other PCMs	0.0	0.0	0.0	0.0	4.3	1.1	2.1	0.6	0.0	0.0	0.0	0.0	0.0	0.0	0.0	0.0

Note: "All NTBs" include: price control measures; finance measures; automatic licensing measures; quantity control measures; and monopolistic measures. "Core" NTBs, which are listed by sector in table 2, encompass "All NTBs" except for finance measures and monopolistic measures. "Hard core" NTBs include QRs and PCMs.

Source: OECD (1995, table 4.1).

Import Cover age Ratios (IC) in table 3.1 are calculated by determining the value of imports of each commodity subject to NTBs, aggregating by applicable HS commodity group, and expressing the value of imports covered as a percentage of total imports in theHS commodity group. The import weights are based on own-country imports for 1988 or an adjacent year. The 1988 import weights are used for the 1993 calculations. A sectoral breakdown for the "Core" NTBs is provided in table 3.2, which includes calculation of unweighted Frequency Ratios (F) and Production (i.e., gross output) weighted Frequency Ratios (PF).[21]

The results reported in table 3.1 suggest that the F and IC ratios for the EU-12, Japan, and Canada declined from 1988 to 1993. The F ratios for the United States declined, but some of the IC ratios increased. It is also evident that QR measures are more commonly used than PCMs in the "Quad" countries, and that there are differences among the countries in their reliance on particular types of NTBs. It appears in table 3.2 that "Core" NTBs are concentrated especially in: agricultural and food products; textiles and apparel; chemicals; nonmetallic mineral products; basic metals; and fabricated metals.[22]

The NTB measures in tables 3.1 and 3.2 are useful primarily in directing attention to the frequency of occurrence of various types of NTBs and the trade/production coverage of NTBs for individual countries and product groups for a given year and through time to the extent that the data are kept continuously. These measures have a number of drawbacks, however. First, according to OECD (1996), the reporting of NTBs is somewhat uneven, and there may be problems arising from how NTBs are defined and the level and type of aggregation used in calculating commodity and sectoral ratios. Second, the F and IC/PF ratios do not provide any information on the possible deterrent effects that NTBs may have upon the pricing or quantity decisions of foreign exporters. Third, the F and IC/PF ratios refer primarily to border measures and thus ignore the entire range of internal governmental measures and the restrictive actions of imperfectly competitive firms that we discussed earlier. Finally, and most importantly, the frequency-type measures provide no information on the economic impact that NTBs may have on prices, production, consumption, and international trade.[23] Worse, they may be positively misleading in this regard, if a large number of relatively small or non-binding NTBs divert attention from a smaller number in other industries or countries that have more serious effects.

Price-Comparison Measures

As indicated in figure 2.1, the effect of any NTB can be gauged in terms of its impact on the domestic price in comparison to some reference price. Because the price impact is a general property of NTBs, such a price comparison can pick up the net effects of all NTBs that are present in a market, without it be-

TABLE 3.2. Pervasiveness of "Core" NTBs in OECD Countries in 1988 and 1993: the "Quad" (Percent)

		United States				EU-12				Japan				Canada			
		Frequency Ratio (F)		Production-weighted Frequency Ratio (PF)		Frequency Ratio (F)		Production-weighted Frequency Ratio (PF)		Frequency Ratio (F)		Production-weighted Frequency Ratio (PF)		Frequency Ratio (F)		Production-weighted Frequency Ratio (PF)	
ISIC	Description	1988	1993	1988	1993	1988	1993	1988	1993	1988	1993	1988	1993	1988	1993	1988	1993
1	Agriculture, Forestry, Fishing	5.5	3.6	-	-	20.6	14.9	-	-	5.9	5.2	-	-	6.0	4.1	-	-
2	Mining and Quarrying	2.3	2.3	-	-	0.0	3.5	-	-	3.1	0.4	-	-	0.4	0.7	-	-
21	Coal Mining	0.0	0.0	-	-	0.0	0.0	-	-	-	-	-	-	8.3	0.0	-	-
22	Crude Petroleum	0.0	0.0	-	-	-	-	-	-	-	-	-	-	0.0	9.1	-	-
23	Metal Ore Mining	0.0	4.0	-	-	-	-			-	-	-	-	0.0	0.0	-	-
29	Other Mining	3.4	2.3	-	-	0.0	3.8	-	-	-	-	-	-	0.0	0.0	-	-
3	Manufacturing	27.3	24.7	17.2	17.9	26.2	22.8	7.7	6.0	7.9	7.4	2.1	1.8	9.4	8.8	8.2	6.8
31	Food, Beverages and Tobacco	14.5	12.1	18.4	15.8	50.7	44.2	0.0	0.0	11.2	6.7	10.8	7.9	14.2	11.4	26.2	22.8
32	Textiles and Apparel	82.6	69.9	84.1	71.8	73.8	76.8	66.5	79.5	21.3	21.4	20.1	20.1	35.2	41.5	40.2	41.6
33	Wood and Wood Products	3.5	0.6	3.9	0.7	0.0	0.0	0.0	0.0	0.0	0.0	0.0	0.0	1.8	3.2	2.4	4.3
34	Paper and Paper Products	1.3	1.3	1.5	1.5	2.7	0.4	1.2	2.6	0.0	0.0	0.0	0.0	1.1	1.2	1.5	1.7
35	Chemicals, Petroleum Products	8.7	5.8	8.6	7.0	5.4	5.1	2.4	5.7	0.8	0.7	1.0	0.8	1.5	0.3	1.8	0.4
36	Non-metallic Mineral Products	9.8	5.3	10.7	7.8	6.6	0.2	5.9	0.0	0.0	0.0	0.0	0.0	1.1	0.4	0.7	0.7
37	Basic Metal Industries	53.4	57.1	48.0	52.3	37.5	19.0	35.3	17.7	0.9	0.9	0.5	0.6	16.6	4.6	16.7	4.7
38	Fabricated Metal Products	10.2	13.8	14.8	20.1	4.1	2.3	4.4	1.8	0.0	0.0	0.0	0.0	1.4	1.4	0.8	0.6
39	Other Manufacturing	4.4	1.1	4.1	1.0	1.4	2.0	0.0	0.0	0.0	0.0	0.0	0.0	0.7	1.2	0.6	1.0
Total	**All Products**	**25.6**	**23.0**	**17.2**	**17.9**	**25.5**	**22.1**	**7.7**	**6.0**	**7.7**	**7.1**	**2.1**	**1.8**	**9.0**	**8.3**	**8.2**	**6.8**

Notes: "Core" NTBs exclude finance measures and monopolistic measures.
Source: OECD (1995, table 5.1).

ing necessary for the investigator to identify what those NTBs are. Thus price comparisons have provided the basis for much of the general empirical work that has tried to quantify them and not just identify where they occur.

We argued in connection with figure 2.1 that the purest measure of an NTB in the price dimension is one that compares p_0 with p_2. The first, p_0, is the price that would prevail without the NTB. The second, p_2, is the price that would prevail domestically in the presence of the NTB if the price paid to suppliers were to remain unchanged. However, because both of these prices are usually impossible to observe, actual measures of NTBs have focused instead on a comparison of the domestic and foreign prices in the presence of the NTB, p_1' and p_1. Letting *upper-case* letters represent the prices themselves, as opposed to their logarithms, these price comparisons are normally reported either as price relatives,

(1) $R = 100 \times P_1'/P_1$,

or as a percentage difference between the prices, comparable to a tariff,

(2) $T = 100 \times [P_1' - P_1]/P_1$.

In the latter form, depending on the particular prices used in the comparison, these measures are commonly referred to as *tariff equivalents, implicit tariffs, or implicit protective rates.*

1. Choosing Appropriate Prices. In order to apply this methodology it is necessary to identify the appropriate prices in data that are available. This is complicated largely because, at least at manageable levels of aggregation, goods of a particular "industry" that are imported into a country are seldom identical to other goods in that industry that are produced domestically. They may also differ from goods that are produced, sold, and perhaps traded elsewhere, abroad. Thus we may identify several different prices of the "good" in question, and these would not necessarily be equal to one another even if trade were perfectly free. It will be useful to give names to some of these prices[24]:

P_d^d—The price of the domestic substitutes for the imported good.

P_d^m—The price on the domestic market of the imported good itself.

P_d—The price of the good on the domestic market, independently of where it was produced; thus an index of P_d^d and P_d^m.

P_c^m—The (c.i.f.) invoice price of the imported good as paid by the domestic importer to the foreign exporter, inclusive of transport costs but excluding tariffs.

P_x^d—The invoice price received by an exporter of the good from the domestic country, exclusive of transport costs and export tax, if any.

In addition to all of these prices that relate to the domestic market, there is a comparable list for each other country of the world. These will be referred to in general with an asterisk (*) or with a country superscript.

Now we would argue that the appropriate prices to use in measuring an NTB are the domestic and invoice prices of the imported good, P_d^m and P_c^m. An example is given in table 3.3 for frozen chickens and frozen turkeys for Canada for 1980–85, taken from Moroz and Brown (1985, table D9). We recognize of course that it may be difficult to find adequate measures of P_d^m and P_c^m, depending on how general and aggregated is the analysis being conducted.[25] Thus domestic price measures typically do not distinguish domestically produced from imported goods. In this event, if P_d^m is not available, it may be necessary to use P_d instead. The "implicit tariff rate" may accordingly by calculated from the formula above for T but using P_d and P_i as the relevant prices:

(3) $IT^1 = 100 \times [P_d - P_c^m]/P_c^m$.

This is a valid measure of an NTB to the extent that the domestic and imported goods that are combined in P_d are perfect substitutes, so that they sell for the same price in the domestic market.[26] But in general, this measure has the serious disadvantage of incorporating information about the apparent substitutability of domestic and foreign goods. For example, a barrier that raises the domestic price of an import good by 10% may raise the price index in the domestic market by much less than that. This will happen if imports are only a small part of the market and if imports are also only a poor substitute for domestically produced goods in the same industry. Furthermore, if domestic varieties are of higher quality than imports, then this measure will find protection even if there is none. This method works best, then, for homogeneous products for which the invoice price of imports can either be observed directly, or constructed from the price on a unified world market.

In case the invoice prices of imports are also unavailable, an alternative is to make do with domestic prices only, but taken from a variety of countries:

(4) $IT^2 = 100 \times [P_d - P_d^*]/P_d^*$.

Here P_d^* may be either the domestic price in a particular foreign exporting country, in which case the measure may be of a bilateral NTB, or it may be the minimum domestic price among all foreign exporters. Thus, suppose that exporting firms are perfectly competitive or otherwise unable to price discriminate, and suppose also that all goods in the industry are perfect substitutes everywhere. Then domestic prices abroad will equal foreign export prices of the same goods, and this will be a valid method of measurement. However, this method will be even more subject to error from imperfect substitutability than the one described in the preceding paragraph, since both P_d and P_d^* will include prices of imperfect substitutes with which the traded good competes. In addition, if foreign suppliers can price discriminate between exports and their own domestic markets, P_d^* will overstate the prices of "dumped" imports and thus IT^2 will understate protection in the importing country. Finally, a basic difference between these two measures is that IT^2 includes transport costs while IT^1 does not.[27]

Examples of the first measure, in equation (3), are provided in table 3.4 for the United States for 1991 and 1993.[28] The results of the so-called price-gap measures for agricultural products may be considered reliable insofar as these products are reasonably homogeneous. The domestic prices used for motor vehicles and maritime transportation seem to us more problematic, however. Estimates of price-gap measures have also been made for several other OECD countries and will be discussed below.[29]

The second measure, in equation (4), can be illustrated in work by Campbell and Cossette (1994) noted in table 3.5. They compared Canadian domestic prices of such supply-managed products as dairy products and eviscerated chicken and turkey with constructed measures of reference prices for low-cost foreign suppliers, New Zealand and the United States. What is noteworthy about the results reported are the adjustments made to achieve comparability even for agricultural products that are ostensibly reasonably homogeneous.[30]

TABLE 3.3. Estimation of Tariff Equivalents for Poultry Products for Canada, 1980-1985

	1980	1981	1982	1983	1984	1985	Average
Estimation of Protection for Poultry Products[a]							
Price of Frozen Chickens[b]							
Canada[c]	70.4¢	91.0	88.8	94.7	103.9	92.4	90.2
U.S. (landed in Toronto)[d]	62.4	65.7	66.5	73.9	85.9	84.5	73.2
Estimate of Price Protection[e]	12.8%	38.5%	33.5%	28.2%	21.1%	9.4%	23.9%
Price of Frozen Turkeys[b]							
Canada[c]	91.7	111.0	115.4	110.3	118.6	132.7	113.3
U.S. (landed in Toronto)[d]	82.1	83.0	87.2	87.6	110.5	118.2	94.8
Estimate of Price Protection[e]	11.7%	33.7%	32.3%	25.9%	7.3%	12.3%	20.5%
Average Price Protection Provided to Poultry Product Producers[f]	12.3%	36.1%	32.9%	27.0%	14.2%	10.8%	22.2%

Notes:

[a]Tariff equivalent estimated by the price-comparison method.
[b]Price in cents per pound.
[c]Price in Toronto.
[d]Price in New York, in Canadian dollars, plus estimated transportation and processing costs.
[e]Estimated as difference between Canadian price and U.S. price, divided by U.S. price, measured in Canadian dollars and expressed in per cent.
[f]Average of estimates of price protection for chickens and turkeys.

Source: Adapted from Moroz and Brown (1985, table D9).

TABLE 3.4. Price-Gap Measures of U.S. Tariff Equivalents, by Sector, 1991 and 1993 (Percent)

Sector	1991	1993
Price-gap measures		
Agricultural sector[a]		
Sugar	124.8	93.7
Butter	26.9	20.8
Cheese	35.4	37.4
Dry/condensed mile products	60.3	60.3
Cream	60.3	60.3
Meat	6.5	5.0
Cotton	-	27.0
Motor vehicles[b]	-	0.4
Maritime transport (Jones Act)[c]	133.0	89.1

Notes:
[a]The price comparisons for the agricultural products were as follows. Sugar -- calculated as the difference between the U.S. price and the world price, inclusive of transport costs and import duties, expressed as a percentage of the world price; data from USDA, *Sugar and Sweetener: Situation and Outlook Yearbook*. Dairy products -- based on domestic and world price data collected by the USDA for whole milk powder, butter, and cheese; for dry/condensed milk products and cream, the price gap for whole milk powder was used as a proxy. Meat -- based on the "market price support" portion of the producer subsidy equivalent (PSE) calculated by the OECD, comparing Sioux Falls (U.S.) cutter prices with New Zealand milk cow prices, and weighted by imports from Australia and New Zealand. Cotton -- based on comparisons of U.S. domestic and world prices of Orleans/Texas "B" index cotton, including adjustments for transportation and marketing costs.
[b]Motor vehicles -- based on an estimated 1.5 percent additional increase above the industrywide U.S. price increase needed in Japanese autos to equate supply and demand in the presence of the auto import restraint; weighted by the percent of Japanese auto imports to total whole imports.
[c]Maritime transport -- calculated as the output-weighted average difference between the U.S. and world price for shipping "wet" and "dry" cargo; for wet cargo, the weighted differences are between the U.S. price for shipping Alaskan North Slope crude petroleum to the U.S. west coast and to the U.S. gulf coast and the average world price for comparable tanker shipments transported equal distances; a separate estimate from the literature was used for the tariff equivalent for dry cargo. Additional estimates of the price gap attributed to the Jones Act can be found in White (1988) and Francois et al. (1996, p. 186).

Sources: USITC (1993, 1995).

TABLE 3.5. Tariff Equivalents for Supply-Managed Products in Canada, 1979-1992

	1979	1988	1992
Dairy			
Cdn. Unit Value of Delivered Milk (C$/T)[a]	258.5	417.2	460.0
Reference Price (C$/T)[b]	136.3	187.2	174.4
Price Difference (C$/T)	122.2	230.2	285.6
Price Difference (%)	89.7	123.0	164.8

20 Measurement of Nontariff Barriers

Chicken			
Cdn. Price Eviscerated (C$/T)[c]	1,190.1	1,526.6	1,560.6
Reference Price (C$/T)[d]	1,004.5	1,286.6	1,221.8
Price Difference (C$/T)	185.6	258.0	338.7
Price Difference (%)	18.5	20.1	27.7
Turkey			
Cdn. Price Eviscerated (C$/T)[e]	1,490.8	1,817.8	1,732.1
Reference Price (C$/T)[f]	1,387.8	1,376.7	1,341.6
Price Difference (C$/T)	103.1	441.1	390.8
Price Difference (%)	7.4	32.0	29.1

[a]Includes fluid milk, industrial milk and cream.
[b]Based on New Zealand price, adjusted to reflect fat content, currency exchange and transportation charges to Canada.
[c]Based on average price for broiler chicken under 2.3 kgs. Data refer to Toronto live price to producer -- 1979 and 1988: *Poultry Market Review*, annual, table 6 - 1992; *Agri-food Perspectives*, July 1992, Agriculture Canada, table 12. Prices converted to an eviscerated basis.
[d]Based on average U.S. live price for 1979. For 1988 and 1992: USDA publication: "Situation and Outlook Report of Livestock and Poultry," May 1992, table 2. Prices adjusted to an eviscerated basis, and to reflect transportation charges to Canada and currency exchange.
[e]Based on average price for broiler turkey under 5.4 kgs. Data refer to Toronto live price to producer -- 1979 and 1988: *Poultry Market Review*, Annual, table 7 -- 1992: *Agri-food Perspectives,* July 1992, Agriculture Canada, table 12. Prices converted to eviscerated basis.
[f]Based on average U.S. live price for 1979. For 1988 and 1992: USDA publication: "Situation Outlook Report of Livestock and Poultry," May 1992, table 13. Prices adjusted to an eviscerated basis, and to reflect transportation charges to Canada and currency exchange.

Source: Adapted from Campbell and Cossette (1994, table 7).

2. Quota-Auction and Quota-Transfer Price Measures. In addition to the foregoing, we should also mention quota-auction and quota-transfer price measures, the latter of which have been calculated in connection with the Multifiber Arrangement (MFA). If rights to import or export under a quota are sold at auction, then the auction price becomes an obvious measure of the quota's restrictiveness. More commonly, as in the MFA, quotas are allocated directly to firms, but the firms are then allowed to transfer these quotas to other firms, and a market develops for their exchange. The market price of these quota-transfers conveys similar information to an auction price, and we will use the term "auction price" to encompass both.

The MFA can be characterized as a voluntary export restraint (VER) in which the import quotas are allocated to foreign suppliers. We have assumed thus far with respect to import quotas that the import licenses are allocated to competitive firms in the importing country, in which case measurement of the price effects of the NTB can be analyzed as already indicated. Alternatively, if the licenses are allocated to foreign suppliers, the import price becomes effectively the domestic price in the importing country, assuming that the foreign supplier captures all the rents involved. To measure the size of the NTB associated with the VER, we therefore need information on the price of the good in the exporting country $\left(P_d^*\right)$ and the auction price of the quota (A). The tariff equivalent of the VER is given by:

$$(5) \qquad IT^{3}_{VER} = 100 \times A/P_d^*$$

In interpreting equation (5), it should be noted that if the VER is not binding, the auction price of the quota should be zero. If the auction price is not zero, then the ostensibly non-binding quota is still having an effect.[31] Furthermore, if market conditions are imperfectly competitive, some of the rents may be captured by importers. The availability of appropriate data also poses serious problems of measurement, although as the name suggests, if the licenses are allocated by a formal and public auction, the auction prices may be public knowledge, making this one of the easiest NTBs to measure. More commonly, however, VERs are allocated directly to firms and measurement of A is problematic, requiring knowledge of the prices charged by these firms in both their domestic and foreign markets.

In some cases as noted, while no auction may be used to allocate the quota initially, a secondary market for the transfer of quota rights may be permitted. The market prices of these transfers may then be used in place of A. One should take care, however, to obtain a representative sample of transfer prices, since they may vary over time and space.

Table 3.6 gives examples of quota-transfer price measures for several types of U.S. imports of textile and apparel products under the MFA for 1991 and 1993. These measures rely heavily on estimates of Hong Kong export prices and quota-transfer prices. Application to other supplying countries is based on adjusting the Hong Kong data to take into account relative differences in labor costs and gross output per worker in the individual MFA product categories.[32]

TABLE 3.6. Quota-Auction Price Measures of U.S. Tariff Equivalents of Textiles and Apparel by Sector, 1991 and 1993 (Percent)

Sector	1991	1993
Quota-auction price measures		
Textiles:		
Broadwoven fabric mills	8.5	9.5
Narrow fabric mills	3.4	3.3
Yarn mills and textile finishing	5.1	3.1
Thread mills	4.6	2.2
Floor coverings	2.8	9.3
Felt and textile goods, n. e. c.	1.0	0.1
Lace and knit fabric goods	3.8	5.9
Coated fabrics, not rubberized	2.0	1.0
Tire cord and fabric	2.3	2.4
Cordage and twine	3.1	1.2
Nonwoven fabric	0.1	0.2
Apparel and fabricated textile products:		
Women's hosiery, except socks	5.4	2.3
Hosiery, n. e. c.	3.5	2.4
Apparel made from purchased materi-	16.8	19.9

22 Measurement of Nontariff Barriers

als		
Curtains and draperies	5.9	12.1
House furnishings, n. e. c.	8.3	13.9
Textile bags	5.9	9.0
Canvas and related products	6.3	5.2
Pleating, stitching, trimmings, and schiffli embroidery	5.2	7.6
Fabricated textile products, n. e. c.	9.2	0.6
Luggage	2.6	10.4
Women's handbags and purses	1.0	3.1

Notes: Tariff equivalents for U.S. imports from Hong Kong were estimated on the basis of average weekly Hong Kong quota prices paid by brokers, using information from International Business and Economic Research Corporation. For countries that do not allocate quota rights in public auctions, export prices were estimated from Hong Kong export prices, with adjustments for differences in labor costs and productivity. It was assumed that

$P_e^o = (W_o/W_{hk})\ (go_{hk}/go_o)P_e^{hk}$, where P_e^o $P_e^o = (W_o/W_{hk})(go_{hk}/go_o)P_e^{hk}$, where P_e^o is the export price of the other exporter country, W_o and W_{hk} are labor costs for apparel in other exporting countries and Hong Kong, go_o and go_{hk} are gross output per worker, and P_e^{hk} is the Hong Kong export price. Assuming that exports from all countries are subject to the same transportation costs and are perfect substitutes, the implied auction price from the other country, A^o, can then be inferred from that for Hong Kong, A^{hk}: $A^o = A^{hk} + P_e^{hk} - P_e^o$, or zero if this expression is negative. Trade weights were used for purposes of aggregation. See USITC (1995, pp. 3-5) for sources of data on labor costs and productivity.

Sources: USITC (1993, 1995).

There have been numerous estimates of the MFA quota tariff equivalents for other OECD countries, some of which will be noted in chapter 4. They are of course subject to the caveats already mentioned. We shall also discuss further aspects of VERs in our treatment of NTB-specific methods of measurement.

3. Measures of Equivalent Nominal Rates of Assistance. While our discussion thus far has focused mainly on border policies that restrict trade, those who have used these measurements for the purpose of estimating assistance to industry have had to take into account other domestic policies. A more comprehensive measure is therefore needed that can aggregate all of the different types of incentives or disincentives that may exist. Two such measures that may be calculated are: (1) the nominal rate of assistance on outputs (NRA); and (2) the nominal rate of assistance on materials (NRM) (intermediate inputs). The NRA of an industry reflects those policies, such as tariffs and other border measures, that raise the price of the industry's output. The NRM of an industry, in contrast, reflects those policies that raise the prices of inputs to the industry, thus taking account of policies in other industries and the input-output interactions among industries. An indication of the component policies included in the NRA and NRM measures by the Industry Commission of the Commonwealth of Australia and definitions of these measures are provided in appendix 2. The NRA and NRM, in turn, provide the basis for calculating the effective rate of assistance (ERA), which is analogous to the effective rate of protection (ERP) and is a measure of the structure of net incentives affecting particular sectors. Under certain specified assumptions, which we shall discuss in more detail below, measures of the ERA can be used to analyze how the structure of net incentives may affect the allocation of labor and capital among the sectors of an economy.

4. Conclusion. Price-comparison measures of tariff equivalents have an intuitive appeal, especially since they give the appearance of having the same properties as nominal tariff rates themselves. This is misleading, however, since, as our discussion suggests, there are some potentially serious conceptual as well as data problems that arise in the estimation and interpretation of tariff equivalents.

Quantity-Impact Measures

We noted in reference to figure 2.1 above that the shift of the import demand curve due to an NTB can be defined in either the price or the quantity dimension. This suggests that the measurement of this shift could also be accomplished by looking at quantities of imports, as an alternative to looking at prices. Indeed Jager and Lanjouw (1977) have argued that a quantity measure is preferable to a price measure in that it comes closer to telling us what we really want to know about the *effects* of an NTB: that is, *by how much it reduces trade*. They argue further that price measures such as tariff equivalents fail to provide this information, since the relationship between the price and quantity effects of an NTB is a complicated one involving all of the elasticities of demand, domestic supply, and foreign supply.[33] Thus a direct measure of the quantity reduction due to an NTB would be desirable, if only as a supplement to the information provided by prices.

Unfortunately, there does not seem to be any way of getting such a direct measure of the quantity effects of an NTB that would be analogous to the price impact measures just discussed. While the quantity that is imported under the NTB is observable, there is usually no other quantity against which to compare it. For particular NTBs, if it is known when they are and are not in effect, it may be possible to build a time-series econometric model of the imports that they cover and thus to estimate what imports would have been without the NTB. But this is an NTB-specific method, and we will discuss it below.[34]

A general approach to measurement of the quantity effects of NTBs is possible, however, using either a cross-commodity or a cross-country regression model to explain trade. Thus the object again is to estimate what trade would have been in the absence of NTBs and to compare this to the trade that actually does occur. To do so requires a satisfactory model of the determinants of trade, as well as data covering a sufficient variety of trading situations. The latter are needed in order to identify, or extrapolate to, a situation in which trade is at least approximately free.

The work that is relevant here stems from the substantial literature on the gravity model that has been developed over the years to investigate the interrelated questions of what determines the size of a nation's foreign sector and/or the flow of trade among or between countries. As Leamer and Stern (1970, pp.

151–52) note, the important determinants involve a nation's GNP, resource endowment, utility structure, and various resistance factors.[35] In the broadest sense, this research can be interpreted as an effort to understand the forces that shape comparative advantage and at the same time to account explicitly or implicitly for a variety of special factors that may diminish or augment a nation's trade.[36] Thus, what we are interested in are the effects of NTBs on trade.

There are several different approaches that have been used to provide the basis for econometric estimates of NTBs. These approaches can be characterized as being based on stylized or formal versions of the Heckscher–Ohlin, Helpman–Krugman, and gravity models of international trade. Essentially, all of these approaches attempt to measure NTBs, either by regarding residuals from the estimated regressions as representing NTBs or by using various dummy variables. That is, the intention is to reflect departures from comparative advantage and thus to identify industries and countries in which trade intervention may possibly diminish or augment trade performance. While it is useful to have such general evidence of the trade impact of policy interventions by industry and country, these approaches share some important drawbacks.[37]

First, by attributing to NTBs all departures of trade from what the included variables can explain, there is a tremendous burden on the model that is used to explain trade. Indeed, the worse is the model of trade flows, the greater—most likely—will be the estimates of NTBs, suggesting a considerable upward bias in their estimation.[38] Second, it can be argued that theoretical trade models are capable of determining patterns of trade only when a series of highly unrealistic assumptions are made. In their absence, such models can only determine patterns of trade in an average sense, and they are not adequate to the task of predicting trade exactly for particular industries and countries. Thus a departure of actual trade from what is predicted by a regression model may reflect only this indeterminacy and not the presence of NTBs. Third, these approaches can really only make comparisons among industries or countries. They cannot tell us how far trading patterns depart from free trade. For if NTBs restrict trade everywhere, that may be imbedded in the parameters of the regressions and will not be reflected in the residuals or coefficients of the dummy variables used to represent unusual circumstances. For these reasons, one should be very cautious in using the results based on estimates of trade models. At best, such estimates may be most helpful for identifying relative levels of nontariff protection across sectors and countries.[39]

Special Purpose Methods

Having reviewed a number of general procedures for measuring NTBs, it may be worth considering some alternative measures that may be promising and that could shed light on some of the particular issues raised in chapter 2 concerning the characteristics of NTBs. These alternative measures include: (1)

elasticity estimation; (2) determinants of variations in elasticity estimates; (3) variations in effects of NTBs over time; (4) binding of NTBs; and (5) risk characteristics of NTBs.[40]

1. Elasticity Estimation. We noted in discussing figure 2.1 that many NTBs are likely to reduce the elasticity of import demand. This suggests that it might be worthwhile to perform a time series estimation of import demand elasticities, in the aggregate or for individual commodities/sectors, using data from several countries and interactive country dummy variables in order to determine how these elasticities may differ across countries. This should provide an indication of the extent to which the price responsiveness of import demand is reduced by NTBs in some countries more than others. Such a measure could be quite general in its coverage, since it would include even cultural barriers and other institutional factors that may restrict trade.

2. Variations in Elasticity Estimates. There is a vast empirical literature in which import demand elasticities have been estimated. Most of the important efforts were surveyed some time ago in Stern, Francis, and Schumacher (1976) and in Goldstein and Khan (1984), but there have not been any more recent surveys. It would nonetheless be worthwhile to review the recent literature to compile the elasticity estimates that may exist for a variety of countries and industries and to use regression methods to explain the variations in these estimates in terms of country and industry characteristics.[41] The regression residuals would then provide another estimate of how the price responsiveness departs from what it would otherwise be, presumably again because of the general existence of NTBs.

3. Effects of NTBs over Time. Our discussion in connection with figure 2.1 was based upon given underlying demand and supply conditions. If these conditions change for any reason, and assuming the NTBs themselves remain intact, then the effects of the NTBs will be altered. In order to determine how these effects vary over time, it might be worth repeating any one or more of the methods noted above for a succession of years. This would apply as well if the NTBs themselves were to change over time.

4. Binding of NTBs. It would be desirable to know to what extent various restrictions are binding, and how this varies over time. This could be done by calculating either the permitted or potential level of imports and then comparing this with actual imports. The comparisons will be significant insofar as the effects of NTBs will surely depend on whether the NTBs are fully or partially binding or not binding at all.[42]

5. Risk characteristics of NTBs. It is widely acknowledged that in the past decade or more there has been an increase in the use of contingent or administered protection, in particular antidumping and countervailing duty actions. Trading firms may thus be confronted with uncertainty over whether they will be subject to NTBs and, if they are, what the size and impact may be. It would be worthwhile accordingly to determine if there are any indicators of the costs that firms face when there is uncertainty regarding the imposition of NTBs. For example, trading firms may adapt their behavior in light of the risks involved, and the question is how they do this and what the costs to them are.[43]

NTB-Specific Methods for Selected NTBs

We turn now to consider measurement problems for some of the most important types of NTBs. Our main objective is to determine the extent to which these NTBs will be adequately captured by the various methods of measurement discussed above. In addition, where possible, we will discuss NTB-specific methods of measurement that may be appropriate to these particular NTBs. To both of these ends, we will begin each case with a brief discussion of how each kind of NTB works, together with a simple theoretical analysis of it.

Before proceeding, we should mention one method of empirical analysis that is applicable to any kind of NTB, but that works only if you know what the NTB is. In many instances, particular NTBs are implemented at a given point in time. With that information alone it may be possible to identify the effects of the NTB just by observing how the price or quantity of imports change at the time of implementation. Or, more elaborately if data are available, one can do a time-series econometric analysis for the periods in which the NTB is in place.[44] Either way, this provides a very straightforward way of analyzing a known barrier to trade.

The method is not without its shortcomings, however. Unless the implementation of the NTB comes as a complete surprise to the public, it is likely to have effects—perhaps perverse ones—long before it is put formally in place. These effects may thus detract from the usefulness of this method of measurement. Also, as always with econometric analysis, the results are only as valid as the model that is used to fit the data. If some other event happens to affect trade simultaneously with the NTB, then this approach may give misleading information unless the importance of that other event is correctly diagnosed.

Quotas

Quotas are the most straightforward of NTBs, and while they are often thought of as the most obvious and typical NTB, their relative simplicity is misleading since it is not shared by other forms of NTB. An import quota is simply a quantitative restriction on imports.[45] That is, a country desiring to restrict imports of a particular good determines the amount that it wishes to let in during a given year, say, and then prohibits any quantity beyond that from entering its borders. We shall assume that those units of the good that do come in do so without a tariff.[46] However, the forced scarcity of imports inevitably raises the price of the good on the domestic market by the amount necessary to sufficiently reduce demand. This in turn means that, somewhere along the chain of transactions that gets the good from the foreign to the domestic market, a premium is added to its price.

This can be illustrated along the same lines as in figure 2.1. Let DD′ in figure 3.1 be the logarithmic demand curve in the absence of any quota. Now impose a quota on the entire industry, prohibiting imports from exceeding the quantity $\hat{q}$. From the point of view of the world market, it appears as though the demand curve has changed to the broken curve DABC, with a kink at A, because at any price below $\hat{p}$ only the demand for $\hat{q}$ will be felt on the world market. Given the supply curve SS′, for imports from the world market, the world price will fall to p_l. However, since demand for the imported good domestically is unchanged, its price on the domestic market must rise to $\hat{p}$, in order to reduce demand to the required level. Since demanders of the good pay $\hat{p}$, only p_l of which reaches the foreign suppliers, the difference $\hat{p}$ -p_l is the premium that must be received by somebody. As we have already mentioned, the exact nature of this premium, and who gets it, both depend on how the quota is administered.

The method of administration that most economists would prefer, but which governments only occasionally use, involves the auctioning of import licenses. That is, at the beginning of each year, say, the government would print up licenses to import the quantity set by the quota for that year, and it then would auction them off in open competitive bidding. Allowing these licenses also to be resold on a secondary market thereafter, competition will establish the price of one of these licenses equal to the anticipated difference between the price of the good on the domestic market and its price on the world market—or $\hat{p} - p_l$, in figure 3.1.[47] As the year goes by, the supply and demand curves are likely to shift and this price will fluctuate. Aside from that fluctuation, however, this method of administering the quota comes close to replicating a tariff equal to the price of the license, since it not only raises the domestic price above the world price, but also allows the government to acquire the price difference as revenue.

A second way of administering a quota is to allocate the rights to import fixed amounts free of charge among importing firms. Once the allocation is made, the firms receive the price difference between the domestic and world markets as a pure rent. If the allocation is made among a sufficiently large number of firms, then they will still compete among themselves on the domestic market and will end up charging a single competitive price. But that price will be $\hat{p}$, enough above the world price to clear the domestic market. The situation is again analogous to a tariff, although here the "revenues" from

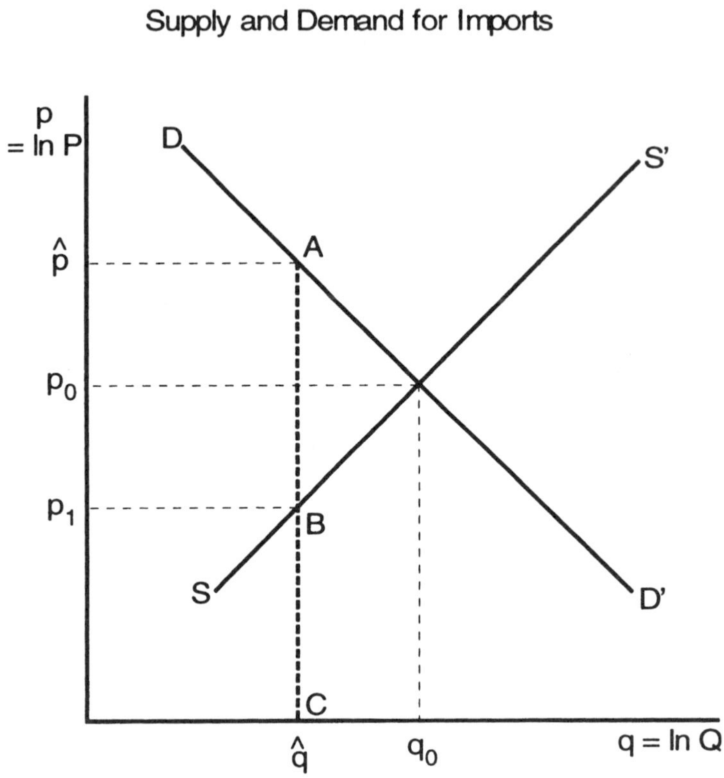

Figure 3.1
The Price and Quantity Effects of a
Quota or a Variable Levy

the NTB, or quota rents, accrue to the firms who were allocated the rights to import.

Additional distortions are possible, however, depending on how the allocation is made among firms. If the allocation is made on a political basis, for example, then potential importing firms will have an incentive to bid for licenses in the political market, by lobbying or whatever other mechanism is acceptable in the country. If the allocation is made on economic grounds, then there is an incentive for firms to distort the behavior that is to be used as an economic indicator. For example, if allocations are to be based on firm size as measured by the book value of capital stocks, then the quota rents become part of their return to capital, and firms have an incentive to over-invest. Or if allocations are on the basis of domestic sales, and if firms have access to a domestic source of supply, then they will expand their domestic supplies beyond even what would be indicated by the elevated domestic price in order to capture more of the quota rents. Clearly there is no end to the list of distortions that could be created by alternative mechanisms of allocating the quota.[48]

There are other ways that a quota could be administered, some of them causing much greater variations in the behavior of the market.[49] The point is merely that the method of administering a quota can make a great deal of difference as to its effects. This underscores the importance that we noted above in chapter 2 of getting as full a characterization as possible of any NTB, since even the seemingly simple quota can be quite complex.

With this sketch of the effects of a quota as background, consider now what difficulties quotas may pose for the methods of general empirical analysis discussed above. That is, can we expect those methods such as the ones reported in tables 3.1–3.6 to do an adequate job of capturing any quotas that are present among the array of NTBs?

Regarding the frequency-type measures, the answer seems to be yes, although of course these measures do not tell us very much. For their purpose, however, quotas have the advantage of being quite visible and easily understood. Because of the formal administrative procedures that they require, it should not be difficult to document the existence of quotas where they occur, as we have already illustrated in tables 3.1 and 3.2.

Regarding the price-comparison measures, however, there are at least three reasons why quotas may pose difficulty in addition to the problems of imperfect substitution with domestic goods discussed above for particular prices used to measure NTBs. Two of these reasons cause price comparisons to understate the severity of a quota, or even miss it entirely, while the third works in the opposite direction.

First, the price $\hat{p}$ in figure 3.1 is the equilibrium price facing domestic demanders of the good, but it is a market price only if these demanders are other than the importers who receive the quota allocations. Not infrequently, though, when quotas are applied to imports of intermediate goods, they are allocated directly to the using firms who are also discouraged from reselling them. In that case, $\hat{p}$ is still a relevant price for measuring the quota, but it is a shadow price and not observable.[50]

Second, other difficulties may arise on the supply side. If foreign supply is really perfectly competitive, and if in addition foreign governments do not change policies in response to the quota, then there is no problem. But if either foreign firms or foreign governments have the power to raise the price at which the good is supplied (the latter perhaps through an export tax), it is clearly in their interest to do so. If that happens, then the invoice price for imports may be not much below $\hat{p}$, even though the quota is no less restrictive. Together, these first two phenomena could completely invalidate at least one of the price-impact measures discussed above in equations (3) and (4).[51]

The third phenomenon works in the opposite direction. This is the well-known tendency for exporters under a quota to upgrade their product lines, exporting higher quality products than before the quota. This enables them to maximize the return on their import licenses and causes their prices to consumers to rise even more than if such upgrading did not take place. In an industry study of a particular NTB this can be taken account of by hedonic pricing methods,[52] but this is impossible in a general study of NTBs across industries. Thus for various reasons price-comparison measures may provide an inexact picture of the tariff equivalent and general incidence of quotas.

The trade-flow regression measures mentioned above fare better with a quota, since these measures tend to focus on quantities rather than prices. Except where smuggling is a serious problem, quantities traded should be more easily measured than prices. The only difficulty we see is that quotas, if they are not always binding, seem to impose such markedly nonlinear behavior that it may be difficult to specify appropriate functional forms for regression models.

Consider finally what specific method would be best if one only wished to measure a particular quota. The quantity to be admitted under the quota is usually readily available information, but by itself it is not very informative. About all it can indicate easily is—by comparing it with actual imports under the quota—whether the quota is binding or not. This is important information, as we noted earlier, but it is not very much.

Other more useful information about a quota may be available depending on the method of administration. Where import licenses are used to allocate the quota, the price of these licenses on the open market—whether purchased from the government or from other firms—can be an excellent source of information on the price impact of the quota. In fact, as already mentioned in connection with the MFA measurements, such information has been used for this purpose.[53]

If quota licenses are not auctioned or marketed, then some sort of price comparison is likely to be the next best alternative. Which particular price comparison is feasible and appropriate depends on the substitutability of the imported good with domestic alternatives, as well as the availability of various price data. Several methods are laid out in appendix 3, and a guide to their use is provided in our concluding chapter 5. The methods include:

(1) comparison of domestic prices with the c.i.f. prices of imports;
(2) comparison of import prices with prices of comparable exports to other countries; and
(3) comparison of domestic prices in the importing and exporting countries.

Whatever may be the most appropriate feasible price comparison, the value of any of these measures will depend on the care that has been taken to collect the needed price data.

If license prices are not available or are not useful because of supply-side responses to the quota, and if price comparisons are infeasible due to lack of data, then there is probably no alternative but to build a careful econometric model of the trade in question and use it to determine, for comparison, what trade would have been without the quota. This of course corresponds to the more general method alluded to above.

Variable Levies

Variable levies are much more specialized than quotas, having been used historically to protect agriculture in the European Community and in Sweden.[54] But we consider them next because they can be thought of as the mirror image of quotas. That is, while a quota fixes the quantity of imports, a variable levy fixes their price. This is done by the mechanism of charging what is essentially a tariff, the size of which varies, however, to achieve the desired domestic price of the import. The variation in the levy is instantaneous, it being left up to the customs officers at the border to charge an amount equal to the difference between the target price and the invoice price.[55]

Formally, figure 3.1 still applies. If the target price of the levy is $\hat{p}$, then again it is as though the world faces a demand for imports that is distorted to the curve DABC. The reason is that a fall in the world price below $\hat{p}$ will just cause the levy to be raised, keeping domestic price at $\hat{p}$ and thus keeping quantity demanded at $\hat{q}$.

This formal equivalence in static terms is misleading, however. There are important differences between the two NTBs if one considers changes in underlying conditions within the importing country.[56] If the demand curve for imports were to shift to the right, for example, a quota would hold quantity constant while forcing the domestic price to rise, whereas a variable levy would hold the domestic price constant and permit the full increase in demand to be imported. Correspondingly, the tariff equivalent of the quota, if it can be measured, will rise due to such an increase in demand, while the tariff equivalent of the variable levy will fall.

If a variable levy could be implemented as easily as just described, the analogue of the rents from a quota would simply go to the importing-country government as revenue from the levy. In fact, however, there is an incentive problem with this scheme that may interfere with the government collecting these revenues in full. Given that the levy will vary to achieve the target domestic price and that the importer knows this, it is a matter of indifference to him what price he pays, up to $\hat{p}$, for the imported good. The foreign exporter therefore faces little constraint in raising his price, even in competition with other exporters, since the importer has no incentive to buy from the cheapest supplier. Presumably the importing-country government can try to prevent such overcharging by monitoring world prices, but this is bound to be difficult. Therefore we expect the invoice price in a market with a variable levy to lie somewhere above p_1.

Empirically, then, the effects of a variable levy may be deceptively difficult to measure. Exactly as in the case of a quota, where foreign suppliers may respond by raising price, the difference between the domestic and invoice prices, if it were known, would not provide an accurate gauge of the size of the barrier that the variable levy entails. For the same reason the size of the levy itself would not be as informative as one would expect.[57] Instead one must get at the effects of a levy more indirectly, perhaps by comparing domestic and world prices as in the formula for IT^2 in equation (4) above. Two such measures are provided in appendix 3.

Voluntary Export Restraints

A form of protection that has been of great importance, especially in the two decades prior to conclusion of the Uruguay Round in 1995, both in the United States and elsewhere, is the Voluntary Export Restraint (VER). Also called a Voluntary Restraint Agreement and similar to an Orderly Marketing Arrangement,[58] a VER is an action undertaken by an exporting-country government to restrict exports of a particular good to a particular importing country, done at the instigation of the importing-country government. Since the restriction is stated in terms of the quantity of exports, it is identical to an export quota except for its political motivation.

A simple model of an export restraint is shown in figure 3.2 under the assumption that there is only a single foreign exporting country supplying the imported good.[59] The free-trade supply and demand curves for imports into the domestic country are SS' and DD' as before, with free-trade equilibrium price and quantity, p_0 and q_0. The VER restricts exports to the quantity $\hat{q}$, and results in a new kinked supply curve SBAC, since foreign exporters will be restrained from supplying more than $\hat{q}$ even at prices higher than p_1. To achieve this reduction on the part of competitive suppliers, either the actual or the shadow price they receive for exports of the good must fall to p_1. This could be accomplished, for example, by auctioning off export licenses, the price of which would then be $\hat{p} - p_1$.

Because a VER is really just an export quota, much of what we said above about quotas applies here as well. In particular, if domestic import firms have any monopsony market power, they will reduce the price paid to foreign exporters below $\hat{p}$, taking part of the quota rents for themselves. Likewise, the shadow price of exports to the foreign firms, p_1, will be difficult to observe since the export licenses will likely be allocated directly to producers, rather than to independent foreign traders who would buy the good on the open market. Thus direct price comparisons will be difficult as a means of measuring the effects of a VER,[60] and a general approach to measuring NTBs by comparing price indices may understate the effects of VERs. Nonetheless, if exporters who are subject to the VER sell in another market as well, either another export market or their own domestic market, then a comparison of prices in these markets may make it possible to circumvent these difficulties. In appendix 3 we provide several such formulas that may be applied, depending on the circumstances.

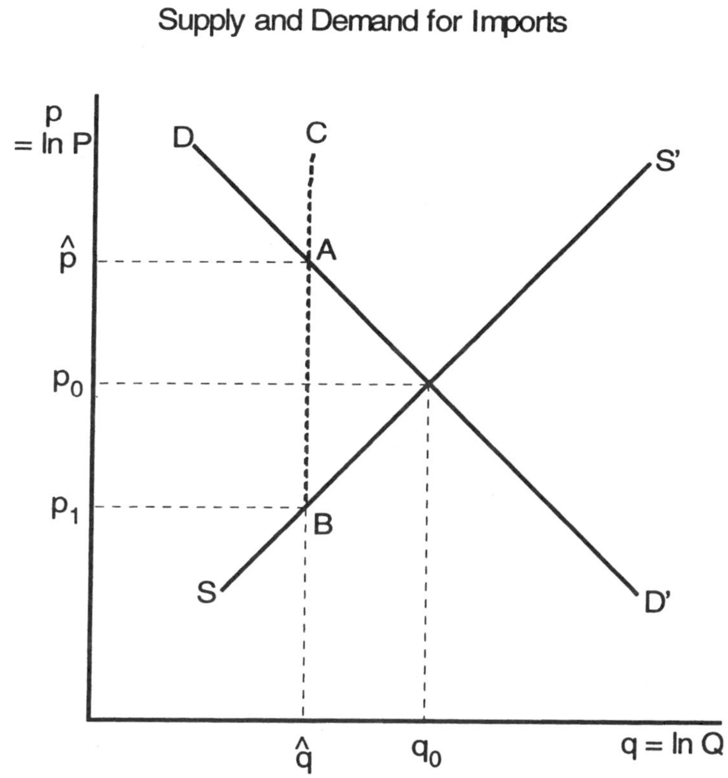

Figure 3.2
The Price and Quantity Effects of a
Voluntary Export Restraint

In some cases of VERs, quantity effects may be easier to get at than prices, since the quantities permitted by the VER and the quantity actually traded are both observable. However to compare either of these to the quantity that would have been traded without the VER requires accurate modeling of the industry's supply and demand behavior over time.[61,62]

Government Procurement Regulations

There are many ways in which demanders in a country may show a nationalistic preference for their own products over imports, either from the world generally or from particular foreign countries. A notable example of such preference is government procurement regulations, which typically may require purchasers for government agencies to show a preference for domestically produced goods. For example, there may be an explicit or tacit requirement that imports be avoided unless they fall below the price of domestic goods by more than a certain stated percentage. This is the kind of NTB that was the subject of one of the codes negotiated in the Tokyo Round and further expanded in coverage in the Uruguay Round. Some governments have as a consequence agreed not to engage in this kind of behavior in a number of areas that were negotiated. Nonetheless, it is still a common practice in most countries and deserves to be analyzed on that account.[63] Also, while government regulations may be more formal than other such prejudices against imports, their effects and problems of measurement are similar. Thus their analysis is actually representative of a much broader class of NTB.

Suppose, therefore, that an identifiable subset (government) of the demanders of a particular good show a preference for domestically produced goods as just described. That is, they undertake to buy domestic products unless imports can be obtained for, say, at least 10% cheaper. How will this affect the market? From the point of view of the subcategory of demanders that are subject to the requirement, decisions are made exactly as though there were a 10% tariff. Furthermore, if they do import, they actually pay only the lower price for the imports, and thus the implicit tariff revenue from the scheme stays within the demanding agency. Since the agency is part of the government, this completes the formal equivalence between a procurement regulation and a tariff.

However, there are two important differences, as well, between a procurement regulation and a tariff, and these have implications for empirical analysis.[64] First, unless the government is the only demander of the good in question, the implicit tariff here is levied on only a subset of demanders of the good within the country. Non-government demand continues to be allocated between domestic and imported goods on the basis of their actual prices. Thus when we aggregate the two groups of demanders to get the effect on the country's total demand for imports, the size of the implicit tariff will be smaller than 10%. That is, it will be approximately equal to 10% times the fraction that the government makes up of the total demand for the good. Also, depending on the nature of the good, the differential treatment of government and non-government demand may lead to a private sector response. That is, firms may increase their imports of the good and resell it to the government after only enough further processing to qualify for the preference for domestically produced goods. If this occurs, the implicit tariff can be reduced even closer to zero. Accordingly, the size of the procurement preference—10% in this example—may considerably overstate the extent of the true barrier that it imposes on international trade.

The second difficulty is that, contrary to what is the case with a tariff, the price on which import decisions are based is not observable. This means that if we use any of the conventional price-comparison methods of measuring NTBs, we may not succeed in capturing the effects of government procurement regulations where they exist. Even if domestically produced goods are perfect substitutes for imports and rise in price by the full amount of the procurement preference, an index of the good's price that includes imports will fail to include the elevated shadow price to which government demanders respond.

Calculations of the tariff equivalents of discriminatory government procurement policies for Canada are presented in Moroz and Brown (1987). Their methodology relied on what they call the "elasticity" approach, which we have discussed above in connection with figure 2.1 and quantity-impact measures of NTBs. The tariff equivalent (TE) here can be expressed as follows:

$$\text{(6)} \qquad TE = \frac{\Delta Q_m}{Q_m} \times \frac{(1+t)}{\eta}$$

where ΔQ_m is the change in imports induced by the NTB, Q_m is the pre-NTB level of imports, t is the nominal tariff rate, and η is the price elasticity of import demand.

Each industry can be divided into a government and private-sector submarket, and the TE for the government sub-market (TEG) is calculated as follows:

$$\text{(7)} \qquad TEG = \frac{APMP\ -\ APMG}{APMP} \times \frac{(1+t)}{\eta}$$

where APMP is the average propensity to import by the private sector and APMG is the average propensity to import by the government.

The foregoing equation assumes that imports and domestic goods are homogeneous, that markets are perfectly competitive, and that APMG and APMP would be identical if there were no discriminatory procurement policies present. It is important to note that private-sector purchases may be sensitive to procurement-induced price changes and that private firms may switch to imports if domestic market prices are increased with discriminatory government procurement. For relatively large economies, discriminatory procurement policies may not have a significant impact.[65,66]

Domestic Subsidies

A major source of complaint in international trade is the subsidization of domestic industry that puts foreign competitors at a perceived disadvantage. Domestic subsidies can take a variety of forms, ranging from credit guarantees to tax breaks on investment, and they are seldom as simple as the cash payments that we shall analyze here.[67] But this simple model can capture the essential features of their effects.

In figure 3.3 we show both the supply and demand on the domestic market, S_d and D_d, in the left panel and the implied excess supply and demand in the right panel.[68] The latter will appear either as the supply of exports, S_x, or the demand for imports, D_m, on the world market depending on the price that prevails there. Assume that a (specific) domestic subsidy equal to AB is now introduced, shifting the domestic supply curve down by the amount of the subsidy to S'_d. This in turn shifts the excess demand curve down also, and has effects in the world market that are analogous to either an export subsidy or a tariff, depending on the direction of trade. Indeed, if the world price happened to be between the old and new intersections of domestic supply and demand, then the subsidy would cause the country to switch from importing to exporting.

Now consider the problem of measuring the trade-distorting effects of this subsidy in a manner that will be comparable to other NTBs. Suppose for simplicity that the world price is fixed at p_w^0, so that the country imports the good, and these imports are reduced by the subsidy. The price on the domestic market will be the same as that on the world market, so that the price-impact measures discussed above will fail completely. Indeed, it is not clear that even conceptually there exists a true tariff equivalent of such a subsidy, since no tariff of any size will have the subsidy's effect of leaving unchanged, or even reducing, the domestic price.[69] On the other hand, the reduction in quantity of imports is analogous to that of tariffs and other NTBs, and regression measures that focus on quantities may pick it up.

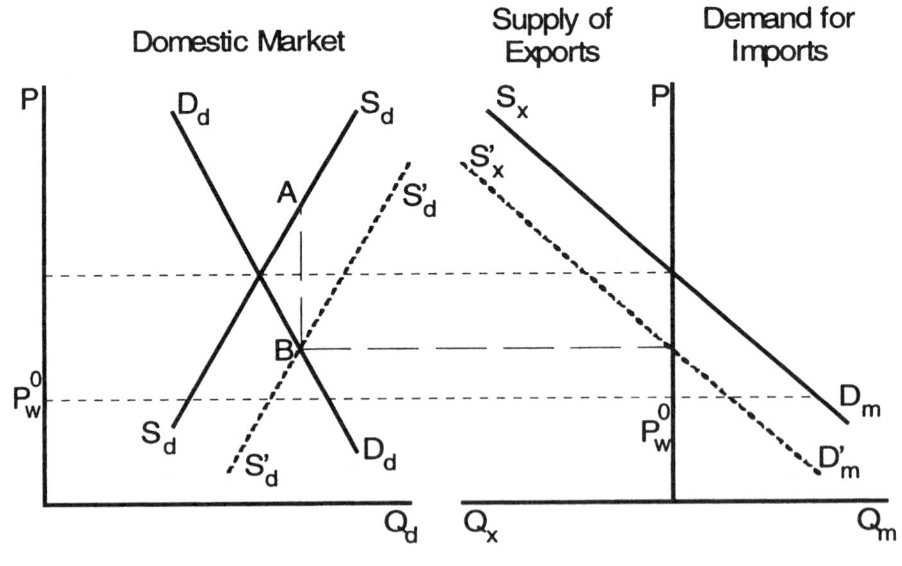

Figure 3.3
Effects of a Domestic Subsidy on
Export Supply and Import Demand

It will be tempting here to look at the domestic subsidy directly and, if its size can be determined, to use that as a measure of the distortion to trade. However it can be seen in figure 3.3 that this would be incorrect. The vertical shift of S_d is necessarily larger than that of the excess demand curve so long as domestic demand and supply are other than vertical and horizontal, respectively. Thus the size of the domestic subsidy provides an overestimate of the size of the implied NTB in terms of its effect on trade. This is true regardless of whether the subsidy serves to reduce imports or to stimulate exports.

Domestic subsidies are too important to ignore completely, however, and our recommendation is that they be measured in terms of their Output Subsidy Equivalent (OSE). This is defined as the direct subsidy to production that would have the same effect on output as the actual subsidy. Thus actual subsidies to output are just measured as their payments per unit of output and as a percent of cost. Subsidies to variable inputs, since these too reduce the marginal cost of additional output, are measured by their percentage cost reduction.[70] Subsidies that are paid over time and that appear to be unrelated to output may nonetheless have an effect on output if they permit a firm or plant to stay in operation instead of closing down. The OSE of such a subsidy can be measured by comparing the amount of the subsidy to costs and prices. One-time subsidies, such as a capital subsidy to finance an initial investment, also have effects on output by increasing firm capacity. Formulas for the OSEs of all of these types of subsidy are provided in appendix 3.

Domestic Content Requirements

These policies typically require that a certain fraction of domestic value added be included in goods sold on the domestic market. This introduces a straightforward trade barrier, to the extent that importers are forced to engage in further expensive processing that adds to their costs. The interesting feature of such a scheme is the way that it distorts the input decisions of producers. As a trade barrier, the increased cost of domestic processing is similar to a tariff, but the revenues that would be implicit in such a tariff are here dissipated in the form of production inefficiency.

Domestic content requirements can be analyzed in terms of the tradeoff between the value of production components that could be imported duty-free once the content requirement was met and the added cost of purchasing the production components from local sources. This is illustrated in figure 3.4, which we have adapted from Industry Commission (1994, p. 19) but interpreted somewhat differently. The line AC traces out the costs of purchasing locally under the content arrangement, with the components arrayed from the most competitive on the left to the least competitive on the right. The area under AC measures the value of domestically produced components. Assuming a small country with tariff, t, that applies to imported components, area E measures the tariff revenue saved by adhering to the content requirement. If the content requirement is adhered to, the firm saves the cost of area F but incurs the additional cost of area D. It will adhere to the requirement if area D is smaller than the sum of areas E+F.[71]

The effect of a domestic content requirement is further complicated because there may be restrictions on the import of the final product that uses both domestically produced and imported components. We shall say more on this below in discussing Australia's content requirements. In appendix 3 we provide a formula for the tariff equivalent for a domestic content requirement in terms of a general benefit provided to the firm in return for compliance. The case of figure 3.4, where the benefit takes the special form of tariff remission on remaining imported inputs, then follows as a special case.

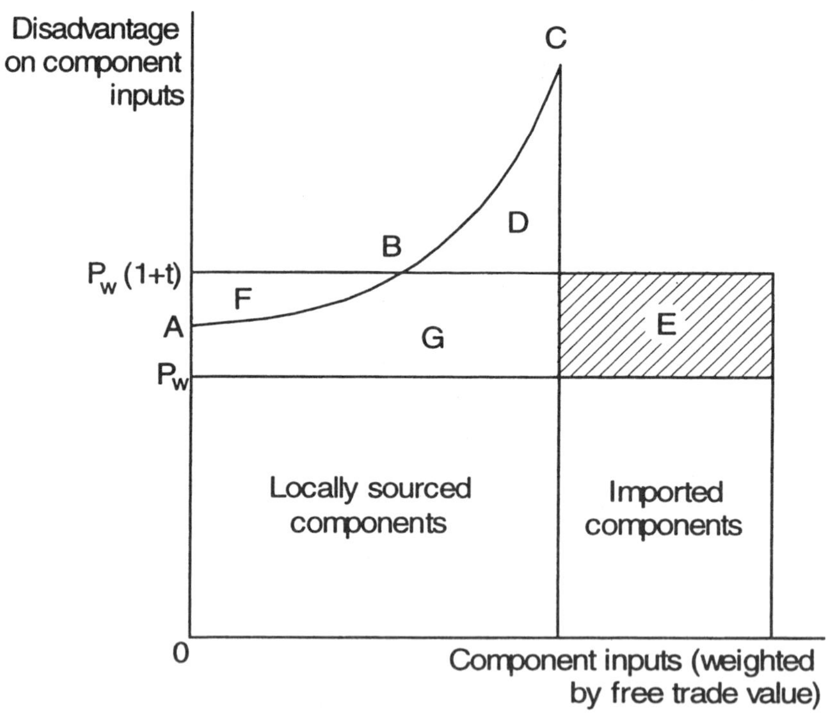

Source: Industry Commission (1994, p. 19)

Figure 3.4
Domestic Content Requirements

Antidumping and Countervailing Duty Measures

Antidumping (AD) duties are intended to offset actions by foreign firms that export for a price that is below the price in their domestic market or below cost. Countervailing duties (CVD) are intended to counteract foreign government subsidies for exports or domestic production.

Once imposed, AD duties and CVDs are simply tariffs and need no special form of analysis. However, an established procedure for imposing such duties will itself distort behavior in international trade even if the duties themselves never have to be levied.[72] That is, the procedure may serve as a signal to foreign producers to raise their prices to an announced level and thus charge higher prices than they otherwise would in hopes of avoiding AD or CVD penalties. Given that dumping and foreign subsidies are an accepted justification for intervention worldwide, it will be very difficult empirically to determine what price exporters would have charged if this were not the case.

There are, however, several cases in which it may be possible to do better than using only the actual duties collected as a measure of the trade restricting effects of AD and CVD laws. In AD cases that are resolved by a settlement rather than by a duty, the settlement itself may provide such a measure. If the settlement is a "price undertaking," then that price, in comparison to previous prices, measures its tariff equivalent. Similarly, a "quantity undertaking" can be translated to a price effect using an import elasticity. Somewhat more generally, if a particular country and sector is suspected to be unusually prone to AD actions, a price comparison similar to those mentioned above for VERs may indicate the effect. All of this is spelled out in somewhat more detail in appendix 3.

An indication of the major users of AD and CVD measures among GATT signatories for 1988–1993 is given in table 3.7. The numbers of AD and CVD measures in force by country and directed at exporting countries for 1990–1993 are shown in table 3.8 and 3.9. Table 3.10 contains a sectoral breakdown of the number of AD and CVD measures. These data are useful in identifying the country and sectoral coverage of AD and CVD measures, but they are subject to the same criticism made above of frequency ratios, which is that they do not convey any information on the economic impacts involved.

Customs Valuation Procedures

Announced levels of tariffs can be misleading if they are levied against a base of an artificially elevated price. This is easily dealt with empirically, however, by comparing tariff revenues with the value of imports and thus inferring what the true tariff percentage must have been. More difficult, however, is the problem that arises when traders do not have a clear idea of the valuation procedure that will be used, well in advance of making their trading decisions. In that case trade can be reduced far beyond what any simple measure of tariff revenues or prices could indicate. Both cases are dealt with briefly in appendix

3, the latter by again comparing export prices to prices charged by the same exporter in other markets.

A further problem arises in dealing with transfer pricing by multinational enterprises (MNEs) since intra-firm prices may be under- or overstated depending on how MNEs seek to minimize their global tax payments. In these circumstances what is needed is some measure of an "arm's-length" price as a reference that can then be compared to the observed import and domestic

TABLE 3.7. Percentage Share of Anti-Dumping (AD) and Countervailing Duty (CVD) Measures in Force by GATT Signatories, 1988-1993

Country	AD Measures	CVD Measures
United States	43.5%	68.0%
European Union-12	26.0	0.5
Canada	13.4	20.5
Australia	7.7	5.2
Mexico	3.4	0.0
Brazil	1.5	4.6
Chile	0.0	1.0
Other	4.5	0.2
Total	**100.0%**	**100.0%**

Source: Adapted from Chapman and Lee (1995, p. 13).

TABLE 3.8. Number of Anti-Dumping (AD) and Countervailing Duty (CVD) Measures in Force by GATT Signatories, 1990-1993

Measures/Country	1990	1991	1992	1993
AD Measures				
United States	201	216	267	304
European Union-12	137	144	159	150
Canada	78	69	73	85
Australia	24	30	44	76
Mexico	6	19	23	28
Brazil	0	2	9	23
Other	12	19	33	38
CVD Measures				
United States	94	87	93	122
European Union-12	--	1	--	2
Canada	31	30	29	29
Australia	1	5	12	12
Brazil	--	1	13	13
Chile	--	2	4	0
New Zealand	--	--	--	1

Source: Adapted from Chapman and Lee (1995, p. 14).

TABLE 3.9. Number and Share of Anti-Dumping (AD) and Countervailing Duty (CVD) Measures Directed at Exporting Countries, 1990-1993

	Number of measures				Share
	1990	1991	1992	1993	1990-1993
AD Measures					
Other	173	176	233	268	32.8%
European Union-12	67	68	74	96	13.4
Japan	79	81	86	86	14.6
China	32	48	62	74	9.5
Korea	28	34	40	48	6.6
United States	18	27	33	48	5.6
Taiwan	26	29	36	37	5.6
Brazil	19	21	28	30	4.3
Canada	16	15	16	17	2.8
Thailand	..	..	..	..	2.1
Mexico	..	..	..	..	1.6
Argentina	..	..	..	..	1.0
Total	..	..	..	..	**100.0%**
CVD Measures					
Other	37	42	42	54	29.6%
European Union-12	43	45	64	73	38.7
Japan	..	..	..	..	0.2
Korea	1	1	1	3	1.0
United States	..	..	..	..	0.3
Taiwan	1	1	1	1	0.7
Brazil	11	11	11	13	7.9
Canada	7	3	6	6	3.8
Thailand	8	9	10	11	6.5
Mexico	8	4	5	5	3.8
Argentina	10	10	11	13	7.6
Total	..	..	..	..	**100.0%**

Not reported.

Source: Adapted from Chapman and Lee (1995, pp. 15-16).

TABLE 3.10. Number and Share of Anti-Dumping (AD) and Countervailing Duty (CVD) Measures in Force by Product, 1990-1993

	Number of Measures				Share
	1990	1991	1992	1993	1990-1993
AD Measures					
Chemicals	94	110	143	155	22.1%
Primary metals	77	88	126	178	20.7
Electrical products	61	76	74	74	12.6
Fabricated metals	55	47	49	53	9.0
Textiles	26	28	41	41	6.0
Food	17	19	22	32	4.0
Printing and publishing	20	23	22	24	3.9
Leather products	..	..	..	..	3.1
Machinery	..	..	..	..	3.1
Agricultural products	..	..	..	..	2.1
Clothing	..	..	..	..	0.5

42 Measurement of Nontariff Barriers

	Number of Measures				Share
	1990	**1991**	**1992**	**1993**	**1990-1993**
Other	108	108	131	147	13.0
Total	..	..	..	..	100.0%
CVD Measures					
Clothing	7	6	7	9	52.0
Food	46	49	70	67	39.9
Primary metals	27	25	26	50	22.0
Textiles	10	12	11	13	7.9
Agricultural products	12	11	10	10	7.4
Fabricated metals	10	10	10	11	7.0
Chemicals	3	3	3	2	1.9%
Machinery	..	..	..	..	1.7
Electrical products	..	..	..	..	0.7
Leather products	2	2	2	2	1.4
Printing and publishing					-
Other	9	8	12	13	5.2
Total	..	..	..	..	**100.0%**

Not reported.
Source: Adapted from Chapman and Lee (1995, pp. 17-18).

prices in the importing country. While the customs authorities may themselves seek information on how imports by MNE affiliates should be valued in levying import duties, it is not altogether clear whether such information is public knowledge. Given the importance of intra-firm MNE trade and the incentives for minimizing tax payments, the existence of transfer pricing raises a host of difficult problems in measuring border protection that are deserving of greater attention.

Technical Barriers to Trade[73]

There is widespread reliance on standards, technical regulations, and certification systems that have been developed to enhance the availability of information and to reduce uncertainties about the quality characteristics of goods and services purchased by firms and households. Standards are generally voluntarily defined by business groups or nongovernmental standardization organizations, whereas technical regulations are legally binding. Certification systems are intended to assure compliance with existing standards or regulations.

To the extent that standards, technical regulations, and certification systems differ across countries, they may act as technical barriers to the flow of trade. What is important, however, is not whether they differ per se, but whether the standards are applied differentially between domestic and foreign goods. The use of price comparisons in assessing inter-country differences in standards may thus be of limited use, since these price differences may not in themselves reflect barriers to trade. What is needed accordingly is information provided by technical experts who are familiar with the details of the standards, regulations, and certification systems applied to particular products or processes. In particular, it may be possible to construct estimates of the added costs involved when: (1) higher standards are applied to imported as compared to domestic goods; (2) regulations are enforced more stringently on imports; and (3) imports are subjected to more cumbersome and costly certification procedures. These considerations are taken into account in the discussion of measuring technical barriers to trade in appendix 3.

Conclusion

Our analysis of NTB-specific problems of measurement in this chapter suggests two general conclusions.

First, the implementation of most NTBs provides only relatively little direct information about their size, and the information available is often misleading. We have seen this with procurement regulations and subsidies, where the formal percentages of preference or subsidy may overstate the true size of their price effects on trade, and this is likely to be true of other NTBs as well. The reason is that markets have an uncanny ability to circumvent attempts to intervene in them, and policies—though often very distorting in unintended ways—seldom achieve the direct effects for which they were intended.[74]

Second, attempts to infer the presence and size of NTBs from observed price differentials between domestic markets and world or foreign markets are fraught with difficulty and will often miss or underestimate many NTBs. We saw this even for relatively straightforward NTBs such as quotas, and the theme was repeated through all of the other examples that we have looked at in this chapter. Thus we remain cautious about the usefulness of price-comparison measures of NTBs except in those cases where the nature and local circumstances of a specific NTB are well understood to be appropriate for this methodology.

On the other hand, while measures based on quantities of trade often appear preferable to price comparisons at a conceptual level, the fact remains that we seldom have a good enough understanding of the quantitative determinants of trade to make these measurements. Therefore price comparisons are likely to be the only viable option for measuring most NTBs. We have outlined here how such comparisons may be undertaken in the various cases, and we provide more detail in appendix 3.

General Methods for Measuring the Effects of NTBs

We have concentrated thus far on issues of measuring the *size* of NTBs. Our discussion would not be complete without also mentioning how NTB measures, once they have been obtained, may be used to assess the effects of NTBs on economic variables of interest, such as domestic resource allocation, trade and economic welfare. We have already discussed calculation of the nominal rate of assistance (NRA), which is commonly used in calculating measures of *effective rates of protection* (ERP) and *effective rates of assistance* (ERA). Measures of ERP and ERA, as will be indicated below, are used to indicate how the structure of net border and domestic incentives may affect the allocation of labor, capital, and land among the sectors of an economy. We shall also discuss calculation of the *Trade Restrictiveness Index* (TRI), which is another method for measuring the effects of the structure of trade policies. Finally, reference will be made to the use of applied general equilibrium (AGE) models that are designed to simulate the economic effects of changes in existing border and domestic policies.

Effective Rates of Protection (ERPs) and Effective Rates of Assistance (ERAs)

Nominal tariff rates and nominal measures of the ad valorem equivalents of NTBs are valuable tools for documenting the presence of trade barriers and for measuring their size on a consistent basis. They are of little use directly, however, for indicating the effects of trade barriers, even in the industries that they ostensibly protect. A major reason is that they refer only to protection of outputs and thus do not take into account the effects of such nominal protection on input costs. Corden (1966) provides the classic reference for the rationale and calculation of ERPs as a means of determining the effects of the entire structure of protection on resource allocation. In order to calculate ERPs, data are needed on both nominal protection in all sectors and the interindustry (input-output) structure of the economy. These data then permit calculation of how sectoral value added is changed due to the structure of protection. Calculation of ERAs is a broader undertaking, since it involves measures of the size of both border and domestic incentives, and it also allows, like the ERP, for input-output interactions.

Trade Restrictiveness Index (TRI)

The TRI, which was developed originally by Anderson and Neary (1991, 1994), is intended to provide a comprehensive measure of NTBs in terms of their welfare effects.[75] An advantage of the TRI is that it provides a single number that characterizes the overall effects of a country's trade policies that apply to a particular aggregate of goods under general equilibrium conditions. But in order to calculate the TRI, information is needed on the prices of imports being protected, world prices, measures of tariff equivalents of products to be included, and measures of own-price elasticity of demand. The TRI may thus require almost as much information about an economy as would be needed for a complete applied general equilibrium (AGE) model. From the standpoint of the present study, which is focused on measuring the size of NTBs, the resultant measures can be directly useful in calculating the TRI.

But because the TRI provides primarily a measure of economic welfare due to changes in trade policies, it seems disadvantageous as compared to a full scale AGE model, which typically would provide economy-wide detail on sectoral changes in trade, output, employment, and other variables of interest.

Applied General Equilibrium (AGE) Model Measures

AGE models provide the most comprehensive framework for quantitative assessments of the economic effects of changes in both trade and domestic policies. As mentioned above, the calculation of ERAs makes it possible to obtain a single overall measure of the net incentives furnished by the structure of existing policies under conditions of partial equilibrium. However, since ERAs do not take into account interactions between industries and countries, they may not provide an accurate indication of how resource allocation and economic welfare may change as trade and domestic policies are changed. Because the TRI is derived under general equilibrium assumptions, it also may be preferable to measurements of ERAs. But if one is interested in the economy-wide impacts of policy changes at the sectoral level, construction of an AGE model should be the preferred methodology.

AGE models have come to be widely used in the past twenty-five years or so especially for analyzing the consequences of trade liberalization and changes in domestic tax structures. Such models can be constructed using a single country multisectoral framework in which trade is treated in the aggregate.[76] There are also numerous multisector, multicountry AGE models in current use.[77]

While AGE models have the advantage of providing comprehensive measurement of the effects of changes in policies, these models require a substantial amount of sectoral data and parameters. Also, to the extent that one is concerned with analysis of selected NTBs, partial equilibrium measures may suffice. In any case, since our present concern is to review existing methodologies for measuring the *size* of NTBs, we can leave aside considerations of which type of framework may be best suited for using such estimates in evaluating the effects of reducing or removing NTBs. Regardless of whether one opts to calculate ERPs or ERAs, to compute the TRI, or to construct a complete AGE model, all of these frameworks require comprehensive and accurate measurements of the NTBs themselves before any calculation of effects can begin.

Notes to Chapter 3

17. For a description of the UNCTAD Database, see OECD (1996, Annex 1).

18. It is also possible to conduct special surveys of how trading firms perceive or experience NTBs, or the number of complaints that firms may file with government agencies. See U.S. Tariff Commission (1974) for survey evidence on the experience and complaints that U.S. trading firms reported about particular NTBs. Frequency distributions were constructed for all NTBs covered in the survey as well as broken down for each type of NTB, country, and commodity group.

19. In addition to these "Quad" countries, results for other OECD countries--former EFTA members (Austria, Finland, and Sweden), EFTA members (Iceland, Norway, and Switzerland), Australia, New Zealand, Mexico, Turkey, and Korea—are presented in OECD (1996).

20. "Core" NTBs are those NTBs normally intended to modify or restrict international trade. "Hard core NTBs" refer to QRs and PCMs.

21. See Greenaway et al. (1995, pp. 11-19) for an analysis of European Union NTBs for 1992 by type of NTB and broken down according to the 2-digit SITC classification. Studies of NTB frequencies and trade coverage for earlier years for the OECD and other countries include Laird and Yeats (1990) and Laird and Vossenar (1991).

22. See OECD (1996) for some other calculations of NTBs, including the extent to which NTBs are escalated according to the degree of processing, substitution or complementarity relations between sectoral tariffs and NTBs, and changes from 1988 to 1993 in the use of NTBs relative to tariffs.

23. See Leamer (1990a,b) for efforts to use the NTB coverage data to assess the impact of NTBs on trade flows in 1983 for the major industrialized and developing countries.

24. The discussion here ignores within country distribution and transport costs. These complications, among others, are taken into account in the formulas of appendix 3.

25. For this reason, Sazanami, Urata, and Kawai (1995), in their study of the cost of protection for Japan, have used "unit values" of imported and domestic goods as proxies for prices. Using unit values is in our view problematic because of obvious difficulties in matching imported and domestic goods and especially controlling for quality differences between these goods. The difficulties would appear to be most serious for manufactured goods in which domestic and imported varieties are imperfect substitutes.

26. Even with perfect substitutes, however, this measure also includes any differences in domestic distribution costs, which we abstract from here. See appendix 3.

27. Again, formulas can be corrected for differences in transport costs, if these are known, using the formulas in appendix 3.

28. For some earlier results, see Baldwin (1975, p. 99), who presented some data on implicit protection on selected commodities in the Philippines for December 1951, using (c.i.f.) import prices and retail prices. He also presented (p. 102) data on U.S. and Philippine wholesale prices for a variety of goods for selected years between 1949 and 1965, and with an adjustment for transport costs, he interpreted the price differences as indicative of Philippine restrictions affecting imports. Bhagwati and Srinivasan (1975, pp. 179-81) provide calculations of implicit tariff rates for India covering 69 products for the years 1963-65 and 1968-69. In some later work, Baldwin (1989, p. 11) noted that price data for 1985 were compiled in Eurostat (1988) for household consumption items and equipment goods for 215 basic headings that covered around 3,000 products. These price data were in turn used by the Commission of the European Communities (1988) to calculate tariff equivalents of NTBs in order to assess the economic effects of the 1992 removal of these barriers. Laird and Yeats (1990, chapter 5) contains a literature survey of a variety of studies in which efforts have been made to calculate ad valorem equivalents by product category and country/region based on differences between domestic and foreign prices for agricultural products, textiles and clothing, steel products, and other manufactured goods.

29. Price-gap measures can also be used to measure the tariff equivalents of quotas on imported inputs for "downstream" and "upstream" sectors. This is referred to as the *cost-push method* in Moroz and Brown (1987) and USITC (1995, p. 7-6). Thus, suppose we have a price-gap estimate for an upstream sector. In this case, we could calculate the tariff equivalent for the downstream sector based on its cost share of production represented by the upstream input. This is the method used for sugar-containing products for the United States for 1991 and 1993. It presumes that the upstream tariff equivalent is calculated accurately and that there is perfect competition in the downstream sector.

30. For some earlier work, see Roningen and Yeats (1976), who compiled price statistics for 1973 covering 90 products in 15 advanced industrialized countries. They assumed the "world" price to be the lowest observed price for a given product specification. Netting out domestic taxes, nominal tariffs and variable levies, and transportation costs in and between countries, they calculated "NTB residuals" for the major product groupings.

31. Linkins and Arce (1994, pp. 4-5) indicate that the extent of coverage and the degree to which MFA quotas were utilized in 1991 varied notably from country to country. This suggests that quota-constrained suppliers may be hesitant to make export commitments, which, if true, can lead to under-utilization of quotas. This does not mean that the quota has no effect, however.

32. For details, see USITC (1995, pp. 7-7 and 7-8).

33. This is evident in figure 2.1 as long as the tariff equivalent is measured using the observable prices, p_1' and p_1.

34. We should mention that, in focusing attention on the quantity effects of an NTB, Jager and Lanjouw (1977) nonetheless looked first at prices. That is, they estimated the tariff equivalent of NTBs in a particular industry, Dutch newsprint, for a number of years in the manner already described. Then they combined the tariff equivalent with separately estimated supply and demand elasticities to derive the implicit quantity effects. This enabled them to illustrate graphically how the relationship between the price and quantity effects of the NTB varied over time, but it does not provide a really distinct quantity-oriented methodology. See also Hufbauer and Elliott (1994), who base their calculation of the costs of protection for 21 U.S. sectors in 1990 on "guesstimates" of demand and supply elasticities and cross-elasticities in determining how trade would respond if existing NTBs were removed.

35. When confronting actual situations, some allowance may have to be made as well for disequilibrium situations and international capital flows.

36. See Deardorff (1998) for a theoretical analysis of the underpinnings of the gravity model.

37. In addition to the points below, quantity measures may be sensitive to disequilibrium exchange rates. This is the case also for price measures. But, since quantities adjust relatively slowly, this should be less of a problem as compared to price measures.

38. This is not to say that bad models of NTBs always somehow overstate their effects. The point here is only that if we infer NTBs from the difference between actual trade flows and those predicted by some model, as this methodology does, then the further the model strays from reality the larger will these differences be, even if there are no NTBs in fact. Of course, a bad model could coincidentally predict exactly the trade flows that NTBs happen to give rise to, but that seems very unlikely.

39. See Saxonhouse and Stern (1989) for an econometric analysis of this kind in an effort to determine whether Japan's trade performance appears unusual in comparison to other countries, in particular the United States and Canada. While the results provide some suggestions about unusual features of each nation's trade performance at the sectoral level, it is not possible to infer unambiguously what the precise sectoral impact is of NTBs.

40. We should also mention the effects of rent seeking which were investigated in the pioneering work of Krueger (1974), who focused attention on the possible costs in the form of wasted resources that might be incurred in competing for the rents arising from import licensing. Krueger's work has been important in changing the way we think about the costs of trade barriers, and it has led to similar theoretical analysis for trade barriers other than quotas, as in Bhagwati and Srinivasan (1980). However, there has been surprisingly little further empirical work on the subject apart from occasional calculations of the rents that are implicit in various NTBs. Hardly any effort seems to have been made to measure directly the rent seeking activities themselves. For one such effort, see Jackson (1984). See also Tarr (1994).

41. See Saxonhouse (1977) for some methodological considerations that are relevant in these circumstances.

42. As mentioned above, Linkins and Arce (1994) have noted in connection with the MFA that quota utilization may vary by country and time period and that less than full utilization of quotas may reflect market uncertainties that constrain exporters. Thus, in measuring the quota-auction price tariff equivalents for MFA quotas in the United States, the USITC (1995) used utilization rates of 80% and 90%. We are not entirely clear, however, as to what role these utilization rates played in their analysis. If the auction price of a quota in a particular market is positive, then the tariff equivalent of the quota is at least that large regardless of the rate of utilization. However, USITC (1995) had auction prices only for imports from Hong Kong, and they used those data to infer tariff equivalents of quotas from other exporters. It was presumably here that they used the utilization rates.

43. It would be interesting to determine if there is any kind of insurance that firms can use to cover themselves against adverse trade policy actions. In this connection, firms are sometimes required to post bond at the beginning of a possible trade action. The size of this bond is itself an NTB, but presumably it also provides some indication of the perceived likelihood that the trade action will be decided against the firm.

44. The work on European Union antidumping (AD) actions by Greenaway et al. (1995), which will be discussed below, is an effort of this kind.

45. Export quotas are also possible, and their analysis is analogous.

46. Actually, it is quite common to have both a tariff and a quota on a given good, so that a tariff is paid on units of the good that are admitted under the quota. This should be distinguished from a "tariff-quota", which is a tariff that increases, discretely, at a certain level or levels of quantity imported. We will confine our attention here, however, to a pure quota that is not accompanied in any way by a tariff. Both accompanying tariffs and tariff quotas will be allowed for in appendix 3.

47. If importers are risk averse and unable to diversify or otherwise offset the risk that their price expectations will be incorrect, then the price of a license will be somewhat less than the expected price difference. This means that part of the price difference will not go to the government as revenue, but will compensate traders for their real loss of utility.

48. On the other hand, some of these "distortions" could be desirable. For example, if the domestic market is already oligopolistic and the quota were allocated in proportion to sales, then the incentive to expand sales would offset somewhat the inefficiencies of the oligopoly. Of course the quota itself is likely to reduce competition substantially, so the net effect of the quota is still likely to be adverse.

49. For example, it is intriguing to consider the administratively simple scheme of allocating the quota on a first-come-first-served basis in each calendar year. With competition, this will cause the domestic price of the import to be lower early in the year than later. How the quantity of imports is altered, and the precise time path followed by the price, depend however on the feasibility

of storing the good. If it is storable and the quota is not too small, for example, one may find the market undistorted during the first part of the year, with the remainder of the quota being imported all at once at some date during the year, and the price rising smoothly thereafter as though the good were an exhaustible resource.

50. If a perfect substitute is produced domestically, then this is not a problem, since the price of the domestic good will equal $\hat{p}$. But if domestic goods in the industry are imperfect substitutes for imports, then the error of using a price index instead of the price of imports will be exacerbated by this failure of directly allocated intermediate imports to be included in the index.

51. The comparison of domestic prices in the two countries, used in IT^2, is not undermined so severely, since presumably foreign governments would not tax their own markets when they tax exports, but we already noted other doubts about the validity of this measure.

52. See Feenstra (1984) for such an approach to the auto industry.

53. See, for example, Bhagwati and Srinivasan (1975, pp. 160-61) for data on premium rates for import licenses in India covering selected products on a monthly basis during 1966. More recent data are to be found in Industry Commission (1995) and Melchior (1993). As discussed earlier in connection with VERs, licenses for exports are sometimes traded freely and the prices for these licenses may be indicative of the impact of the quota. In particular, information from Hong Kong has been used to calculate the quota rents on textiles and clothing subject to the MFA.

54. Studies of variable levies and related policies include Sampson and Snape (1980) and Sampson and Yeats (1976, 1977). Additional references can be found in Laird and Yeats (1990).

55. Variable levies have been only one part of the European Community's Common Agricultural Policy, which has also involved domestic price supports for certain goods and adjustments of target prices to take intercountry exchange-rate changes into account. As a result of the Uruguay Round, these and other border measures have been converted into equivalent tariffs. For further discussion and details, see especially Hathaway and Ingco (1996).

56. There is no difference in responses to changes abroad. Since both policies lead to the same distorted demand curve, they also cause identical responses to shifts of foreign supply.

57. In fact only the target price, and not the size of the levy collected, is normally publicly available anyway.

58. The latter may differ from both of the former by involving both a more formal institutional structure and a larger number of participating countries.

59. Or, equivalently, that the VER is negotiated with all foreign exporters. The case of a VER implemented by only a subset of exporters is more interesting, as we will note below, but it is also more complicated and is beyond what we can pursue in any detail here.

60. See our earlier discussion of the quota-auction price method.

61. One further complication is left out of the analysis in figure 3, but may be quite important. As noted above, in practice VERs are often negotiated with only a subset of foreign suppliers, and one of their effects is to stimulate increases in supply from other sources. The most straightforward way of evaluating a VER, by simply comparing the permitted quantity to that which was coming in immediately before the VER was put in place, will considerably overstate the importance of the VER if this effect is neglected. A similar source of bias arises if the VER fails to cover exports of close substitutes even from the same country. Producers are quite adept at changing their product lines to penetrate loopholes in a negotiated restraint.

62. An indication of how complicated this can be, especially for imports of a differentiated product, may be found in Berry et al. (1995) who estimate the effects of the VER on autos imported by the United States from Japan.

63. See Hoekman (1997) for data and analysis for 1983-93 of various aspects of actual procurement by government entities in the major industrialized countries that are subject to the Government Procurement Agreement (GPA). He concludes that the GPA has not accomplished a great

deal thus far in opening markets. Since government procurement accounts for a sizable proportion of total expenditures in many countries, there appears to be considerable potential for removing existing barriers in both the major industrialized and developing countries. It should be noted that the GPA was one of the few parts of the Uruguay Round agreements that was not to be applied automatically to all members of the World Trade Organization.

64. Lowinger (1976) has assessed the effects of government procurement restrictions by calculating what government imports would be if the government had the same import propensities as the private sector. This assumption was also used by Moroz and Brown (1987) for Canada, as will be noted below. Another noteworthy study of the discriminatory impacts of government procurement policies is Baldwin and Richardson (1972). For a discussion of the methodology used in these and other studies, see Francois, Nelson, and Palmeter (1997).

65. This is the case in Canada insofar as government nondefense purchases of goods accounted for a small proportion of total purchases. As noted in table 4.12 below, only fourteen of the ninety-two Canadian industries covered had a calculated tariff equivalent in excess of one percent. A similar conclusion was reached by Francois, Nelson, and Palmeter (1997) for the United States, based on 1992 data. They suggested, however, that this conclusion may not carry over to services since government nondefense procurement is relatively sizable in a number of services sectors. See also Deltas and Evenett (1997) for theoretical analysis and simulation results for the effects of government preference policies on firm profits and procurement costs and implications for future liberalization of government procurement practices.

66. The import price elasticities used in calculating the tariff equivalents for Canadian government procurement for fourteen sectors are listed in table 4.12. The elasticity estimates for all ninety-two sectors are given in table D2 of Moroz and Brown (1987). These estimates came from the Canadian Department of Finance.

67. Perhaps the most ambitious efforts to measure subsidies are those described in OECD (1986) for the agricultural sector in the major OECD countries. These include measures of producer and consumer subsidy equivalents. The producer subsidy equivalents (PSEs) are a measure of the payment or subsidy that would be required to compensate producers for the removal of government agricultural assistance programs of various kinds. The consumer subsidy equivalents (CSEs) measure the implicit tax on consumption from agricultural policy measures as well as subsidies to consumption.

68. In this figure the quantities themselves are graphed, rather than their logarithms as were used in the preceding figures. This is necessary, since the excess demand curve takes on both positive and negative values, and incidentally therefore cannot have constant elasticity as was assumed before.

69. A tariff equivalent would exist if equivalence were defined in terms of, say, effect on quantity of trade or assistance to domestic industry. We do not pursue these options here, having decided that for most trade barriers equivalence in terms of effects on domestic prices provides the most useful measure. Subsidies, where they exist, must therefore be handled separately.

70. Subsidies to inputs have additional effects, of course, in addition to their effect on output, since they alter the mix of inputs that are employed. Thus two subsidies with the same OSE may not be equivalent in terms of their effects on things other than output, just as two NTBs with the same tariff equivalents may have different effects on variables other than price.

71. Note that area G cancels out for the firm, being a tariff cost without compliance and a real input cost with compliance. The country as a whole, however, would have retained the tariff revenue. From the country's point of view, compliance causes only the real resource loss of areas G+D.

72. For some empirical evidence on this point, see Messerlin (1988).

73. See Hoekman and Kostecki (1995, esp. pp. 112-20) for a discussion of technical regulations and standards with reference especially to the economic issues involved, GATT/WTO rules and procedures, and the Uruguay Round Agreement on the Application of Sanitary and Phyto–Sanitary Measures.

74. This is the theme of Baldwin's (1982) Graham lecture.

75. A useful introduction to the calculation and interpretation of the TRI is provided in USITC (1995, pp. 7–10 – 7-13).

76. Among the many single-country AGE models in current use, the best known and by far most sophisticated model is the ORANI model of the Australian economy, details of which can be found in Dixon, Parmenter, Sutton, and Vincent (1982) and in the publications and working papers of the IMPACT project which is currently located at Monash University in Melbourne. An AGE model for the United States is maintained by the USITC (1995) and has been used periodically to assess the economic effects of existing U.S. tariffs and NTBs.

77. Applications of these models can be found in the quantitative assessments of the Uruguay Round negotiations reported in Martin and Winters (1996). These assessments include the effects of tariff reductions, tariffication of agricultural protection and domestic production subsidies and other supports, reduction/removal of NTBs, including the MFA, and the potential for liberalization of international trade in services.

APPENDIX 3

Formulas for Measuring NTBs

Note Regarding Country Size:

In all of the formulas of this appendix, the notation represents prices, costs, etc., that prevail in an equilibrium in the presence of NTBs, and there is no assumption that any of these would necessarily remain the same if the NTBs were removed. Thus the formulas can be applied equally well to a country that is large enough for its trade to influence world prices as to a country that is too small to have such an effect.

Notation:

For a good that is not traded:

MC	= Marginal cost in production
r_p	= Producer rent (markup over marginal cost)
$P_e = MC + r_p$	= Ex-factory price
C_w	= Cost of wholesale distribution
$P_w = P_e + C_w$	= Wholesale price
C_r	= Cost of retail distribution
$P_r = P_w + C_r$	= Retail price
$C_d = C_w + C_r$	= Total cost of distribution

Thus: $P_r = P_e + C_d = MC + r_p + C_d$

For a good that is traded:

MC	= Marginal cost in production
r_p	= Producer rent (may include some rent from NTB)
$P_e = MC + r_p$	= Ex-factory price
C_s	= Cost of getting good from factory onto ship
r_x	= Exporting-country post-factory rent per unit of NTB, built into f.o.b. price (ad valorem $\rho_x = r_x/P_c$)
$P_f = P_e + C_s + r_x$	= F.o.b. price
C_t	= Cost of transport and insurance
$P_c = P_f + C_t$	= C.i.f. price
t	= Tariff in specific terms (ad valorem $\tau = t/P_c$)

r_m = Importing-country rent per unit of NTB (ad valorem $\rho_m = r_m / P_c$)

$P_i = P_c + t + r_m$ = "Inside border" price

$= P_c + (\tau + \rho_m)P_c = (1 + \tau + \rho_m)(P_f + C_t)$

C_w = Cost of wholesale distribution

$P_w = P_i + C_w$ = Wholesale price

C_r, C_d, P_r = Same as for nontraded good

Thus $P_r = P_e + C_s + r_x + C_t + t + r_m + C_d$

$= MC + r_p + C_s + r_x + C_t + t + r_m + C_d$

Thus an NTB, by creating rents $r = r_x + r_m$ (plus a portion of r_p in some cases), drives a wedge between marginal cost, MC, and the inside-border price, P_i, analogous to a tariff. The tariff equivalent, TE, of the NTB, as we define it, is the *ad valorem* tariff that, if it replaced the NTB, would lead to the same value of this inside-border price (or, for some NTBs that are thought to work by making distribution more difficult, that lead to the same wholesale or retail price, adjusted for any legitimate differences in distribution costs). In ad valorem terms relative to the c.i.f. price,[1] if rents from the NTB change prices in the same way as a tariff of the same size, then the tariff equivalent of the NTB is

$$TE = \rho = \frac{r}{P_c} = \frac{r_x + r_m}{P_c}$$

The problem is to infer these rents (to the extent that they do alter prices) from other information and assumptions. Note that since the c.i.f. price and tariff are observable, a part of this problem—the measurement of rents in the importing country, r_m—would be trivial if the inside-border price were observable. To an extent, therefore, the problem of measuring the TE is the problem of measuring this inside-border price.

In the formula above, as in all those below, we measure TE as a fraction. All of the formulas should be multiplied by 100 to obtain percentages.

All of the prices and costs above, if they carry a superscript, m, will refer to the imported good whose tariff equivalent is being sought. Other superscripts indicate other goods, as follows (examples show retail prices, but other costs and prices for the same goods are indicated similarly).

P_r^m = Retail price of imported good

P_r^d = Retail price of domestic comparable good ($P_r^d = P_r^m$ if they are perfect substitutes)

P_r^x = Retail price of import good in another export market

P_r^o = Retail price of import good in exporter's own domestic market

All prices and costs are expressed in importing country's currency at the prevailing exchange rate.

Formulas: Motivation and Application

I. Import Quotas

A. If quotas are auctioned

1. If the auction is plausibly competitive, the auction price per unit of quota $A = r$ and can be used to measure the *TE*:

$$TE^{AUC} = \frac{A}{P_c} \qquad \text{(I.A.1)}$$

If bids are stated in ad valorem rather than specific form, then the bid itself is the tariff equivalent. In both cases, care should be taken to observe variations in auction prices across time, and to use a suitable average of prices for a period of time. If an auction at the beginning of a time period is followed by secondary market sales at transfer prices different from the auction price, then these transfer prices should be used, also averaged over time, rather than just the auction price.

If the unit of the auction is not a one-time unit of import quota, but a recurring right to import a unit each year for a period of years, then it is necessary to convert the auction price to a price per unit of one-time quota using a discount rate that takes account of both the interest rate and the uncertainty of future trade and quotas. This is sufficiently difficult to do with any accuracy that we recommend not using auction prices at all in this situation.

2. It is possible that auctions may be conducted for the quotas that apply to some exporters of a product, such as Hong Kong, but not others. In that case this method can still be applied to those other exporters if their auction prices can first be inferred from the Hong Kong auction price together with differences in labor costs and productivity between the exporting countries and Hong Kong. Thus, letting P_e^{hk} and P_e^{o} be the ex-factory prices of exports from Hong Kong and the other exporter respectively, it can be assumed that these two prices differ primarily by measurable differences in wages, W^{hk} and W^{o}, and in labor productivity, go^{hk} and go^{o}, measured as gross output per worker. Thus

$$P_e^{o} = \left(\frac{W^{o}}{W^{hk}}\right)\left(\frac{go^{hk}}{go^{o}}\right)P_e^{hk}$$

Assuming that products of the two exporters are perfect substitutes (hence $P_c^{hk} = P_c^o$) and that transport and other distribution costs are also identical, the auction price for the other exporter can be estimated as

$$A^o = A^{hk} + (P_e^{hk} - P_e^o)$$

and this can be used in the formula above for TE^{AUC}. Of course if A^o turns out to be negative in this calculation, then one of the assumptions is evidently incorrect. If A^o is negative and not too large, however, one can probably safely assume that the tariff equivalent for the other country is simply zero.

3. If the auction is thought to be significantly less than perfectly competitive, then the auction price is of no value, except as an indication of how rent is shared with the government. Use the same techniques listed below for quotas that are given away.

B. If quotas are exchanged (transferred) on a plausibly competitive secondary market, use the transfer price in place of A in TE^{AUC} (I.A.), with the same caveats mentioned there.

C. If quotas are allocated to (a large number of) domestic residents (hence $r_x = 0$), and if there are enough sellers in the relevant markets to justify assuming perfect competition, do the following, depending on availability of markets for goods with comparable characteristics or distribution costs:

1. For a good with a perfect domestic substitute (hence $P_r^d = P_r^m$), use comparison of c.i.f. price with ex-factory price of domestic substitute:

$$TE^{SUBST} = \frac{P_e^d - P_c^m}{P_c^m} + \frac{C_d^d - C_d^m}{P_c^m} - \tau \qquad \text{(I.C.1)}$$

Note, that if the import and its perfect substitute on the domestic market are presumed to have the same distribution costs ($C_d^d = C_d^m$), then the tariff equivalent is obtained simply by comparing the ex-factory price of the domestic substitute to the c.i.f. price of the import, and subtracting the ad valorem tariff, τ.

If distribution costs are not the same, then these need to be accounted for as shown. In particular, if the import has higher distribution costs for some reason, this can explain part or all of a gap between the ex-factory and c.i.f. prices, which then do not necessarily indicate the effects of only the quota and tariff.

If an excess distribution cost of the imported good is itself regarded as an NTB (in addition to the quota), then failing to account for it as above will implicitly attribute its effect to the quota. If the concern is the total barrier to trade and not how it is divided between quota and distribution costs, this would be acceptable.

2. If the imported good is a discounted perfect substitute for a domestic good, then the formula above needs to be reduced by the size of the discount. That is, suppose that the import is comparable to the domestic good but is known to sell at a discount due to certain natural disadvantages of imported goods (referred to in Industry Commission 1994 Attachment A, pp. 6-7 as "natural protection"–a discount that covers "a range of uncertainties associated with importing and because of the ease of contacting local suppliers if difficulties arose"–and as "local advantage"). Then if the size of that discount, δ, can be estimated separately from knowledge of the industry, a tariff equivalent can be derived from the same price comparison as above but starting with $P_r^d = P_r^m/(1-\delta)$:

$$TE^{DISC} = TE^{SUBST} - \delta\frac{P_r^d}{P_c^m} \tag{I.C.2}$$

3. If a good has no perfect domestic substitute but is itself also exported by the foreign producers to another country where there is no quota, then assuming that foreign producers require the same ex-factory price for both destinations ($P_e^x = P_e^m$), one can infer the tariff equivalent from a comparison of prices at the same stage of distribution (wholesale or retail) across countries, together with differences in distribution costs and tariffs in the two markets. That is,

$$TE^{EXP} = \frac{P_r^m - P_r^x}{P_c^m} - \frac{C^m - C^x}{P_c^m} - \frac{t^m - t^x}{P_c^m} \tag{I.C.3}$$

where the unsubscripted C's are the sums ($C_s + C_t + C_d$) of the costs to the two markets. (To use wholesale prices, change P_r to P_w and C_d to C_w.) Thus one can use differences across countries in the same traded good's retail or wholesale prices to indicate the restrictiveness of a quota if distribution costs and tariff costs can be assumed to be the same, or exactly offsetting, along the two routes. And if these costs are different but can be measured, they can be accounted for as indicated. However, if there is no market that is quota-free, this will not work.

If more than one unconstrained foreign market is available for comparison, replace the export prices and costs above with averages across countries. Note also that estimates of C^m and C^x separately are not necessary for this calculation. Only their difference is needed. The expression $C^m - C^x$ can be replaced by an estimate of the difference in distribution costs, so that accuracy in measuring absolute levels of C^m and C^x is not an issue.

4. If a perfect domestic substitute does not exist, but there is an imperfect domestic substitute for which domestic distribution costs are deemed likely to be similar to those of the imported good (or linearly related to those costs, as in $C_d^m = a + bC_d^d$ where a,b are known constants), then

$$TE^{IMP} = \frac{(P_r^m - P_c^m) - [a + b(P_r^d - P_e^d)]}{P_c^m} - \tau \qquad \text{(I.C.4)}$$

Note that if distribution costs are thought to differ, but if that difference is itself regarded as an NTB, then setting a=0 and b=1 above will include that distributional NTB in the measured *TE*, along with the effect of the quota.

If it is not the total distribution costs, $C_d = C_w + C_r$, that are known to be related, but only the wholesale distribution costs, $C_w^m = a + bC_w^d$, then the above equation for *TE* holds with P_w's replacing P_r's.

D. If import quotas are allocated to a small number of domestic residents, so that quota holders have some market power, it may be that they will raise the price of the import above what would be needed to reduce demand only to the level of the quota. In that case, the quota will be underutilized, but this will not mean that the quota has not restricted trade. On the contrary, it has restricted trade more than it would have if the quota holders had been competitive. Each of the methods described above for allocations to a large number of domestic residents (formulas for TE^{SUB}, TE^{EXP}, and TE^{IMP}) will still be valid for measuring the tariff equivalent of the quota. It is important that the exporters of the good be perfectly competitive (so that $P_e^x = P_e^m$ in TE^{EXP}), but otherwise the same formulas apply.

E. If import quotas are allocated to foreigners, then the export prices (P_f and P_c) both include some quota rents as indicated above, and TE^{SUB} and TE^{IMP} that compare to P_c cannot be used.

   1. So long as the quotas are not allocated to the foreign producers themselves, and if these producers are competitive, then the formula for TE^{EXP} can still be applied, since the ex-factory prices, P_e, to different destinations would be equal and would not include rents.

2. If quotas are allocated to foreign producers, then formula TE^{EXP} can be adapted if these foreign producers also sell the same product in another NTB-free export market. It will not now be the case that $P_e^x = P_e^m$, since the producers will incorporate their rents from the NTB into their ex-factory price destined for the importing-country market. But if they sell the same product in both markets, then their marginal production costs will be the same, $MC^x = MC^m$. If producers are perfectly competitive without the NTB, then $r_p^x = 0$ and r_p^m is entirely due to the NTB (whether or not the producer is able to raise price above the demand price for the quantity permitted by the quota). These assumptions then again yield the formula for TE^{EXP}.

   If producers are not perfectly competitive, but can be assumed to earn the same monopoly rents per unit in both markets without the quota, so that rents due to the quota are $r = (r_p^m - r_p^x) + r_x^m + r_m^m$, then the same expression holds.

   Note again that the C's in the formula for TE^{EXP} (I.C.3) include all costs, from shipping inside the producing country through retail distribution in the importing and other export markets. Analogous formulas are possible comparing wholesale prices, as before. In addition, if it is certain that all rents from the quota are confined to the producer, then comparisons may also be made between c.i.f. prices, f.o.b. prices, or even ex-factory prices, making appropriate adjustments in the C's and tariffs. The formula in this last case will be the same as TE^{OWN} below with export country replacing own country.

3. If quotas are allocated to foreign producers who do not export to a third country market, but who do sell the same product (with $MC^o = MC^m$) in their own domestic market, and if market power can be assumed the same in both markets absent the quota so that $r = r_p^m - r_p^o$, then the TE can be inferred from a comparison of ex-factory prices to both destinations:

$$TE^{OWN} = \frac{P_e^m - P_e^o}{P_c^m} \qquad \text{(I.E.3)}$$

   If ex-factory prices are not available, or if quota rents are thought to accrue partly at later stages of distribution, then comparison of own-country and import prices at later stages may be attempted. However, these comparisons require rather detailed data on shipping, transportation, and distribution costs plus tariffs. For example, the formula for comparing retail prices in the own and import markets, assuming $MC^o = MC^m$ and $r = (r_p^m - r_p^o) + r_x^m + r_m^m$, is

$$TE^{OWN^*} = \frac{P_r^m - P_r^o}{P_c^m} - \frac{C_x^m - C_t^m - t}{P_c^m} - \frac{C_d^m - C_d^o}{P_c^m} \quad \text{(I.E.3*)}$$

None of these additional terms is likely to be negligible, since even the two distribution costs, C_d^m and C_d^o, occur in different countries and are likely to be different. The main hope would be that some other unprotected good with similar costs in both countries might be used as the basis for comparison. This seems sufficiently tenuous that we do not devote space and notation to illustrating the possibility, which would be somewhat analogous to the formula for TE^{IMP} in (I.C.4) above.

F. If the rents due to a quota are thought to be shared by resident individuals or firms in both the exporting country and the importing country, then TE^{EXP}–comparing retail or wholesale prices in the domestic market with another quota-free export market, and taking account of differences in distribution costs and tariffs–can still be used, since it includes rents in both countries.

G. If there are no imports at all under a quota, as in the case of an embargo, then no import price will be observed and none of the above formulas can be applied. Participants in the market may nonetheless know fairly accurately the prices at which imports would be available if there were no restrictions, and thus estimates of c.i.f. and f.o.b. prices in the formula for TE^{SUBST} may still be used. Alternatively, such estimates may be constructed from f.o.b. prices to other export markets and estimates of transportation costs. That is, if $P_f^m = P_f^e$ and goods are perfect substitutes, then

$$TE^{EMBARG} = \frac{P_e^d - P_c^x}{P_c^x} + \frac{C_t^x - C_t^m}{P_c^x} + \frac{C_d^d - C_d^m}{P_c^x} - \tau \quad \text{(I.G)}$$

If it can be assumed that the embargoed imports would face the same transportation costs to the domestic market as to an existing export market, and that their domestic distribution costs would be the same as domestic goods, then this formula yields a *TE* with only minimal information.

H. Tariff-Quotas: A tariff-quota permits imports in excess of the quota but only at a higher tariff rate, τ^* than the rate τ that applies to imports within the quota. If imports in excess of the quota do *not* occur, then the tariff-quota is the same as any other quota. If imports in excess of the quota *do* occur, then the market behaves at the margin as though it were subject only to a tariff, at the higher rate τ^*. Thus the tariff equivalent of a tariff-quota cannot exceed τ*. Unless it is known with confidence whether imports above quota have occurred, the *TE* should be measured using the most appropriate of the methods listed above for simple quotas, yielding TE^{QEST} as the estimated *TE* of the quota alone. Then the *TE* of the tariff-quota should be taken as the minimum of that and τ*:

$$TE^{T\text{-}Q} = \min(TE^{QEST}, \tau^*) \tag{I.H}$$

II. Variable Levies

Even though the effects of variable levies are in many ways different from those of a quota or a tariff, in terms of the way they change over time as conditions change, the measurement of their tariff equivalent could be quite straightforward as long as the full effect of the variable levy can be assumed to accrue to the importing country government as revenue from the levy itself. The first method below just uses these revenues to measure the average tariff equivalent over a period. On the other hand, if knowledge of the variable levy leads foreign exporters to raise their prices in order to capture some of these rents, then the revenues will understate the *TE*. The second and third methods therefore use comparison prices instead for this purpose.

A. If there is reason to believe that foreign exporters *do not* raise prices in response to the variable levy, then use the revenues from the levy relative to the value of trade to measure its tariff equivalent. Letting *REV* be the revenues collected from the variable levy on a particular product over a period of time, and letting *M* be the f.o.b. value of imports subject to the levy, the tariff equivalent is

$$TE^{VAR1} = \frac{REV}{M} \tag{II.A}$$

There is no objective indicator that will tell whether export prices have been raised by a variable levy. However, it seems likely that export prices are more likely to be raised the fewer foreign exporters there are in competition. Thus this formula is best applied when the export market is reasonably competitive.

B. If there is reason to believe that foreign exporters *do* raise prices in response to the variable levy, then use comparisons of f.o.b. prices into the import market with f.o.b. prices into other export markets, together with the levy revenues, to infer the size of the levy.

$$TE^{VAR2} = \frac{P_f^m - P_f^x}{P_c^m} + \frac{REV}{M} \tag{II.B}$$

C. Alternatively, if these prices are difficult to observe, one can compare inside-border prices in the import market (which in this case are those prices mandated by the variable levy) with inside border prices in other markets. Assuming that competitive foreign suppliers require the same f.o.b. prices to all destinations ($P_f^x = P_f^m$) except when altered by the variable levy, the latter can be constructed from c.i.f. prices, tariffs, and the difference between transport costs, if there are no NTBs in these other markets:

$$TE^{VAR3} = \frac{P_i^m - P_c^x - t^x}{P_c^x} - \frac{C_i^m - C_i^x}{P_c^x} \qquad \text{(II.C)}$$

III. Voluntary Export Restraints

These are normally implemented as quantitative restrictions, allocated to producers in the exporting country. Their tariff equivalents are given by the same formulas listed above for quotas that are allocated to foreigners.

IV. Government Procurement Regulations

A. If the regulation takes the form of an explicit preference (buy domestic goods unless imports are at least *x%* cheaper), then the tariff equivalent is just the size of that preference times the share of demand (government plus non-government) that is subject to the preference:

$$TE^{GOV1} = x \frac{D_g}{D_p + D_g} \qquad \text{(IV.A)}$$

This also assumes that imports cannot qualify for the preference with only minimal domestic processing. To the extent that is possible, the tariff equivalent is reduced to the percentage excess cost of that processing.

B. If the regulation is only implicit, then it is necessary to estimate the proportion of government expenditures that would have been imported in the absence of the regulation. This is commonly done by comparison with the import share of the same or a comparable category of private expenditure. Let θ_g^m be the import share of government expenditure and θ_p^m be the import share of private expenditure. Then

$$TE^{GOV2} = \left(1 - \frac{\theta_g^m}{\theta_p^m}\right)\left(\frac{D_g}{D_p + D_g}\right)\frac{(1+\tau)}{\eta} \qquad \text{(IV.B)}$$

where τ is the ad valorem nominal tariff rate and η is the (positive) elasticity of demand for imports, to be estimated econometrically or taken from the literature.[2]

V. Countervailing Duties

Countervailing duties (CVDs) are just tariffs, and they can be measured as such. It is true that the threat of a CVD, even if never implemented, might have some effect in restricting trade, but to the extent that this occurs only through a reduction in a countervailable subsidy, it is not clear that this effect should be regarded as an NTB. Likewise, the availability in the law of CVDs and a demonstrated tendency to use them could have a dampening effect on trade. But we know of no obvious way to quantify either of these possible effects.

CVDs should therefore be measured directly from the sizes of the duties as they are levied. The only special concern here is that these duties may not appear in the regular tariff schedules, and therefore it is necessary to look for them directly, in the records of the outcomes of CVD cases.

VI. Anti-Dumping Duties

Anti-dumping duties (ADDs) are similar to CVDs in many, but not all, respects. Because they are levied against private firms instead of governments, they may induce changes in firm behavior that a CVD would not. Thus in addition to simply measuring the ADDs themselves as tariffs, one must also examine any settlements that are reached in AD cases that alter firm behavior in prescribed ways. It is also plausible that the active use of an AD statute by a country will have effects on trade in sectors where actual cases are never filed, and these effects in principle could be large and should be measured, although we know of no general useful way to do this.[3]

A. All duties that are currently being levied as a result of past and present AD cases should be recorded, converted if necessary to ad valorem terms, and included in any general quantification of NTBs. If these duties have already been included along with other tariffs, then they must not be double-counted. But it is desirable to separate them from other tariffs because they have somewhat different effects. (An ordinary tariff will normally, like any tax, be absorbed partially by the exporting firm or industry. However, exporters that are subject to an ADD know that if they lower price at all, the dumping margin and the ADD itself will simply be increased. Thus the true tariff equivalent of an ADD in terms of its effect on the domestic price of imports is somewhat larger than the size of the duty itself. However, the extent of this understatement is difficult to know, since it requires knowledge about market size and structure that is not readily available. We therefore recommend that ADDs be reported in terms of the simple ad valorem duties that are levied, but that they be reported separately from other tariffs.)

In order to include all current ADDs, note that it is necessary to examine not only AD cases from the current year, but also cases going back arbitrarily far in time since, under current WTO rules, ADDs can be renewed indefinitely if removal would cause material injury. It would be best if countries would maintain an inventory of all AD cases, including all for which ADDs are still being levied, and then update that inventory each year.

B. All AD cases should be examined for this purpose, not just those that have led to a positive determination and the levying of a duty. All cases that were settled prior to a final determination should also be included, and the nature of any settlement should be quantified and included in the measure of AD as an NTB. Such settlements can take many forms, and their quantification will seldom be straightforward. The following are two examples that could be used as guides to actual cases:

1. If the settlement takes the form of a "price undertaking," in which the foreign exporter agrees to keep price at some higher level, a comparison of the promised price with recent past prices will yield a percentage difference that can be taken as the *TE* of the undertaking.

2. If the settlement takes the form of a "quantity undertaking" or a "market share undertaking," in which the foreign exporter agrees in some fashion to limit sales in the domestic market, this can be quantified with an elasticity approach. First calculate the percentage reduction in quantity of exports to which the exporter has agreed, say $\%\Delta M$. The let the *TE* be the percentage price increase that would reduce demand for the good by that amount. That is, assuming a (positive) elasticity of demand of η,

$$TE^{SET} = \frac{\%\Delta M}{\eta} \qquad \text{(VI.B.2)}$$

C. While there is no general way to infer the trade reducing effects of a whole complex of AD laws in many countries, it is possible that if a particular country and sector is suspected of being especially prone to AD actions, the resulting discouraging effect on trade may be picked up by using price comparisons. Since exporters to that country would be hesitant to charge low prices, a comparison of export prices to other export prices destined for other country markets may reveal a differential. If so, then the formula for TE^{EXP} in (I.C.4) will provide the tariff equivalent.

VII. Domestic Content Requirements

Domestic content requirements can take many forms, and it is therefore essential that they be examined closely to determine exactly how they are constructed and what effects they are likely to have. Our analysis follows Industry Commission (1995, pp. 91-93).

A. A content requirement typically says that some percentage, c, of a good's content that must be sourced domestically, in return for which the firm producing the good will be given some benefit. If the firm opts not to satisfy the requirement, then the requirement has had no effect at all. Similarly, if the firm opts to include more than c percent of domestic content in its product, then again the requirement has had no effect. Only if the firm satisfies the requirement and finds it binding, has the requirement had any protective effect (on the input industry). Thus the first step in quantifying the effects of content requirement schemes is to identify those cases in which this is true.

B. Let b be the benefit given to the firm if it satisfies the requirement, per unit quantity of its output, and let C be its cost per unit in the presence of the local content requirement. To the extent that the content requirement is binding, it raises the cost of domestic inputs by some percent, TE, which is therefore the tariff equivalent of the content requirement. (That is, if a tariff of TE had been levied on all such inputs, their domestically-produced substitutes would have risen in price by this amount.) For the using firm to break even while satisfying the requirement, the increased cost of these inputs, $CcTE/(1+TE)$, must be equal to the benefit provided:

$$b = \frac{TE}{1+TE} cC$$

Thus

$$TE^{CON1} = \frac{b}{cC - b} = \frac{\beta}{c - \beta} \qquad \text{(VII.B)}$$

where $\beta = b/C$ is the benefit expressed in *ad valorem* terms.

C. In the case considered by the Industry Commission, satisfying the content requirement entitles the using firm to import its remaining inputs tariff-free. Letting t be the percentage tariff on inputs, the benefit from satisfying the content requirement is a reduction in cost of $t/(1+t)$ on its inputs (the fraction $(1-c)$ are now tariff free, and the tariff on the fraction c has been replaced by the cost of domestic inputs included in the TE), or $b = tC/(1+t)$. Thus

$$TE^{CON2} = \frac{t}{c(1+t) - t} \qquad \text{(VII.C)}$$

VIII. Customs Valuation Procedures

In order for a country's tariff rates to be comparable to those of other countries, they should be calculated as a percentage of the f.o.b. price of the import, and this f.o.b. price should be based on a free-market transaction. If imports are valued on any other basis for the application of ad valorem tariffs, then the difference can be viewed as an NTB. Since the Customs Valuation Code of the Tokyo Round, however, countries have foresworn the arbitrary use of valuation procedures in order to restrict trade, and the extent to which such procedures currently cause problems is primarily a result of the difficulty of estimating free-market prices for goods that do not themselves go through markets, such as intra-firm trade. Such difficulties will typically make it equally difficult to calculate the size of the implicit NTB that may be present, and therefore it is not expected that customs valuation procedures will, for most countries, constitute a major source of measurable NTBs. The formulas that we give here, therefore, are not expected to be widely used.

A. If valuation procedures are well defined, but do not accord with the standard of valuing at the f.o.b. free-market price, then the preferred method of dealing with them is not to calculate any NTB at all, but rather to recalculate the true ad valorem tariff rates relative to f.o.b. free-market prices.

B. If for some reason the recalculation of tariff rates is not possible, then the *TE* of customs valuation procedures can be calculated as follows. Let P_v be the value placed on imports by the valuation procedure and P_f, as above, be the f.o.b. free-market price. Then

$$TE^{VAL} = \frac{P_v}{P_c} t - t \qquad \text{(VIII.B)}$$

Note that only the excess of the actual ad valorem incidence of the tariff over the announced tariff rate t is regarded as an NTB, since the tariff t is already included in the measure of the country's tariff protection.

C. Valuation procedures become true NTBs when they are not well-defined, so that importers do not know until they reach the border what the duty will be. The trade restricting impact of such uncertainty is difficult to determine, but in cases where it is clear that such an impact exists, it should somehow be accounted for. One way would simply be to increase the value of the tariff arbitrarily, as in the above formula. Alternatively one could try to infer from other prices how much extra is being charged in this market to compensate for the uncertainty. Thus if the producing firm sells the product also in another export market that is subject neither to this uncertainty nor to other

NTBs, or if it sells the product in its own domestic market, then the formulas given above for TE^{EXP} or TE^{OWN} can be used. The analogue to the quota rent in the discussion there of quotas allocated to foreigners is not here a rent at all, but rather a compensation for uncertainty.

IX. Technical Barriers to Trade

Technical barriers to trade are regulatory and certification mechanisms that are designed in a way that puts imports at a disadvantage relative to domestic goods. Like customs valuation procedures, these have been limited by agreements under both the Tokyo and Uruguay Rounds of trade negotiations. Nonetheless, new needs for regulation and certification are constantly arising, and the possibility that these will be handled in discriminatory ways will continue to exist. Unfortunately, they are one of the most difficult NTBs imaginable to quantify. Our only general suggestion, aside from trying to extract credible assessments of their costs from experts in the affected industries, is again to use the formulas given above for TE^{EXP} or TE^{OWN} for quantifying quotas based on comparisons with other export markets or with the own domestic market of the exporter.

For a specific technical barrier that is thought to exist in a specific industry, the best approach is to collect information from experts in the industry itself. What information is needed depends somewhat on the nature of the barrier. As noted in the text, technical standards, regulations, and certification requirements can constitute barriers to trade in several different ways:

A. If more stringent standards are applied to imported as compared to domestically produced goods, then one must determine how much more costly it is to satisfy those more stringent standards. Letting the (per unit) cost of satisfying domestic standards be denoted C_{StandD} and the cost of satisfying the standard on imports be C_{StandM}, the tariff equivalent of the standards is

$$TE^{STAND1} = \frac{C_{StandM} - C_{StandD}}{P_c} \qquad \text{(IX.A)}$$

B. If identical regulations are enforced more stringently on imports than on domestic goods, then of course one needs to compare the costs to the two groups of producers of satisfying the standards. If these costs are identifiably different, then the formula for TE^{STAND1} can be used directly. Alternatively, if the measurable difference is in the fractions of product units that are made to satisfy a single standard at a cost of C_{Stand}, then letting θ_D and θ_M be the fractions of output satisfying the standard, we have

$$TE^{STAND2} = \frac{(\theta_M - \theta_D)\, C_{Stand}}{P_c} \qquad \text{(IX.B)}$$

C. Finally, if imports are subjected to more costly certification procedures than domestically produced goods, then TE^{STAND1} can again be used directly but with the two costs measuring costs of certification rather than of satisfying the standards.

X. Domestic Subsidies

As illustrated in Figure 3.3 and discussed in Chapter 3, domestic subsidies can affect trade, but not in a way that is equivalent to a tariff in terms of its effect on prices. Therefore we cannot usefully define a tariff equivalent of a domestic subsidy. Nonetheless, the measure of subsidies is important, and we recommend that a separate measure be used for them, the Output Subsidy Equivalent, OSE. It is defined as the ongoing cash payment, per unit of output and as a percent of cost, that would be equivalent to the actual subsidy in terms of its effect on output. Thus, an actual cash subsidy to output is just measured as a percent of cost. Similarly, for a subsidy to variable inputs (inputs of which more is needed to produce more output), one should calculate the OSE as the cost reduction per unit of output, but since the cost reduction is just the subsidy itself, this too is the subsidy as percent of cost.

More difficult are subsidies that do not appear to be related to output. For example, an ongoing cash payment to a firm that is truly unrelated to its outputs or its inputs does not change the amount the firm will supply to the market at prices for which it would have covered costs even without the subsidy. But at lower prices, at which the firm would have shut down and supplied nothing, the OSE is either the excess of cost over price or the subsidy payment divided by output, whichever is smaller. Thus the OSE of such a subsidy depends upon the prevailing price in the market, being zero for prices above cost and positive for prices below cost. Whether to use long run average cost, LAC, or short run average variable cost, VAC, for these purposes depends on the circumstances. If the subsidy is paid every year indefinitely, thus permitting the firm to survive in the long run, then LAC is the appropriate cost measure. However, if the subsidy is temporary, then it matters for output in the short run only if price is below VAC, so that the firm would otherwise have stopped producing.

What then of a one-time subsidy that is unrelated to current or future output?[4] Such a subsidy is equivalent to a permanent interest-free loan, and thus to an ongoing payment each year of the one-time subsidy times the interest rate. However, because this benefit is received regardless of whether the firm produces or not, it has no effect on output and its OSE is zero.

We summarize and elaborate these suggestions in the formulas below, using the following notation:

S = Total subsidy payments per unit time

S_0 = One-time subsidy payment

Q = Output per unit time

C_a = Long-run average cost per unit output

C_v = Short-run variable cost per unit output

P_{av} = Average ex-factory price over time

A. If subsidies are paid directly for output, or if they are paid for inputs that vary with output, then

$$OSE^{OUT} = \frac{S}{C_a Q} \qquad \text{(X.A)}$$

B. If an ongoing subsidy per unit time is paid independently of the size of output as long as output is positive, then

$$OSE^{IND1} = \begin{cases} 0 & \text{if } P_{av} > C_a \\ \min\left(C_a - P_{av}, \dfrac{S}{C_a Q}\right) & \text{if } P_{av} < C_a \end{cases} \qquad \text{(X.B)}$$

C. If a temporary subsidy per unit time is paid independently of the size of output as long as output is positive, then for the periods in which the subsidy is paid (with P_e the ex-factory price in the period),

$$OSE^{IND2} = \begin{cases} 0 & \text{if } P_e > C_v \\ \min\left(C_v - P_e, \dfrac{S}{C_v Q}\right) & \text{if } P_e < C_v \end{cases} \qquad \text{(X.C)}$$

D. If a one-time subsidy is paid that is related to output, such as a capital subsidy, then the amount of the subsidy should be converted to an equivalent ongoing flow using the real interest rate, i:

$$OSE^{OUT0} = \frac{iS_0}{C_a Q} \qquad \text{(X.D)}$$

E. If a one-time subsidy is not related to output, then its OSE is zero:

$$OSE^{IND0} = 0 \qquad \text{(X.E)}$$

Notes

1. Most countries report tariffs as percent of the c.i.f. price. For the few other countries, such as the United States, that instead report relative to the f.o.b. price, this and all other formulas in this appendix should be multiplied by P_c/P_f, which in most cases just means replacing P_c with P_f.

2. See, for example, Moroz and Brown (1987, Table D2).

3. Greenaway et al. (1995) employ an econometric method to quantify the trade-reducing effects of potential ADDs, but their method does not always succeed, even for them, and we do not regard it as a generally applicable methodology.

4. A subsidy to expanding capital *is* related to output and can be dealt with as above. It should be converted from a stock to a flow, however, by multiplying by the interest rate. See (X.D) below.